Hydra of Carnage

The International Linkages of Terrorism and Other Low-Intensity Operations

The Witnesses Speak

Uri Ra'anan
Robert L. Pfaltzgraff, Jr.
Richard H. Shultz
Ernst Halperin
Igor Lukes

The Fletcher School of Law and Diplomacy
Tufts University

Lexington Books
D.C. Heath and Company/Lexington, Massachusetts/Toronto

Library of Congress Cataloging-in-Publication Data
Main entry under title:

Hydra of carnage.

  Includes index.
  1. Terrorism—Addresses, essays, lectures.
I. Ra'anan, Uri, 1926–
HV6431.H93 1985   303.6'25   85-45430
ISBN 0–669–11135–X (alk. paper)
ISBN 0–669–11136–8 (pbk. : alk. paper)

Published simultaneously in Canada
Printed in the United States of America
Casebound International Standard Book Number: 0-669-11135-X
Paperbound International Standard Book Number: 0-669-11136-8
Library of Congress Catalog Card Number: 85-45430

The paper used in this publication meets the minimum requirements of American National
Standard for Information Sciences—Permanence of Paper for Printed Library Materials,
ANSI Z39.48-1984.
∞(TM)

The last numbers on the right below indicate the number and date of printing.

10 9 8 7 6 5 4 3 2 1

95 94 93 92 91 90 89 88 87 86

Hydra

"A serpent or monster slain by
Hercules. It had nine heads, any of
which, when cut off, was succeeded
by two others, *unless the wound was
cauterized.*"

Webster's New Collegiate Dictionary
1961 Edition
emphasis added

Contents

Tables and Figures

Tables

Figures

Introduction

T he open societies of the contemporary global arena are confronted
by a form of warfare which, while not altogether new in itself, is
unprecedented both in its dimensions and in its linkages, reflecting a
common thread between episodes of violence that are threatening stability in
areas as far apart as South Asia, the Middle East, Southern Africa, Western
Europe, and the Western Hemisphere. To date, mysterious immunity to this
epidemic appears to have been acquired by one type of regime only, and that
prevails generally in the closed societies which follow the Leninist doctrine.
Interestingly, however, at least in some of the regions infected, the immune
regimes appear to be located in close proximity to the open societies which
are under attack.

It would appear that the exigencies of a thermonuclear age render direct
military confrontations rather risky in areas where the Western and Soviet
military alliance structures stand eyeball to eyeball, that is to say, Central
Europe and the Pacific rimland. The dialectic, however, abhors static situations, and, if "movement" (that is, conflict) is restricted in one part of the
globe, clearly it must be diverted elsewhere, into arenas that appear to be less
fraught with peril. The term "diversionary" comes to mind and, indeed, the
forms of surrogate warfare being waged today in the other regions mentioned
conform essentially to this category, including not merely rural insurgency
and other forms of societal destabilization, but terrorism, whether waged in
urban centers and/or sophisticated facilities on the ground or in the air.

The editors of this work felt that an in-depth analysis of the international
linkages of what is generally known as "low-intensity operations" was overdue. This does not mean, of course, that the publication lists are wanting as
far as works on terrorism are concerned. On the contrary, a veritable flood
has descended upon the reading public of books reviewing the ostensible
causes and political aims of terrorists, their "psychological profile," sermons
on how to negotiate with terrorists, examinations of the state of mind of
hostages during and after a hijacking, discussions of passive and defensive

countermeasures, and, most of all, regurgitations of morally neutral definitions of terrorism (along the lines of "one man's terrorist is another man's freedom fighter").

The present book does not address itself to any of these issues; rather, it looks upon terrorism as part of a wider problem of surrogate warfare against Western and pro-Western governments, with the primary aim of destabilization and eventual delegitimation (reducing certain countries even to the status of "pariah states"). The growing tendency to view terrorists and their victims in colors of moral and ethical neutrality (resorting to terminology which treats them as essentially equivalent) helps, of course, to reduce legal governments to a position no higher—and, in some cases, even lower—than is occupied by those who assail them. That is not to say that the editors assume the existence of one single center controlling, orchestrating, and sending surrogate combat units into action. The contemporary political arena is simply not that neat or uncomplicated. Nor is this work intended to deny that various insurgent and terrorist organizations pursue political aims that are far from identical or that serious friction between them, often of a very lethal nature, can and does occur.

However, what the analysis of the highly experienced contributors to this book shows (and they have all dealt with the phenomenon in an operational or an analytical capacity), and what the astonishing plethora of accessible witnesses (former initiators and controllers of terrorist and other low-intensity combat), as well as primary source documentation, demonstrates, is the degree of international linkage that exists in terms of coordination of political as well as military actions, financing, communications, movement of men and materiel across frontiers, training, and organization. Those involved are, first and foremost, states supporting terrorism and insurgency, particularly the USSR, its allies, and clients—both communist and Third World states, especially in the Middle East. Others are the "low-intensity" combatants themselves, with an amazing range of links between them, spanning whole continents, from the Caribbean to the Middle East and to Bangladesh, Japan, Italy, and many other areas. In the jet age, it is no major effort to train operatives in one continent and to send them into action several thousand miles away.

In examining these linkages, it is essential to avoid becoming preoccupied with purely military matters; ideological coordination, propaganda and disinformation campaigns, other "active measures," including the political, moral, and even physical annihilation of outstanding adversaries, are no less important, albeit given far less attention by most analysts. Of equal weight is the growing involvement of insurgent and terrorist groups with criminal enterprises, particularly the "Nark-Intern" (Narcotics International), the organized crime entities running international drug traffic, which provide an almost ideal modality for other entities that require an existing channel for transporting explosives, weapons, and combat units across international frontiers, while at the same time financing themselves from the proceeds of the sale of narcotics. It appears that ordinary and political crime have become almost inextricably interwoven.

Given the variety of these manifestations, and the relative impotence displayed so far by the societies under attack, it would not be stretching the imagination too far to speak of combat with "low intensity, albeit with high lethality and frequency, but low jeopardy."

While rejecting the assumption that the organizations in question are mere disparate bands of social misfits whose problems could be eradicated by appropriate reforms, the editors refuse to accept the theory that these entities, and particularly international terrorism, are as mysterious and unknowable as Churchill's USSR or Kant's *Ding an sich*. For one, it was found that material in the public domain demonstrates the increasingly central role occupied by this form of warfare by indirection in such basic documents as the current Program of the Communist Party of the Soviet Union, which devotes a major section to the "National Liberation Movement" and the support it must be given, as well as the present "Brezhnev" Constitution of the USSR, which states in Article 28 that "the foreign policy of the USSR shall be aimed at . . . supporting the struggle of peoples for national liberation . . ." (The previous "Stalin" Constitution did not deal with foreign policy at all.) Clearly, Soviet assistance for "low-intensity operations" is regarded as constituting an essential part of the duty of the Soviet state. In 1975 the late Marshal Grechko left little doubt as to the operational meaning of these documents, stressing the "division of wars into just and progressive if they pursue liberating goals, and unjust and reactionary if they are based on imperialist goals . . . it would be an unjust, reactionary war *in all cases* on the part of imperialist powers . . . [and] just and progressive on the part of the Soviet Union and other socialist states" (Our emphasis).

Article 12 of the Cuban Constitution of 1976 states "the Republic of Cuba espouses . . . the combative solidarity of the peoples and . . . aspires to establish along with the other countries of Latin America and of the Caribbean—freed from foreign domination and internal oppression—one large community of nations joined by . . . the common struggle against colonialism, neocolonialism and imperialism . . ." In April, 1985 the Secretary General of the Communist Party of El Salvador, Shafik Handal, stated in a seminal piece in *Problems of Peace and Socialism,* published in Prague, Czechoslovakia, that "experienced Party workers who are in North America, Latin America and in Europe have begun conducting far-reaching international activities . . . We have come to realize that the essence of revolution as a historical process is *offensive* . . ." (our emphasis).

It may be asked why those who deal with these delicate matters as part of a combined Leninist–Clausewitzian approach to "total politics" should be so candid about the role of such operations in their doctrine and strategy.

The fact is that any organization, no matter how structured and how covert in its actions, must communicate with its supporters, and they, in turn, with one another. Given, moreover, the role of doctrine as a motivating and legitimating factor in the states and movements concerned, manifestoes, declarations, and even highly theoretical articles are an essential ingredient of the conduct of policy. Moreover, they have learned that they can afford to be outspoken, since there appears to be no penalty for frankness. To the contrary, open intimidation elicits trepidation, which manifests itself in a rejection of counter-action by the West. The governments and societies that are the targets of low-intensity warfare seem intent upon ignoring even the material in the public domain.

However, in addition to these open and accessible documents, there are others that have become available, for the simple reason that the operations in question are not immune to occasional setbacks. Significant documents and other forms of evidence can be captured, and have been in such areas as Grenada and southern Lebanon. Others become available because of indigenous resistance to regimes that support destabilization operations in general and terrorism in particular, such as Iran. For the same reason it has been possible to tap former leading practitioners who have "come over from the other side," and without whose eye and ear witness testimonies, the editors of this work would have the bare bones, but not the flesh and blood, of the *Gestalt* we are confronting.

The editors were surprised to what extent those witnesses were approachable (albeit living under pseudonyms and observing strict precautions), and to what degree earlier debriefings had failed to elicit information that is highly relevant to the topic of this book. As a result of the formidable documentation acquired in this way, the editors found themselves convinced, beyond a reasonable doubt, of the vital role played by the international linkages that are increasingly pervasive in the arena of terrorism and related phenomena. This was all the more important since the work was approached without preconceived notions and with little anticipation of the treasures that could be discovered.

The International Security Studies Program of The Fletcher School of Law and Diplomacy was so fortunate as to obtain a grant for the implementation of an Oral History Project that was intended, in the first place, to tap the memories of leading statesmen before the passage of time rendered this impossible. The members of the Program increasingly became convinced that it was more useful to implement this work in a collective rather than an individual manner, and it was decided to interview personalities who had come over from closed societies and had been near to the decision-making process or to operations that reflected that process. At the same time, emigrés from such societies were to be interviewed also, to the extent that their former professions had been in sufficiently significant areas, particularly in science and technology, to make their work the object of decision making at a relatively high level and in a manner that was likely to be observed by them. In a word, we wanted to view the decision-making process "from above and from below." In preparation for these interviews, we gathered a group of particularly talented and knowledgeable graduate students to examine extant literature with a view to compiling a protocol, that is, a highly detailed and carefully documented questionnaire, which would ensure that the interviewees were asked the most relevant questions, in the most precise manner, covering lacunae in the available publications, as well as elucidating contradictions in that literature. As this instrastructure work proceeded, however, more and more interviewees became accessible, and we discovered that our group of graduate researchers had become expert to a degree which enabled them to be most valuable participants in the interviews and in the subsequent work on this volume, particularly Part II, "The Witnesses Speak." The fact that a number of the interviewees happened to have first-hand knowledge, from "the other side," of the support, coordination, and direction given by regimes sponsoring "low intensity operations," actually was an unanticipated boon. (Part I of the work was the result of a gathering of leading personalities, engaged operationally or analytically in combatting the "Hydra of Carnage" which constitutes the title of this book. That meeting, covering a period of some two and a half days, took place in April of 1985.)

The editors acknowledge with gratitude and with great satisfaction the work of these graduates: Messrs. Nicholas Dujmovic, Randall J. Scheunemann, Steven L. Wilensky, Walter A. Levin, Mark D. Edington, Mark H. Dawson, Ronald J. Czarnetzky, Shah Y. Azmi, Roger H. Rotondi, Dale A. Baker, and Martin B. Swartz. We believe that their contribution demonstrates that genuine education depends on much more than merely the material taught in the classroom.

The International Security Studies Program of The Fletcher School of Law and Diplomacy acknowledges with deep appreciation and gratitude the support granted so generously, from its inception, by the Sarah Scaife Foundation, Inc., and, particularly for the Oral History Project, by the Howard J. Pew Freedom Trust. The editors wish to express their appreciation for the dedicated work done by Mrs. Freda Kilgallen, Mrs. Roberta Breen, Ms. Geraldine Wilson, and Mrs. Jean Noble-Neal.

Part I
The International Linkages of Terrorism and Other Low-Intensity Operations

Section A
The Nature of the Problem

1
The International Linkages—What Do We Know?

William J. Casey

The work of the Fletcher School's International Security Studies Program has provided an appropriate forum for us to grapple with the grim and sobering reality of world terrorism. International terrorism has become a perpetual war without borders. To the extent that I can, I shall explain how the American Intelligence Community assesses this dreadful scourge and how I think we should deal with it.

In just a few years we have witnessed the bombings of our embassies in Beirut and Kuwait, the attack on United States and French forces in Beirut, the vicious attack on the South Korean Cabinet which took place in Rangoon, the assassinations of President Bashir Gemayel and Prime Minister Indira Gandhi, the attempted assassination against Prime Minister Margaret Thatcher, and the attempt that was made against Pope John Paul II in St. Peter's Square.

In confronting the challenge of international terrorism, the first step is to call things by their proper names, to see clearly and say plainly who the terrorists are, what goals they seek, and which governments support them. What the terrorist does is kill, maim, kidnap, and torture. His or her victims may be children in the schoolroom, innocent travelers on airplanes, businessmen returning home from work, political leaders—diplomats in Paris, London, Los Angeles—or legislators like those on whom machine guns were turned in the 1950s here in Washington. The terrorist's victims may have no particular political identity, or they may be political symbols, like Aldo Moro or, perhaps, Pope John Paul II. They may be kidnapped and held for ransom, maimed, or simply blown to bits. One defining characteristic of the terrorist is the choice of method: the terrorist chooses violence as the instrument of first resort.

We are engaged in a new form of low intensity conflict against an enemy that is hard to find and harder still to defend against. The number of recorded international terrorist incidents rose from about 500 in 1983 to more than 700 in 1984. Last year 355 international terrorist bombings occurred, nearly one for every day of the entire year.

U.S. citizens and property have always been among the most popular targets of international terrorists. Last year a large number of attacks also were directed at the French, the Jordanians, and the Israelis. The Middle East remains a fertile ground for terrorism. There were ominous developments in West Germany, where leftwing terrorist groups combined forces and began attacking NATO targets.

Terrorism has been with us for a long time. But it once manifested itself in fundamentally different forms than those we see today. Earlier in this century we saw forms of terrorism that usually had their roots in ethnic or separatist groups and confined themselves to a small geographic area and to very selective targets. Even today, remnants of this brand of terrorism still are with us—the Basque Separatists in Spain, the Irish Nationalists in Northern Ireland, the Moro Tribesmen in the Philippines, and other ethnic terrorist groups.

Since the late 1960s we have witnessed the birth and rapid development of a new stripe of terrorism which is primarily urban and for the most part ideological in nature. In Europe, for example, extreme leftwing ideology has spawned such urban terrorist groups as the Red Army Faction in West Germany, the Communist Combat Cells in Belgium, the Direct Action in France, and the Red Brigades in Italy. In the Middle East, we may mention several extremist Palestinian groups—including some factions of the Palestine Liberation Organization (PLO). In South America, which has been relatively peaceful on the terrorist front for the past decade or so, similar groups seem to be maturing in countries such as Chile, Colombia, Ecuador, and Peru.

Today we also have state-supported terrorism used as an instrument of foreign policy. The chief protagonists of this new departure in international murder are Iran, Syria, and Libya. Probably more blood has been shed by Iranian-sponsored terrorists during the last few years than by all other terrorists combined.

Tehran uses terrorism as a major element of its ongoing campaign to export the Iranian revolution throughout the Muslim world and to reduce Western influence—especially that of the United States—in the Middle East. In 1983, we identified as many as fifty terrorist attacks with a confirmed or suspected Iranian involvement. Most of these incidents occurred in Lebanon, where radical Shiites of the Hezballah operated with *direct Iranian support* from terrorist bases in the Syrian-controlled Bekaa Valley. To protect themselves from direct retribution, they try to mask their acts under the nom de plume "Islamic Jihad."

Iranian-sponsored terrorism was a major factor elsewhere in the Middle East in 1983 as well. Members of the Islamic Call Party—who received training and direction from Tehran—successfully carried out six bombings on 12 December, including one blast that severely damaged the U.S. Embassy in Kuwait.

Iran also continued its active recruitment and training program for Muslims from the Persian Gulf, Africa, and even Asia. Many of these individuals will be available for subversive or terrorist operations in the future, particularly in the oil-rich Persian Gulf states. Most alarming in 1984 was the accumulating evidence that Iranian-sponsored terrorism was increasing in scope and effectiveness in Western Europe. For example, in July the French arrested three individuals suspected of being Iranian agents, and an Air France flight was hijacked from West Germany to Iran. In August and September, Islamic Jihad claimed credit for armed attacks on Saudi and Kuwaiti nationals in Spain, and in November seven pro-Iranian Lebanese students in Italy were arrested after plotting an attack on the U.S. Embassy in Rome. We believe that agents working out of Iranian embassies and Islamic cultural or student centers in several European nations will continue to attempt such operations in the future.

Although Libya's Mu'ammar Qadhafi is not in the Ayatollah Khomeini's league, still his reliance on and support for terrorists is well known and must go unchallenged no longer. We identified at least 25 terrorist incidents last year involving Libyan agents or surrogates. The main target of Libyan terrorism was anti-Qadhafi exiles in Western Europe and the Middle East. In March the British arrested a number of Libyan agents following a series of bombings that injured at least 30 people in London and Manchester. Most of the victims were innocent bystanders. In April, a gunman firing from the Libyan People's Bureau killed a British policewoman and wounded 11 anti-Qadhafi demonstrators. Following the siege of the People's Bureau, British police found weapons in the building, documenting once again Libya's practice of stocking weapons and explosives in its embassies—a clear violation of international diplomatic conventions.

Some of the many factions of the PLO also practice terrorism. The PLO is actually something of an umbrella organization for eight or nine often-warring factions with varying ideologies and competing sponsors such as Iraq and Syria. Although the PLO's influence is somewhat diminished in recent years—due primarily to its defeat in Lebanon in 1982 and heightened factionalism—many of its member groups remain a credible threat to Israel and many Western governments. Syria controls or at least influences many of the radical splinter groups of the PLO that are believed to be behind recent terrorist attacks on moderate Palestinians and other Arabs—especially Jordanian officials.

For several years, various European left-wing terrorist groups have called for the establishment of an international united front against "Western Imperialism," and particularly against its most powerful symbols—NATO and the American presence in Europe. Since the summer of 1984, at least three of these groups—the West German Red Army faction, the French group Direct Action, and the Belgian Communist Combat Cells—have apparently collaborated in a terrorist offensive against NATO that reached a fever pitch of violence by early February, 1985.

The offensive seems to have begun in August with terrorist attacks in Paris on the Atlantic Institute, the West European Union, and the European Space Agency—all targets that a Direct Action communique wrongly asserted were associated with NATO. Then, in October, the Belgian Communist Combatant Cells bombed several multinational firms because of their connection with NATO military activities.

More and increasingly coordinated violence ensued in December. Belgian terrorists bombed the NATO pipeline system at six points. At the same time, the Red Army Faction and its supporters in West Germany began a long-planned offensive—more than 30 imprisoned terrorists began a hunger strike, while dozens of bombing attacks against targets associated with NATO were carried out in solidarity with the hunger strikes.

In late January/early February 1985, the offensive reached its zenith. In Belgium, the Communist Combat Cells bombed a U.S. military recreational facility and declared its intention to inflict casualties as well as property damage in future attacks. In West Germany, the Red Army Faction continued its bombing campaign and assassinated industrialist Dr. Ernst Zimmerman. In France, Direct Action assassinated a senior official of the Ministry of Defense, General Rene Audran. At the same time, French Direct Action prisoners began a hunger strike in sympathy with their German terrorist colleagues. Following the Audran and Zimmerman killings, the West German and French terrorists ended their hunger strikes and the wave of anti-NATO terrorist attacks in northern Europe abruptly stopped—probably only temporarily.

Now, to turn for a moment to the Soviet connection. It may seem shadowy to some, but it seems very close to me. Iran and the Soviet Union are hardly allies, but they both share a fundamental hostility to the West. When Libya and the PLO provide arms and training to the communists in Central America, they are aiding Soviet-supported Cuban efforts to undermine our security in that vital region.

In the Middle East, the Soviets and their East European allies have provided intelligence, weapons, funds and training at camps in the Soviet Union and elsewhere in Eastern Europe. Those passing through these training camps receive indoctrination in Marxism-Leninism which provides a rationale for terrorism and violence against civilian targets—all in the name of wars of national liberation.

To give the devil his due, we have seen only indirect evidence of East Bloc involvement in the murders and bombings now carried out by the Europeans themselves. Publicly, the Soviets posture loudly and pietistically that they disapprove of terrorism and that terrorism is "leftist adventurism" and "simplistic ideology." At the same time, I don't see the Soviets taking any action whatsoever to assist victimized governments in curbing terrorist activities.

Moreover, the USSR and its East European allies have allowed West European terrorists to transit those countries en route to the Middle East. Some East European countries have also been uncooperative in the extradition of terrorists under international arrest warrants. It is also interesting to note that relatively few Soviet targets worldwide have become the victims of terrorist attacks. Moreover, rarely do we hear of a terrorist attack taking place in the Soviet Union or in a Soviet-dominated country where there is totalitarian control. Only four terrorist incidents were reported for 1984 for the whole of Soviet-dominated Europe.

The fact is that over recent years the Soviets have changed their operational techniques and have become increasingly sophisticated in their use of "active measures" against the West. The USSR can now achieve its aims quite well *indirectly* by providing training to selected individuals and very small groups, by providing logistical support to the groups, and upon occasion, by providing weapons and explosives to various groups. It does not have to provide much, if any, money. The terrorists obtain all they need from armed robberies of banks, ransoms from kidnappings, and thefts of materials and weapons from Western European governments and private enterprises; they are able to purchase weapons—including Soviet-made weapons—on the black market.

The Soviet Union makes little attempt to conceal the extent of its financial and military aid for countries like Libya and Syria—countries that have adopted terrorism as part of their state policy. The Soviet leaders are quite willing to sell Libya any weapons it requires. The Syrians also receive considerable quantities of arms from the Soviet Union. Many of these weapons are passed along to the Palestinian groups for use in Lebanon or Israel. Some of these weapons find their way to radical groups far from the hills of Lebanon.

Even more serious is the continuing willingness of Moscow and its allies to allow radical groups to maintain offices in Eastern Europe and to grant safe passage to operatives traveling to Western Europe or elsewhere to commit terrorist acts. No one can seriously believe that these activities—which have gone on for at least fifteen years—have escaped the notice of the Communist authorities.

The chain extends around the globe. Part of the subversive threat we face in Central America is stimulated by outsiders who are well-versed in terrorism. For example, Italian Prime Minister Craxi stated in early February that Nicaragua hosts 44 of Italy's most dangerous terrorists—a statement corroborated in part by a former Red Brigade terrorist who stated that at least five of his former comrades now serve as noncommissioned officers in the Sandinista Army. Nicaragua, by the way, is a major recipient of aid from Libya, and recently played host to Iranian Prime Minister Musavi. Strange how the same names and faces keep turning up whenever the subject is international terrorism!

I would now like to turn briefly to the murky area of collusion between the big drug dealers and the terrorists and their supporters. These two groups have radically differing goals. Drug dealers are after one thing only—money, and lots of it. They are, above all, merchants who wish to preserve their trade. Drug dealers see their interest as being the corruption and gradual control or manipulation of the established regime—to include the buying of policemen, security agents, judges, members of parliaments, and even premiers. Money is the means and also the object for the narcotics pushers.

Terrorists, on the other hand, are out to *destroy* the existing system. If they had their way, they would not corrupt the policemen and judges—they would kill them. Moreover, money is useful for buying weapons, paying operational expenses, and perhaps for buying intelligence and other information. But the terrorist is above all ideological, not mercenary. He or she is committed to overthrowing the established system.

This said, there is cooperation between some terrorist and narcotics groups for at least tactical reasons. A symbiotic relationship has grown up between the narcotics dealers along the Caribbean Coast and the Revolutionary Armed Forces of Colombia, two groups who ordinarily would have little to do with one another. The drug merchant needs a secure transit point for his goods to reach markets in the United States. One such transit point is Cuba. The Cubans funnel arms and money to the guerrilla groups through drug merchant channels. Although Fidel Castro roundly denies having dealings with drug merchants, in interviews with American journalists, we've caught him red-handed. By helping drug dealers push cocaine and marijuana, Castro gains improved access to the Cuban community in South Florida, contributes to crime and disorder in the United States, and aids his revolutionary offspring in Colombia. Similarly, we caught the Sandinista government in Nicaragua red-handed in narcotic production and trafficking between Colombia and Miami, apparently looking for money which we have seen deposited in Panama and used to bolster their sagging economy.

Terrorist methods are becoming more sophisticated. Explosives that are remotely detonated or set off by a fanatical suicidal vehicle driver are examples of both technical and tactical innovation. All of the risks associated with terrorism by small groups are greatly enhanced by the involvement of certain states in the planning, financing, training, documentation, and provision of safe haven for terrorist groups.

With the help of a sponsoring state, they are able to use more sophisticated techniques, to draw on state-funded training programs, and amass equipment and arms that are more violent, more deadly, and more difficult to detect. Such sponsorship provides them also with improved intelligence gathering and their planning, official travel documents, and sometimes the use of diplomatic cover to mask their true identities, movements, and munitions deliveries. Finally, they find safe haven in a sponsoring state after an attack.

Radical states see in terrorism the potential of obtaining concessions from other states that could never be obtained by traditional diplomatic means. Our ability to endure in our policies is being called into question and confused by terrorism. Our decision-making processes are disrupted by terrorism. Confidence in the workability of our institutions is eroded. And unless we deal effectively with it, our international credibility will be seriously weakened, as happened at the time of the Iranian hostage crisis some five years ago. Perhaps worst of all, terrorism has become a tempting instrument to accelerate social, political, and economic collapse.

In several European and Latin American states, small numbers of revolutionaries, disdainful of the electoral process and unable to win popular support through the ballot box in any case, have indeed succeeded in converting the climate of opinion from one that sustains parliamentary debate into one that encourages blows and counterblows, violence and counterviolence, and a resultant breakdown in parliamentary institutions.

Clearly, the Soviet Union and its allies all have grasped the potential of terrorist movements for disrupting societies, particularly in the so-called Third World. Clearly, they have recognized that throughout Asia, Africa and Latin America there are weak governments with low levels of legitimacy and high levels of instability. To a degree far greater than is generally realized, these governments are acutely vulnerable to terrorist disruptions, and are therefore inviting targets to terrorist campaigns. In providing terrorist movements with arms, training, and political support, the Soviet Union and its allies have thus discovered a highly "cost-effective" way of making the point that in today's world it is not safe to practice democracy.

"National liberation movements" is the name given to groups supported by the Soviet Union and associated states seeking power by violence. Some have become confused about the differences between insurgency and terrorism. An insurgency—that is, openly using armed conflict as a means for seeking movement or concessions from a dictatorial or totaliarian government that has denied peaceful forms or redress of grievance or civic change—can readily be distinguished from a group that attacks a democratic society by taking hostages or by placing suitcases filled with explosives on board airliners full of innocent people. The distinction between terror used in defense of society and terror used to destroy society is really not so difficult. Many, however, have become confused by the semantics of totalitarianism, by the specialists in propaganda.

The level of training and organization that has enabled international terrorism to challenge established governments is simply beyond the reach of local, isolated terrorist groups. International terrorism is inconceivable apart from the financial support, military training, and sanctuary provided to terrorists by certain states. To seek the causes of terrorism in the behavior of societies victimized by terrorism is thus to look in the wrong place. Rather, these causes are to be found in the convictions and expectations of the terrorists themselves and in the activities of those states that find it in their interest to support international terrorism—the Soviet Union and its satellite states in Eastern Europe, Libya, Syria, Iran, Iraq, North Korea, the People's Democratic Republic of Yemen, Cuba, and Nicaragua.

How do we cope with these small bands of highly trained people, most of them fanatics, many ready to give up life itself to do their evil work, increasingly sophisticated as they move around the world crossing borders with officially and professionally prepared papers, knowing that they will have no trouble obtaining weapons, explosives, and whatever else they need near the site of their intended attack, knowing too that they will be able to find protection and sanctuary pre-arranged for them? We can combat this only with the highest professionalism, dedication, and diligence.

We need to know and understand the various terrorist groups, their style and operating methods, their support structures, the training camps which sprout up around the world. This is a task of continuing collection and analysis of intelligence in which the civilized nations of the world must cooperate. We need to provide security and protection for our people and our facilities. We need to provide the most advanced security and police methods. But against a threat which can move so quickly, widely and quietly, none of us can do it alone. With increasing tempo and effectiveness, we are developing a worldwide counterterrorist network, made up of the intelligence, security, and police organizations of the threatened nations. They exchange intelligence, share data banks, work together operationally, provide training and technical capabilities to the less advanced of their number, undertake surveillance and other intelligence assignments for each other, report their findings, and transmit alerts and warnings.

Terrorist groups are a very tough nut for intelligence to crack. They are small and not easily penetrated. Their operations are closely held and compartmented. They move quickly and place a high premium on secrecy and surprise. Yet prompt reporting and prompt follow-up action does frequently forestall terrorist incidents. The most common example is forewarning to U.S. and foreign embassies or other institutions, of actual threat or strong indications of planning for attack on installations or individuals. The usual response is heightened alert, increase in protective measures, or change in plans and schedules. Recently, for example, intelligence on a threatened hijacking of a foreign commercial airliner resulted in a change in travel plans and police work which prevented the intended hijacking. In other instances in Europe, the Middle East, Africa, and Latin America, U.S. officials and businessmen directly targeted by terrorists have been temporarily removed from their posts. On several occasions, our warning and detailed intelligence have directly assisted foreign authorities in capturing terrorists. Through timely intelligence work, two sophisticated suitcase bombs were intercepted and disabled and warnings on the nature of these types of bombs were provided promptly to intended and potential victims worldwide. This warning led to the discovery of two more such devices by cooperating services.

On the other hand, there are many false alarms. The volume of threat reporting has almost invariably escalated dramatically in the wake of a headline-making terrorist incident. At such a time, some individuals seek to market "information" they know has become salable. At the same time, our own intelligence collectors are energized by major terrorist events to ferret out any information, even seemingly marginal, concerning possible planning for attacks that could threaten U.S. lives and property. The flip side of this is that when such threat reporting rises, more reports of dubious credibility than normal tend to make it through the system that is designed to filter them out. This can also produce false confirmations. We have made very good progress in developing a system of very rapid communications to gather assessments, have reports tested by intelligence experts in our other governments and pass conclusions quickly to the point of threat.

What is our policy in dealing with terrorism? The practice of international terrorism must be resisted by all legal means. State-sponsored terrorist acts or threats are hostile acts and the perpetrators or sponsors must be held accountable. Whenever we obtain evidence that an act of terrorism is about to be mounted against us, we will take measures to warn and protect our citizens, property and interests and our friends and allies as well. Terrorism is a common problem for all democratic nations and we must work intensively with other countries to eliminate this threat to free and open societies. We will use every possible diplomatic and political avenue to persuade those now practicing or supporting terrorism to desist. Acts of state-sponsored and organized terrorism are to be appropriately exposed and condemned in every available forum.

Our own government is now engaged in large-scale efforts to improve the physical security of our diplomatic missions and overseas facilities. Training programs are now mandatory for sensitizing our diplomatic and military personnel to the nature of the terrorist threat and the steps that every individual can take to improve personal protection from terrorist attack. We are working closely with many other governments to improve the quality and quantity of the security that is provided to our personnel and facilities abroad, and we are expanding our capabilities to provide additional protection to foreign diplomats and dignitaries, as well as visitors here in our own country.

The United States does not use force indiscriminately. But we must be free to consider an armed strike against terrorists and those who support them where elimination or moderation of the threat does not appear to be feasible by any other means. We face very difficult and sensitive problems in choosing appropriate instruments of response in each case. Yet, we cannot allow this to freeze us into paralysis. That is exactly what the terrorists now expect. Just as we will not bargain—and that, as you know, has been for some years our declared policy.

We cannot and will not abstain from forcible action to prevent, preempt, or respond to terrorist acts where conditions merit the use of force. Many countries, including the United States, have the specific forces and capabilities we need to carry out operations against terrorist groups. If we do not use those forces where their use is clearly justified, we lose both the direct benefits of action and the deterrent value of having the capability to retaliate. We need that deterrent. We cannot permit terrorist groups or their sponsors to feel they can make free and unopposed use of violence against us. We must demonstrate our will to meet a terrorist challenge with measured force applied quickly when the evidence warrants. We cannot permit terrorists and their sponsoring states to feel that we are inhibited from responding or that our response will be so bogged down in interminable consultations or debate that we, in fact, do not have a deterrent.

International terrorism is the ultimate abuse of human rights. We should be prepared to direct a proportional military response against bona fide military targets in a state which directs terrorist actions against us. We need not insist on absolute evidence that the targets were used solely to support terrorism. Nor should we need to prove beyond all reasonable doubt that a particular element or individual in that state is responsible for specific terrorist acts. There is today, for example, sufficient evidence that radical Shia terrorists are responsive to Iranian guidance for us to hold Tehran responsible for their attacks against U.S. citizens, property, and interests.

The legitimacy of using force against terrorism depends on our also making strong efforts to deal with this challenge by means short of force. Physical security, training, diplomatic efforts, the improvement of institutions for sharing our resources and knowledge with other countries, the force of law—all these measures must also be applied in an integrated fashion as rigorously as possible. We must continue to prove our ability to wield all of these elements of national power—political, economic, diplomatic, military, informational, and covert—against the scourge of terrorism.

In my view, Western nations have, on the whole, been weak in applying economic, political and diplomatic measures to check state terrorism. Sanctions, when exercised in concert with other nations, can help to isolate, weaken, or punish states that sponsor terrorism against us. Too often, countries are inhibited by fear of losing commercial opportunities or by fear of provoking further terrorism. Economic sanctions and other forms of countervailing pressure impose costs and risks on the nations that apply them, but some sacrifices will be necessary if we are not to suffer even greater costs down the road.

Examples of how the international community can move in concert are the 1973 Convention for the Suppression of Unlawful Acts Against the Safety of Civil Aviation (the Montreal Convention) popularly known as the Anti-Hijacking Convention, and the 1979 International Convention Against the Taking of Hostages. The international community should put teeth in existing agreements of this sort by severely punishing violators.

Today, there are additional initiatives that must be taken bilaterally and multilaterally if we are to deal with this problem effectively. For example:

We should review international treaties and agreements that define diplomatic privilege to identify standards of diplomatic practice and behavior which could be more vigorously enforced. We may need new international measures to counter misuse of diplomatic privileges by states sponsoring terrorist activities.

Although the issue of extradition is dealt with bilaterally under normal circumstances, terrorism violates all civilized norms. We should think about developing international treaties whereby 1) persons who commit terrorist acts against citizens of signatory states could be routinely extradited, 2) individuals who use false passports or other documentation and who cross international boundaries can be detained to permit investigation of the purpose of such travel, and 3) individuals known to be involved in terrorism can be prevented from entering any signatory states.

It would be an important signal for those nations signatory to existing counterterrorism conventions and agreements to proceed to ratify those agreements. Five European nations, for example, have yet to ratify the Strasbourg Convention (European Convention on the Suppression of Terrorism).

Terrorism aims at the very heart of civilization. We have no realistic choice but to meet it, and that means head on, when nothing else works. The aim of terrorists and the ultimate objective of those who sponsor, train, and supply them is to undermine our values, to shatter our self-confidence, and to blunt our response.

In the absence of a national will to fight terrorism at its roots, we must be content only to cope with terrorism's effects—not its cause. A strong beginning has been made. Parliaments have begun to authorize funds and governments to establish effective counterterrorist units. Intelligence and security services are developing new capabilities and improving their methods and performance. A work such as this goes far to air the tough issues in dealing with terrorism and directs public attention to this vital subject.

Section B
Historical and Contemporary Manifestations

2
Political Warfare in Totalitarian and Traditional Societies: A Comparison

Adda B. Bozeman

T he occurrences which we group in such categories as terrorism, political warfare and low-intensity conflicts or operations have been normal aspects of internal and external statecraft in all cultures with which I am familiar—except that of the West. The reason why we in the West did not formulate this important new vocabulary earlier is found in history.

There was no world-spanning political system before the seventeenth century. Rather, societies existed and interacted for centuries, even millennia, in "closed systems," that is, systems that are regionally and culturally separate. Most if not all of these were conflict systems in the sense that peace and war were interpenetrating and generation after generation was conditioned to tolerate high levels of conflict and violence.

The European order started out as simply one among many. However, it was the only one that deliberately distinguished—conceptually and practically—between peace and war. Each of these conditions was carefully circumscribed and regulated by an objective law that purported to speak to everyman. This factor, together with the expansion of the West's power and culture, explains why the Orient and Africa were gradually drawn into the so-called Modern European States System, and why many in the West, notably in the United States, became persuaded that diversity—and therewith international anarchy—had been superseded once and for all.

These expectations were cancelled, however, from about the middle of this century onward under pressure of several closely related circumstances:

1. The steady development and diffusion of Marxist–Leninist totalitarianism and the consequent rise and expansion of three communist totalitarian empires—those of the Soviet Union, Mainland China, and North Vietnam;

2. The decline of the West's power and prestige throughout the world;

3. The dramatic resurgence, throughout the Orient, Africa, and Latin America, of traditional dispositions in matters of internal and external statecraft, and with them, of conflict systems which we had deemed defunct.

It is with these developments in world affairs in mind that I welcome this important volume, with the editors' challenging agenda and invitation to come to terms with the new concepts and realities of terrorism, political warfare, and the varieties of so-called "low-intensity conflict" which bring such high-intensity violence to nations throughout the world.

The four questions I addressed in this chapter are as follows: 1) How did rulers in traditional closed societies employ political warfare and extreme forms of violence against foreign adversaries? 2) Did they also employ surrogates and mercenaries for these purposes? 3) Did these rulers establish guidelines for utilizing these measures? 4) What continuity exists between the ways in which traditional rulers employed these techniques and how they are exercised by present-day governments?

Several premises are implicit in these questions, one of which is communicated explicitly in the following terms: the direct and indirect use of these techniques by contemporary totalitarian states is not a new development, but can be traced back to earlier times. It cannot be denied that international history is dense with records of political warfare, extreme forms of violence, and low-intensity conflicts as defined by Richard Shultz in a recent paper on this subject.[1] It is also true that some elements of this conflict syndrome—that is, the psychopolitical penetration of adversaries, wars of nerves, limited or irregular military engagements, and the employment of surrogates and mercenaries—have often been essential ingredients of political and military arsenals in Europe and North America. A noteworthy example from the period of the French and Indian wars is "Roger's Rules of Rangering or Ranger's Standing Rules for Rangering" (1756)—a complete and forthright primer on the craft of covert and guerrilla warfare that stood earlier generations of fighting Americans in good stead, and that would make healthy reading for present-day members of congress and other citizens who lapse into trauma at the mere thought of an American involvement in that so-called "illegal" and "immoral" covert war in Nicaragua.[2]

It is an indisputable fact that generations of nations in diverse cultures have known institutionalized terror. However, its sources and forms, as well as the actual human experiences induced by it, are so strikingly various that they can hardly be covered by any one definition. For example, *Safire's Political Dictionary* identifies "terrorism" as "persuasion by fear; the intimidation of society by a small group, using as its weapon that society's repugnance at the murder of innocents."[3] This definition may be appropriate for contemporary western opinion, even though it does not make allowance for psychological and mental techniques of political terrorism. However, it does not come to terms with the heavy incidence of institutionalized yet arbitrary violence in traditional non-Western societies. Killings on an elaborate scale, as for example human sacrifices, have been essential aspects of statecraft—both religious and secular—in several high civilizations of the Near and Far East as well as in the American Indian empires and Africa's folk societies and kingdoms. What one learns from available records is that levels of tolerance for conflict, violence, terror, and death have traditionally been higher in the Orient, Africa, and Indian America than in the Occident, and that the regular enactment of awesomely violent rites and punishments was characteristic of many ancient non-Western cultures.[4]

In short, the precedents for violent statecraft had indeed been set in earlier times. Whether these precedents are relevant for an understanding of modern totalitarian techniques and whether they entitle us to speak of continuities is another question. The answer will be affirmative if we can identify the societies or cultural spheres in which these techniques were steadily employed, and if we can conclude that the present complex of terrorism, irregular armed struggles, insurgency, and so forth repeats patterns previously set in the same society or at least in the same culture. In other words, I disagree with the assumption, implicit in question 1, that techniques advanced by modern totalitarian states can be traced automatically to precedents set by earlier societies. Further, I see no justification in international history for identifying all of the latter with "rulers in traditional closed societies".

It cannot be denied that non-Western, noncommunist perspectives on time—specifically on the relation between past, present and future—accentuate the supremacy of the past in ways alien to the Western, so-called Promethean view. However, nowhere in the world has the remembrance or the dominion of the past been absolute. Rather, life everywhere has had a way of interpenetrating with the past by bringing forth new ideas or new mutations of old ideas and therewith new approaches to the governance of internal and external affairs.

This has changed with the advent of twentieth-century hardcore totalitarianism, which is Marxist-Leninist in essence and which constitutes, in my view, an entirely new development in thought and statecraft.[5] Whether viewed as ideology or political system, communist totalitarianism stands for the legitimacy of total power over human life and thought, the human past, and human conceptualizations of realities and facts. Two diverse experiences illustrate this propostion. A Czech historian's reflections on the Soviet Union's relentless campaign to impose Leninist totalitarianism on his native land brought this poignant unassailable judgment:

> The first step in liquidating a people is to erase its memory. Destroy its books, its culture, its history. Then have somebody write new books, manufacture a new culture, invent a new history. Before long the nation will begin to forget what it is and what it was.[6]

A young Chinese, buffetted by Maoist "struggle sessions" to recognize as "truth" only what the party leadership established from occasion to occasion, gave this analysis of her experience: "If the leader says of such and such an event, "it never happened"—well, it never happened. If he says that two and two are five, well, two and two are five. This prospect frightens me much more than bombs."[7]

In addition to staking out absolutist control over time, Marxism–Leninism demands total power over space. Communist statecraft is thus committed to limitless territorial expansion, and therewith to the abolition of "bourgeois" notions of the sovereign state and distinctions between "foreign" and "domestic" matters. It is also committed to the liquidation of democracy, law, and other noncommunist forms of government, and the invalidation of non-Leninist international systems.

Lastly, the totalitarian ideology was conceived of, and is being administered as, a combat doctrine on all levels of life and human relations. The "adversary" here is therefore not identified primarily with a threatening or aggressive foreign state. Rather, all human beings—whether within or without the nominal frontiers of today's Gulag state—are "the enemy" because they may not be trusted by the ruling clique of the day. Leninist totalitarianism thus stands for hatred, violence, and war. Its logic stipulates that the dictatorial command post, whether embodied in the politburo, the KGB, the *nomenclatura*, or their surrogate equivalents, has the unrestrained right to invent, select, and deploy whichever tactics are best suited for advancing its "cause" and increasing the power of its imperialist directorate.

A review of the steady and ongoing realization of these doctrinal theses throughout the world supports the case for the uniqueness of Marxism–Leninism in the history of international political thought. However, it is also true that three forces not of communist making have lent considerable momentum to the evolution and consolidation of hardcore totalitarianism in this century. One is the revolution in communication, which facilitates territorial expansion and political control. The second is the scientific revolution in biology, genetics, chemistry, physics, medicine, and technology, which provides protagonists of totalitarianism with the ultimate techniques to effect the total subjugation of man. The third force that favored totalitarianism in this century is the West's political, moral, and intellectual inattentiveness to the development of Marxism–Leninism in thought and statecraft. This oversight on the part of the West explains why the Soviet Union, acting under the protective auspices of the Modern States System, could go on cancelling the independence of states (beginning with those in Eastern and Central Europe) by masterminding low-intensity conflicts, including terrorism; why it could succeed in invalidating international law with its neat distinctions between internal war and interstate war; and why, in short, we no longer know how to think about war.[8]

The Totalitarian Phenomenon

Hardcore totalitarianism today is indentified with the Soviet Union and each of its nominally sovereign but actually dependent satellite states in Europe and Asia: mainland China; the new (North) Vietnamese empire, which includes the formerly independent states of South Vietnam, Laos, and Cambodia; North Korea; Cuba; Nicaragua; Ethiopia; Zimbabwe; Angola; Mozambique; and numerous terrorist nonstate bands that are internationally operative across political frontiers. Milder, essentially non-Leninist forms of totalitarianism are represented today by Libya (which I view as an emanation of Colonel Mu'ammar Qadhafi's personality); the Shiite theocracy of Iran, which is rooted in religious fanaticism rather than in secular ideology; and the majority of Black Africa's despotic states. Here, too, one must make allowance for the force of ancient religious beliefs which sanction what we regard as wanton abuses of human integrity. Further, and unlike other non-Western societies in modern times, in light of repeated regime changes, it is difficult to formulate reliable estimates of an African state's political and ideological configuration.

What was the incidence of violence, terrorism, low-intensity operations, and war in these provinces of the world before the advent of Leninism? Did ruling establishments employ surrogates or mercenaries in the conduct of their foreign relations? In short, can we speak in terms of either continuities in patterns of statecraft or compatibilities between traditional patterns of statecraft and those fashioned in this century by totalitarian thought and tactics?

Answers to most of these complex questions can only be found in history. But since history is neither science nor ideology, and since it instructs different historical minds differently, it may not provide all the answers. The past existence of the Inca Empire in what is today Peru is a well-documented fact, and so is the present-day existence in Peru of the Sendero Luminoso (Shining Path) terrorist group. This is a Maoist split from the Peruvian Communist Party which follows totalitarian strategies of terror while fighting the usual Leninist–Maoist "protracted people's war" with subsidies from foreign communist principals. However, the guerrillas also think of themselves as heirs to the pre-Colombian Inca empire, a formidable military power which was administered by a religious bureaucracy wielding awesome powers over men. To "revive" the Inca splendor and prestige after its five-hundred-year lapse, but to do so on the model of communist totalitarianism, is one of the avowed objectives of the Shining Path.[9]

A comparison of the Shining Path with the Incas in terms of past and present lifestyles, propensities for violence, and techniques of political warfare does point to certain concordances, but not, in my opinion, to continuities. The same conclusion suggested itself when I examined the relation between the totalitarian Khmer Rouge of Kampuchea, their illustrious forbears, the Khmer of Cambodia, and *their* immediate predecessors, who created the unique civilization of Angkor in Indochina as well as an expansionist yet deeply religious kingdom—one destined to be severely tested throughout its long history.[10]

Do these visions and uses of the past express a genuine longing for continuity in time, or are they tactics of deception and exercises in disinformation on behalf of the totalitarian principle that time and history mean what the communist apparatus says they mean? Questions such as these illustrate the plurality of time perspectives, the occasional waywardness of the historical imagination, and the ambiguities of historical references in today's international discourse. Nevertheless, they are too important to remain unanswered. Not only do they affect the integrity of history, which is a strategically vital academic discipline especially in the West, but they are also critically relevant to present-day U.S. decision making in foreign affairs.

Twentieth-century records show, however, that this dimension of statecraft has been uncongenial to Americans because they tend to identify politically significant time with the last two hundred years—the timespan of their own existence as a separate state—rather than with the last two thousand five hundred years. Yet, it is this latter time frame which should be our major reference when we speak of "earlier times," since it is the gestation period not only of western civilization and thus of the main idea systems that sustain the U.S. today, but also of all the other culturally distinct contemporary societies with which we are involved.

This decidedly ahistorical American frame of reference explains why we overlook the obvious fact that all politically organized nontotalitarian societies in the world are not only older by centuries if not millennia but are also more consciously attuned to the past. Further, when seen in conjunction with the trend to think materialistically about the destinies of nations, it explains why we cannot satisfy the elementary requirement of statecraft—namely, that of understanding "the other" on his own terms.

Understanding in a general sense is well-defined by the German historian Wilhelm Dilthey as insight into the working of human minds and therewith as the ability to penetrate the mental states or processes which lie behind outer manifestations. In the framework of diplomacy and intelligence, "understanding" thus means that one knows the mainsprings and patterns of thought of foreign societies and that one is able therefore to assess and influence their plans and movements, detect deception, and distinguish singular occurrences from regularities and continuities in conduct.

This kind of challenge was illustrated by Herodotus in his account of direct and indirect warfare between the Persians and the Greeks. This type of "understanding" is also the main theme in the long history of the Venetian intelligence system. At the core of this establishment were erudite, highly disciplined envoys and secret agents who knew how to evaluate the long-range significance of events, whether recorded in Europe or Asia; how to recruit reliable informants; and how to size up the character traits and political dispositions of influential personages, whether in the Papal court in Rome, the Byzantine Christian empire, the capitals of Europe, or the far-flung domains of Mongols, Turks, Persians, and Arabs. The information thus collected was regularly submitted to the Venetian government in the form of official ambassadorial reports (*relazioni*). These were carefully preserved over the centuries in well-organized, readily accessible archives that had the ultimate function of conditioning successive generations to understand foreign societies realistically on their own terms and to develop unifying time-transcendent perspectives on the republic's national interests in world affairs.

This unusual conception of statecraft and intelligence could be concretized successfully even in the most stressful periods of any type of conflict or war because the Venetian databanks did not simply contain summaries of recent developments, biographical profiles, accounts of a given area's geography, local laws, and governmental institutions. Rather, and most importantly, they were replete with precise references to historical precedents for each of the phenomena to which an envoy had drawn the Senate's attention so as to establish politically significant continuities.

History, then, was deliberately used here as the primary tool of political analysis both at home and abroad because it "contributed to the reputation of states" and because it instructed rulers "in the management of their daily business," thus assisting them "to foresee with greater prudence the things to come . . ." This was the main reasoning in a Decree of 1530 which stipulated the appointment of an official historian who would guard the abiding values and traditions that sustained the identity of the Republic in both time and space.[11] This reasoning also persuaded the Florentine historian Guicciardini to take note of the conviction shared by "certain of the oldest and most reputable members of the Venetian Senate that Venice enjoyed a particular advantage in her ability to wait for the opportunity of times and the maturity of occasions."[12]

Since the mind of Venice seems reincarnated in the minds of the editors of this volume, and since the position of Venice in the world environment from the thirteenth to about the seventeenth century is not unlike that of the United States today, I do not hesitate to follow some Venetian guidelines for probing the relation between "then" and "now" and for tracking international linkages between principal powers and their surrogates. This led me to focus on today's principal totalitarian power—the Soviet Union—and the precedents for its techniques of statecraft in "earlier times."

The question is *which* earlier times? I could not very well relate Moscow's "active measures" to the Incas and their human sacrifices, or the Fulani divines and their fierce jihads in the Sudan and the Sahara, or to the orders of the Shiite Assassins and the Hebrew Zealots. Although all of these phenomena are relevant for the general problems which this work addresses, as well as for the particular problem of understanding the warring ways of specific peoples in the Middle East, Black Africa, and parts of the Americas, they are irrelevant to the case at hand.[13] Reflections made it clear that I had to stay *within* the culture zones in which the Soviet Union evolved, and this led to linking it to the Byzantine Empire. Given more space, one could add a discussion of the linkages between Maoist China and Imperial China. Such a "dual focus" would be useful, since 1) the two "earlier times" coincided at least for one millennium (Byzantium was extinguished in 1453 when it was "tunnelled" into defeat by the Turks); 2) both traditional empires were hard pressed, and greatly influenced, by the Mongols; and 3) Russia and China are jointly responsible for the evolution of North Vietnam and North Korea—Imperial China tutored them as its hedge-guarding satellites while the Soviet Union converted them into totalitarian surrogates that specialize today in deploying terrorism as state policy. But for the sake of brevity, linkages between Maoist and Imperial China will only be discussed briefly at the end of the chapter.

The Byzantine Empire

The Byzantine Empire excelled in developing and deploying most of the political techniques under discussion here.[14] Indeed, it endured from the fifth to the fifteenth century by dint of its mastery in psychopolitical warfare and diplomacy. Throughout these turbulent centuries, it was a superpower coexisting with other expansive superpowers, among them the Western Christian Commonwealth, Persia, a variety of powerful Islamic caliphates (from the seventh century onward) and, farther East, the Sinocentric universe.

The Empire itself consisted of a complex array of European, African, and Asian provinces. It was a Middle Kingdom, for beyond its periphery and separating it from the broad circle of other empires was a ring of lesser entities—some settled, some nomadic. Among these restless peoples were the Bulgars, Avars, Petchenegs, Russians, and Seljuk Turks who never ceased transgressing imperial boundaries, laying waste to state areas, and threatening the capital. Checking these intrusions after they had occurred was one challenge. But the experience of these ongoing encounters made it clear that the interest of the Empire required not only military vigilance but also long-range policies that would control the population movements on the periphery and, if necessary, accommodate those foreign elements that seemed intent upon settling in the close vicinity of the imperial state. Byzantium responded to these conditions by creating gradually an intricate system of political controls in which secondary states came to serve as clients and surrogates capable of holding each other in check and keeping the great powers at bay. In neither of these concentric rings of state could Byzantium rely solely on its military forces as an adequate shield against its foes. Aggressive moves on the part of one or several foreign nations had to be anticipated, forestalled, or weakened whenever possible if the Eastern Christian Empire was to gain mastery over the adverse elements of its geographic and political position.

This Byzantine design was formulated and deployed by a corps of scholarly bureaucrats who represented all governmental services, including the imperial establishment, the Church, the treasury, the army, and above all a comprehensive foreign intelligence system. They were the persons who found the ways and means of making the central government generally respected within the orbit of imperial power, who assured the stability of the nation's social life by maintaining the rule of law, and who protected the mystique of the imperial establishment by controlling an elaborate court ceremonial. It is interesting to note that they were recruited from all ethnic and cultural components of the cosmopolitan Byzantine state.

Quite in contrast to the Holy Roman Empire of the German nation, where theory and policy converged on clear distinctions between peace and war—Byzantine Eastern Rome was conditioned to regard war as an ever-present possibility and to trust the standing army as the chief instrument for the survival of the state. Yet the army was deliberately kept small, the theory being that its real strength did not lie so much in its numbers as in the intelligence with which it faced the Empire's enemies. It was then the business of military administrators to learn each opponent's particular method of warfare and to assemble a whole arsenal of stratagems and tricks that could be employed to demoralize, weaken, or outmaneuver possible antagonists. Only when the enemy's defences had been thoroughly undermined would Byzantium employ its fighting forces. The army would then be guided by elaborate instructions outlining techniques for the feigning of flights, staging of night attacks and ambushes, and the conduct of truce negotiations for the purpose of winning time. Similar principles guided the operations of the navy until the eleventh century, when Byzantine naval strength was permitted to decline.[15]

All Byzantine conceptions of the function of war and the uses of the armed forces were made possible by the Empire's successful establishment of a money economy and a permanent fisc or state treasury, which had an apparently inexhaustible capacity to make payments.[16] This achievement explains why the emperor could pay salaries, that is, why he did not have to remunerate his vassals for their military aid by granting them land.

Whereas the imperial government was most economical in the use of the military, it was lavish in its expenditure on the arts of diplomacy. Vanquished nations—whether Bulgaria or conquered parts of southern Italy—were treated with calculated mildness and given latitude in self-government, albeit under the strict control of imperial commissioners. Except for extreme cases in which the defeated proved to be entirely intractable and were removed to other districts, the government ruled by indirect and devious means, skillfully exploiting such human foibles as ambition, pride, cupidity, and jealousy. New tribes invading the domain were appeased by grants of territory or of political status, while settled nations were often kept from rebellion and aggression simply by the annual payment of subsidies, or by fixed remunerations in return for some useful political function. For example, Justinian subsidized the Utigurs as long as they kept the Huns from attacking Cherson and Bosporus. Such arrangements were not restricted to the so-called "barbarians." In the tenth century, Byzantium paid Venice for policing the Adriatic, Syria for protecting the eastern frontiers, and various Armenian states for replenishing the ranks of the imperial army.

This particular political method of utilizing lesser nations also proved profitable when Byzantium had to cope with great powers that could neither be bought nor defeated. When Justinian wished to divert Persia's attention from the imperial boundaries, he found ways of persuading the Huns and Arabs of the desert to harass this enemy. Indeed, the Byzantines discovered in the course of their international dealings that most people could be induced to quarrel with their neighbors. This inexpensive diplomatic tactic proved particularly effective among the undeveloped, unsophisticated barbarians whose predatory designs the government had reason to fear. Byzantine diplomats were therefore continuously engaged in sowing the seeds of suspicion and discord among the lesser nations in the immediate vicinity.

However, the general diplomatic record shows that the imperial agents were also acutely conscious of the intellectual and cultural vacuum that existed in most border regions. They were therefore committed to the task of filling this vacuum by diffusing Byzantine jurisprudence, literature, and art, and by conducting special orientation programs for kings and other leaders. Under the terms of this policy (it was initiated by Justinian), young chiefs arrived at the imperial court either as guests or as hostages; others, exiled from their home country, were granted asylum or educated as pretenders to native thrones. Quite contrary to the miserable treatment usually meted out to envoys from great powers who were enemies by definition, those from the satellites were befriended, protected, educated, and entertained during their sojourns in Constantinople.[17] Also, and since the Byzantines were masters in the art of evolving forms—whether in architecture, liturgy, court etiquette, or diplomacy—the lesser emissaries or chiefs were deliberately drawn into the empire's courtly system, where they were decorated, titled, given crowns, sceptres, and, if their services were deemed especially desirable, even Byzantine princesses in marriage.[18] Indeed, symbolism, as employed by the Eastern Empire, became an international political language through which the government could convey the power and the unity of the empire to its multifarious component groups, whether literate or non-literate.

This policy of acculturation reached its greatest moral and intellectual depth in the missionary activities of the Eastern Christian Church, which penetrated the interior of all surrounding areas, specifically those inhabited by Slavic peoples. The missionaries seemed to have known as well as the empire's secular intelligence agents that the leadership principle was the pivotal point in the political organization of most barbarian nations. Their proselytizing efforts were therefore usually initiated by attempts to convert the native chief and his entourage. Vladimir of Kiev, for example, received baptism after his capture of Cherson in 988, and his conversion was followed by Vladimir's marriage to the Byzantine princess Anna and the collective baptism of his pagan subjects.

Most carriers of the orthodox faith did not confine their efforts to the titled and illustrious. Rather, as illustrated by the so-called apostles to the Slavs in the ninth century, they were determined to bring the illiterate simple folk into the orbit of the church. The wide-spread diffusion of Byzantine theology, jurisprudence, literature, and art that followed in the wake of these efforts was thus eventually tantamount to the creation of a more or less ideologically unified orbit.

At its epogee, the Byzantine system encompassed great powers and ancient civilizations as well as small nations and culturally undeveloped societies. It also addressed a great variety of goals. Most of these pertained to that inner ring of nations which separated the state from the other great powers of the world. Here Byzantine diplomats had the mandate of maintaining the empire's existing spheres of influence and of coping with the steady pressure of barbarian tribes by drawing the new arrivals into the circle of hedge-guarding imperial client states that was meant to serve as an outer line of defense.[19] This design was translated into fact by the establishment of a complex constituency of satellites, vassals, and surrogates in all quarters of the Eurasian world.

Within the fluctuating boundaries of this great orbit, Byzantine diplomacy was required to ascertain the degree of control that could be exercised over each separate community and to supervise the evolution of each particular relationship. It also had to counter whatever competitive appeals rival great powers might address to these lesser states or tribes, to keep abreast of native movements toward independence, and if need be, to modify or discard outworn terms of suzerainty. A summary view of the entire diplomatic record shows that the Byzantines were able to execute most of these intricate assignments. Indeed, in regard to culturally less developed and politically weaker nations, they displayed such an ingenuity in finding patterns of both accord and control that one is justified in defining their statecraft as the science of managing barbarians.[20]

Byzantine political theory assumed that the emperors themselves were most qualified to deploy this science. But even the most proficient emperor needed assistants if the empire's foreign policy was to be systematically transacted. This service was rendered by a special department of external affairs and an elaborately organized and highly trained body of agents whose status and prestige in the society were fixed in all details.[21] While on duty abroad, they were to collect as much information as possible about the domestic affairs of the host country. Envoys to barbarian courts were always instructed to study the habits, morals, and institutions of all tribes in the vicinity, ascertain their military strength and weakness, follow the flow of commerce and the trends of intertribal and regional relationships, watch for and investigate internecine quarrels, identify existing and prospective leaders in the district, and analyze vulnerable traits in the personalities of barbarian chiefs.[22]

The Second Rome, that is, Byzantium, declined steadily even as it celebrated some of its greatest triumphs. Its power was sapped steadily on each of its frontiers because it was locked in conflicts with the rival Christian commonwealth in the West; because it could not cope militarily with the stream of determined Islamic conquerors;[23] because it was unable to manage all of the incoming aggressive barbarians all of the time; and because many satellite states composed of erstwhile barbarians had themselves become ambitious aspirants for super power status. The end came in 1453 when the Islamic Ottoman Turks succeeded, after numerous attempts, to take possession of Constantinople.

As preceding references have indicated, Byzantine influences had by that time permeated all neighboring realms. However, most of these realms, including the Turks and other Islamized peoples as well as Venice, proceeded to fashion their own identities and techniques of statecraft, often in stark counterpoint to the legacies received from the Second Rome. In that context we can therefore not speak of meaningful continuities between "then" and "now." The situation is altogether different when we turn to the Russians, who were a steady presence in Byzantium's orbit.

Prominent as mercenaries, surrogates, and even as "surrogate allies" in later times, Russians were also feared as aggressive, unprincipled traders who routinely engaged in piracy and plunder when they were thwarted in their designs. This militant commercialism came to constitute state policy after the Russians took control of Kiev and then established their first state. The focus of their militant commercial expeditions was Constantinople. At least six such semiwars, or "high-intensity operations," were staged against the city of their desires between 860 and 1043, some of which had devastating effects upon the imperial capital, where the Russians continued to be viewed as inferior barbarians and their princes deemed to be vassals. Some treaties, however, were nonetheless concluded in the course of this ambivalent relationship.[24]

These ever-latent animosities and conflicts were offset by mutual goodwill when it came to the legal resolution of disputes. After all, the Russians had become thoroughly "byzantinized" in this respect, and Kievan jurists collaborated effectively with their imperial counterparts in formulating legal provisions for the treatment of civil and criminal offences as well as a clause binding the contracting parties to aid shipwrecked merchants. Yet nothing in the records on either side suggests the acceptance of an international law that distinguished between "peace" and "war."

The linkage with Byzantium ceased officially when the first Russian state was subjugated by the Mongols. However, it revived after the overthrow of the Tartar yoke in the fourteenth and fifteenth centuries, the establishment of the Muscovite Tsardom, and the extinction of the Second Roman Empire when the Tsars conceived their own imperial designs.

Not suprisingly, these designs were in many respects modeled on Byzantine precedents. Two spiritual principles in particular appealed to the Russians as techniques for empire building: the idea of the church-state and the idea of the unity of the orthodox world. Both could be used to justify and sublimate the territorial and personal aspirations of the tsars. Further, and since it was being realized that the Russian people had become deeply susceptible to the myths, symbols, and rites associated with policies of the fallen empire, the leaders became adept practitioners of the art of manipulating these phenomena on behalf of their own ambitions. Indeed, several legends and symbols were invented—and history distorted—to bolster trust in Moscow's divinely ordained mission to become the new Constantinople,[25] and also the legitimate heir of the First (imperial classical) Rome, and therewith superior over the rest of the European states. These claims were announced in doctrinal form in the early part of the sixteenth century when an orthodox monk proclaimed that Moscow was the Third Rome, charged with the sacred mission of saving mankind—a mission in which both Western Rome and Eastern Rome had failed.[26] This doctrine could become the principal consolidating force in the early Russian state as well as one of the chief determinants of the Russian orientation toward other states and peoples, because it was linked from the beginning of the country's history with the power of the national state and the ambitions of its autocratic rulers. It is in this essentially nonspiritual rendition that the idea of Moscow as the Third Rome found expression in the Tsardom of Moscow, thereafter in the Empire, and in the end, in the Third International.[27]

Most scholars of precommunist Russia have acknowledged the continuance of Byzantine traditions of statecraft and diplomacy in their homeland.[28] Soviet studies affirm the influence of both Byzantines and Mongols on the evolution of the Russian state.[29] R. Vipper extols the centralized military monarchy of the Mongols in which all social forces were effectively organized for war, but he also pays tribute to Byzantium.[30] Indeed, and as Kluchevsky confirms,[31] the Russians of the Mongol era were adept practitioners of the Byzantine art of influencing people. Muscovite princes thus never dreamt of openly resisting the Mongolian overlord, since they knew very well that the Horde could be dealt with more easily by "peaceful cunning" ("détente" in our times) than by force of arms. Liberation was achieved because the Muscovites managed the Mongolian himself as the instrument of their schemes.

These brief surveys of Byzantine and Russian methods of statecraft suggest the following answers to the four questions outlined above. 1) Although the Eastern Christian Empire certainly cannot be described as a traditional closed society—a term more appropriate to its different Russian progenies—it did employ political warfare. In fact, in my opinion, its mastery of this diplomatic method has never been surpassed or even equalled. "Resort to extreme forms of violence against foreign adversaries," by contrast, was avoided. 2) The use of surrogates and mercenaries constituted the essence of Byzantine statecraft. 3) The records are replete with guidelines on how to manage low-intensity conflicts.

In reply to the fourth, and main question—What continuity exists between the ways in which traditional rulers employed these techniques and how they are exercised by present-day governments?—I have come to the following conclusions. There are indeed definite parallels or near analogies between Byzantine and Soviet techniques of political warfare, low-intensity operations, the use of surrogates, and so forth. However, the significance of these affinities or continuities cannot be estimated unless one remembers that orientations to foreign affairs are everywhere reflections of a given society's basic internal norms and values. In the case at hand it is unquestionably true that Russians have sought and cultivated the Byzantine connection for over one thousand years, and that Kievan Russia is the root from which the later tsarist empire grew. But as the preceding section of this chapter suggests, documentary records of thought and behavior in domestic as well as foreign affairs also show that successive Russian states have deviated substantially from the models set by the Eastern Christian Empire, that the ancient root system of concepts and values were severely disturbed by the Mongols and their immediate tsarist successors, and that it has been decisively sapped in our century by Marxist–Leninist rule.[32] (The only order of ideas that has so far withstood destruction is Russia's version of the Greek Orthodox faith).

In light of the radical transposition, and even the eradication, of some fundamental principles of persuasion, it should not be assumed therefore that the two sets of political techniques, however similar in their surface manifestations, originate in similar modes of reasoning or are meant to serve similar strategic purposes. Thus it should be remembered that the Eastern Christian

Empire had at no time been a gulag-state (and, as I suggested earlier, never could have been), and that governmental power, however authoritarian, was firmly and openly kept in check by several factors which have absolutely no equivalents in the totalitarian Soviet empire. For example, in the general context of the Greco-Christian tradition it was assumed that the monarch would always honor the dictates of *philanthropia*—an unwritten moral obligation that required him to serve his subjects in a humane way. This commitment was buttressed by the classical Roman theory that government is an obligation, not a privilege, by the express precepts of the Greek Orthodox faith which was the state's religion, and by the ecclesiastical establishment's highly respected "oversight" function in all governmental matters. Now it is true that the imperial policies and actions of the orientalized Eastern Christian Empire were not decisively affected by the kind of constitutional law that was formulated in the Western Christian Empire on the model of the classical Roman law. For example, Justinian codified the civil law of Rome, and most of his successors—aided by a corps of dedicated jurists—saw to it that Eastern Rome remained a "law state," in contrast not just to all other contemporary Near Eastern empires but also to the present Soviet Russian empire.[33]

There is a second reason why Byzantine and Leninist political reasonings differ significantly. Whereas Byzantium's strategic design was fashioned to assure the identity, security, and survival of the state in an international society of entities that were highly diverse both culturally and politically, the Leninist imperium is built to achieve global hegemony. It should be noted that the two designs agree with all eastern traditions—including those of Kievan, Mongol, and Muscovite Russia—in *not* polarizing conditions called "peace" and "war", and are thus in opposition to ruling Western concepts of international order. The Occidental law of nations, which is rooted in such a juxtaposition, therefore has no equivalent in either of the eastern domains.

This agreement on the interpenetration of war and peace explains why political warfare and "irregular" military operations could become leading themes in the foreign policies of two quite disparate imperial societies. Yet it is almost irrelevant for a study of continuities in statecraft, because war and all its subspecies are associated with functions in Soviet ideology and practice that would not have been consonant with the self-image, world view, and strategic design of the Eastern Christian Empire, and that are therefore missing from Byzantine records.

In stark contrast to Marxist-Leninist doctrines, Byzantium was not seized either by hatred for all that is other than the party line as defined on a given day or by lust for total power and trust in total destruction. Nor did it subscribe to theories of permanent war and revolution or of the absolute need for armed struggle and armed victory. Rather, it sought to reduce the threat of war to dimensions that would allow for the effective management of low-intensity conflicts. Genocidal wars aimed at total subjugation, on the order of those fought by the Soviet Union in Afghanistan or by Sovietized Vietnam in Cambodia and the rest of Indochina, would not have been fathomed in Constantinople. Nor would state-sponsored terrorism have been condoned as either a legitimate or an effective weapon against foreign adversaries. In these, as in many other respects, Eastern Christian Rome simply did not become just another Oriental despot on the order of the Assyrian, Mongol, or radical Islamic prototypes. This may explain why no auspices were provided either for the kind of terrorist fraternities represented by the Assassins and the Zealots, who operated in early times, or for the kind of Leninist terrorist "action groups" and bands of urban guerrillas that prove to be effective instruments of communist policymaking in our times.

Other Soviet deviations from Byzantine norms can be isolated if the following factors are borne in mind. Byzantium was an authoritarian church-state. Its governing institutions were what they openly professed to be. All of them were superbly served by intelligence services which had a variety of far-flung tasks, but they were at no time functions or expressions of a covert system of administration on the order of the communist party, its special buros, policing organs, local cells, and globe-spanning secret networks. Front organizations of the type set up by Leninist regimes in noncommunist countries singled out for destabilization, revolution, or takeover, therefore had no precedents here. On the other hand, it is certainly true that psychological and political warfare was as common in Byzantine as it is in Soviet statecraft. Further, it is incontestable that the different Russias, including the Soviet Union, learned how to camouflage weakness and wield power inexpensively from the Byzantines. The Soviet tactic of intimidating and humiliating emissaries of "great" powers while nursing the egos of the weak through flattery may thus be viewed as a replay of Byzantine statecraft.

Further, and as set forth in earlier pages, one finds in both systems a heavy reliance on satellites, surrogates, and mercenaries. However—and this is in my view the chief area of Soviet deviations from Byzantine patterns—the relationships between the imperial center on the one hand and the Soviet Union's satellites and foreign agent-nations on the other were fashioned in radically different manners and served entirely different purposes. Contrary to the Soviet design—which requires the same absolute ideological and political conformity from its political dependencies that it requires from its individual subjects at home—the Byzantine design called for a form of tutelage or trusteeship not unlike the one instituted first by the West's modern colonial administrations and thereafter by the charter of the United Nations. Being a cosmopolitan civilization renowned among contemporaries as the foremost center of learning, Constantinople relied mainly on acculturation rather than obedience to heavy-handed controls to keep its hedge-guarding satellites in order. Literacy, Christianity, law, and education were thus implanted in several areas, but policies to re-Christianize Islamic Arabs or turn Catholic Italians into Greek Orthodox Italians were not pursued.[34] Indeed, upward mobility was the theme in the Eastern Roman Empire's orbit of vassalage. Dependencies—whether civilized or barbarian—could retain and develop their own traditions even as they were enriched by Byzantium's deliberate promotion of art and learning, the rise of commerce, and the consolidation of urban life. However, neither their status of inferiority nor the functions they served in the context of Byzantium's strategic design went unacknowledged.

All this stands in stark contrast to the administration of the multicultural Soviet imperium. In Eastern and Central Europe—the area of greatest strategic importance for the USSR—war diplomacy, coups d'état, and low-intensity operations were skillfully managed from the 1940s to the 1960s to reduce once independent states to the status of Soviet provinces. Moscow's communist party apparatus recruits and controls the leading personalities in each local government while its armed forces are firmly ensconced along the long North/South frontier now separating the Leninist imperium from what is left of Western Europe. Yet each of these dependencies retains statehood as a camouflage on the scene of world politics so that it can cast its pro-Soviet vote in negotiations and debates with noncommunist or anti-Soviet states. This double game assures the Soviet Bloc superiority in the United Nations and other international organizations set up on Western constitutional foundations. It also legitimizes the Warsaw Pact as an alliance of sovereign self-determining states equal to that of NATO, and it provides the underpinning for such other multilateral but anti-Western compacts as the Helsinki accords, which ratified the Soviet conquests in 1975.

The imperial center's relationship with Eastern Europe has a special poignancy not found in its relations with other satellites. Quite unlike Byzantium, the Soviet Union is culturally less developed than most if not all of its European provinces.[35] Not only does it lack princesses to give away, it has nothing to teach or suggest either in aesthetics, letters and art, or urban and economic development. Having left the shores of humanism, cast off the precommunist Russian heritage, and opted for totalitarian politics and the garrison state, Moscow rests its case for leadership on providing compulsory education in subversion and all categories of regular and irregular warfare and on deploying and guiding surrogates—specifically Bulgaria and East Germany—in the transaction of low-intensity operations and terrorist business.

The basic Soviet game plans that are operational today in non-Western regions of the world are the same as the ones just reviewed. However, the records accumulated in the last decades in the Caribbean, Central America, the Middle East, and Africa show that the tactics employed in these regions have striking affinities with some of the methods put into play by the Eastern

Roman Empire in so-called "barbarian" lands. In fact, I tend to think that the Byzantines would not have been as adept in their dealings with Black Africa as the Muscovites are today.

The theme of convergence and continuity here as in some other traditional but undeveloped areas of the so-called Third World is knowing how to select a few local personages for surrogate status and how to shape their minds and characters in desired molds. Marked divergences from Byzantine patterns emerge, however, as one reflects on the biographies of several generations of African leadership and their relations with the Soviet master-mentor. For in the Soviet context the task requires producing totalitarian regimes subservient to Moscow's brand of Leninism by 1) knocking out some traditional loyalties and inhibitions while exploiting such deeply rooted beliefs as trust in magic and ancestral power; 2) stirring up jealousies, suspicions, and above all antagonisms to the West; 3) exacerbating ever latent tribal warring dispositions; and 4) modernizing customary guerrilla warfare.

By and large the Soviet Union has succeeded in each of these respects. That is to say, it has been well served by those who came to wield totalitarian power over Ghana, Guinea, Guinea-Bissau, Congo-Brazzaville, Ethiopia, Angola, Mozambique, Zimbabwe and others. The losers here are the societies that are forced to serve the dual communist tyranny. Deprived of their African heritage and identity, poorer and more conflicted than ever before, they exist today as battlefields for alien causes and as "Kingdoms of Death" for their own human kind.[36]

The same brand of "individualization" (and needless to say it is an expression as well as a tactic of Leninist totalitarianism) marks the Soviet play in the Middle East and Central America. The Islamic states of West Asia and North Africa are not "first class" as either satellites or surrogates. Yet Moscow has been successful in conditioning several of the despotic regimes so that they will act reliably in surrogate capacities. Well served by the KGB and its dense web of international agents, Moscow knows not only how to capitalize on inter-Islamic conflicts and the regionally shared enmity to Israel but also how to key into the fanatical hatred of the United States that consumes the Ayatollah Khomeini and other radical Shiites, and how to give covert guidance and support to Colonel Qadhafi's transterritorial designs for murder—in short—how to delegate the task of terrorizing the rest of the world.[37]

The pattern of depending on ruthless, power-seeking personalities to whom active (that is, unsavory) measures can be safely entrusted also marks Soviet statecraft in the Caribbean and Central America. Here however, as in Eastern Europe and the newly communized states of Black Africa (foremost among them Ethiopia), the chief clients are Marxist–Leninist hardliners. Further, and as revealed by the *Grenada Documents: An Overview and Selection,* the Soviet Union itself has been calling most of the shots in the entire region because its long-range strategic plan requires the transformation of the states adjacent to the United States into Soviet satellites on the model of those in Eastern Europe.

This plan was initiated several decades ago with the conversion of Fidel Castro into an ardent and imaginative propagator of Moscow's brand of Leninism and the concomitant casting of Cuba as chief ideological and military training ground for the Third World's younger generation, supplier of mercenaries for revolutionary battle service in Latin America and Africa, and principal base of operations for planning and enacting psychopolitical warfare, guerilla wars, coups d'état, and all other manner of low-intensity operations in disparate parts of the noncommunist world. Most of these interventions are carried out openly. An interesting exception is the protracted, but ultimately strikingly successful, ideological campaign of transposing Christianity into a subspecies of Marxism, during which scores of Jesuit priests and exponents of other Christian orders and churches in the two American hemispheres were induced to become willing agents of an atheist empire.

Castro's Cuba occupies a unique position in the Soviet Union's hierarchical imperial order. It is no satellite, but it is dependent on Moscow—it receives guidelines and fulfills surrogate, even mercenary, functions. Yet it outranks such states as Mengistu's Ethiopia and probably also North Korea. The question of whether the Soviet/Cuban connection has an analogue in the history of Byzantine statecraft arises naturally in the context of this paper. Venice comes to mind, but must be ruled out because Eastern Rome was not an ideologically unified system and Christianity then was not the ideology it appears to be now. Further, and most importantly, Venice never surrendered its national, religious, and intellectual identity. In the limited context of comparing relations between principal centers of power and their surrogates, however, it may be argued that the status of the Adriatic republic resembles that which the communist Vietnamese empire in Indochina occupies today in the Soviet design. For while it has been serving Moscow in important surrogate functions, it has retained the characteristics of what used to be North Vietnam and therewith also those that link its long precommunist history to that of precommunist China.

China

Mainland China today is a totalitarian empire built on Marxist–Leninist–Stalinist principles. But contrary to the Soviet Union, which can be identified only with this political ideology and the operational code it spawned, communist China is also heir to the Han, Sui, T'ang, Ming, and Manchu dynasties. That is to say, it continues to rest on an authentic, self-contained, and creative civilization which had endured for at least twenty-five hundred years before it underwent its transformation in the middle of this century under the aegis of the Soviet motherland of socialism. The theme of continuity is thus being rendered differently here.

Successive generations of Chinese have thought of the space they occupied not as a territorially bounded state but as the abode of "civilization" writ large. As such it fancied itself absolutely and perennially superior to all other societies. Contrary to Russia, which began its career in history as an inferior first to Constantinople and then to the Mongol conquerors, China started out as Asia's superpower in 221 B.C. after the victory of the state of Ch'in over all other warring states had led to the establishment of a unified empire.

The intellectual force that determined these political achievements emanated from a school of thought known as the Realists or Legalists. The essence of this science, fully developed in the fourth and third centuries B.C. in the writings of Sun Tzu, Lord Shang, and Han Fei Tzu, is the uncompromising recognition that war and organization for war are the mainstays of government, and that people are best subdued by busying them in war and agriculture and by threatening them with punishment. Peace, by contrast, is presented in this literature as a misfortune bound to breed "the Six Maggots," among them detraction of warfare and shame at taking part in it.

In the Realist context, then, China is cast in the mold of an imperial despotism in which unity and order are sought through the principle of absolute subordination to the emperor in his role as carrier of heaven's mandate, and in which lesser peoples are by definition subject to imperial tutelage, chastisement by punitive war, and conquest when this is deemed necessary and possible. In the Confucian context, by contrast, the empire is experienced as a family of nations, analogous to the classical Confucian model of the natural family, in which inferior peoples had assigned roles. Yet here, too, the emphasis is on the duty to punish badly ruled states and to chastise unruly barbarians on the periphery of the Middle Kingdom.[38] It goes without saying that this concept of the righteous war often served as a moral cloak for open acts of aggression, and these were usually undertaken after atrocity stories concerning the society singled out for punishment had been spread.

The steady interpenetration of these two schools of thought[39] provided the underpinning for China's remarkable system of managing low-intensity conflicts and waging political warfare. Quite apart from the fact that the latter can raise no serious political and moral problems if war in its general sense is a cultural given, two characteristics seem noteworthy. One is that all Chinese regimes, including the present, have accepted history as a source of statecraft—a striking divergence from the ahistorical bent of the Soviet mind. However, the two communist regimes are at one in their commitment to control human understanding of the past and put historiography in the service of strictly ideological purposes. Indeed, Mao Tse-tung had an advantage over his Russian counterparts when he silenced millions of thinkers after the "Hundred Flowers Period" and during the "Cultural Revolution" because he could legitimize his totalitarian programs by referring to those of China's first unifier, the Emperor Shih Huang Ti, which included the notorious "Burning of the Books" (also of some scholars) in 213 B.C.

The other characteristic in Chinese statecraft that has traditionally assured successful political warfare is the purposeful stress on ideas and on ways of manipulating human minds. This was well illustrated in Maoist China by the determined effort to resolve the controversy between Confucianist and Legalist Schools so as to bring it into a dialectically satisfying relationship to Marxism/Leninism/Maoism and thus give "history its proper place as a science."[40] In other words, the freedom to falsify and "disinform" in the service of power politics was taken for granted here as in Tsarist and Soviet Russia.

What is unique to China is an unwavering commitment not to compromise the integrity of its basic norms and institutions. This was well illustrated in the seventeenth century when most of the "red" barbarians (that is, the Europeans, including the Russians) were induced to relinquish their own commitments to the principle of state sovereignty and equality and to comply instead with the requirements of the Chinese tribute system. Between the mid-nineteenth and early twentieth centuries, by contrast, when the Chinese position in world affairs had weakened, and when Peking felt impelled to accommodate Western notions of international law, their diplomats proceeded as follows. They officially "received" Martin's translation of Wheaton's text on the subject, but they provided it with a foreword which announced that even though the practices set out in the work might not be followed by China, the book would nonetheless serve as a useful aid to Peking in planning "border defense"—that is, as a manual for dealing with western "barbarians."

These and earlier episodes in imperial China's statecraft corroborate Jean Escarra's observation[41] that the Chinese invariably returned to the wisdom of the Legalists when they felt threatened by foreign influences. And the core of that wisdom is that it is necessary to wage indirect as well as direct warfare if the country and the people are to be preserved.

This challenge was not as easily met in reality as it was in theory. For China, not unlike Byzantium, was actually a "middle kingdom" which bordered several established realms and always had to contend with aggressive (or simply nomadic) peoples, chief among them the Mongols and the Russians. Nonetheless, traditional China could expand and sustain itself in ever-changing circumstances because successive dynasties knew, from the period of the warring states onward, how to apply Legalist guidelines for military and psychopolitical warfare. As expounded by Sun Tzu in his classic work on *The Art of War*[42], these included the following maxims:

All warfare is based on deception.

Thus, those skilled at making the enemy move do so by creating a situation to which he must conform.

He who knows the art of the direct and indirect approach will be victorious.

The philosophy underlying these and numerous other instructions is presented in Chapter 3 on "Offensive Strategy":

When you are ignorant of the enemy but know yourself, your chances of winning or losing are equal.

If ignorant both of your enemy and of yourself, you are certain in every battle to be in peril.

Therefore I say: Know the enemy and know yourself; in a hundred battles you will never be in peril.

The Chinese thus learned early that only double knowing of this kind can assure successful strategic deception—and therewith maximum victory—on the interlocking planes of psychological, intellectual, political, and military operations. However, and as Scott A. Boorman reminds us[43], the art of attacking by stratagem is not merely outwitting an enemy—whether in internal or external statecraft. Rather, it aims at breaking his will without fighting by manipulating his view of the world and inducing him to contribute to his own encirclement.[44] Accounts from the long period of the Warring States thus tell us in great detail how to create false impressions, use divination as a ploy in psychological warfare, and exploit the vanity of opponents. We also learn that trusted defectors served as intelligence collectors, that alliances in the enemy camp were skillfully disrupted, and that states were neutralized. In one significant episode an aggressive large state got at its real opponent by striking at the most accessible satellite of that opponent.[45]

As the Chinese heartland moved southward and dependence on barbarian border peoples increased, China was often forced to deploy indirect tactics. These included matrimonial alliances with strategically placed tribes, dividing potential enemies, recruiting surrogate tribes, military manpower and intelligence operatives, and taking hostages. The latter evolved into standard practice during later dynasties and has remained a fixture also in Communist China as the Maoist use of Tibet's Panchen Lama and Cambodia's Prince Sihanook illustrates.[46]

Other enduring traits in the Chinese art of direct and indirect war were exemplified in imperial responses to offensive actions of Japanese "marauders" in the sixteenth century. As listed by Fairbank[47] the repertoire included offers of pardon, patronizing friendship, subornation of colleagues, poisoned wine, moral principles, false intelligence, procrastination, beautiful women, bribery, banquets, threats, lies, assassination, and deployment of troops.

In short, history shows that peace and war were not neatly distinguished in this civilization. The Chinese did not either "declare" war or proclaim martial law, and international relations were not conceptualized as relations between equal states. This explains why military warfare was usually attended by what would be called in the West "excessive violence," why diplomacy was rendered in terms of political warfare, and why no orderly system of diplomatic representation evolved. Envoys were sent to barbarians, it is true, but their missions consisted of scouting, observing, and spying, and their safety was nowhere assured. It goes without saying that envoys *from* barbarian lands were viewed as hostile agents bent on ferreting out Chinese secrets.

The classical Chinese approach to the conduct of foreign affairs proved inadequate in relations with Japan (whose leaders had learned from experience as well as from Sun Tzu that the arts of war and peace were the two sides of the coin of statecraft), Russia, and the West.[48] However, it had been impressively successful in fashioning a sinocentric universe which included Korea, sections of Southeast Asia, among them Annam and Laos, as well as vast stretches of Inner Asia that were controlled by diverse Mongol societies. Although Sino-Mongol syncretisms evolved naturally in the course of 2000 years of coexistence, the area was not absorbed territorially until the Manchu administration chose the military solution.[49]

All of these outlying societies together constituted the emperor's international family even as they formed a belt of tributary states which was consistently viewed as merely the outer fringe of the Middle Kingdom. Control over this vast area was exercised on an ad hoc basis, we learn from Immanuel C. Y. Hsü,[50] by reliance mainly on the principle of playing the barbarians off against each other. When serious hostilities erupted either on the frontiers or in the interior, the government had to opt for one of two responses: a straightforward military solution, called "extermination"; or an indirect political solution, called "pacification," supported by threats of military action.[51]

The tribute system which required periodic missions to and from the imperial court, in conjunction with the powerful concept of membership in a culturally superior imperial family, provided ideal support for observing and penetrating barbarian societies. Also, it made it possible to select and control the operatives best suited to guide dependent peoples into functions supportive of the imperial cause. Not surprisingly, such agents were frequently chosen from one barbarian people for the purpose of subverting or fighting another inferior people. Likewise, in strictly military affairs, mercenaries as well as surrogates were carefully selected with an eye to exploiting interbarbarian relations.[52]

Buddhist Tibet presented special challenges in each of these respects. All dynasties had intricate designs for controlling this geopolitically vital region, or for inducing Tibet to function as China's agent. Indeed, Buddhism itself appealed to Chinese strategists as a "surrogate" system of ideas in 1570 when a Ming emperor was advised that this barbarian religion should be spread deliberately among the troublesome Mongols in the North in the hope of "pacifying" their aggressive instincts.

History shows incontrovertibly that classical China could not subdue either the Tibetans or Buddhism. But it is relevant to note that Leninist China did. The policy of extermination was brutally initiated in the early 1950s when Mao Tse-tung prepared his design for the total subjugation of Tibet by encircling and neutralizing Jawaharlal Nehru and his India. The instruments deployed in this psychological operation were Buddhism and international law—two systems of ideas that carried no substantive validity for dedicated Asian Marxist–Leninists.[53]

A western-type agreement on trade with Tibet was nonetheless concluded in April 1954, and explicit obeisance was pledged in its preamble to the *panca sila,* five precepts of interpersonal Buddhist ethics which have no relevance to the political matters at issue. This maneuver to deceiving a somnolent Indian neighbor was promptly followed by mainland China's genocidal take-over of Tibet, the humiliation of India, and soon thereafter by the Sino-Indian border war. However, and as in earlier times, elimination worked in tandem with pacification. Peking had set up a Chinese-Buddhist Association for the purpose of courting foreign Buddhists just before unleashing state terrorism onto Tibet. Soon after this success it proceeded to rally Buddhists in a Pan-Buddhist Congress. Similar low intensity operations were staged some years later in Vietnam with a view to penetrating the Buddhist "apparatus." According to captured documents (September 1964) communist cadres were ordered to join Buddhist organizations after severing party links.

In short and by way of conclusion: China's conversion to Marxism–Leninism stands in marked contrast to its earlier experiences in political and intellectual history. It has had the effect, in this writer's view, of cancelling the integrity of China as a civilization, but it did assure continuity, albeit in a new key, because Marxism–Leninism was Sinified effectively in terms of Legalism. "Scratch a Mao and you find one of the better known traditional Ch'in despots" is thus, in this context, a justifiable prognosis.

Conclusion

The United States and other nations in the West cannot hope to cope successfully with the belligerent ideologies and techniques of statecraft that are associated with today's totalitarian systems unless they revise their present understandings of the nature of war and its relation to peace. A survey of our times indicates clearly that law states are persuasively outnumbered and out-fought by power states, and that international law as understood in the pres-ent-day United States is politically irrelevant. The sovereign, territorially de-fined nation state is no longer the sole or primary unit in world politics. Peace is not the norm in international relations and war is nowhere viewed as either abnormal or immoral except in the rarefied strata of Occidental academe. All basic themes identifiable in non-Western and communist provinces of the world converge on military and nonmilitary conflict as the major norm-set-ting reality.

The world society, then, lacks the kind of order and cohesion with which the modern West, specifically the United States, has imbued it in the brief era of its preponderance in international history. It is therefore illusionist to as-sume that we can count on a common understanding of the law of war—which is the "pièce de resistance" of international law. Further, and as reflec-tions on earlier times in the history of the West reveal conclusively, peace and war could not be surgically separated from each other even in the European Christian realm. Quite in counterpoint to the belief of international lawyers at the end of the twentieth century, Hugo Grotius, the father of the European law of nations, made it eloquently clear that war and peace interpenetrate in the minds of men and therefore also in the policies of nations. Peace does not emerge from *De Jure Belli ac Pacis* (1625) as a readily attainable or easily definable condition, and war, he notes, "is a name for a situation which can exist even when warlike operations are not being carried on" (Book III: xxxi, 10).

Notes

1. Richard Shultz, "Low Intensity Conflict," in *Mandate for Leadership II*, ed. Stuart M. Butler, Michael Sanera, and W. Bruce Weinrod (Washington, D.C.: Heritage Foundation, 1984). According to the author, "low-intensity conflict includes guerrilla war, revolution, insurgency, civil war, and coup d'etat. Terrorism which often is treated as a separate subject, also can be considered as a type of low intensity warfare" (p. 264.).

2. See 19 basic "rules" in Army Field Manual, *Ranger Training and Operation*, 1756. I am indebted to Senator Barry Goldwater for this reference.

3. William Safire, *Safire's Political Dictionary* (New York: Ballantine Books, 1978).

4. The Safire definition refers to the Jewish Zealots, the Shi'ite Assassins and the Indian Thugs as three sects whose resort to terrorism has become synonymous with "violence or irrationality." The suggestion here is that terrorism exists when it is "irregular," that is, not consonant with established custom. See David C. Rapoport, "Fear and Trembling: Terrorism in Three Religious Traditions," *The American Polit-ical Science Review*, 78 (1984): 658–677 for a lucid comparison of these three sects.

5. Here I find myself in agreement with Aleksandr Solzhenitsyn when he writes that "Communism is a force such as the world has never known. It is anti-human and even metaphysical: its very defects, absurdities and failures tend to strengthen it the more." See his "Three Key Moments in Modern Japanese History," *National Review,* 9 Dec. 1983; and, with Alain Besancon, *The Rise of the Gulag: Intellectual Origins of Leninism,* trans. Sarah Matthews. (New York: Seabury, 1981). Besancon argues that it is ideology, namely Leninism, that makes the difference between the present Gulag State and classic dictatorships or bureaucratic despotisms.

6. "The Legacy of 1968" in Silnitsky, Franktisek et al., *Communism and Eastern Europe,* trans. Cynthia Stone (New York: Karsk), pp. 25–32. This paper also discusses a pre-Leninist Chinese precedent.

7. From Fox Butterfield, *China Alive in the Bitter Sea,* (1982), p. 405.

8. The well-coordinated assassinations and terrorist policies recently identified with communist action groups in France, Germany, Italy, Belgium, Portugal, and Greece have persuaded Italy's Interior Minister that "terrorism is no longer guerrilla fighting. This is war, fought in another way" (*The Wall Street Journal,* 4 February 1985, p. 27). Commenting on the problem of estimating enemy strength during the Vietnam war, which was "part conventional, part terrorist, part psychological and part political," Paul Nitze noted that he was as uncertain in 1967 as he is today of what importance to attach to forces "that could be one thing one day" and "the next day be something else" (*New York Times,* 5 December 1984, excerpts from testimony in General William C. Westmoreland's libel suit against CBS).

9. Michael S. Radu identified the Shining Path as "the most brutal of all contemporary Latin American groups," in "Terror, Terrorism, and Insurgency in Latin America," *Orbis,* 28 (Spring 1984), p. 31. Founded by a Peruvian philosopher-teacher in the 1960s who proclaimed himself the "Fourth Sword of Marxism" (the others being Marx, Lenin, and Mao), the Shining Path has a large and fanatical following among students. All accept the founder's message which combines Mao's personality myth with the God-Sun adoration for the Inca rulers, the promise of a utopia modelled after the Inca state with the projection of himself as maximum leader worthy of adoration. Being totalitarians who admit that human life is irrelevant since only ideology counts, members of the group also proclaimed it their right to speak and act in the name of the non–Spanish-speaking Indians of the Peruvian highlands. If the latter did not understand or accept Sendero's aims (which seems to have been generally the case), punishment or death could follow.

10. For one of the best evocations of Cambodia's past see Christopher Pym, *The Ancient Civilization on Angkor* (New York: New American Library 1968).

11. For the text of the Decree, see Archivio Veneto, 3d ser., 9(1905): 332 ff.

12. See Francesco Guicciardini, *History of Italy* (Florence, Italy: 1561), bk. 3, ch. 4. For a full analysis of Venetian diplomacy, see Adda B. Bozeman, *Politics and Culture in International History* (Princeton: Princeton Univ. Press, 1960), pp. 464–498, and "Covert Action and Foreign Policy" in *Intelligence Requirements for the 1980's: Covert Action,* ed. Roy Godson (1981), pp. 15–78; see in particular pp. 63–73, "Venice and the United States," and authorities cited in these two works.

13. Another reason for not examining the incidence of political warfare and terrorism in the histories of the Arabs, Turks, pre-Islamic Persians, Hindu Indians, and Black Africans is the general absence of modern totalitarianism (apart from societies

expressly identified in the first section of this paper), and the consequent inability to develop the theme of continuity along the lines mapped out in the sections on totalitarian Russian/Byzantium and totalitarian China/imperial China. However, I have analyzed the issues in these sections of the world in several rather recent publications, among them "Moral and Political Perspectives on War and Its Relation to Peace: A Background Paper on the Nuclear Freeze Movement," *Conflict, An International Journal* 5(4) pp. 271–307; "Statecraft and Intelligence in the Non-Western World," *Conflict, An International Journal* 6 (1) pp. 1–35; "U.S. Foreign Policy and the Prospects for Democracy, National Security and World Peace" *Comparative Strategy* (Spring 1985); "War and the Clash of Ideas," *Orbis* 20 (Spring 1976) pp. 61–103; "Iran: U.S. Foreign Policy and the Tradition of Persian Statecraft," *Orbis* 23 (Summer 1979) pp. 387–402; "Covert Action and Foreign Policy," in Roy Godson, ed., *Intelligence Requirements for the 1980's: Covert Action*, 1981, pp. 15–78. See "Case Studies" on the Middle East and India; and several chapters in *Conflict in Africa: Concepts and Realities.*

14. See Bozeman, *Politics and Culture*, ch. 9, "The Byzantine Realm," pp. 298–356, and authorities there cited for an examination of Byzantine history and statecraft.

15. See Bozeman, *Politics and Culture*, p. 321, note 59, for the suggestion that the fourth crusade might have been directed against Egypt and not against Constantinople had the Eastern Empire maintained a fleet. This paper also discusses equivalent Chinese principles.

16. M. Gelzer, *Studien zur Byzantinischen Verwaltung Egyptens* (1909), as quoted in Norman H. Baynes, *The Byzantine Empire* (London: William and Norgate 1925), pp. 130–131.

17. The parallel to Soviet diplomatic techniques is obvious.

18. In order to conciliate the Bulgarians when they were particularly threatening, the Tsar was even given permission to call himself "Basileus."

19. Compare this political arrangement with the organization of China's imperial orbit.

20. See J. B. Bury, "Roman Empire, Later," in *Encyclopedia Britannica*, 1944, p. 444.

21. Their qualifications were first enumerated in the fifth century during the reign of Theodoric, the Ostrogothic king of Rome who had been imbued with Byzantinism while a hostage at the imperial court in Constantinople. See Bozeman, *Politics and Culture*, p. 329, for particulars. It must be noted that Byzantium did not maintain permanent embassies abroad.

22. For these notations see S. Bakhrouchine, A. Ephimov, E. Kosminski, A. Narotchnitski, V. Serguiev, S. Skazkine, V. Khvostov and E. Tarlé, *Histoire de la Diplomatie*, 3 vols., tome premier, publié sous la direction de M. Potiemkine, Paris, 1947, pp. 86 ff' hereafter cited as Tarlé, *Histoire*. The fact that the authors are Soviet historians is relevant for comparative studies of the Byzantine and Soviet empires.

23. For a poignant record of relations between the two Romes and the conflict's weakening effect on Christendom's relations with Islam see *Memoirs of a Renaissance Pope: The Commentaries of Pius II*, an abridgement; transl. by Florence A. Gragg; ed. by Leona C. Gabel, (New York: Capricorn Books, 1962).

24. For a discussion of this relationship see Bozeman, *Politics and Culture*, pp.

340–356, "The Continuance of the Byzantine Tradition in Diplomacy; The Russian Realm" and authorities there cited.

25. See ibid., 351–354.

26. Ibid., 354–355 for excerpts of the text.

27. For this conclusion see Nicholas Berdyaev, *The Russian Idea* (New York, 1948), p. 9.

28. See for example A.A. Vasiliev, *History of the Byzantine Empire, 324–1453,* Engl. ed., rev., (Madison, Wis: Univ. of Wisconsin Press 1952), pp. 32 ff, for a review of Russian historical opinion; V.O. Kluchevsky, *A History of Russia,* tr. C.J. Hogarth, 3 vols., (London and New York, 1911–12), particularly vol. I, p. 84, for comments on the cultural significance of Byzantine tutelage over the evolution of Kievan law. Nicholas Berdyaev, *The Origins of Russian Communism,* London, 1937), and *The Russian Idea,* (New York, 1948), as well as Russian authorities cited in Bozeman, *Politics and Culture,* p. 342. See also James A. Duran Jr., "Russian Nationalism in the Cultural Policy of Catherine the Great", (in press), which concludes that "To the Empress and contemporary intellectuals, the recovery of the pre-Petrine Russia was a mission executed in defense of the Fatherland." To them, "Kiev Rus was a key element in establishing an antiquity for Russia comparable to that of West European states." (p. 8)

29. See M. V. Levchenko, *History of Byzantium,* (Moscow and Leningrad, 1940), p. 4.

30. *Ivan Grozny,* (Moscow, 1947), p. 169. See also, Tarlé, *Histoire,* pp. 100ff.

31. See Kluchevsky, *A History of Russia,* vol. I, p. 285.

32. I have developed some of the ideas here in play in "Decline of the West? Spengler Reconsidered", *The Virginia Quarterly Review,* Spring 1983, vol. 59, No. 2, pp. 181–208, see pp. 199 ff; and in "Do Educational and Cultural Exchanges Have Political Relevance?", in *International Educational and Cultural Exchange,* Fall 1969, vol. V, No. 2, pp. 7–21.

33. See earlier references in this paper and Bozeman, *Politics and Culture in International History,* pp. 302ff, for an account of Constantinople's treatment of Bishop Liutprandt who came to the rival Christian capital in mid-tenth century as a special envoy of Otto the Great, charged with negotiating a marriage of Otto's son to the Byzantine princess Theophano.

34. It is noteworthy that Ethiopia was Christianized in the 4th century AD, i.e., several centuries before the advent of Islam, and that the missionary effort issued directly from Egypt, then part of Eastern Rome.

35. Bulgaria is an important exception, mainly, I believe, because it belongs to the Slavic ethnicities that were Christianized by Constantinople. Poles, Czechs, Croats, Hungarians, Lithuanians, Letts, Esthonians were Christianized by Rome and maintained close relations with the West.

36. See Francis X. Maier, "Kingdoms of Death: A Reporter's African Journal," in *This World,* Spring/Summer 1984, no. 8, pp. 27–46.

37. See also Bozeman, "Covert Action and Foreign Policy", section on the Middle East; Bozeman, "Intelligence and Statecraft in the Non-Western World" in *Conflict, An International Journal,* vol. VI, No. 1, (1985) pp. 1–35.

38. For a first class exposition of Chinese philosophies see Arthur Waley, *Three*

Ways of Thought in Ancient China (London, Allen & Unwin, 1939). Also Edward L. Dryer, "Military Continuities: The PLA and Imperial China", ch. 1 in William W. Whitson, ed., *The Military and Political Power in China in the 1970's* (New York: Praeger, 1972), pp. 3–24.

39. King-chuan Hsiao, "Legalism and Autocracy in Traditional China" in Li Yuning, ed., *Shang Yang's Reforms and State Control in China* (White Plains, N.Y.: M.E. Sharpe, 1977), pp. 125–143.

40. "On New Democracy", *Selected Works*, Engl. ed., vol. II, (Peking, 1967), p. 381.

41. *Le Droit Chinois*, Libr. du Recueil Sirey, Paris, 1936, pp. 69 ff. On this issue see also Adda B. Bozeman, "On the Relevance of Hugo Grotius and *De Jure Belli Ac Pacis* for Our Times", *Grotiana* vol. I, no. 1, 1980, The Hague, pp. 65–124, and "Human Rights and National Security" in *The Yale Journal of World Public Order*, vol. 9, no. 1, Fall 1982 (publ. 1984), pp. 40–77.

42. (New York: Oxford Univ. Press, 1963), transl. and edited by Samuel B. Griffith. See the editor's remarks on the diffusion of the work and the relation between Sun Tzu and Mao Tse-tung, p. 45 ff, and appendix III. For an American comment on these two issues see Vernon A. Walters, *Silent Missions*, (Garden City, N.J.: Doubleday, 1978), p. 546. Reporting on his meetings with the Chinese Ambassador to France in Jan. 1971 when President Nixon's trip to China was being prepared, Walters writes: "we then discussed the famous Chinese writer on the art of war, Sun-tzu, and the Ambassador told me that his writings were required reading in all Chinese military schools." Walters summarizes the Sun Tzu on p. 614 f.

43. See his essay on "Deception in Chinese Strategy: Some theoretical notes on the Sun-Tzu and Game Theory" in William W. Whitson, Ed., *The Military and Political Power in China* (New York: Praeger, 1972), Ch. 16, pp. 313–337. Mao Tse-tung's works are replete with citations or paraphrases of the *Sun-Tzu*. However, it is significant for studies of "continuity" in Chinese thought to note that Sun-Tzu—contrary to Mao Tse-tung—does not believe either in annihilating enemy states and armies or in protracted military warfare.

44. The Chinese idea of war is persuasively rendered in the *wei-ch'i* ("Go" in Japan) game. For an interpretation of the game and its relevance in Chinese politics see Scott A. Boorman, *The Protracted Game: A wei-ch'i Interpretation of Maoist Revolutionary Strategy* (New York: Oxford Univ. Press, 1969). See pp. 6 f. for suggestion that Sun-Tzu's theories bear a distinct similarity to *wei-ch'i*, see p. 208, n.8. His thesis is significant: Chinese communist policies and the game are products of the same strategic tradition—one without parallel either in Occidental military tradition or in the game of chess. He views *wei-ch'i* as an important, if little recognized, model of the Maoist system of insurgency.

45. See Frank A. Kiernan, Jr., "Phases and Modes of Combat in Early China" in Frank A. Kiernan, Jr. and John K. Fairbank eds., *Chinese Ways in Warfare*, (Cambridge, Mass: Harvard Univ. Press, 1974), pp. 37–66. Michael Loewe, "The Campaigns of Han Wu-ti" in Kiernan, Jr. and Fairbank, eds., *Chinese Ways*, pp. 67–110; see specifically pp. 89, 102 and p. 78 for the following passage: "When weak, Han had to submit to the demands of the other party and to purchase peace at the price of valuables. When strong, Han was ready not only to launch large-scale campaigns

but also to take other violent measures, for instance, the butchery of the population of Lun-t'ai (ca. 100 B.C.) or the instigation of plots to murder or replace the kings of the oasis communities."

46. See Lien-sheng Yang, "Hostages in Chinese History" in *Studies in Chinese Institutional History,* Harvard-Yenching Institute Studies, vol. XX, (1963); p. 45 to the effect that "Taking hostages was a standard practice of the Han Dynasty for controlling small barbarian states." P. 43 for the exchange of hostages between Chou and Cheng recorded in the *Tso chuan* and the sending of Korean hostages to the Manchu rulers between 1637–1645. See also Loewe, "The Campaigns," p. 102, to the effect that Han generals were rewarded for their services by their success in capturing important personages, such as kings, members of royal families, or other leaders.

47. John K. Fairbank, "Introduction: Varieties of the Chinese Military Experience" in Kiernan Jr. and Fairbank, eds., *Chinese Ways,* p. 1–26; see particularly p. 23. For analytical studies of Chinese tactics see Charles O. Hucker, "Hu Tsung-hsien's Campaign Against Hsu Hai, 1556", ibid., pp. 273–307, and Herbert Franke, "Siege and Defense of Towns in Medieval China", ibid., pp. 151–202.

48. See Immanuel C. Y Hsü, *China's Entrance into the Family of Nations: The Diplomatic Phase 1858–1880,* (Cambridge, Mass.: Harvard Univ. Press, 1960); L. Carrington Goodrich, *A Short History of the Chinese People* (New York: Harper, 1951), pp. 11–113; Melvin Frederic Nelson, *Korea and the Old Order in Eastern Asia* (Baton Rouge, La., 1945).

49. John K. Fairbank, "Introduction: Varieties," p. 12; Frederick W. Mote, "The T'u-mu Incident of 1449" in Kiernan, Jr. and Fairbank, eds., *Chinese Ways,* pp. 243–272. See pp. 244 ff on the rise of the Mongol nation.

50. Immanuel C. Y. Hsü, *China's Entrance,* p. 115.

51. Charles O. Hucker, "Hu Tsung-hsien's Campaign," p. 274.

52. Note the striking parallels to the Byzantine "science of managing barbarians."

53. See "A Vast Sea of Chinese Threatens Tibet" by the Dalai Lama in *The New York Times,* August 9, 1985, p. A27.

3
The State of the Art

Claire Sterling

In the introductory chapter of this book, William Casey presents a broad outline of a problem, one aspect of which I believe deserves more careful and precise investigation: state-sponsored terrorism as a form of surrogate warfare. The international terrorism phenomenon of the 1980s constitutes a continuation of what the West has experienced since the beginning of the 1970s. However, while the general focus, in my estimation, is not new, today it is more pointed and starker than anything we experienced during the 1970s.

Let us start with the kidnapping of General Dozier in Italy by the Red in the winter of 1982. This was the first time that the Red Brigades, which had been operating on the scene actively since the beginning of the 1970s, took on a foreign target—an American target. He was the highest ranking NATO officer present on Italian soil, and the communique was issued by the Red Brigades at the time (the first after the kidnapping), stated that they kidnapped General Dozier as part of their new strategy to drive the multinational imperialist state out of Europe, to block the installation of the Cruise and Pershing missiles in Italy and throughout Europe, and especially in Germany—the ideal territory for a land-based attack on the Soviet Union. This is the first time in all the years the Red Brigades had been operating in Italy that they so clearly expressed their parallel objectives with those of the Soviet Union. In effect, we find Moscow's security interests vis-à-vis NATO serving as the rationale for acts of violence carried out by one of Western Europe's most active and violent terrorist factions. The Red Brigades presented the following challenge to the Western Alliance: we have taken this American NATO general so that we can help the Soviet Union's campaign against the installation of Cruise and Pershing missiles. We believe the installation of these missiles, especially the Pershing in West Germany, threatens Soviet security in Europe. Directly after this case one began to see the same line being taken by other groups operating in the free societies of Western Europe, the perimeter of the western part of the European continent, and, of course, the area containing the European part of the NATO Alliance. This culminated during December 1984–January 1985, with 60 bombings of U.S. military installations in West Germany.

According to Italian newspaper reports in January 1985, a joint proclamation of the French terrorist group *Action Directe* and the German RAF (Rote Armee Fraktion) stressed the need to prevent the installation of the Euro-missiles. At the time a new group called the "Communist Combat Cells" bombed the NATO pipeline across Belgium. Within the same two or three weeks' period there were two bombings of the pipeline running from Torrejon to Saragossa in Spain which served U.S. and Spanish military forces. Additionally, just a few months before that time, we had the assassination in Italy of Leaman Hunt, an American civilian who was the Director of the Multi-National Peace-Keeping Force in the Sinai. "Credit" for this execution was taken by the Red Brigades and the Revolutionary Armed Faction of Lebanon, which is an extreme Left Leninist formation operating in West Europe.

Throughout the following period, there have been some forty bombing attacks in France, primarily addressed toward defense-related industrial establishments, and the assassination, a week later in West Germany, of a defense-related industrialist. There also has been a continuing series of attacks in Portugal, a bombing of a six-ship NATO squadron outside of Lisbon, and four other bombing attacks inside Portugal. Now we hear of a new attack in Madrid, a frightful attack on the restaurant generally serving as a gathering place for Americans from the U.S. Air Base at Torrejon.[1]

Remarkably, in each of these cases we have continued to hear from the countries concerned that, while these were troubling events, they almost certainly were unrelated national episodes, that is, they were not related and integrated assaults by a covert network linked to Moscow. In the course of observing this developing strategy, I have seen indications of common operational footprints. Additionally, there was a formal announcement on 15 January in Paris of the operational merger of Direct Action and the offspring of the German Baader-Meinhof Gang, the Red Army Faction. Their announcement—published in French, Turkish, and Arabic—that they had merged in order to combat NATO and the American military presence in Western Europe was analyzed by experts who found it to be a translation from the German. This episode reveals a four-part international terrorist connection. It is a matter of public knowledge that two of the groups, Direct Action and the German Red Army Faction, have been working directly with the Belgian Communist Combat Cells which emerged only in the course of this past winter. Recently in West Germany, a member of the RAF has been arrested with documents of military installations in the Federal Republic for which bombings were being planned and prepared.

In Rome, we have had seven Lebanese who call themselves the Islamic Holy War. It may be that this is their real affiliation. However, they also may be connected to other Lebanese Marxist-Leninist groups. In any case, they were found with very detailed plans of the American Embassy in Rome, including the important security points which would indicate where it would be more or less practicable to penetrate with a truck or car bomb. In this case the authorities caught the seven Lebanese, who are not talking. Italian officials do not believe that it was possible for these seven Lebanese students to acquire this kind of information on the interior arrangements of the American Embassy without the assistance of Soviet Bloc intelligence services, Italians who were able to penetrate the American Embassy, or both.

At the same time, there have been a number of attacks on the U.S. Embassy in Portugal, as well as a series of assaults in the past year against American personnel and installations in the Middle East. The point of recounting these frequently described "national episodes" is to demonstrate that they are anything but unrelated events. To the contrary, the emerging pattern seems to be unmistakably one of far more open reliance upon and willingness to defend State interests, starting, but not ending, with the Soviet Union. I believe that when we talk about state-supported terrorism, there are many instances in which the linkages are easier to establish, particularly when the connections are to the Syrians, the Libyans, and especially the Iranians. It is surprising, therefore, that the existence of state-sponsored international terrorist linkages is questioned at all.

Libya, for example, has announced many times over in the last year or two, either through Colonel Qadhafi or through his radio and press, that it has every intention of continuing to provide full logistical support, training, weapons, and so forth, to what it calls the "liberating groups" of Europe.[2] The Libyans are not talking here about other Middle Eastern "liberation groups," which they also assist in a major way. Indeed, they have been indicted by two Italian courts as having supplied (over a period of several years) massive quantitites of armaments to the West European groups, including the Italian terrorists,[3] the Red Brigades, and the Sardinian separatists who are now on trial. An international arms ring including Libyans, Lebanese, Palestinians, and Egyptians was supplying weapons to the Red Brigades for their own use and for distribution to other terrorist groups throughout West Europe, including Direct Action, the Spanish Basques, the Germans, the IRA, and so on. The investigating magistrate discovered that there was a KGB liason with this group—Maurizio Folini. An international warrant for his arrest has been issued and he is now a fugitive believed to be hiding in Mozambique. The investigation also uncovered the name of an Italian who worked with Folini—Oreste Scalzone. He was let out of prison by the Italians because of poor health, and promptly skipped to Paris, where he enjoys a free existence. There is an arrest warrant from Italy, but extradition has been refused by the French.

Thus we have Folini and Scalzone, the former designated by the Italian court as a KGB agent distributing Libyan and Soviet Bloc weapons, while the latter has not been so designated by the court, and is living freely in Paris—the great center for terrorist operations in Europe today. The two are connected, according to another Italian court investigation, to a language institute called the Hyperion Institute, located in Paris;[4] it is currently inoperative because of the investigations of the Italian court, but formerly it served as a center—a gathering place—for Italian terrorist groups, the Germans, the French, the Spanish, the IRA, the Belgians, the PLO, and other Palestinian operational groups. Again, these meetings took place in the presence of a KGB liaison who, according to an Italian Investigation Magistrate, was one of three Italians who were running the Hyperion Language Institute. The point is that, when we talk about the States who are openly seen to have been supporting terrorist attacks in Europe through training and the supply of weapons, as in the case of Libya, we cannot stop with Qadhafi. From this evidence we can proceed to what is thought to be that last unmentionable step—the involvement and commitment of the Soviet Union in ensuring the possibility of such a supply.

In the case of the Hyperion Institute, Folini, and the two court investigations, we do have direct evidence of names and organizations. But there are other ways of coming to the same conclusion through the Hyperion Institute. One of the Italian court investigations which brought these other facts to light was conducted by Judge Mastelloni in Venice. He issued an international warrant for the arrest of Yasser Arafat and for Arafat's chief lieutenant Abu Iyad on the basis of documents found in the possession of Italian Red Brigade terrorists in their safe-houses. These included, among other things, the minutes of meetings in Paris at the Hyperion Institute attended by Abu Iyad in the name of Arafat, in which Abu Iyad undertook to provide weapons through a series of shipments. These were discovered, still wrapped, by the way, in Arab language newspapers, in different hiding places in Italy, and Abu Iyad then said (in the minutes of these meetings) that he would have to check back with Arafat to see if the arrangements for these shipments were okay. Then, in another meeting, the minutes indicate that he had checked with Arafat and that Arafat had said "yes" and therefore the agreement was sealed and the arms were delivered for use, not just by the Red Brigades in Italy, but by every important group operating against the free societies of Western Europe and especially the West European members of NATO.

In the course of this investigation, Judge Mastelloni heard the testimony of three defectors from the Red Brigades, Antonio Savasta, Michele Galati, and Carlo Brogi. Independently of each other, all three confirmed that in the Autumn of 1978 a meeting between representatives of the PLO and of the Red Brigades had taken place in Paris, and that this had resulted in an agreement by which the PLO would furnish arms, free of charge, to the Red Brigades. In compensation for this, the Red Brigades would commit anti-American and anti-Israeli terrorist acts on Italian soil. From Brogi's testimony Judge Mastelloni drew the conclusion that the PLO functioned "as a political and military point of reference for all the European terrorist organizations (IRA, RAF, ETA, etc.) above all as regards the delivery of arms."[5]

To summarize, during the last year or so, a common and recurring pattern has emerged in the direction of strategy, the targets chosen, and the methods used by each of the different terrorist groups mentioned. This escalation in the state-sponsored strategy of terrorism came just at the time when the Soviet Union agreed to sit down with the United States at the bargaining table in Geneva to discuss arms control. It would seem that this is such a classic case of timing that it does not need much comment, except for the persistence of what we might call "resolute disbelief" on the part of the Western powers. I have encountered this attitude frequently in my attempts to explain what I have uncovered in studying the problem of Soviet-supported terrorism. The posture of almost tragic unwillingness to recognize the patterns described above is seen over and over again because the evidence creates such difficulties and embarrassment for proponents of arms control and detente. This has resulted, in my opinion, in an extraordinary degree of blindness toward what our principal adversary has been doing over the last fifteen years. Consequently, while we now have a more coherent military policy and while the campaign to block the Cruise and Pershing missiles by the "peace movement" has failed (with the installation of the Pershing in West Germany), we have yet to come to grips with the next line of attack—Soviet-sponsored terrorist attacks on military personnel and military installations in Western Europe. And yet, because the Soviet Union has agreed to negotiate on arms control, we find every major government in Western Europe, with the honorable exception of Italy,[6] denying that there is any essential connection between what is happening in one country and any other. Spokesmen of the Kohl government, in West Germany state that the escalation of terrorism they are experiencing is an unfortunate resurgence of the old Baader-Meinhof problem in the Federal Republic, and assert that there is no indication, no evidence, of any Soviet involvement or connection in any way with sixty bombings of American military installations in Western Germany during a two-month period. We have had similar statements from the Spanish Government, which has chosen to believe that there is no proof that the bombing of the restaurant frequented by U.S. military personnel was the work of groups linked to the USSR, even though the explosive used was the same as that used by GRAPO, a Spanish insurgent guerrilla group. GRAPO has used exactly the same tactics in the past to attack the California Restaurant in Madrid; the same explosives and tactics had also been used at the time of emerging democracy in Spain. We have seen an unwillingness on the part of the Spanish Government to concede that there would be the same inclination, the same desire, and the same strategy among the Basques and the GRAPO urban guerrillas to use extreme violence, not simply for their own considerations, but for the larger strategic objectives of the USSR. This common concern between the terrorist group and Moscow is aptly described by the Italian paraphrase, "the parallel convergency." Now, I don't mean by this that these groups meet in a room with Soviet agents and receive specific orders concerning specific operations on any given day. What I do mean is that when you take a case like Arafat and Abu Iyad sanctioning the distribution of weapons to Western Europe, and you include Libya running a huge arms ring in support of these Euro-terrorist groups (and you see that, in the Libyan case, there is a direct KGB connection), the evidence becomes indisputable. In the case of Arafat, you have Palestinian weapons being delivered to the terrorists of Western Europe, and you have one of the leaders of the Italian terrorist movement, now a repentant terrorist, in prison saying, "Never, and again, never, could these Palestinians have given us these weapons, which are from the Soviet Bloc, without the knowledge and consent of Soviet leadership." When you have these two now clearly defined paths of logistic support for an operation which is unmistakably a strategic operation serving Soviet interests, it is inconceivable that the countries of Western Europe can continue to refuse to concede that there is a Soviet connection. There you have what I think is our major problem in the question of how to combat terrorism.

I believe that the primary reason for our having arrived at this very unhappy stage in the development of international terrorism in our time is this perverse unwillingness on the part of the Western powers to face the reality of what is known by the authorities of the Western world (and to the intelligence services in the governments of the Western establishment) about the responsibility of the states who sponsor terrorism. While in the case of Iran we can point to direct training of extremist groups, this is only part of the story. Because they make available the wherewithal which makes it possible to continually increase both expertise and the technological level of attack, as well as to influence the choice of targets and the development of strategy, we must talk about the Soviet Union and its clients in the Soviet Bloc and not simply hide behind Libya, Syria, and Iran. It is true, of course, that there are distinctions between the forms of Iranian terrorism and those used by, let us say, the Lebanese revolutionary armed factions. One can argue about the degree to which the Soviet Union is able to influence what Khomeini does with the Iranian terrorists. Certainly there is a very special problem with the kind of suicide missions which seem unique to the Islamic Fundamentalist form of terrorism. However, it seems to me that although the suicide squadron and the Kamikaze squad presents a very serious and very difficult new aspect of the problem for the West, in the long run the more serious challenge comes from those whom we continue to accept as negotiating partners in the arms control process. We continue to see a national context used to explain Soviet-sponsored terrorism, rather than viewing it as a form of surrogate warfare that is as old as the ages but has taken on its most sophisticated form in the last fifteen years.

The degree to which this resolute disbelief has overtaken the Western states can be seen in the attempted assassination of the Pope. This case is related directly to the question of state-sponsored terrorism in the sense that I have discussed it, that is, in the disposition of the Soviet Union to provide the wherewithal and logistic support for various forms of terrorist action directed against Western society. In the case of the Papal shooting, we have had, as one example, an article in *Problems of Communism* which, as you all know, is a U.S. Information Agency publication paid for by the United States Government and read very widely by experts and specialists in Europe, who regard it as a voice of the United States on delicate matters involving the Soviet Union. In this publication William Hood, who was, I believe, a former high-ranking counterintelligence official of the CIA, wrote that it is ridiculous to say the USSR could have been behind the plot to shoot the Pope because the Kremlin leaders would not be so inefficient. Additionally, Moscow is cautious and conservative, as we all know, and therefore does not take risks.[7] If you put that together with what has been stated in other publications by authoritative spokesmen of the CIA, you will see that they say, "It is possible that the Turk who shot the Pope was working with some Bulgarian." That does not necessarily mean that the Bulgarian was working on the orders of the Bulgarian Secret Service, or, if he was working on the orders of the Secret Service, that the Secret Service was necessarily operating under the order of the Bulgarian Government, or, if the Bulgarian Government had given the orders, that the order came from the Soviet Union. And even if it did come from some level of the Soviet Union, it must have been a middle level of the KGB. Finally, even if all of this is true, it does not mean that the order would have come from Andropov who, at the time, was the head of the KGB. Or if it came from Andropov, it was not known to the Politburo. Now there we have, in very short, encapsulated form, a point of view addressed to the entire question of low-intensity surrogate warfare directed against the West. This sums up the position taken by the West since the beginning, and I believe we never would have come to the real answers if this position had not been challenged. Furthermore, I do not believe that the Soviet Union would have even contemplated an act like attempting to assassinate the head of the Roman Catholic Church in 1981, if it had not been quite sure that, in the preceding nine or ten years, every act accelerating the phenomenon of terrorism in the West had been forgiven, excused, or ignored by all the Western powers, bar none. Therefore, the Soviet leadership could assume (and correctly so) that if and when the Pope was assassinated on Soviet orders—but indirectly through whatever means were chosen—the West could close its eyes again and say, "Well, it is not possible that the USSR did it" and therefore any Soviet risk would be reduced to the point of being minimal. Indeed, I believe there was no risk at all, because, although we now have a formal indictment from an Italian judge and the commencement of a trial of three Bulgarians charged with complicity, to this very day not one government in the West—not one— is willing to say "It is now possible to imagine that the Soviet Union was responsible for the attempted assassination of the Pope."

To summarize, through the resurgence of a now clearly defined new terrorist wave in Western Europe designed to separate the United States from its European allies, Moscow seeks directly to weaken the NATO installations in Europe, and indirectly to frighten, for example, the Dutch and the Belgians, who are the waverers on the Cruise and Pershing missiles, by the kind of paramilitary terrorist activity currently underway. While this is being directed against the members of the Alliance, our explanations continue to focus on local sociological discontent. This assumes that, unless and until we solve the problems of Belgium or Spain or Portugal or Turkey or Italy or West Germany, we will not come to grips with (state-sponsored) terrorism. In fact, however, without the kind of sustenance and support the terrorists have had from the governments opposed to us, they could not function in any way that presents a serious menace to our own security. This is the "objective reality," to use Soviet parlance, that the West has failed to recognize.

Notes

1. See "Dopo la strage anti-USA di Madrid" in *Corriere de la Sera,* Milano 4.15.85.
2. See "Gheddafi minaccia aiuti ai terroristi" in *Giornale di Sicilia,* Palermo 4.4.85.
3. See "Le armi di Gheddafi ai terroristi" in *Corriere de la Sera,* Milano, 10.1.81.
4. See "La vecchia pista dell' "Hyperion," in *Corriere de la Sera,* Milano, 9.27.84.
5. See "Procura Generale della Republica presso la Corte di Cassazione," Statement by Prosecutor General dated April 10, 1985. The Court later sustained Arafat's appeal against the warrant on the grounds that the evidence against him personally was insufficient.
6. See, for instance, Address by Prime Minister Craxi to the Italian Parliament on 11.22.84, in *Camera dei Diputati - Senato della Republica,* IX Legislatura-Documenti.
7. See William Hood, "Unlikely Conspiracy," in *Problems of Communism,* Washington, D.C., March–April 1984, pp. 67–70.

Section C
Operational Principles

4
Political Doctrine and Apparatus

Herbert Romerstein

War between nations, low-intensity warfare, and influence operations (active measures) are all intertwined in Leninist theory. As Lenin paraphrased the Clausewitz dictum, "War is simply the continuation of politics by other (i.e., violent) means."[1] Therefore, all forms of struggle, violent and political, are combined to achieve the goals of the Soviet state. The role of that state was outlined by Lenin in 1915: "The victory of socialism is possible first in several or even in one capitalist country alone. After expropriating the capitalists and organizing their own socialist production, the victorious proletariat of that country will arise against the rest of the world—the capitalist world—attracting to its cause the oppressed classes of other countries, stirring uprisings in those countries against the capitalists, and in case of need using even armed force against the exploiting classes and their states."[2]

To provide mutual support for such uprisings, the Communist International (Comintern) was established in Moscow in 1919. Lenin looked upon the establishment of the Comintern as the signal for the imminent world revolution. Addressing the First Congress, he said, "The victory of the proletarian revolution on a world scale is assured. The founding of an international Soviet republic is on the way."[3]

The short-lived Hungarian Soviet Republic and the violence in various European countries were looked upon as indicators of the coming world revolution. A one-thousand man Russian battalion was sent to join an international brigade to defend Bela Kun's Communist regime in Hungary.[4] They were of course unsuccessful.

The methods encouraged for foreign revolutionaries were based on the Bolshevik experience—low-intensity warfare, preferably carried out by others, to lead to a general uprising and thus to victory. During the 1905 Russian revolution, Lenin had instructed the Combat Committee of the St. Petersburg Bolsheviks on methods to be used. He wrote, "You must proceed to propaganda on a wide scale. Let five or ten people make the round of hundreds of workers' and students' study circles in a week, penetrate wherever they can, and everywhere propose a clear, brief, direct, and simple plan: organise combat groups immediately . . ."[5]

Lenin's instructions were detailed:

> The propagandists must supply each group with brief and simple recipes for making bombs, give them an elementary explanation of the type of the work, and then leave it all to them. Squads must at once begin military training by launching operations immediately, at once. Some may at once undertake to kill a spy or blow up a police station, others to raid a bank to confiscate funds for the insurrection. . . . Let every group learn, if it is only by beating up policemen: a score or so victims will be more than compensated for by the fact that this will train hundreds of experienced fighters, who tomorrow will be leading hundreds of thousands.[6]

Similar methods were taught by the Comintern to foreign revolutionaries. The Comintern role was to provide political support to the revolutionary groups. However, physical support was also available.

The Second World Congress of the Comintern took place in 1920. Its manifesto, signed by Communists from various countries, including Lenin and Trotsky—proclaimed: "All over the world Civil War is the order of the day. Its watchword is—All power to the Soviets!"[7]

After the Second Congress, the Comintern formed the Young Communist International (YCI) to assist in the revolutionary struggle. The Third Congress of the YCI, held in 1922, ordered the creation of nuclei in the imperialist armies and navies as "the only means for the fight against war and its transformation into the civil war and revolution."[8]

In its report on activities two years later, the YCI made a frank admission as to how Moscow controlled its apparatus: "When the white press and the social democrats write about 'Moscow Orders', they are very badly informed on the character of these 'orders', but the Moscow leadership is a fact, a leadership through letters, directions, delegation(s), which reach the various countries despite the guards of the bourgeoisie and the social democrats."[9]

Direct Soviet assistance to insurrections and guerrilla warfare was provided. The Hamburg uprising in 1923 is an example. Erich Wollenberg, then a Comintern apparatchik and member of the German Communist Party, was the Military-Political commander in Hamburg's southwest district. He revealed many years later that his Soviet advisor had been Alexei M. Stetzky, subsequently a Central Committee member of the Communist Party of the Soviet Union. The northwest district had as its advisor Soviet general Moishe Stern, who was later to distinguish himself in Spain under the nom de guerre "General Kleber." The insurrection was a failure, but lessons were drawn from it.

In 1928, Wollenberg was working in Moscow for the Comintern. He was called to the office of Osip Piatnitsky, the Organizational Secretary. The purpose of the meeting was to organize the publication of a training manual on armed insurrection. The book, published in German as *Der Bewaffnete Aufstand* in 1928 and *L'insurrection armee* in French in 1931, had a number of distinguished authors, including Marshall Tukhachevsky, Ho Chi Minh, Piatnitsky, and Hans Kippenberger, the military leader of the Hamburg insurrection. The book was signed "A. Neuberg."[10] The book included analyses of the Hamburg uprising of 1923, the Reval revolt in 1924, and the 1926 and 1927 uprisings in China, as well as general chapters on how to conduct an insurrection.

All of these attempts were unsuccessful, as were the 1923 and 1925 uprisings in Bulgaria. The first was led by George Dimitrov, later Secretary General of the Comintern, and Vassil Kolarov.[11] According to Dimitrov, the uprising took place because a month earlier a "sound Marxist nucleus had taken power in the Party" with the aid of the Comintern.[12]

After the failure, Dimitrov fled to the Soviet Union, where he served as Secretary of the Balkan Communist Federation and leader of the West European Bureau of the Comintern.[13]

On 16 April 1925, a terrorist bomb exploded in the Sofia Cathedral during the funeral of a general who had been assassinated. The Comintern immediately denied responsibility claiming, "It is not the work of the party."[14] Over a week before the murder and bombing, the Sofia press had carried the text of an alleged Comintern document ordering an insurrection in Bulgaria to start on 15 April. The Comintern branded the document a forgery. Coincidently, the terrorism and attempted insurrection began on just that date. A declaration of the Balkan Communist Federation, signed by Dimitrov and dated April 23, called the bombing "an act of self-defence."[15] Twenty-four years later, as head of the Bulgarian government Dimitrov admitted to a Community Party Congress that indeed the terrorist acts were committed by the Communist Party. Dimitrov referred to "the desperate acts of the leaders of the Party's military organization, culminating in the attempt at the Sofia Cathedral."[16]

The important role of disrupting the enemy's armies was given to the YCI. In June 1925, a conference was held in Berlin of the European Young Communist Leagues to "lay down the tasks, which the Communists had to carry out" in regard to the French War in Morocco and the events in China. All sections of the YCI were given a series of practical tasks. Special tasks were given to the YCIs of Great Britain, France, Italy, America, and Japan regarding work among soldiers and sailors serving on battleships. The French League appealed to the French soldiers to fraternise with the Cabyles of the Riff and to turn their weapons against their own exploiters.[17] That the Communist support for liberation of the colonies was not purely altruistic could be seen by the speech of Dimitri Manuilsky at the Fifth Congress of the Comintern in 1924. Addressing the French Communists, he said:

> In your army there are 250,000 black soldiers. Do you think you will be able to make a social revolution if these 250,000 are on the other side of the barricades? Will you working class be able to win a single strike if the bourgeoisie have at their disposal these black reserve troops which they can incite any minute against your heroic proletariat? Have you carried on any anti-militaristic propaganda among these black troops? (From the French section: Yes, yes yes.)[18]

From 1927 to 1935, the Comintern maintained a front called the "League Against Imperialism." The First Congress of the League was held in Brussels in 1927, the second in Frankfurt in 1929.[19] This front had been created by Willi Muenzenberg, the Comintern's mastermind of the front apparatus.[20] The 1929 Frankfurt Congress heard a speech by American Communist official James W. Ford, the Communist Party USA's leading Negro functionary. Ford called upon Negro soldiers to "organize," saying, "Negro workers, peasants and soldiers, turn the imperialist war into a civil war against your oppressors! Fight to defeat 'your' imperialist country in the war! Negro soldiers, in the event of war, fraternize with the soldiers of the opposing armies! Down with race war, long live the class war! Negro workers, peasants and soldiers, defend the Soviet Union against imperialism!"[21]

The Comintern's major efforts in the late 1920s were in support of the revolution in China. So significant was this activity that Stalin personally spoke at a meeting of the Chinese commission of the Comintern on 30 November 1926 to lay down the line to be followed by the Chinese Communists.[22] The Communist attempt to secure China at that time was unsuccessful, and a Communist uprising in Canton was drowned in blood.

M. N. Roy, an Indian Communist, served as a Comintern representative in China in 1927. He later wrote, "Ever since 1923 the C.P. of China had been under Russian guidance. It's leading cadre was trained by Russian Communists."[23] Roy attributed the 1927 defeat to the misleadership of Mikhail Borodin, a Soviet Party and government official who virtually ran the Chinese Communist Party from 1923 to 1927.[24]

In 1980, during the course of the polemics against the Chinese Communist Party, the Soviets published, *Soviet Volunteers in China, 1925–1945*, which provided significant information on the role of Borodin in China as well as on the exploits of Soviet General Vasily Blyucher, who under the name Galen served as the Soviet military chief in China.[25] Many of the Soviet military personnel listed in the book, including Blyucher, died in the purges of 1936–38.

The military defeat of the Chinese Communists resulted in the disruption of the Comintern's operations in China. In the early 1930s a new crew, many of them German Communists, were assigned as both military and political advisors. Among those who operated in Shanghai were Gerhardt Eisler and Arthur Ewert. American Communists who worked in the Comintern apparatus in China included Earl Browder and Eugene Dennis, both of whom later served as general secretaries of the Communist Party USA.[26] Otto Braun served as military advisor; his wife of the time, Olga Benario, also worked for the Comintern.

The cover used by the Comintern for its political operations in China, India, and Indo–China was the Pan Pacific Trade Union Secretariat of the Comintern's trade union front, the Red International of Labor Unions. The magazine "Pan-Pacific Worker" and a number of pamphlets carried instructions to Comintern operators in the East.[27]

The contact man in the United States for the Pan Pacific Trade Union Secretariat was Harrison George. He edited the organization's magazine in San Francisco. For a time Eugene Dennis served as his assistant before being assigned by the Comintern to activities in the Far East.[28]

The Seventh World Congress of the Comintern held in Moscow in the summer of 1935 is best known for the instructions it gave the World Communist Movement to organize a united front against fascism. But it did other things as well. Soviet Communist Party official Otto Kuusinen frankly explained the role of youth in the Communist movement. He said,

> We want to attack our class enemies in the rear when they start war against the Soviet Union. But how can we do so if the majority of the working youth follow not us but, for instance the Catholic priests or the liberal chameleons. We often repeat the slogan of transforming the imperialist war into a civil war against the bourgeoisie. In itself, the slogan is a good one; but it becomes an empty and harmful phrase if we do not do everything today to create a united youth front.[29]

The Seventh Congress of the Comintern also heard the report of the Chinese Communist official, Wang Ming, on the revolutionary movement in the colonies. He reported that in Brazil the Communists had formed the "National Liberation Alliance" and that CP leader Prestes ". . . in the name of the entire Brazilian people, has unfurled the banner of struggle under the slogan: 'All power to the National Liberation Alliance!'."[30]

Despite the heroic paraphrase of Lenin's "all power to the Soviets," the Brazilian Communists were defeated. Prestes was captured and with him a number of Comintern agents, including Arthur Ewert, fresh from China, the wife of Prestes (and formerly of Otto Braun), German Communist Olga Benario, and the young American Communist, Victor Barron.[31]

Benario was returned to Nazi Germany, where she died at the Ravens-brueck Concentration Camp. The East German government issued a postage stamp in her honor in 1959.[32] Ewert was so badly treated that he was never again in any condition to continue his Comintern work. Victor Barron fell or was pushed out of a window in police headquarters. After his death the Communists identified him as the son of Harrison George.[33] The Comintern's use of the same cadre in China and then in Brazil indicates how few trained people were available to the Comintern during this period.

The Spanish Civil War, although a defeat for the Communists, allowed them to train a large number of people in military and paramilitary activities and to utilize their own military personnel.

"The International Brigades are selected units formed of anti-fascist volunteers from all over the world in reply to the call of the Communist International . . ." boasted Franz Dahlem, German Communist functionary in the Communist International's magazine for May, 1938. According to Dahlem, "The 11th International Brigade with its basic battalions—the Thaelmann and Edgar Andre—was made up in the first months almost exclusively of Communists, mainly Party functionaries and Red Front Fighters of Germany, and of strong units of Austrian Schutsbundlers [*sic*] and of Polish, Bulgarian and Jugoslavian [*sic*] Communists."

Thousands of volunteers came from all over the world to fight for the Spanish Republic. Organized by the Communists, they soon found themselves commanded by both military leaders and political commissars. The Soviet Union played a major role in both the International Brigades and the Spanish Army. A 1975 Soviet book listed dozens of Soviet military advisers and boasted "The Soviet Government recommended experienced military men as advisers. The post of chief adviser was held consecutively by Y.K. Berzin (1936–37), G.M. Stern (1937–38) and K.M. Kachanov (1938–39)."[34] What the Soviets neglected to say was that Berzin and Stern were both killed in the purges. Berzin, former head of the NKVD, was killed in 1937. Stern was killed in 1941 after leading Soviet troops against the Japanese in the 1938 battle of Lake Hassan and speaking at the Eighteenth Congress of the Community Party of the Soviet Union. His brother, M. Stern, led the International Brigades in their first battle to defend Madrid. Using the nom de guerre "General Kleber," Stern was first heralded as a Comintern hero and then quietly killed.[35] The Comintern magazine, *International Press Correspondence*, reported on 19 December 1936:

General Kleber, who is responsible to the Republican General Staff for the whole Northern Madrid front, is the Commander-in-Chief of the International Column. General Kleber is a man of few words, but an excellent linguist. He is a born general with long experience of wars and civil wars. When he was a prisoner of war in Russia he was released by the revolution and offered his services to the Soviet government. While in command of important units he first became well known for his victories over Kolchak and the French general Janin. After having participated in the organisation of the Hamburg insurrection he became one of the military leaders of the anti-imperialist struggle in China.

The two Sterns were later rehabilitated and were listed in the 1975 Soviet book.[36] M. Stern was also listed in a 1966 Austrian Communist pamphlet[37] but the 1956 East German history of the Eleventh Brigade ignored him.[38]

Some members of the International Brigade were trained in guerrilla warfare. At least two Americans received this training. William Aalto and Irving Goff described their experiences in the American Communist magazine *Soviet Russia Today* in October, 1941:

> Our Soviet advisers, as our previous article pointed out, not only put at our disposal their experience, but also practical aid. In our guerrilla schools, lessons from the Red Army's experience were taught to us, verbally and through Spanish translations of Red Army manuals. The mines, and the trick apparatus we used in Spain were constructed from patterns given to us by our Soviet advisers . . . The whole Spanish army and especially the guerrillas were reminded of the support of the Soviet Union every time they loaded a gun—for the bullets so often were Soviet.

Many of those who received such training served in underground guerrilla units fighting against the Nazis after the Soviet Union was attacked in 1941. Of course during the Soviet-Nazi Pact the Communists did not fight the Nazis.

Guerrilla units in the Soviet Union were organized by bypassed Soviet troops (often NKVD) and by party organizers deliberately left behind. A. Fyodorov, a Communist Party organizer in the Ukraine, described how in one area the district chief of the NKVD had organized a guerrilla unit. In one remarkably frank passage, Fyodorov wrote,

> There was an extermination battalion consisting of volunteers operating in his district. Comrade Kurochka correctly decided that the men of this battalion, who had already acquired a certain amount of experience in fighting the enemy in the woods, under conditions approximating those the partisans would be in, might make up the core of a detachment. All the two hundred and forty men of the extermination battalion agreed to remain behind in the enemy rear and enlist as partisans.[39]

The most dramatic and highly publicized guerrilla movement of World War II was the partisan movement headed by Marshall Tito. However, Tito admitted that the entry of the Yugoslav Communists into combat was delayed until two months after the conquest of their country. Tito wrote, "On June 22nd, 1941, Hitler's fascist hordes carried out a sneak attack on the Soviet Union. The Politbureau had a session the same day and the new situation as well as the measures our Party had to take in this connection were discussed. It was determined that the CC CPY and other central and provincial committees would publish proclamations, calling the people to armed struggle, to a general people's uprising."[40]

The popular image is one of the Yugoslav Communists liberating their country from the Nazis with no help. However, the exchange of letters between the Communist Party of Yugoslavia and the Communist Party of the Soviet Union, which resulted in Tito's break with the Cominform in 1948, provides a valuable insight. The Soviet Communists wrote that "after the Headquarters of the Yugoslav partizans had been routed by the German paratroops, at a moment when the national liberation movement of Yugoslavia was experiencing a serious crisis, the Soviet Army came to the help of the Yugoslav people, routed the German occupier, liberated Beograd and thus created the conditions indispensable to the Communist Party for taking power."[41]

Although the Yugoslavs denied the Soviet claim, Milovan Djilas, once Tito's closest associate but later a dissident, subsequently revealed:

> . . . the Germans had carried out a surprise attack on the Supreme Staff of the Yugloslav Army of People's Liberation in Drvar. Tito and the military missions had to flee into the hills . . . I was in complete agreement with Stalin's insistence on Tito's need, in view of the serious and complicated circumstances and tasks, to find himself a more permanent headquarters and to free himself of daily insecurity. There is no doubt that Stalin also transmitted this view to the Soviet Mission, for it was just at that time, on their insistence, that Tito agreed to evacuate to Italy, and from there to the island of Vis, where he remained until the Red Army got to Yugoslavia.[42]

Tito's propaganda radio station actually broadcast from the Soviet Union. Another Tito associate, Edvard Kardelji, wrote in his memoirs, "The 'Slobodna Jugoslavija' (Free Yugoslavia) Radio Station was set up on December 11th, 1941, in Ufa, USSR. It broadcasted news within the system of the Comintern Radio Station. From April 1942 until it ceased operating in January 1945, the Station broadcasted programmes from Moscow. Its broadcasts were in Serbo-Croatian and Slovene, and, from mid–1944, in Macedonian. From 1943, it broadcasted news in different languages for the people in occupied Europe."[43] Kardelji disingenuously wrote that "throughout the war, there was a direct radio communication between the Supreme Command and Moscow. However, formally, this was a contact with the Comintern, rather than with the Soviet government which had its ambassador to the Yugoslav Royal Government in London . . ."[44]

In 1943 Stalin dissolved the Comintern, but not its apparatus. As Djilas pointed out, Dimitrov, the Comintern's General Secretary, and Manuilsky, the Comintern Organizational Secretary, shared the direction of the section of the Soviet Central Committee for Foreign Communist Parties.[45]

In the postwar period, the Soviet apparatus for support for low-intensity warfare as well as influence operations has been led since 1958 by the International Department of the Central Committee of the Communist Party of the Soviet Union. The magazine *Problems of Peace and Socialism* or *World Marxist Review (WMR)* serves as the international theoretical organ. Conferences of the editorial board are held instead of meetings of the Comintern executive. A secret publication of the Workers Party of Jamaica (the communist party of that country) revealed in 1982 that while

> there is presently no formal centre of the International Communist Movement . . . The Journal and its regular Conferences, therefore, play an important role of providing for contact, exchange of views and formulation of international policy. Through their representatives in the Journal at Prague (very often CC members) and in these conferences now being held every four years, important international questions can be tackled. This has to be done, unfortunately, without any formal aknowledgement of its role, which would intensify the charges that the WMR is acting as a 'centre' of the movement.[46]

At another level and also under the direction of the International Department, the International Soviet Fronts meet annually to plan their strategy. The October 1983 meeting included, in addition to a representative of *World Marxist Review,* officials of all of the major International Soviet Fronts.[47]

The Soviet controlled Afro-Asian Peoples' Solidarity Organization (AAPSO) and the Cuban-controlled Organization of Solidarity With The People of Asia, Africa and Latin America (OSPAAL) work closely together in support of low-intensity warfare throughout the world. Shortly after the Prague meeting, AAPSO and OSPAAL met in Cairo to plan future operations.[48]

Other International Soviet Fronts also provide support for violent activities. As the World Federation of Democratic Youth pointed out in 1965, "Peaceful coexistence presupposes also the continuous development of the national liberation movement, going as far as armed struggle."[49] Khrushchev boasted in 1963 that "many peoples have used our armaments in their liberation struggles and have been victorious . . ."[50] As one Soviet writer explained it: "Each nation has the sacred right to wage liberation war against the colonialists, and there can be no coexistence as far as this question is concerned. As before, the Soviet Union is providing all-round support to the national-liberation movements, thus demonstrating the profound sense of internationalism typical of the Soviet people."[57]

A mysterious element in the Soviet support apparatus for international terrorism was the existence of a group in France led by Henri Curiel, formerly a leader of the Egyptian Communist Party. The Curiel apparat provided support to terrorist groups in Africa and Latin America until the murder of Curiel in 1978. One of Curiel's followers, Breyten Breytenbach, who had been captured in South Africa while on a mission for the apparat, revealed in a recent book that he himself believed that Curiel was a KGB operative and that he certainly was an orthodox Soviet Communist or Stalinist.[52]

Another of Curiel's followers was the French Communist Party member, Michele Firk, who committed suicide when captured by police in Guatemala after participating in the murder of the U.S. Ambassador to that country in 1968. Firk was eulogized in *Granma* the official Communist Party newspaper in Cuba, in its issues of October 13 and 20, 1968. According to the Cubans, she joined the Communist Party in 1958 and operated on behalf of the Algerian Liberation Movement, "For more than 3 years she acted as a messenger, hiding and carrying weapons, collecting money and false documents, participating in public demonstrations." In 1963 she visited Cuba, where she met the Guatemalan terrorists and joined their ranks. She was identified as a member of the Curiel apparat in the French magazine *Le Point* on 21 June 1976.

Small violence-prone groups in the Caribbean received the support of the regime in Grenada led by the late Maurice Bishop. In April, 1983, Bishop met with Andrei Gromyko in the Kremlin. Bishop explained that he had organized meetings of fifteen Marxist-Leninist Parties from the Caribbean and had provided "airline tickets, subsistance etc. plus direct financial grants." According to Bishop, this had already cost $500,000. He said, "The USSR needs to get involved in providing some material support—through the most appropriate channel, to ensure the survival and development of these progressive organizations." Gromyko promised to help.[53]

The primary supporter of low-intensity warfare in the Western Hemisphere is Cuba, which serves as a Soviet surrogate. In 1967 a headline in the Cuban Communist Party newspaper *Granma* proclaimed "The guerrillas are destined to be the basic nucleus of the revolutionary movement" (20 August 1967).

OSPAAL was established at the first Tri-Continental Congress held in Havana in January 1966. It serves as the Cuban apparatus to coordinate support for low-intensity warfare. Its magazine, *Tricontinental,* published in Havana in Spanish, English, and French, provides both theoretical justification and practical instructions in terrorism and insurgency. The entire November 1970 issue was devoted to the text of Carlos Marighella's "Minimanual of the Urban Guerrilla." This booklet contained detailed instructions on assassination, bank robbery, kidnappings, and other terrorist acts, even describing the appropriate weapons to use. Terrorist organizations throughout the world reprinted this document, including the New World Liberation Front in the United States. Every issue carries glowing reports of the activities of terrorist organizations from every part of the world.

On 5 October 1969 *Granma* headlined "Brazilian Revolutionaries Released in Exchange for Yankee Ambassador Arrive in Cuba—Fidel Welcomed them at the Airport on Behalf of our People." This of course was a report about a group of terrorist kidnappers who were welcomed in Cuba.

The Cuban Communist Party's apparatus to support these activities is the America Department of the Central Committee of the Communist Party of Cuba, headed by Manuel Pineiro, the former head of the Cuban intelligence service. On 26–28 April 1982, a secret conference was held in Havana organized by the Cuban Communist Party to discuss the subject, "general and particular characteristics of the revolutionary process in Latin America and the Caribbean." A letter of invitation was sent to "Communist Parties and other revolutionary organizations in Latin America and the Caribbean." A copy of the letter in Spanish was found in the Grenada archives. Pineiro made a major speech at the conference which was later published in the Communist magazine, *Cuba Socialista*. According to Pineiro, "The revolutions in Cuba, Nicaragua, and Grenada present well-known differences, but among other similar elements, have the common stamp of the use of arms. At the same time, along with specific common bases (especially in the cases of Cuba and Nicaragua), they show difference in military employed, in insurrectional forms, etc. For example, in El Salvador creative revolutionary formulas are being applied in the use of arms . . ."[54]

The insurgency in El Salvador is not only supplied with arms by the Soviet Union through Cuba and Nicaragua (as was well documented in the State Department white paper of 23 February 1981 and the large collection of documents released with it), but Castro and Pineiro played a major role in bringing together the small terrorist groups in El Salvador into one insurgent force. Documents captured in El Salvador in 1980 contain reports written by the Salvador rebels to Pineiro detailing their operations.

The technique of providing support to terrorist groups when they agree to work together in an insurgency has been used by the Cubans elsewhere in Latin America. On 8 February 1982 Agence France Press reported the merger of a number of small terrorist groups in Guatemala. On 12 February 1982 *Prensa Latina* reported that diplomatic representatives from the Communist Bloc expressed their support at a meeting of the Guatamalen United Force at OSPAAL headquarters in Havana. Lastly, the Nicaraguan Communist newspaper, *El Nuevo Diario* reported the merger of the small terrorist groups in Honduras on 20 April 1983.

Even violence-prone Americans have received training in Cuba. Some members of the Venceremos Brigade received such training. In 1970 a Cuban report outlined one such class: "Susan wants to clear up some confused points of Marighela's 'Mini-manual of urban guerrilla'; Bob would like to know how the Tupamaros function and organize themselves because 'we could do the same in many cities of the United States'; a blond long-haired young man worries about 'What actions could we carry out to cooperate with Latin American revolutionaries in their struggle against Yankee imperialism?'."[55]

One group of Venceremos Brigaders heard a talk by Julian Rizo, a Cuban intelligence officer assigned to the America Department and later Cuban ambassador to Grenada. Rizo told them ". . . the first thing that a U.S. revolutionary must be convinced of is precisely the fact that he does come from a decadent society, that he comes from a society that must be destroyed . . ."[56]

Cuban support has also been provided to the Puerto Rican terrorist organization, FALN, which has been guilty of a number of murders. An FALN communique of 27 October 1975 stated, "We especially acknowledge the moral support given to our organization by the Cuban people and government in a speech made by Prime Minister Fidel Castro in August in which he said that the Cuban government would do all it could to support the FALN."

Many of the violence-prone Americans were radicalized during the Vietnam War, when a major effort was made by the international Communist movement to provide political support as well as Soviet arms to the Vietcong. Special bulletins were published in North Vietnam to organize worldwide support for the Vietcong. Coordinated demonstrations were conducted throughout the world to provide political support. One letter sent from North Vietnam to its American supporters dated 30 December 1970 said, "Carrying out successfully your Spring activities, you will make big contributions in raising the political consciousness of the people, in embracing the much more larger participation of the masses in the anti-war movement."

An international support apparatus is currently functioning on behalf of the Communist insurrgency in El Salvador. Headquartered in Mexico, it is called *Frente Mundial De Solidaridad Con El Pueblo Salvadoren* (World Front in Solidarity with the People of El Salvador). The letterhead of this group shows as a member of the permanent buro, Sandy Pollack, a leading functionary of the CPUSA.

In 1980, a Salvadorian Communist, Farid Handel, visited the United States to organize a support apparatus. His trip report was captured in El Salvador. According to Handel, he met with people from the Cuban mission to the United Nations and officials of the American Communist Party. One of the American Communists was Sandy Pollack, whom Handel identified as a member of the Central Committee of the Communist Party. She helped them organize a support apparatus, which eventually came to be known as the U.S. Committee in Solidarity with the People of El Salvador (CISPES).

CISPES serves the Salvador insurgency by organizing demonstrations as well as by circulating forgeries and disinformation. For example, CISPES published the text of a supposed State Department dissent paper, which the FBI branded a Soviet forgery in congressional testimony.[57]

On 8 April 1981 CISPES issued a press release charging that the Salvador national guard had massacred fifteen hundred peasants in a particular town. Three weeks later on 28 April 1981, the *Washington Post* reported that the massacre was hard to verify since there was no such town or cave as the one described by CISPES.

The accidental deaths of two American Communist women two years apart provided some valuable information on the apparatus. On 11 December 1982, the Communist Party newspaper in New York *The Daily World* reported on the death in a fire of Communist Party member Terry Santana. According to the Communists, one of her jobs for the Party was the solidarity operation in support of the revolt in El Salvador.

On 19 January 19 1985 Sandy Pollack died in the crash of a Cubana Airlines plane flying from Havana to Managua. According to the *Daily World* of 23 January 1985, "She was a member of the National Council and International and Peace and Solidarity commissions of the Communist Party, USA and responsible for international solidarity work for the U.S. Peace Council."

The 22 January 1985 issue of the *Daily World* provided still more information reporting that

she first visited Cuba in 1969 and traveled there many times over the years, becoming a leader in the U.S. movement in defense of the Cuban revolution. She served on the national committee of the Venceremos Brigade, which sent many hundreds of Americans to cut sugar cane and build housing and schools, in defiance of U.S. travel bans. Every year for over a decade she helped organize the coalitions commemorating July 26, Cuba's revolutionary holiday. She co-founded Tri-Continental News Service, which broke the information black-out by distributing Cuban and Latin American political writing and art in the U.S. As a natural outgrowth of her Cuba work, Ms. Pollack became deeply involved in the Chile solidarity movement following the overthrow of Allende; the movement in support of Puerto Rican independence; defense of revolutionary Grenada and, especially, the anti-interventionist movements in support of the Nicaraguan and Salvadoran revolutions. In all of these struggles she combined serving on their executive committees with doing the kind of nuts and bolts day to day work of which lasting movements are made. Tributes to Ms. Pollack published this week in the Nicaraguan and Cuban media and issued by the Salvadoran revolutionary leadership attest to the magnitude of her achievements, and the respect and affection she had gained.

The Palestine Liberation Organization (PLO) serves as both a terrorist organization in its own right and a surrogate for Soviet military and political support to other terrorist groups. It describes itself as: "The Palestinian resistance movement which leads the struggle of the Palestinian people is an organic part of the forces of world revolution: the socialist countries, the international liberation movement, and the working class parties in the capitalist countries."[58]

One of the most bizarre terrorist groups associated with the PLO is the Japanese Red Army (JRA). The JRA's own description is "a volunteer army dependent on the Palestinian revolution." This description was given in 1979 on the seventh anniversary of the JRA massacre of innocent people at Lod Airport.[59]

Not only leftwing terrorists but even neo-Nazis find their way to the PLO camps. In an interview with *Der Spiegel* of 13 July 1981, PLO official Abu Iyad admitted that members of the neo-Nazi Hoffman terrorist group from West Germany had trained at a PLO camp.

Even American terrorists have shown up at those camps. In September, 1981, Judy Clark, who was later convicted in the Brinks robbery case, attended a PLO conference in Lebanon. In a report to the May 19th Communist Organization, Clark wrote, "The struggle of the Palestinian people is to liberate Palestine from the forces of zionism, imperialism and Arab reaction. In waging the national liberation struggle to free Palestine they must overcome all the forces of imperialism and the local bourgeoisies that are trying to maintain dominance in the region. The so-called state of 'Israel' is a creation of imperialism, established because of the imperialist's need to control this incredibly rich and strategic region."[60]

Lenin's policy of encouraging others to engage in terrorist acts has borne fruit throughout the world—even in the United States. The small terrorist groups operating in this country repeat the slogans of the international Communist movement. A 17 August 1983 communique of the Armed Resistance Unit began, "Tonight we attacked the computer operations complex at the Washington navy Yard. We have acted in solidarity with the revolutionary struggles of the peoples of Central America and the Caribbean." The communique of the same group, dated 7 November 1983 began, "Tonight we bombed the U.S. Capitol building. We attacked the U.S. government to retaliate against imperialist aggression that has sent the marines, the CIA and the army to invade sovereign nations, to trample and lay waste the lives and rights of the peoples of Grenada, Lebanon, El Salvador, and Nicaragua, to carry out imperialism's need to dominate, oppress, and exploit."

Low-intensity warfare, often carried out by others, is an important element in Communist strategy. Over the years the Soviet government has maintained an apparatus to provide political and ideological support to such activity. The names have been changed—Comintern, Cominform, *World*

Marxist Review, International Department—but the policy remains the same. It is the policy of combining war and peace and conducting war as a continuation of politics.

Notes

1. V.I. Lenin, "The Collapse of The Second International," 1915, *Collected Works,* vol. 21 (Moscow: Progress Publishers, 1964) p. 219.

2. V.I. Lenin, "On The Slogan For A United States of Europe," August 1915, *Collected Works,* vol. 21 (Moscow: Progress Publishing, 1964), p. 342.

3. V.I. Lenin, "Concluding Speech at First Congress of the Communist International," 6 March 1919, *Collected Works,* vol. 28 (Moscow: Progress Publishers, 1964), p. 476–477.

4. Major General V. Matsulenko, "The Liberation Mission of The Soviet Armed Forces," *Mezhdunarodnia Zhizn* (Jan. 1985): 84.

5. V.I. Lenin, "To The Combat Committee of the St. Petersburg Committee," 16 Oct. 1905, *Collected Works,* vol. 9 (Moscow: Progress Publishers, 1964), p. 345.

6. Lenin, "To The Combat Committee," pp. 345–46.

7. *The Communist International* Petrograd, 2, (13), pp. 2330, 2338.

8. *From Third to Fourth, A Report on the Activities of the YCI Since Its Third World Congress* (Sweden: Executive Committee of the Young Communist International, May 1929), p. 54 A. Neuberg.

9. *From Third to Fourth,* p. 40.

10. *Armed Insurrection,* intro. Erich Wollenberg, (London: NLB, 1970), pp. 9–23.

11. *Data for a Report on the Life and Work of George Dimitrov,* (Sofia: Sofia Press, 1972), pp. 10–11.

12. George Dimitrov, *Political Report V,* (Sofia: Congress of the Bulgarian Communist Party, Sofia, 1949), p. 17.

13. *Data,* pp. 11 and 12.

14. *International Press Correspondence,* Vienna, 23 April 1925, p. 475.

15. *International Press Correspondence,* Vienna, 7 May 1925, pp. 541–43.

16. Dimitrov, *Political Report V,* p. 21.

17. *The Communist Youth International,* Report of Activity Between the 4th and 5th Congress 1924–1928, (New York: Young Workers [Communist] League of America, and Communist Party of Great Britain, 1928), pp. 8–9, 25f.

18. *Fifth Congress of the Communist International, Abridged Report of Meetings Held at Moscow, June 17 to July 8, 1924* (London: Published for the Communist International by the Communist Party of Great Britain, 1924), p. 192.

19. *William Dubois, Scholar, Humanitarian, Freedom Fighter,* (Moscow: Novosti, 1971), p. 49.

20. See Babette Gross, *Willi Muenzenberg: A Political Biography* (Mich.: Michigan State Univ. Press, 1974) and R.N. Carew Hunt, *Willi Muenzenberg,* (Carbondale, Ill.: Southern Illinois Univ. Press, 1960), St. Antony's Papers, no. 9.

21. Two editions contain this speech: *Negro's Struggle Against Imperialism,* (the

Provisional International Trade Union Committee of Negro Workers, 1930) and the other was entitled *The Communists and the Struggle for Negro Liberation* (New York: The Harlem Division of the Communist Party, circa 1936).

22. *China in Revolt: Speeches by Stalin et al.* (New York: Daily Worker Publishing Co., circa 1927).

23. M. N. Roy, *My Experience in China* (Calcutta: Renaissance Publishers, 1945), p. 19.

24. Roy, *My Experience,* pp. 31, 53.

25. *Soviet Volunteers in China, 1925–1945* (Moscow: Progress Publishers, 1980.

26. See *A Partial Documentation of the Sorge Espionage Case* (privately printed in Japan in 1951 by Gen. Charles A. Willoughby for the use of the House Committee on Unamerican Activities); and Charles A. Willoughby, *Shanghai Conspiracy* (New York: E.P. Dutton & Co., 1952.

27. See, for example, Orgwald, "Tactical and Organizational Questions of the Communist Parties of India and Indo-China," *The Pan-Pacific Worker,* no place, no date.

28. Peggy Dennis, *The Autobiography of an American Communist* (Westport, Conn.: Lawrence Hill & Co., 1977), p. 39.

29. *VII Congress of the Communist International* (Moscow: Foreign Languages Publishing House, 1939), p. 489.

30. Ibid., p. 295.

31. *International Press Correspondence,* London, 15 Feb. 1936, p. 231; 11 April 1936, pp. 484–485; 25 April 1936, pp. 556–558; 12 May 1936, p. 50.

32. East German folder of stamps to commemorate the concentration camp at Ravensbrueck, 1959.

33. Luis Carlos Prestes, *The Struggle for Liberation in Brazil* (New York: Workers Library Publishers, 1936), pp. 3–5; and Harrison George, *The Crisis in the C.P.U.S.A.,* privately printed in Los Angeles, 1947, p. 4.

34. *International Solidarity with the Spanish Republic* (Moscow: Progress Publishers, 1975), p. 327.

35. Robert Conquest, *The Great Terror* (New York: Macmillan, 1968), pp. 60, 230, and K. Voroshilov et al. *The Red Army Today* (Moscow: Foreign Languages Publishing House, 1939), p. 64f.

36. *International Solidarity,* p. 46.

37. Max Stern, *Spaniens Himmel* (Vienna: Schoenbrunn-Verlag, 1966), p. 34.

38. Gustav Szinda, *Die XI. Brigade* (Berlin: Verlag Des Ministeriums für Nationale Verteidigung [East German Ministry of National Defense], 1956).

39. A. Fyodorov, *The Underground R.C. Carries On* (Moscow: Foreign Languages Publishing House, 1950), pp. 103, 28.

40. Josip Broz Tito, *Political Report of the Central Committee of the Communist Party of Yugoslavia* (Beograd, 1948), pp. 49, 51.

41. *Letters of the CC CPY and the CC CPSU (b)* (Beograd, 1948), pp. 86–87.

42. Milovan Djilas, *Conversations with Stalin* (New York: Harcourt, Brace, 1962), pp. 68 and 72.

43. Edvard Kardelj, "The Struggle For Recognition of The National Liberation Movement of Yugoslavia," *Macedonian Review* 11, (1981):201.

44. Ibid., p. 202.

45. Djilas, *Conversations*, p. 24.

46. *Party Life* (Kingston: Workers Party of Jamaica, circa 1982). This is an internal publication, for members only.

47. "Communique," issued in Prague 9 Oct. 1983.

48. Circular Letter of the Afro-Asian People's Solidarity Organisation, 16 Oct. 1983.

49. *Executive Committee of the WFDY*, Accra, 15–19 April 1965; WFDY, Budapest, 1965, p. 20.

50. *Nikita Khrushchov's Speech At the Sixth Congress of the Socialist Unity Party of Germany* (London: Soviet Booklet, 1963), p. 27.

51. I. Shatalov et al. *Lenin and Revolution in the East* (Moscow: Novosti Press Agency Publishing House, 1969), pp. 88–89.

52. Breyten Breytenbach, *The True Confessions of an Albino Terrorist* (New York: Farrar Straus Girous, 1985), p. 89.

53. Grenada Archive at U.S. National Archives, Washington, D.C.

54. *New International,* a publication of the Socialist Workers Party (Spring-Summer 1984) contains a translation of the speech of Manuel Pineiro.

55. *Direct from Cuba*, Havana, 30 Oct. 1970, "Venceremos Brigade Imposes Its Rhythm."

56. *Venceremos Brigade Preparation Course* (New York: Venceremos Brigade, no date), Sec. 2, p. 3.

57. *Soviet Active Measures,* Hearings before the Permanent Select Committee on Intelligence, House of Representatives, 13 and 14 July, 1982, pp. 215 and 230.

58. *The Palestinian Resistance: A National Liberation Movement* (No place: Palestine Liberation Organization, Political Department, no date), p. 3.

59. The Japanese Red Army, *Let's Consolidate our Standpoint of Internationalism and Self-Reliance!* (No place, 30 May, 1979), p. 16.

60. *Death to the Klan!,* Newsletter of the John Brown Anti-Klan Committee, Chicago, October-November 1981, p. 4.

5
Military Doctrine and Structure

John J. Dziak

From the earliest years of the Bolshevik Party's struggle for power, reliance on special categories of military force absorbed a great deal of attention. Since the Party viewed itself as the herald of a new revolutionary future attainable only by bloody struggle, it endeavored to devise politically reliable and unique military instruments to advance that struggle.[1]

In order to secure the Party's exclusive claims to power while at the same time foisting a revolutionary socioeconomic program on a war-weary Russia Lenin saw to the creation of the CHEKA, the All-Russian Extraordinary Commission for Combatting Counterrevolution and Sabotage. The CHEKA, formed even before the creation of the Red Army, was granted special administrative and extralegal powers, making it the principal action arm of the Party. This preferred position in the Party-State amalgam continues with today's KGB, or Committee for State Security.

While the Armed Forces may be viewed as the third pillar in the triangle of Party, Police, and Army, its subordinate position relative to the other two was evident from its birth. Though the Red Army earned the victory laurels for defeating the various White forces, non-Bolshevik revolutionaries, and foreign armies, the Red Army itself was subject to a dual system of penetration and control from the CHEKA and the Party, the other two pillars of the system. This unique symbiosis between the Party and the police—a relationship which not only eluded the military but indeed made it a target—is best illustrated by Lenin's dictum ". . . a good Communist is . . . a good Chekist."[2] The Party and the CHEKA were the only two institutions in the new system unhindered and unbounded by anything approaching a constitutional or moral check. Such freedom from any bonds of higher restraint explains in part a tendency toward state-sponsored terror, first against their own domestic "class enemies" and then against international "enemies" in Moscow's bids to revolutionize the international system.

The views expressed or implied in this paper are solely those of the author and do not necessarily represent the views of the Defense Intelligence Agency or the Department of Defense.

While Trotsky and the Party saw to the formation of the Red Army, Dzer-zhinskiy, with Lenin's approval and encouragement, created specialized military units drawn to a great extent (according to Party accounts) from loyal Party cadres. One of these, originally labeled CHON (Chasti Osobogo Naz-nacheniya or Units of Special Purpose) was created by a Central Committee resolution in April 1919. These units served several purposes: 1) as special guard troops, 2) for the suppression of uprisings, and 3) for working with other categories of CHEKA troops known as OSNAZ (Otryad Osobogo Naznacheniya or Detachments of Special Purpose). They also operated on Party orders in enemy territory organizing partisan warfare and sundry clandestine activities.[3] In 1924 the Party formally disbanded CHON units, but they were actually reorganized, along with OSNAZ, into a Division of Special Designation. Following Dzerzhinskiy's death in 1926, the Division was re-dubbed OMSDON (Imeni Dzerzhinskogo or the Dzerzhinskiy Detached Motorized Infantry Division of Special Purpose).[4] The unit still exists as the First Dzerzhinskiy Motorized Infantry Division nominally subordinated to the MVD (Ministry of Internal Affairs), but in reality is an elite unit of state security for suppressing uprisings, coups, and rebellions against the Party.[5]

It should be noted that these special tasks or missions and the units specially formed for their fulfillment were not subordinated to the regular military. Indeed, the CHON units were organized and controlled by the Party Central Committee, although in practice they worked closely with state security and in many cases were run by the latter. Because they were highly trusted, they, rather than the regular military, were granted the politically sensitive missions of internal suppression and external partisan warfare activities. Indeed, with the exception of the partisan warfare experience of the Russian Civil War, there is no evidence of large-scale "diversionary" activities associated with the regular military, or more precisely, military intelligence, until the period immediately prior to World War II.

Soviet military doctrinal writings are far less explicit about "diversionary" or special operations-type activities than they are with other categories of military science, military art, or military strategy. This is to be expected, given the political sensitivity associated with such actions and the fact that the forces charged with these missions are subordinated to the intelligence and security services—the "organs" of the USSR. However, diversionary activities particularly during World War II have been lionized as part of the Soviet historical experience. Hence, and as with so many other openly discussed Soviet military topics, a convoluted Aesopian quality characterizes what the Soviets say about the subject of diversion and related activities. While they will admit to their own use of diversion historically, contemporary use is ascribed only to the "imperalists." This is best illustrated by their discussion of diversion and related entries in the authoritative *Soviet Military Encyclopedia*. Under the entry for *diversiya* (diversion), we find:

> The action of groups (sub-units) or individuals in the rear of the enemy to put out of action military, industrial, and other installations, disrupting troop control, disrupting of signal communications, lines and centers, manpower and military-materiel destruction, influencing the morale-psychological state of an opponent. Diversion primarily is accomplished by small forces for confusing an opponent, distracting his attention and forces from the main axis. The Russian military and naval leaders A.V. Suvorov, M.I. Kutuzov, F.F. Ushakov and others skillfully used such applications of diversion. *Later, diversion was used for the solution of more varied tasks....*
>
> In the Revolutionary Liberation War of the Spanish People of 1936–39, in the composition of the Republican 14th Corps, designated for activity in the enemy rear, there were diversionary brigades and detachments, subunits of which accomplished diversions along the rail and highway routes, telegraph and telephone communications....
>
> The Soviet command devoted major attention to the organization of mass diversionary actions in the rear of the Fascist predators.... Diversionary actions occupied a leading place in the combat activity of partisans and the underground. They utilized small forces with nominal or no losses to inflict significant losses on the enemy....
>
> Diversion was widely implemented by partisans in Yugoslavia, France, Poland and other countries occupied by the Fascists and after the Second World War in the National Liberation Wars of the peoples of colonial and independent countries. Special units and sub-units, dedicated to the accomplishment of diversionary and terrorist acts, have been created in the USA and a number of other capitalist countries within the composition of the armed forces.[6]

Thus, we see an admission that diversion was practiced by Tsarist military heroes, by Soviet-supported revolutionaries—the Spanish Republicans, 1936–39—by the Soviets themselves against the Germans in World War II, by European partisans against the occupying Germans and Italians, and by anti-colonial forces since World War II. While the Soviets do not eschew the practice in the contemporary period, neither do they readily admit to it. Only the capitalists now indulge in "diversionary and terrorist" acts. Still, no effort is made explicitly to distance themselves from the practice.

In another entry in the *Soviet Military Encyclopedia* the Soviets offer a rather pointed definition of a military term actually current in the Soviet lexicon. As with the previous entry, they conclude this definition by linking the actions described to the U.S. and its allies. But each action more precisely correlates with what is known of the missions, organization, and functions of contemporary Soviet special purpose forces under the KGB and GRU (Chief Intelligence Directorate of the Soviet General Staff). The Aesopian veneer thins somewhat under careful scrutiny. The term is *"spetsal'naya razvedka,"* special reconnaissance:

> Reconnaissance conducted to subvert the political, economic, military and moral potential of a probable or actual enemy. The primary missions of special reconnaissance are: acquiring intelligence on major economic and military installations and either destroying them or putting them out of action; organizing of sabotage and acts of subversion and terrorism; carrying out punitive operations against patriotic forces; conducting hostile propaganda; forming and training insurgent detachments, etc. Special reconnaissance is set-up by military organs and special services and is conducted by the forces of *covert intelligence and special designation troops.* Special models of weapons, supplies and equipment are utilized in performing special reconnaissance, including firearms with silencers, mines and demolition equipment, radio, and other special equipment, as well as biological weapons, narcotics, poisons, etc.[7]

Notwithstanding the linkage of such activities to the West, virtually all of the actions described above are not only admitted to by the Soviets but glorified in numerous accounts extolling the Soviet partisan struggle during World War II. A trail of first-hand testimony, ranging from KGB and GRU defectors, to captured terrorists trained in Soviet or Soviet-supported camps to refugees and Western doctors from Afghanistan, and so on, clearly establishes that the above activities are still conducted by the special designation forces of the military's GRU and the direct action elements of the KGB.

The weightier tomes of open Soviet military literature are likewise rather disingenuous in their discussions of diversion, partisan warfare, and other types of direct action. As in the *Encyclopedia* entries, considerable space is devoted to extolling such Soviet operations in World War II. But in one of the more consistently reliable guides to official Soviet doctrinal and strategic thinking, Marshal Sokolovskiy's *Military Strategy,* the pertinence of these activities to contemporary Soviet strategic requirements is adduced with a minimum of indirection:

> . . . the work of the Soviet partisans in the rear of the enemy had important strategic significance. . . . The past war had again shown that the partisan movement is a characteristic feature of war in the defense of our socialist Fatherland and that *it is one of the most powerful factors in the victory of our people in their just, liberating wars against alien usurpers.*[8]

This same prestigious work also heralded a significant change in Soviet military policy: a more assertive role for the Soviet armed forces in Third

World "national liberation" struggles. Heretofore, Soviet support to these struggles had not involved direct, open applications of Soviet military power. Sokolovskiy's 1968 edition of his book added "military support" to the political and material aid Moscow would render to "national liberation" struggles.[9] By the 1970s this doctrinal modification was more publicly expanded upon with announcements from senior political-military spokesmen of a much enhanced "external" mission for the Soviet armed forces.[10] Capability soon followed doctrinal prescription as the Soviet Union began deploying its growing projection forces beyond the traditional confines of the USSR's continental periphery.

Parallel changes occurred in those intelligence and security organs responsible for diversion and special operations/direct action. By the early 1970s it had become evident that the General Staff's Chief Intelligence Directorate, the GRU, had expanded its capabilities for working with so-called "national liberation" movements and terrorist organizations.[11]

Concurrently, however, information seemed to dry up about the KGB's notorious "Wet Affairs" Department, or Department V, following the 1971 defection of one of its officers in England. This element had been the KGB's principal action arm for kidnappings, sabotage, and political murders.[12] It wasn't until years later that it became known that in the wake of a 1971 defection in England and the resultant scandal in KGB headquarters, Department V was disbanded and then reconstituted as Department Eight of the highly sensitive Illegals Directorate, or Directorate S. Evidence surfaced in 1982 that Department Eight planned and led the special operation which resulted in President Amin's assassination in Afghanistan in 1979.[13] This rather unique event followed actions that demonstrated that Moscow was prepared to make bold moves involving quick, decisive military aid or interference in volatile situations where decisiveness could decide the issue in Moscow's favor. Soviet Bloc and surrogate operations in Angola, Ethiopia, and the Seychelles, among others, pointed to a convergence of doctrine, capability, and will—a convergence in which special operations elements of Soviet intelligence and security were at the leading edge.

Soviet Forces for Low-Intensity Combat Operations

KGB and MVD

While the foregoing discussion made a case for the primacy of the Party and the KGB over the military in politically sensitive activities such as diversion, terrorism, or direct action, the KGB *is* considered to be part of the Soviet Armed Forces and deploys forces larger than those found in many sizeable countries. Hence, the KGB has the mandate and the means to engage in military and quasi-military operations, domestically and externally. It simply answers to the Politburo and Central Committee rather than to the Ministry of Defense or General Staff.

The largest and most clearly identifiable troop elements of the KGB are those of the Border Guard Directorate, whose strength has been estimated as anywhere from 250,000 to 400,000.[14] Obviously the bulk of these forces are used for the sealing of Soviet frontiers, but such duties necessarily include cross-border missions comprised of actions included under "special reconnaissance." During various counterguerilla campaigns against the so-called "Basmachi"—or more correctly the "Beklar Hareketi," The Freeman's Movement among the Muslem Turks—in Central Asia from the 1920s through the early 1930s, Border Guard and other state security units ran significant punitive operations including cross-border incursions against Afghanistan sanctuaries. A half-century later a defecting KGB-trained Afghan secret police general reported on Afghan rebel raids into the USSR.[15] The defense against such activities is a duty of the KGB Border Guard and encompasses the authority to strike across the frontier. Given the massive Soviet presence in Afghanistan, this is a moot point, and it must be assumed that these KGB troops are integrated into both "special reconnaissance" actions and the more regular security activities of overall Soviet military operations there.

There are also other KGB troop elements—exclusive of the Ninth or Guards Directorate and the Communications Troops—about which little is known. These may well be hidden under other organizational entities, possibly military or, more likely, MVD. The MVD, headed by a former KGB officer, Gen. Fedorchuk, employs roughly a quarter million of its own Internal Security troops, which are also technically a part of the Soviet armed forces but operationally independent of the Ministry of Defense and answerable to the Party. Historically, many of these MVD troop units were state security forces with pedigrees dating to the Civil War and the 1920s. Of these, the "Feliks Edmundovich Dzerzhinskiy Order of Lenin, Red Banner Division" is one of the more likely candidates for the "hidden" KGB forces, along with its sister division, the Second Motorized Infantry Division of Internal Troops.[16] The Dzerzhinskiy Division was used in numerous special operations against the "Kulaks" during collectivization, the Basmachi in Central Asia in the 1930s, the Germans in World War II, and the anti-Soviet partisans and occupied East European countries during and after the war.[17] There are, then, extant specialized state security troop elements with a tradition of diversionary and other special operations and on which the KGB most certainly draws for sensitive missions.

But the organizational focal point within the KGB for diversionary activity, including terrorism and terrorist support, is Department Eight, Directorate S of the First Chief Directorate (mentioned earlier). This entity has its own diversionary and terrorist training school near Moscow at Balashika, a site traditionally associated with the KGB.[18] Since the 1979 Soviet coup against President Amin in Afghanistan and subsequent military operations there, an upsurge of activity at the Balashika complex has been reported suggesting heavier future KGB involvement in sabotage, terrorism and other diversionary operations.[19]

Department Eight's *institutional* roots go back at least to 1936 when the NKVD formed its "Administration for Special Tasks." Prior to that time, assassinations and other diversionary tasks were handled by state security through an as-needed tasking system with initiatives frequently originating from the highest political leadership (the tradition still holds—Amin's assassination was ordered by Brezhnev's Politburo). Over the years the unit's title changed several times, the last one being "Department V" as recently as the early 1970s.

According to the U.S. Department of Defense, the "KGB is assessed to have responsibility, under Central Committee guidance, for operational planning, coordination and political control of special purpose forces that operate abroad in peacetime."[20] For wartime, Department Eight maintains its own capabilities in clandestine assets for assassination and sabotage.[21] Both Afghanistan in 1979 and Czechoslovakia in 1968 witnessed *joint* KGB and military SPETSNAZ (Spetsalnaya Naznacheniya or Special Purpose/Special Designation) operations under overall KGB guidance and control, a traditional style of operation especially common to the World War II experience.

Department Eight is also the most likely KGB focal point for working with Bloc and surrogate counterpart diversionary/terrorist elements and for connections to various terrorist, revolutionary, and so-called "national liberation" groups outside the Soviet Bloc.[22] Originally, camps for foreign diversionists and terrorists seemed to be concentrated in the USSR itself; as early as 1919–20 camps were set up in Soviet Central Asia for operations against Western colonial holdings in the Middle East. Balashika seems to have been a training site for foreigners for many years prior to its current notoriety. The Spanish Civil War appears to have been the first major state security and military venture in the large-scale training of foreign terrorists outside the USSR.[23] Both General Orlov of the NKVD and former General Berzin of the GRU were heavily involved in such work in Republican Spain. Orlov identified Konev (later Marshal Konev) as one of the officers conducting terrorist training in Spain; actual sabotage and guerrilla operations behind Nationalist lines were controlled by Orlov's assistant, General Kotov (alias Eitingon). Ramon Mercador, the son of Kotov's mistress, Caridad Mercades del Rio, was the assassin of Leon Trotsky. Upon release from his Mexican prison in 1960, Mercador headed east and was decorated by Moscow for his action and his silence. From Beria's Administration for Special Tasks to Andropov's Department Eight, state-sponsored terrorism has been an organic element of Soviet foreign policy.

GRU and the Military

The Soviet military has several elite force groupings on which it can draw for conducting state-ordered diversionary activities. These forces range from elements of the seven airborne divisions to naval infantry brigades in the four Soviet fleet areas. Similar units can be found in most non-Soviet Warsaw Pact countries as well.

The most clearly identified military units specially dedicated to conducting sensitive reconnaissance, sabotage, and other diversionary missions are the GRU's SPETSNAZ. In wartime these units have a theoretical capability to operate in the full depth of the military theater—that is, throughout the enemy homeland—conducting reconnaissance, sabotage, and direct action on a wide spectrum of military and political targets, in support of frontal or fleet operations.[24]

In peacetime, aside from training, exercises, and other standard duties, GRU SPETSNAZ forces actively pursue Party-directed missions of a sensitive, covert nature. As discussed earlier, joint KGB/SPETSNAZ teams were at the leading edge of Soviet forces in the 1968 Czech and 1979 Afghanistan invasions. Since 1979, GRU SPETSNAZ units have been operating in Afghanistan performing missions similar (not surprisingly) to Soviet partisan and anti-partisan operations during and immediately after World War II in Western Russia and Eastern Europe and the anti-Basmachi campaigns in Central Asia throughout the 1920s and early 1930s.

Another probable peacetime mission of GRU SPETSNAZ forces involves Moscow's support to various Western and Third World terrorist groups, sundry revolutionaries, and so-called "national liberation" movements. "Probable" is used because, while there is ample evidence to point to KGB and Soviet military connections to these groups, it is less clear that the military elements involved are GRU SPETSNAZ. At a minimum, the GRU, the General Staff's Tenth Directorate (foreign military aid), and regular military units are connected to training and support activities at KGB/military facilities within the USSR and to training camps scattered throughout the Middle East, Africa, and Latin America.[25] But given the overall missions and capabilities of GRU SPETSNAZ units, we would expect to find their expertise being employed for such operations. The Soviet camps frequently mentioned as providing foreigners with terrorist/diversionary training—Baku, Balashika, Simferopol, Odessa, Tashkent, and Batumi[26]—have long been associated with state security (KGB), GRU, and other military facilities. Similarly, the camps most often reported as terrorist-associated in Eastern Europe—Prague, Karlovy Vary, Doupov and Ostrava in Czechoslovakia, Pankow and Finsterwalde in East Germany, Varna in Bulgaria, and near Lake Balaton in Hungary[27]—are connected to Bloc security services and/or the military, which in turn are linked to the KGB, the GRU, and the Soviet military; some of these camps are reported to be actually run by the Soviet Union.[28]

GRU SPETSNAZ are believed to be organized as brigades, with an estimate of one brigade each assigned to most military districts, groups of forces outside the USSR, and the four fleets.[29] Victor Suvorov, a former Soviet officer, credits each brigade with between 900 and 1,300 officers and men in a total force of 16 brigades; he also calculates 41 separate companies, but doesn't offer company strength figures. In all, he counts 27,000 to 30,000 men in the GRU SPETSNAZ order of battle, exclusive of reserves. According to him, mobilization will increase that figure by a factor of 4-to-5. These figures do appear excessively high, especially since it is not at all certain that 16 brigades can be accounted for, or that most military districts each possess a brigade. Mobilization figures likewise appear excessive, although the Soviet reserve system is very large compared to the American system and has a greater surger capacity. Even a mobilization factor of 2 would generate respectable numbers of SPETSNAZ reservists, albeit with reduced readiness. Finally, Soviet SPETSNAZ forces will be augmented by counterpart units from other Warsaw Pact countries, although little open-source data is available on the order of battle of these units, either collectively or by individual country. One source estimates that 20,000 East European special purpose troops, mainly from East Germany, Poland, and Czechoslovakia are available to the Soviets for rear area special reconnaissance/diversionary missions.[30] Other allied and surrogate countries are likewise reported to have their own special purpose forces; the lead element of Cuba's expeditionary force in Angola in 1975 was rumored to be a special purpose commando unit which had to be withdrawn after being mauled by the South Africans.

In war or crisis situations SPETSNAZ brigades are expected to infiltrate the enemy rear and fight as small teams (6 or more members per team), with each brigade fielding around 100 teams. A standard team would be led by an officer with a warrant officer or NCO as second in command. Other team members would possess radio, demolitions, and weapons expertise. Frequently, the teams would draw assistance from illegal support agents in the target countries. Identified training includes: infiltration tactics, airborne operations, sabotage/demolitions methods and techniques, reconnaissance and target location, hand-to-hand combat and silent killing techniques, clandestine communications, psychological operations, survival, and language and customs of the target country. One former KGB officer believes that nuclear, biological, and chemical weapons are included in the SPETSNAZ inventory.[31] To facilitate realistic training, SPETSNAZ brigades work with full-scale mock-ups of enemy installations and weapons systems: airfields, command, and communications facilities, nuclear storage sites, aircraft and nuclear delivery systems such as LANCE, PERSHING and Ground Launched Cruise missiles (GLCM).

In sum, the USSR has built a respectable standing low-intensify warfare capability with significant potential for Third World intervention (of the type in Afghanistan and in terrorist training) in peacetime and a major disruptive potential in wartime. The combined forces of the KGB/MVD and the GRU are subject to the highest party authority, with the KGB serving as the Party's legate to ensure control, responsiveness, and decisiveness in sensitive operations.

Historical and Contemporary Cases: The Continuity of Low-Intensity Combat in Theory and Practice

From the very beginning of the Soviet experience, low-intensity combat had a clear state security focus, responsive to Party control in the tradition of what should properly be called the "counterintelligence state." State-sponsored diversion, assassination, and sabotage have always been viewed as legitimate political instruments of the Party and its principal action arm, state security. The military, a tertiary partner in this enterprise, periodically found itself a target of the other two; a more amicable and mutually reinforcing condominum of interest among all three now seems to be the operative style. The following cases are illustrative of low-intensity conflict in this unique Soviet tradition:

1. Special CHEKA forces (CHON) stiffened a pensive Red Army in brutally supressing the rebelling Red Sailors of Kronstadt in 1921. Party cadres were thrown in to stiffen the CHEKA. This is an early example of the developing symbiosis between the Party and state security.

2. Special Designation Troops of state security figured prominently in enforcing collectivization and in hunting down recalcitrant peasants (so-called "Kulaks") who opposed those disastrous policies. The KGB/MVD Dzerzhinskiy Division took part in these punitive operations and claims them as a favored chapter in its unit history.[32] Other state security internal troops and border guards carried out similar punitive operations, including hot pursuit and elimination of peasant families who fled from the Soviet Caucasus Republics across the frontier into Iran.[33] This brutal exercise in forced socialization is comparable in many ways to what the Soviets are now doing in Afghanistan.[34] The parallels are truly striking but little remarked upon in the West. In both events state security forces exercised a critical and central role.

3. Another antecedent to Afghanistan (indeed, maybe a continuation) was the more than decade-long low-intensity counterinsurgency campaign, carried out in Soviet Central Asia from the time of the Civil War to the early 1930s. This was the "Basmachi" uprising—or more correctly the "Beklar Hareketi," the Freeman's Movement against the Moslem Turks—which spread throughout Soviet Turkestan. Several major campaigns were required to crush the movement. State security special designation units, including the Dzerzhinskiy Division, were brought in to spearhead the various operations. As late as 1931 the 63rd OGPU Division fought a pitched battle for control

of the city of Krasnovodsk.[35] It wasn't until 1933 that the last elements of the Basmachi were defeated by special purpose troops. Afghanistan had played a key cross-border support role for the Basmachi throughout much of the insurgency. When the KGB spearheaded the 1979 invasion, it was rumored to have arrest lists of Basmachi principals it had been seeking since the 1930s. Afghan refugees report that KGB interrogators referred to arrested Afghans as "Basmachi."[36]

4. The Spanish Civil War offers a pre–World War II instance of concurrent NKVD and GRU terrorist and guerrilla operations at Stalin's orders. Former GRU Chief Jan Berzin, the head of the Soviet military aid effort, was ordered by Stalin to hold aside a select group of officers and men to seize military control of Madrid as a "key point" in a diversionary operation should the Republicans win the Civil War.[37] As discussed earlier, the NKVD "rezident," General Orlov, identified Marshal Konev as having a terrorist training role in Spain and NKVD General Kotov (Eitingon) as actually running terrorist and guerrilla operations behind Nationalist lines.

5. In one of the first known instances of a specifically identified military special designation unit before World War II, a unit of fifty men were brought to the front during the Russo-Finnish War of 1939–40 in an unsuccessful attempt to capture Finnish prisoners. This unit was subordinated to the Fifth Department (Otdel) of the GRU and was openly referred to as the "Otdel diversiya" ("diversionary department").[38]

6. Following the creation of the NKVD's "Administration of Special Tasks" in 1936, assassinations and kidnappings outside the USSR increased in both volume and tempo. The most prominent victim of the surge was Leon Trotsky, who was assassinated in 1940 in Mexico by a Spanish NKVD agent. Numerous other Soviet officials, Western communists, and Russian emigres were among the victims. This unit remained in existence, under various titles, within the KGB down to the present. It is now known as Department Eight of Directorate S.

7. Soviet Partisan operations of World War II served as a major formative laboratory for subsequent Soviet state security and military entities and for supporting post-war terrorist and guerrilla movements. Although a Partisan Directorate at the High Command level oversaw all partisan operations, Party and state security cadres were the actual controlling elements. While the announced purpose of the operation was the harassment of the German rear areas,[39] the real objective was to reintroduce Party control in occupied territories. This involved deceptions and provocations to identify, surface, and eliminate real and potential opponents to the reimposition of Soviet rule. It also included the neutralization and compromise of non-Soviet resistance and Partisan groups. A major means for accomplishing all this was the provoking of terror and German counterterror with the ultimate object of intimidation of the local population. Still later, many loyal partisan commanders

and subordinates were executed or shipped off to the GULAG at the end of the war. Stalin apparently feared that their small taste of independence boded ill for the system. Other core Party and NKVD cadres were reorganized under NKVD General Sudoplatov for the planning of diversion and terror behind the lines of what was to become NATO.

8. From the end of World War II through the late 1940s and early 1950s, state security prosecuted major counterinsurgency campaigns against anti-Soviet guerrilla groups in the Baltic and the Western Ukraine. Special state security, border guard, and selected army units ran punitive operations comparable in some ways to current Soviet operations in Afghanistan. Village bashing, scorched earth, mass summary executions, and mass deportations characterized state security operations. In a certain sense, Moscow's prowess in low-intensity combat is in *counterinsurgency* rather than insurgency operations. There are pitifully few success stories of countries overthrowing Soviet or Soviet-sponsored control.

9. In Hungary in 1956 and Czechoslovakia in 1968, state security and special designation military units seized "key points," echoing Berzin's guidance from Stalin during the Spanish Civil War. In Czechoslovakia, KGB resident agents in Czech state security collaborated with the KGB in those seizures and in the arrests of Czech officials. One of these agents guided a KGB-led assault team to the Czech Central Committee building where the leadership was arrested.[40] Similar techniques were followed in Afghanistan and would be repeated in future target countries.

10. In Sweden there were reports for years of repeated incursions by Soviet submarines and/or minisubs. These reported penetrations actually have increased following the sensation caused by the running aground of the Soviet WHISKEY-class submarine #137 well inside Swedish territorial waters, inside a military security zone and almost within sight of the Swedish Naval Base at Karlskrona. According to Arkady Shevchenko, a high ranking defector from the Soviet foreign ministry, in 1970 the Kremlin decided to initiate submarine probes into Swedish and Norwegian territorial waters, despite Prime Minister Palme's efforts to regularize relations with Moscow.[41] It has been speculated that these violations of Swedish waters involve a combination of strategic reconnaissance and real-world exercises of Soviet naval SPETSNAZ elements. One experienced observer states that ". . . in considering the effectiveness of the Soviet Navy's SPETSNAZ operations in the Northern TVD theater of military operations, it is important not to lose sight of the fact that bases in the United Kingdom and particularly in Scotland could easily be targets for such activities. . . . It is but a short jump, then, to make the same considerations with respect to such teams operating against the U.S. . . ."[42]

11. Finally, there is Afghanistan—the ongoing Soviet operational laboratory where we are witnessing a contemporary re-enactment of:

a) The Basmachi episode with the full repertoire of the Soviet counter-insurgency tradition, including participation of Soviet state security cadres in arrests, interrogations, torture, and executions of real or imagined opponents of the Soviets and their puppet president Karmal.[43]

b) The horrors of collectivization, which revolutionized the social, population, and agricultural structure of the Soviet Union. A similar social revolution is being imposed on traditional Afghan society with no concern for human suffering bordering on genocide. Though Stalin is long gone, his successors are repeating policies of the late 1920s–early 1930s.

c) The long tradition of diversion, terrorism, and direct action conducted by the Soviet intelligence and security services under Party direction. In Afghanistan the Soviets have a "controlled" environment in which to refine their special operations capability and to work on the effective fusing of the talents of the KGB with those of the GRU SPETSNAZ and other special military units.[44] Such "joint" KGB/GRU/military operations will serve as operational models for preserving and expanding Soviet gains.

Conclusions

The Soviet system is the world's premier example of the counterintelligence state. Its very idiom and medium of operation is struggle, with an accent on military metaphors. The USSR is uniquely and temperamentally well-equipped for pursuing conflicts of varying intensity, especially those in the shadows. The very raison d'etre of the counterintelligence state causes it to put a premium on those instruments of struggle which prosecute diversion, terrorism, direct action, and other types of low-intensify conflict. Soviet military doctrine does not see these instruments of conflict as negative social overhead, but as a desired end-product of the Soviet system. The experiences Moscow gleaned from operations in Afghanistan, its own history, and its activities in support of international terrorism and Third World revolutionary movements have provided the new Soviet leadership with an operational confidence reminiscent of an earlier Soviet era.

Notes

1. For some earlier analyses of these instruments, see John J. Dziak, "Soviet Intelligence and Security Services in the 1980's: The Paramilitary Dimension" in *Intelligence Requirements for the 1980's: Counterintelligence*, ed. Roy Godson (Washington, D.C.: National Strategy Information Center, 1980), pp. 95–121 and "The

Soviet Approach to Special Operations" in *Special Operations in U.S. Strategy,* ed. Frank R. Barnett, B. Hugh Tovar, and Richard H. Shultz (Washington, D.C.: National Strategy Information Center and National Defense Univ. Press, 1984), pp. 95–133.

2. V.I. Lenin, 3 April 1920 Speech at the Eleventh Party Congress *Protokoly IX Sezd RKP (B)* (Moscow, 1934), p. 398; and *Collected Works,* vol. 30 (Moscow: Progress Publishers, 1965), p. 483.

3. P.G. Sofinov, *Ocherki Istorii Vserossiiskoy Chrezvychaynoy Komissi* (1917–1922gg.) (Moscow: Politizdat, 1960), p. 152.

4. Peter Deriabin, *Watchdogs of Terror,* 2nd ed., revised and updated (Frederick, Md.: University Publications of America, 1984), p. 265.

5. I.G. Belikov et al., *Imeni Dzerzhinskogo* or In the Name of Dzerghinskiy (Moscow: Voyenizdat, 1976).

6. V.E. Bystrov, "Diversiya" (Diversion), *Sovetskaya Voyennaya Entsiklopedia,* vol. 3 (Moscow: Voyenizdat, 1977), pp. 177–78, emphasis added.

7. "Spetsal'naya Razvedka" (Special Reconnaissance), *Sovetskaya Voyennaya Entsiklopediya,* vol. 7 (Moscow: Voyenizdat, 1979), p. 493, emphasis in original.

8. Marshal V.D. Sokolovkiy, ed., *Voyennaya Strategiya* (Military Strategy), 3rd ed. (Moscow: Voyenizdat, 1968), p. 201, emphasis added.

9. Ibid., p. 222.

10. Gen. A.A. Yepishev in *Kommunist* (Communist), no. 7 (May 1972), p. 62; Marshal A.A. Grechko in *Voprosy Istorii KPSS* (Problems of History of the Communist Party of the Soviet Union), no. 5 (May 1974), pp. 30–47.

11. Viktor Suvorov, *Soviet Military Intelligence* (London: Hamish Hamilton, 1984). Suvorov is a former Soviet military officer apparently with some knowledge of military intelligence. On pages 57–58 he identifies the pertinent element as the "Third Direction" of the GRU.

12. John Barron, *KGB* (New York: Reader's Digest Press, 1974), p. 78.

13. John Barron, *KGB Today: The Hidden Hand* (New York: Reader's Digest Press, 1983), pp. 15–16, 445.

14. James T. Reitz, "The Soviet Security Troops—The Kremlin's Other Armies," in *Soviet Armed Forces Review Annual,* ed. David R. Jones, vol. 6 (Gulk Breeze, Fla.: Academic International Press, 1982), pp. 279–327. Reitz feels that KGB troop levels are probably well over 250,000. John Barron estimates the levels as between 300,000 and 400,000 in *KGB Today,* p. 451.

15. *Foreign Report* (published by the *Economist*), 21 December 1982, pp. 1–2.

16. Deriabin, *Watchdogs of Terror,* pp. 328, 365.

17. For a glorified history of these operations, see Belikov, *Imeni Dzerzhinskogo,* chs. 2, 3, and 4.

18. Barron, *KGB Today,* pp. 15–16, 445; "Coups and Killings in Kabul," *Time* 22 November 1982, pp. 33–34.

19. Barron, *KGB Today.* Barron cites as his sources for this information a former KGB major, Stanislav Lenchenko, who came out in 1979, and Western intelligence services. Very similar information given in the *Time* article above is attributed to another KGB major, this one from Directorate S, Vladimir Kuzichkin, who fled to the British from his post in Iran. Their information is reinforced by refugees and others from Afghanistan. See *"Tears, Blood and Cries," Human Rights in Afghanistan Since*

the Invasion, 1979–1984, A Helsinki Watch Report (New York and Washington, D.C.: Helsinki Watch Committee, December 1984).

20. U.S. Department of Defense, *Soviet Military Power,* 4th ed. (Washington, D.C., GPO, 1985), p. 72.

21. Ibid., pp. 72–73.

22. For a highly detailed study of such KGB links, see Roberta Goren, *The Soviet Union and Terrorism,* ed. Jillian Becker (London: George Allen and Unwin, 1984), especially Ch. 5.

23. See U.S. Congress, Senate Committee on the Judiciary, *The Legacy of Alexander Orlov,* 93rd Congress, 1st sess., August 1973 (Washington, D.C.: Government Printing Office, 1973); and U.S. Congress, Senate Committee on the Judiciary, *Hearings, Testimony of Alexander Orlov,* 85th Congress, 1st sess., 1957, Pt. 51 (Washington, D.C.: GPO, 1957), p. 342.

24. U.S. Dept. of Defense, *Soviet Military Power,* pp. 72–73.

25. For discussions of these camps, see: Goren, *The Soviet Union and Terrorism,* Ch. 5; Ray S. Cline and Yonah Alexander, *Terrorism: The Soviet Connection* (New York: Crane Russak, 1984), Chs. 4 and 5, Appendix A; Benjamin Netanyahu, ed., *International Terrorism: Challenge and Response,* Proceedings of the Jerusalem Conference in International Terrorism, July 2–5, 1979, (Jerusalem: The Jonathan Institute, 1979), passim.

26. Ibid.; *Foreign Report* (published by the *Economist*), 11 July 1979.

27. Cline and Alexander, *Terrorism,* p. 46.

28. Ibid., pp. 45–46. On the nature of Soviet control of, and coordination with, Bloc security and intelligence service, see Barron, *KGB,* Chs. 4 and 8; Barron, *KGB Today,* Appendix B; Jan Sejna, *We Will Bury You* (London: Sidgwick & Jackson, 1982); Suvorov, *Soviet Military Intelligence,* pp. 34, 44–44.

29. For a general discussion of GRU SPETSNAZ brigades, see the author's two articles cited in note one. More recent and detailed work is found in Suvorov, *Soviet Military Intelligence,* passim.; Suvorov, "SPETSNAZ: The Soviet Union's Special Forces," *International Defense Review* 16 (1983): 1209–16; Suvorov, "SPETSNAZ and Sport," *International Defense Review* 17 (1984): 687. The most detailed open work on Soviet naval SPETSNAZ is Lynn M. Hansen's *Soviet Navy SPETSNAZ Operations on the Northern Flank: Implications for the Defense of Western Europe* (College Station, Texas: Center for Strategic Technology, the Texas A&M University, April 1984). The remainder of the discussion of GRU SPETSNAZ is drawn principally from the above works and from *Soviet Military Power* (1985), pp. 72–73.

30. C.N. Donnelly, "Operations in the Enemy Rear," *International Defense Review* 13 (1980): 37.

31. A. Myagkov, "Soviet Sabotage Training for World War III," *Soviet Analyst* (9 January 1980), p. 5.

32. Belikov, *Imeni Dzerzhinskogo,* Ch. 2.

33. Ismail Akhmedov, *In and Out of Stalin's GRU* (Frederick, MD: University Publications of America, 1984), pp. 80–81.

34. Helsinki Watch Report *Tears, Blood and Cries.*

35. Martha B. Olcott, "The Basmachi or Freemen's Revolt in Turkestan," *Soviet Studies* (June 1981): 362.

36. Helsinki Watch Report *Tears, Blood and Cries.*

37. John Erickson, *The Soviet High Command* (London: St. Martin's Press, 1962), pp. 429–30; Walter G. Krivitskiy, *I Was Stalin's Agent* (London: Hamish Hamilton, 1939), pp. 99–100.

38. From an interview with Ismail Akhmedov, former GRU officer, 7 June 1985. Used with permission.

39. For a recent Soviet account which glorifies the Partisan movement, see N.F. Yudin, comp., *Pervaya Partizanskaya* (The First Partisan Division) (Moscow: Izdatel'stvo Moskovskiy Rabochiy, 1983).

40. Sascha Demidow, "Wir Schosen Besser Als Cowboys" (We Shot Better Than The Cowboys), *Der Spiegel* (20 July 1970): 86–93.

41. Arkady Schevchenko, *Breaking With Moscow* (New York: Alfred A. Knopf, 1984), p. 179.

42. Hansen, *Soviet Navy SPETSNAZ Operations on the Northern Flank*, p. 34.

43. Helsinki Watch Report *Tears, Blood and Cries* pp. 5, 137–138, 140–41, 143, 146–50, 155–56, 165, 181–82.

44. See Ibid., pp. 182–84 for an account of a Soviet commando operation which resulted in the capture of one of the French doctors of *Medecins sans Frontieres.*

Section D
Political Orchestration

6
Recent Regional Patterns

Richard H. Shultz

Over the last fifteen years the Third World has been the scene of a growing number of low intensity or unconventional conflicts, including guerrilla insurgency and terrorism. While due, in part, to a myriad of internal and regional political, social, and economic cleavages, this instability has been fostered by various international actors. Recently, for instance, the Ayatollah Khomeini and his followers have promoted fanatic violence in the Middle East through their interpretation of Islam. Under the rule of Qadhafi, Libya has assisted a number of terrorist factions, including the Popular Front for the Liberation of Palestine and the Irish Republican Army.

However, among the states involved, the Soviet Union has played the most active role. Beginning in the early 1970s, the Kremlin escalated its involvement in Third World conflicts. By the end of the decade they increased dramatically their capacity to promote insurgency and terrorism, either directly or through surrogate forces, including Czech, North Korean, Vietnamese, Libyan, South Yemeni, and PLO assets. To accomplish policy objectives the Soviet Union employs an array of tactics. Now termed "active measures," these include political and paramilitary techniques. Through the integrated application of these measures, Moscow has assisted a number of successful insurgent factions.[1]

A number of studies have assessed how the paramilitary elements of active measures, particularly arms transfers, have been utilized by Moscow to assist guerrilla movements. For instance, based on documents captured by the Israelis in Lebanon, Cline and Alexander delineate the extent to which close Soviet–PLO relations resulted in extensive arms transfers and military training for Palestinian forces.[2] Documents captured in southern Africa disclose a similar if less extensive arrangement between the USSR and the South West African People's Organization (SWAPO).[3]

The extent to which Moscow employs the political tactics of active measures in support of insurgent movements, however, has been generally overlooked by Western scholars. Consequently, foreign propaganda, the activities of international front organizations, and political action within international organizations have not been the subject of comprehensive and systematic analysis. This is surprising in light of the historical commitment, as well as the extensive organizational and financial resources presently devoted by the Kremlin leadership to conducting these activities.

The purpose of this study is to begin to fill this gap in the literature by highlighting the ways in which Moscow employs propaganda and other political techniques within its overall strategy of promoting and assisting Third World insurgent movements. Through the selective case study approach, the findings from a systematic examination of how the Soviets utilized these tactics to promote insurgency in Vietnam, Namibia, Nicaragua, and El Salvador will be presented. The study is divided into the following sections. First, we will describe briefly Soviet policy and strategy for promoting low-intensity conflict. This will be followed by an overview of the four cases examined. The main body of the study will synthesize our findings in order to identify common patterns and differences in how the Soviet Union uses propaganda and political activities as part of its overall strategy for assisting insurgent movements. Common thematic approaches, methods, and the targets of these tactics will be identified. Additionally, the interrelationship and coordination of instruments in the four examples will be described.

Soviet Policy and Strategy

Support for national liberation movements has been a basic element of Moscow's foreign policy since the first years of rule by the Communist Party of the Soviet Union (CPSU). Lenin and his followers portrayed the USSR as the champion of self determination for all people and an uncompromising opponent of colonialism. This was a natural outgrowth of his theory of imperialism.

However, theoretical precepts and the priorities of policy are not always perfectly correlated. For a variety of reasons discussed in the literature on Soviet foreign policy, from the Stalin period through the late 1960s, Kremlin leaders were cautious and restrained in their adherence to Lenin's exhortation.[4] Beginning in the early 1970s Soviet policy began to change, and by the end of the decade Moscow was in the midst of an unprecedented involvement in Third World conflicts. This included the promotion of instability in Southern Africa, the southern part of the Arabian Peninsula, and by the end of the 1970s, in Central and South America.

In effect, support for insurgent movements, a principle facet of Soviet Third World policy since the inception of the regime, received unprecedented operational emphasis during the 1970s. This has continued in the 1980s.

The Twenty-Fourth Congress and Wars of National Liberation

While it is unclear precisely when the USSR decided to undertake this change in policy, officially it was set forth in Brezhnev's report to the Twenty-Fourth Congress of the CPSU in March 1971. According to the CPSU General Secretary, "Lenin's prediction that the peoples of the colonies and dependent countries, starting with a struggle for national liberation, would go on to fight against the very foundations of the exploitative system is coming true. Success in the struggle," according to Brezhnev, "largely depends on the cohesion of the anti-imperialist forces, above all the world communist movement, their vanguard." He then pledged the USSR to "give undeviating support to the people's struggle for democracy, national liberation and socialism," and "further to invigorate the worldwide anti-imperialist struggle."[5] This official pronouncement gave authoritative endorsement to a policy already being implemented in the field. Since the 24th Congress, considerable official commentary has been devoted to the subject. In addition to frequent declarations by top party leaders and other official pronouncements, this change in policy has been discussed in great detail by leading CPSU foreign policy experts, as well as in the professional military literature.

Examination of this material suggests that the following factors contributed to Moscow's decision. First, by the early 1970s the USSR's enormous investment in defense altered the military correlation of forces. As they reached parity with the West in both strategic and conventional terms, the leadership appeared less constrained in proclaiming its right to project power into Third World conflicts. Furthermore, the growth of certain military capabilities, particularly sea and air lift, enhanced the capacity to employ force in this way; Gromyko's confident assertion at the 24th Congress is illustrative of this. Commenting on the current power balance in world politics, the former Foreign Minister stated that "there is no question of any significance which can be decided without the Soviet Union or in opposition to it."[6]

It is important to note that non-military factors contribute to changes in the overall correlation of forces.[7] Included are a wide range of what Moscow terms "active measures," such as propaganda, agents of influence, the activities of international fronts, disinformation, and similar instruments of deception and subversion. At the time of the 24th Congress, the KGB and Central Committee departments responsible for conducting active measures were in the midst of major campaigns initiated following the decision in 1958 to enter a "new phase" in political warfare operations.[8] It seems reasonable to assume that these developments contributed to Moscow's perception during the early 1970s that the correlation of forces was shifting in its favor.[9]

A lack of resolve and splits in the Western camp also contributed, according to Soviet commentary, to the new power equation. Consequently, the declining willingness of the United States to maintain commitments, exemplified by the withdrawal from Vietnam, as well as reduced defense spending and cleavages in the alliance were factored into the Kremlin's new assessment of the East-West balance of power.

These assertions and their relationship to expanding Soviet support for national liberation movements have been articulated by leading foreign policy specialists from the Central Committee's International Department (ID). During the last decade there has been considerable debate over whether the Ministry of Foreign Affairs (MFA) or the ID plays the major role in foreign affairs. This has been disputed among Western specialists and former Soviet officials. Based on a number of factors, succinctly discussed by Schapiro and Teague, the ID appears to have a more decisive influence, subject to Politburo approval.[10] This is the case especially with respect to national liberation movements. It is not surprising, therefore, that the underlying rationale for this new policy has been authoritatively recounted by the leadership of the ID.

The major theoretician is the ID's de facto Chief, Boris Ponomarev. The "elder statesman" of Soviet foreign policy, Ponomarev's publications over the years have established him as the leading official voice on theoretical issues related to Soviet international relations doctrine, including national liberation movements. His pronouncements on national liberation conflicts and Soviet policy (which included books, articles, and speeches) accelerated during the 1970s. Among the most important are *Some Problems of the Revolutionary Movement* and *Lenin and the World Revolutionary Process*, both of which mirror those factors identified previously as underlying Moscow's decision to escalate support for insurgent and terrorist groups.[11] Thus, in *Kommunist* of November 1977, Pomonarev asserted that the worldwide "national liberation movement has entered a qualitatively new stage." While noting that "imperialism and the local oligarchy were able to deal major blows at the liberation movements in Chile, Uruguay, Brazil and some other countries . . . the liberation movement was not extinguished."[12] By 1980 the head of the International Department pronounced the 1970s the decade of significant "progress of the world revolutionary process," as a result of the "merciless objective laws of social development."[13]

The 1970s witnessed a new considerable progress of the anti-imperialist movement in many parts of the world. This included the victory of the Vietnamese people and unification of Vietnam, the strengthening of the people's system in Laos and the elimination of the Pol Pot regime in Kampuchae. Ethiopia, Angola, and Mozambique freed themselves from the chains of imperialism. Their peoples . . . are bridgeheads for socialist orientation in Africa. In this respect South Yemen is playing an important role. The dictatorial regime in Nicaragua was overthrown. The revolution in Afghanistan, the overthrow of the monarchy of the Shah in Iran, and the victory of the Zimbabwe patriots were blows struck at imperialism.[14]

The theme of declining U.S. influence in the world also permeates Ponomarev's reflections: "American imperialism has always been and continues to be the chief bulwark of tyrannical and mercenary regimes. Today, under the onslaught of the liberation forces, which are rapidly increasing both on a national and international scale, American imperialism is no longer capable of protecting its proteges and puppets against being overthrown."[15]

In sum, Ponomarev makes clear that the overthrow of Third World governments through protracted armed struggle contributes to the overall East-West balance of power. While stressing that radical indigenous elements must advance the protracted revolutionary struggle, and not the "hand of Moscow," in recent commentary the head of the ID has stated that the USSR offers both its "solidarity and support": "Whenever such forces exist and fight, they can rightfully count on our solidarity and support. Those who raise the banner of struggle . . . are considered by us to be representatives of a just cause."[16]

In light of the importance of the ID, Ponomarev's statements have both theoretical and operational implications. In addition to serving as the leading official voice on issues related to conflict in the Third World, during 1978–80 he met personally with many of the leaders of the national liberation movements supported by the USSR.[17] For example, in Moscow on 13 November 1979 Ponomarev and Foreign Minister Gromyko met with a PLO delegation headed by Yasser Arafat and including representatives from Sa'iqa, Popular Front for the Liberation of Palestine (PFLP), Popular Front for the Liberation of Palestine-General Command (PFLP-GC), Democratic Front for the Liberation of Palestine (DFLP), and the Arab Liberation Front. During the meeting, Ponomarev described the purpose of a recently founded Committee for Friendship and Solidarity with the Palestinian People. Comparing it with a similar ID-sponsored organization established during the Vietnam War, Ponomarev described in operational terms a new instrument to be employed as part of the international political warfare effort waged against Israel and the United States. In sum, as the head of the ID, Ponomarev has principle responsibility for formulating, coordinating, and conducting Soviet political warfare operations, including those in support of national liberation movements.[18]

In addition to Ponomarev, three of the Deputy Chiefs of the ID—Rostislav Ulyanovsky, Karen Brutents, and Petr Manchka—are considered leading specialists on national liberation movements. Ulyanovsky appears to be the senior expert of the three, specializing on Afro-Asian movements. A former Deputy Director of the Institute of Oriental Studies, he has authored numerous essays on the subject, including *National Liberation,* an examination of "liberation struggles" in Africa and Asia.[19] Brutents supervises the activities of the Middle East and Latin American sections of the ID, and it appears that he will replace Ulyanovsky as the CPSU's leading specialist on national liberation movements. In his best known work, the two-volume study entitled *National Liberation Revolutions Today,* Brutents outlines the role of the USSR in this process:

> In accordance with the whole course of the world revolutionary process, the question of alliance with the national liberation movement . . . has now acquired both objectively and subjectively—in the light of the struggle between the two social systems—a largely different meaning than it had, say, in the early period of the Soviet state. At that time, it was largely a matter of *defense* of the first socialist revolution against imperialism, whereas today it is a question of carrying on the *offensive* against imperialism and world capitalism as a whole to do away with them.[20]

Manchka, who specializes in African affairs, takes a similar approach in his book, *In the Vanguard of the Revolutionary Struggle in Africa.*[21]

By the mid-1970s, Soviet military professionals began to assert that the armed forces of the USSR also would play an active role in this policy. According to leading Western experts Harriet Scott and William Scott, "1974 marked a doctrinal shift" in Moscow's view of the role of military force as an instrument of statecraft:

> Soviet leaders announced that the responsibilities of the Soviet Armed Forces were no longer restricted to defense of the fatherland and other Socialist states. Henceforth imperialist aggression would be repulsed wherever found. This was called a new "external" role for the Armed Forces. In the early 1980s it is receiving more and more attention . . . Since they first began to emphasize "external" functions on the power projection role, Soviet spokesmen have stated that the Armed Forces must be prepared to resist imperialist aggression wherever it may appear.[22]

Beginning in the mid-1970s both the senior leadership of the Soviet Armed Forces and the professional military literature reiterated this point. Apparently, this was to include both direct support to insurgent movements and assistance to newly established Marxist—Leninist regimes seeking to consolidate power.

In 1974, Marshal A. A. Grechko, then Minister of Defense, described this new role in the following terms: "At the present stage the historic function of the Soviet armed forces is not restricted merely to their function of defending our Motherland . . . In its foreign policy activity the Soviet state actively and purposefully opposes the export of counterrevolution . . . supports the national liberation struggle, and resolutely resists imperialist aggression in whatever distant region it may appear."[23] Along the same lines, Marshal N. V. Ogarkov, until recently the chief of the General Staff, stated in an essay contained in the *Soviet Military Encyclopedia:* "Soviet military strategy takes into account the possibility of local wars rising . . . according to the classic positions and Leninist theses on just and unjust wars. While supporting national liberation wars, the Soviet Union decisively opposes the unleashing by imperialists of local wars."[24]

This new emphasis on external power projection is the subject of frequent discussion in the Soviet military periodicals. For example, in the second of a two-part essay entitled, "Documents and Materials: Long-Range Subjects for Military Historical Research in 1981–1990," the following subjects were listed under the heading of "Developing Countries":

1. Strategy and tactics of counterinsurgency actions of American imperialism in Indochina (1960–1975).

2. The art of war of warring nations and their armies in modern national liberation rebellions and wars.

3. Unique features of military development in countries assuming the path of revolutionary transformation of society.

4. Pressing problems in organizations of the armed defense of people's liberation revolutions.[25]

This list reflects the dual concern of the Kremlin leadership. On the one hand, the USSR seeks to assist certain insurgent factions in seizing power through protracted revolutionary warfare. On the other hand, Moscow provides military and security support to newly established pro-Soviet Marxist–Leninist regimes threatened by noncommunist insurgent movements. In the case of the former the policy objective is the seizure of power, while the latter concentrates on the consolidation and institutionalization of control. These two themes run simultaneously through Soviet military literature.[26] Katz summarized these developments in Soviet military strategy during the 1970s in the following terms:

> At first, in the late 1950s and early 1960s, Soviet military thinkers said nothing specific about the role of the USSR in local conflicts. In the middle and late 1960s, they discussed arms transfers and then in the early 1970s, the role of Cuban armed forces and treaties of friendship and cooperation were discussed. Even some hints of the use of Soviet armed forces were given, though no explicit advocating this as a general policy have yet been made. Thus, in these statements there has occurred a progression over time toward increasing Soviet involvement in Third World conflict.[27]

In sum, what was authorized by Brezhnev at the 24th Congress of the CPSU and explicitly reaffirmed at the 25th and 26th Congresses—a new policy of power projection to influence the course of Third World conflicts—has been the subject of extensive commentary by key CPSU foreign affairs specialists and military professionals. In the next section we will briefly describe how this new policy fostered the development of strategy and capabilities for its execution "on the ground." Finally, it should be noted that Moscow saw no contradiction between detente/peaceful coexistence and expanding involvement in Third World conflicts. Detente did not alter the USSR's understanding of war and politics in international relations. Soviet writers stated that peaceful coexistence and support for national liberation struggles were not incompatible.[28] In fact, the conditions of detente created an atmosphere in which these struggles could flourish. If we return once again to the 24th Party Congress, one can find Brezhnev and other leading CPSU officials declaring that peaceful coexistence with the West was not incompatible with Soviet assistance to "progressive forces in wars of national and social liberation."[29] These themes run concurrently in Soviet pronouncements following the 24th Party Congress of the CPSU.

Active Measures and Insurgency

To pursue the policy described above, the Kremlin employs a complex and integrated political-military strategy. The instruments range from propaganda and political influence techniques to paramilitary assistance. Specifically, these include:

Political Measures	Paramilitary Measures
Foreign Propaganda	Arms and Logistical Support
International Front Organizations	Political-Military Training
Political Activities Within International and	Advisory Assistance
Regional Organizations	Deployment of Forces

The Soviets appear to use the term "active measures" to describe political and paramilitary techniques for influencing events and behavior in, and the actions of, foreign states.[30] In terms of support for insurgent movements, both elements of active measures are important for achieving policy objectives. Political measures are utilized to champion the cause and objectives of the insurgents in the international arena. International acceptance of the "just cause" of the insurgency and the "repressive-immoral" character of the incumbent regime can play an important role at each stage of insurgent development. Paramilitary assistance, on the other hand, seeks to improve the political-military proficiency of the insurgents to conduct operations against the target government.[31]

The political component of Soviet active measures constitutes an array of overt and covert techniques. The former includes officially sponsored propaganda and the activities of friendship and cultural societies, as well as attempts to manipulate statelike national and international relations. Disinformation, manipulation and control of media assets, agent of influence operations, the activities of international front organizations, clandestine radios, and related activities are among the covert tactics. What follows is a brief examination of three of these techniques—foreign propaganda, international front organizations, and political activities within international and regional organizations—and an identification of those parts of the Soviet apparatus charged with their planning and implementation.

Among the Soviet political techniques employed to promote the cause of insurgent movements in the international arena, *Foreign Propaganda* is of primary importance. Since the period prior to the Bolshevik seizure of power, propaganda has been an important instrument of policy. According to one leading authority, "Lenin established a tradition within which Bolshevik professional revolutionaries and, later, specially trained functionaries of the Soviet state . . . have systematically employed modern communications techniques."[32]

Escalation in propaganda coverage of an insurgent movement often indicates that it has become a more consequential policy issue for Moscow. It also triggers the initiation of a broader political warfare campaign, in which other instruments are brought into play (such as the activation of international front organizations).

The Soviet message is transmitted through a vast and coordinated array of propaganda channels, including international broadcasts, numerous publications circulated worldwide, and two major news services.[33] An examination of this output reveals the degree to which Moscow can mobilize and integrate specific propaganda campaigns. They are characterized by the Soviet technique of "Kombinatsia," the combining and integrating of multiple issues in support of a specific policy. Other general features include intensity and concentration, flexibility and adaptivity, deception and manipulation, and centralized control and coordination.[34]

Because campaigns are conducted on an international scale, they are broad in scope. This is due in part to the fact that multiple audiences are targeted. The Soviet campaign in support of the North Vietnamese and Vietcong is a case in point. What is interesting about the Vietnam case, as well as a number of subsequent ones, is the extent to which the United States is characterized as a major cause of the conflict. The degree or even absence of U.S. involvement appears to have no apparent impact on the way in which

Soviet propaganda covers the subject. Consequently, there was little variance in the Soviet propaganda pattern.

Within the Soviet apparatus, the International Information Department (IID) of the CPSU Central Committee was established in 1978 to improve the coordination of what was already an impressive program of foreign propaganda activities. Not a great deal is known about the IID, and there are conflicting opinions regarding its purpose and scope of responsibilities. Available evidence, however, suggests that it neither sets the propaganda line nor has responsibility for programmatic guidance. These appear to be the duty of the International Department of the CPSU Central Committee (under Politburo direction).[35] The IID, on the other hand, concentrates on improving the coordination of the various overt propaganda channels.

A second political technique for promoting internationally the cause of insurgent movements is through the activities of Soviet directed *International Front Organizations*. As with many other aspects of Soviet policy and organization, the use of international fronts can be traced back to the early days of the regime. Lenin saw the importance of advancing Soviet foreign policy objectives through broad organizations which, because of their ostensibly idealistic objectives, would attract greater support than openly communist parties.[36] The Comintern was assigned responsibility for organizing and directing the fronts, and during the 1920s–30s a number came into existence.[37]

Soviet overt propaganda themes in support of insurgent movements are promoted and enhanced through the Kremlin's major international fronts. Their techniques include propaganda and international conference diplomacy.[38] The latter is the more action oriented of the two techniques and can take the following forms:

Meetings of the Front Organization. The fronts use their own deliberations as international forums to promote the cause of different insurgent movements. Once the meeting is completed, a communique is released and a final report published. The representatives of the national level affiliates of the fronts are then expected to promote the themes of the meeting back home.

International and Regional Conferences Sponsored by one or more Fronts. The fronts will use international and regional conferences, which are attended by both front and non-front individuals and organizations, to promote insurgent causes. These may be either regionally or internationally focused.

International Conferences Involving the UN or Regional Organizations. The major fronts will attempt to link themselves to different UN committees and organizations. This includes participating in and even cosponsoring UN international and regional conference activity.

They also will do this with other non-governmental and regional organizations.

The purpose of each of these techniques is to reach a much larger audience than the USSR could hope to influence on its own. In the case of SWAPO, for instance, two of Moscow's major international fronts—the World Peace Council (WPC) and the Afro-Asian People's Solidarity Organization (AAPSO)—utilized all three techniques. Other cases examined in this study will disclose different ways in which Moscow configures and employs its front groups.

Through publications the fronts conduct propaganda campaigns in support of insurgent movements. In almost every respect the general thematic pattern mirrors Soviet commentary. However, some differences can be detected. For example, in the case of Central America the number of themes covered were fewer and the treatment of issues more simplistic in approach and vitriolic in tone than that found in Soviet overt propaganda. The front campaign focused on audiences in the region and carried a basically simple message that it played back through international and regional conference activities.

The ID has responsibility for directing the front organizations as well as conducting relations with nonruling Communist parties. However, as we noted above, its duties appear to extend far beyond those publicly identified and, as Dziak observes, can be traced back to the Comintern.[39]

In addition to planning and coordinating active measures, as well as implementing them through over a dozen major international fronts and several non-ruling Communist parties, the ID "has its own representatives in a number of Soviet embassies under special Central Committee tasking." These include "such sensitive areas as relations with the United States, the Middle East, and West Europe, among others."[40] This has been substantiated by former Soviet officials, including Vladimir Sakharov of the Ministry of Foreign Affairs and ex-KGB officer Stanislav Levchenko.[41]

A third technique utilized by Moscow since the early 1970s is *political action within the UN and other international and regional organizations*. The Kremlin has sought to align itself (and its Bloc and surrogate states) with radical and anti-Western Afro-Asian states in these organizations to promote "revolutionary" alternatives in the Third World.[42]

By the mid-1970s, this appears to have paid dividends in various ways within the UN. The PLO, SWAPO, Popular Movement for the Liberation of Angola (MPLA) and the African National Congress (ANC) have been recipients of these developments. With the encouragement and direct involvement of the Soviet Union and its surrogates, the increasingly militant Afro–Asian bloc has pressed the initiative in the UN to support and assist such movements. One important result—among many—has been the granting of permanent observer status in the UN to SWAPO, the PLO, and similar groups, and their recognition as the sole legitimate representative of the "people" they claim to be fighting for.

In sum, the Soviet Union approaches the UN and other international organizations as arenas for conducting political warfare.[43] This appears to be true for Soviet promotion of a number of insurgent movements. Moscow uses these regional and international forums to promote the insurgents' cause and to enhance their influence with Third World states.

Of the three political warfare instruments examined, this appears to be the most difficult to employ, due to the environment in which the USSR and its surrogates have to operate. These are not controlled situations, and the degree to which the Kremlin can successfully employ political influence techniques is limited. Nevertheless, the UN, the nonaligned movement, the Organization of African Unity, the Socialist International and similar organizations are arenas in which Moscow conducts political influence activities in support of insurgent groups.

In terms of the apparatus, existing evidence suggests a large KGB and Bloc intelligence role at the UN. In 1983, R. Jean Gray, head of the FBI's New York section, estimated that there are 1,100 communist bloc officials in New York, including 150 Soviets in the UN Missions and about 180 in the Secretariat.[44] Arkady Shevchenko, a former Soviet Ministry of Foreign Affairs Official who served as Under-Secretary General of the United Nations in 1973–78, estimates that a significant percent of Soviet UN employees, including Missions and Secretariat, are skilled KGB officers.[45] In Moscow, Service A, located within the KGB's First Chief Directorate, has responsibility for planning and overseeing such covert active measures.[46]

The ID also is involved in political active measures at the UN. Several Soviet controlled international front groups (such as the World Peace Council), officially recognized as nongoverning organizations (NGO), take part in UN deliberations. These organizations can be employed for influence operations. Whether or not the ID has officials at the Soviet UN mission similar to its representatives at embassies in the US and Western Europe is uncertain. Some believe that given the importance of the active measures effort in the UN, the ID is likely to have its own representatives in place.[47] Others suggest that while the ID plans and coordinates active measures, their officials are not operationally involved at the UN.

Moscow calls upon surrogate assets to perform specialized tasks beyond its own capabilities. It appears that the East European bloc and other surrogates perform distinct political and paramilitary functions that parallel and augment Soviet strategy. One Western expert has characterized this as a "communist division of labor."[48] In southern Africa, for instance, the East Germans and Cubans serve various functions. According to Western specialists, "the security mission of the East Germans in Africa has been broadly defined . . . there are about 2,500 East Germans training the Angolan army and the Namibian insurgents, the South West African People's Organization (SWAPO)."[49] Evidently, East German troops stationed in Angola have also "participated in search and destroy missions against the Unita insurgents and challenged the spearhead of South African columns deep inside Angola in November 1981."[50] In addition to training, advising, and limited combat support, during the postinsurgency period of power consolidation the East Germans provide sophisticated knowledge of the military and intelligence sciences. In Angola, a core of advisors are training the regime's intelligence and security services.[51] Cuba likewise plays multiple paramilitary roles in southern Africa and elsewhere in the developing world.

In terms of political techniques, Cuban and East German personnel are active in the front organizations and promote insurgent movements through political action in the UN and other international organizations (such as the Cuban role in the nonaligned movement). Their overt propaganda also is targeted to support these efforts. Other Soviet clients play similar roles in supplementing Moscow's propaganda and political efforts in support of insurgent movements. For instance, former high-level Sandinista officials have provided first hand accounts of PLO and Bulgarian activities in Nicaragua.[52]

The importance of the multiple political warfare measures discussed above has been overlooked in Western analysis of Soviet strategy. This is surprising, given the fact that few insurgencies have been unaffected by the international situation; few have succeeded or failed exclusively on their own. Since they are almost always weaker than the incumbents, one way to offset this and allow the insurgents to continue to expand is by acquiring various forms of international assistance. This includes the active championing of the strategic goals of the insurgency within the international arena. International acknowledgement of the "just cause" of the insurgents and the "repressive-immoral" character of the incumbent regime can play an important role during each stage of insurgent development. During the initial period, when recruitment and cadre cell expansion lays the foundation of the guerrilla political-military infrastructure, international political support can be replayed internally to advertise and popularize the movement. This support may also encourage uncommitted nations to back the insurgents. Such support also may be directed at isolating the incumbent regime internationally. Finally, political support may lead to other forms of paramilitary assistance from outside powers. This assistance will be of particular importance once the insurgents increase the scale and intensity of their activities.

Case Studies

The insurgencies examined include Vietnam, Namibia, Nicaragua, and El Salvador. In each case an assessment was undertaken of how Moscow utilized the instruments described above to promote the cause of the insurgents in the international arena. The remainder of this study identifies common thematic approaches, methods, and targets, and also describes the interrelationship and orchestration of these active measures techniques. Before turning to these matters, a brief note is necessary about both the roots of Moscow's involvement and its policy objectives in each of the cases.

During 1965, Soviet involvement in the Vietnam conflict changed dramatically as the Kremlin began to demonstrate a greater readiness to support insurgency in the Third World. This was reflected in the marked growth in the quantity and sophistication of arms transferred to Hanoi. By mid-1967 this included 200 SAM sites, 7,000 anti-aircraft weapons, numerous early-warning and ground-control intercept radars, and MIG-15, MIG-17, and MIG-18 fighters.[53] In conjunction with the acceleration of military assistance, during 1965 Moscow also escalated the use of political warfare measures to promote internationally the cause of the North Vietnamese and Vietcong. Soviet objectives included providing Hanoi with the means of ensnaring the United States in the Vietnam quagmire and eventually defeating it. They also sought to gain greater influence over the North Vietnamese to draw it away from China and demonstrate to the Third World their willingness to assist and promote national liberation movements.

In retrospect, this change in Soviet policy was a harbinger of things to come. It marked the beginning of a greater readiness on the part of Moscow to become involved in low-intensity conflict. The withdrawal of the United States from Vietnam and the impact of the war on the American body politic apparently influenced the Soviet decision to escalate its support for insurgent movements during the 1970s.

The events in Angola in the mid-1970s contributed to the extension of the policy into southern Africa. Until 1974, the region appears to have been considered relatively unimportant when compared with other parts of the Third World. It was dominated by South Africa, Portugal, and Rhodesia. While Moscow did not ignore guerrilla movements challenging these powers, the assistance provided was on a relatively small scale. This changed with the overthrow of the military dictatorship in Portugal in April 1974. The political situation in the region was transformed and the Kremlin intensified its support for insurgent movements, especially the MPLA. The subsequent consolidation of power by the MPLA, due to extensive Soviet and Cuban assistance, further altered politics in southern Africa. This resulted in increased Soviet international political support and paramilitary assistance for SWAPO, the Namibian guerrilla movement fighting South Africa.

The expansion of support for SWAPO served several Soviet policy objectives. It permitted Moscow to strengthen its ties with the Organization of African Unity (OAU), nonaligned movement, and African states, as well as to seize the moral high ground against the Western nations. Support for SWAPO also is part of a larger Soviet policy in southern Africa which seeks to enhance its geostrategic position and eventually deny access to this region, to the United States and the West Europeans.

During the late 1970s, the development and implementation of an increasingly aggressive Soviet strategy for fomenting insurrection and a rapidly changing political situation in Central America resulted in a drastic modification of Soviet policy for the region. Events in Nicaragua in the late 1970s provided the opportunity for Moscow to extend its low-intensity strategy.[54] Principally through its Cuban surrogate, Moscow stepped up military support to the Sandinista National Liberation Front (FSLN) during 1978. In 1979, Havana helped organize, arm, and transport an "international brigade" to fight alongside Sandinista forces and also transferred more sophisticated weapons. In conjunction with this escalation in military assistance, Moscow expanded its international political activities to promote the FSLN. The insurgent victory in Nicaragua resulted in a further extension of Soviet support for other members in the region. The major effort since the FSLN victory has been directed toward El Salvador. As in the other cases, this involves the activation and integration of both political and paramilitary support.

Soviet objectives in Central America, in large part, resemble those in other Third World regions where they actively assisted insurgent movements. Thus, a principle goal is to mire the United States in a costly protracted war similar to Vietnam but much closer to its borders. If these movements seize power, Moscow can acquire new client states from which similar conflicts can be promoted. This is what has transpired in Nicaragua. Finally, new clients may provide the Kremlin with future naval and land bases necessary to a global power with geostrategic goals.

Common Patterns and Comparative Generalizations

An examination of how Moscow employed foreign propaganda, international front organizations, and political activities within international organizations to promote insurgency and revolution in Vietnam, Namibia, Nicaragua, and El Salvador reveals several common methods, patterns, and targets. What follows is a comparative summary of findings for each of the three instruments, as well a description of how they are integrated within Soviet strategy.[55]

Soviet Foreign Propaganda

Soviet foreign propaganda is an important instrument of power, policy, and political warfare. In conjunction with other overt and covert techniques of active measures, propaganda seeks to influence other governments' policies, undermine confidence in their leaders and institutions, disrupt relations between other nations, and discredit and weaken major opponents. Since the early days of the post–World War II period, the United States has been the main target of Soviet propaganda. Since the late 1950s, Moscow has accelerated the quality, quantity, and intensity of the propaganda campaign directed against the United States. As this study demonstrates, Soviet propaganda campaigns in support of insurgent movements are part of this long term operation. In each of the insurgencies examined, the United States was one of the major Soviet propaganda targets. Consequently, the linkage is tightly drawn between the long term campaign conducted against the "main enemy" and these more intermediate efforts in support of insurgency movements.

The general features of Soviet foreign propaganda, as noted above, include intensity and concentration, flexibility and adaptivity, deception and manipulation, and centralized control and coordination. Additionally, reflecting the Soviet technique of "Kombinatsia," propaganda campaigns combine and interrelate multiple issues to support a set of specific themes. The use of this technique was apparent in each of the four case studies, particularly with respect to American involvement in Vietnam.

A brief examination of the growth and development over the last twenty years of the wide variety of Soviet foreign propaganda outlets provides one important indicator of the importance CPSU leaders place in this instrument of foreign policy. Consequently, given the historical importance of propaganda as a tool of statecraft and the development of a large organizational mechanism for conducting operations, it is not surprising that it has played an important role in Soviet strategy for promoting and assisting Third World insurgent movements. Major channels include the foreign radio broadcast system, two news agencies, the prestige press, various publications, and approximately 500 Soviet journalists stationed in foreign countries. These capabilities are supplemented by the East European bloc and other Soviet surrogates. Surrogate capabilities appear critical to overall Soviet strategy for promoting and assisting insurgent movements, as was quite apparent in the two Central American cases.

An analysis of the Soviet use of foreign propaganda to promote the cause of an insurgency in Vietnam, Namibia, Nicaragua, and El Salvador reveals the following common developments:

1. An analysis of Soviet foreign propaganda provides insights into Moscow's foreign policy objectives. In each of the four cases examined, an escalation in foreign propaganda coverage signalled that the insurgency had become an important policy issue for Moscow. This resulted, in turn, in an expansion of support and assistance for the guerrillas.

2. The initiation of the Soviet overt propaganda campaign in support of the insurgent movements examined signalled the beginning of a broader political warfare campaign, in which other instruments were brought into play. For example, as foreign propaganda coverage expanded and began to actively promote the cause of the North Vietnamese (DRV) and Vietcong (VC) and to denigrate U.S. policy, international front organizations were activated. Their propaganda and international conference diplomacy increased significantly from what it was before the Soviet propaganda campaign began. This was followed by an increase in Soviet political action to promote the cause of the DRV/VC in the U.N. In effect, an escalation of foreign propaganda in each case served to set in motion a broader political warfare campaign in which other instruments of power and influence were immediately brought into play.

3. In each of the cases investigated, Soviet overt propaganda set the thematic pattern that was followed by the international front organizations and also guided the political action conducted within international organizations. While not a perfect congruence, it is accurate to say that overt propaganda established the thematic framework from which the other instruments took their cues. One main difference was that the international fronts did not concentrate on as many themes as did Soviet propaganda, and their treatment of issues was generally more simplistic in approach and vitriolic in tone. This may be the result of the target audience and of the instrument itself. Soviet overt propaganda examined in this study was targeted worldwide, and is the official voice of the government. Multiple targets may account for thematic complexity. The somewhat less strident tone, on the other hand, is probably due to the official status of Soviet propaganda.

4. Of the three political warfare instruments examined in this study, overt propaganda reflected the Soviet technique of Kombinatsia in the most sophisticated manner. It combined and interrelated multiple issues in support of a number of central themes. For example, in the case of the Soviet propaganda in support of SWAPO, six specific themes, with multiple sub-themes subsumed under them, were integrated and combined into the overall international campaign.

5. Campaigns conducted on an international basis can be expected to be broader and more complex because there are various audiences targeted. The Soviet propaganda campaign in support of the DRV/VC is a case in point. To the Third World the Soviets wanted to communicate that it was aligned with and actively supporting the cause of national liberation. Additionally, they sought to present an image of the United States as the new colonial power. To the Europeans its objective was to characterize the United States as warlike and recklessly aggressive, and to convince

them that such behavior could plunge Europe into war. The emphasis on worldwide opposition to U.S. policy in Vietnam was part of the post–World War II Soviet propaganda effort aimed at characterizing the United States as the greatest threat to world peace. Given the multiple objectives, it is little wonder the propaganda campaign manifests the characteristics described above. More specifically targeted foreign propaganda channels will take a narrower approach. For instance, radio broadcasts targeted on specific regional audiences in southern Africa (in an African dialect) would not reflect the complex number of themes in Soviet worldwide broadcasts. The topics covered would be those more germane to the region.

6. Measuring the immediate impact of the various instruments of active measures is very difficult. This is especially true of overt propaganda conducted on an international basis. However, according to Western specialists, as well as former Soviet block intelligence officers, the Communist approach to questions of effectiveness is different from that in the West. Their concern is more with the overall cumulative effect over time. Furthermore, their view of time is much different. So, concern with measuring the specific effectiveness of each type of active measures operation, many of which are difficult to evaluate, is not emphasized to the degree it is in the West. It is the cumulative impact that is important.[56] From an operational perspective, this may be defined as the evolution of a specific situation in the direction favoring Soviet objectives.

In addition to these recurring patterns, there are a number of other similarities in the case studies. The overall objective of Soviet overt propaganda, as well as that of the other instruments of political warfare, is to promote the cause and program of the insurgent movement while discrediting and isolating the government against which the insurgency is directed. Nevertheless, as was noted previously, in each case the United States is the major target of the propaganda effort. It receives, at minimum, as much attention as the government against which the insurgency is directed.

In each of the insurgencies examined, regardless of whether or not the United States was involved (as well as the degree to which it was assisting the government experiencing the insurgency), Soviet propaganda characterized the United States as a major cause of the conflict. The reason for this is readily apparent. The propaganda campaigns conducted in support of insurgency movements in the Third World are combined with the major and long term campaign directed against the United States over the last three decades. A major facet of this campaign is the assertion that U.S. policies are incompatible with those of the developing nations, and are based on aggressive, militaristic, and imperial motives.

The degree of U.S. involvement in the conflict had no apparent impact on the way in which Soviet propaganda covered the subject. Regardless of whether it was Vietnam, Namibia, Nicaragua, or El Salvador, there was very little variance in the pattern. This was the case even though American involvement differed significantly in these four cases. The difference between Vietnam and Namibia, for instance, is of immense proportion. Furthermore, during the final years of the Somoza government the Carter administration sought to distance itself from that regime. As the "main enemy" of the USSR, however, such distinctions are not germane to the pursuit of policy objectives.

The specific propaganda themes directed against the United States were what the informed student of Soviet political warfare might expect. The tone was harsh and there was little variation in the overall message. For example, in the case of Namibia the Soviets asserted that the United States employed every maneuver (from the most benign to the most insidious) to maintain its imperial interests in southern Africa. To this end the government of South Africa was employed as a surrogate force for maintaining and protecting Western interests. The United States provided Pretoria with every form of assistance, including nuclear weapons, in order to maintain it in power. In this case, the United States placed in the hands of the South Africans the means for brutal repression of all opposition. In other cases, most notably Vietnam, the United States is charged directly with carrying out repression and atrocities. Currently, El Salvador is presented as a mirror-image of the early years of the American involvement in Vietnam. Washington has intervened directly and, according to Moscow, is responsible for unleashing through its client forces a brutal campaign of repression to maintain its interests. There is no need to recite further examples. The major point, to reiterate, is the degree to which the United States is placed at the center of Soviet propaganda campaigns and characterized as a primary source of conflict.

One also finds a high degree of continuity in other aspects of each of these campaigns. For instance, each of the insurgent movements examined was presented as the sole legitimate representative of the people, to the exclusion of other political parties. The insurgent political program was praised and their military actions justified on the grounds that the policy of the United States and its clients permitted no alternative. Finally, the USSR and the Socialist bloc were characterized as the natural allies of these insurgent movements. There was nothing surprising about those thematic patterns. However, once under way, each campaign reflected the ability of Soviet propaganda to intensify and concentrate the effort. Additionally, each campaign was characterized by deception and manipulation of the facts, as well as by the Soviet technique of Kombinatsia, the combining and interrelating of multiple themes.

International Front Organizations

The Kremlin employs overt and covert political techniques to strengthen allies and weaken opponents, and to create a favorable environment for the successful execution of operations and the achievement of objectives. These techniques are centrally coordinated and intensively and systematically implemented. The themes of Soviet overt propaganda in support of insurgents do not stand alone—they are promoted and amplified through the Kremlin's major international front organizations.

As was noted previously, the methods of Soviet-directed international fronts are two-fold. Reflecting the Kremlin's approach to political warfare, fronts combine "words" (propaganda) and "deeds" (political action). The international front organizations utilize the instruments of propaganda and conference diplomacy. In the case of the latter, it can take a number of forms. Front involvement in conference diplomacy may serve the Soviet foreign policy objective of supporting and promoting the cause of selected insurgency movements in a number of ways:

1. Their meetings are often attended by the educated elites of Third World and Western countries. If Moscow can indirectly or directly help fashion the agenda of the meetings (and the conference recommendations) in ways supportive of its foreign policy objectives, these elites may be favorably influenced. Thus, the conference can be used for propaganda purposes.

2. International conferences are also used for conducting political influence operations. The fronts seek to persuade conference participants to take action on behalf of Soviet policy.

3. The proceedings and documents of the conference are generally reproduced and circulated on both a regional and international basis for propaganda purposes.

The USSR controls a number of different international front groups, and through them promotes the cause of insurgent movements in the world arena. However, in each of the four cases examined, the World Peace Council (WPC) played a key role in the overall front campaign. This is not surprising in light of the fact that the WPC takes the lead in almost all major front programs and activities. In addition to the WPC, which played the central role in the Vietnam campaign, the other three examples disclose a pattern of activity in which more than one front played a key part. For instance, in the case of Namibia the Afro-Asian People's Solidarity Organization (AAPSO) was as involved as the WPC in the Soviet front campaign in support of SWAPO. In the Central American examples, much broader campaigns were conducted in which a wider coalition of fronts were mobilized. In sum, the four case studies reveal the following two general patterns: 1) one or two of the major fronts take individual or joint responsibility for directing the campaign and conducting the majority of conference operations (Vietnam and Namibia) or 2) the campaign is decentralized with a number of the front organizations brought into play, but with no one organization conducting the majority of operations (Nicaragua and El Salvador).

In terms of front propaganda campaigns, in almost every respect their general thematic pattern mirrored Soviet commentary. In each of the case studies the difference between Soviet and front group propaganda was in tone (front propaganda is harsher) and the fact that the fronts tended to concentrate their efforts on a fewer number of themes. Front propaganda campaigns were not as broad in scope or targeted against as many audiences as their Soviet counterpart.

In the case of Vietnam, for instance, while WPC propaganda followed the Soviet line and focused on condemning U.S. policy as criminal and praising that of the DRV/VC, the major subject of WPC commentary focused on the "rapidly growing" and worldwide opposition to America's role in Vietnam. This was, of course, also a Soviet theme. Proportionally, however, it received much wider coverage in WPC propaganda. This dovetailed, as we shall explain below, with the major thrust of WPC conference diplomacy.

Similarly, in the case of international front commentary focused on insurgency in Central America, the number of themes covered were fewer and the treatment of issues generally more simplistic in approach and vitriolic in tone than that found in Soviet overt propaganda. The overt propaganda effort of the fronts focused on audiences in the region and carried a basically simple message that it played back through its international and regional conference activities. They concentrated on U.S. policy in the region in general, and toward Nicaragua and El Salvador in particular. The Vietnam analogy remains an important element of this line. In light of the regional audiences targeted through front conference diplomacy, the focus on the U.S. policy in Central America demonstrates the link between front propaganda and political action.

Finally, in the case of Namibia the thematic pattern of front group propaganda, unlike the previous cases, was as broad in scope as that of its Soviet counterpart. Additionally, in this case two major fronts—WPC and AAPSO—both played central roles in the international campaign to mobilize support for SWAPO. Their international conference activities since the mid-1970s have been extensive, reflecting the multiple themes amplified through Moscow's propaganda network.

International propaganda is only one of the methods an international front organization employs. Of equal importance is the tactic of international conference diplomacy. International conferences, as was noted earlier, may be divided into the following categories: meetings of the front organizations; international and regional conferences and meetings sponsored by one or more of the fronts; and international conferences sponsored by other international organizations in which the fronts play an active role. In each of the four case studies examined in this report, an escalation in international conference activity in support of a particular insurgent movement coincided with the activation of the other political warfare measures. However, the particular kind of conference action employed differed from case to case. For instance, all three approaches were utilized by the WPC and AAPSO in their campaign in support of SWAPO, including major programs conducted in cooperation with different UN committees. Their conference activity provided a means through which to observe how fronts combine propaganda with political action. Perhaps the most important development that emerged from the assessment of this case is the degree to which the WPC and AAPSO attempted to surround their activities with the legitimacy gained through interaction with the UN, OAU, and nonaligned movement. Especially through their recognition by the UN, the WPC and AAPSO sought to place their activities within the mainstream of world public opinion. The Namibian case depicted how the WPC and AAPSO play to the active interest of certain specialized UN committees in Namibia in order to broaden the base of their political operations in support of SWAPO. The circumstances were appropriate in the Namibian situation to allow for this.

In the other case studies the approach taken was different. For example, of the three variations identified above, "international conferences sponsored by a front" was, by far, the primary international conference technique employed by the WPC during the Vietnam war. The Stockholm Conference (which began in 1967) and its national level spinoffs became the vehicle through which the WPC sought to coordinate and organize West European and American opposition to U.S. policy in Vietnam. As the study on Vietnam reveals, this was a classic example of how a front combines "words and deeds" in a large and extended operation targeted against multiple audiences—in this case those in Western Europe and the United States opposed to the Vietnam War.

International front conference diplomacy conducted in support of insurgency in Central America reveals still another pattern. Unlike the previous two case studies, these conferences and meetings were smaller in size and scope, and were regionally focused. Perhaps the most interesting development in the Nicaraguan and Salvadoran examples were the number of fronts involved in the campaign. Evidently, given the limited assets of the fronts in this area the decision was made to try and offset this problem by mobilizing a number of the fronts to devote a portion of their time to these causes, rather than assigning the Central American "account" to any one organization. These included the WPC, World Federation of Trade Unions (WFTU), World Federation of Democratic Youth (WFDY), International Organization of Journalists (IOJ), International Union of Students (IUS), and Afro-Asian and Latin American Peoples Solidarity Organization (AALAPSO). In other words, the assets of a number of the fronts would be stretched to cover Central America until new capabilities were mobilized. The regional target focus of conference activity in Central America is not always the case. For instance, in the Vietnam case the WPC conference activity was focused on West European targets.

The political action campaigns conducted by Moscow's front organizations in the international arena are introduced at the state level by the front's national affiliates. This was true of each of the cases examined. The national level activities even extended into the United States. Over the last five years the U.S. Peace Council (USPC) has been increasingly active in the movement opposing the Reagan administration's policies in Central America. The USPC, whose leadership is drawn from the Communist Party USA (CPUSA), was instrumental in establishing the Committee in Solidarity with the People of El Salvador (CISPES). The latter, whose leadership is drawn from the USPC and CPUSA, has been very active since 1981 in conducting operations against American policies in El Salvador. This has included, among other activities, involvement in the May 3, 1981 march on the Pentagon, distribution of a State Department forgery on El Salvador, civil disobedience actions in 1983 and 1984 in a number of cities, and planning and organizing major annual demonstrations in Washington, D.C. in 1983–85.

Political Activities within International Organizations

Earlier we observed that during the 1960s Moscow shifted from a defensive to an offensive strategy in its approach to international organizations. They aggressively staked out a position in UN deliberations that placed it on the side of anticolonialism and newly established Third World states. As the new states became increasingly radical and anti-Western, Moscow maneuvered to take political advantage of these developments.

Since the early 1960s, either in the General Assembly or specialized UN committees, Moscow has cooperated with and supported the activities of the radical Afro-Asian bloc. This is reflected in their policy toward the PLO, MPLA, SWAPO, ANC, and other Third World insurgency movements. The increasingly militant African and Asian states in the UN have pressed the initiative both to recognize and to assist these national liberation movements, with the support and encouragement of Moscow.

The growing domination of the General Assembly by Third World states has allowed the Kremlin to utilize this forum to align itself with this bloc in ways that strengthened its position. Thus, the Soviet Union approaches the UN and other international organizations as arenas in which to conduct political warfare. This has been the case in Soviet support for certain Third World insurgency movements. Moscow has, in conjunction with the radical bloc, sought to use the UN and other international organizations as forums for promoting the cause and enhancing the reputation and credibility of these insurgent movements.

In each of the cases examined, to different degrees, the USSR employed this technique. Consequently, there are important variations in the degree to which the Kremlin has been able to make use of this technique. For example, in conjunction with the initiation of the Soviet propaganda campaign and international front political action in support of the DRV/VC, Moscow sought in the latter half of the 1960s to maneuver the UN to take up the issue of American involvement in Vietnam. However, at that time the power balance in the UN was not as anti-Western as it became in the 1970s and 1980s. Furthermore, there was no specialized committee through which the Soviets could maneuver to achieve their objectives in the General Assembly. As the case study of SWAPO demonstrates, such a base is essential. Soviet-sponsored support for the PLO in the UN is an equally important example of the need for a base. No such foundation existed for addressing the Vietnam question. This severely limited the opportunities for success. Thus, while Moscow brought the question before the General Assembly in 1965, the US was able to block passage of the Soviet resolution. With no specialized committee to penetrate and the General Assembly in an unreceptive mood, the Soviets could only use the UN as a public forum from which to criticize American policy, and between 1965 and 1972 it did just that. However, it was unable to move from propaganda to political action in order to mobilize the General Assembly against U.S. policy.

The case of SWAPO and the UN stands in sharp contrast. In this instance a specialized UN committee—The Committee of 24—existed, and Moscow was actively involved in its day-to-day deliberations. The Soviet Union and its surrogates have played an active part in the Committee's work since the very early days of its existence. As the Committee became increasingly militant and anti-Western by the early 1970s, the United States and the British withdrew.

This militant and radical stance can be attributed to the power balance within the Committee. When the radical elements from the Afro-Asian bloc aligned with the Commitee's communist members, it is not surprising that the Committee moved in an anti-Western direction. During the 1970s the Committee of 24 played an instrumental role in the recognition by the General Assembly of certain national liberation movements as the authentic representatives of the people for whom they claimed to fight. In conjunction with this, through the General Assembly, the Committee of 24 was able to have regularly budgeted UN funds allocated either directly or indirectly to these insurgent movements. In some cases, this financial assistance has not been inconsequential. This is certainly true in the case of SWAPO. Committee of 24 activities on behalf of SWAPO and other insurgent groups fit into the categories of publicity and procurement of assistance. SWAPO benefited greatly from both forms of assistance.

In sum, here we see a classic political operation in which the Soviets align with a like-minded coalition to promote its objectives in southern Africa. This is not meant to suggest that the Soviets control the activities of the Committee of 24, for this does not appear to be the case. They have, however, formed an alliance with likeminded Afro-Asian states, and this serves the same objectives as those promoted through overt propaganda and international front group activities. Of the four cases examined, UN support for SWAPO was by far the most extensive and successful.

In the Central American cases the Soviets appear to have decided to bypass the UN and to focus their efforts on the nonaligned movement. As the Kremlin began to concentrate on insurgent movements in Nicaragua, El Salvador, and elsewhere, they faced the problem of having no specialized committee structure in the UN through which to promote the cause of the guerrillas. As a result of this, Moscow seems to have chosen to use their Cuban surrogate to maneuver the nonaligned movement to promote the cause and program of "national liberation" movements in Central America. Soviet strategy seeks to use all avenues for building international support for selected insurgent groups. The nonaligned movement was potentially one such avenue. In 1979, at the Havana Summit of the nonaligned movement, this strategy was achieved as the member states widened their support of national liberation movements to include Latin America.

Havana was able to place this theme on the nonaligned agenda, therefore broadening the issue of national liberation in Latin America from a regional to an international one. In the years following the Havana Summit, the dual issues of US imperialism and national liberation in Latin America have remained an important agenda item for the nonaligned states. As the head of the nonaligned movement in 1979, Cuba played an instrumental role in moving the nonaligned movement to more actively support national liberation movements in Latin America. This is a good example of how shared interests can be maneuvered to serve the objectives of the USSR and their Cuban surrogate. However, because of Cuban heavy-handedness they were not able to follow up this initial success with the nonaligned movement.

Documents captured in Grenada after October 1983 reveal an attempt on the part of Moscow's surrogates to intervene directly in the Socialist International (SI) to influence the course of the debate on Central American questions. The documents describe how the New Jewel Movement of Maurice Bishop joined a secret pro-Soviet faction in the SI that included the Nicaraguan FSLN. The secret faction, which operated under the guidance of the Cuban Communist Party, sought to influence the SI to support a resolution to the conflict in El Salvador along Marxist-Leninist lines.[57]

Conclusion

We have examined the ways in which Moscow coordinates and employs propaganda, international fronts, and political action within international organizations to promote the cause of insurgent movements in the world arena. These techniques, which constitute the political elements of active measures, are only one part of the overall Soviet political-military strategy. There is also an important military aspect which cannot be separated from the political measures. Political and military techniques are combined by Moscow and employed simultaneously to achieve policy objectives. Although not within the purview of this study, the evidence shows how closely political and military measures are coordinated once Moscow decides to escalate its support for an insurgent movement. Policy objectives are achieved not by any one instrument, but through the utilization of the political-military techniques described above. The coordination of all means deemed effective is the sine qua non of the Soviet approach.

The coordination of propaganda, international fronts, and political action within international organizations can be observed in each of the cases examined in the study. In each instance, once the decision was made by the Kremlin to escalate its involvement with a particular insurgent movement, each of these political instruments was activated. The initiation of the Soviet foreign propaganda offensive signaled the beginning of a broader political warfare campaign and set the themes and targets for the other political instruments. While the specific themes differed in each case, the general pattern and objectives were quite similar.

Will the Soviets continue to employ these instruments in the 1980s? What changes in policy and strategy can we expect? Will Moscow escalate its activities? While prediction is always difficult, the trends of the 1970s and early 1980s suggest increased Soviet activism in support for insurgent movements. We say this for the following reasons:

1. The decision in the early 1970s to escalate political and military support for insurgent movements occurred within the context of a Soviet perception of a favorable shift in the overall correlation of forces. If the Soviets continue to believe that the strategic and theater military balances are shifting to their advantage, it is quite likely they will escalate support for insurgent movements. Under this umbrella a more assertive policy in the Third World can be expected.

2. During the past two decades, the Soviets have made significant improvements in their capabilities to project military power in Third World areas. They also have demonstrated a willingness to employ these means, in conjunction with political instruments, as part of an integrated political-military strategy. In effect, Moscow has developed the experience and infrastructure that will allow them to maintain and escalate support for the insurgents in the 1980s.

3. In conjunction with extensive Soviet assets is the development of a wide range of surrogate capabilities for assisting Third World insurgent movements. These capabilities will remain at the Kremlin's disposal in the 1980s. In light of growing Soviet reliance on surrogates over the last decade and the important contributions they have made, it would seem likely that these will continue to be mobilized and employed in the 1980s.

4. Since the early 1970s a number of Soviet-backed insurgent movements have come to power, and this has been advantageous to Moscow's political and geostrategic position in the Third World. When combined with the factors listed above, this is an added impetus motivating Moscow to continue (if not escalate) its policy of assisting and promoting insurgent movements.

6. Finally, the radicalism that is increasingly evident in many parts of the Third World constitutes a political trend that will continue to present Moscow with opportunities for exploitation and expansion.

With respect to the political measures examined in this study, we can expect a general continuation of the patterns described above. The organizational infrastructure is in place and has been employed effectively over the last decade. It would seem likely that these will be utilized by Moscow. Of course, if the Kremlin escalates its support for insurgents in the 1980s, one can expect these political instruments to follow suit. There also are possible new trends that could emerge in the next few years especially in the use of surrogate political instruments. Given the growing importance of Central America, Moscow may expand the role of its Cuban surrogate. In light of these factors, Moscow's continued promotion of insurrection in the Third World appears quite likely. Rather than de-escalation, an escalation of such activity seems to be more probable.

Notes

1. Donald Zagoria, "Into the Breach: New Soviet Alliances in the Third World," *Foreign Affairs* (Spring, 1979); Frank Fukuyama, "The New Marxist-Leninist States and Internal Conflict in the Third World," in *Vulnerabilities of Third World Marxist-Leninist Regimes: Implications for U.S. Policy* (New York: Pergamon-Brassey, 1985).

2. Ray Cline and Yonah Alexander, *Terrorism: The Soviet Connection* (New York: Crane Russak, 1984).

3. U.S. Congress, Senate Committee on the Judiciary, Subcommittee on Security and Terrorism, *The Role of the Soviet Union, Cuba, and East Germany in Fomenting Terrorism in Southern Africa,* vols. 1–11, 97th Congress, 2nd sess. (Washington, D.C.: GPO, 1982).

4. Stephen Hosmer and Thomas Wolfe, *Soviet Policy and Practice Toward Third Conflicts* (Lexington, Mass.: Lexington Books, 1983); Raymond Duncan, *Soviet Policy in the Third World* (New York: Pergamon, 1980); Adam Ulam, *Expansion and Coexistence* (New York: Praeger, 1973).

5. Leonid Brezhnev, *Report of the CPSU Central Committee to the 24th Congress of the Communist Party of the Soviet Union* (Moscow: Novosti Press Agency, 1971). For the complete Congress materials see *Foreign Broadcast Information Service (FBIS)/Daily Report—Soviet Union* (5–9 April 1971).

6. *FBIS/Daily Report—Soviet Union* (6 April 1971 Supplement), pp. 76–83.

7. Vernon Aspaturian, "Soviet Global Power and the Correlation of Forces," *Problems of Communism* (May–June, 1980).

8. For a discussion of the decision to expand the use of disinformation as an instrument of Soviet strategy, see Anatoliy Golitsyn, *New Lies for Old* (New York: Dodd, Mead & Co., 1984), chs. 5–12.

9. See Richard Shultz and Roy Godson, *Dezinformatsia: Active Measures in Soviet Strategy* (New York: Pergamon-Brassey, 1984).

10. Leonid Schapiro, "The International Department of the CPSU: Key to Soviet Policy," *International Journal* (Winter, 1976–77); Elizabeth Teague, "The Foreign Departments of the Central Committee of the CPSU," *Radio Liberty Research Bulletin* (27 Oct. 1980). For the perspective of former Soviet officials on this question, see Arkady Schevchenko, *Breaking with Moscow* (New York: Alfred Knopf, 1985) and the interview with Stanislav Levchenko in Shultz and Godson, *Dezinformatsia*, ch. 5.

11. Boris Ponomarev, *Some Problems of the Revolutionary Movement* (Moscow: Progress Publishers, 1975) and *Lenin and the World Revolutionary Process* (Moscow: Progress Publishers, 1980).

12. Boris Ponomarev, "Universal-Historical Significance of the Great October Socialist Revolution," *Kommunist* (Nov. 1977), trans. in JPRS/USSR Report (January 1978), pp. 42, 46.

13. Boris Ponomarev, "Great Vital Force of Leninism," *Kommunist* (May 1980), trans. in JPRS/USSR Report (July 1980), p. 11.

14. Ibid.

15. Boris Ponomarev, "Invincibility of the Liberation Movement," *Kommunist* (January 1980), trans. in JPRS/USSR Report (March 1980), pp. 29–30.

16. Ibid., pp. 14–15.

17. See *Appearances of Soviet Leaders* (Washington, D.C.: CIA/National Foreign Assessment Centre, 1978, 1979, 1980).

18. For the complete text, see document 1, "Protocol of Talks Between PLO and Soviet Delegations in Moscow," contained in Cline and Alexander, *Terrorism: The Soviet Connection,* pp. 83–106. For excerpts from this meeting see document 4 in the Middle East section of Part II in this study.

19. Rostislav Ulyanovsky, *National Liberation* (Moscow: Progress Publishers, 1978).

20. Karen Brutents, *National Liberation Revolutions Today,* vol. 1 (Moscow: Progress Publishers, 1977), p. 16.

21. Pete Manchka, *In the Vanguard of the Revolutionary Struggle in Africa* (Moscow: Political Literature Publishers, 1975).

22. Harriet Scott and William Scott, *The Soviet Art of War* (Boulder, Colo.: Westview, 1982), p. 291.

23. A.A. Grechko, "The Leading Role of the CPSU in Building the Army of a Developed Socialist Society," *Voprosy Istorii KSPP* (Problems of History of the CPSU), trans. FBIS, (May 1974). Also cited in Scott and Scott, *Soviet Art of War,* p. 243.

24. N.V. Ogarkov, "Military Strategy," *Sovetskaya Voyennaya Entsiklopedia (Soviet Military Encyclopedia),* vol. 7 (Moscow: Voyenizdat, 1979), p. 564.

25. "Documents and Materials: Long-Range Subjects for Military-Historical Research in 1981–1990," *Voyenno-Istroicheskiy Zhurnal* (June 1981), trans. in JPRS/ USSR Report (Military Affairs), September 1981, pp. 65–66.

26. For instance, in a 1981 article by Capt. N. Chikhachev, the author underscores Brezhnev's report to the 26th Party Congress, stressing the Soviet role in "Guarding the Progressive Conquests" that have occurred "in a number of Afro-Asian and Latin American nations." See "Guarding the Progressive Conquests," *Kommunist Vooruzhennykh Sil* (July 1981), trans. in JPRS/USSR Reports (Military Affairs), Dec. 1981. In an article in the same periodical by Maj. Gen. V. Khalipov the author concentrates on those documents from the 26th Congress concerned with the "national liberation struggles" and Soviet Policy. See "Irreversible Process of Revolutionary Renewal of the World," *Kommunist Voorushennykh Sil* (May 1981), trans. in JPRS/ USSR Report (Military Affairs), August 1981.

27. Mark Katz, *The Third World in Soviet Military Thought* (Baltimore: Johns Hopkins Univ. Press, 1982), pp. 123–25.

28. Henry Trofimenko, "America, Russia, and the Third World," *Foreign Affairs* (Summer 1981).

29. *FBIS/Daily Reports—Soviet Union* (5–9 April 1971). The most thoughtful early examination can be found in Foy Kohler et al. *Soviet Strategy for the Seventies* (Miami: Center for Advanced International Studies, Univ. of Miami, 1973).

30. For detailed discussion, see Richard Shultz, "Soviet Strategy and Organization: Active Measures and Insurgency," in *The Red Orchestra,* ed. Dennis Bark (Stanford, Calif.: Hoover Institution Press, 1985).

31. Since this study is concerned only with Soviet propaganda and political support of insurgent movements, a discussion of the paramilitary instruments is not included. For this see Shultz, above.

32. Frederick Barghoorn, *Soviet Foreign Propaganda* (Princeton, N.J.: Princeton Univ. Press, 1964), pp. 4–5.

33. Shultz and Godson, *Dezinformatsia,* chs. 2–3.

34. Ibid.

35. Ibid., pp. 25–31.

36. For background on the fronts, see Witold Sworakowski, *The Communist International and Its Front Organizations* (Stanford, Calif.: Hoover Institution Press, 1965); James Atkinson, *The Politics of Struggle* (Chicago: Regnery, 1966); John Roche, *The History and Impact of Marxist-Leninist Organizational Theory* (Cambridge, Mass.: Institute for Foreign Policy Analysis, 1984).

37. Franz Borkenau, *World Communism* (reprint, Ann Arbor, Mich.: Univ. of Michigan Press, 1962).

38. This term is borrowed from Arieh Eilan, "Conference Diplomacy," *The Washington Quarterly* (Autumn 1981).

39. John Dziak, *Soviet Perception of Military Power: The Interaction of Theory and Practice* (New York: National Strategy Information Center, 1981), p. 40.

40. Ibid., pp. 40–41.

41. See Testimony of Vladimer Sahkarov later in this volume. Levchenko's commentary on the ID can be found in Shultz and Godson, *Dezinformatsia,* ch. 5.

42. Alvin Rubinstein, *Soviet Foreign Policy Since World War II* (Cambridge, Mass.: Winthrop, 1981), chs. 9–10.

43. Rubinstein notes that "conflict, not cooperation is the dynamic that impels Soviet behavior in international organization." They are "battlefields" (Ibid).

44. Cited in Julian Pilon, "The UN and the USSR," *Survey* (Autumn-Winter 1983), pp. 95–96.

45. Shevchenko, *Breaking With Moscow.*

46. Shultz and Godson, *Dezinformatsia,* pp. 31–33.

47. See the testimony of Vladimer Sahkarov later in this volume.

48. U.S. Congress, Senate, Subcommittee on Security and Terrorism, Committee on the Judiciary, *Soviet, East German, and Cuban Involvement in Fomenting Terrorism in Southern Africa,* vol. 1, p. 26.

49. Peter Vanneman and W. Martin James, *Soviet Foreign Policy in Southern Africa* (Pretoria: Africa Institute of South Africa, 1982), pp. 38–39.

50. Ibid.

51. Gavriel Ra'anan, "Surrogate Forces and Power Projection," in *Projection of Power,* ed. Uri Ra'anan, Robert L. Pfaltzgraff, Jr., and Geoffrey Kemp (Hamden, Conn.: Archon Books, 1982).

52. See testimony by Eden Pastora Gomez and Miguel Bolonas Hunter later in this volume.

53. William Zimmerman, "The Korean and Vietnam Wars," in *Diplomacy of Power,* ed. Stephen Kaplan (Washington, D.C.: The Brookings Institutions, 1981), pp. 336–351.

54. See testimony by Pastora and Bolonas later in this volume.

55. The author has, in draft form, individual chapters on each of these cases which are part of a larger study the author has undertaken on Soviet political and military support for six insurgent movements.

56. Shultz and Godson, *Dezinformatsia,* ch. 5.

57. The appropriate documents and relevant analysis can be found in Paul Seabury and Walter McDougall, eds., *The Grenada Papers* (San Francisco: Institute for Contemporary Studies, 1984).

7

Central America: The Role of Cuba and of the Soviet Union

Ernst Halperin

The Caribbean Basin is noted not only for the proliferation of dictatorships, but also for the eccentricities (to put it mildly) of some of
these dictators. The great American writer Eugene O'Neill even devoted one of his plays to the subject—*Emperor Jones*. The model for this
figure was probably Christophe, the early nineteenth-century ruler of Haiti
who was said to have amused himself by having serried ranks of his army
march over the top of a cliff.

In our century we have, among others, the case of Trujillo of the Dominican Republic, whose madness became so dangerous to all around him that
his closest associates organized his assassination. There is a jubilant Dominican folk-song—a *merengue*—celebrating this event, which contains the line,
"Han matado al chivo—en la carretera!" (They have killed the madman—on
the highway!).

Another case of insanity among Caribbean dictators—a clinical case of
megalomania—is that of the ruler who in 1976 dictated a Constitution,
unanimously adopted by an obedient Assembly, which declares the elimination of all U.S. political, economic, and cultural influence in Latin America
and the Caribbean to be the foreign policy aim of his small island country.
Article 12 of the Cuban Constitution of 1976 states:

> The Republic of Cuba espouses the principles of proletarian internationalism
> and of the combative solidarity of the peoples and . . .
>
> c) . . . considers that its help to those under attack and to the peoples
> that struggle for their liberation constitutes its internationalist right and
> duty . . .
>
> g) aspires to establish along with the other countries of Latin America
> and the Caribbean—freed from foreign domination and internal oppres-
> sion—one large community of nations joined by the fraternal ties of histor-
> ical tradition and the common struggle against colonialism, neocolonial-
> ism and imperialism, in the same desire to foster national and social
> progress . . ."

The Constitution thus calls upon the peoples of Latin America and the Caribbean to wage, with Cuban support, a "liberation struggle" against "foreign domination," that is, the alliance of their countries with the United States, and against "internal oppression," that is, the governments, be they dictatorial or democratic, that maintain this alliance. In other words, the aim of the struggle is to dismantle the Interamerican Alliance and break all ties with the United States—in brief, to expel the United States from the Organization of American States (OAS). Once the dominoes—the pro-American governments—have fallen, a new community forged in the struggle against "imperialism" will emerge. One need hardly spell out who would be the leader of this "anti-imperialist" Latin American Alliance.

Similar declarations abound in Castro's speeches and in other official documents of the Cuban revolutionary regime. Already the Second Declaration of Havana, authored by Castro and unanimously adopted by a "Cuban People's Assembly" on 4 February 1962—twenty-three years ago—invokes the names of Bolivar, San Martin, and the other leaders of the independence struggle against Spain, and then continues:

> Great as was the epic of the independence of Latin America, heroic as was that struggle, to the present generation of Latin Americans there has fallen an even greater and more decisive task. Because that struggle was to liberate itself from the Spanish colonial power, a decadent Spain, invaded by the armies of Napoleon. *Today it is faced with the struggle for liberation from the most powerful imperial metropolis in the world, from the most important power of the imperialist world system,* and in order to render a service to humanity even greater than that rendered by our ancestors.[1]

In our "gringo" arrogance we might be tempted to dismiss such statements as empty rhetoric typical of the region in which it originated—the Caribbean with its luxuriant tropical vegetation. Fidel Castro's rhetoric is indeed luxuriant and ornate, but it is by no means empty, especially not when it promises violence.

Castro is the man who launched his career as a revolutionary leader by attacking the Moncada Barracks at Santiago de Cuba with a contingent of one hundred and fifteen men. There followed, two and a half years after this failed attempt, Castro's invasion of Cuba at the head of eighty-four men. Eighty-four against a well-equipped army of twenty-three thousand! And this invasion was successful, after a two-year guerrilla war waged by Castro—as the historian Hugh Thomas has put it—as a political campaign surrounded by armed men, rather than as a military campaign.

Once securely ensconced in power, Castro soon flung down the gauntlet to the United States and to the OAS. Already in the first Declaration of Havana, pronounced on September 26, 1960, he promised that "Latin America will soon march united and victorious, free of the chains that convert its economies into wealth appropriated by North American imperialism, and which prevent it from making its true voice heard in the meetings where domesticated Ministers of Foreign Affairs provide a shameful chorus for the despotic master."[2]

There followed the long series of Castroite guerrilla campaigns of the 1960s—prolonged campaigns in Guatemala, Venezuela, Colombia, and Peru, with lesser attempts in Mexico, the Dominican Republic, Nicaragua, Panama, Brazil, Argentina, and Paraguay. Then, after Che Guevara's disastrous failure in Bolivia, there came the campaigns of terrorism—"urban guerrilla warfare," as it is euphemistically called by its protagonists—in Brazil, Uruguay, and Argentina.

By the mid-1970s these attempts had also failed. It is typical of Castro, however, that defeat only inspires him to new and greater efforts. Although it is doubtful that in all the guerrilla and terrorist campaigns of the 1960s and early 1970s put together a total of more than four or five thousand fighters had been employed, these campaigns created the impression of an entire continent in flames. But in 1976, Castro began to despatch whole brigades and divisions to new battlefields—this time across the ocean, in Africa.

With this action, little Cuba, a Caribbean island of ten million inhabitants, began to play a role in intercontinental politics—an absurdity, a whim of history, or better said, the whim of one man alone—Fidel Castro. This demonstrates the inadequacy of the quantitative method of analysis in the study of politics. By all quantitative measures, the President of Brazil should be playing Castro's role in Africa, and the President of Mexico Castro's role in Central America. You cannot quantify Fidel Castro. His example illustrates the decisive role of personality in politics.

Then, in 1979, one of the Fidelista revolutionary groups formed in the early 1960s managed to conquer power—the Sandinista National Liberation Front in Nicaragua. This organization was founded in 1961 through the merger of a group of young communists led by Carlos Fonseca Amador, Tomas Borge, and Silvio Mayorga with a group of noncommunist anti-Somocistas under the leadership of a former lieutenant of the national hero Sandino, Colonel Santos Lopez. Noncommunist participation in the Sandinista movement was at times high, especially in the last phase of the armed struggle, in 1978–79, but after the victory, the noncommunist elements in the leadership were pushed out one by one, until the state and its ruling Sandinista Movement were totally under the control of loyal Fidelista communists.

In a remarkable interview published by the weekly *Cromos* of Bogota, Colombia, on 3 January 1984, Tomas Borge, one of the founders of the Sandinista Movement and today Minister of the Interior in the revolutionary government of Nicaragua, describes Fidel Castro in terms that reveal Borge to be a worshipful disciple: "Fidel is a great human being, a most sensitive, extraordinary person. We all hold him in a very special admiration. . . . He is a man of exquisite sensitivity, full of affection for the people. He has won the love of all his people and ours as well. It moves me to think of him." In the same interview Borge relates that already in the summer of 1961 he had a meeting with Che Guevara in Havana in which Che "agreed to give us the economic assistance we were asking for."

Massive Cuban arms deliveries were decisive for the victory of the Sandinista rising in the summer of 1979. Today there are literally thousands of Cuban advisors in the military, the economy, and the cultural institutions of Nicaragua. Nicaragua is Cuba's closest ally. Only tact prevents us from describing it as Cuba's satellite.

Fidel Castro has thus been remarkably successful in his defiance of the American superpower. He has not only managed to maintain himself in power for a full quarter of a century, but he has also succeeded, after many years of struggle, in establishing a beachhead on the mainland of our continent. Do these successes refute our diagnosis of megalomania? I think not.

In my view, Castro's case is a case of what I am tempted to call the "Napoleon Syndrome," that is, megalomania coupled with genius—the genius facilitating successes impossible for normal human beings and thus obscuring the underlying insanity. In Napoleon's case, victory after victory on the battlefield obscured the fact that the impulse behind his conquests was irrational, that he had to move from conquest to conquest, that he simply could not stop himself, until he embarked on the mad adventure of invading Russia. One of the facets of Fidel Castro's political genius is his ability to mobilize, to win the devotion of thousands of disciples who are willing to lay down their lives for him. But who are these followers?

Inequities in the distribution of wealth, especially in land tenure, are often cited as the main cause of the revolutionary movement in Central America. A glance at the relevant statistics indeed tempts one to conclude that this is indeed the case. Yet here it is necessary to pronounce a caveat: if the Central American revolution is a rural revolution—the revolt of a landhungry, exploited peasantry—then where are the peasant leaders of this peasant uprising?

If the Mexican Revolution produced an Emiliano Zapata, a Doroteo Arango (Pancho Villa) and scores of other gifted, though illiterate or semiliterate leaders, why is there not a single peasant in the top leadership of the Sandinista Movement in Nicaragua? And why is it that, as Father Ernesto Cardenal, Minister of Culture in the Sandinista government of Nicaragua, has stated in an interview published by *Playboy Magazine* in September 1983: "I can't think of another country where there has ever been such a large sector of the upper bourgeoisie that has so identified itself with revolution. There are even some *comandantes* from millionaire families."[3] The comandantes are, of course, the very summit of the Sandinista leadership—the men in power.

Father Cardenal is in error in assuming that in its social composition—the elitist and middle-class background of its leadership and cadres—the Sandinista Movement is exceptional among contemporary Latin American revolutionary movements. The composition of the Salvadorean revolutionary groups is very similar. All their leaders are of upper- or middle-class background and have a college education. The only proletarian among the Salvadorean revolutionary leaders, Salvador Caetano Carpio, was eliminated—one might call it "suicided"—under mysterious circumstances two years ago.

This brings us to the one specifically internal factor among the causes of the Central American revolution that is, strangely enough, never or hardly ever mentioned: *the rebellion of the children of privilege*—the rejection of the existing social and political system by a considerable proportion of the youth of the political, economic, and social elite (the "upper bourgeoisie," as Father Ernesto Cardenal would put it) and of the urban middle classes.

The social composition of today's Latin American, and specifically Central American, revolutionary movements is strikingly similar to that of the Fascist movements of the 1930s in Europe and in Latin America as well, even though their ideologies are diametrically opposed. Today's Latin American revolutionary movements—the *Fidelista* movements, as they may justly be called—are centered in the universities, not in the shantytowns of the working class, precisely as was the case with the Fascist movements of the Thirties.

The alienation of a considerable portion of the youth of the Latin American and specifically Central American elites and middle classes cannot be explained by economic causes alone. Poor employment prospects may perhaps turn some middle-class university students into revolutionaries, but millionaires' sons, such as the Sandinista comandantes mentioned by Father Cardenal, do not have such problems.

The causes of this alienation, this rebellion of Latin American upper- and middle-class youth, undoubtedly lie deeper. Their alienation is a symptom of a cultural crisis, a crisis of faith which our social scientists have not yet even begun to examine, to analyze, and to debate. Needless to say we cannot attempt to do so within the scope of this modest paper. What can be said here is that today as in the Thirties the question of whether the causes of the revolutionary movement are internal or external is based on a false alternative.

The root cause of the Fascist movements of the Thirties was the Depression, the slump that hit a society already demoralized by the slaughter of the First World War. This does not mean, however, that one can safely ignore or dismiss as nonexistent or irrelevant all the evidence pointing to the instigation and coordination of Fascist movements from centers in Berlin and Rome.

What the United States is faced with in Central America today is *not* a series of spontaneous uprisings by a peasantry driven to desperation by lack of land or by workers who will no longer stand the misery and degradation of life in the shantytowns. Today in Central America we have a revolutionary crisis due first and foremost to the rebellion of children of privilege against the very system that has granted them their privilege—the rebellion of a sizeable sector, though probably not a majority, of the youth of the elites and middle classes. At the same time there is ample evidence of the instigation and coordination of the revolutionary movements from a center—in Havana! And today, as in the Thirties and in earlier revolutionary crises, there is a revered leader who provides example and inspiration to a myriad of devoted followers.

Castro is undoubtedly a genius, but he is not a magician. He has not transformed a Caribbean island into a power on the world scene by waving a magic wand, but by winning the support of Russia. It is only because of Soviet backing that Cuba can play the role it does today in the Western Hemisphere and across the ocean.

It is sometimes proposed that the United States could "buy Castro off," move him out of the Soviet camp by resuming trade relations and offering aid. This proposition is based on the false premise that he is a responsible statesman concerned with the welfare of his people. His entire record shows that that is *not* his concern. Under his rule, the Cuban economy stagnates and, according to some statistics, is even in a decline. He has never allowed this to hamper him in the pursuit of his political plans, his quest for glory.

Without Soviet protection Castro would have to withdraw his troops from Africa, renounce his Central American ambitions, and give up his big-power role. He would sink to the position of just another Caribbean tyrant, a Trujillo or Batista. That is far too high a price to ask of him. Thus, resumption of U.S. commerce with Cuba would simply mean a lightening of the Soviet burden, without moving Cuba out of the Soviet camp or persuading Castro to give up his anti-American policy, his efforts to expel the United States from Latin America.

This does not mean that Castro has become a mere instrument, agent, or puppet of the Soviets. He is a largely independent actor, his freedom of action being, of course, limited by his dependence on Soviet military, economic, and political support. In other words, he pursues his own goal and is supported by Moscow as long as his activities in pursuit of this goal are considered to be useful by the Soviets.

Today, the Soviet Union is no longer ruled by fanatics dedicated to the single aim of world revolution. Its rulers are professional administrators, bureaucrats, and many of them are tired, old, and ailing. It is highly unlikely that these men share Castro's dream, that they believe him capable of expelling the United States from Latin America. Then why do they support him? Obviously because of his value as a troublemaker. They have their problems in Poland and Afghanistan; it is only appropriate in their view that the United States should have equivalent problems in its own hemisphere. The Cuban presence in Africa is a further reason for Soviet support of Castro. If Castro withdrew his troops, the Soviet position in Angola would probably be lost, and even the Soviet position in Ethiopia would be seriously threatened.

The most obvious reason for Soviet support of Castro is, of course, the strategic importance of the Caribbean Basin. This seems self-evident, but we must introduce a note of caution: Soviet interest in the strategic possibilities offered by the Caribbean Basin is certainly very high today, but this is a rather recent development, and Soviet priorities may well change again.

It was certainly not because of the military, strategic importance of Cuba that Khrushchev and Mikoyan began wooing Castro in 1960. Indeed, Khrushchev strove hard to keep Castro in the position of an expendable ally, and Castro almost had to crash his way into the "Socialist Camp" by force. The outcome of the Missile Crisis of October 1962 brought about a serious deterioration of Cuban–Soviet relations, and friction continued for several years after Khrushchev's removal from office. It was only after Castro's approval of the Soviet invasion of Czechoslovakia in 1968 that Soviet–Cuban relations rapidly improved. Presumably as a reward for this approval, Soviet Defense Minister Marshal Grechko visited Cuba—the first such visit by a Defense Minister or high-ranking military personality. Certain events of the following years allow us to deduce with some degree of probability what arrangements Grechko and Castro arrived at in their talks.

The attempt to establish a facility for the servicing of nuclear submarines in the Cuban port of Cienfuegos was blocked by President Nixon in 1970, but in the following years Soviet naval visits to Cuba were stepped up to such an extent that today they amount to a de facto permanent Soviet naval presence—not to mention the unit of ground troops whose presence on the island caused such commotion during the Carter Administration.

Nevertheless, throughout most of the Seventies the Caribbean Basin was not a region of high priority for the Soviet strategists. This became clearly evident when two of Castro's friends in the area, Prime Ministers Manley of Jamaica and Burnham of Guyana, visited Moscow to solicit aid. Both Premiers were sent home with mere token gifts. The Soviets at the time were content to use Cuba as a base for their submarines and did not feel that they needed anything more. In their eyes, the Caribbean and the adjacent Atlantic waters were not of the same strategic importance as, say, the Indian Ocean, the Persian Gulf, or the Red Sea.

There is reason to believe that Castro's success in Nicaragua has caused the Soviet strategists to change their view. A Soviet military base on the Central American mainland, with only an unarmed Costa Rica and militarily weak Panama separating it from the Panama Canal—that is certainly an enticing prospect for the strategic planners of the Soviet High Command.

Researchers from the Oral History Project of our Fletcher International Security Studies Program recently interviewed the former Commander-in-Chief of the Sandinista Armed Forces, Eden Pastora Gomez. Commander Pastora stated categorically that when arms negotiations between the Soviets and the Nicaraguan revolutionary government began, it was the Soviets who insisted that Nicaragua must accept, as part of the arms delivered by Moscow, Soviet tanks—an offensive weapon. Pastora added that Castro was not at all happy with this: he did not think that the Nicaraguan army needed tanks.

This indicates that the interests of Castro and Moscow in Nicaragua do not quite coincide. Castro is interested in Nicaragua as a base from which to foment insurrection and revolution, first in El Salvador and then in other countries of the area; the headquarters of the Salvadorean revolutionary coalition, the "Farabundo Marti National Liberation Front," are in Managua. Moscow, on the other hand, is interested in the purely military, strategic possibilities. The acceptance of Soviet tanks is only a first step: Soviet aircraft and Soviet trainers will follow, and one day the United States will be confronted with a permanent Soviet military presence, a Soviet military base in Nicaragua. It is Soviet policy constantly to probe, explore, and test what the opponent will accept. If there is a sharp response, the Soviet leaders can easily retreat: they do not have to face criticism by a public, vocal, organized opposition at home.

I need hardly stress that I do not claim that the Soviet leadership or Military Command is seriously contemplating a land war in Central America in which Soviet tank units or Soviet-trained Nicaraguan tank units would make a dash for the Canal. Military bases do not become effective only in the event of actual war. They are useful instruments of policy in situations which fall far short of armed conflict. Their role may be compared to the role of certain squares on a chessboard which may be occupied not in order to checkmate the opponent, but just to oblige him to resign or at least force him to a draw. Thus, to give just one example, the 1962 Cuban Missile Crisis might well have ended in a shameful defeat for the United States if at that time there had already been a substantial Soviet naval presence in Cuban waters. A Soviet military base in Nicaragua threatening the Canal could play a decisive role in a future show-down with the Soviets far short of actual war.

It is of course anything but certain that the Soviets will actually manage to establish a military base in Nicaragua. That will depend partly on the determination of our government to prevent it, and partly on possible changes in Soviet priorities. As already pointed out, these priorities have changed before, and they may change again.

But here we are entering the realm of speculation. To end this with an appropriate phrase borrowed from my favorite political philosopher, the *New York Times* columnist Russell Baker: Whether there will be any change in Soviet foreign policy in general or Soviet–Cuban relations in particular— *only time will tell!*

Notes

1. Translated from Fidel Castro, *La Revolución Cubana*, 2nd ed., (Mexico: Ediciones Era, 1975), p. 484.
2. Ibid., p. 244.
3. *The Sandinistas*, interview in *Playboy*, 30, (September 1983): 60.

Section E
The Infrastructure

8

The Impact of Technological Innovation

Neil C. Livingstone

F ormer President Lyndon Johnson once observed that "Today the problem is not making miracles—but managing them."[1] In this connection, one of the scientific truths of the modern world is that technology is a double-edged sword and that every scientific advance generally contains inherent dangers and problems which, while not always immediately evident, are nonetheless there and require both diligence and careful management to ensure that they do not outweigh the anticipated benefits of the technology. Some have described this as the "law of unforeseen consequences," and note that a careless moment, an instant's distraction, or a single error of judgment by someone in command of one of our precocious technologies can mean the difference between life and death, so narrow are the margins of safety in our complex, overbuilt, postindustrial societies. The 1984 disasters in Bhopal, India, where an estimated 2,500 people perished as the result of a leak at the Union Carbide pesticide plant on the edge of the city, and in Mexico City, that took 452 lives and injured 4,248 when liquefied gas tanks in a heavily populated area exploded, are grim testimony to the fragility of our modern technologies.

Technological innovation is one of the most powerful engines of change in the contemporary world, and in no place is this change more of a mixed blessing than in the context of terrorism and low-intensity conflict. Not only does technological innovation enhance the arsenals available to terrorists, but it provides violence-prone nonstate actors with an almost limitless universe of targets and vulnerabilities to attack. Terrorists, albeit slowly, are learning this fact, and while the modern world has so far escaped a major catastrophe produced by techno-terrorists striking at the very heart of our technological civilization or employing some kind of hi-tech weapon of mass destruction, it is too much to believe that this situation will continue indefinitely.

It is not my goal in this chapter to be a Cassandra conjuring up apocalyptic visions of terrorist mayhem, but only after the current threat landscape has been identified can steps be taken to protect our critical networks and nodes of vulnerability and to deny terrorists the weapons and means they need to constitute a real threat. A century ago this was not the case. A single terrorist was limited in the amount of damage he could inflict by the comparatively rudimentary weapons available to him and by the absence of what we today know as high consequence targets.[2] As Walter Lacqueur has noted, "One hundred fifty years ago if someone wanted to put out all of the lights in a village, he had to go from house to house to do it. Now he blows up one generator and all the lights in the city go out."[3] As illustration, in December 1984 a $300,000.00 electrical transformer belonging to the Flathead Irrigation Project in Montana was destroyed by one bullet, which caused an estimated 1,500 gallons of oil to leak out onto the ground, resulting in a nine-hour power blackout in a fifty-mile radius.

As our world has become ever more urban and complex, we have correspondingly become ever more vulnerable to the designs of small groups, or even single individuals, bent on disrupting the lives of or inflicting their will on, the majority. Our slender lifelines of water, energy, transportation, communication, and sanitation are all at the mercy of sophisticated terrorists and saboteurs; a mere handful of people who know how the system works can inflict tremendous damage on it, perhaps even bring it to a standstill. Like a stone thrown into a quiet pond, the disruption of even one basic service or critical node ripples outward in ever widening circles to impact on other activities and vulnerabilities with a domino effect known as "cascading failures." The closure of a single major international airport anywhere in the world by a terrorist bombing or hostage drama is capable of disrupting the entire global civil aviation system, producing overloads in some places and underloads in others, late or canceled flights, planes without passengers and passengers without planes, uneaten meals, and idle crews.

Terrorist Weapons

The one constant in the evolution of modern weaponry is its ever increasing lethality. As a result of technological advances—especially in the fields of micro-miniaturization and advanced electronics—one man can command more killing technology than ever before. One individual in the age of technology is potentially the equal of an army in what Trevor N. Dupuy refers to as "the age of muscle," when the chief weapons of war were the sword, the bow, and the spear.[4] This is one of the chief reasons why terrorists represent such a threat to the contemporary world.

As scientific advances of the industrial revolution were applied to military needs, a whole array of new killing technologies evolved and older ones underwent substantial refinement. While the basic theory of small arms has not changed, improvements in metallurgy, ballistics, chemistry, and even electronics have meant that firearms became ever more portable, durable, simple to operate and maintain, and lethal. As a measure of this improvement, one leading study observes:

> During the Napoleonic Wars an infantry battalion could fire about 200 bullets per minute; by World War II, a battalion could fire about 30,000 bullets per minute. Between 1923 and 1968 the amount of metal which could be fired in a single salvo by a Soviet rifle division increased expotentially from 336 kg to 53,000 kg; from 1945 to 1968 alone, *fire power increased 25 times.*[5]

Today weapons such as the .22 calibre AM180 fire at the rate of 1,800 rounds per minute, or 25 per second, and are capable of chewing up concrete blocks and even penetrating heavy metal sheets since so much firepower can be directed at a single spot. And like many modern submachine guns, the AM180 is small enough to fit into a briefcase. Indeed, one model on the market is completely contained inside what appears to be a normal briefcase; a small trigger is concealed beneath the briefcase handle and the weapon fires through a port in the side of the case. Outfitted with a silencer, the AM180 can be fired with virtually no sound or flash and is the perfect assassination weapon.

Added to new weapons improvements and technologies are corresponding advances in ammunition and overall ballistics characteristics. Newer high-velocity hollow-point bullets have far greater wounding power than older style ammunition, and KTW armor piercing ammo even penetrates the ballistic nylon or Kevlar body armor worn by many police. As the promotional literature for KTW metal piercing ammunition exudes: "When you need to shoot through concrete block, an automobile engine block, barricades or armor plate you'll be glad you have some KTW metal piercers."

Virtually all terrorist organizations have access to bulk explosives, automatic weapons, and hand grenades,[6] and it is not uncommon to find RPG2 anti-tank missile launchers in terrorist and insurgent arsenals. While fewer groups possess the more sophisticated Soviet-made RPG7 and RPG7V anti-tank grenade launchers, the list of those who do includes most of the Palestinian (who reportedly even have their own manufacturing facility) and Iranian militias in Lebanon, the German Red Army Faction, the Irish Republican Army (IRA),[7] and various African and Central American insurgents. At least a dozen terrorist and insurgent groups are known to possess Soviet-built SA-7 anti-aircraft guided missiles, including various Cuban surrogates, Colombian drug dealers, the U.S.-backed "contras" in Nicaragua, and a number of African, European, and Palestinian revolutionary organizations.

As an example of the sophisticated arms supply networks operated by many terrorist organizations, in September, 1984, the Irish navy interdicted a trawler off the Irish coast with seven tons of weapons on board destined for the IRA. The list of weapons seized included pistols, rifles, submachine guns, rockets, and hand grenades, along with flak jackets, telescopic sights, and other military equipment. The weapons had all been procured in the United States, where a small number of Americans of Irish descent continue to support the murderous activities of the IRA out of a misguided sense of romantic attachment to the "old country."

When in 1978 the IRA put on display one of several stolen U.S.-made M60 machine guns that the terrorist organization had acquired in the Middle East, it created a stir in Great Britain and was the subject of news stories around the globe. While such an acquisition by a terrorist group today would still be the source of concern to authorities, it would not be particularly newsworthy in view of the many other sophisticated weapons and technologies flowing into terrorist arsenals.

Imagination is still the best weapon available to modern terrorists. Imaginative terrorists can turn almost any technology—however seemingly benign—into a weapon that can serve their purposes. In March, 1984, for example, it was revealed that Libya had acquired a small fleet of remotely controlled speedboats that could be packed with high explosives and used in Kamikaze-style attacks on U.S. naval vessels and port facilities. Similar scenarios utilizing small airplanes were a matter of concern to U.S. military and intelligence personnel in Beirut during the period American Marines were stationed there. Libya was also implicated in sowing the Red Sea with mines during August, 1984. In this connection, terrorists could fabricate their own mines or possibly even steal sophisticated naval mines in an effort to close harbors and block shipping channels.

Nothing so symbolizes modern terrorism as bombings, with all of their impersonality and horror. Indeed, everyone is familiar with the nineteenth-century caricature of the anarchist/terrorist as an individual wearing a long black coat and broad-brimmed hat and carrying a large round black bomb with a fuse protruding from the top. Regrettably, the terrorist and the bomb still form a unique symbiosis. One half of all attacks on diplomats in 1983 were bombings, and by 1984, 49 percent of all terrorist attacks, on a global basis, involved explosives. Today the bomb is the terrorist weapon of choice, largely because explosives and bomb technology are more accessible than ever before. Moreover, from the terrorist point of view, bombings involve far less risk to the terrorist since he/she can be far from the scene of the attack when the explosive device goes off.

The October 1983 blast that leveled the U.S. Marine headquarters in Beirut was a first-rate piece of engineering. Acetylene enhanced and possessing an explosive force of something between 12,000 and 18,000 pounds of TNT, it was—pound for pound—one of the most powerful conventional bombs ever built, and perhaps the largest terrorist bomb in history. During a military briefing on the subject, it was observed that had a terrorist driven a similar bomb into one of the bus tunnels underneath the Pentagon, which are now blocked off, the explosion would have collapsed a whole wing of the building and possibly even destroyed the entire structure. So large and well-constructed was the bomb that there is widespread speculation that the Islamic terrorists who launched the attack had outside assistance in preparing the device.

Terrorist vehicle bombs have become a worldwide phenomenon, although it is in Lebanon that the problem is most acute. Nothing so symbolizes the long Lebanese civil war as the ubiquitous car bomb. Vehicle bombs have been almost a weekly occurrence in Lebanon during the past several years. In addition to the Beirut attacks on the U.S. Embassy, the embassy annex, and the U.S. Marine headquarters, numerous other targets have been hit by vehicle bombs including French and Israeli military posts, the Palestine Research Center, and the Iraqui Embassy. Such bombs have killed and injured everyone from Lebanese political leaders to foreign diplomats and ordinary citizens on the street. In March 1985, nearly 300 people were killed and wounded when a car bomb exploded near the home of Mohammed Hussein Fadlallah, a Shiite Moslem leader and reputed head of the fundamentalist Hezbollah (Party of God) terrorist movement.

In view of recent history, we can expect ever larger and more disastrous terrorist bombs in the future, in keeping with the motto of Spanish terrorists who once observed, "The worse, the better."

Weapons of Mass Destruction

One of the most often cited technological nightmares is that terrorists or revolutionary insurgents will somehow build a weapon of mass destruction capable of wiping out thousands, perhaps even hundreds of thousands, of innocent people. Proponents of such scenarios most frequently focus on fissionable weapons and postulate that terrorists might fabricate everything from so-called "suitcase nuclear bombs" to crude clandestine nuclear devices that could be secretly spirited into the heart of a major American city and then detonated. Quite frankly, such speculation is at best premature by several decades, if not altogether implausible for the indefinite future.

Experts are in general agreement that extraordinary resources would be required on the part of any nonstate group desiring to construct such a device. In addition to fissionable material, the terrorists would require accurate design information, a machine shop, a large secret facility, high explosives, unusual physical and technological capabilities, probably years of single-minded effort, and tens, if not hundreds, of millions of dollars.[8] Although there have been a variety of diversion rumors in recent years, including $2.5 million worth of uranium ore smuggled out of the Juaduguda, India, storage facility in the early 1970s, and various Israeli diversions (with the complicity of at least three Western governments), there is no known black market at the present time in fissionable material, especially with respect to plutonium-239. Nevertheless, a junkyard owner in Rome was apprehended by Italian authorities in May 1983 after he attempted to sell what was described as 10.5 ounces of "enriched uranium" to a "Middle East country."[9] Even if terrorists were able to get their hands on an adequate amount of uranium ore or other basic fissionable material, the refinement and enrichment processes are extraordinarily expensive, difficult, and demanding, and most of the necessary hardware and technology are closely monitored and regulated on an international level. Construction of a clandestine nuclear device, moreover, not to mention any effort to recover plutonium from spent reactor fuel or to produce enriched uranium, is fraught with grave risks to the bomb builders. Finally, presuming that the terrorists could overcome all of the hurdles described, any device is likely to be a dud since testing presumably will be impossible.

Thus, the likelihood of terrorists building a workable fissionable device is so remote as to be beyond the interest of this study. By contrast, a real danger exists that terrorists or other nonstate actors might be able to divert an intact nuclear weapon; the possession alone of such a weapon would create an unprecedented international crisis, even if the terrorists could not overcome the various internal protective systems (permissive action links) required to make it operational. This is a particularly serious threat in Europe, where NATO installations have come under renewed terrorist attack. In addition, the prospect that U.S. commando teams have been equipped with backpack-sized nuclear weapons that can be clandestinely planted at key facilities in Warsaw Pact nations and later set off by remote control has also raised fears that such weapons could potentially fall into the hands of terrorists.

To date there have been no known instances of terrorists or other nonstate actors making a serious attempt to steal fissionable material or to fabricate a bomb. But nuclear weapons represent only one dimension of the problem. Other weapons of mass destruction include those of a chemical or biological nature. There have been more than fifty chemical/biological incidents involving terrorists or other nonstate actors in recent years, a figure which reportedly represents only the so-called "tip of the iceberg" since federal authorities in the United States believe that there have been far more incidents, but that most have gone unrecognized for what they really were.

In November 1980 French and German authorities raided a Paris apartment rented by terrorists and discovered inside a miniature laboratory designed to produce the spore-forming bacterium *Clostridium botulinum*, which secretes botulinal toxin, without a doubt one of the deadliest substances known to man. To appreciate the toxicity of botulinal toxin, the amount needed to kill one human being can be likened to "a flea on a hundred-mile long freight train, the flea's presence being able to derail the train."[10] So deadly is it that only eight ounces—if properly dispersed—would be enough to kill every man, woman, and child in the world.[11] Of course, dispersal on that scale would be impossible, but there is little question that botulinal toxin in the hands of a terrorist group as vicious as the German Red Army, which was implicated in the raid on the Paris apartment, would represent a serious threat to public health and safety.

Another potential misuse of a botulism-producing culture took place in the fall of 1984 when two Canadians allegedly ordered unfrozen tetanus and botulism cultures from the American Type Culture Collection (ATCC) in Rockville, Maryland. Due to inadequate procedures for screening orders, this was the second order from the two bogus researchers. An earlier order, for one ampule of a frozen tetanus culture, was filled in September 1984 and sent to a suburban Buffalo, New York, address. Thus, the range of lethal chemical compounds, pathogenic organisms, and toxins available to terrorists bent on mayhem is extensive. Most can be purchased, stolen, isolated from nature, or manufactured by the terrorists themselves. There is even the danger that foreign nations might supply terrorists with deadly cultures. It is known, for example, that the PLO has received training in chemical and biological warfare.

It is almost impossible to prevent people from producing or obtaining such substances if they are clever and know where to look. As one recent study has noted, "Any resourceful person with a Master's degree in chemistry or microbiology and access to fairly common raw materials could, in the privacy of a kitchen or garage, brew up a chemical or biological weapon of mass destruction capable of wiping out thousands of innocent people."[12] Not only are such substances relatively easy to manufacture, but they are cheap. According to one estimate, the cost of producing 1,000 kilograms of GB (nerve agent), based on small laboratory purchases of raw materials, would be in the neighborhood of $200,000.00[13]

It is not unreasonable to fear that one of the next vehicle attacks on a U.S. embassy in the Middle East might actually involve a chemical or biological poison instead of explosives. Anthrax is particularly well-suited to aerosol dissemination, as are numerous organophosphorous compounds, and terrorists could drive by an embassy or through a U.S. military compound releasing the deadly substance by means of an internal generator mounted inside a car or truck. Similarly, a truck loaded with drums or canisters containing a nerve agent like VX or Sarin could be crashed into an embassy and exploded, turning the deadly substance into a fine mist which would envelop the entire facility.[14]

In view of recent terrorist attacks on U.S. military personnel in Europe, NATO pipelines, and U.S. military facilities, the prospect of U.S. military bases in Europe coming under chemical or biological attack by terrorists is not farfetched. Not only could water systems be poisoned or dried agents released upwind of a base or airfield, but terrorists could surreptitiously launch an attack on a target using mortars embedded in sand-filled trucks outside the defensive perimeter of the base. The mortar bombs, if filled with a V-series nerve agent, would force the evacuation of the entire area and probably inflict a large number of casualties. If the target were an airbase, it would, in all likelihood, be shut down for a matter of days. In the event that anthrax were used, the airfield might be rendered unserviceable for months, even years, inasmuch as anthrax spores have been known to remain alive in the soil for over twenty years.[15] An attack using a similar modus operandi occurred in late February 1985 in Northern Ireland, though it did not involve a lethal chemical agent. IRA terrorists mounted homemade mortar tubes on the back of a stolen truck and parked it on a hill overlooking a fortified police base. Nine mortar rounds were fired electronically, six of which struck the base. A crowded canteen was hit, killing nine police officers in one of the bloodiest attacks in several years.

Many more subtle and clandestine opportunities for terrorist mischief involving chemical and biological substances also exist, including product tampering such as that witnessed in the Tylenol deaths and the attempts to poison candy in Great Britain and Japan; the surreptitious spraying of crops with herbicides; and the theft and misuse of dangerous chemicals from toxic waste sites. It would not be difficult for terrorists to set themselves up as a toxic waste disposal firm and simply to stockpile the chemical wastes until a sufficient amount was accumulated to threaten society.

Infectious diseases could be introduced into countries as a terrorist weapon. The very threat on the part of terrorists to do so would likely cause serious public alarm. There are some reports that link Cuba to the introduction of AIDS into the United States. According to these reports, Cuban troops in Angola first contracted the disease and then transmitted it to others in Cuba, who ultimately were sent to the United States as a part of the so-called "Mariel Boatlift." Whether true or not, it is certainly possible, and the United States would be extremely vulnerable to a plot of this kind.

Hi-Tech Targets

Terrorists will not necessarily have to cross the threshold to weapons of mass destruction in order to achieve horrific results. It is more than likely that they will increasingly seek out so-called high-consequence targets or critical nodes of our civilization whose disruption will have a cascading effect throughout the entire system. Such targets offer the advantage that many can be hit with relatively low-tech weapons or simply sabotaged by utilizing ingenuity and a knowledge of the technology itself. The disaster at Bhopal, India, clearly demonstrates the advantages—from a terrorist perspective—of striking at a deadly chemical production facility, rather than simply bombing a public building which would be unlikely to involve significant secondary or tertiary consequences. Senator Frank R. Lautenberg recently observed that the chemical industry in the United States has a demonstrated "potential for catastrophe" greater than that of the nuclear power industry.[16] Terrorists could produce mishaps similar to the tragedy at Bhopal by means of sabotage from within or by forceably taking over a chemical manufacturing facility and venting hazardous chemicals. Explosives could also be used to breach containment walls and storage tanks, poisoning the neighborhoods and communities that often lie adjacent to chemical manufacturing facilities.

Another inviting target for terrorists is the storage and transport of liquefied natural gas (LNG). A 4,200-cubic metre LNG storage tank located in Cleveland ruptured during World War II. Vapor engulfed the surrounding area and was ignited. A second LNG storage tank also fractured in the resulting fires and explosions, and when it was all over 130 people were dead and 225 injured.

Following the Cleveland disaster, LNG storage and handling technology was greatly improved. However, the potential for disaster still exists. LNG gas carriers are thought to be particularly vulnerable on the high seas to attack or hijacking. In his study, "Frost and Fire: The Maritime LNG Sabotage Threat," Paul Shemella offers a unique and wholly plausible scenario involving the seizure by antiKhomeini terrorists of an LNG transport vessel:

> One option available to Azadegan [an antiKhomeini opposition group] would be to capture an LNG tanker somewhere in the Persian Gulf and use it to threaten the Iranian coastline. Since Iran's LNG industry is not yet functioning, the ideal place for such an operation would be near the port of Abu Dhabi. There is an enormous amount of LNG entering and leaving the port, and its proximity to the Strait of Hormuz would add much to the impact of a hijacking executed in the area. The Iranian naval port of Bandar Abbas, just across the Gulf at the mouth of the strait, would offer the terrorists a valuable bargaining chip to be wielded in its struggle to bring down the embattled Teheran regime.[17]

The seizure of an LNG tanker would be far more effective than an attack on the vessel using PGMs (precision guided munitions) inasmuch as the LNG holding tanks are below decks on most vessels and therefore fairly safe from projectiles and explosives. If terrorists were able to breach the tanks, moreover, the result would most likely be a raging fire and explosion, and while the ship would probably be destroyed, there would be little threat to or impact on the surrounding area. What the terrorists, ideally, must try to achieve is a rupturing of the tanks or a release of their contents without ignition. Only in this way can a vast vapor cloud be produced which, depending on ambient weather conditions, would threaten a major population center or naval base in the event that it was ignited. Once in control of the vessel, terrorists could force a crew member—if they themselves lacked the necessary expertise—to tamper with safety valves or to overpressurize the system in order to force a significant release of the cargo. Even simpler, perhaps, would be to pump the LNG overboard. Whatever method of discharging the cargo was used, given proper atmospheric conditions, writes Shemella, "the terrorist could assume full control of a developing crisis from the cargo control room of the LNG tanker."[18]

Our growing dependency on computers clearly presents technologically minded terrorists with a dazzling array of new opportunities. As R. James Woolsey has observed, much of our money and information have been "reduced to electrons."[19] Computers are essential to the nation's defense, banking, communications, and transportation systems, and food production and distribution networks. They are becoming increasingly common features of daily life in every sector of the U.S. economy.

Computer crime is already a serious problem in the United States, partly because it is extremely hard to detect. The accessing of supposedly secure computers by gifted "hackers" is evidence of what computer terrorists could do if they set their minds to it. Using a computer to steal funds from banks and corporations to finance the "revolution" would certainly be easier and less risky than holding up banks or kidnapping their executives.

The loss, moreover, of a few strategically placed computer control centers would shut down many of the natural gas pipelines in the country, idling thousands of industrial workers and depriving millions of homes of heat and cooking fuel. Indeed, one of the features that makes our major energy, transportation, and communications networks such inviting targets is that there are too few redundancies built into the system. The failure of a single electrical transformer can black out a major municipality, and utility companies rarely have additional units stockpiled because of their high cost, nonstandardized design, and differing voltage combinations. Most transformers are manufactured overseas, and this also complicates speedy replacement of damaged units.

Another example of our lack of redundancies and alternatives was described in *America's Hidden Vulnerabilities*, the final report of a panel investigating this topic at the Center for Strategic and International Studies (CSIS). The report noted the fact that the Air Florida flight that crashed in Washington, D.C., in January 1982 narrowly missed hitting a railroad bridge spanning the Potomac River. Had the bridge been damaged, contends the report, all north-south rail traffic on the east coast would have had to be rerouted through Cincinnati, Ohio, producing enormous delays and disruptions within the economy.[20]

During the past several years there has been a trend toward ever bloodier terrorist attacks, chiefly because Western societies have grown increasingly indifferent to violence, both on television and in real life, and therefore terrorists must strive to launch ever more spectacular and deadly attacks in order to capture sustained news coverage, especially by the television networks. Accordingly, we should be prepared for more terrorist strikes at high consequence targets where both the impact and the number of casualties can be multiplied by the strategic value and inherent characteristics of the target.

Puerto Rican FALN terrorists, for example, have been suspected of plotting to blow up a nineteenth-century railroad tunnel link to Manhattan. The tunnel, located beneath the Hudson River, is already in poor condition—a part of the aging U.S. infrastructure—and it would take very little in the way of explosives to drop it on a commuter train filled with hundreds of passengers. While U.S. authorities were fortunate to obtain intelligence in advance concerning the suspected FALN plot, Italian police were not so lucky in December 1984. Two explosions planted by terrorists ripped through a crowded holiday train as it passed through the 11.6 mile long Apennine Tunnel between Naples and Milan. Nearly seventy people were killed and injured, and rescue efforts were hampered by the fact that the train was 3.6 miles inside the tunnel when the blasts went off.

By contrast to guerrilla warfare, which is predominantly rural, its nameless engagements far from the glare of television cameras, terrorism is essentially an urban phenomenon. Terrorist acts increasingly occur in media centers such as Tokyo, Paris, Washington, New York, London, Frankfurt, and Rome where the terrorist is confident that his message of death and intimidation will be transmitted to the largest possible audience. The day may not be too far off when terrorists, reluctant to depend exclusively on the media to convey and define their message, decide instead to become skilled in media techniques and learn to use the technology so that they can not only make news but package it themselves. At the present time, the media generally show us only the aftermath of an attack; they do not show the actual incident, because to do so would mean that the media had advance notice of the attack. Just as the terrorists prepared a videotape of American hostages in Lebanon for propaganda purposes and to demonstrate that they were still alive, terrorists may soon videotape their actual bombings and other acts of terror to make certain that the full horror of each attack is captured in visual images that can be transmitted into the living rooms of ordinary citizens everywhere. By showing people dying in explosions and other attacks, their limbs torn from their bodies, and conveying their screams of terror, terrorists will not necessarily need bigger bombs to get their message across, but will be able to maximize the impact of whatever weapons and targets are at their disposal. While some television stations will responsibly refrain from showing such footage, there will always be at least one station that will succumb to the temptation to air the tape. Once that happens, no station will be able to resist doing the same because of the purported "news value" of the footage and the fear of losing out to the competition.

Other novel scenarios involving the media might include terrorists seizing an uplink station and threatening to execute hostages on camera if their demands are not met, sending pirate signals to satellites, or even hijacking one of the major television networks and broadcasting live to the entire country. Security at most network studios is fairly rudimentary and consists mainly of poorly paid and inadequately trained security guards who would be no match for a well-equipped terrorist force.

Terrorists could also co-opt the media as an unwitting accessory in the public dissemination of elaborately crafted hoaxes. They might, for example, videotape someone dumping a fifty-five gallon drum of corn starch off the top of a tall building in the financial district of New York. Several dozen copies of the tape might then be sent to television stations in the area with an attached note alleging that "a drum of yellowcake [unenriched uranium] was spread over lower Manhattan today" and that "everyone who inhaled it will develop cancer." Despite the fact that corn starch does not look very much like yellowcake or that actual unenriched uranium only represents a moderate health hazard, the public's fear of anything nuclear or even faintly radioactive is such that a hoax of this kind would likely produce a near panic in the New York metropolitan area. In sum, credible hi-tech hoaxes will remain a serious terrorist problem for the indefinite future. And if the group perpetrating the hoax has a well-established reputation for violence already, every time they cry "wolf" the authorities will probably regard the threat as credible and react accordingly.

Hi-Tech Counterterrorism

"A weapon is defensive or offensive depending on which end is pointing at you," Aristide Briand reportedly once said. In this connection, while modern technologies clearly aid terrorists in terms of their weapons and choice of targets and provide them with unprecedented mobility and communications, nevertheless, technology can also be turned against them and become the ally of the embattled West and other states in opposition.

Surprise is still a great advantage in warfare and one of the terrorist's chief weapons. Thus, good intelligence remains the first line of defense against terrorism. Computers play a large role in assisting Western governments keep track of terrorists and their movements around the globe, although severe restraints still exist in the United States with respect to the collection and sharing of intelligence data about domestic terrorists.[21] Electronic collection methods and signals intelligence permit the United States and other Western governments to eavesdrop on and intercept terrorist communications, and therefore to better predict their attacks. After the hijacking of a Kuwaiti jetliner to Tehran in late 1984, during which two American passengers were brutally murdered and two others abused and tortured, Iran's sympathy and cooperation with the hijackers was firmly established by means of U.S. intercepts of transmissions between the tower and the hijackers in command of the hostage jetliner. U.S. signals intelligence also confirmed Iran's complicity in the bombings of the U.S. Embassy Annex and the U.S. Marine headquarters in Beirut.[22]

A good example of hi-tech aerial reconnaissance and intelligence gathering took place in September 1984, after authorities were tipped off by an informer about a forthcoming shipment of weapons from the United States to the IRA. A ship carrying seven tons of arms and military supplies destined for the IRA was tracked by an American spy satellite as it crossed the Atlantic, and the transfer of the arms to a sixty-seven-foot trawler was photographed. An RAF (Royal Air Force) Nimrod then took up the surveillance until the trawler was intercepted by two Irish naval vessels.

Terrorists, however, are becoming increasingly aware of the electronic wizardry of Western nations, and in some cases are taking steps to prevent their communications from being compromised. According to some reports, members of the so-called Islamic Jihad have all but abandoned the use of the telephone, telex, and even radio transmitters for their communications and have instead resorted to communicating by old-fashioned methods like messages written on pieces of paper (which can then be destroyed) and face-to-face communications.

New technologies also assist those threatened by terrorists with improving their static defenses. Electronic sensors, closed-circuit cameras, pop-up barriers, new building materials and techniques, various detection and screening devices, and dozens of other new products all provide enhanced physical security to buildings and facilities. Automobiles and other vehicles, similarly, can also be protected, or "hardened," to make them more impervious to terrorist attack.

Modern technology has provided counterterrorist commandos with a wide variety of new paraphernalia for striking back at terrorists, ranging from flash grenades (to temporarily blind terrorists in hostage situations where the rescue force must take great care not to injure the hostages), long-range sniper rifles, night vision equipment, and incapacitating chemicals such as those carried by the U.S. Delta force on its abortive raid into Iran in 1980 to rescue American embassy personnel. The chemical aerosol they carried purportedly lowered the blood pressures of anyone who inhaled it, and any rapid movement on their part would cause them to black out. One new weapons system on the market called "Synco-Fire," described in its promotional literature as "a powerful new tool for aggressively dealing with criminal and terrorist violence," electronically links all SWAT marksmen together under the control of their commander and ensures that they will all fire simultaneously at hostagetakers. A new generation of helicopters and navigation systems, moreover, provides counterterrorist forces with enhanced mobility, range, and surprise. It is even reported that two aging Polaris nuclear submarines are being refitted to carry U.S. counterterrorist commandos secretly to any corner of the world.

In the final analysis, imagination will remain the terrorist's best weapon. Accordingly, we must set our minds to outthinking terrorists, and in this way devise appropriate strategies to neutralize their advantages and ultimately to defeat them. We should always strive to avoid the trap of technological fetishism that the United States fell into during the Vietnam War, when we attempted to substitute hi-tech weapons and massive firepower for good tactics and realistic objectives. Moreover, we must adapt our military doctrines, weapons, and forces to meet the terrorist challenge, for terrorists will not adapt to us or schedule their attacks for our convenience. We can even take advantage of terrorists' increasing technological dependency and turn it against them. For example, in Lebanon and elsewhere the United States, Israel, and other Western nations are engaged in an ongoing effort to disrupt terrorist operations by means of so-called "black work" and "dirty tricks." In one instance, Western intelligence operatives, acting as illicit arms merchants, sold terrorists defective bomb detonators. In another instance, the bomb detonators were ultrasensitive and triggered a devastating premature explosion as the terrorists were attempting to load the bomb into a vehicle.

If counterterrorism is becoming an intellectual kind of war, it also involves a good deal of common sense—a fact we should never lose sight of. It does not require, for example, a particularly astute or experienced security officer to realize that the most essential element in protecting a building like the U.S. Embassy Annex in Beirut from car bombs is to keep all vehicles at a safe distance from the structure. Since nearly all embassies and other target installations are likely to be located in proximity to a road or highway, it is vital that trucks and vans capable of carrying a large amount of explosives— since they represent the greatest threat—be prevented from approaching the structure. Indeed, all explosives have impulse pressure. Even at seventy-five yards away, the detonation of 10,000 pounds of explosive will demolish the front of a large building. Thus, the further away the bomb is detonated, the better. If steel gates and pop-up barriers are not available, dump trucks filled with sand or tanks and armored personnel carriers can be used to block off an approach. In Vietnam, tanks and other armored vehicles were regularly parked in front of entrances to high-priority buildings to discourage attacks. Another inexpensive and relatively simple method of keeping trucks and vans from using a particular roadway is to erect an "I" beam across the roadway at a desired height that will permit passage of autos underneath but not of larger vehicles.

Exception, therefore, must be taken to those who regularly complain that it is almost impossible to prevent terrorist attacks, especially those involving imaginative and technologically proficient terrorists. The combination of aggressive tactics, good technology, and common sense will always be a formidable strategy in combatting terrorism.

Conclusion

The "Carlos" of the future may more likely be armed with an Apple II home computer than a Polish-made WZ63 machine pistol, and we must be prepared for him. It is necessary to seize the initiative from the terrorists whenever and wherever possible, and to this end technology will be a valuable ally to the United States and other Western governments. But while terrorism can be defeated, there will always be a cost associated with doing so, and in some cases it may be more than we are willing or prepared to pay. Totalitarian nations experience relatively little terrorism because of the level of social control maintained by the state, the absence of personal rights and freedoms, and the ruthlessness with which such governments usually respond to opposition. Democratic nations, on the other hand, generally will have to tolerate some level of violence and terrorism rather than undermine the fundamental tenets on which they are based by adopting draconian measures to suppress and control terrorism. In the past, such tradeoffs were sensible; terrorists could pose no threat so serious as to justify any erosion of our Constitutional framework and Bill of Rights. But recent technological advances have created new vulnerabilities and complicated what was heretofore an easy equation.

For the most part, potentially dangerous technologies are a necessary and indispensable feature of the contemporary world, and we must continue to live with the associated risks. However, some of our new technologies—such as genetic engineering and nuclear power—are potentially so perilous if misused or deliberately sabotaged as to justify the adoption by governments of safeguards and protective measures that conflict with some of the hallmarks and traditions of Western pluralistic societies.

Notes

1. Lyndon Johnson, quoted by Neil Livingstone in "Megadeath: Radioactive Terrorism," in *Political Terrorism and Energy,* ed. Yonah Alexander and Charles K. Ebinger (New York: Praeger Publishers, 1982), p. 141.

2. See Neil C. Livingstone, "Low-Level Violence and Future Targets," *Conflict* 2, (4), 1980.

3. Walter Lacqueur, quoted by David M. Alpern, "More Outrages," *Newsweek,* 26 December 1977.

4. Trevor N. Dupuy, *The Evolution of Weapons and Warfare* (Fairfax, Va.: HERO Books, 1984), p. 290.

5. Stockholm International Peace Research Institute (SIPRI), *Anti-Personnel Weapons* (New York: Crane, Russak & Co. 1978), p. 45.

6. Robert K. Mullen, "Mass Destruction and Terrorism," draft of article for *Journal of International Affairs,* 1978. (xeroxed)

7. The IRA reportedly obtained their RPG7's from Libya.

8. See Mullen, "Mass Destruction and Terrorism," p. 4, and Neil C. Livingstone and Joseph D. Douglass, Jr., *CBW: The Poor Man's Atomic Bomb,* (Cambridge, Mass.: Institute for Foreign Policy Analysis, Inc., 1984).

9. Robert K. Mullen, "Nuclear Incidents (Excluding Espionage) 1966–1983," unpublished study, no date, no page numbers.

10. Letter from Dr. N.J. Holter of the Holter Research Foundation, 21 January 1977.

11. Seymour N. Hersh, *Chemical and Biological Warfare* (Garden City, N.J.: Doubleday, 1969), p. 83.

12. Livingstone and Douglass, *CBW,* p. 4.

13. Harvey J. McGeorge, "Six Scenarios for the Employment of CBW Agents by Adversary Groups," unpublished study, no date, no page number.

14. Harvey J. McGeorge, "Terrorist Use of Chemical and Biological Agents to Attack United States Air Force Facilities," a preliminary analysis prepared for Jaycor, 27 February 1984, p. 19.

15. Hersh, *Chemical and Biological Warfare,* p. 82.

16. "Lautenberg Urges Control of U.S. Chemical Industry," *New York Times,* 19 February 1985.

17. Paul Shemella, "Frost and Fire: The Maritime LNG Sabotage Threat," (Thesis, Naval Postgraduate School, Monterey, Calif. 1982), p. 63.

18. Ibid., p. 97.

19. Statement to the author, Center for Strategic and International Studies, December, 1984.

20. Panel on Crisis Management of the CSIS Science and Technology Committee, *America's Hidden Vulnerabilities: Crisis Management in a Society of Networks* (Washington, D.C.: The Center for Strategic and International Studies, 1984), p. 10.

21. West Germany's GSG-9 counterterrorist commando unit has computerized the interior configuration of every major jetliner in the world so that in the event of a hijacking they will have a blueprint of the plane indicating all of its emergency exits and other vital data.

22. Such intelligence will not always produce a response, however, since to act on it might compromise sources and methods. Or, as in the case of Iran's involvement in a massive campaign of terror against the United States, this country is simply not prepared to deal with the secondary and tertiary consequences that might flow from a counterattack. After the bombing of the embassy annex, the U.S. military recom-

mended potential targets for air strikes in Iran and elsewhere, but a decision was made not to carry them out since they might produce a new round of escalation—such as an attack on Saudi Arabia or suicide bombers in the United States—which would go beyond effective resolution.

9
Intelligence, Training, and Support Components

Michael A. Ledeen

T wo significant articles in the press have direct bearing on the topic of this chapter. The first was published in the Hearst chain on 7 March 1985 written by John P. Wallach, who states in part:

> The Soviet Union . . . has just completed terrorist training of 35 Lebanese Shiites who are members of Amal . . . This was disclosed by Israeli intelligence sources who revealed that the 35 Shiites returned to southern Lebanon late last month from Simferopol, capital of the Soviet Crimea, where they had completed a three-month training course in the use of explosives and small arms.

The second comes from the Washington *Times*, 5 April 1985, written by Alan McConagha, who states:

> A National Security Council staff analysis completed this week says the slaying of a U.S. officer in East Germany was part of a Soviet intelligence campaign of active measures against U.S. forces in West and East Germany . . . the NSC analysis lists 40 acts of terrorism committed against U.S. forces in West Germany and West Berlin or against West German connections with NATO between Nov. 4 and Feb. 28. . . .

If the NSC (National Security Council) has come to the conclusion that the Soviet Union has sponsored terrorist organizations in a systematic effort to destabilize and weaken the West, it is in good company, for this conclusion has been reached, slowly and reluctantly to be sure, by several Western countries. The one I know best is Italy, where by the late 1970s many of the best minds in the country in and out of the government concluded that the considerable wave of terrorism at that time had considerable outside support, and that the Soviet Union played a substantial role in the support and command network. They based this conclusion on a substantial body of circumstantial evidence:

1. For over half a century, clandestine revolutionary organizations have existed in Italy. And, although they have operated within the general context of Italian Communism, they have often been at odds with the official leadership of the Italian Communist Party (PCI). These organizations have often turned out to have had at least a significant covert input from the Soviet Bloc. Italian intelligence officials in the second half of the 1970s studied trials of leftwing assassins from the immediate postwar period, and found that many of them had been trained and recruited in the East: in Yugoslavia prior to the Tito split, and later in Czechoslovakia.

2. In the late 1940s, the *Volante Rossa,* a group with considerable similarity to the Red Brigades, came into existence. This group carried out political assassinations, organized the Communist Party's security service (including the important task of protecting foreign dignitaries when they came to Italy on invitation from the Party), and inflicted physical beatings—and on occasion carried out assassinations—on selected enemies. Although its members held Communist Party cards, they acted with considerable autonomy while providing the security for top Party members. When the government cracked down on them, *Volante Rossa* members fled into exile in Eastern Europe, most notably Czechoslovakia.

3. During the same period, the PCI maintained a substantial covert paramilitary organization (estimated at over 100,000 armed men by the National Security Council in the early 1950s) that stored weapons in secret warehouses and trained in preparation for what they believed would be the inevitable armed conflict with their capitalist enemies. This apparatus was under the control of Pietro Secchia, the PCI official in charge of "Organization." Secchia's group was a classic Russian-style clandestine apparat, down to such details as the use of female "swallows" to recruit agents and the pairing of male and female agents—sometimes ordering them to marry—in order to avoid hostile penetration. In the fall of 1948, when Italy appeared to be on the verge of civil war following the attempted assassination attempt against PCI Secretary-General Palmiro Togliatti, Secchia's clandestine network surfaced for a few days, occupying central piazzas in northern cities, taking charge of the national telephone network for a while, and generally carrying out—apparently without specific order from Party headquarters—a prearranged military plan.

4. Secchia was purged in 1953 following a scandal involving one of his top assistants, and many of his collaborators went to Prague. This was no accident: Prague was a center for the Soviet control of the PCI. The archives of the Party were kept in Prague at least until the mid-1950s; PCI couriers regularly carried documents to, and money and instructions back from, Prague. Further, in 1968 some twenty-nine Czech and Soviet agents were expelled from Western Europe on the basis of information obtained from an Italian working as a Czech agent in Italy. In short, Prague served as a center

for Soviet clandestine operations in Italy, sometimes involving the Communist Party, sometimes not. It was therefore significant that many of the first generation leaders of the Red Brigades went regularly to Prague, and that they were in contact in Italy with the survivors of the Secchia group from a previous generation. The celebrated Italian playboy/publisher/terrorist Giangiacomo Feltrinelli went to Czechoslovakia twenty-two times between December 1969 and his death in March 1972. Carlo Curcio, the first leader of the Red Brigades, went often to Prague—as did his right-hand man, Franceschini—and Curcio was in close contact with the Genovese Giovanbattista Lazagna, one of Secchia's former associates.

5. All this suggested that, at a minimum, the founders of the Italian terrorist movement of the Left in the 1960s went to Prague to get in touch with those people who had actual experience in running a clandestine paramilitary network in Italy. To Italian security officials, this was highly suggestive: if the Russians had operated in Italy through Prague in the past, was it unreasonable to fear that they were doing it again, especially with a movement that bore such striking resemblance to their previous operations?

While evidence for foreign involvement in Italian terrorism of the Left in the 1970s was in large part circumstantial, there was hard evidence for such involvement on the Right. Italian officials knew that Libya funnelled money and provided training and weapons to such neo-Nazi organizations as *Ordine Nero,* and to various separatist movements in Sicily (a particular target of Qadhafi's) and Sardinia. Moreover, Libya was developing ever closer ties to the Soviet Union, leading Italian officials to wonder if this Libyan support for terrorism could be a second strand of a Soviet plan to destabilize the country.

The notion that terrorism in Italy might be part of a larger whole, with significant Soviet support (and possibly a degree of Soviet control as well) was supported by three bits of direct evidence, one of which remains controversial: 1) the Badawi (Lebanon) terrorist conference of 1972 (which is often viewed as a follow-up to the Tricontinental Congress of the mid-1960s; 2) the role of the PLO in international terrorism; and 3) the testimony of General Jan Sejna. Each of these requires separate treatment.

The Badawi Conference

The Badawi Conference of international terrorist movements was organized by George Habbash, head of the Popular Front for the Liberation of Palestine (PFLP), in May 1972. Representatives of most of the leading terrorist groups attended the meeting, held in great secrecy in a Palestinian refugee camp outside Tripoli, Lebanon. At the conclusion of the discussions, Habbash happily announced that "we have created organic supports between the Palestinians and the revolutionaries of the entire world." In the following years, these "organic supports," from the Middle East to Western Europe, became evident. In September 1972, for example, Black September carried out the firebombing of the oil refineries in Trieste, Italy, at the request of the Red Brigades. Some years later an extremist cell in Rome was discovered transporting SAM-7 missiles for the PFLP (and the connection was open enough for Habbash to send a letter to the Italian court, accepting PFLP responsibility, and asking for the return of the missiles). Similar ties were demonstrated in the case of the German terrorist organizations, from the Baader-Meinhof group to the Red Army Fraction.

A formal agreement between the PFLP and other terrorist organizations was considered especially significant because of the presence of two high-level officials from the PLO: Abu Iyad and Fouad Chemali. Since the decisions at Badawi were all unanimous, the international terrorist network could fairly be said to have benefitted from the substantial funds and connections of Arafat's organization. To be sure, this raised many questions for Western analysts who had long argued that the PLO should not be considered a "terrorist organization" but rather a "liberation movement." This distinction is an important one, especially in evaluating the Soviet role in international terrorism, for the links between the PLO and the USSR are well-established and substantial.

The Role of the PLO

The Soviet-PLO connection hardly needs documentation; not only have thousands of *Fedayeen* (fighters) trained in the Soviet Union, but the PLO has been granted special diplomatic status by the Soviets. The PLO thus enjoys the benefits of easy movement throughout Eastern Europe, and operated with similar ease out of Beirut during its "state-within-a-state" period in Lebanon. This meant that the Palestinians had the equivalent of a diplomatic pouch service, with all of the convenience this entails for the movement of money and weapons, as well as access to facilities for forged documents of all sorts.*

Had the PLO been determined to be a "terrorist organization," it would have been necessary to investigate its many ties with the Soviet Union and with the Democratic Republic of Germany; but once the investigation of "terrorism" in the Palestinian camp was limited to the so-called "radical" organizations (PFLP, PFLP/General Command, Saiqa, Black September, Black June, and so forth), the Fatah—Arafat's core group—was not subjected to this kind of investigation. Moreover, with regard to the possibility that the

---

*The best recent work on the PLO, including some excellent firsthand reportage from Lebanon, is Jillian Becker, *The PLO*, (London, United Kingdom: Weidenfeld and Nicolson, 1984).

Soviet Union was directly involved in international terrorism, there was no firsthand evidence of Soviet agents active within a Palestinian organization, radical or otherwise. This reinforced the notion that the PLO should be treated as a political and paramilitary organization and added to the general conviction that Arab terrorism was generated by its own internal dynamic and was neither fostered nor substantially controlled by outside forces. Such a view also fit with the overall conviction that terrorism in general was primarily the product of local problems and should not be viewed as an overall phenomenon, even though analysts recognized—as in the case of Badawi (and the earlier Cuban-based Tricontinental Congress)—that there were considerable connections among the various terrorist groups.

The Testimony of General Jan Sejna

With this background, it is perhaps possible to understand the resistance of many American experts to the claims by former Czechoslovakian General Jan Sejna that he had personally been involved in the training of foreign terrorists in Czechoslovakia in a program under the direct control of Soviet Military Intelligence (GRU). Sejna's statements—published in an interview with Michael Ledeen in *il Giornale nuovo* of Milan—were contested by some American intelligence officials, even though Sejna had proved to be an extremely good resource for military information. Sejna not only provided details on the training of foreign terrorists in Czechoslovakia, but gave the names of a dozen or so Italians who had gone through the program. Some of these were names of fairly well-known figures in the Red Brigades (Feltrinelli, Franceschini, and so forth); but others were unknown, and subsequently turned out to be significant terrorists. Moreover, some of the names given by Sejna turned out later to have been associated with the Hyperion Institute in Paris, which was believed by some top Italian and French intelligence officials to have been run by the KGB as a coordinating center for European-based terrorists. Information pointing in this direction appeared in a report prepared by the Italian military intelligence service (SISMI) in the spring of 1984 and reprinted by *La Nazione* (Florence) later in the year.

According to this document, sent from SISMI to two separate Parliamentary Commissions in May 1983, as early as 1978 the Italians had compiled a list of Italian terrorists who were believed to have undergone terrorist training in Czechoslovakia. This document also includes the interesting case of Roberto Viel, a leftwing extremist accused of murder, who fled Italy to Czechoslovakia in 1971, accompanied by Giangiacomo Feltrinelli. As noted in the document, this trip "would have been impossible without Czech security officials' approval . . ." More importantly, to those Italian analysts who had studied the postwar period, the Viel case seemed to be a replay of the many earlier ones in which Soviet Bloc-supported terrorist groups were able to send comrades in trouble to sanctuaries in the East.

Indeed, as recently as January 1980, an on-the-record interview with Mr. Costantino Belluscio, head of the office of security and public order, reported that "at least four top Italian guerrilla leaders and possibly more than two dozen of their followers trained at top secret Czech bases near the towns of Karlovy Vary and Doupov. He said the camps were set up by the Czech MV and the Soviet KGB intelligence services." And two years earlier, in an official Parliamentary inquiry, the former head of military intelligence, General Vito Miceli, said that he had reported in 1972 to the Minister of Defense that there was proof of contacts between Giangiacomo Feltrinelli, extremist subversive groups, and KGB agents working under cover in the Soviet Embassy in Rome. According to Miceli, the proof was serious enough for him to recommend the expulsion of twenty-two Soviet agents from Italy, a recommendation that was supported by the Foreign Minister and the Interior Minister of the time.

Contacts with Hyperion were maintained for the Red Brigades (BR) by Mario Moretti, the leader of the BR until his arrest in 1981, and it is significant that Moretti was captured in Italy upon his return there from exile in Libya, where he had taken refuge. Hyperion was also one of Toni Negri's points of contact in Paris; he also worked closely with the Curiel organization, which was in the KGB loop as well. It was the conclusion of several of the Italians who came in contact with the Hyperion Institute that it was the "long arm of the KGB." Finally, some analysts suggested that the timing of the Dozier kidnapping, following hard on the heels of the attempt against General Kroesen, indicated a desire on the part of Moscow to escalate the campaign against American Cruise and Pershing missiles in Europe. But there is no hard evidence, as far as we know, to support this interesting theory.

The Palestinians performed much of the work of coordinating the activities of the Red Brigades—as in the case of the German RAF according to the SISMI report. And it was the conviction of Senzani, the last major leader of the Red Brigades, who was arrested after the liberation of General Dozier that the KGB was in a position to guide the major European and Palestinian terrorist organizations in an anti-Western direction. According to a document captured at the time of Senzani's arrest that was quoted in the SISMI report, Senzani also believed that the KGB could manipulate extreme rightwing groups, and was convinced that the Soviets had effectively infiltrated the "militarist wing" of the Red Brigades.

One can say, then, that there is solid evidence that the KGB has been extremely active in West European terrorism, sometimes directly, sometimes through their PLO intermediary, sometimes through other Warsaw Pact intelligence services. Finally, there is one further firsthand source: Ion Mihai Pacepa, the former deputy director of the Rumanian intelligence service who defected in 1978, has said that Italian Red Brigades terrorists were being trained in Bulgaria as of the time of his defection.

The debate over the Soviet connection to international terrorism was important not only for intellectual reasons, but also for operational ones—the United States during the Carter administration could not provide assistance to a foreign country to fight "national" terrorism; aid could only be given for a fight against "international" terrorism. The debate over certain movements was predictably lively, such as the one over the Spanish Basque terrorist movement, ETA. As late as 1978–79, there was still considerable dispute over the nature of ETA (and the more violent group known as ETA Militar), even though a movement that kills in Spain, lives in France, and trains in Algeria ought to be considered "international." It took quite some time, however, before the American Government certified this conclusion—not until the second half of the Carter administration. In the meantime, Spanish Foreign Minister Marcellino Oreja was treated to a remarkable proposal from the Soviets: Gromyko told Oreja that if the Spaniards stayed out of NATO, they would have far less trouble with the Basque terrorists. The Spaniards took this to be proof positive that the Russians exercised considerable control over ETA (a believe that was subsequently reinforced by the Spaniards' discovery that nine ETA terrorists were training in Nicaragua in the summer of 1983). Oreja confirmed this story to Flora Lewis of the New York Times as well as to Spanish columnists from *ABC* and *El Pais,* in 1982–83.

The Dozier case reopened the discussion of Soviet Bloc connections to Italian terrorism, this time in the form of the "Bulgarian connection." It was discovered that the Red Brigades had entered into discussions with the Bulgarian intelligence service during the Dozier affair, and that the Bulgarians had recruited at least one high-level agent in the Italian trade union movement. This latter discovery was of no small importance, for the particular trade union official—Luigi Scricciolo—had apparently been recruited from an extremist youth organization in the late 1960s, during the peak years of communist-inspired demonstrations in Italy against American Vietnam policy and against specific Italian practices. Finally, Scricciolo and his wife were major liasons between the Italian trade unions and the Polish *Solidarnosc* organization. Thus the information gathered from and about the Scricciolos (all of which will eventually become public when the texts of the interrogations of the Scricciolos and others involved in the case by Judge Ferdinando Imposimato are made public as part of the formal accusation against the two Scricciolos) played into another major event in international terrorism: the attempt to kill Pope John Paul II in Rome.

For intelligence officials of the Italian Government—some of whom had worked on these problems for a very long time—the "Bulgarian Connection" was not analyzed as a single event, but was viewed against the background of decades of documented Soviet activity with paramilitary groups in Italy.

The Italians' analysis was not limited to groups of the political Left, for they knew that in the 1960s a so-called "Nazi–Maoist" extremist group had been created in Italy by the Czechoslovakian intelligence service (this revelation came from General Sejna, and was confirmed by American intelligence in the late 1960s). Hence the notion that the Bulgarian service might be working through an ostensibly rightwing Turkish group (the Grey Wolves) was not inconceivable.

Other Theaters of Action

In 1974 an automobile carrying two known KGB agents through the streets of Brussels had an "accident" (arranged by European security services), and Belgian security officials found in the automobile a collection of documents that demonstrated the existence of an "autonomous central" for terrorism operating in Vienna. This "central" carried out liaison operations with terrorist groups in Belgium, England, Holland, and Italy. These contacts and assistance involved terrorists ranging from the Red Brigades to elements of the Japanese Red Army moving through Europe. Within hours of the "accident," the Vienna "central" was closed and moved to Libya. This incident was described in an article on the op-ed page of the *Washington Post* by Arnaud de Borchgrave and Michael Ledeen in February 1981.

Not only was there considerable evidence about direct Soviet involvement in terrorism in Western Europe and the Middle East, there was little question about the Soviet hand in Latin America. Several major terrorist groups in countries ranging from Argentina and Uruguay to Bolivia and Venezuela operated with considerable Cuban assistance and, increasingly, PLO and Libyan support as well. The Cuban connection was unambiguous, since the KGB's control over the Cuban DGI (General Directorate of State Security) had been well established in the 1960s. And although there was a certain lull in Latin American terrorism for a decade or so following the defeat of the Tupamaros, Montaneros, and Che himself, terrorists returned to the forefront with a vengeance in the late 1970s with the success of the Sandinistas in Nicaragua. Prior to the Sandinistas, the older generation of terrorists had simply been integrated into the various national structures overseas; thus one heard of Latin American terrorists showing up in Italy during the heyday of the Red Brigades, or in various Arab countries (as in the celebrated case of Carlos).

Here again, as in the case of the PLO, there was the question of drawing distinctions between "terrorist movements" and "movements of national liberation." Superficially, it seemed that the distinction was a matter of approval or opposition ("one man's terrorist is another's freedom fighter"). Thus, refusal to call a given movement "terrorist" generally signified some sort of approval, or at least toleration. The terrorists themselves insisted that terrorism was simply the first stage in a general assault against the State. And every terrorist movement claimed to be acting against an institutionalized evil, so that there was always ideological justification for those with the desire to classify a given movement "national liberation."

There have been two major recent developments in Latin America: 1) the emergence of the Sandinista regime in Nicaragua as a staging base for terrorism in Central America; and 2) the development of a major drug-smuggling and arms-running operation based in Cuba as an adjunct to Cuban activities in behalf of terrorism in Latin America, and particularly in Colombia. There is also an interesting problem for future analysis concerning the "Maoist" terrorist movement in Peru known as *Sendero Luminoso.*

The basic information on the Central American guerrilla movement was assembled by the Carter administration, and the assessment made in late 1980 is still basically correct. Additional information has only confirmed those conclusions:

1. There is very little popular support for the FMLN in El Salvador, and its real base lies outside the country, in Nicaragua and Cuba.

2. The FMLN (Farabundo Marti National Liberation Front) is fully integrated into the international terrorist network, thanks to its close working relationship with Cuba and Nicaragua. Thus, just as the Sandinistas obtained money, expertise, training, and weapons from such diverse sources as the Tupamaros, the Montoneros, the PLO, Libya, Bulgaria, and Cuba, so the Salvadorean guerrillas draw upon the same sources.

3. A rich variety of sources, ranging from defectors to emigres, has demonstrated that the command and control center of the Salvadorean guerrillas is in Nicaragua, and that Cuban officials are in key positions in the command and control structure.

4. The connection between Nicaragua/Cuba and El Salvador (and other countries, notably Honduras) is a replay of the successful methods used by the Sandinistas in their campaign against Somoza. During the Nicaraguan struggle, the Sandinistas used Costa Rica as a staging base for both military and propaganda actions against Somoza, and as in the more recent Salvadorean guerrilla movement, this was achieved with help from other members of the "terrorist international," most notably the survivors of the Uruguayan and Argentinian campaigns, the Tupamaros and Montoneros, along with Cuban advisers and intelligence officials.

5. In a broader context, the Nicaraguan role is clearly subordinate to the Cuban role, since the Cubans manage the operation. Cuba is the transit point for Salvadorean and Nicaraguan men and women headed toward East Germany and Bulgaria for military and intelligence training; it is

also the transit point for East European officials, PLO agents, Libyans, and the like who are headed for Managua and work with and/or supply the Salvadorean guerrillas. Moreover, Nicaragua is now a haven for European terrorists, as witnessed by the discovery that Red Brigades leaders are now at terrorist training camps there. In all probability, these individuals are serving as advisors and instructors in Nicaragua, waiting for an opportune moment to repatriate.

6. As in the case of the PLO's role in Western Europe, Cuba's activities in Central America (and more broadly in this hemisphere) raise the question of ultimate Soviet responsibility. This issue is often misdescribed: one does not have to believe that the Soviets are puppeteers and the terrorists marionettes in order to ascribe a large share of responsibility for the scale and success of terrorism to the Kremlin. Unless one believes that the guerrillas represent a substantial segment of the population of Salvador, and that they could continue to represent a serious fighting force without sanctuary, assistance, and guidance from Cuba and Nicaragua, one must seriously contemplate the Russians' responsibility. Finally, there is mounting testimony of a direct Soviet role in Nicaragua, particularly in command and control functions. At least one Nicaraguan defector, Miguel Bollanos, has been quoted to this effect.

Drug-Smuggling and Terrorism

The Cubans have not only continued their traditional support for terrorists in the hemisphere and revived the Guevarist method in Salvador; they have recently organized a major drug-smuggling and arms-running operation with its center in Cuba and its extremities in the Southeastern United States, on the one hand, and Latin America (particularly Colombia), on the other. Despite its official rhetoric against drugs, and its long-standing reputation as a country that did not tolerate drug traffickers, Cuba has now placed itself at the center of hemispheric drug movements.

The drugs typically come from Colombia, whence they are transported by small boat to Cuban waters. Once there, they are placed on a Cuban "mother ship" and, in the fullness of time, transferred to another boat headed for the United States (usually southern Florida). On the return trip, the proceeds of the sale are divided up to purchase weapons, to pay the Cubans, to line the pockets of the traffickers, and to aid other terrorists in Latin America. The evidence of Cuban activities in this area is so solid that four members of the Central Committee of the Cuban Communist Party have been indicted by a federal grand jury in Dade County, Florida for their role in drug trafficking. The Cuban involvement in turning the profits into money for arms and terrorism is equally well documented in a lengthy article in *Reader's Digest,* in a four-part series in the New York *Post* by Arnaud de Borchgrave and Robert Moss, and in an article in the *New Republic* by Michael Ledeen.

The decision to enter the drug-smuggling business is an interesting one for Castro, because it greatly increases the risk of discovery, of penetration from hostile countries, of substantial corruption within his own system, and of loss of control over his own people. Indeed, he has already suffered several major embarrassments as a result of the exposure of his drug-running activities in the United States (the Johnny Krump case, which led to the indictments of the four Central Committee members, was particularly damaging).

It may be significant that Castro is not the only element of the terrorist network to engage in drug smuggling on a substantial scale. In the past there has been massive trafficking between Bulgaria and Turkey run along lines similar to those discovered in the Caribbean, and in recent years similar operations have been discovered in Italy. At least two of these have been documented by Italian magistrates and security and narcotics officials: one running through Sicily, the other through Trent and Trieste in the North. In all three of these cases, the Bulgarians have played a role of some importance (greatest in the Turkish case, still undefined—although apparently established—in the Italian cases), and in the Italian operations the Red Brigades were involved. Indeed, in the kidnapping of American General James Dozier in Italy in 1981, the kidnappers were finally located because some of them were in the drug network. This marked the first time that important elements of the Red Brigades were caught through the drug pipeline, and demonstrated a working relationship between the traditional Mafia and the terrorists that was new to Italian officials.

The willingness of terrorists with some ties to the Soviet Bloc to engage in drug smuggling raises a series of questions. The appearance of this pattern in three separate theatres of terrorist activity suggests that we are dealing with a general decision, rather than three individual ones. Was this decision taken totally without reference to Soviet authorities? Or, is it not probable that the Soviets gave at least some sort of approval for such a fundamental shift in tactics? And if that is so, what might be the reason for the shift?

The most obvious explanation is a need for money. While it is often said—with considerable truth—that terrorist organizations can finance themselves through kidnappings and bank robberies, and hence have no urgent need of money from outside sources, it nonetheless remains true that such methods are risky, and any professional terrorist organization would prefer to have its money come from reliable and secure sources. Moreover, we probably are not in a position to accurately calculate the real costs of running a terrorist organization. There may well be a costly infrastructure to maintain, and this infrastructure could be separate from the activists, and hence not have easy access to the money raised through robbery, blackmail, and kidnapping. In any event, this is not simply a hypothetical question, for we know that the Cubans are heavily subsidized by the Soviet Union to the tune of 3–4 billion dollars annually, just as we know that in Colombia, at the other end of the pipeline, M-19's late leader, Jaime Bateman, was trained in Moscow.

In recent years, the Soviets have found themselves periodically short of hard currency. In the most celebrated recent case, they were unable (or unwilling) to make good on Polish foreign debt, and risked having Warsaw declared in default by Western banks and governments. They have resorted to dumping commodities from gold to aluminum over the past twenty-four months in order to raise hard currency, and in their dealings with Castro the Soviets have—for the first time in memory—been quite exigent, demanding that he meet deadlines for repayment and refusing to discount sugar prices in favor of Cuba. All of this suggests that Moscow may have encountered cash flow problems for the financing of at least some of the terrorist operations they were supporting, and this matches the picture of the terrorists engaging in risky drug trafficking to generate large sums of money.

Whatever the explanation, a surprisingly close working relationship between terrorists and traditional organized crime now exists in all three theatres. In Turkey, the organized criminals in some cases operate with the assistance of the Bulgarian Secret Service; in Italy, the terrorists are working with the Mafia (and local organizations not part of the "family structure"); in the Caribbean and South Florida the Cuban-sponsored drug and arms network similarly works with the Mafia (these connections may be confirmed as part of the spectacular breakthrough in the Italian anti-Mafia campaign, and thanks to the growing cooperation between the United States and Italy, this information should be made available to American officials in a timely manner). To be sure, once the terrorists elected to go into the drug-smuggling business, it was inevitable that they would have to come to terms with the Mafia, but the relationship in certain cases became remarkably close. In some Italian operations, professional (Mafia) killers carried out "hits" on behalf of the terrorists, and the terrorists in return moved drug shipments for the Mafia. While this was superficially attractive to the Red Brigades, the joint venture had some defects: when Italian authorities launched a major anti-crime operation in Sicily following the assassination of *Carabiniere* General dalla Chiesa in 1982, the Mafia simply turned over members of the Red Brigades to the government.

The final observation about the current state of affairs in Latin America concerns the Peruvian *Sendero Luminoso*, a Maoist terrorist organization in which at least one foreign national (a West Germany woman) is involved. Maoist terrorist organizations have always been rare, and now that Maoism has been discredited even in the People's Republic of China, the emergence of such an organization in Peru is bizarre. On the other hand, we know of at least one instance in which the USSR has created a "Maoist" movement (a so-called "Nazi–Maoist" Party in Italy in the 1960s). This possibility should be considered in the case of *Sendero Luminoso*.

Armenian Terrorism: The Secret Army

In Beirut, Secret Army for the Liberation of Armenia (ASALA) was part of the same network of terrorist organizations that trained under PLO supervision and benefitted from the terrorist infrastructure of the PLO's "state-within-a-state" in Lebanon. Many antiterrorist officials in Western countries believe that the Soviet Embassy in Beirut was actively involved in this infrastructure, although hard evidence is lacking. The most suggestive element in this hypothesis concerns the Soviet Ambassador to Lebanon since 1974, Alexei Alexeyevitch Soldatov who, unlike most Soviet ambassadors, is a member of the KGB. Recruited in 1940, Soldatov has spent his career in the diplomatic service, and has often been involved in major espionage cases. Ambassador to London from 1960 to 1966, he organized the network that led to the expulsion of one hundred five Soviet diplomats. After a year at home, Soldatov was then sent to Havana in the spring of 1968, where he organized the KGB's takeover of the Cuban DGI, with its attendant network of terrorist activities throughout the world. His passage to Beirut—where so much of international terrorism found sanctuary, an operational base, and funds—was a logical step. Similarly, the current Soviet Ambassador to Bulgaria, Nikita Pavlovitch Tolubeyev, was in Cuba from 1970–79, where he is said to have taken an active role in setting up the Cuban terrorist activities, including recruiting, training, and then running terrorists from third countries. Tolubeyev is a member of the Central Committee of the Soviet Communist Party, and served in the Soviet Embassy in Cyprus prior to going to Havana.

From all indications, ASALA is now based in Paris and Germany, with considerable support coming from Syrian-based terrorists (until the past year or so, this support came primarily from the Abu Nidal group, but with the leader out of action, or perhaps even dead, this relationship may have changed). There is a close working relationship between ASALA and *Action Direct* in France.

Section F
Nark-Intern (Narcotics International)

10
Organized Crime and Drug Linkages

Paul B. Henze

We have come a long way toward understanding terrorism as a mechanism for political destabilization in the present decade. Some of the things we now take for granted—such as the Bulgarian role in drug and arms traffic—were long overlooked. Even when they were first exposed, it was not realized that they were an intrinsic part of the whole spectrum of low-intensity warfare. "Until the beginning of the 1980s, no evidence had surfaced of Bulgarian clandestine operations in Italy other than espionage," observes a recent survey of terrorism in Italy.[1] How the situation has changed in a very brief time! Hundreds of thousands of pages of testimony and investigative reporting have now been collected by Italian judges who have been exposing the Bulgarian connection with three major interlocking cases that are still in process: the plot to kill the Pope, the Scricciolo case (originally exposed as a result of the kidnapping of General Dozier) and the vast, complex arms- and drug-smuggling operations centered in Trento. Even a good summary of what is now known of Bulgarian activities in Italy would require a thick volume, and much more is bound to come to light. Retrospective analysis is already producing valuable insights, including substantial evidence of what is still somewhat euphemistically called left–right collaboration, but which might more accurately be termed leftist exploitation of the right.[2]

Until an already known Turkish terrorist, Mehmet Ali Agca, was exposed as the principal actor in the plot to kill the Polish Pope in May 1981 and the Bulgarian connection with this sordid scheme became publicly known a year and a half later, the full importance of the Bulgarian role in destabilizing Turkey in the 1970s was also not realized. Agca has admitted that he knew he was working for the Bulgarians as early as 1978, when he was only 20. In 1983 he told Turkish interrogators in Rome that he went to Syria with a well-known Turkish communist, Teslim Töre, head of the pro-Moscow Turkish People's Liberation Army that summer and ". . . we were trained by Bulgarian specialists. This training involved use of weapons, explosives, cold war concepts, how to carry out coups d'état and related revolutionary theory.

There were not only Europeans there but people from many other parts of the world, especially terrorists from Central and South America."[3]

Before they returned to Turkey, Töre and Agca were given money by Bulgarian agents in Damascus to take back to two extreme-left labor groups in Istanbul. There they worked under the direct sponsorship of Abuzer Ugurlu, already well known as the Turkish Mafia "Godfather." He was overlord of drug- and arms-smuggling operations extending from the Middle East and South Asia to Western Europe and America—*through Bulgaria*. Again, Agca's own words sum up the essentials of the story:

> . . . I was well known to the Bulgarian secret services. With Abuzer Ugurlu acting as intermediary, I and other members of my organization . . . did reports for the Bulgarian authorities relating to how the Turkish state would develop in the future . . . From a political point of view we had relations with hundreds of members of both the right and the left as well as the Mafia.[4]

Both as cover and to draw rightists into supporting anti-Western goals, Agca developed a wide range of associations with the National Action Party of Colonel Alparslan Türkes, especially the youth wing called the Gray Wolves, but he never joined this group. He was busy in other directions at the same time:

> I took part in meetings of the Gray Wolves, but I always went alone. I also followed the activity of the Maoist-leaning Turkish Peasants' and Workers' Party (TIKP). In the fall of 1978 I had contacts with a member of the Dutch Communist Party . . . to work out a relationship between this party and the TIKP. Basically both parties were Maoist. Their activities were having the effect of dividing leftist forces. I was charged with finding out whether there were common points between these two organizations. Teslim Töre had given me this task and he himself was acting in behalf of the Bulgarians.[5]

We see here in Agca's revelations most of the key elements of the low-intensity warfare spectrum: terrorist training; leftist infiltration and exploitation of rightist nationalists; movement of money; the symbiosis between political destabilization and crime; propaganda and political action with short- and long-term goals. And, as always, the Bulgarian connection. It takes a great deal of naiveté to harbor any illusions about the Bulgarians' ultimate masters.

It is worth remembering that Agca was not a major figure on the Turkish scene at this time—he was one of thousands. He may even have given his interrogators an exaggerated impression of his role. But he may also have been selected as especially promising, for a few months later he would play a key part in the shooting of the prestigious newspaper editor, Abdi Ipekçi, and then go on, after a still partially unexplained process of being caught, confessing, being put on trial, retracting his confession, and escaping, to become even more famous in Rome. Because of his connection to the plot to kill Pope John Paul II, Agca's testimony about his early involvement in terrorism is especially useful to highlight the astonishing scope of the low-intensity warfare that was being conducted in Turkey—and far beyond—at that time. There are remarkable parallels with Italy in connection with episodes such as the murder of Aldo Moro. To review both situations in a single chapter would be impossible. Therefore the next phase of this discussion is focused primarily on Turkey, because that country's experience with destabilization and terror has still been insufficiently studied and because we find examples there of almost every feature of the program of destabilization which the Kremlin has long been implementing.[6]

The Strategy to Destabilize Turkey

Turkey was a prime target for the kind of low-intensity warfare to which the USSR began to give higher priority in the 1960s. There were several basic reasons for Moscow's actions. These extend back deep into Russian history and involve the Turkish Straits and unrequited territorial ambitions. They also reflect Soviet concern about its own rapidly growing Muslim population. A successfully modernizing, democratic Turkey sets an example of an alternate future which Azeris and Uzbeks might decide would be more to their liking than becoming "new Soviet men," a prospect which many Russians themselves seem not to relish greatly. There was, of course, the more immediate goal of weakening Turkey as a NATO outpost and major U.S. ally. The propaganda infrastructure began to take shape with the inauguration of the clandestine "Bizim Radyo" in 1958.[7]

To some men in Moscow, Turkey probably looked like a better candidate for destabilization in the 1960s than Iran did. This was because its freewheeling democracy gave Moscow ample openings to meddle in politics without being visible. Long-forbidden leftist publications and discussion groups now proliferated. The colonels who overthrew Adnan Menderes in 1960 had introduced a more liberal political system, with more checks on executive authority and proportional representation, that almost guaranteed political instability. Major disinformation operations were launched by Moscow to exploit the resentment that developed in Turkey over Cyprus in 1964–65 as a result of the "Johnson Letter."[8] For a brief period the Turkish Labor Party looked promising to Moscow, but it proved to be a difficult instrument to guide and collapsed in the wake of ferment generated by the Soviet invasion of Czechoslovakia in August 1968. By this time Andropov had taken over the KGB and Moscow was ready for a rougher game. A second clandestine radio station, the Voice of the Turkish Communist Party, began broadcasting from East Germany and Romania in 1968.

The first wave of terrorism in Turkey built up rapidly in 1969, continued through 1970, and provoked a modified form of military intervention in 1971. The campaign centered on leftist students, enough of whom were eager to imitate their rampaging European and American cousins to provide cadres for violent activist groups. These engaged in a great deal of propaganda and agitation aimed at exploiting anti-American and anti-Western feeling that had developed as a result of frustrations over Cyprus and other frictions natural at the midstage of an alliance which, like a passionate marraige, had been too warm during its early years to continue without disappointments. Violence was directed at disrupting Turkey's alliance relationships and her constructive relations with Israel. American, British, and Canadian military personnel were kidnapped and killed, and an Israeli Consul-General was murdered. Weak governments had difficulty mustering enough resolve to deal firmly with terrorism. The military leadership grew impatient and forced formation of an "above-parties government" that declared martial law and began a crackdown on terrorists in March 1971. Over 4,000 terrorists and supporters were rounded up and over 2,000 eventually imprisoned.[9]

Even with the military leaders exercising substantial influence, Turkey was not unaffected by the political naiveté and willful refusal to face unpleasant facts which characterized the entire Western world at the beginning of the 1970s. Eager to avoid the opprobrium of too long or too direct intervention in the democratic political process, the military leaders made no basic changes in the political system and set multiparty competition in motion again in 1973. A great deal of evidence of foreign—that is, Soviet Bloc—involvement in support of terrorism had been gathered during two years of investigations and trials of incarcerated terrorists. An impressive summary was issued on 30 June 1973, but in classified form—not released to the public![10] It had no effect on the national debate that soon developed about granting amnesty to the imprisoned terrorists.

Bülent Ecevit, who emerged as Prime Minister of an incongruous coalition put together after long delay combining his now left-leaning Republican People's Party and religious demagogue Necmettin Erbakan's National Salvation Party, had promised a quick amnesty during the election campaign. Getting the amnesty issue through parliament almost wrecked the coalition, but enough votes were gathered and most of the imprisoned terrorists were released in the summer of 1974. Thus the groundwork was laid for the second phase of the massive destabilization effort which began to take shape in 1975.

What had the first wave accomplished? Little, in terms of apparent short-term goals. Turkey's NATO relationship was probably strengthened. But a whole group of terrorist leaders had been battle hardened, a few had been killed to become heroes for the future, and a great deal of experience had been gained on the basis of which new plans could be developed for a more massive effort as soon as circumstances were judged opportune. The first wave had concentrated on students as activists and foreigners as targets. There was no effort to undermine the economy or the society. The Turkish military and even the police were seldom the object of attack. The criminal element in Turkish society was only incidentally involved. A substantial group of drug traffickers had burgeoned in Turkey during the 1960s, when illicit opium processing had mushroomed. Here was a new source of tension between Turkey and the United States. On American urging, poppy growing was banned during the period of above-party governments. As soon as Ecevit won on the amnesty issue, he revoked the ban. Though controls were strict and illicit production of opium derivatives was never resumed on a large scale in Turkey, the network of drug traffickers and smugglers who had steadily expanded their activities took heart. They were already enjoying Bulgarian facilitation of their operations.

The multipurpose state trading agency Kintex had been set up in Sofia in 1965 and had steadily expanded its activities in both legal and illegal fields—Communist governments, unlike their Western counterparts, being little interested in distinctions between the two.[11] During the same period, Bulgaria had begun international trucking operations, rapidly expanding from serving its own parochial requirements to providing efficient transport services from Europe to the Middle East. Along with tomato paste and machinery, Bulgarian trucks carried arms to the insatiable markets of the Middle East and—as the smugglers' operations expanded—were ready to bring back shipments of drugs originating from sources as distant as the Golden Triangle, Pakistan, and Afghanistan. All of this well-oiled and smoothly running infrastructure was in place and operating dependably by the time a new destabilization effort in Turkey was ready for launching.

Lessons were applied and techniques refined by the time the second great wave of terrorism got under way at the end of 1975. Students were still useful, but the operation no longer revolved about them. Leftists were favored, but the right now loomed as a major factor in the situation. The role of the right was complex. It would serve as a foil and a goad for the left and, with intellectuals, as an excuse for reinforcing leftist loyalties and excusing leftist excesses. The concept was by no means entirely new. Examples can be found in Tsarist Russia in the early twentieth century. More directly relevant is the history of Germany in the period when Hitler was being helped to power by the communists—posing as his arch enemies.[12] Frustration and insecurity drove many nationalists, religious individuals and sincere but narrow provincial politicians toward the right in Turkey in the 1970s. The arms embargo enacted by the U.S. Congress in the wake of the Cyprus crisis of 1974 lowered confidence in democracy—which seemed to lead only to stalemate—and in the United States—which appeared incapable of understanding where its own best interests lay. The older generation which turned rightward was of less direct use in whipping up terrorism than the younger men who joined rightist movements and became available as streetfighters.

Leftist organizations multiplied. Some claimed to be direct heirs of those active a few years before and dedicated themselves to the memory of heroes who were killed or executed in the early 1970s. The Turkish Communist Party remained outlawed even in this permissive period, but five small legal parties competed for leftist votes and served to mask the more subversive movements operating in their shadows. Their leaders enjoyed international respectability. The proliferation of leftist groups served several overtly contradictory but covertly compatible purposes. They created the impression of a great upsurge of leftist ideology, especially among youth. They diverted academics, journalists, and security officials into endless, hair-splitting analyses of supposed ideological differences between them which came to be of less and less importance as the level of violence rose. The wide variety of groups through which to operate gave terrorist managers the advantage of compartmentation when they needed it, improved the security of financial and supply operations, and at times fostered the illusion of massive grassroots support. The situation was spiced with separatists championing Kurdish autonomy and sectarians espousing particular religious viewpoints. These groups could be used to generate tension and clashes in which it sometimes became difficult to determine who was on the left and who on the right. At other times, cooperation could be facilitated when larger aims were to be served by it.[13]

We see many of these general characteristics of the destabilization program reflected in the quotations from Mehmet Ali Agca above. These quotations also reflect the broader objective of the second great wave of terrorism: the disruption of Turkish governmental processes and economic and social cohesiveness. No longer was the aim limited to spoiling Turkey's relations with the United States and NATO. It was to create so much turmoil in Turkey that all basis for a NATO relationship would be destroyed: other NATO countries would not want a country with so much internal turbulence as a member of the Alliance.[14]

As terrorism spread in 1976 and 1977, the economy became a direct target. The country had been plunged into economic chaos by the oil price hike following the 1973 Arab–Israeli War. Weak coalition governments took the easy course by increasing subsidies for petroleum and basic commodities instead of permitting prices to rise. Both left and right used state economic enterprises as devices for buying short-term political favors. Much of the country's most productive economic activity was driven underground. Labor unions and workers were major targets of leftist agitators, who encouraged a historically passive Turkish labor force to make extreme demands. Workers returning from the Federal Republic of Germany were not easily drawn into this kind of activity (being predominantly of rural origin), so they were exploited from the right.

The presence of more than a million Turkish laborers in Germany and other Western European countries proved useful to the instigators of destabilization in many ways. They were more accessible to communist operatives than those in Turkey itself. But here again, leftist appeals were a minor theme, the major theme was rightist extremism. Rightist organizations were easier to exploit for narcotics operations. Profits from narcotics trafficking could be channeled back into Turkey through smuggling networks, as could arms ostensibly purchased with drug earnings. As these operations expanded, they became more complex, and a symbiosis between narcotics traffickers and terrorists of all political colorations developed. As Agca described it: "Even if there were contradictions between them, Teslim Töre [head of the communist Turkish People's Liberation Army] and Abuzer Ugurlu [Turkish Mafia 'Godfather'] were in partnership for different reasons: [Töre] was working for purely revolutionary reasons; [Ugurlu] to make money off the weapons traffic."[15] Worker remittances—averaging a billion and a half dollars yearly through legal channels alone by the mid-1970s—could also be used as a device for getting money to all kinds of propaganda and terrorist organizations in Turkey.

Turkey in the Late 1970s: The Roots of Instability

Much of what we now know about the manner in which terrorism in Turkey was supported to destabilize the society and make democratic government ineffective was not realized, or at least not acknowledged, when the process was at its height in the late 1970s. In many ways, democracy worked to hinder open recognition of what was really happening to the country. Moderate leftist Ecevit, prime minister again from January 1978 until October 1979, persisted in believing that persuasion and toleration would bring terrorists to see the error of their ways. He encouraged his own party to adopt the view that rightist politicians were more responsible for violence than leftists. He abhorred taking responsibility for declaring martial law. His principal rival, Suleyman Demirel, leader of the moderate right Justice Party, was equally determined not to invite the military back into the governing process, having been the prime minister set aside by the military when violence reached its earlier peak in 1971. To make matters worse, Ecevit and Demirel had an extreme personal antipathy toward each other. During 1977, with Demirel in office, political killings had totaled 231. Ecevit expected violence to abate when he took office. But during his first month back in office, 51 persons were killed and 444 wounded; there were also 129 bombings and 20 terrorist robberies. By the end of 1978 political killings had climbed to 832. Moderate leftist leadership was clearly no better than moderate rightist in dealing with terrorism. By this time the sponsors of destabilization in Turkey had come to regard all moderates as enemies to be exploited and undermined. By the end of 1978, mounting left–right clashes reached a peak in the southeastern town of Kahramanmaras, where several days of rioting not only reflected senseless left–right rivalry, but also fed on religious (Sunni–Shia) and separatist (Kurdish) tensions.

Ecevit had to admit failure of persuasion and ask the Council of Ministers to declare martial law—but only in 13 of Turkey's 67 provinces. If Turkey's generals had been thirsting to take power, the Kahramanmaras riots alone would have offered more than sufficient excuse. Instead they stood aside, urged by a well-intentioned but passive President (Korutürk, a former admiral) to avoid interference in the democratic process. They continued to remain in the background throughout 1979, despite the worsening situation and the fact that the police and the military more frequently became targets of violence themselves. What was not known—or admitted—at the time was that the police and the security services (and to some degree the military at lower levels) were increasingly penetrated by subversive influences, bribed, coerced, and entrapped into taking sides in favor of one terrorist group over another. Leftists concentrated on setting up "liberated areas," primarily in the working-class quarters of larger cities. These became havens for terrorists and distribution points for money, arms, and explosives. DISK, the leftist labor confederation, and TÖBDER, the teachers' association, became major channels for managing terrorist operations. Vast quantities of propaganda, predominantly leftist, poured out of presses whose sources of income were obscure. Arms and drug traffickers had meanwhile extended their operations into remote corners of the country and were so active in corrupting members of the police, border guards, and customs services that they sometimes exercised more direct authority over their operations than the government's ministers in Ankara.[16]

A major episode in the advance of the demoralization which took a deep hold on the country during 1979 as inflation accelerated and the economy began to falter was the mysterious murder of liberal newspaper editor Abdi Ipekçi on the evening of 1 February of that year. The murder was immediately blamed on rightists, although evidence of rightist sponsorship was sparse. When Mehmet Ali Agca was apprehended and immediately confessed to the crime at the end of June, he claimed to be neither leftist nor rightist and persisted in this position throughout his trial and escape in November. The leftist bias of the press both in Turkey and abroad served Agca's sponsors well, for the Ipekçi killing and Agca's more spectacular assassination effort later in Rome in 1981 were immediately attributed to exactly those obscure elements his sponsors hoped to see blamed: "Fascists," Islamic fundamentalists, and the Gray Wolves.[17] These concepts have become anchored in intellectual consciousness, and continue to be repeated even today, at times in the most unlikely outlets and despite the lack of any confirmatory evidence while massive evidence of Soviet Bloc sponsorship of Agca has accumulated.

As citations already given from the 1983 Turkish interrogation report of Agca demonstrate, there was never any solid basis for attributing his crimes to rightist political forces. Subtle and not-so-subtle disinformation efforts served their purpose and exploited the natural tendency of intellectual establishments everywhere in the Western world to credit extreme leftists with noble motives and to condemn as thugs all who are regarded as rightists.[18] Agca was a talented young opportunist willingly adopted by conspiratorial pro-Moscow leftists who were operating under Bulgarian direction. An adjunct of their operations so essential as to be considered an integral part of them was the relationship with the Turkish mafia, with all its drug- and arms-smuggling ramifications. Although only a small part of the entire picture of terrorism in Turkey during the 1970s, the international drama of the Agca case makes it appropriate for highlighting most features of the terrorist destabilization process in Turkey as well as terrorism in a much broader international context. There is still more to be learned about Agca, even though the process has advanced very far and is likely to lead to the publication of extensive new details and full legal confirmation of most of what has already come to light.[19] It also demonstrates that terrorism was by no means brought to a definitive end when the Turkish military leaders finally lost patience and hope that ordinary political processes could restore stability to their country and took power into their own hands on 12 September 1980.

Narcotics Traffickers, Terrorists, and the Communist Bloc: A Symbiotic Relationship

During the final year before the Turkish General Staff designated itself the National Security Council and took charge of the government, terrorist and subversive incidents registered on police records totaled 23,841, and 2,812 people were killed in terrorist violence. Several prominent figures were deliberately targeted for assassination. Attacks against Americans became frequent, although unlike the situation a decade earlier, they were a minor target in the broad offensive aimed at paralyzing the country and generating civil war.

In what had seemed like an endless process of musical chairs, Demirel had again succeeded Ecevit as prime minister in November 1979. Partial parliamentary elections in October had demonstrated popular disillusionment with Ecevit's policies as well as a decline in the strength of Islamic fundamentalists. The economy had deteriorated to the point where the World Bank insisted on decisive corrective action as a condition of further assistance. Turgut Özal had a series of fundamental reforms ready to lay before Demirel, who knew that procrastination was no longer feasible and could lead only to an accelerating downward economic spiral. He proclaimed these reforms on 24 January 1980, laying the basis for a sharp turn toward an open, free market economy—a break with more than half a century of economic tradition.

The effect of the economic reforms was almost instantaneous. But terrorism, instead of declining, intensified. Its sponsors saw nothing to lose in ordering a test of strength between the terrorists and the politicians. There would be no need to change course until the military moved—and perhaps, if they waited too long, it would be too late. The Turkish criminal world—the Mafia—had reached a peak of power and influence. Their operations had become international, with links to Lebanon and Syria, to Armenians working in both the Middle East and in Europe, to Italy, Germany, France, and Great Britain. Only the vaguest hints of Bulgarian sponsorship of terrorism and links with the Turkish Mafia had surfaced. The press never pursued them. What is even more surprising is the fact that intelligence services seem to have learned so little about such things—they did not rank high in their priorities. So during the first two-thirds of 1980, money, arms, drugs, and contraband of all kinds flowed more freely in and out of Turkey than ever before. Moscow had invested heavily in operations that had to some extent become self-sustaining as well as self-financing. They would be reduced in scope only in the face of concrete and irresistible counteraction.

By the summer of 1980 at least one Turk was being killed every hour countrywide—an average of 28 per day. International confidence in Turkey, encouraged by economic reforms, was again declining and the economic reforms were coming under heavy propaganda assault from the leftist press and leftist publicists, as well as from the two clandestine radio stations broadcasting from Eastern Europe. The military leaders planned their takeover carefully. They expected, and received, no opposition. Instead the country heaved a massive, collective sigh of relief.

In retrospect we can see that the fact that Turkey proved able to endure the onslaught of extreme terrorism in 1979–80 demonstrates the exact opposite of what the terrorists' sponsors were hoping to prove. Far from being a country so rent with tensions and cursed with contradictions that it could not hope to practice democracy or fulfill its obligations to the Western Alliance, Turkey turned out to be remarkably sound. Turks had been able to withstand what had amounted to sustained subversive attack. Low-intensity warfare verged on high-intensity warfare but, except for those unfortunate victims of terrorism who were killed and wounded, the Turkish people suffered no irreversible trauma. Order was restored with extraordinary speed as soon as the military leadership displayed determination. Contrary to what fleeing terrorists, their supporters, and centers of anti-Turkish propaganda abroad claimed at the time, and have elaborated upon ever since, military rule was comparatively soft-gloved and even-handed. Only those who had been involved in terrorism and subversion had anything to fear from it.

The military leaders immediately announced a commitment to restore democracy and honored it. A new constitution ensuring an open society, but with better means of protecting itself from assault by its enemies, was drawn up. It was adopted by a surprisingly large percentage of citizens at the end of 1982. This and subsequent developments form a separate story which deserves to be better understood than it has been by the Western press and public.[20] For the purposes of this chapter we can deal only with what came to light as the Turkish authorities proceeded to restore order, destroy the infrastructure that had supported terrorism, and bring to justice those who had participated in it.[21]

The quantity of arms and ammunition—the most important tools of terrorism—that came into the hands of the Turkish military and security services was enormous. No one expected so much. During the first 18 months of military administration, more than 800,000 weapons were confiscated. Most of these were pistols, but the total included 64,000 high-powered rifles, over 6,300 automatic rifles, and over 6,000 machine guns and pistols. The military also captured or uncovered 23,200 bombs, grenades, mines, and other explosive devices, 26,240 stabbing and cutting instruments, 24 rocket launchers, and 94 two-way radio communications sets. More than 5,300,000 rounds of unused ammunition were collected. This materiel was varied enough in origin to provide samples for the catalogues of the most versatile international weapons dealers. Only a few of the weapons were of Turkish manufacture, and only a few of foreign make had been stolen from Turkish military or police arsenals. There was no normal source in Turkey for most of them. They had to be smuggled in, primarily from Bulgaria and Syria, sometimes through Mafia channels, sometimes via less roundabout routes. Some had been transferred from seagoing ships onto smaller coastal vessels and unloaded at obscure points along the Black Sea and Marmara coasts. Supplies from Syria often came overland via returning Bulgarian-registered international transport trucks, as well as by other means of transport. The value of this initial haul of arms and ammunition on the international market was conservatively estimated at $300 million, a large-scale military aid program if it had been carried out overtly. This was by no means the whole story. Interrogation of terrorists and examination of captured records provided enough information on finances for propaganda, and the travel, living, and operating expenses of terrorists to justify the conclusion that the terrorist assault of the late 1970s in Turkey could have cost no less than $1 billion.

Weapons, ammunition, and other terrorist equipment continue to be surrendered, uncovered, and captured in Turkey, although naturally in much smaller quantities. A great deal of terrorist manpower was required to utilize all this weaponry. During the first year of military administration, 43,140 terrorists and terrorist supporters were taken into custody—ten times as many as had been arrested when the first great wave of terrorism was brought to a halt in 1971–72. Large numbers of terrorists and terrorist supporters escaped abroad to European countries where many were granted asylum and some assumed other identities. Other went into hiding in Turkey. In subsequent years many surrendered or were captured. As of the end of 1983, estimates of the total number of individuals implicated in some way in terrorist activities of all kinds in Turkey based on all information available to security authorities were as follows:[22]

Leftists	113,099
Rightists	78,147
Separatists	31,931
Total	223,177

Destabilization operations involving this many people, even in a country whose population exceeded 40 million at the time, had gone beyond the point where they could be considered low-intensity warfare. With so large a group to work on, Turkish investigators have compiled an enormous amount of data and have published a significant sampling of it. What is surprising is that so little use has so far been made of this information by scholars of terrorism.

After taking power in September 1980, Turkey's military leaders understandably gave highest priority to rounding up active terrorists and breaking up conspiratorial organizations. But they lost little time in cracking down on smugglers. There was a great deal to do in Turkey itself, but the full job required international cooperation. Drug and arms smuggling had become a truly multinational business. All major figures carried several passports, had several residences in different countries, and had established companies which served in part as fronts, in part as real operating entities. Many foreign officials had been deceived, intimidated, and bribed. During this period coordination between police and security and intelligence services in Europe left a great deal to be desired. It is all the more remarkable, therefore, that Turkish authorities succeeded in obtaining extradition of Mafia Godfather Abuzer Ugurlu from Germany in March 1981, two months before Agca was to attempt to kill the Pope in Rome. No one—except Agca and his closest associates, if they knew of Ugurlu's misfortune—can have realized at that time how momentous that extradition would turn out to be.[23] Ugurlu refused to talk when brought back to Turkey and has reportedly volunteered very little information to Turkish interrogators even though he is still a defendant in three judicial processes which remain to be concluded. Nevertheless, diligent investigation, pursuit of Ugurlu's associates and collaborators in Turkey, development of leads resulting from Italian investigations and Agca's confessions, and information obtained from other European countries have gradually enabled Turkish prosecutors to reconstruct a comprehensive picture of Ugurlu's operations. What emerges is a multibillion-dollar network with all the strands merging in Bulgaria, where Ugurlu, like his associate Bekir Çelenk, enjoyed the highest favors of the Bulgarian regime.[24]

One of the strangest developments in this whole sequence of events is the appearance in late 1981 of a sensationally written book entitled *Weapons Smuggling and Terror* by one of Turkey's most clever leftist journalists, Ugur Mumcu.[25] A columnist for the Istanbul daily *Cumhuriyet,* which had advocated neutralist positions during the 1970s, and self-proclaimed socialist and strong critic of Turkey's Western orientation, Mumcu had time and again given credence and publicity to Soviet disinformation during the 1970s. Now, in the wake of military takeover and crackdown on terrorism and smuggling, he produced a book full of details of the operations of the smugglers and their close links to Bulgaria. The book was less curious, however, when read to the end, for its main themes were two: 1) the smugglers were all closely linked to rightist politicians in Turkey, and 2) Bulgaria itself was the victim of exploitation by a loose consortium of international arms traffickers and businessmen (including the famous Adnan Khashoggi) and NATO intelligence agencies (including, of course, the CIA). Since the weapons smuggled into Turkey to support terrorism originated for the most part in NATO countries, Mumcu implied that terrorism had been the creation of NATO. Analysis of the Bulgarian–Soviet relationship was mysteriously lacking.

In the wake of Agca's attack on the Pope, Mumcu quickly produced another book designed to show that Agca had been the tool of rightists in Turkey, was a dyed-in-the-wool rightist himself and probably a fanatical Muslim, and that Bulgaria was again primarily the gullible victim of exploitation by nefarious Western criminal and political elements.[26] Even in face of steadily accumulating contrary evidence, Mumcu persisted in attempting to divert attention from Soviet complicity in the plot to kill the Pope and Soviet support of terrorism in Turkey. A second book expanding upon these themes appeared in 1984.[27] What we seem to have here is a remarkably bold and complex disinformation operation. With Ugurlu's extradition to Turkey, some of the facts about Bulgarian sponsorship of drug and arms smuggling were bound to emerge. So they were conceded—but with an attempt to lay ultimate responsibility on the West and deflect it from the Soviet Union. When the assassination attempt on the Pope failed and Agca was caught, another pre-emptive damage-limiting operation—parallel to that which Moscow itself has tried to implement through Yona Andronov's articles in *Literaturnaya Gazeta*—had to be improvised. In the face of steady exposure of basic facts, it, too, has tended to crumble. Only the "Denial Syndrome"—still very prevalent in Europe and America and by no means absent among Turkish intellectuals—sustains Moscow's efforts.

The Soviet Union and Low-Intensity Warfare in the 1980s

It is a stimulating intellectual exercise to speculate about whether the linkage between drugs, arms, and destabilization as revealed in the Turkish experience may be evidence of a master plan developed in Moscow in the 1960s. Is implementation of the scheme and the shielding of it by deception and disinformation operations a manifestation of the evil genius of Yuri Andropov, head of the KGB from 1967 to 1982? Was the flooding of the West with drugs fostered as a device for social and political destabilization? Was the experience gained in the Middle East and Europe then transferred to the Caribbean and Latin America? Or was it all simply a response to opportunity, the result of readiness to build on initial success and take advantage of an exploitable correlation of subversive forces? It is more likely the latter. The vast complex of drug- and arms-smuggling operations exposed by Judge Palermo at Trento points in this direction.[28] The Soviets did not need to plan their involvement with this kind of activity in advance, except in the general sense of being ready to capitalize on it and encourage it as opportunities arose. In this their operators have displayed a perverted sense of enterprise that seems lacking in almost all other aspects of their system, except perhaps certain areas of space and weapons research.

A few years ago, questions about the Soviet approach to terrorism and destabilization could not have been posed without being dismissed by an overwhelming portion of the journalistic and scholarly community, and perhaps even the intelligence community, as evidence of paranoia on the part of the asker. We have now reached the point where such subjects must form part of any serious debate. It is like dealing with a pernicious disease: as long as we refuse to recognize the need for investigating its causative and contributing factors, we cannot expect to start devising a cure. But, as with many diseases, a cure will not spring automatically from a correct diagnosis. If a discovery is possible at all, it will only come through steady, cumulative effort entailing prevention and precaution as well as direct counteraction. There is, unfortunately, little reason to believe that the Soviets have abandoned terrorism and destabilization or that they have foresworn exploitation of the criminal underworld for their purposes. As the chronic problems of their system deepen, as the intractibility of the crises they face in Poland and Afghanistan becomes more apparent, they are likely to be increasingly driven to desperate negative actions simply to preserve their power and the privileges of the *nomenklatura*.[29]

From the Western Hemisphere we have mounting evidence of alliances of convenience with criminal networks and encouragement of trafficking in narcotics by communist and Soviet-friendly movements. Both Cuba and Nicaragua are deeply implicated, as testimony before U.S. Congressional committees has indicated.[30]

There is some reason to believe that Bulgaria's arms- and drug-smuggling operations may have become economically essential to the regime. Meanwhile we see a new upsurge of allegedly Shi'a-inspired terrorism in the Middle East and the utilization of a wide variety of small groups to bomb NATO facilities and U.S. military installations in Western Europe, assassinate executives of defence industries, and engage in various other forms of propaganda by deed. Cui bono? That should be the first, not the last, question to be asked as we try to cope with these challenges. What we already know of Soviet destabilization operations and utilization of narcotics traffickers, criminals, and underworld operatives provides all we need to develop models that can be tested and applied to new situations as they develop.

Notes

1. Vittorfranco Pisano, *Terrorism and Security: The Italian Experience*, Report of the Subcommittee on Security and Terrorism of the Committee on the Judiciary, U.S. Senate, November 1984 (Washington, D.C.: GPO), p. 33.

2. Examples include Vittorfranco Pisano, "Clandestine Operations in Italy: the Bulgarian Connection," *Journal of Conflict Studies* University of New Brunswick (Winter 1984): 28–38; and Christopher C. Harmon, "Left Meets Right in Terrorism: a Focus on Italy," *Strategic Review* (Winter 1985).

3. The citations are from an 88–page Turkish interrogation report which has not yet been publicly released but which was printed in part in the 1 February 1985 edition of the Istanbul daily, *Hürriyet*.

4. Ibid.

5. Ibid.

6. One of the most recent, and most thorough, books about Soviet support of international terrorism has, surprisingly, no serious discussion of terrorism in Turkey at all: Robert Goren, *The Soviet Union and Terrorism* (London: Allen & Unwin, 1984).

7. I have covered these developments at greater length in *Goal: Destabilization, Soviet Agitational Propaganda, Instability and Terrorism in NATO South,* (Marina del Rey, Calif.: European American Institute for Security Research, 1981).

8. These and many other strains in the Turkish–American relationship are well analyzed in George S. Harris, *Troubled Alliance* (Stanford, Calif.: AEI/Hoover, 1972).

9. The best study of the major incidents of the period has been done by Margaret Krahenbuhl, *Political Kidnappings in Turkey, 1971–72* (Santa Monica, Calif.: Rand Corp., no. R-2105-DOS/ARPA, July 1977).

10. *Türkiye'de Yikici Faaliyetler*, General Staff, Ankara. This study was the sub-

ject of a long article in *Hürriyet* on 10 September 1981 by Cuneyt Arcayürek, entitled "The White Book Revealed it all but . . ." which sums up the main conclusions of the report and argues that taking them seriously would have made it possible to avoid the deterioration of the latter part of the 1970s.

11. "Bulgaria is a Key Link in Drug Trade," *Wall Street Journal,* 13 May 1983; Nathan Adams, "Drugs for Guns," *Reader's Digest,* January 1984.

12. Paul Johnson, *Modern Times, the World from the Twenties to the Eighties* (New York: Harper & Row, 1983), p. 278 ff.

13. A compendium issued by the General Secretariat of the National Security Council, Ankara, in 1982, entitled *12 September in Turkey, Before and After,* with extensive citations from documents and many photographs, provides a vivid impression of the massive confusion which was generated.

14. If the masterminds behind the destabilization campaign in Turkey had calculated on the Western press to serve their purposes well, they were not mistaken. Consider the following headlines of stories in the *Washington Post* on 5 February 1979: "Political Violence, Economic Ills, Stir Fears for Turkey's Future;" "Turkey's Political, Economic Woes Worry NATO Allies;" "Editor's Murder Stirs Talk of Slide into Anarchy."

15. *Hürriyet,* 1 February 1985.

16. I have described the evolution of terrorism in Turkey at greater length and in a broader political context in Chapter 3 of my book, *The Plot to Kill the Pope* (New York: Scribners; London: Croom Helm, 1983). I know of no other comprehensive treatment of the subject, though it merits attention as an extraordinary case study of destabilization on a massive scale.

17. The *New York Times* headlined a full-page story to which ten of its reporters contributed on 25 May 1981: "Trail of Mehmet Ali Agca: Six Years of Neo-Fascist Ties." In light of what we now know about Agca, practically everything in this story can be demonstrated to be wrong in its political implications.

18. Rightist extremists deserve no sympathy and much opprobrium for letting themselves be so duped and exploited by the very people which they claim—and in many cases believe—to be their archenemies. The enmity of both versions of extremist authoritarian ideology for an open, pluralist society and for democratic processes drives them together. From what we now know of terrorist practice in Turkey, there is ample evidence that the two extremes often cooperated; the same has been true in Italy.

19. I first called attention to the likelihood of Agca's Soviet sponsorship in a report for the *Reader's Digest,* "Mehmet Ali Agca—Whose Agent?" 5 September 1981. The postscript chapter to the paperback edition of my *Plot to Kill the Pope* sums up what we now know of Agca's involvement with Turkish leftists and drug smugglers, including the evolution of the plan to kill Abdi Ipekçi; this edition will be off the press in late spring 1985. A condensed version of this chapter will appear in *Problems of Communism* (May–June 1985).

20. See my "Turkey on the Rebound," *Wilson Quarterly* (Special Issue 1982): 108–125.

21. Much of the information which follows is taken from a 1982 Turkish Government publication, *Türkiye'deki Anarşi ve Terörün Gelişmesi, Sonuçlari ve Güven-*

lik Kuvvetleri Önlenmesi. The full account of terrorism remains, of course, to be written, for trials and investigations in Turkey are still bringing new information to light and terrorists' confessions are adding background providing insight into support sources and methods of operation.

22. These statistics are taken from tables accompanying an article by Turan Itil, "Terrorism in Turkey with Special Consideration of Armenian Terrorism," in *International Terrorism and the Drug Connection* (Ankara: Ankara Univ. Press, 1984), pp. 29–48.

23. The interesting question arises, did the Bulgarians consider the implications of Ugurlu's arrest and extradition to Turkey, which can hardly have escaped their notice, in implementing the plot to kill the Pope? They must have had confidence in Ugurlu's ability to resist interrogation. They must also have assumed that his relationship with Agca was so sufficiently obscured that there would be no danger of its emerging. Perhaps the key factor was simply confidence that Agca would accomplish his mission and that they would succeed in either eliminating him or getting him safely back to Bulgaria—as appears to have happened with his associate, Oral Çelik.

24. Çelenk, who was more closely linked to Agca during the implementation of the plot to kill the Pope than Ugurlu, fled from London to Sofia as soon as the Bulgarian connection was exposed in Rome at the end of 1982 and has remained there ever since.

25. *Silah Kaçakçiligi ve Terör* (Istanbul: Tekin Yayinevi, 1981).

26. *Agca Dosyasi* (Istanbul: Tekin Yayinevi, 1982).

27. *Papa, Agca, Mafya* (Istanbul: Tekin Yayinevi, 1984). Mumcu's books are all printed in large editions, frequently reprinted, and widely circulated through distribution channels which even in post-1980 Turkey remain leftist dominated.

28. Like the Turkish experience, the Italian revelations have yet to be summarized in a single, comprehensive account. Examples of the voluminous press reporting include *Il Giornale* accounts such as "'Pista Bulgara' anche a Trento," 23 December 1982, and "Anche Siria e Pakistan sarebbero implicati nel traffico di droga er armi della pista bulgara," 7 March 1983; "How South Africa bought a Red Arsenal," *Observer*, 29 April 1984; "Ein Netz Illegalen Waffenhandles in Italien," *Neue Zuerche Zeitung*, 8 June 1984; "Bulgarian Connection to Illicit Arms Trade is Found," *Wall Street Journal*, 10 August 1984; "Italian Case Uncovers an Alpine Heart of Darkness," *New York Times*, 24 November 1984.

29. As defined and analyzed by Michael Voslensky, *Nomenklatura: Anatomy of the Soviet Ruling Class,* (New York: Doubleday and Company, 1984).

30. *Drugs and Terrorism, 1984,* Record of Hearings before the Subcommittee on Alcoholism and Drug Abuse of the Committee on Labor and Human Resources, U.S. Senate, 98th Congress, 2d sess., 2 August 1984, (Washington, D.C.: GPO, 1984).

11

Drug Trafficking, Organized Crime, and Terrorism: The International Cash Connection

Charles C. Frost

Drug Abuse and Drug Demand

Americans have a voracious appetite for illicit drugs. According to the latest annual report of the House Committee on Narcotics Abuse and Control, more than twenty million Americans use marijuana regularly, roughly eight to twenty million are regular cocaine users, about half a million are heroin addicts, one million use hallucinogens and approximately six million abuse prescription drugs.[1] Why so many indulge in drug abuse is largely beyond the scope of this paper. Perhaps the reasons lie in the breakdown of societal and family restraints, peer pressure, media encouragement of instant gratification and a low tolerance of pain or hardship, and the belief that there is a quick fix for every difficulty from pimples to bad moods. If neuropharmacologists and psychologists really know the answer—and this is doubtful—their knowledge has not yet been translated into a clear policy prescription for dealing with the malaise. We would delude ourselves, however, if we attributed the drug abuse problem essentially to an external cause. With the possible exception of veterans exposed to heroin and marijuana use in Vietnam, there is little credible evidence that foreign enemies have substantially influenced Americans' demand for illicit drugs. Our national disgrace is of our own making.

This massive demand for illegal drugs puts enormous amounts of cash into the hands of drug traffickers. The quantities of drugs consumed and the profits they generate can be only roughly estimated. Table 11–1 has been constructed on the basis of tonnage figures and price data from the most recent U.S. Government assessment of the world drug trafficking situation. A range of $45–49 billion may be too conservative and, in any event, does not include abuse of prescription drugs. Former Attorney General William French Smith used a figure of $76 billion last fall[2] and, according to the Rangel Committee report, sales of illegal drugs reached $110 billion in 1984.[3]

Table 11–1

Retail Value of Illicit Drugs Consumed in the United States, 1983
(an approximation based on official data)

Illicit Drug	Official Estimate of Quantities of Illicit Drugs Consumed in 1983	1983 Retail Prices from the Official Estimate	Retail Value in 1983 Prices (billion $)
Cocaine	50–61 metric tons[a] (pure basis)	$75–100/gm.[b] (average 35% pure)	12.5–15.3
Marihuana	13,600–14,000 metric tons	59% @ $58/oz (average)[c] 11% @ $75/oz (average)[c] 30% @ $60/oz (average)[c]	29.0–29.9
Heroin	4.1 metric tons (pure basis)	$5/bag (100 mg.)[d] (average 5.2% pure)[d]	3.9
Total			45.4–49.1

Source: National Narcotics Intelligence Consumers Committee, *Narcotics Intelligence Estimate: 1983.*

[a]This is a consumption-based estimate. Supply-based data indicate that a total of 54–71 metric tons of illicit cocaine entered the country and was available for consumption in 1983. This difference was assessed to be consistent with indicators suggesting that the supply of cocaine exceeded the demand (pp. 2, 16 and Figure 7).

[b]Equivalent to $214–286 per gram of pure cocaine ($250 per gram average).

[c]Market shares are Colombian (59 percent), domestic (11 percent) and other (30 percent) (p. 9 figure 4).

[d]Equivalent to $0.96 per milligram of pure heroin.

Pernicious Effects of Drug Profits

Drug profits have become by far the largest single source of revenue for organized crime in advanced countries. A study done by the Royal Canadian Mounted Police found that drug trafficking accounted for 87 percent of the cash income of organized crime from all types of consensual crime.[4] In Japan, organized crime derived an estimated one-half of its 1978 revenues from peddling illicit amphetamine drugs.[5]

With multimillions in cash at their disposal, traffickers can hire thugs, smugglers, lawyers, and bankers to work for them; lease boats, aircraft, and real estate; and, as necessary, bribe policemen, jail wardens, and even judges to protect their nefarious activities. It is not difficult to find evidence of drug-related corruption of foreign officials. A few examples will suffice. Corruption of local police figured in the recent abduction and murder of an agent of the Drug Enforcement Administration (DEA) in Mexico and the escape (for a time) of the prime suspect. Prior to the extradition of that suspect from Costa Rica, U.S. officials had complained that not a single major trafficker was arrested in Mexico in eight years despite more than $110 million in American narcotics control assistance to that country. A royal commission in the Bahamas found evidence that drug-related corruption ranges from policemen patrolling remote islands to cabinet officials. The chief minister of the Turks and Caicos Islands was caught red-handed in an undercover investigation initiated with the permission of the British governor. In this country, patrolmen on the beat and county sheriffs are occasionally suborned to turn a blind eye to drug trafficking and smuggling. The DEA, the FBI, and the Customs Service must be prepared to run operations against their own agents to maintain the integrity of their investigations. Corruption in private institutions has lately surfaced, with allegations of collusion of employees of domestic banks in laundering money for organized crime.[6]

Money Laundering

Even gigantic drug profits are worthless to organized crime if they can be readily traced and seized by drug enforcement authorities. Organized crime must, therefore, have the means for disguising their ill-gotten gains. The volume of cash apparently exceeds that which organized crime can satisfactorily launder by the myriad transactions of money couriers who handle just under $10,000 each day, the present reporting threshold. Criminal enterprises have had to rely on legitimate financial channels to accept large cash deposits, which may then be used to buy stock, be transferred to accounts in other domestic banks, or be moved out of the country. Officials of banks, currency exchanges, brokerage houses, and casinos are involved in these money-laundering schemes, often unwittingly, but sometimes knowingly. The President's Commission on Organized Crime has estimated that the narcotics traffic alone is the source for $5–15 billion in illegal profits channeled abroad, two-thirds of which transits through domestic financial institutions.[7] Concluding from its investigations that the Bank Secrecy Act does not provide sufficient authority to prosecute and to penalize money laundering activity, the Commission recommended that money laundering be made a criminal offense and that casinos be made subject to the Act.[8]

Concern Over Security Implications of Drug Trafficking

The UN International Narcotics Control Board (INCB) voiced grave concern for the effects of rampant drug abuse and drug-related crime on the security of member countries in its Report for 1984. Illegal drug production and trafficking activities, the INCB states, "are so pervasive and generate such vast volumes of capital that countries' economies are disrupted, legal institutions menaced and *the very security of some States is threatened.*"[9]

Senator Paula Hawkins's Subcommittee on Alcoholism and Drug Abuse explored the links between drug traffic and terrorism in hearings in August

1984. The State Department has somewhat of a conceptual problem with the term "terrorism" in this context. In their view, terrorism means the use of violence (or the threat of violence) as a political weapon to achieve control, to influence government policy and/or to destabilize and even to overthrow governments. By this definition, most of the activities of narcotics organizations, however violent, do not qualify as terrorism in the true sense.

Purism aside, the Department noted numerous instances wherein *insurgent organizations,* which frequently use terrorist tactics, have become involved directly or indirectly with narcotics production and trafficking. Some highlights of their testimony are as follows:

1. Burmese insurgent groups run the gamut from ideological revolutionaries such as the Burmese Communist Party, to ethnic separatists such as the Karen Independence Organization, to "opium warlord" bands such as the Shan United Army who are dedicated only to profit. These groups control the areas producing the opium, tax the crop or take a share of it, in some cases process opium, and make direct sales to middlemen.

2. "There are clear connections between Colombian guerrilla groups and narcotics production/smuggling operations," the State Department reported.[10] Two principal insurgent organizations are the Revolutionary Armed Forces of Colombia (FARC) and the 19th of April Movement, better known as M-19. The FARC, the largest and oldest of the country's guerrilla groups, has a rural base. Half of its fronts operate in coca- and marijuana-growing areas. Fronts have direct arrangements with traffickers in their respective areas. FARC collects protection payments from the coca growers but provides warning of the approach of antinarcotics police or military patrols. Because of their control of a number of strategic river points in the interior, the guerrillas can impede travel by the police. The FARC guarantees a number of clandestine airfields for the use of traffickers. In exchange, the guerrillas receive money from the traffickers to buy weapons and supplies. Such goods are often smuggled in on return drug flights. Drug trafficker–guerrilla alliances can be turbulent at times, however. Serious interorganizational friction leading to several deaths erupted in 1983.[11]

3. The clearest evidence of a Cuban narcotics–terrorism link surfaced in connection with the Jaime Guillot Lara case in Federal District court in Miami in November 1982. Fourteen persons were indicted in that case, including a former ambassador and a former deputy chief of mission of the Cuban Embassy in Bogota and a vice admiral of the Cuban Navy. The case documented Cuban Government involvement in actions to provide haven for Colombian drug smuggling vessels en route to the United States and the shipping of arms to the M-19 guerrilla forces in Colombia. Guillot agreed to pay the Cubans for their cooperation.[12]

Since 1982 there have been tenuous indications from nautical charts and logs seized aboard smuggling vessels, as well as evidence taken from a plane that crashed in Colombia, that Cuba continues to facilitate the trans-Caribbean narcotics traffic. Colombian officials were quoted in March 1984 as saying that aircraft carrying drugs out of the country returned with cargoes of weapons for the FARC. The State Department acknowledged, however, that these and other claims that Cuba is currently engaged in drugs-for-arms deals have not been confirmed.[13]

4. The Maoist terrorist group *Sendero Luminoso* (SL), or Shining Path, has established close ties to international narcotics traffickers, according to State Department testimony. Cocaine traffickers reportedly supply arms and money to the terrorists in return for protection against law enforcement authorities. The motives for SL cooperation with the traffickers may be complex, however. The SL are engaged in a vigorous campaign to recruit new followers to their cause among the indigenous Quechua-speaking people, with whom they have linguistic and cultural affinities. A number of these people have migrated to the Upper Huallaga Valley to grow coca. Many of the growers perceive coca eradication efforts funded by the United States to be a threat to their livelihood. Thus, the SL may make common cause with the cocaine traffickers not only to obtain money and weapons but also to capitalize on the peasants' grievances in order to promote agrarian revolution. The Peruvian Government has been convinced of a firm link between cocaine traffickers and the SL insurgency at least since early 1984.

In his submission to the Hawkins Subcommittee, the head of the Drug Enforcement Administration acknowledged trafficker–terrorist cooperation but minimized its importance, at least for the drug traffic.

> This emerging relationship between drug trafficking and terrorism is not a reflection of any ideological coalition or conspiracy. What we find in most cases is more of an accommodation or cooperative effort for the mutual benefit of both trafficker and terrorist. Each will take advantage of the experience, equipment, and contacts of the other in order to pursue its own ends. With the possible exceptions of the FARC and the Shan United Army, there is no evidence of wholesale participation by terrorist groups in drug trafficking, or of large scale involvement by various terrorist group leaders. Although DEA believes the terrorist connection to drug trafficking is increasing, we do not believe that it has had a significant impact on drug availability in the United States. At this time, terrorist groups are not in a position to compete with established drug smuggling organizations and are not a threat to their operations.[14]

Comment on DEA and State Department Positions

The DEA does not dispute the facts presented by the State Department. Indeed, much of the language used by the two agencies in their testimony before the Hawkins Subcommittee is identical. There is, however, a somewhat different emphasis in the DEA's perception of the drug–terrorism link. The State Department focuses on the extent to which a movement cooperating with drug traffickers has supplanted government authority in a part of the country. State has a dual concern: in the short term, whether this cooperation will increase the flow of illicit drugs to the United States; and in the longer term, how will such cooperation strengthen the insurgents in their struggle against the government, and will American interests be caught in the crossfire.

The DEA is not particularly concerned with the reasons why a movement cooperates with drug traffickers. It looks at the entire spectrum of political violence—from agrarian revolution to separatism, urban terrorism, subversion, dissidence, and general lawlessness—but only from the standpoint of how it affects the supply of illicit drugs. By this stand both the DEA and the State Department might be faulted for not giving more attention to the effects of the poorly organized but fairly effective regional autonomy movement in the Northwest Frontier Province of Pakistan. Afghanistan is also not mentioned in the context of the drug–terrorism link. This appears to be a matter of convenient definition, since the Afghan *mujaheddin* are officially regarded as anti-Soviet "freedom fighters" rather than as insurgents or terrorists. The omission is all the more curious because Afghanistan produces, by U.S. estimates, a whopping 400–575 metric tons of opium.[15] It seems likely that a considerable amount of this sizable tonnage is produced with the approval and encouragement of leaders of *mujheddin* groups.

Increased Sophistication in the Use of Political Violence

A development that was almost entirely overlooked in the hearings on drug–terrorism linkages is the increasing use by criminal organizations of violence *for political effect,* that is, classical terrorism. If the focus is shifted from the form of the organization or how it is defined or classified to the substance of drug-related terrorist incidents, some rather interesting shifts appear. Table 11–2 lists a series of recent incidents that represent what might be considered the traditional form of battle between the trafficking organizations and government enforcement agencies.[16] Sadly, such incidents are all too common. And the list could have included earlier assassinations of judges in Colombia, as well as the 1982 Mafia murder in Palermo, Sicily, of General Carlo Alberto Dalla Chiesa, one of the highest-ranking police officials in Italy. It will also be noted that the list indicates that the Colombian traffickers are bringing the battle to DEA's home ground.

Table 11–2
Terrorist Incidents Aimed Primarily at Host and U.S. Governments
(Purpose: Reduce Resolve to Pursue Vigorous Law Enforcement)

Date	Event
February 1984	Murder of Eduardo Gonzalez, Colombian Justice Ministry official who actively and publicly supported implementation of the U.S.–Colombian extradition treaty
April 1984	Assassination of Colombian Justice Minister Rodrigo Lara Bonilla
14 November 1984	U.S. Embassy in Bogota reportedly received message from cocaine traffickers threatening to kill five Americans for every Colombian extradited to the United States to face drug charges
19 November 1984	Jungle coca eradication campsite in Peru is sprayed with machine gun fire, killing 15 local workers. (The $30 million U.S.-financed project was immediately suspended.)
26 November 1984	Car bomb exploded outside U.S. Embassy in Bogota, Colombia, killing a woman and wounding six others.
November 1984	(17 Embassy officials and their families withdrawn from Colombia)
1 February 1985	DEA office in Boston reported to be taking extra precautions to protect its personnel and buildings in the face of threats by Colombian drug traffickers
7 February 1985	DEA agent Enrique Camarena Salazar and Mexican drug eradication pilot kidnapped in Guadalajara, Mexico
February 15	(U.S. Customs initiated intensified searches at border crossings)
18 February 1985	DEA acknowledged that it had received reports Colombian traffickers were offering up to $350,000 for kidnapping Administrator Mullen or other high agency official
2 March 1985	Nine small U.S. border crossings closed on the grounds that "credible threats" against American customs agents had been received
6 March 1985	Tortured and beaten bodies of Camarena and Mexican pilot found under suspicious circumstances

The incidents listed in table 11–3 represent a startling new departure by criminal organizations—an effort to gain public sympathy for their activities. Surely, it is too soon to say much about the effect of such propaganda on public opinion. Likewise, one can only speculate at this point on the expectations of the initiators of such actions. One can presume, for example, that organization leaders who are not averse to murder and bombings might welcome an opportunity to salve their consciences somewhat by wrapping their deeds in a moral cloak, as terrorists often do.

Table 11–4 lists incidents in which U.S. business firms operating in drug source countries have been subjected to criminally inspired attack. This suggests an ominous trend toward retaliation against American business for losses sustained through host government law enforcement cooperation with

Table 11–3
Use of Terrorist Incident and Media Aimed at Public Opinion
(Purpose: Clothe Criminal Activity With National Interest)

Date	Event
July 1984	Bomb exploded on campus of the University of the Atlantic in Barranquilla, Colombia. The Urban Insurrection Front, a previously unknown group, claimed responsibility, stating that it was protesting the spraying of marijuana crops in the Sierra Nevada mountains.
March 1985	Filmed interview with accused Colombian drug trafficker Carlos Lehder Rivas aired on Bogota TV station. "Cocaine and marijuana," Lehder declared, "have become an arm of [the] struggle against American imperialism. We have the same responsibility in this—he who takes up a rifle, he who plants coca, [and] he who goes to the public plaza and denounces imperialism. . . . [Justice Minister] Lara Bonilla, [American Ambassador] Tambs and [President] Betancur united to conspire against the interests of this country. Lara Bonilla was executed by the people."

Table 11–4
Terrorist Incidents Sited at U.S. Business Firms Overseas
(Purpose: Bring Indirect Pressure Against U.S. and Host Governments to Lessen Law Enforcement Efforts)

Date	Event
January 1985	American scholar visiting Ecuador's Napo region reported that American oil company officials fear that Colombian coca traffickers will retaliate against their workers, holdings, and pipelines for losses sustained in U.S.-backed eradication on the Colombian side of the border.
9 February 1985	Bombs exploded at one-hour intervals outside the offices of IBM, Union Carbide, and Xerox in Medellin, Colombia. A private guard was killed at the IBM headquarters. The city's mayor blamed leftwing guerrillas for the bombings.

the United States. U.S. overseas firms are convenient targets, and occasional attacks on them would be a logical extension of the criminal organizations' campaign against government law enforcement.

Conclusions

1. Selective but deliberate use of terror by organized crime against U.S. targets to accomplish its objectives is a possibility that must be reckoned with.

2. It is to organized crime's advantage to clothe their nefarious activities with the national interest. This pose portrays host government coopera-

tion with the United States in suppression of the drug traffic as treasonous and prepares a favorable climate of public opinion for actions against American officials and installations and U.S.-sponsored programs.

3. Mutual assistance between guerrilla groups and organized crime may well strengthen insurgencies and act as a destabilizing influence against local governments. By the same token, a government's one-sided response to an insurgency threat while reacting only at U.S. urging against drug traffickers may be self-defeating.

4. American business firms in drug-producing countries may find themselves convenient targets for criminally inspired terrorism because they are an American presence in the area of operations and because they may be used to bring pressure against the U.S. and host governments.

Notes

1. U.S. House of Representatives, Select Committee on Narcotics Abuse and Control, *Annual Report for the Year 1984* (Report 98-1199), p. 8.

2. *Washington Times*, 14 September 1984.

3. House Select Committee Report, p. 9. Rep. Charles B. Rangel (D-NY) is Chairman of the Select Committee on Narcotics Abuse and Control.

4. Canada, Solicitor General's Department, *RCMP National Drug Intelligence Estimate: 1983*, p. 76. See also the article by RCMP drug enforcement officials Rodney T. Stamler and Robert C. Fahlman in UN *Bulletin on Narcotics*, vol. 25, no. 2, pp. 61–70.

5. Sadahiko Takahasi and Carl B. Becker, "Organized Crime in Japan" (Paper presented at the 1985 annual meeting of the Academy of Criminal Justice Sciences), p. 16.

6. See, for example, the following articles in the *Washington Post:* "Bank Fined $500,000 in Currency Case," 8 February 1985, p. B1; "Bank Regulators Track Paper Trails in Search of Laundered Transactions," 3 March 1985, p. F5; "Laundering Cash" (editorial), 22 February 1985, p. A18; "Bank of Boston in Spotlight," 3 March 1985, p. F1.

7. President's Commission on Organized Crime, *The Cash Connection: Organized Crime, Financial Institutions and Money Laundering* (Washington, D.C.: GPO, 1984). See also *New York Times*, 31 October 1984, pp. A1, A24; *Washington Post*, 30 November 1984; *Time*, 12 November 1984.

8. The Federal Bank Secrecy Act, passed in 1970, requires banks to file reports with the Treasury Department whenever a transaction exceeds $10,000 but provides fines of only $1,000 for each failure to comply. Under Customs regulations a person leaving the United States must declare cash or negotiable instruments if the amount exceeds $5,000. The intent of this requirement can be easily circumvented by purchasing cashier's checks and money orders in the United States and mailing them to accomplices in Panama.

9. E/INCB/1984/1, p. 2, emphasis added.

10. Testimony of Acting Assistant Secretary of State Clyde D. Taylor in U.S. Senate, August 1984, Committee on Labor and Human Resources, Subcommittee on Alcoholism and Drug Abuse, *Drugs and Terrorism, 1984* (Hearing Report 98-1046), pp. 27–49.

11. *RCMP National Drug Intelligence Estimate: 1983*, p. 38.

12. U.S. National Narcotics Intelligence Consumers Committee, *Narcotics Intelligence Estimate: 1982* (Washington, D.C.: GPO, 1983), pp. 15–16. See also Cuban American National Foundation, *Castro and the Narcotics Connection* (Washington, D.C., 1983).

13. Testimony of Clyde D. Taylor, *Drugs and Terrorism, 1984*, p. 43.

14. Testimony of DEA Administrator Francis M. Mullen, Jr., 2 August 1984, in *Drugs and Terrorism, 1984*, pp. 14–23. For an earlier discussion of drug–terrorist links by a DEA official with executive experience in Europe and the Middle East, see John Warner, "Terrorists and Drug Traffickers Develop Working Alliances; Trend Expected to Continue," in *Narcotics Control Digest*, 12 October 1983.

15. U.S. National Narcotics Intelligence Consumers Committee, *Narcotics Intelligence Estimate: 1983* (Washington, D.C.: GPO, 1984), figure 23.

16. Material enclosed in parentheses represents U.S. reactions to criminally perpetrated events and U.S. actions that may have provoked reaction by criminal organizations.

Section G
The Open Society: Response Options

12
Defensive Responses

Sam C. Sarkesian

errorism and unconventional conflicts are now a permanent feature of the international landscape.* In the long run, the dangers that such conflicts pose to open societies may be as serious as those posed by nuclear conflict. And as recent history has demonstrated, open societies are least prepared to respond to terrorism and unconventional conflicts.

The purpose of this chapter is to study the nature of unconventional conflicts, analyze the challenges these pose to an open society, and identify defensive measures necessary to respond effectively to such conflicts. The goal, however, is not to design an operational directive, but to develop concepts and guidelines that can be the basis for policy and strategy. As a preliminary step, we need to clarify the conceptual basis of unconventional conflict and the various terms associated with it. Without clarity and coherence, it is difficult to see how purposeful policies can be formulated and effective strategy designed to respond to terrorism and unconventional conflicts.

Concepts and Terminology

There is a considerable degree of confusion and disagreement regarding definitions and concepts of unconventional conflicts. In the United States, one school of thought has emerged which places all such conflicts under the rubric of special operations. A number of organizations reflect this perspective, such as the First Special Operations Command. A related theme, but one which has a different perspective, is the use of the term "low-intensity conflict" for all unconventional conflicts. This theme is reflected in the definition contained in the U.S. Army Field Manual, which describes low-intensity conflicts as "Conflicts ranging from terrorism, revolution, and counterrevolution

---

*The term unconventional conflict is used here as an introduction to the subject. Later, a clarification of this term and others will be the basis for developing a different set of categories and concepts.

to limited small war operations conducted by a political group to achieve a major political goal that can include the overthrow of the existing system and replacing it with a new leadership and political–social order."[1] Another school of thought gives little credence to the special nature of unconventional conflicts and places all conflicts of a lesser magnitude in the category of "small wars."[2]

Although there may be a degree of overlap and commonality, the differing perspectives of these various "schools" tend not only to confuse the distinction between unconventional and conventional conflicts, but also to perpetuate the mismatch between policy, strategy, and capability. While there are some corrective efforts underway, the danger is that the mismatch may become institutionalized before complete corrective action can be effective.

Even though unconventional conflicts may include a broad range of unorthodox conflicts, the most common and dangerous forms are terrorism and revolution, and their antitheses, counterterror and counterrevolution. These are the mainstays of unconventional conflicts, and need to be addressed in detail in any serious study of problems and dilemmas facing an open system.

Revolution and Counterrevolution

Even a cursory view of the literature reveals a variety of perspectives and conceptual formulations on revolution and counterrevolution.[3] Guerrilla war, partisan warfare, insurgency, wars of national liberation, people's war, internal war, and civil war are some of the terms used, many of them synonymously, to describe revolutionary and counterrevolutionary conflicts.

However, as Sir Robert Thompson points out: "Revolutionary war is most confused with guerrilla or partisan warfare. The main difference is that guerrilla warfare is designed merely to harass and distract the enemy so that the regular forces can reach a decision in conventional battles. . . . Revolutionary war on the other hand is designed to reach a decisive result on its own."[4]

Bernard Fall argued persuasively about the need to distinguish between various concepts associated with unconventional conflicts. According to Fall, "Just about anybody can start a 'little war' . . . even a New York street gang. Almost anybody can raid somebody else's territory . . . But all this has rarely produced the kind of revolutionary ground swell which simply swept away the existing government."[5]

These observations are the basis for the conceptual formulation used in this study. Revolution is a political-social challenge to the existing system in which unconventional warfare is employed along with any other means to change the fundamental political and social order. In brief, a revolutionary leadership and cadre, articulating a particular ideology that is "rooted" in the political-social grievances of the populace, undertakes to overthrow the existing system and its ruling elite for the purposes of institutionalizing a revolutionary system and ideology.

Terrorism

Terrorism is a fundamental part of the revolutionary and counterrevolutionary process. It is also a strategic and tactical concept of its own. As with the terms "revolution" and "counterrevolution," there is much disagreement on the meaning and concept of terrorism. A useful definition is offered by one scholar: "Terrorism . . . is violence, or threats of violence . . . designed to intimidate and sow fear throughout a target population in an effort to produce a pervasive atmosphere of insecurity, a widespread condition of anxiety."[6]

Terrorism is usually characterized by a variety of tactics, such as assassination, hijacking, kidnapping, sabotage, and the use of "innocent" victims to affect a third party. Terrorism, in short, is the creation of fear in a population in order to force the existing system to respond to the terrorists' demands and/or objectives.

Conflict Spectrum

These initial observations constitute important starting points in the systematic study of unconventional conflicts. However, the development of an effective response to such conflicts must be seen in a broader context. There can be (and usually are) linkages and interdependencies between most conflicts of varying degrees of magnitude. The Conflict Spectrum as shown in figure 12–1 provides a schematic categorization of conflicts, in general.[7]

On one end of the conflict spectrum are those conflicts least likely to develop into armed conflict, that is, acts of individual terrorists. On the opposite end is the ultimate in conflict—major nuclear war. For a clearer distinction between unconventional and other types of conflicts, the conflict spectrum identifies two major dimensions of unconventional conflicts from the U.S. perspective: special operations (terror and counterterror) and low-intensity conflicts (revolution and counterrevolution). Other types of conflicts are grouped into "conventional" and "nuclear." Figure 12–2 provides details of the unconventional conflict categories.

A clear delineation is difficult to make in categorizing conflicts in general and low-intensity conflicts in particular. Many times it is difficult to distinguish clearly between counterrevolutionary conflict and limited conventional wars, for example. Moreover, counterrevolutionary conflicts may include periodic limited conventional operations. Similarly, on the low intensity end of

Noncombat	Unconventional	Limited	Major
Shows of Force	Special Operations	Conventional	Conventional
Assistance	Low-Intensity Conflicts	Nuclear (?)	Nuclear

Figure 12–1. The Contemporary Conflict Spectrum

the conflict spectrum, it is not always easy to delineate the act of an individual terrorist from those conducted by revolutionary systems. Indeed, it is conceivable that a particular low-intensity conflict will include all categories in the low-intensity conflict spectrum. Further, these categorizations are not necessarily comprehensive descriptions of the nature of the conflict. The individual combatant in a low-intensity conflict may be exposed to intense conflict, and for such individuals, there is nothing "low" about the intensity of the conflict.

These categorizations are policy distinctions, designed to point out the political-military posture and perceptions of open societies with respect to low-intensity conflict. Additionally, the spectrum is intended to show general conceptual considerations. Thus, while counterrevolutions may include limited conventional operations and terrorism, the main thrust of such conflicts is to counter the revolutionary system and maintain and protect the existing political system and its socioeconomic underpinnings.

Special Operations and Low-Intensity Conflicts; Policy and Strategy

The distinctions between special operations and low-intensity conflicts need to be examined in detail for a clearer understanding of what these mean with respect to defensive measures implemented by open systems. Moreover, the conceptual basis for these categories must be studied regarding their relationship to terror and revolution. (See figure 12–2).

Special Operations

In the main, there are three patterns of terrorism; terror qua terror, revolutionary terror, and state-supported terrorism. "Terror qua terror" is generally the term applied to terrorist groups whose primary goal is the act itself and

*Noncombat	**Special Operations	Low-Intensity Conflicts	Conventional	Nuclear
		Revolution/ Counterrevolution	Limited Major	Limited Strategic
		················		
		***I II III IV		

---------------------------------- Most likely contingencies ----|

*Shows of force; Economic assistance and military advisors

**Hit-run raids, counterterror, rescue, spearhead

***Phase I: Combined economic and other nonmilitary assistance; weapons training teams, military advisory groups; beyond noncombat assistance

Phase II: Special forces teams + Phase I

Phase III: Special forces B, C, and D teams, U.S. ground troop commitment—defensive role + Phases I and II

Phase IV: Vietnam-type involvement

Figure 12–2. Revised Conflict Spectrum

whose principal purpose is the conduct of terror for the sake of terror. This pattern is seen, for example, in the Baader-Meinhof Gang and Japanese Red Army. Although there may be some immediate political goal attached to the act, there is rarely a coherent, purposeful, long-range political policy to which such terrorist groups adhere, except for rather hazy notions of equality for all people.

Revolutionary terror is a tactical concept that is employed by revolutionary systems. The terrorist act or the groups performing such acts are normally under the direction of a revolutionary system whose political purpose and objectives are relatively clear, such as the PLO, the IRA, the Vietcong. The terrorist act in this context is an extension of the revolution and is performed to assist the revolutionary struggle.

State-supported terrorism is a not so much a different terror concept as it is a means for a state to achieve certain political goals. Thus, a state may support any terrorist group if its objectives or tactics serve the state. Moreover, it is conceivable that a state may create a terrorist group for the specific purpose of serving the state. Support may range from financial resources to training facilities and actual operational direction. There are a variety of purposes for state-supported terrorism, including destabilization of a state or region, intimidation or threat, or coercive diplomacy.

Although specifically designed for counterterror operations, special operations evolve primarily from conventional roots employing Ranger- and

Commando-type units. Special operations missions include hit-and-run raids, hostage rescue, and spearhead operations such as Grenada. Many special operations can be conducted as a joint civilian-military undertaking. In brief, special operations tend to be "quick strike and withdrawal" in character, on a target or targets that are identifiable and limited in scope. This also characterizes the missions of units engaged in special operations—limited to achieve a particular short-range military or political-military purpose.[8]

Low-Intensity Conflicts

Low-intensity conflicts are revolutionary and counterrevolutionary situations that are usually protracted and differ considerably from conventional conflicts and special operations. Revolutions are aimed at overthrowing the existing system and putting into place a revolutionary leadership and ideology. The general strategy includes unconventional warfare combined with political mobilization and psychological warfare. The center of gravity of revolution is in the political-social milieu of society. Moreover, revolution contains its own morality and ethics. Success of the revolution is the ultimate morality—any means used to achieve this goal is ipso facto held to be moral and ethical.

Counterrevolution is difficult to conceptualize except as strategy in response to revolution. Although evolving from the same patterns as revolution, counterrevolution differs in purpose, organization, targets, and political-strategic posture. The most effective counterrevolutionary strategy is effective government and all that this entails with respect to leadership, effectiveness of governing instruments, and responsiveness to popular grievances.

The effectiveness of defensive measures undertaken by open societies in response to terror and low-intensity conflicts must evolve directly from the understanding of these concepts and distinctions. Otherwise, as has been emphasized earlier, policy, strategy, and organizational response are likely to be misdirected. What is equally important, passive measures taken under misconceived notions of the nature and character of the threat can lead to unanticipated and unacceptable consequences, such as the attack on the U.S. Marine Peacekeeping force in Beirut.

Nature and Character of Open Systems

A serious study of political systems, their ideologies, and their internal styles reveals a variety of "types" of open and closed systems. A more realistic formulation should include those systems that are striving to establish democratic foundations even though they are not currently "open" to the same degree as liberal democracies. Systems that have not developed all of the institutions or cultural requisites of a democracy may be seriously pursuing such objectives. It is conceivable, for example, that existing military systems are precursors of more democratic systems, as has been the case in several states in the Southern Hemisphere, in particular, Uruguay. It is also important to note that a number of military and "rightwing" systems have been replaced by fledging democracies. But as yet, no established Marxist–Leninist system has been replaced by popular democracies or more open systems. Nonetheless, such leftwing authoritarian systems are vulnerable to, and can be influenced by, internal as well as external forces.

Requisites of an Open System

There are a variety of ways in which political systems can be studied according to their open or closed nature. Edward Shils has published one excellent study.[9] Using four elements as a framework—nature of the elite, focus of authority, civil order, and public opinion—Shils identifies five types of systems: political democracy, tutelary democracy, traditional oligarchy, modernizing oligarchy, and totalitarian oligarchy. An analysis of these systems reveals a number of important characteristics of open systems.

First, the commitment to the rule of law is essential. This does not mean that all of the values that are part of Western liberal democracies must be incorporated into a particular system. It does mean, however, that the actions of officials and political-military instruments must adhere to some standard of law that is widely accepted and recognized. Not only does such a condition create the basis for developing a comprehensive rule of law, but it creates a sense of predictability based on the idea that one need not "fear" the government. This implies of course that unacceptable action by the instruments of government can be challenged in a court of law, through other institutions, or by nonviolent political actions.

Second, there must be a critical mass of officials, bureaucrats, police, and military leaders who are committed to the idea of an open society. From this a leadership elite can evolve at all levels that insures control and proper behavior of instruments designed to implement policy.

Third, there must be a general sense on the part of the populace, especially major political actors (such as labor union leaders, church officials, and opposition leaders, for example) that the system can be changed peacefully and that there is some stake in maintaining the system's existence as it moves toward more "openness."

Fourth, the government's police and intelligence instruments must operate in accord with some basic rules of law and sensitivity to individual rights. At the same time the populace and major political actors must have a sense of confidence in the government's ability to control such instruments. Further, there must be some degree of confidence by nongovernment political actors that there is legitimate recourse should governmental actors break the law.

Fifth and finally, a clear movement toward a pluralistic system is a key sign of "openness." This does not necessarily mean ethnic or racial pluralism, but political pluralism. There must be an accepted legal basis supporting the evolution of political groups who can challenge the rulers in accordance with the accepted "rules of the game." In brief, there must be some movement toward broadening the political base and expanding the meaning of legal political activity. This in turn must be accompanied by a general acceptance of rational "rules of the game."

Obviously no system, regardless of how open it may be, is perfect in any of these ways. But the essential point is the commitment of a critical mass of leaders, elite, and major political actors to these (or most of these) characteristics. Moreover, in liberal democracies, there are many other considerations that institutionalize the rule of law, justice, individual worth, and control of governmental institutions. But the characteristics noted here are minimum in categorizing systems with respect to their "openness." Political democracy is clearly an open system. It can also be argued that tutelary democracy is a type of open system, albeit in a much narrower sense.

Compared to closed systems, open systems are constrained to varying degrees in dealing with terrorism and revolution. In brief, if such systems expect to maintain their legitimacy and direction, they must adhere to democratic characteristics to some degree, even under the most severe crises. Only in terms of perceived national survival can such systems change their character without threatening their legitimacy. The problems, therefore, in trying to adopt measures in response to terrorism and revolution are compounded by the very nature of open systems. In the case of tutelary democracies, there is always the danger that heavy-handed response to terrorism and revolution will lead to repressive measures throughout the system. This, in turn, not only tends to lead to ineffective counterrevolutionary strategies, but usually establishes the basis for authoritarianism. In the case of political democracies such as the United States, the problems of dealing with unconventional conflicts are particularly difficult and complex, even though the possibility of repression and authoritarian response is considerably less, if not nonexistent.

The American Perspective

Many Americans, as is the case of virtually all open societies, have not been able to grasp the essentials of unconventional conflict. Conflicts tend to be seen through conventional lenses and evolve from historical experiences associated with "big battles" and wars reminiscent of World War II. Consequently, a great deal of intellectual effort, policy planning, and defense expenditures are aimed at strategic nuclear scenarios or major conventional battles across Europe. While there is some attention now being given to "small wars," these also tend to be seen through conventional lenses. Indeed, the very label of "small war" is in itself a version of limited conventional wars. It is used as a "catchall" by some to cover both conventional conflicts of a lesser magnitude and unconventional conflicts.[10]

The American experience in war tends to perpetuate a "Pearl Harbor" mentality. Thus, the outbreak of war is usually associated with a visible and major attack or critical event in which the United States is a major actor. In turn, there are expectations that the enemy must be clearly identifiable, the challenge must be serious and immediate, America's policy and purpose clear, and the goals conclusive.

Open Systems: Conflicts, Contradictions, and Dilemmas

The policy and strategy of an open system's defensive measures in response to unconventional conflicts are conditioned by the contradictory and dialectical impact created by two fundamental forces: the nature of an open society and the character of terrorism and revolution. In brief, open systems must adhere to certain norms in determining policy ends, means (strategy), operational doctrine, and behavior of its representatives and soldiers. The socialization process within society determines to a great extent the mindsets and behavior patterns of those charged with planning and carrying out political-military policy. Equally important, performance criteria evolve from democratic principles. Finally, the socialization process of open systems reflects democratic values, creates restraints on government, and conditions its public servants accordingly.

As a result, open systems that are engaged in special operations and low-intensity conflicts, particularly in a third-power role in a host state, are placed in highly disadvantageous positions. On the one hand, the purpose of those engaged in terrorism and revolution is to overthrow the existing system or, at the least, to achieve a particular political goal outside of the existing system. The strategy and doctrine designed to carry out such goals are bound neither by conventional "rules of the game" nor by the dictates of open systems. Such conflicts are "no-holds-barred" struggles which are usually protracted and unconventional.

Because open systems, conditioned by the norms of democracy and the close relationship between ends and means, tend to perceive unconventional conflicts through conventional lenses they are not well postured to engage in protracted and unconventional conflicts. The same is true for systems of varying degrees of openness, even though the constraints and limitations on such systems may be less rigid or more narrowly defined. In the final analysis, these contradictions create a fundamental dilemma for open societies that are trying to implement effective defensive measures against terrorism and revolution.

Defensive Measures

Generally speaking, defensive measures are primarily those that are designed to create a protective barrier or security screen around critical targets and political actors of the state in order to raise the stakes and increase the costs for those engaged in terrorism or revolution. Most authorities agree that such passive measures alone are not enough to succeed against determined adversaries. However, defensive measures can provide the base upon which policies and strategies can be designed and implemented to counter those who are arrayed against open societies. Thus, both active and defensive measures must be components of any effective policy and strategy.

America in a Third-Power Role

Many times open systems become involved in special operations and low-intensity conflicts in support of other states, known as host states. In such circumstances, the role of open systems must evolve from political-military policy and strategy aimed at reinforcing the effectiveness of the existing system, that is, the host state. This includes a commitment to increasing the degree of openness. Thus, the third-power role must be seen as supportive, with an emphasis upon economic development, political-psychological support, and increasing governmental efficiency. In contrast to special operations, support in low-intensity conflicts must be conceived in terms of long-range policy and encompass virtually the entire political-social system of the host state.

The international aspects of special operations and low-intensity conflicts can place the United States in several roles, encompassing a number of dimensions. With respect to special operations, the United States usually acts as a third power conducting joint special operations with other friendly states against terrorists or as conducting unilateral special operations against terrorists with the agreement or acquiescence of a third state(s), which may include acting in an advisory role. In low-intensity conflicts, the United States is likely to be involved as a third power intervening on behalf and in support of an existing system (host state) or as a primary partner involved in one degree or another in support of those conducting low-intensity conflict in a third-country environment. The study of defensive measures in their international dimensions must be seen in this context. Further, open systems other than the United States may be faced with similar issues, even though such systems may be "qualified" open systems (or even reflect some characteristics of authoritarian systems) and conditioned by less rigid standards of conduct than liberal democracies.

There are at least four major dimensions of defensive measures associated with open societies: policy coherency, the intelligence component, organizational strategy, and multinational efforts. Each of these has its equivalent active dimension.

Policy Coherency

The basis for any coherent policy rests on a number of considerations, including perceptions of the threat, the development of policy and strategy within the bounds of open systems, and the need to explain clearly the nature of the threat to the populace at large in order to establish support for policy and strategy. If the most effective means to respond in special operations and low-intensity conflicts, even in their defensive dimensions, requires greater latitude in terms of policy and strategy, how can this be done or supported in open systems?

According to one authority, the protection and survival of open systems requires a morality that transcends legalistic notions and hypermoralism.[11] The problem is that the most effective policies and strategies, even in their defensive dimensions, may appear to some to violate or threaten the notion of democratic morality and ethics. For example, collecting information on possible terrorist groups may require close scrutiny of a variety of groups, some of which may be nonterrorist groups. Yet the very act of information collection by intelligence agencies on legitimate groups runs counter to democratic norms. Unless there is some fundamental understanding of the nature and character of unconventional conflicts, strategies such as information collection can be so interpreted and constrained as to make them useless. The problems are compounded when applying these considerations to the whole range of defensive measures across the unconventional conflict spectrum. Without some degree of agreement within the governing circles and without some understanding and acceptance by major political actors of the nature of terrorism and revolution, it is unlikely that reasonably effective defensive measures can be implemented.

An important task, therefore, for elected officials and policy makers of open systems is to provide the necessary information regarding the nature of terrorism and revolution so that these can be articulated, assessed, and understood by political actors. The long-range commitment (staying power) of open systems to engage in special operations and low-intensity conflicts is in no small measure based on the ability of elected officials and policymakers to articulate policies and strategies that develop a consensus within the body politic. Advocacy and political mobilization by those in government is probably necessary to achieve even a minimal consensus. But this in turn may incur political costs over the long run, depending upon the outcome of the involvement.

In brief, open systems contain a variety of countervailing powers—for example, the War Powers Act, budgetary control, and Congressional oversight—arrayed against the executive power, the military, and other operational instruments that can considerably limit or constrain the scope of defensive measures and the aggressiveness with which these are pursued. In order to engage in conflicts that stretch the notion of democracy and are likely to be protracted, a consensus must be developed within the populace in general regarding the nature of the threat and the policy and strategy designed to respond to it. This consensus must be based on realistic views regarding morality, ethics, and the survival of the open system. This is particularly the case with respect to the role of intelligence.

The Intelligence Component

It is self-evident that knowledge of the "enemy" is necessary before effective defensive measures can be developed and implemented. Thus, an effective intelligence system is the *sine qua non* of effective defensive measures. Therefore, it is commonplace to declare that the ability of an open system to respond to terrorism and revolution is a function of its intelligence capability. In actual practice, however, it is usually the case that intelligence operations must be balanced with the demands of an open system. It is the attempt to balance these notions, which are at times quite contradictory, that creates difficult problems with respect to policy, strategy, and effective implementation of countermeasures.

America's Intelligence System. The intelligence community in the United States includes a variety of intelligence agencies, such as the Defense Intelligence Agency and those of the various services. However, the Central Intelligence Agency (CIA) is the most well known to the American public as well as to foreigners, and is the focal point of most strategic intelligence.

Although some changes have been made in the Central Intelligence Agency's organizational structure since its creation in 1947, the basic structure has remained intact. As one authority, Stafford Thomas, concludes:

> The internal composition of the CIA changes from time to time. While it is not always in a state of flux, no description of CIA structures is immutable. Likewise, the activities or functions of the Agency expand and contract over time, especially in terms of emphasis. The salience of any one part of the CIA will vary with the importance of the activity it performs. So, the internal dynamics of the CIA are not rigid. Despite this dynamic character, certain

structures and functions are constant, although names and jurisdictions may change.[12]

The general organization of the CIA is shown in figure 12–3. The main concern here is the Directorate of Operations, since this includes the Counterintelligence Staff.

The Deputy Director of Operations (DDO) has three staffs under his jurisdiction: the Foreign Intelligence Staff, the Counterintelligence Staff, and the Covert Action Staff. Thomas states:

> The Foreign Intelligence Staff is concerned with espionage especially HUMINT or the collection of information by human means . . . The Counterintelligence Staff is primarily concerned with protecting U.S. intelligence, and especially the CIA, from "penetration" by foreign intelligence services, especially the Soviet KGB . . . The Covert Action Staff is responsible for planning and executing the actions against foreign governments or other actors . . . which the U.S. government, and especially the President, wants to deny undertaking.[13]

As noted earlier, counterintelligence and covert operations are closely linked, particularly since most experts agree that defensive measures alone (counterintelligence information) are insufficient to deter a determined adversary. There has been a continuing controversy in the United States regarding covert operations and the extent to which passive measures are inextricably linked to active measures. It is the area of counterintelligence and covert operations that raises the greatest controversy. Thus, the Directorate of Operations remains the most controversial part of the CIA, and the DDO usually is on the "hot seat" with respect to oversight and intelligence activities. The dilemmas and problems of intelligence, particularly counterintelligence, evolving from its relationship to the system are part of the larger problem faced by open systems in trying to respond to terrorism and revolution.

America's Intelligence Dilemma. The experience of the United States over the past decade in trying to cope with external unconventional threats is illustrative of the problems faced by open systems in general. The public and governmental reaction to the Watergate Affair and Vietnam, carrying well over into the Carter administration, created virtual chaos in the intelligence community, particularly in the counterintelligence effort.

During the period from the end of the Vietnam War to the end of 1970, the intelligence community was under constant pressure from a variety of sources. First, the Executive Branch attempted to implement strict controls over intelligence activities. Second, Congress established a series of rules and oversight procedures intended to create broad legislative supervision over the

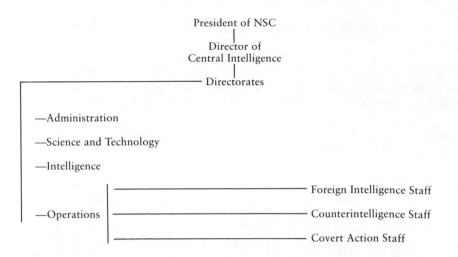

For a detailed description see Stafford T. Thomas, *The U.S. Intelligence Community* (Lanham, Md.: University Press of America, 1983), ch. 4. See also Ray S. Cline, *The CIA Under Reagan, Bush & Casey* (Washington, D.C.: Acropolis Books, 1981), ch. 7.

Figure 12–3. CIA Organization—The Directorates

intelligence community. Third, the American people were exposed to a barrage of media criticism of intelligence activities. Combined with the attempt by a variety of groups to discredit the intelligence community, a high degree of mistrust and skepticism developed within the body politic of intelligence operations, as Thomas writes:

> In 1975 the community was the object of intense public scrutiny unparalleled in history. No country had ever subjected its secret organs of government to such open and extensive review . . . The Congressional Committees conducted their business openly and publicly, adopted an adversarial, accusatory, an investigative approach, and, perhaps, inevitably and irresistibly, dramatized its proceedings . . . It rarely acknowledged any legitimate reasons for clandestine operations and operated under the assumptions that most clandestine or secret activities were indefensible.[14]

The effectiveness of the Central Intelligence Agency was eroded considerably under the Carter administration, not only as a result of diminished human resources, but also because of the impact of events on the morale and prestige of the Agency. Moreover, a series of constraints, both legal and political, were put into place, many of which remain today. This tended to create a "chilling effect" on operations and developed a cautious and legalistic intelligence mindset. Thus, many intelligence personnel became more concerned with operating according to a strict interpretation of the law, than with developing innovative and imaginative concepts and procedures. It is safe to say that this was (and is) part of the larger problem of the role of intelligence in an open system. One authority concludes:

> The US is on the horns of a dilemma. Foreign intelligence agents operate in our midst, and we are faced with a hostile adversary. Defensive measures remain inadequate in the face of criticism by those who view them as endangering civil liberties. Counterintelligence is thus hamstrung, ill-defined and misunderstood, organizationally fragmented and unequal to the task of protecting our institutions.[15]

The intelligence community is partly to blame for some of these problems. Throughout the community, various intelligence agencies hesitate to share information, much less cooperate in the intelligence function. Not only is this a result of bureaucratic "turf" protection, but it also reflects the natural reluctance of the "intelligence" mind to expose information sources and the tendency to apply a rigid "need to know" doctrine even in dealing with other friendly intelligence agencies.

This creates real operational problems. As one authority noted with respect to the "putative discovery of the Soviet brigade in Cuba . . . The (intelligence) community's performance during this episode . . . epitomizes the tendency of each agency to expand its own collection and processing capability and to restrict dissemination of the product."[16]

Compounding the problem is the fact that very few Americans, including many elected officials and policymakers, recognize the importance of counterintelligence to the entire intelligence component. Fewer still would accept the proposition that aggressive counterintelligence and covert operations institutionalized within appropriate governing institutions are essential to the maintenance of an open system.

Counterintelligence. Counterintelligence epitomizes the problems of intelligence in an open system. Yet, even for experts in the field, trying to define counterintelligence is difficult. "Unfortunately there seems to be no easy way to explain counterintelligence . . . effective counterintelligence is a combination of so many aspects of the intelligence business and other political, military, economic and social factors . . ." one expert states.[17]

Therefore, any definition of counterintelligence must be broad and encompassing. In this respect, counterintelligence can be seen as

> The art of examining the entire spectrum of enemy intelligence activities in the light of enemy intelligence strategy, our own national objectives and the performance of our own and allied intelligence and counterintelligence ser-

vices, for the purpose of devising better means of advancing our policies and protecting our nation from espionage, subversion, disinformation and deception and adverse military and political and economic actions.[18]

In specific terms, counterintelligence is the element within the intelligence component that is most critical to defensive measures since it encompasses personnel security, physical security, and counterespionage. The first two parts are self-explanatory and do not generally evoke a great deal of controversy, except when these are carried so far as to violate the "individual" and intrude upon his/her sense of dignity. However, most authorities do not believe that these alone can provide long-term effective defensive measures. According to one view,

> Protection of personnel and facilities is essentially passive in nature. Experience has shown that these measures alone will ultimately be defeated by a determined and resourceful enemy. The third component of counterintelligence is concerned with the penetration of the intelligence organization of the enemy in order to ascertain what he is trying to accomplish, how he is doing it, and how successful he has become.[19]

It is the third part—counterespionage—that reinforces the first two parts and is the "cutting edge" of defensive measures. It is also the part that creates the most controversy because of its highly secretive nature and its tendency to develop directly into active measures, particularly covert operations.

In sum, because counterintelligence is a response to attempts by "others" to penetrate and affect the American government, it is seen by many outside the field of intelligence specialists as a passive measure. Nonetheless, even the most "aggressive" passive measures cannot be realistically separated from active measures. The intensity with which passive measures are implemented and the aggressiveness with which the means are employed to penetrate enemy structures may necessarily require an active strategy and doctrine.

Guidelines for Effective Defensive Measures

The study of passive measures undertaken by open systems against terrorism and revolution includes the analysis of at least three components: the nature and character of terrorism and revolution, the nature of open systems, and the relationship between active and passive measures.

The first component requires conceptual coherency regarding the nature of the threats and their relationship to other conflicts along the conflict spectrum. The second component requires an understanding not only of the meaning of open systems, but also of their nature and character, and what these mean with respect to policy, strategy, and doctrine. The third component focuses attention on the meaning of passive and active measures, and their various linkages.

The conclusion to be drawn from this analysis is that the systems that are the most open are in the most vulnerable and disadvantageous position with respect to special operations and low-intensity conflicts. While a variety of passive measures can be undertaken, there is compelling evidence that such measures by themselves are not enough to "win" against a determined adversary.

The close connection between passive and active measures tends to trigger a counterreaction by a variety of political actors in an open system, particularly with respect to human rights and moral and ethical norms. This becomes acute if passive measures are carried out purposefully and aggressively since they tend naturally to spill over into active measures. Not only is such activity likely to trigger domestic reaction, it is also likely to cause serious concern among various groups in Congress, leading to pressure on the intelligence community to limit and rigidly control operations. Overall, such reaction is likely to have a "chilling effect" on the aggressiveness with which intelligence functions are undertaken.

Only if the international security situation or specific aspects of American policy are seen as "crises" or as clear threats to American security interests is it likely that intelligence agencies will be in a position to broaden their activities. Nonetheless, there is sufficient concern within the American political system about adversaries and a recognition of the importance of intelligence to provide a basis for developing an effective intelligence structure within the context of democracy. But this is contingent upon the ability to develop conceptual coherency about the nature and character of the threat, the design of instrumentalities within the political system capable of developing and implementing coherent policies to respond to such threats, the clear articulation of these to the American people, and the effective implementation of strategies for special operations and low-intensity conflicts.

While there are a number of recommendations that evolve from this chapter, four are particularly important. First and foremost, there must develop within political and military policymaking circles a realistic understanding of the nature and character of terrorism and revolution, and their antitheses. This must translate into congruent policy, strategy, and operational capability. Further, clear and comprehensible policy and strategy options must be articulated to major political actors within domestic politics. To be sure, this necessitates "prudent" advocacy. Such advocacy may not insure the acceptance of the policy or develop the necessary political consensus in support of special operations and low-intensity conflicts. But at a minimum, it may affect the direction of the debate, broaden the understanding of the public, and shape the agenda toward a more concerted effort in responding to terrorism and revolution.

Second, policymakers, both civilian and military, as well as those in the operational component, must develop a realistic understanding of the nature and character of open systems (for instance, their moral and ethical underpinnings) and how these affect the ability to conduct special operations and low-intensity conflicts. The relationships and dynamics between open systems and the demands of special operations and low-intensity conflicts must, in turn, be projected into the public realm, and particularly to major political actors.

Third, since terrorism and low-intensity conflicts are not the exclusive responsibility of either the military or the civilian sector, there must be a joint planning and operational structure that effectively coordinates all military and civilian agencies for implementing special operations for low-intensity conflicts. Organizational strategy and the institutionalization of counterintelligence within such a strategy are in themselves important passive measures.

Fourth, the concept of counterintelligence and its passive and active dimensions must be institutionalized within the intelligence community as well as within policymaking circles. This is not a call for a central counterintelligence function (as defined in this chapter). Rather, it is simply the recognition that counterintelligence is a fundamental part of the intelligence function and must be part of every intelligence activity, particularly special operations and low-intensity conflicts.

Finally, defensive measures undertaken by open societies can include everything associated with "good" government. Clearly there are a number of specific defensive measures—such as intelligence collection, physical security, and security of personnel. Most of these are reasonably well known. But as has been suggested repeatedly, by themselves these measures are inadequate to defeat a determined adversary. Passive measures are considerably strengthened simply by the process of study and dialogue triggered by the analysis of the concepts of special operations and low-intensity conflicts as suggested here. If nothing more, the dialogue and analysis created by such an effort increases the awareness and broadens the sensitivity of policymakers and the American people. Such efforts can be important components of defensive measures.

It is still not certain that the United States has recovered from earlier intelligence failures and self-destruction. Nor is there any assurance that the emerging intelligence system and American political-military posture will be effective in undertaking special operations or low-intensity conflicts. The ends/means morality and ethical linkages remain critical in assessing American policy and strategy, as they do in open systems in general. Yet it is also true that terrorism and revolution are strategic conflicts that are likely to be part of the international security landscape for years to come. As such, they must be seen in long-range terms. Moreover, the increase in international terrorism and the continuing revolutionary and counterrevolutionary conflicts in Southeast Asia, Central America, Black Africa, and Afghanistan have sensitized a number of major political actors in the United States to the need for a more effective political-military posture and intelligence effort. There are bounds beyond which political-military and intelligence instruments cannot go without fear of destroying their credibility and legitimacy in the eyes of many Americans. Unless measured against these broader dimensions, the passive measures employed by open systems are likely to be misdirected, misunderstood, and ineffective.

To presume, however, that democracies must rigidly adhere to strict application of law, even to the point of self-destruction, is the height of immorality. Equally presumptuous is the view that democracy should take no action unless a clear and present danger exists. The very nature of terrorism, revolution, counterterror, and counterrevolution precludes the notion of clear and present danger in conventional terms. The onset of such conflicts usually indicates the existence of well-established groups already enmeshed within the political-social system. In other words, if we wait until there is a clear and present danger, it may be too late. Even if it is not too late, waiting for a clear outbreak of conflict may place the open system in an extremely disadvantageous position, considerably raising the costs of effective response.

Defensive measures, therefore, must go beyond filling sandbags and placing them around embassies or putting on bulletproof vests. Effective measures must also include recognition of the nature of unconventional threats, conceptual coherency underlying policy and strategy, a broad view of the role of intelligence, a strategy of public education, appropriate organizational design and capabilities, and broad-ranging multinational efforts.

The traditions of governmental responsibility and accountability together with the other fundamental values of the United States can furnish the basis for developing effective arrangements for oversight, control, and accountability of the political-military instruments that are a part of special operations and low-intensity conflicts. To do anything less is to create a self-destructive syndrome in which the United States and other pluralistic societies would be destroyed by the perpetrators of terrorism representating antithetical political systems and values.

Notes

1. *Low Intensity Conflict,* FM 100-20 (Washington, D.C.: Department of the Army, January, 1981).

2. See, for example, Eliot A. Cohen, "Constraints on America's Conduct of Small Wars," *International Security* 9 (Fall 1984): 151–81.

3. See, for example, Sam C. Sarkesian, "American Policy on Revolution an Counterrevolution: A Review of the Themes in the Literature," *Conflict 5*, no. 2 (1984): 137–84.

4. Sir Robert Thompson, *Revolutionary Wars in World Strategy 1945–1969* (New York: Taplinger Publishing Co., 1970), pp. 16–17.

5. Bernard Fall, *Street Without Joy: Insurgency in Indochina, 1946–63*, 3rd rev. ed. (Harrisburg, Pa.: The Stackpole Co., 1963), p. 356.

6. Neil C. Livingstone, *The War Against Terrorism* (Lexington, Mass.: Lexington Books, 1982), p. 4.

7. For a more detailed study of the conflict spectrum, see Sam C. Sarkesian, *America's Forgotten Wars; The Counterrevolutionary Past and Lessons for the Future,* (Westport, Conn.: Greenwood Press, 1984), pp. 229–48.

8. For an excellent overview of the problems posed to the United States with respect to terrorism and response, see Brian Michael Jenkins, "The US Response to Terrorism: A Policy Dilemma," in *Armed Forces Journal International* (April 1985): 39–45. The author states, for example, "The US needs to improve its machinery for planning and orchestrating a campaign against state-sponsored terrorism. The US has the components, each with its own specific responsibilities and expertise, but who puts the whole thing together?" (p. 45).

9. Edward Shils, *Political Development in New States* (The Hague: Mouton and Co., 1965).

10. See, for example, Cohen, "Constraints."

11. Claes G. Ryn, "The Ethical Problem of Democratic Statecraft," in *Power, Principles & Interests; A Reader in World Politics* ed. Jeffrey Salmon, James P. O'Leary, and Richard Shultz (Lexington, Mass.: Ginn Press, 1985), p. 119. See also Jean-Francois Revel, *How Democracies Perish* (Garden City, N.J.: Doubleday & Co., 1983).

12. Stafford T. Thomas, *The U.S. Intelligence Community* (Lanham, Md.: University Press of America, 1983), p. 46.

13. Ibid., p. 60.

14. Ibid., p. 82.

15. Newton S. Miller, "Counterintelligence at the Crossroads," in *Intelligence Requirements for the 1980's: Elements of Intelligence*, ed. Roy C. Godson, Rev. ed. (Washington, D.C.: National Strategy Information Center, 1983), p. 45.

16. Allan E. Goodman, "Fixing the Intelligence Mess," in *Foreign Policy*, no. 57 (Winter 1984–85): 177.

17. Roy C. Godson, ed., *Intelligence Requirements for the 1980s: Counterintelligence* (Washington, D.C.: National Strategy Information Center, 1980), p. 41.

18. Ibid.

19. Norman L. Smith, "Counterintelligence Organization and Operational Security in the 1980s," *Intelligence Requirements for the 1980's: Counterintelligence,* ed. Roy C. Godson (Washington, D.C.: National Strategy Information Center, 1980), p. 214.

13
Vulnerabilities of the International Support Apparatus

Uri Ra'anan

My focus is primarily on operations in the Third World, conducted by states and/or movements, assisted by Soviet surrogates and/or Soviet military and security elements themselves, and underpinned by Soviet hardware, logistics, and training. The other aspect of this work—the predominantly urban warfare carried on in primarily developed areas—is addressed in other chapters. The reason for my approach is that I believe it to be difficult and possibly counterproductive to come up with hard and fast definitions and distinctions between Soviet-supported "Local Wars," Soviet and/or surrogate-assisted "National Liberation Movements," and terrorist activities in the more narrow and classical sense of the term. Indeed, Soviet politico-military strategic literature does not draw any rigid distinctions between this welter of generally nonconventional activities supported by the USSR, and it behooves us, therefore, to present the role of all of this *Gestalt* in Soviet concepts and plans.

It may be appropriate first to emphasize how high a place on the agenda of Soviet operations and policies is given to this gamut of activities. During the addresses heard in Moscow at the time of Konstantin Chernenko's demise, an especially prominent role was played by the concept and the term "revolutionary democracies"—the code word since the 1960s for Soviet-supported states and movements outside the immediate confines of the Bloc itself.

However, there are indicators of a more solemn and durable kind as to the significance of this topic in the eyes of the Soviet leadership. Both the CPSU Party Program, dating back to Khrushchev's time, and the much more recent "Brezhnev" Constitution (Article 28), address this aspect of Soviet overall strategy. The latter states that "The foreign policy of the USSR is directed at . . . supporting the struggle of peoples for national liberation and social progress, at preventing aggressive wars . . ." This can be understood fully only in the context of the fact that, in other basic Soviet documents, including Marshal Grechko's last work, "aggressive wars" are defined by their *class* content, and not by the question: Who initiated a particular conflict and who is attempting the existing balance? All wars, according to this definition, are "just" as far as members of the Soviet Bloc and their Third World clients are concerned, whereas all attempts by the other side to resist are "unjust." Moreover, the issue of whether a struggle should or should not be deemed supportive of "national liberation and social progress" is decided subjectively, that is by the Soviet leadership itself. It is hardly necessary to emphasize how thin a dividing line separates "struggles" marked by terrorist operations from those that are described by many as "guerrilla" warfare.

There are other indicators of the constant intensification of the Soviet commitment to this particular aspect of an unrelenting (if not uniformly successful) drive for what the Chinese leadership has described so elegantly as "global hegemonism." Particular attention should be devoted to the geographical extension of the "Brezhnev Doctrine" (defined perhaps more precisely as the "Doctrine of Irreversibility," meaning that the overthrow or replacement of pro-Soviet regimes or the defeat of a pro-Soviet movement "in the field" constitute in themselves unacceptable "aggression" irrespective of where such a regime or movement may be located). In effect, that extension preceeded even the actual enunciation of the Doctrine and the rise to power of Brezhnev himself, since, to be historically accurate, this is what lay at the core of the Cuban Missile Crisis. It has become accepted wisdom that this Crisis terminated in a Western victory; what seems to be overlooked is that Khrushchev's publicly declared aim was to ensure that the implantation of a Soviet client regime in the Western Hemisphere could not be undone, and the upshot of the October 1962 confrontation was precisely a perceived commitment by the Administration that the United States would not use force to remove Castro from power. Thus, in effect, the Doctrine of Irreversibility received a Western imprimatur even before it was formally articulated.

Equally significant is the fact that this geographical extension of the countries and movements covered by the Doctrine has been underpinned ideologically by the practice, begun in the 1961 CPSU Twenty-Second Congress, of inviting (Third World) leaders and parties that are not communist themselves to participate as candidate members, so to speak, in gatherings that were confined previously to communist parties and leaders alone. The clear implication of this departure is that, by virtue of the recognition of their new status, these movements and states were to be considered sufficiently close to the international communist movement iself to merit the "umbrella" provided by the Doctrine. To assume otherwise is to ignore the importance in Soviet eyes of the symbolism highlighted in this manner.

Other indicators which illustrate the steady expansion of the outer parameters of Soviet operations and commitments to support the "National Liberation Movement" in all its emanations can be seen in the directives of the Soviet Navy—the most visible of the armed services directly involved in such activities—particularly where logistics, including sea lift, are concerned.

As is so often the case in the USSR, these operational directives find expression in slogans that are published on such occasions as Red Navy Day, in midsummer, and on other appropriate dates. It is notable that the Navy's mission slogan, which spoke of "Defense of the Motherland" in Stalin's time and changed to "Defense of Soviet State Interests" in the Khrushchev period, was escalated subsequently to read "The Enhancement of Soviet Prestige and Influence," a concept reminiscent of British Gunboat Diplomacy in the period during which that country truly was the world's hegemonial power. The new mission relates particularly to support for the National Liberation Movement, that is, quantum jumps in "soviet prestige and influence" by means of significant accretions to the Soviet "sphere."

There are two other indicators of intensification of Soviet operations in the Third World: 1) the absolute and relative escalation of the quality of Soviet military hardware transferred to "revolutionary democratic" states and movements, as well as the quantity of such arms; and 2) the injection by Communist regimes of combat personnel into areas of sharp East–West conflict outside the immediate Warsaw Pact–NATO Central Front. To repeat, these regions provide the stage for the National Liberation Movement in all its emanations: "local war," "movements" fighting in the bush, and terrorism proper.

Thus, weapons transferred to Third World recipients in the mid-1950s consisted of World War II hardware that was beginning to be phased out as obsolete from the arsenals of the Red Army and its allies. By the end of that decade, arms shipped to the Middle East and elsewhere still were in use in Warsaw Pact countries, although beginning to be obsolescent and due to be replaced in the not-too-distant future. By the 1960s, the materiel in question still was in full use in the Bloc, even though more modern prototypes had made their appearance. By the 1970s, and, especially in the last five years, the USSR has been equipping countries such as Syria, Libya, and Iraq with items that, in many instances, have not yet been received by Moscow's allies in the Warsaw Pact, and which the Soviet Union itself has only just deployed. Consequently, today such Third World conflict arenas hardly lag behind the European Central Theater itself where weapons sophistication (excepting nuclear weapons) is concerned.

In quantitative terms, it is noteworthy that the arsenal, in armor alone, of a country such as Syria now exceeds in size the number of tanks employed in the world's largest armored battle heretofore—the Battle of Kursk, between the Red Army and the German Reichswehr. This situation is extremely worrisome. These quantities exceed the current absorptive capacity of the recipient's armed forces (probably even after expansion of manpower). Consequently, one has to assume that such weapons are being prepositioned for transfer to various National Liberation Movements or for use by communist surrogates or even by Soviet combat units themselves. In this context it may be worth recalling the situation of October 24–25, 1973, when several Soviet airborne divisions took off in the general direction of the Middle East (in a very noisy and demonstrative fashion, by the way), but without the air lift capacity to make this demonstration truly credible since only the men and not the hardware, could be transported rapidly. Prepositioning, under some double key system, would take care of this problem, of course, and suggests the grim prospect of Soviet combat units being deployed in such centers of instability. Even without this factor, however, the developments described have sinister implications, if only because the USSR has always boasted that, unlike the United States, it transfers weapons "without strings attached"— that is, without the prohibition imposed by Congressional legislation that such hardware may be used only for legitimate self-defense and internal security. In other words, if you want to launch an offensive against your neighbor or your government, the USSR will not veto such use of Soviet-manufactured arms.

These developments, moreover, have to be viewed within the context of another form of Soviet escalation in which the resort to surrogates has played an important role. With our very limited institutional memories, many may have forgotten by now the June 22, 1973 *Agreement Between the United States of America and the Union of Soviet Socialist Republics on the Prevention of Nuclear War*, which stated, in part, that "The parties agree . . . that each party will refrain from the threat or use of force against . . . the allies of the other party and against other countries in circumstances which may endanger international peace and security." This codified the "Basic Principles" endorsed by the two superpowers, acting on behalf of the two opposing blocs, on May 29, 1972 during the Moscow Summit which was crowned by SALT I and the ABM Treaty. These "Principles" committed the parties to refrain from exploiting crisis situations, particularly in the Third World, for unilateral gains.

In the period immediately following the 1973 Agreement, the Soviet Union found modalities for circumventing the spirit without violating the letter of the understanding that was reached. In fact, the USSR established a military presence precisely in the areas that had been the object of the Agreement by means of the military and security elements from communist countries that were *not* members of the Warsaw Pact—Cuba, Vietnam, and North Korea (three regimes, small numbers of whose forces appeared in the Middle East battle zone during and immediately after the October 1973 War)— which could be viewed as falling outside the parameters of the texts in question.

A major consideration, evidently, was that the use of these particular proxies could serve, if not directly to "disinform" opponents, at least to provide them with the "ammunition" with which to deceive themselves. Thus, from 1975 onward, a Vietnam-weary United States was presented with the picture of an incursion into Angola by elements from a Caribbean island state with a population of less than 10 million. Had the USSR adopted an overt combat role instead of confining itself more discreetly to logistical tasks, one wonders, could the Clark Amendment have been passed or could an American diplomat have remained in office after describing the Soviet Union as "a stabilizing force in Africa"? Yet, from the Western point of view, is the potential impact upon vital sea lines of communication really less because "only" Cubans were involved rather than the Red Army? Not only did Moscow pay no price when the USSR utilized Cubans to achieve Soviet goals, but Fidel Castro did not forfeit his role among the "nonaligned," and still garnered plaudits from the American Ambassador to the United Nations.

It was the tepid Western reaction to the initial phase of proxy warfare that encouraged the Soviet leadership to escalate to a new level by introducing Warsaw Pact elements, if only because Cuban efficiency left something to be desired, even if Fidel's men blended in better with their surroundings than blond East Germans. (Incidentally, Cubans encountering South Africans for the first time hardly distinguished themselves.) It seems fair to speculate that the relative apathy with which this step was received less than half a decade after the 1972–73 agreements persuaded Moscow that one could move one step further and introduce the Red Army itself—in Afghanistan. (To be sure, Soviet combat elements had appeared prior to 1972, particularly in Egypt, and had flown combat missions over the Suez Canal, but were withdrawn in 1972.) Again, these developments acquire an additional dimension when viewed in the context of the apparent prepositioning of Soviet hardware in countries like Syria.

Paradoxically enough, the aspects considered thus far point not only to the degree and intensification of Soviet involvement in these areas of armed struggle and related instability, but may indicate also potential vulnerabilities in the network of international linkages which may be of interest to those of my colleagues whose task it is to address potential active responses of open societies to low-intensity operations of various types.

The first of such exploitable stresses in the Soviet-organized international support apparatus stems precisely from Russia's utilization of surrogates in a combat capacity. The very fact that these clients, like the USSR itself, operate as closed societies appears as a source of strength, but only at first sight. It is true that this factor enables the regimes in question to persist in relatively costly operations carried out in far-off areas, without pressure from the media or from a restive Congress. Yet, precisely because these are closed societies, the population reacts with inbred distrust to everything that "they" (the rulers) publish or do not reveal. In other words, the masses assume that spokesmen of the regime, indeed of all regimes, lie through their teeth. Now in the Cuban case, a relatively large proportion of a rather small population of call-up age is serving in far off countries of which most Cubans know extremely little, and the regime, of course, does not publish casualty rates. The families of the young men involved, and, indeed, other portions of the population, assume the worst, and the resulting rumor mill (which is extremely effective in such societies, serving as a substitute, so to speak, for free and open communications) no doubt wildly exaggerates Cuban losses, if only because no credible information is published. Of course, there *have* been casualties (many due to disease and barroom brawls, incidentally, as well as combat) but probably nowhere near the dimensions rampant in the popular mind.

The Soviet regime would be wise to consider whether it may not be contributing, at least marginally, to the destabilization such client states, by "exporting" to them these particular tasks. Clearly, this is recognized at least to some extent, since the USSR has decided not merely to subsidize the Cuban economy to the tune of some $3–4 billion annually, but to send interceptors to "fly interference" over Havana, and to assist in setting up a Praetorian Guard to defend Castro in case of "eventualities." It is an extremely appropriate question, therefore, whether, from the Soviet point of view, it would be worth "exchanging Cuba for Angola"—if the West were minded to exploit such destabilization, for instance, by recognizing a government in exile in Miami, where some of the more heroic of Fidel's former associates may be found who have no taint of association with the Battista period. As the Chinese say, "Cuba is the largest country in the world, with its government in Moscow, its troops in Africa, and its population in Miami Beach." They have discerned, correctly, that this is not exactly a sound prescription for a stable regime.

Such vulnerabilities are evident not merely in the Cuban case, but even in instances that relate to the employment of Warsaw Pact allies as surrogates, including East Germany, where, years ago, the communist press was impelled to publish "Letters to the Editor" asking "What are our boys doing near the Red Sea?" This occurred, furthermore, despite the fact that the numbers involved in the East German case are much smaller, with a larger population base, and, in most instances, the entities involved are security elements rather than combat units. Obviously the reason for permitting the issue to be aired in public at all was to provide some response to persistent rumors about East Germans dying in obscure and alien localities, as well as to offer an explanation along the lines of "we cannot permit imperialism to export counter-revolution with impunity."

The question is whether the USSR feels secure enough about the situation in its various client states to subject them even to this mild degree of potential destabilization. Again, the answer is positive only if the Soviet Union believes that it may take for granted total Western abstinence from any measures likely to exploit such vulnerabilities (even if this means only actions of a political/psychological, rather than military, nature).

Nor is the USSR itself totally immune to such problems. These derive from two separate sources. One is Afghanistan; in this context, to a very limited degree, the Soviet population is beginning to display some of the tendencies that were described earlier in relation to Cuba's ventures in Angola: there are persistent rumors of really major Soviet casualties, and sealed coffins arriving with the bodies of young men burned or hacked beyond recognition are unlikely to allay such anxieties. However, in this instance we are dealing only with the very beginning of the process, and it remains to be seen what another year or two may do. The possibility should not be discounted that the ever-increasing brutality of Soviet actions in Afghanistan relates at least in a small way to a desire to terminate the affair before reverberations "from below" become an item on the agenda of Soviet "administrative measures." Of course, in the Soviet case, "termination" does not mean the exit of Soviet troops, but rather the annihilation of all segments of the Afghan population capable of resistance.

An entirely different problem emanates from the very strong chauvinistic, indeed xenophobic and racist, attitude, persisting especially among the Great Russians, as well as from a concomitant isolationist, "anti–foreign aid," sentiment which in the past has expressed itself in food riots when vessels were being laden at Black Sea ports with supplies for Cuba. Other aspects of this mood have surfaced in physical assaults by Russians upon African and Asian students and trainees on street cars, either because they were accompanying Russian girls or because their presence precipitated resentful remarks such as "Why are you here eating our bread?" These problems, as well as the normal Soviet preoccupation with security, have led to special measures to segregate such trainees from exposure to the realities of life in the USSR, with the consequence that Africans renamed the Soviet Lumumba University "Apartheid University." It is known that, from time to time, certain of the Soviet leaders have objected to what they viewed as a diversion of resources to "ungrateful" Third World regimes and movements to the point at which some of Khrushchev's rivals were forced to stand up and accuse themselves, at the 21st Special CPSU Congress in 1959, of having opposed "helping the partly developed and developing countries of Asia and the Near East" and of having "behaved like people blinded by narrow-minded national insularism." After Khrushchev's overthrow, *Pravda* carried articles reminding readers that Lenin had always placed the accent upon investing in more rather than less developed areas as the best way of obtaining a rapid return and that, in the long run, making developed regions more viable was the best way of enabling them to assist the underdeveloped areas!

East European countries, particularly Czechoslovakia, compelled to act as surrogates or even as funnels for Soviet military shipments to various Third World clients, have been even less enthusiastic. They have found various subtle ways of indicating that the recipients are less than grateful and expect a great deal without being willing to provide an adequate return.

Needless to say, the still relatively marginal problems, contradictions, and tensions described, could amount to real vulnerabilities and to potential sources of destabilization *only* if the price paid for increasing covert and overt Soviet intervention activities in the areas mentioned were to become more tangible, that is, were to start to precipitate penalties that are really painful to Soviet decision makers. In other words, the West would have to demonstrate that it can exploit these vulnerabilities to the point of initiating significant destabilization, particularly in the surrogate countries and regimes. In that case, there will be inevitable "fallout" upon Moscow itself. As was mentioned earlier in this paper, there are signs that Soviet leaders are far from unanimous on the whole gamut of Third World ventures. This does not mean, of course, that some are "doves" and some are "hawks," as the more simple-minded Western analysts would like to believe. It does mean, however, that despite all its efforts the Soviet leadership is not entirely monolithic, being divided along lines of personal allegiance and support, rather than over policy, as my late son Gavriel and I have attempted to demonstrate in various publications. That implies that one or other of the rival factions might be happy to pounce upon an adversary within the Kremlin who has proven himself to be an "adventurist," that is, a leader who indulged in irresponsible and injudicious enterprises which turned out to be far from risk free. The fact that this phenomenon has little to do with any long-term factional commitment to a specific policy line, but is due rather to the irresistable urge to damage a competitor politically, is not important from our point of view. What does matter is that the phenomenon may provide options for leverage on the Soviet decision-making process, so long as the West shows awareness of this factor and develops the determination to exploit stresses, contradictions, vulnerabilities, and potential instabilities within the other camp.

For that matter, open societies are not condemned necessarily to supine inactivity even in the face of the most dramatic—indeed traumatic—emanation of the whole *Gestalt* of surrogate warfare against them, namely terrorism, including highjacking. In dealing with the options available, lamentable confusion is evidenced between three very different forms of active countermeasures: a) preemptive operations, b) rescue missions, and c) retribution. Particularly by forgetting entirely about the first, and probably the least problematic, possibility and blurring the distinction between the other two, the societies targeted frighten themselves into paralysis, focusing upon the risks with which actions are fraught that, of necessity, will have to be implemented at a time and place almost entirely of the adversary's choice. This is true particularly of rescue missions, but, to a fair degree, even of retaliation, at least to the extent that the inhibitions of open societies do not permit enough time to elapse for public indignation to cool (about the last outrage)—indeed for memory to fade—or for penalties to be inflicted at any distance from the scene of the crime. On the other hand, preemptive operations, which, unlike retribution, do not have to be dramatic or public, may be carried out with initiative and consequent surprise, on the side of the antiterrorist, since he can chose the propitious locale and time period. This reduces drastically the risk element and can be far more devastating than a single blow, however spectacular. Moreover, given the very character of terrorist movements with the constant fear of betrayal attendant upon outlaw activities of a particularly furtive and bloody nature and the consequent suspicions that each must harbor of his colleagues, it becomes especially effective to engage in disinformation activities that play upon these emotions to the point of precipitating splits and the consequent internecine warfare between rival chiefs and respective gangs. At that stage it becomes easier to infiltrate one, or several, of the splinters which desperately need reinforcements when their membership becomes depleted and falls below critical mass. Both to cause and to exploit such developments requires an effective intelligence infrastructure which is enhanced, of course, when infiltration becomes feasible. At that point, options for rendering terrorist organizations impotent increase geometrically: rivals can be induced to squander their forces in combat with one another, indeed effectively to decapitate one another's command structures; leaders can be trapped in ambush and captured; operations against the open society can be anticipated and pinpointed, eventuating in total failure and in the capture of the perpetrators; and, if necessary, sporadic meetings of the main figures can be ascertained with just enough warning time to render possible the dream of those who think of retribution—namely, a surgical strike with little or no collateral damage (implemented by commandos, from the air, the sea, or any other appropriate variation). The main requirement is *strategic* intelligence, shedding light upon the structure, linkages, leadership and personality conflicts, power and succession struggles, subgroups, and, indeed, the whole modus operandi of what is essentially a miniature closed society. While terrorism exploits cruelly the vulnerabilities of the open society, paradoxically it is also one of the more vulnerable of the surrogates addressed in this chapter for all of the reasons mentioned above. As in the other instances referred to, these vulnerabilities become relevant only when exploited by a West able and willing to move toward "active defense" in the place of a purely reactive, essentially passive posture.

14
Active Responses

B. Hugh Tovar

T he arsenal of democracy has yet to refine the weapons systems required to wage war at the low end of the spectrum of conflict. Over
years, the United States has displayed some mastery of improvisa-
tion. Old weapons have been adapted to new purposes. Old institutions have
likewise shown flexibility in the face of new challenges. Yet in recent decades,
as the prospect of large-scale conventional war has receded only to be replaced by the spread of low-intensity conflict in a host of countries we consider important, American success in coping with these affronts has been
limited.

Conversely, the record of our adversaries, particularly during the past
dozen or so years, ought by now to have forced us into intensive questioning
of our old methods. Most of those adversarial successes have involved the
instigation and support of revolutionary guerrilla warfare. Add to this terrorism, which, ageless though it be as a phenomenon of human history, has
introduced a new and bitter element to the equation of struggle for the United
States. Moreover, terrorism has barely scratched the surface of modern technology and new weaponry, which open possibilities undreamt of by the
bomb-throwing anarchists of earlier days.

Are we, then, already out of our depth in thinking it feasible to meet the
modern challenges of revolutionary insurgency, proxy warfare, and terrorism
vitalized by Soviet active measures on a global scale? At first blush, that
would appear to be the case. Debate in the American political arena today is
focused sharply on one of the rare current instances where the United States
is actively engaged in attempting to halt revolutionary guerrilla warfare in a
friendly country (El Salvador) while curtailing aggression exported from a
Soviet client state (Nicaragua). The use of force in this process is a central
issue of the debate. If the politicians are about equally divided, opponents of
the policy seem strongest among academics, religious leaders, and the press.
Attitudes of the general public do not emerge clearly on this spectrum, but
we should not forget the dramatic registration of public support for the Pres-

ident on Grenada at a ratio of ten to one, certainly far in excess of what he could have counted on from any of the specific groups mentioned.

Turning to the literature on the subject, it is interesting to note that more than ever before publicists who address the issues of conflict in today's world point toward the spread of warfare at the lower reaches of the so-called spectrum of conflict, and hail it as the challenge most likely to be faced by the United States between now and the end of the century. Terrorism is recognized as an important element in this pattern.

Those same publicists generally urge vigorous efforts to strengthen U.S. capability to cope with conflict at those levels. They are, of course, vague in suggesting exactly when and under what circumstances force is to be employed. Legal and political considerations weigh heavily in their equations, and nonviolent solutions are to be preferred at almost any cost. Although in principle the use of force does not seem to be ruled out, there is great fear that once used, it will lead to uncontrollable escalation—the Vietnam syndrome—and ever deeper U.S. involvement. Critics of the Administration deplore acts of terrorism, although they are prompt to exploit the hue and cry for other reasons. Public attitudes would probably favor a vigorous response to the terrorist attacks.

John Q. Public, however, receives very little encouragement from those who write on terrorism. Both American and European publicists treat the subject more circumspectly than they do other gradations of low-intensity conflict. Very few of those experts ever come to grips with the question of force. They utter the words "preemption" and "retaliation" in rather hushed tones. The name of the game has been, and still is, defense. Some writers would endorse the use of force against the terrorists if it were predicated upon hard information as to identities and locations, thus permitting pinpoint targetting for penetration of strike units.[1] A case can be made for this approach, but there is also a likelihood that the unending quest for intelligence will insure in the end that no action is taken. This reluctance to come to terms with the use of force clearly inhibits the U.S. ability to deal effectively with both revolutionary warfare and terrorism.

The Dilemma of the Open Society

As an open society committed to the rule of law both at home and abroad, the United States faces special problems in responding to political-military challenges at low-intensity levels. Our government needs and generally seeks public endorsement for its foreign operations. At times it fails to explain the issues or clarify its goals sufficiently to win that endorsement.

As a society predicated upon a sense of "decent respect for the opinions of mankind," we are reluctant to take liberties with the law. We believe in a moral order which is intended to protect everyone. We are always somewhat inhibited in our dealings with outlaws. Although we manage this reasonably well here at home, we face increasing difficulties abroad owing to the aggressive, ruthless behavior on the part of people who play by different rules, or only by rules of expediency. Under Soviet aegis, the promotion of revolutionary guerrilla warfare has infested one vulnerable country after another. Again under Soviet aegis, terrorism—which displays affinity for totalitarianism as both a source of supply and a model to be emulated—has followed suit. These phenomena represent systematic exploitation of what their authors deem to be American weaknesses.

Both revolutionaries and the terrorists aim to impose their will by force, thereby creating conditions of fear and hopelessness. Violence is their primary weapon, and they recognize no such thing as an innocent bystander. Their goal is the destruction of whatever moral order exists in our world today.

If there is to be a moral order within which an open society can survive, it has to be protected. There is both a right and an obligation to act in self-defense. The use of violence against us, against the moral order of which we are a part, is increasingly unrestricted, and our preference for nonviolence is being exploited with great skill. This is not to advocate outright recourse to the full panoply of terrorist or revolutionary methods. On the contrary. We continue to hold that the end justifies the means only within narrowly defined limits. But *certain* ends justify certain means.

The conditions of daily life in many parts of our world today are hard to distinguish from warfare. Force is being used blatantly to achieve political goals. Our preference is for political means to achieve our political goals. But when these are countered with force, we cannot logically eschew force as an instrumentality to be used at least in parallel with the preferred political means.

Although both common sense and history tell us that a static defense wins few wars, our instincts continue to lean toward defensive measures. If we retreat to a defensive posture, it may give us temporary security, but it means we abandon the battlefield and allow "him" to determine when, where, and with what he will hit us next. The Carter administration learned that this did not work well with the Sandinistas. As regards terrorists, negotiating means giving in to their demands, usually at the expense of those we would presume to protect against their assaults.

The historical precedents for the use of force by the United States against insurgency are of course numerous. There are also precedents for an aggressive response when the lives of Americans were jeopardized in local upheavals or by what today would be called terrorists. The earliest of these was the Decatur expedition of 1801 against the Barbary pirates. At the time, President Jefferson did not ask for a public consensus to support his action. He knew he had it. Closer to our own day, Pershing's incursion into Mexico in pursuit of Pancho Villa in 1916 was in retaliation for the murder of numerous American citizens and as a response to Villa's raids into American territory. President Wilson acted because the Mexican Government was incapable of preventing attacks on U.S. citizens.

A Case for Positive Response

The best defense is a good offense. This applies to what is seen as a present responsibility to forestall further communist (Soviet) exploitation of revolutionary guerrilla warfare and to quell the scourge of terrorism; both of these aspects represent a threat to the stability of the free world and the survival of the moral order as we know it. For the purposes of this chapter, attention will be confined to the positive, admittedly aggressive, action that can be taken to reduce the willingness of the Soviets and their proxies to support what they call "wars of national liberation." A similar approach will be taken toward terrorism, with the focus on the use of force in coping with it. Defensive measures will be left to others' discussion.

The problem is not to make the Soviets stop exporting the Marxist–Leninist ideology. We can live with that; given a fair shake, we can defeat it, even though it may capitalize on real local grievances. The problem arises when the Soviets arm their ideologues and use guerrilla insurgency or terrorism against the society of which the latter are a part, including the local democratic opposition. We see how they have accomplished this in Nicaragua, and also in Afghanistan where the Soviets resorted to outright invasion to insure victory. In Ethiopia, it was accomplished brutally, with the help of Cuban proxies and without regard for the human cost.

Angola offers another classic example of the effective use of a proxy army to facilitate takeover. It could not have been done, however, without help from the U.S. Congress, which terminated support for rebel factions competing with the MPLA. South Yemen, in contrast, went down the garden path hardly noticed, succumbing to a combination of subversion and proxy involvement. The Southeast Asian picture is only too well known. The communist victory in Vietnam added three previously free countries to the Soviet orbit.

This is not a pretty picture. And there is no reason to think that communist pressure has eased. El Salvador, as only one example, faces critical problems. Yet the picture has its bright side. Consolidation of the revolutionary regimes in those eight countries has a long way to go before the local leadership can sleep easily. Some are pressed by insurgencies of their own.

Can these conditions be exacerbated? Yes. To what end? In some instances, to reverse the situation. In others, to ameliorate conditions. In all instances, to put pressure on the Soviets, to assure them that they cannot get away with it again. Another goal would be to show our friends in the Third World that we are reliable, that we can be counted on to stand fast beside them. Many of them need to hear this.

Encouragement of insurgency entails obvious dangers. To succeed, it must be an integral element of a larger policy framework, predicated on principles to which the United States is known to be committed. The Monroe Doctrine certainly has not outlived either its validity or its usefulness. The Kennedy inaugural proclamation of our devotion to liberty wherever it is under attack still evokes deep feelings. And can we deny that injustice elsewhere in the world affects us deeply, whether it is civil rights in South Africa or human rights in Poland or Cambodia? If these considerations are well understood, we need not solicit world endorsement for every application of policy aimed at reversal of communist inroads. The less said or proclaimed, the better. As for strategy and tactics, there is no obligation whatsoever to announce them. Some measure of secrecy is imperative for the implementation of an activist policy.

This is not to suggest that only clandestine or covert techniques would be involved in a positive response. We must insure that covert action not be substituted for a comprehensive and coherent policy. An aggressive policy designed to make life difficult for the communists in countries newly under their control should incorporate energetic measures in the diplomatic sector and other areas of political maneuver, both national and international. As an element of a comprehensive whole, it can succeed. As a hedge against policy inaction, it will prove costly and ineffective.

It would do no harm to take a page out of the Soviet book in this field. Active measures, or *dezinformatsia* in Soviet parlance, run the gamut of overt and covert techniques, diplomacy, public information, propaganda, economic and military assistance, and the use of military force to achieve political goals. This is a very mixed bag of tricks, adaptable to virtually all conditions.[2]

Resistance to the idea of a positive response will come from familiar quarters and draw upon familiar arguments. Intervention in the internal affairs of sovereign states is naturally denounced, even by those who practice it most vigorously. Indeed, all states intervene to one degree or another when and if they can.[3]

Assisting Anticommunist Insurgents

Although the United States today is assisting insurgencies challenging Soviet-sponsored regimes in both Afghanistan and Nicaragua, it may be argued that we do not have a *policy* of active assistance. Would such a policy—designed for a long term and applicable to all anticommunist insurgencies—be thinkable? Yes, even though long-term programs do not always fare well in the

American scheme of things. It might also become a viable adjunct to our continuing efforts to sustain the moral order in a world beset by communist efforts to remake it.

An activist policy so designed should have two main thrusts—one to support insurgencies already in existence; the other to instigate insurgencies against communist-supported regimes where the *potential* exists. Here, we might differentiate among the various categories of Soviet-supported communist regimes.

> Regimes, newly communist, which exist precariously and only by virtue of sustained Soviet support. These are Nicaragua, Ethiopia, Afghanistan, Angola and Laos.

> Regimes which are comparatively well established and fully allied with the Soviet Union, but where Soviet support is vital to the survival of the regime. Cuba, South Yemen, Vietnam, and Cambodia as an adjunct to Vietnam are in this category.

> Regimes where communism is fully established and which are not only supported by the Soviet Union but are also integral elements of the Soviet system. These are the countries of Eastern Europe, and perhaps Outer Mongolia.

The risks entailed in such categorizations are obvious. We might go on to note that the sensitivity attaching to each increases with proximity to the Soviet Union itself.

It is hard to resist pondering the implications of Soviet involvement in the Afghanistan morass and the threat it poses for the hitherto tightly barricaded Soviet Central Asia. To date, no other Muslim community has been able to immunize itself from the pervasive and growing influence of Islamic radicalism, fundamentalism, or whatever else one might call the Islamic revolt against the twentieth century. It would be folly for the Soviet Union to assume impregnability on this score. It would therefore behoove us to look hard at the equities and to weigh the available means of affecting them.

Focusing on categories A and B, prospects for increasing the discomfiture of some Soviet-supported regimes appear to be good. A policy directed toward that end should complement an equally active counterinsurgency policy supporting friendly regimes currently under communist pressure. The Soviet leaders have achieved remarkable success in combining political subversion with guerrilla insurgency, and sometimes outright invasion, in wreaking havoc with U.S. interests around the world. To this less than rosy picture we must add the often synergistic drive of Islamic agitation, which poses imminent danger to a dozen friendly countries already faced with internal problems exploitable by the communists. If within their councils the ayatollahs declare communists to be anathema, externally they are prompt to throw their weight behind any Soviet policy thrust to thwart the aims of the real "Satan," the United States. This is a dilemma that we will probably not resolve in the near future, given certain facts of life—namely, that we are not likely to desert our Israeli allies, and we have little hope of inventing an internal combustion engine that runs on water.

Further procrastination on our part will redound to the advantage of the Soviet leaders as—overtly or covertly, directly or through their surrogates—they move to soften up and eventually topple target countries of their choosing. To counterbalance this, the United States should initiate a policy of aggressive response, focused on the most vulnerable of the Soviet-supported communist regimes mentioned above. It should be synchronized with support to other states threatened by communist-instigated revolutionary guerrilla warfare. An activist policy of this nature cannot come into being full-blown. It must be developed and implemented selectively.

Initial Objectives and Requirements

Although U.S. resources are now heavily committed in Central America (and also, we presume, in Afghanistan), it should not be beyond our powers to extend this effort to include two countries where present opportunities are ripe.

Cambodia

The horrors that have beset this country since the Khmer Rouge takeover in 1975 defy belief. That was literally true during the Pol Pot ascendancy, when Americans in general chose to ignore what was known to be taking place in Cambodia. U.S. policy has been schizophrenic. We chastise the Vietnamese for their invasion while being secretly relieved that Pol Pot and his gang have been ousted. Pol Pot, under Chinese sponsorship, is a continuing presence on the Thai-Cambodian border. Miraculously, an alternative to both Pol Pot and the Vietnamese occupiers exists, although it has barely survived the recent Vietnamese dry-season offensive.

Son Sann and his Khmer People's National Liberation Force (KPNLF) are members of an uneasy coalition that includes Prince Sihanouk and the Khmer Rouge. Their common ground is resistance to the Vietnamese. The coalition is favored by the United States because the inclusion of Pol Pot legitimizes the claim of the KPNLF to be the legal government of Democratic Kampuchea.[4] At some point Son Sann and Sihanouk must unite seriously. Also, at some point Pol Pot and the Khmer Rouge leadership must be scuttled.

A careful policy of political, financial, and military support to Son Sann and Sihanouk would be applauded in Southeast Asia. The Association of Southeast Asian Nations (ASEAN) has made this clear. ASEAN endorses armed resistance to the Vietnamese occupation—not aimed at defeating the Vietnamese on the battlefield but at preventing Vietnam from consolidating its hold on Cambodia—while at the same time offering Vietnam an "honorable" exit.[5]

Within the United States, opinion has been veering in the same direction. Devotees of nonintervention such as *The New York Times* and *The Washington Post* will now countenance assistance to Son Sann. Influenced by Rep. Stephen Solarz (D-NY), the *Post* recently indicated willingness to consider military assistance to the KPNLF in support of American strategic interests, to contain Soviet power, and to reassure America's friends.[6] On 3 April 1985 the House Foreign Affairs Committee voted to authorize $5 million in military aid to noncommunist forces resisting the Vietnamese occupation. A modest step, surely, but at least a step in the right direction.

This comes in the wake of reports that military supplies have reached the Cambodian resistance via Thailand—from the Chinese to Pol Pot, and presumably from the United States to Son Sann. If so, it should be comparatively easy to step up support with Thai cooperation, assuming that Thailand has reasonable assurance that it will not be left in the lurch. Assets in the form of U.S. personnel to sustain this endeavor are probably available in components of the Department of Defense and CIA. Equipment could be drawn from stocks of captured Vietnamese materiel if available, or from other sources, that is, China, if it cooperates. Transportation of materiel—again, assuming Thai cooperation—might be conducted through military assistance channels initially, and then through covert arrangements developed in the field. The sensitive question of advisors to the resistance forces might likewise be obviated if the Thai army will take the lead.

This broad-brush approach would have to be supplemented by efforts in other sectors. The prospect of eventual diplomatic recognition and economic assistance should figure in dealing with the Vietnamese. If the Chinese wish to forestall Vietnamese hegemony over Indochina, they may see their way toward judicious application of additional pressure along their common border.

Within Laos, similar pressures could be applied to the Vietnamese and their Pathet Lao clients. South Laos is particularly vulnerable. With very little encouragement, dissident elements now living in Thailand or France might create a low-key insurgency situation in the central and southern provinces of Laos. Assisted, say, by the Thais, this could become a fairly serious problem for the Lao communist government, and would add to the problems the Vietnamese face in maintaining their presence in both Cambodia and Laos.

The mechanisms required to implement the operations indicated above for Cambodia could be adapted readily to a parallel effort in Laos.

Thinking further along unthinkable lines, Vietnam itself ought not to remain immune. Within that country there are doubless many centers of potential dissidence. Problems of distance, internal security controls, and the absence of an identifiable external resistance group similar to the KPNLF would make it significantly more difficult, but not impossible, to exploit.

Angola

The fortunes of Agostinho Neto and the MPLA have not fared as well as expected during the years since the Clark Amendment assured him of victory. Jonas Savimbi and the Union for the Total Independence of Angola (UNITA) are still alive and doing well; the Angolan government, with Cuban support, is shaky and struggling.

However, the Cubans are still there in great numbers, and they remain a force for mischief on the African scene. They are also more vulnerable in Angola than in Ethiopia. Savimbi's forces have taken their measure more than once. Removal of the Cubans would represent a legitimate objective. An opportunity for Savimbi to share in the government would be another.

To pursue those objectives through other than diplomatic channels is of course out of the question under the Clark Amendment. A logical first step would be rescission of that law. Indeed, quiet rescission on grounds that it no longer serves a useful purpose would signal to the Angolans and the Soviets that we are growing impatient and changing our tactics.

Resumption of contact with Savimbi should be easy. He would probably welcome it although, deserted once before, he might be somewhat chary of running the risk again. Zaire would almost certainly be available once more as a staging area for transshipping supplies to UNITA. Conditions in Zaire being as they are, plausible cover for both personnel and the movement of materiel would have to be devised.

In the years since the CIA was known to have been active in paramilitary activity of this kind, its resources have undoubtedly undergone substantial change. Without detailed information regarding its capabilities today—only partially reflected in press coverage of Nicaragua—we may assume that the Agency is in much better shape than at any time since 1975. Its key problems will doubtless revolve around experience, manpower, cover, and the capability to transport materiel securely and expeditiously. One would hope that in deploying its own resources today in on-going operations the CIA is also in a position to draw upon the capabilities of the Department of Defense (DOD), specifically those of the Special Operations Command (SOCOM). Close collaboration between the DOD and the CIA is essential, not only from the intelligence support standpoint but in terms of effective utilization of men and equipment. There are indications that such collaboration is now taking place.[7]

Cover for covert paramilitary operations is difficult enough for the CIA itself to arrange and implement. For the U.S. military, operating independently, it is next to impossible. A simpler solution is for the CIA to draw upon military manpower resources as needed for insertion into Agency-controller mechanisms. Intelligence support is another factor militating against a unilateral military approach. The Agency's knowledge of foreign areas is generally far deeper than that of the military, and it is better equipped to bring all intelligence community resources to bear upon an operation. In certain situations a primarily military undertaking, drawing upon CIA resources, should also be feasible.

To conclude this speculative examination of the feasibility of assisting insurgencies challenging Soviet-supported communist regimes, it would seem sensible to suggest that anything beyond the indicated scope is unrealistic at this time, especially given the uncertainty of public endorsement and the availability of funds. We assume that the Administration's efforts in Nicaragua will continue to be pressed, and that whatever is being done in Afghanistan will probably continue at its present level. Against that backdrop, South Yemen can be allowed to steam under the desert sun for a while longer. As for Ethiopia, the terrible conditions of famine in that country must command primary attention.

Striking Hard At Terrorism

There is a difference between the Reagan administration's approach to terrorism and its approach to other forms of low-intensity conflict. In the latter, action taken to date has been ad hoc, aimed at particular targets—El Salvador, Nicaragua, Afghanistan. There is little indication of a national strategy predicated on a clear concept and directed toward certain objectives. True, our actions have been explained repeatedly in the case of Central America. Yet beneath all rhetoric the identification of objectives has left much to be desired. Perhaps it is too much to expect that all of this be formulated under a single encompassing rubric. The anxiety neurosis that has afflicted us since the collapse of Vietnam in 1975 makes us reluctant to project involvement beyond the very short term. Unfortunately this tends to weaken the will to act. It also invites criticism, which weakens the will further. Afghanistan is a curious anomaly in this context. The Administration has simply supported the rebels. There has been no debate. In the Congress, support for the Afghan rebels has been enthusiastic, even among those who on other issues are professed anti-interventionists. There seems to be no doubt that the American public endorses the President's action.

The Administration's reaction to repeated acts of terrorism against Americans has been perplexing. High officials from the President on down have regularly excoriated terrorism, terrorists, and the people who support them. Yet in the face of such rhetoric, force has never been used to redress the situation. All visible measures undertaken have been defensive. If this incongruity is disconcerting, it has its positive side. For the past year the Administration has been laying the groundwork for a counter-terrorism policy, at least as far as the declaratory aspects are concerned, which will include the use of armed force to prevent, preempt, and even retaliate against terrorist attack. In so doing the case has been presented to the public with notable clarity, in part for the purpose of informing the public of its position, and at the same time eliciting the latter's reaction.

Dimensions of a Strategy

Countering terrorism is only one of the obligations facing us in our efforts to deal systematically with the military and quasi-military provocations erupting at the lower end of the conflict spectrum. As with other such provocations, it is essential that terrorism be recognized for what it is—a form of warfare. Noting also that in its political overtones it is exceedingly complex and sometimes related to valid causes, we must focus on the aspects of terrorism most offensive to us and most unconscionable, namely, indiscriminate violence in noncombat situations. Our goal is therefore to stop the violence, and, by punishing the violators where possible, to insure against its recrudescence.

The terrorists operate currently on two basic assumptions. One is that the West, specifically the United States, so abhors violence and fears so much for its world "image" that it will never bring itself to concerted use of force against terrorism. The other is that the West, though given to expressions of mutual concern and revulsion against terrorist violence, will never subordinate parochial interests in a cooperative effort to suppress terrorism. We see much these days that would support those assumptions.

Selective use of force against terrorism is imperative if the United States is to be taken seriously. Its purpose—to halt terrorist attacks—must supplement diplomatic and other action aimed at solving the more complex issues of which terrorism is an extreme manifestation. It will be argued that force should only be used as a last resort. In practical terms that means that it will never be employed. If we are serious about stopping terrorism, we will use force whenever we deem it justified and feasible. To do otherwise would be to lose any deterrent value it might offer and to give the terrorists a clear field for another shot at us.

International support for terrorism means Soviet support for terrorists. It is one more proxy operation targeted against the West in general and the United States in particular. As with other Soviet proxy efforts to undermine U.S. interests, the stakes are not large enough to warrant going to war over them. And just as the Soviets hedge their bets in such maneuvers, we can afford to do likewise. If our interests and resources have limits, so do theirs. We should take their measure over sponsorship of terrorism, and there is no better way to do so than by putting the terrorists effectively out of business.

A Tactical Approach

Soviet Union. If Soviet support and sponsorship for terrorism in the form of training, equipment, funds, and political backing did not exist, there might still be terrorism. But without Soviet sponsorship and the benefits accruing from it, the terrorists would be much harder pressed than they are today. Were the Soviets actually to cooperate with the West in terrorist suppression, the advantages would be enormous. It is therefore important that pressure be kept on the Soviets to change their cynical policy. There are many ways to accomplish this.

> We should advertise Soviet performances. Even if the "world" chooses to look askance, a drumbeat of factual information supplemented by covert propaganda should carry the message.

> Other interested parties, such as the Italian judicial system, should be encouraged to investigate Soviet complicity in terrorist acts.

> Intelligence collection should concentrate on verification of direct or indirect Soviet complicity or sponsorship.

> Diplomatic pressure should be included in other Soviet–American exchanges. It is at the heart of the question of good faith, which is fundamental to any agreement. If the Soviets cannot be dissuaded from promoting the international gangsterism we call terrorism, they must pay for it.

Libya. After the Soviet Union, there is Libya—by any rational criteria an outlaw state. The consensus under international law that endorsed Jefferson's action against the Pasha of Tripoli in 1801 could be matched easily today against the Pasha's successor tyrant. The mythology of Arab solidarity is an obstacle, but not insurmountable. Plausible steps to end this plague of the Maghreb would include:

> First, consolidating the opposition to Qadhafi, both within Libya and in the Libyan diaspora, that has developed as a consequence of Qadhafi's

tyranny. Clandestine contact with oppositionists is imperative, but it need not exclude open contact, protection, and support for legitimate leaders.

Second, a concerted effort to effect a change of government in Libya, employing a broad range of overt and covert techniques.

Third, a covert commando strike against a Libyan port facility—on the occasion of the next major terrorist attack in the Middle East, Africa, or Europe, in which Libyan complicity is indicated.

Iran. The Khomeini government of Iran, owing to its support and guidance of the Shiite Muslims in Lebanon and elsewhere in the Middle East, is another sustaining force for terrorism. Khomeini has clearly declared war on the United States, while encouraging others to fight his battles. Since Iran is thus almost certainly responsible for the murder of a great number of Americans, and probably for the kidnapping of many others in Lebanon today, Khomeini should be told that no more will be tolerated—that henceforth any action against a U.S. diplomat akin to that perpetrated in Teheran in 1979 will be treated as an act of war and that any public affront (such as a trial) or physical harm to the U.S. diplomats and other Americans kidnapped by Shiite terrorists in Lebanon encouraged and supported by Iran will evoke immediate retaliation against Iran. As of this writing, press reports indicate that a message along these lines has been sent through diplomatic channels. If it is disregarded, then there is ample justification for an action such as the destruction of a major Iranian installation by air attack. The Kharg Island facility comes immediately to mind; there may be other targets equally suitable.

The Terrorists Themselves. The measures outlined above all focus on the terrorists' main sources of support. They must be matched by equally vigorous action against the terrorists themselves. The Libyan role is not confined to sponsorship—they are practitioners, and should be treated accordingly. This may also be true of the Iranians.

Employment of force to prevent, preempt, or even retaliate against a terrorist attack is difficult to discuss without indulging in heavy speculation. It may be presumptious for a private person to do so while ignorant of what our government may actually be doing in this field. Risking this, we suggest that there are two ways in which the U.S. might proceed unilaterally.

First, through direct action by U.S. ground forces against known terrorist installations. This would involve Special Operations Forces, Marines or other ground elements, in uniform, without effort to conceal their American identity, using commando tactics of speed and surprise via air or ground penetration. An alternative would be naval gunfire or air attack against discrete targets, less attractive because of the near-impossibility of confirming the impact to the terrorist target. The advantages and disadvantages of this approach would vary enormously as factors of location, access, strength of opposition, and so on. One consideration worth weighing bears on the concept of "proportionate" action—the use of force adequate to need yet not likely to produce disproportionate side effects, such as casualties among "innocent bystanders." The American way of war is not renowned for its lightness of touch. In the military lexicon of the United States, the "discrete surgical strike" has relatively few historical precedents.

An alternative to direct activity is the use of small-scale covert commando raids against known terrorist installations, civilian or military in composition, using resources of personnel, equipment, and transport not readily identifiable with the United States. A decision to attempt a covert operation would depend on its feasibility and on the importance of concealing U.S. involvement.

Both of these strategies are risky. Still another way of striking at a terrorist target would be in collaboration with a friendly government. This might entail such action as deployment of a combined force from an appropriate point of line of departure. It might be undertaken covertly, reflecting a sponsorship other than the participating governments, or under the ostensible sole sponsorship of one of the two. Some form of collaboration with Israel thus presents itself for consideration. Similar arrangements with certain friendly Arab governments are at least conceivable.

Some Requirements for Striking at Terrorism

Maximum stress must be placed on developing and fine-tuning elements which together comprise the sine qua non of active response. One of these elements is military strike capability. During the past year the media has carried a steady flow of reporting and speculating about the expansion and improvement of U.S. Special Operations Forces and other units designed for unconventional warfare. Much of this has related to the Delta Force. Observations made by Assistant Secretary of Defense Noel C. Koch were particularly interesting as a reflection of the progress being made as well as of the problems still besetting U.S. planners.[8] In any event, the military strike capability should include:

1. Resources of the U.S. Special Operations Command, which, while they are certain to be heavily committed in counterinsurgency operations, offer enormous potential for use in counterterrorist strikes. If, as Koch has stated, the Special Forces mission includes sabotage, subversion, and psychological operations (PSYOPS), they risk being spread too thin. Why not drop subversion and PSYOPS and instead stress development of an independent intelligence collection capability?

2. The U.S. Navy Sea-Air-Land (SEAL) Forces, with capability for under-water warfare with submarine support plus special infiltration craft and hi-speed multimission patrol boats. Recalling some excellent civic action work by the U.S. Marines in Vietnam, one wonders whether there is any planning for a Marine role in counterinsurgency, if not in counterterrorist operations.

3. Resources of the U.S. Air Force, which include special operations forces and air transport equipment. Although designed for rescue missions, USAF special forces could handle counterterrorist operations, using special equipment for silent infiltration under cover of darkness and low-altitude navigation with terrain-following radar. It would seem advisable to designate a specially trained air assault squadron, capable of launch from a carrier, to be available for use against identified terrorist targets or targets controlled by terrorist sponsors.

A second element of active response is civilian penetration/strike teams for covert or clandestine deployment against identified terrorist installations. If it has not been done already, the CIA should be given this responsibility. The Agency's institutional memory goes back to World War II, and there has been enough continuity since then to transcend the dismantling of Agency paramilitary resources in 1975. Resistance, of course, is to be expected. At the middle levels of Agency leadership today there is comparatively little paramilitary experience. Also, disaffection within the CIA over the exposures of the seventies, most of which were in the realm of covert action, has not enhanced the internal popularity of the latter as a channel for career development.

These considerations are unimportant, however, weighed against the necessity of acquiring a strike capability that can be used expeditiously. Vastly greater resources of men and equipment are of course available in military channels. And, as emphasized above, the latter must be developed and prepared for use. At the same time it should be recognized that internal factors—not least of which is an inflexible command and control system, coupled with a less than forward-looking attitude toward special operations on the part of many of the most senior military officers—will often make it difficult to effect a military response as promptly as required. In time this consideration should become less important, especially if the CIA and the military commands develop the pattern of close collaboration mentioned earlier.

Further, parallel preparations should be made for the selective introduction of third-country nationals or, alternatively, for joint training with other national forces. Special security considerations arise in this connection, but they are manageable.

A third element involves continuing, intensive training, which is imperative for all personnel involved in counterterrorist operations. The obvious contours of such training encompass infiltration, commando attack, demolition, exfiltration, and so on. It is equally imperative to remember that training cannot go on forever: the weapon has to be fired if we are to be sure it works.

Another element of active response is intelligence, which is cited as the overriding consideration in all discussions of countering terrorism. Lack of hard intelligence has been cited repeatedly, whether correctly or incorrectly, as the reason why we have not been able to forestall terrorist attacks and as the reason for our hesitation in striking back at terrorists presumably responsible for the attacks. Intelligence is indeed an overriding consideration. But it is not *the* overriding consideration. We must also possess the means of taking action—that is, of gaining access to the terrorist target, striking it with force proportionate to need and with due cognizance of possible side effects (casualties among "innocent bystanders"), and exiting safely. Intelligence thus entails:

1. Penetration of terrorist organizations. This proposition is not well understood. Just as penetration of narcotics trafficking means that the agent must appear to be a trafficker, penetration of a terrorist organization means that the agent must appear to be a terrorist. If he does not act like a bona fide terrorist, he will either be unable to penetrate the organization or have his throat cut soon after presenting his credentials. Thus, if we truly expect to acquire intelligence from within a terrorist organization, it may be necessary to look the other way regarding some questionable behavior on the part of our agent.

2. Exploitation of information from all sources, including technically acquired data and information from allied or friendly intelligence services. All analytic resources should be brought to bear on the subject. There should be exchanges of information with cooperating foreign intelligence and security services.

3. A joint targeting center should be established to service all U.S. elements sharing responsibility for counterterrorist action. It should be "all-source" in composition and operate under heavy security controls.

Another element of active response is the fact that if cooperation with certain allied governments is to be taken seriously, joint training in operations will be just as important as exchange of intelligence. Many factors will militate against the concept of a joint operational effort, including visceral inclinations on both sides. It should nonetheless receive careful consideration.

In addition, the provision for rewards as an inducement to terrorists to defect or provide information could become an important means of acquiring intelligence. Last year, new legislation including this policy was requested by the President and was passed by the Congress. The rewards, clearly, must involve "big money." A foreseeable danger is that, as with defectors from the Soviet Bloc, our techniques for handling such people securely and productively beyond the initial debriefing period leave much to be desired. Serious advance planning may enable us to avoid the more obvious pitfalls.

Also in the context of requirements of effective active response, some attention should be given to a factor affecting the morale of participants, military and civilian. On the military side, the component likely to bear the brunt of the endeavor—the Special Operations Forces—still struggles for recognition within its system. Some progress has been made in recent years. It is reflected in the Defense Guidance of 1981 which directed the U.S. armed services to develop a special operations force capability, and in the numerous accounts published since then which describe substantial forward movement in this field. That is all to the good. However, it is not enough. The doctrine to guide the deployment of special operations forces remains undeveloped. Attention given to the subject in the senior command and staff colleges is minimal. Prejudice on the part of conventional-war-oriented senior officers plays a heavy role in restricting development of this nonmainstream capability. One symptom is the paucity of promotions to general-officer rank, which compares unfavorably with that of the highly regarded British counterpart of the U.S. Special Operations Forces, the Special Air Service (SAS). People who undertake dangerous missions under special conditions qualify as an elite. But elites fare rather badly in the American system.

CIA experiences some of the same problems. Its predecessor organization, the Office of Strategic Services (OSS), acquired the "elite" label from its inception, to the discomfiture of the armed services. Inheriting the mantle from the OSS, the Agency became the presidential "troubleshooter," and enjoyed what many saw as favored treatment. Following two decades of "exposures," that is hardly the case any longer. Indeed, the "rogue elephant" bears some of the earmarks of a whipping boy. If, therefore, the CIA people appear gun-shy in the face of assignments with a high flap potential, it should be no surprise.

The Impact of Positive Response

By themselves, the policy proposals outlined in these pages will not relieve the United States of all anxieties associated with either terrorism or the export of revolution by the Soviet Union. Implemented, however, within a larger policy framework of national objectives supported by adequate means, they will help considerably in the long and the short run.

Initiatives at the lower intensity conflict levels are in the grand strategy of the Soviet Union. Like everything else, they have a price calibrated as a balance of ends and means. The United States and the Soviet Union are now engaged in complex negotiations over nuclear weapons. Non-nuclear issues will not only be affected by, but may also affect, those proceedings. The price tag, therefore, on the initiatives under discussion here may vary widely; their value is certainly not unlimited. Our aim is to increase the cost to the Soviets of their intrusion into so-called "wars of national liberation," to the point, we hope, of convincing them that there are better ways to apply their finite resources. In the process, we may refurbish our own prestige, which has been badly eroded by Soviet political and paramilitary warfare.

The Soviets, once they see that the United States means business, may think twice before trying to penetrate a region of importance in the American scheme of things. In the Philippines, for example, it might be assumed that a golden opportunity invites Soviet exploitation today. Yet a combination of vigorous counterinsurgency assistance to the Philippines, coupled with the instigation of trouble for the Soviets in the Indochina area, might reverse at least a local trend.

The bystanders of this world must wonder how good the Soviets are at bailing out their clients when the tide is against them. To date, the Soviets have not really been tested. In the case of Nicaragua, they must know that the cards are stacked against them. When the Sandinistas are finally run out, there will be little the Soviets or the Cubans can do about it except fulminate. A similar defeat in, say, Angola, might have a therapeutic effect at a time when the new Soviet leadership must be weighing its equities carefully.

Even in the face of actions such as these, if they can be carried out successfully, it is perhaps too much to expect that the Soviets will desist entirely from adventures in the realm of low-intensity conflict—at least not until they have experienced the embarrassment of failure. But it may slow them down. And prospective dissidents in countries important to U.S. interests may be obliged to think twice before making their moves if they cannot be assured of Soviet assistance.

The cost of sponsoring terrorism is negligible compared to supporting insurgency or sustaining a client regime. For the Soviets it is warfare on the cheap, and will continue to be so unless their feet can be held to the fire. For other governments abetting or sponsoring terrorists—specifically Libya and Iran—the situation is different. They have no guaranteed immunity. They pay most of the heavy cost of current terrorist activity, and the price tag, with comparatively little effort on our part, could be made excessively large.

Quite apart from considerations of sponsorship, whether Soviet, Libyan, and Iranian, most terrorist acts these days seem to depend heavily on the willingness of the terrorists to die in the attempt. The mind of the driver at the wheel of the truck-bomb is an unfathomable force. Yet the success of the first undoubtedly made it easier to recruit the second. When one is finally thwarted and seen to have died in vain, his successor may be less inclined to follow suit. The terrorist organization itself may also have to weigh the over-all costs once it realizes that its immunity to forcible response has ended.

It will be argued that none of these measures guarantees success, and that they all entail heavy risk. True. In an ideal world we might rely in toto on diplomacy to convey our message. In truth, we have largely done that over recent decades, with little success. Instead, we have seen our values under-mined and our self-confidence corroded. The time is long overdue to move forward using all elements of our national power against terrorists and other disruptive forces similarly inspired.

Notes

1. Neil C. Livingstone, *The War Against Terrorism* (Lexington, Mass.: Lexington Books, 1982).

2. Richard H. Shultz and Roy Godson, *Dezinformatsia: Active Measures in Soviet Strategy* (New York: Pergamon, 1984).

3. For an instructive debate on the subject of intervention, see comments by Leslie Gelb, Ray S. Cline, George W. Ball, William E. Colby, and Morton Halperin et al. in *Harper's* (September 1984).

4. An illuminating account of the circumstances underlying this strange coalition is presented in "The Lesser Evil, An Interview with Norodum Sihanouk," by David Ablen and Marlowe Wood, *New York Review of Books*, 14 March 1985, pp. 21–26.

5. See the address of H.E. Tommy T. B. Koh, Ambassador of Singapore to the United States, delivered on 12 February 1985, as the Second Jackson H. Relston lecture.

6. Editorial, *The Washington Post*, 24 March 1985.

7. See "CIA, Military Training Foreign Squads," *The Washington Post*, 24 March 1985.

8. See interview with Noel C. Koch in *Armed Forces Journal*, also, Koch testimony before the Hutto panel on special forces, U.S. House of Representatives, quoted by Robert Toth, *Los Angeles Times*, 18 November 1984.

15
The Role of Congress

Malcolm Wallop

During my eight years of responsibility for the intelligence budget of the United States, my duties included decisions about how we ought to counter terrorism and help friendly resistance movements in communist-held territory. Here I will briefly share some reflections on why I think that these vital tasks have proven too difficult for the U.S. Government to accomplish competently. I will also discuss two measures that I have joined some of my colleagues in proposing, which we hope will ameliorate the situation somewhat.

Let there be no illusion that these measures—by themselves—will enable us competently to use low-intensity conflict offensively and defensively. The intellectual, moral, and organizational insufficiencies that prevent us from doing this are too formidable to be vanquished except by first-class leadership at the State and Defense Departments and the CIA—and that clearly is not now in place. If we simply list in our minds the things that our enemies have done to us and to our interests in peacetime, either with their own special forces or by providing materials and training to individuals inclined to use them against us, imagine what they could do in war. Then, if we survey our own intelligence agencies and military forces for the means to counter such actions, we cannot help but be struck by a sense of disproportion.

Think, for example, of the chaos that several Soviet SPETSNAZ battalions—air landed or infiltrated—could wreak in the United States in the early stages of a war. Our military has lost the habit of thinking about how to defend against, or even to carry out, such classic cavalry missions. Our military is not prepared for simple special operations such as turning out the lights in enemy capitals. Much less is it prepared for sophisticated special operations, the most difficult of which involve building bases for insurgencies in enemy territory. Tragic? Without question. Theoretically, we could do more unto our enemies by special operations than they do to us. Given equal preparations, our societies should be more resistant to special operations than theirs because communist regimes govern populations that are generally quite hostile to them. But our preparations have *not* been equal. We simply have not invested the proper planning, moral conviction, and resources. The disorganized state of our meager 15,000 special forces (as opposed to about 500,000 from which the Soviets can draw for conducting these activities) was recently detailed in *Newsweek,* which even identified one of the principal causes for this state of affairs—a lack of overall military strategy in the service of which special operations would make sense.

Had *Newsweek* looked further into the issue, it might have found a deeper cause in the statement of Lt. General Eugene Tighe, former director of the Defense Intelligence Agency, that the world's complexities have made it "increasingly difficult to recognize friends and foes." Obviously, firm, clear convictions about who is on our side in this world and who is not are the sine qua non of military strategy. But it seems that our intelligence officers are now too sophisticated to tell the difference between friends and enemies, and so conscious of complexities as to be wary of engaging opponents until they have proven their enmity beyond the shadow of a doubt. It is indeed a perverse sophistication that would immobilize us until clouds of Soviet warheads rain down on our high plains. At any rate, whether by inaction or ineptitude, or both, this country has racked up a near-zero batting average in helping friendly movements. Elsewhere I have argued that the medium by which we have given this aid—the CIA's covert action—has become an issue in itself, obscuring fundamental choices about policy in the minds of lawmakers and presidents alike.* But why?

In my estimation there are two fundamental reasons for this failure in the most difficult kind of special operations. The first and most basic is intellectual and moral confusion. The words, "One man's terrorist is another man's freedom fighter," from a national intelligence estimate on terrorism in 1979, express the conventional wisdom in the Executive Branch of the U.S. Government and, to a lesser extent, on Capitol Hill. They are also the most concise symbol of philosophic and moral illiteracy that one could imagine. In the minds of the officials who carry such words in their very bones, the differences between a Jonas Savimbi and an Idi Admin, between the Khmer Rouge and the Khmer People's National Liberation Front, between the Sandinistas, the Contras, and Salvador's Farabundo Marti Front, indeed the differences between Gorbachev and Solzhenitzyn, are matters of taste: a dilettante's distinction of distractingly empty thought processes. Such officials will not dispute that it may be in the interest of the United States, at any given time, to ally with any of these symbols against others, or that in our body politic the "values" of some lead to certain preferences, while the use of others lead elsewhere. But they affirm that it is futile to try to decide which "values" are better and which are worse. Above all, they aggressively refuse

---

*See Malcom Wallop, "U.S. Covert Action: Policy Tool or Policy Hedge?" *Strategic Review* (Summer 1984).

to be drawn into deliberations on such matters. I once asked a senior official of the FBI why he had not followed up on the many leads that had pointed to the People's Temple as a dangerous organization. He answered with some vehemence that the People's Temple claimed it was a religious organization, and that infiltrating it would have been no different than infiltrating the Catholic Church!

Indeed, for the overwhelming majority of senior officials, the sole moral and intellectual compass—aside from their tastes, prejudices, or personal interest—is the aggressive "know-nothingism" of one who will not think and therefore cannot judge. This intellectual and moral emptiness is not a guarantee against abuses. On the contrary, the absence of intellectual and moral principles allows tastes and personal considerations to drive American officials into doing some awful things. Today they want to give military aid to the communist government of Mozambique to crush a democratic resistance. Today, these officials aid Afghanistan's Mujahedin against the Soviets with the same conviction with which they aided the Kurds aginst Iraq. Today some of the highest officials in the CIA rejoice that they are finally rid of the burden of supplying arms to Nicaragua's contras. Indeed, for several years they have been discussing with lawmakers who share their tastes at what point the contras should be "dumped." There is no passion for the Sandinistas at the CIA or the State Department, just a dull desire to be rid of the arduous task of confronting them and to return to routine. Their "reputation," meaning their ease, represents a higher scale of values than their mission.

No wonder that such officials are uncomfortable discussing right and wrong, better and worse as though these terms mean something objectively. Thus last year the CIA refused my request to compile sets of unclassified biographies of the Sandinista leaders and of the contras because, responsible officials said, they did not want to be party to a debate about which side in that civil war is inherently preferable! So much for the words of Christ so proudly carved on the CIA's building, "You shall know the truth, and the truth shall make you free." The biographies of the contras finally compiled, I put them into the Congressional Record. This year a few dedicated foreign service officers expanded the set. But the State Department's Bureau of Public Affairs blocked their publication until pressure from the White House allowed it to proceed. There is no reason for surprise here. If the Contras are indeed "Our Brothers," as the President said, if their cause is objectively better than that of their foes, then the duty we have in their regard is both clear and strict. After all is said and done, we simply cannot allow them to be crushed and the bad side to triumph. If this be so, then there is at last an objective standard against which the performance of the CIA and the State Department can be judged. That standard makes accommodation with the Sandinistas impossible. But that standard is inconvenient, because living by it displeases friends of so many high officials. For that reason, such officials describe the world as too complex to be painted black and white. Within a standardless spectrum of grey, they can indulge their emptiness.

Another manifestation of this emptiness is the ability of so many high officials to give good causes their due in speech, but to betray them in action. Secretary of State George Shultz is as good an example as any of one who rejects the Brezhnev Doctrine with eloquent words, but has never been known to oppose it with any concrete actions. Such officials have learned from Helmut Sonnenfelt's experience in 1976 that when their words reflect their de facto preference for accommodation with totalitarians, the American political system will produce a Ronald Reagan who will discredit them before the American people and make it impossible for them to hold public office. So they talk brave talk, formulate half-baked plans, and present them to the Congress in ways that subtly signal that they would not be very upset if the Congress disapproved. Thus they project upon the Congress and on the American people their own confusion and lethargy. Thus do they bring out the worst in the Congress. Regrettably, that is easy to do.

The second reason flows from the first. In the absence of intellectual and moral compasses in working order, the bureaucracies that form the U.S. Government have gone their own way. The U.S. Military has traditionally distrusted special operations (OPS). There is nothing unusual in this. Conventional military forces around the world accept special units in their midst only when forced to by higher authority. In the United States, higher authorities have interfered with the military's attitude toward special OPS only sporadically. After World War II, the Joint Chiefs of Staff did not contest the National Security Council's decision to assign to the CIA the mission of providing paramilitary assistance. They did not think that the CIA would ever have enough resources in effect to fight unconventional wars. They just did not want the mission. When the Kennedy administration decided to contest the Soviet Union in the Third World, it realized that the CIA's paramilitary apparatus was insufficient, and quickly directed the Army to build special forces as a set of teams, each of which would raise and direct a battalion of indigenous forces.

Vietnam was the first and major test of the special forces. They performed well, both militarily and politically. But as the enemy's pressure increased, the Joint Chiefs of Staff and the Johnson administration chose to meet it by a massive conventional presence in South Vietnam and with limited air strikes in the north, instead of with an increase of special forces in the south and a conventional attack on the north. The special forces became a sideshow, as did the CIA's most brilliant and effective operation ever—the arming of General Vang Pao's H'Mong in Laos. But the abject failure of the approach used by the Joint Chiefs of Staff and the White House toward Vietnam resulted in discrediting of paramilitary support forces within both the Armed Forces and the CIA.

When President Carter reached for a force able to rescue Americans in Tehran, he found that the items in the cupboard were not only few, but above all, ill-designed for action. Essentially, there were more than enough men who had practiced living off the land, crawling through difficult places, and shooting very well. But there were none who had practiced going into a strange country illegally to gather information and set up the support network and sabotage that would make forcible entry on a small scale possible. Much less did we have people trained to go into countries like Iran clandestinely and raise indigenous forces. It is a high tribute to American ingenuity that such a group was assembled ad hoc and performed well. But no sooner had the group which performed in Iran been constituted as the intelligence support activity (ISA) then the regular forces and their supporters in Congress attacked the ISA. Men in a group like the ISA, if they are to do their jobs, must be intimately familiar with the language and customs of the places where they might operate. That means they have to travel, undercover—perhaps as tourists with their wives. This was excuse enough for the Army to abolish the ISA.

Today, we have more special troops than a few years ago, and many can operate more wonderful gadgets than ever, including terminals for the global positioning system. But we are almost back to where we were in the late 1970s in terms of the usefulness of special forces in missions that require illegal entry into hostile countries, gathering intelligence, contacting indigenous people, and perhaps sabotage. Why? Because in the absence of strategy, the Military Services just do not care very much about such things. And they appear to care even less about confronting the basic issues of developing strategy. But why? One set of answers leads us back to moral and intellectual illiteracy. Another set has to do with the reticence, fatal for soldiers, to look on war as a real possibility. It is not strange that when the possibility most clearly exists, its likelihood is most remote—but how easily that fact is lost on fainthearted planners. Of all the reasons why the President and the Secretary of Defense do not impose a military strategy upon the services—even if they felt competent to do so—the most justifiable reason by far is that they felt bound by the network of legal restrictions that the Congress placed on the Executive Branch in the 1970s. First among these is the War Powers Act, which prohibits a president from using military power abroad without an affirmative vote by both Houses of Congress. Although such an affirmation has never been denied when requested, and the Act might never be upheld by the Supreme Court if the President chose to contest it, its existence has made presidents leery of using small amounts of force abroad. Especially when, as happens so often, administrations have not rigorously defined the policy they will follow, and therefore do not feel confident, the existence of the War Powers Act has proved to be a powerful deterrent to action. Second among these deterrents is the Section 600 of the Foreign Assistance Act, which bans foreign aid from being used to help train foreign police forces. This was enacted as an emotional reaction to the murder of an Agency for International Development (AID) officer in Uruguay, and after a long campaign by the KGB against this very effective program. Without it, the U.S. Government is forced to rely on the military or the CIA.

The list of restrictions is long. The Case–Church Amendment prohibited presidents from using any kind of force in, over, or near Indochina. Indochina fell. The Clark and Tunney Amendments stopped covert aid to Angola. It fell. The Boland Amendment, which this Administration too cleverly endorsed in 1982, has practically wrecked covert aid to Nicaragua. None of these provisions, I might add, made it impossible for determined presidents to do their jobs successfully. But, singly and all together, they have raised the political ante beyond the ability to presidents, beset with weak subordinates and ill-supported by the bureaucracy, to meet it.

Small wonder, then, that presidents have tended to rely on secrecy for the application of small amounts of force here and there in the world. But as I have argued in the past, reliance on wholly covert means has a bad effect, obverse to that of the War Powers Act—it gives policymakers the illusion that they can dispense with making policy. It also has tended to concentrate the public's attention on the fact of covert action rather than on the problem that the covert action is addressing. Finally, the CIA's bureaucracy has shown that it wants no part of paramilitary covert action. It has leaked and lobbied against every one that ever came up during my years on the Intelligence Committee.

So much for the bad news. Perhaps, just perhaps, the following two measures will prove to be more than drops in the bucket. First, I will propose an amendment to the Defense Authorization Act to give the Department of Defense (DOD) primary authority for providing military or paramilitary assistance, overt or covert. The CIA will not want to lose its exclusive charter, but, in fact, it has not done the job. Perhaps if the law gives that job wholeheartedly to the DOD, the Military Services will see an opportunity to build a capability of which they can be proud. Second, I have joined with Senator Humphrey in a request to the White House that it establish an office to advise the President—and to advise the Executive Branch on the President's behalf—about the many things that the United States can do to help friendly resistance movements. These things may be military, but they may also be diplomatic or economic.

These two measures fall under the category of concentrating the mind—that is, trying to make sure that the right question is asked at the right time in a place where asking it can do some good. As I said at the beginning, our foreign and defense apparatus suffers from major intellectual and moral failings on the part of senior officials, and from the effects of bureaucracies left to steer by their own bureaucratic instincts. Special operations are useful only as the finely wielded tool of a government that has picked its policies wisely and pursues them intelligently and steadfastly. The rebirth of American special operations will have to await such a government.

16
The Role of the Media

Sander Vanocur

I feel half qualified to address the subject, "Terrorism and the Media"—I know too little about terrorism and too much about the media, especially television, the focus of my chapter. Normally, I subscribe to Ken Galbraith's dictum, expressed in his book *An Ambassador's Journal,* that self-modesty is a highly overrated virtue. In the present context, however, modesty is required, since I am unable to provide the assurance many may seek—namely, that the aid of the media can be enlisted in the battle against international terrorism. I do not think this can be done, not because most journalists do not wish to help, but rather because our functions—it should be noted that I do not load the argument by the use of terms like "duties" or "responsibilities"—are just not the same.

In instances where what we do in this business and how we do it are under scrutiny, too many of my colleagues have a tendency to wrap themselves unduly in the First Amendment and solemnly pontificate about "the people's right to know." The First Amendment, as I understand it, simply states that Congress shall make no law abridging freedom of speech or of the press. It says nothing about "the people's right to know."

We are in a business, the business of information. Whatever anyone else may claim for us, that is what we are supposed to do—pass on information, as best we can, as quickly as we can, as accurately as we can. We are not, at least I am not, in the enlightenment or education business. If that results from what I or my colleagues do, it is a by-product, perhaps even a laudable by-product. But it is not our primary function.

There is a tendency on the part of many in television to think of television in literal terms—that what you see (and this is especially true of live television) represents a pretty close approximation of reality. Indeed, it has been said that the camera never blinks, implying that unlike other eyes which do blink, a camera brings you unblinking truth or unblinking reality.

Having been around longer than most of my colleagues, I tend to think of television not in optical terms, but rather in caloric terms. In the book, *Terrorism and the Media,* I was surprised and flattered to find Professor Robert Friedlander of Ohio Northern University citing a remark I made at my alma mater, Northwestern University, in April 1980, to the effect that television news can be likened to an omniverous carnivore which requires fresh raw meat on a daily basis. Since making that analogy, I have changed my views somewhat. A carnivore, even those that are not especially bright, reaches a saturation point. Since I am no longer sure that is the case with television, I have altered the imagery somewhat, now likening television not to a carnivore, but rather to an immense tapeworm.

Consider these realities. Television, especially in this country, is virtually on around the clock. In the case of the Cable News Network it *is* on around the clock. Consider also that television now has the capacity to be almost everywhere almost at once. In the earlier days of television's coverage of world events, when radio was still supreme, network correspondents sent their reports back on film, to be edited back at their network headquarters. The process, especially in the days of piston-engine aircraft, took time. There was no conscious claim that what one was doing was immediate. In effect, what you were sending back was a night letter, or cable, in which the very process of time—the difference in time between when you reported the event and when it appeared—took some of the immediacy away from the report. Your viewers had probably heard about the event on radio or read about it in newspapers. But matters changed quickly, first with satellites, then with light mobile equipment, all of which allowed you to see events as they happened or soon after they happened—for example, a suspected presidential assassin gunned down in a Dallas police station, astronauts walking on the moon, and battles in Vietnam that had occurred only hours before. In short, because of technology, television has become virtually omnipresent.

This is well known. I know it and most terrorists know it, and those who don't soon make it their business to know it. We all have this in common—we all agree that television is powerful. Mao said power flows from the barrel of a gun. Today, power flows from the end of a cathode tube. It does not really matter if television is as powerful as people claim it to be. If enough persons think it is powerful and if those persons act as if it is powerful, then it is powerful.

When I was a young journalist, newly arrived in Washington, I had this quaint notion, no doubt derived from experience in Europe, that persons with real power seldom displayed it. That was the secret of their power. They had it, they knew they had it, hence there was no reason for display. But as years passed and the television tapeworm grew, political figures assumed, not unreasonably, that less was not more, more was more, and that more persons viewing meant that more political power could be gained by mass exposure. The most telling political phrase to emerge from the turbulence of the 1968 Democratic convention was: "The whole world is watching." (That may not have been entirely true. But America was certainly watching and, to the degree it was watching, most of it probably approved of the way in which the Chicago police force was beating up on a lot of upper-middle-class youth and, on occasion, a few upper-middle-class journalists.)

Those who followed Eugene McCarthy at Chicago and before were in no sense terrorists, and their attempts to make sure, through television, that the whole world was watching backfired in terms of advancing their cause. They were blamed, and, I might add, so were those of us covering that convention, for the violence unleashed. And that marked a real crossover for those of us in television—namely, that we became, in the eyes of many, part of the problem itself, which brings us to the focus of this book.

I have been reading a good deal of material on the problem of terrorism and the media's role in reporting it—some critics would say aiding and abetting it. I have read about guidelines and about restraint on the part of reporters, producers, and executives. And most of all, I have read complaints about how the press in general fails to understand the threat of international terrorism. It is very tiring. First, I yield to no one in my concern over our failings. I tend to align myself with Gene McCarthy who, when asked in 1970 what he thought about Spiro Agnew's attacks on the television networks, replied: "I agree with everything he says. I just deny him his right to say it." But what I don't go along with is "media bashing," which has figured rather prominently in what I have read in this field.

The critics want us, depending on which of them you read, to be: neoconservatives, terrorist experts, law enforcement officials, government officials, legal scholars, or philosophers. That is really not our function. It was once said by the late Eddie Lahey of the *Chicago Daily News,* a product of the "Front Page" school of journalists (who, in the first Neiman Fellows class at Harvard, delighted Felix Frankfurter) that every good general-assignment reporter ought to have the depth of a one-pound box of candy. By that, Lahey meant that every good reporter should have the capacity to cover any story, any time, under all circumstances. That is why, as someone who has always been a general-assignment reporter, I doubt very much if one will ever see, as has been advocated, reporters who are "terrorism experts" employed full-time by network, local stations, or newspapers on a wide scale, who can be deployed in print or on the air to report terrorist activity whenever and wherever it occurs.

Even if such a plan were feasible, and then even if it were adopted on a widespread basis, I am not certain how useful it would prove to be. I am of an age where I am skeptical of all well-made plans about almost everything, especially those designed to deal with news events that may or may not occur. I tend to think that each event, if and when it finally takes place, has conditions peculiar to itself and must be handled, if not on an ad hoc basis, then at least in a relatively flexible manner.

I would not like to guarantee now how I would act individually, or how any news organization to which I may be attached would react to a variety of hypothetical situations. Each one would, I imagine, present different challenges and elicit differing responses. I also would not like to lay down guidelines on how we in the news-gathering business would cooperate with police, security forces, military personnel, government officials, and so on, when it comes time to report on a terrorist incident that is threatened, in progress, or has just ended.

In principle, I think too much is asked of us when it is recommended that we enter into formal, binding arrangements with security forces and government officials in matters of this kind. My instinct is that when it comes to dealing with governmental authority, at whatever level, most journalists (and surely this is most evident in Washington) are not, as we are charged, adversarial, but rather that we are too compliant with governmental authority. And this disturbs me, not because I have disdain for governmental authority—I do not—but simply because government is in one business and I am in another. Thus, while I would be most reluctant, as a general rule, to take part in any arrangement whereby I or my colleagues would be used in an attempt by authorities to resolve a terrorist undertaking, at the same time, I would be equally reluctant to be used by the terrorists for their purposes.

Again, each case is different. Take the Baader-Meinhof kidnapping of Western Berlin mayoral candidate Peter Lorenz, when the terrorists virtually dictated, for as much as seventy-two hours, how West German television operated. That incident was surely different from how local Washington television stations operated in the Hanafi Muslim takeover of the B'nai B'rith headquarters in Washington, even though in the latter, at least one local anchorman figured prominently in a conversation with the leader of the Hanafi Muslims—an action which produced, almost immediately, an offer from two publishers to the local anchorman to write a book and one other offer from a man volunteering to be his agent for book and film projects.

The issue with which this chapter deals, and with which we journalists deal, is not the existence of terrorist activity by itself. The issue is how terrorist activities are reported and the role that journalists play in the reporting of these activities. I am not at all persuaded that if news organizations stopped reporting terrorist activities aimed solely at influencing public opinion and governmental behavior, then terrorist activities would stop. They would not. They would merely change. As Abraham H. Miller has said: "It would be impractical for the media to ignore terrorist events. And even if it were not, the withholding of this kind of information from the public would ultimately have some negative and unanticipated consequences. Ultimately, the terrorists would increase the scope of their activities or select such prominent targets that the media could no longer afford to ignore them."

The greatest problem facing those who would wish to reduce the capacity of news organizations to be used, albeit in most cases unwillingly, for the purposes of the terrorists, is the competition that exists between news organizations, especially those in television and radio. There are more news networks, television and radio, than ever before. There are more large stations, most affiliated with networks, that have large news departments because, unlike, say, twenty years ago, local news has become a major source of profit for these local stations. They have excellent modern equipment, in some cases better than the network news departments, and they do not hesitate to use this equipment when the occasion demands it. They are in fact, and this is especially true here in the United States, increasingly in competition with the network news departments, even those news departments to which they are affiliated.

Two relevant examples will illustrate this point. First, in the late winter of 1981, when I was on the diplomatic beat for ABC News, I became interested in the proposals to sell five AWACs aircraft to Saudi Arabia. There were very few other reporters, in print, radio, or television, covering the story at that time. Finally, in the fall, on the night the vote was taken, when I went out to do my report on the lawn outside the capitol, there must have been in addition to the cameras of ABC, NBC, CBS, CNN, and INN, at least three or four from local stations in the D.C. area and possibly about a dozen others from various local news stations around the country. Second, at both the Democratic convention in San Francisco and at the Republican convention in Dallas, it was startling to see, in addition to the network booths, the large number of smaller booths with the call letters of either local stations or broadcast groups that included several local stations.

I am not trying to offer a seminar in the growth prospects of local television, but, in terms of this country, that is a reality of television news. We will have increasing numbers of what I call "SONY sherpas" lugging around very light, very mobile, very sophisticated electronic gear to cover every form of activity, including terrorist activity. And even if many—even if all—of these local "SONY sherpas" work for organizations that do have, as the networks have, rather stringent guidelines, I can promise that this critical competitive mass will have a difficult time not playing into the hands of terrorists who are probably going to become just as sophisticated as the technology that is being used to cover them.

I am sorry to have to say that. But I believe that is what is likely to happen in the future. No one, I believe, can prevent it. The competition is too intense. And what is worse, the individuals engaged in the reporting of the events, especially if the coverage is live and continuing, may not be able to apply any judicious editing safeguards to their reporting. All the guidelines that have been drawn up, all the advance understandings with local police or local government officials, all the understandings that are negotiated while a terrorist activity may be under way, are going to be strained to their limits by the sheer mass and density of this age of electronic communications.

This does not mean that those officials charged with tackling terrorist activity should not seek ongoing liaison with news organizations about the problem, so long as it is done on a generally ad hoc basis. I think that there has been enormous benefit to both sides when this has been done. And I must say, at least on the level at which I work, I think there is a great sense of responsibility about how we have proceeded in the past and there will be a greater sense of responsibility on how we proceed in the future.

But having said that, I would not like to leave anyone with the impression that there is some foolproof way for the news media to avoid being used by terrorist organizations in the future—used against their will, but used nevertheless. There is no perfect preventative. If we become more sophisticated and if the police become more sophisticated, my guess is that the terrorist organizations—especially if their ranks are filled with "Atari assassins," that is, the children of the television and computer age—will also become increasingly sophisticated.

For myself, I don't mind if the press is used as a whipping boy for a great many matters that don't go as many would wish. I never entered this line of work because I thought it was a rhinestone-laden path of popularity. But what I do mind and what I will challenge, even at the risk of offering unintentional offense, is that I can do the authorities' work for them, even in such an ugly business as terrorism. I can't. I can try to help, consistent with what I think are my journalistic functions and limitations. But I can't go much beyond that, nor can most of my responsible colleagues. If, once, you do cross over the line that will always divide the governmental function from the journalistic function, you create a precedent. If you do it twice, you create a pattern. And if you do it the third time, you create an expectation, one that in time could compromise journalism in a way that no one would ultimately like.

All that I have written may be, as the English would put it, "small beer." And while we may be part of the problem and while we may be part of the solution, I would insult the reader's intelligence and my own self-respect if I agreed that we are *the* problem and we are *the* solution. I wish that it were all that simple. Unfortunately it is not.

17
International Responses

Douglas J. Feith

Terrorist organizations devote a great deal of effort to participating in international conferences, cultivating diplomatic relations with governments, and, in the course thereof, capitalizing on their own earnest invocations of international law as the source and the sign of the legitimacy of their struggles. That terrorist organizations take international law seriously (which is not at all to say that they comply with it) is evident from the history of the Geneva Diplomatic Conference on the Reaffirmation and Development of International Humanitarian Law Applicable in Armed Conflict (the Diplomatic Conference), which met from 1974 to 1977. Conducted under the auspices of the International Committee for the Red Cross (ICRC), the Diplomatic Conference negotiated two protocols[1] that revised and augmented the 1949 Geneva Conventions for the Protection of War Victims.[2]

The record of the Diplomatic Conference sheds light on how terrorism, law, and politics tie together. It calls attention to the gulf that divides Western liberal political culture from that of totalitarian and so-called Third World powers with respect to conceptions of law and of human rights. It reveals the pitfalls of dialogue in the absence of common values, common interests, and common usage of words. And it opens for examination the negotiating techniques Westerners routinely employ in international forums, techniques rooted in the conviction that there are things more important than principle.

Humanitarian Law and the Diplomatic Conference

The law of armed conflict has traditionally been divided into Hague rules,[3] which limit the means and methods of allowable warfare (such as what may be targeted and what weapons and techniques may be used), and Geneva rules, which mandate human treatment of war victims. The four Geneva Conventions of 1949 form the crux of international humanitarian law.

The sporadic efforts of parties in the years after 1949 to promote conferences to modify the Geneva Conventions bore little fruit before 1974. But by then the ground had become amply fertile, largely by means of United Nations General Assembly (UNGA) resolutions that supported "national liberation movements" (NLMs) and thereby highlighted the failure of the Geneva Conventions to sanction the kind of warfare such movements usually wage. Interest in creating rights for irregulars combined with other interests—for example, that of the ICRC in increasing protection for its medical personnel and that of the United States in pressuring North Vietnam regarding U.S. prisoners of war and the remains of fallen U.S. soldiers—to draw 126 states in February 1974 to participate in the first session of the Diplomatic Conference.[4]

Notwithstanding its humanitarian subject matter and the legal nature of its mission, the Diplomatic Conference from its inception operated as most United Nations forums then did (and do)—as a theater for harshly expounded, highly ideological politics. The major international events and circumstances of the period—the successful wars against Portugese rule in southern Africa; the North Vietnamese conquest of South Vietnam; the assertion of power by Third World oil-exporting states, in particular Arab states; the PLO's inspirational alchemic accomplishment in converting terrorism into broadly based diplomatic stature; the Soviet Union's rapidly increasing military power and its growing role in "national liberation wars" outside Russia's historical sphere of activity; and the traumas inflicted on the United States by Vietnam and Watergate—tended to embolden many non-Western conference participants and therefore proved unconducive to sober disinterestedness and to deference to traditional principles of international order.

Liberation Law Promoted

The Diplomatic Conference's work on updating the 1949 Conventions was based on two draft protocols, the first covering "international" and the second "non-international" armed conflicts. How to categorize "wars of national liberation" was a heated issue with weighty legal and diplomatic ramifications, and it arose at the outset.

The Diplomatic Conference lost little time in adopting a resolution that invited the participation of NLMs from around the world.[5] The following groups accepted and, though they lacked entitlement to vote, helped rewrite the international community's humanitarian law:[6]

African National Congress (South Africa) (1st, 2d, 3d sessions)

African National Council of Zimbabwe (Rhodesia) (3d, 4th)

Angola National Liberation Front (FNLA) (1st, 2d)

Mozambique Liberation Front (1st)
Palestine Liberation Organization (all sessions)
Panafricanist Congress (South Africa) (1st, 2d, 4th)
People's Movement for the Liberation of Angola (MPLA) (1st, 2d)
Seychelles People's United Party (1st)
South West Africa People's Organization (all sessions)
Zimbabwe African National Union (1st, 2d)
Zimbabwe African People's Union (1st, 2d)

The original working draft stated simply that Protocol I applies to those situations that the 1949 Geneva Conventions classified as international conflicts. At the Diplomatic Conference, amendments were proposed to specify that such situations include wars of national liberation, defined with reference to the struggles of "peoples" against "colonial domination," "alien occupation," and "racist regimes."[7] Most struggles of that kind, entailing the direct involvement of only one sovereign state, had for years commonly been deemed internal or noninternational matters. On the establishment of the opposite proposition, however, hung the legitimacy of all the many foreign interventions, diplomatic and material, made on behalf of the various NLMs. As the East German representative explained:

> [T]he General Assembly . . . [has] declared that "armed conflicts involving the struggle of peoples against colonial and alien domination and racist regimes are to be regarded as international armed conflicts in the sense of the 1949 Geneva Conventions." That resolution was extremely important because it confirmed that the colonial Power had no rights of sovereignty over colonial territories and peoples, [and] that assistance by foreign States to the liberation struggle of colonial peoples did not constitute interference in the domestic affairs of the colonial Power. . . .[8]

Proponents of applying Protocol I to national liberation conflicts contended that the treaty should affirm both "the right of peoples to self-determination,"[9] and the "lawfulness" of armed conflict to realize that right.[10] The characterization of self-determination as a right was repeatedly attributed to the United Nations Charter.[11] Wars fought for that "right" were often referred to as "just"[12] or "legitimate."[13] The failure of the Diplomatic Conference to consecrate such wars, it was said, would amount to a denial of both political reality and current law. According to the USSR representative, the "sole object" of the proposed national liberation war language was to "embody in humanitarian law a rule which was already in existence and which took into account the realities of the times."[14] Opposition to such language could be attributed only to mean self-interest on the part of Western imperialists. The Tanzanian representative declared that his delegation "was not prepared to accept a humanitarian law drawn up solely in the interest of the imperialist powers."[15] The Nigerian representative later added that "if the Conference did not agree that the national liberation struggles were governed by draft Protocol I, his delegation's fears would be confirmed: the problems would be dealt with solely from the point of view of the western Powers, in defiance of the principles of international law . . . ."[16]

The Senegalese representative warned that a wrong decision on this issue by the Diplomatic Conference could aggravate the problem of terrorism:

> To deny the international character of [wars of national liberation] was to trample on the most sacred rights of the peoples who were fighting.
>
> It was the feeling of injustice so engendered which was mainly responsible for what was described as "international terrorism". When thousands of innocent people were daily being slaughtered in many parts of the world, it was difficult for people to be shocked at the few dozen innocent victims of the hijacking or sabotage of airliners. Without justice, humanitarian law was merely an empty word.[17]

Liberation Law Dispraised

Opponents of the national liberation war amendments denounced them as destructive not only of humanitarian law, but of the prohibition against war promulgated in Article 2(4) of the United Nations Charter,[18] the first principle of international law since World War II. They argued that the amendments would legally sanction the resurrection of the medieval "just war" doctrine[19] and effectively abolish the distinction between international and noninternational conflicts. Furthermore, the most important terms in the amendments lacked definition, so the application of humanitarian law would depend on subjective judgments rooted in politics.

The British representative expressed "surprise" at the text of the amendments:

> The 1949 Conventions had been carefully drafted on the basis of a distinction between international and non-international armed conflicts. If the systems of those Conventions were to be disrupted, all the Conventions would have to be revised. . . . [S]truggles for national liberation fell within the ambit of Protocol II [dealing with non-international conflicts].
>
> The various arguments had presented no convincing case for considering an internal struggle as an international one. Moreover, it was a basic principle of the Geneva Conventions, The Hague Regulations and other instruments that legal and humanitarian protection should never vary accord-

ing to the motives of those engaged in a particular armed struggle. Deviation from that principle would mean damaging the structure of The Hague and Geneva Conventions and would involve the need to reconstruct the whole of humanitarian law. Moreover, to discriminate between the motives of those engaged in the struggle would violate essential principles of human rights.

It was true that self-determination was mentioned in the Charter of the United Nations, but as principle, not as a right. Nowhere in the Charter did the right to engage in armed struggle appear. No resolution of the United Nations could amend the Charter, which would remain inviolate until amended in the proper manner. Terms like "struggle for the self-determination of peoples" were all too vague. What was a "people"? Such terms were elastic, as Biafra and Bangladesh had shown. They could not be used as a basis for law-making.[20]

The Swiss delegate elaborated further on the distinction between law and politics:

[The amendments] tended to establish a particular category of conflicts on the basis of subjective criteria stemming from the causes of those conflicts and the aims of the parties. That entailed a move from the field of *jus in bello* to a zone which held dangers for the Conference, namely, *jus ad bellum*. . . . [I]t would be very dangerous, and against the spirit of humanitarian law, to classify armed conflicts on the basis of non-objective and non-legal criteria. In adopting that position, his delegation was not expressing an opinion on the legitimacy of national liberation struggles with which people in Switzerland felt in sympathy. That question lay within the province of other forums; the task of the Conference was to provide the greatest possible protection for the victims of those conflicts.[21]

States like Iraq, Nigeria, the Soviet Union, and Yugoslavia, which can be (and have been) charged with denying the right of self-determination to certain of their national and ethnic groups, supported the national-liberation-war amendments without evincing concern that such groups would derive any aid or comfort therefrom. The amendments' opponents pointed out that there existed no objective standards for judging whether a group qualified as a NLM. "Any separatist band of armed criminals in a colonial territory might claim to be engaged in an armed struggle in furtherance of their people's right to self-determination," observed the Irish representative.[22] The amendments' supporters, however, saw the matter not primarily as one of definitive standards but international recognition; the prevailing view was that a NLM is any group recognized as such by "the regional intergovernmental organizations concerned"—for example, by the Arab League or the Organization of African Unity (OAU).[23] Indeed, it was on that basis that the movements listed above were invited to participate in the Diplomatic Conference.[24] Given the nature and record of the relevant regional intergovernmental organizations, one could confidently predict whether a given armed group would obtain recognition as an authentic NLM or whether, for reasons of its unprogressiveness or the inadvisability of crossing its antagonist, it would be denied the protections of Protocol I.

Several states objected that extending Protocol I to "national liberation wars" would discriminate invidiously against sovereign states in favor of irregular forces fighting them in their own territory. The problem would arise because both the irregular force and its state-enemy would enjoy rights under Protocol I and the 1949 Geneva Conventions, but only the latter would command the kind of resources (for example, law courts and medical facilities) required for the fulfillment of the corresponding obligations. The Italian representative commented:

> [T]he word "Powers" used in the . . . Geneva Conventions could only mean States and not authorities other than States. That fact was borne out not only by the letter and spirit of the Conventions, but also by the circumstances that application of many provisions of the Geneva Conventions called for complicated machinery which was, generally speaking, available only to States.[25]

The United States representative later added:

> Liberation movements could not fulfill all their obligations under the Conventions and would thus be branded as being in violation of those Conventions. The only benefit which those movements would receive from labeling their struggle as international would be enhanced political status, but nothing on the humanitarian plane.[26]

Treating the issue as one of good intentions, respect for law, and willingness to do all one can do, rather than as a matter of objective capability to perform an extensive list of specified duties, the representatives of the Mozambique Liberation Front and the PLO dismissed the competency question. In this connection, the former deemed it relevant to assert that "[c]ases were known where States had departed from the established rules far more grossly than the liberation movements."[27]

The last major argument against extending Protocol I to "national liberation wars" invoked the practical principle that humanitarian law should be crafted to encourage compliance. If the law's applicability to a group of fighters hinged on their cause's legitimacy, a state battling a NLM will refuse to apply the law, lest it make a fatal political concession. In the words of the Israeli representative: "[Protocol I's national-liberation-war provision] had within it a built-in non-applicability clause, since a party would have to admit that it was either racist, alien or colonial. . . . [S]uch language . . . ensured that no State by its own volition would ever apply that article."[28]

Ends and Means

A very large portion of the Diplomatic Conference—which spanned more than three years—was spent in this debate over the status of "national liberation wars." Though it generated its share of heat, the debate is remarkable for the dearth of actual engagement between the sides. They generally talked past one another.

The participants that adhered to the traditional concepts underlying the 1949 Geneva Conventions, whom for ease of reference and with general accuracy we label "Western," distinguished between considerations appropriate for a political body, such as the UNGA, and those suitable for either a humanitarian organization like the ICRC or a treaty-drafting body like the Diplomatic Conference.[29] Accordingly, as we have seen, they made their case against the national-liberation-war amendments with arguments of a legal nature.

Their concept of law derived from that body of philosophy, the pride of Western Civilization, whose appendages include the Magna Carta, the United States Constitution, and the Declaration of the Rights of Man. In brief, it is law as impartial principle, expressed in objective phraseology, duly defined, to be applied to specific cases by disinterested judges. Its essence is fair procedure—due process of law—which binds all elements of society, including the government. Its purpose is to safeguard the rights of individuals from the depredations of other private actors and of the government. Hence, where this conception prevails, law imposes limitations on all political activity within the state, even that of the party in power, which is held accountable for any violations. In such circumstances, the notion of the common good is derived from the ground up—that is, from the protection of the rights of individuals. This Western view of law does not allow for a group to invoke "the people's interest" to justify depriving an individual, without due process of law, of his life, liberty, or property. Nor does it allow for action in the name of the people in the absence of their express consent.

Small wonder that the Western representatives' legal arguments failed to resonate among their interlocutors from the Socialist camp and from much of the so-called Third World. In most of the world outside the West, law does not constrain governments; indeed, it often serves merely as a device by which ruling parties suppress their opponents. Adherents of the view that collective interests—described as those of the ruling party, the state, the people, or whatever—necessarily outweigh the interests of individuals have understandable difficulty in conceiving of law as it is known in the West. As the record of the Diplomatic Conference makes plain, the idea of law as separate from and above politics is the light and delight of a small minority of states.

This helps account for much of the ships-passing-in-the-night nature of the Article I debate. The Western representatives wanted to weigh the merits of competing legal formulations. The non-Westerners wanted to use the Protocol to make political points in support of their favorite NLMs. The Westerners argued that such points may do for a political resolution of the United Nations, but not for a legal document. The non-Westerners rejected the distinction and continually made erroneous reference to UNGA resolutions as international law.[30] The Westerners warned that vague and subjective wording would make humanitarian law a tool of politics. The non-Westerners already viewed it as such and evidently considered the circumstances desirable; none expressed qualms about making the applicability of the law to irregulars a matter for decision by the Arab League, the OAU, and other such political forums.

The Westerners defended the merit of the political neutrality of the UN Charter and the 1949 Geneva Conventions. They explained that amending and reinterpreting so as to politicize those treaties would negate the advance (rare and valuable, albeit largely theoretical) which they effected in the direction of world peace and respect for human rights. Certain states and causes, to be sure, could reap quick benefits from such mischief, but these would likely prove fleeting in a world where international law, having lost its neutrality lost its moral force, and therefore much of its sway over those states that heed it.

Such high-minded metaphysics had no apparent effect on its targets, many of whom denied that existing international law was neutral and described it as pro-imperialist or pro-Western. Moreover, a number spoke as if there were no such thing as a neutral principle of law. They seemed to view international law as a zero-sum game: If a provision is supported by the West, it must be undesirable for the Third World.

Liberation Law Ascendant

The debate, in short, produced no meeting of the minds on the fundamentals. The Westerners presented their case forcefully and generally emphasized the points that most deserved emphasis—that the proposed national-liberation-war language would legitimate certain types of war, license belligerent foreign meddling in the sovereign domain of certain states, and politicize humanitarian law, thereby rendering it even less sturdy a shield for its intended beneficiaries. In light of this critique, it may surprise the reader to learn that Article

1 of Protocol I, as ultimately adopted by the Diplomatic Conference with but one negative vote, reads (in relevant part) as follows:

> 4. The situations [to which Protocol I applies] include armed conflicts in which peoples are fighting against colonial domination and alien occupation and against racist regimes in the exercise of their right of self-determination, as enshrined in the Charter of the United Nations and the Declaration on Principles of International Law concerning Friendly Relations and Co-operation among States in accordance with the Charter of the United Nations.[31]

The March 1974 vote in committee on that paragraph was 70 votes in favor and 21 against (Belgium, Canada, Denmark, Federal Republic of Germany, France, Israel, Italy, Japan, Liechtenstein, Luxemburg, Monaco, Netherlands, New Zealand, Portugal, Republic of Korea, South Africa, Spain, Switzerland, United Kingdom, United States, and Uruguay), with 13 abstentions (Australia, Austria, Brazil, Burma, Chile, Colombia, Greece, Guatemala, Holy See, Ireland, Philippines, Sweden, and Turkey).

The May 1977 final vote in plenary on Article 1 was 87 in favor and one against (Israel), with 11 abstentions (Canada, Federal Republic of Germany, France, Guatemala, Ireland, Italy, Japan, Monaco, Spain, United Kingdom, and the United States).

The PLO representative was gratified, "[He expressed] deep satisfaction at the result of the vote, by which the international community had re-confirmed the legitimacy of the struggles of peoples exercising their right to self-determination."[32] The record of the Diplomatic Conference is silent on why many of the negative votes became abstentions three years later. In fact, several members, in explaining their plenary abstentions, cited the very objections to Article 1 on which they had justified their earlier negative votes.[33]

The British representative recalled that "the main reason for [UK] opposition . . . was that [paragraph 4] introduced the regrettable innovation of making the motives behind a conflict a criterion for the application of humanitarian law." He stated that his delegation had "not wish[ed] to see the Protocol founder on that difference of opinion" and, because "the cardinal principle of equality of application to all participants had been respected," his delegation felt "relieved."[34] The relief seems, however, to flow from begging the question, for the determination as to which fighting group qualifies as a "participant" remains under Protocol I a political judgment.

The United States offered no formal explanation of its plenary vote. It is noteworthy that certain U.S. government lawyers involved in the negotiations recommended in a 1977 "working group review and analysis" that the U.S. government sign and ratify Protocol I, refrain from making any reservation regarding Article 1(4), and mitigate the problems inherent in that provision through a strict construction. They observed that "[t]he kinds of conflict that nations deemed covered by the general phrase wars of national liberation were those fought against the foreign element in Vietnam, Guinea-Bissau, Angola, Palestine, southern Africa, and Mozambique," and concluded: "The narrow interpretation suggested above appears to be one that is in the United States interest."[35]

The Uniform and the Irregular

Establishing the international character of "national liberation struggles" was a necessary step toward exempting the participants from the municipal law of their sovereign enemies. Under the 1949 Geneva Convention on Prisoners of War (GPW), combatants in international conflicts are deemed entitled to commit acts of belligerency that would be punishable if committed by an ordinary individual.[36] And such combatants, if captured by their enemy, have a right to special treatment as prisoners of war. But the GPW does not bestow combatant status on just any fighter, guerrilla, terrorist, or irregular engaged in an international conflict. The conditions for qualification set forth in the GPW favor the interests of noncombatants above those of irregular forces.

Article 4 of the GPW affords combatant status to regular uniformed soldiers (whether nor not the power for which they fight is recognized by its enemy as a Party to the conflict) and in subparagraph A(2), to:

> Members of other militias and members of other volunteer corps, including those of organized resistance movements, belonging to a Party to the conflict . . . provided that such militias or volunteer corps, including such resistance movements, fulfill the following conditions:
>
> (a) that of being commanded by a person responsible for his subordinates;
> (b) that of having a fixed distinctive sign recognizable at a distance;
> (c) that of carrying arms openly;
> (d) that of conducting their operations in accordance with the laws and customs of war.

These conditions have roots in the laws of war that reach back at least to The Hague Conventions of 1907 and 1899, the Brussels Declaration of 1874, and the American Civil War. They effectively preclude nonuniformed paramilitary bands like the typical terrorist group or NLM from qualifying for combatant/POW status. Such a force ordinarily is not recognized as a Party to the conflict. Unless it has a secure base in a region beyond the writ of the government it is fighting, wearing uniforms and openly carrying arms would be suicidal. And, as previously discussed, such forces usually lack the facilities needed to fulfill the formidable obligations the Geneva Conventions impose on Parties.

In attempting to explain the stringency of the GPW's standards, some commentators have alleged that the drafters were largely oblivious to guerrilla warfare.[37] The evidence is abundantly to the contrary, however.[38]

The rationale for the conditions, especially the "openness" requirements in subsections (b) and (c), can easily be found in the traditional solicitude for civilians that is the primary raison d'etre of international humanitarian law. If one had to render all of humanitarian law while standing on one leg, one might well proclaim: Combatants are to be distinguished from noncombatants; the rest is commentary. In a war in which the participants appear openly as soldiers, each soldier may reasonably assume that people who look like civilians are civilians and that they pose no threat and may safely be spared attack. On the other hand, as Draper has noted:

> Once the . . . man with the bomb who is a civilian in all outward appearances but can blow you to smithereens as you pass him by, once you bring such a person within the framework of the protection given to regular armed combatants under article 4 of the Geneva Prisoners-of-War Convention, you make life for every single civilian hang upon a thread. . . .[39]

Traditional considerations of the rights and interests of individuals, however, conflicted with the conception of humanitarian law dominant among the Socialist/Third World majority at the Diplomatic Conference. In that conception, humanitarian law is not about individuals, but causes. If a rule that protects innocent bystanders impedes the success of a humanitarian cause— one aimed at liberating a territory from "colonialists," "aliens," or "racists"— it is not a humanitarian rule.

It was clear to all that the respective interests of the civilian and the irregular fighter conflict. "Openness" requirements are invaluable to the former and dangerous for the latter. Whereas the drafters of the CPW interpreted their charter in conformity with traditional individualist ideas of human rights and chose to reaffirm those requirements, the majority at the Diplomatic Conference were intent on shifting the balance of the law in favor of the nonuniformed fighter. Articles 43 and 44 of Protocol I,[40] as adopted by the Diplomatic Conference,[41] make this radical shift.

The Protocol I standards for irregular forces deviate from the long-standing rules in several respects, among the most important of which are: 1) There is no requirement for a "fixed distinctive sign"—that is, a uniform;[42] 2) The general requirement to carry arms openly has been dropped—one must do so only during certain military operations; and 3) a combatant forfeits his right to be a POW only if he violates the narrow "openness" rule of the second sentence of Article 44(3), but even then he retains all the POW protections afforded by the GPW.[43]

It is not difficult to grasp why the PLO representative declared Article 44's adoption in committee "encouraging" and "an important step forward in the growing recognition, through international instruments, of the legitimacy of the struggle of national liberation movements and the need to guarantee their fighters adequate protection;"[44] and one easily comprehends his statement, following its adoption in plenary, that "national liberation movements. . . . could not fail to welcome the protection accorded to their combatants by [Article 44] . . ."[45] What may be less obvious is why the United States, breaking ranks with a number of its allies and other states, voted in favor of the Article and praised it as "an important advance in the law."

If You Can't Get the Law You Want, Love the Law You Get

Early on at the Diplomatic Conference the United States cosponsored a draft article that would have granted POW status to captured members of irregular forces only if they "distinguish themselves from the civilian population in their military operations by carrying arms openly or by a distinctive sign recognizable at a distance or by any other equally effective means" and otherwise complied with the laws of war. The draft article would have denied POW status to an individual irregular only if he failed to fulfill the broad "openness" condition. Nonfulfillment of the two conditions by individual irregulars would not have deprived other members of their irregular force of POW status upon capture.[46]

That proposed article would have relaxed the GPW "openness" requirements by allowing irregular forces to choose their own means of distinguishing themselves from civilians, but, as a U.S. representative explained, "[t]he single important issue is that combatants be distinguished from civilians—how it is done is not so important as the fact that it is done."[47] The unique importance of openness in all military operations would have been reflected in the provision that made violation of that requirement the sole exception to the rule in favor of POW status. In justification of the proposed exception, the U.S. representative stated:

> This requirement that they distinguish themselves from civilians is so fundamental to the purposes of Protocol I—so essential, if we are to give meaning to the protected status that we have conferred on civilians—so basic if we are to give credibility to [other articles intended to protect civilians from attack], for all of these reasons, it is vital that Protocol I deny a privileged status to combatants who violated the requirement that they must in some

manner distinguish themselves from civilians in their military operations. . . . In our view, a combatant who deliberately fails to distinguish himself from other civilians while engaging in combat operations has committed such an extraordinary violation of the laws of war and so prejudices the protection for civilians that he loses his entitlement to be a prisoner of war. . . . The desire and urgency to protect the civilians is no different today than it was in 1907—or 1949—and the lives of civilians are no less important today than they were then.[48]

The gap between that initial U.S. stand on the POW issue and the provision of Protocol I is difficult to bridge. Article 44, after all, does not condition POW status for irregulars on their distinguishing themselves from civilians during all military operations, and Article 43 fails to make an irregular force's compliance with the laws of war a condition for combatant status.

In explaining his delegation's support for Articles 43 and 44, U.S. Ambassador George Aldrich attributed much weight to the first sentence in Article 44(3), which he described as a "basic rule" that "meant that throughout their military operations combatants must distinguish themselves in a clearly recognized manner."[49] The paramount justification, however, was the belief that Protocol I might induce groups like the PLO, South West Africa People's Organization, and the other "movements" participating in the Diplomatic Conference to comply with the laws of war:

> [Article 44] conferred no protection on terrorists. It did not authorize soldiers to conduct military operations while disguised as civilians. However, it did give members of the armed forces who were operating in occupied territory an incentive to distinguish themselves from the civilian population when preparing for and carrying out an attack.[50]

I Swear, But Don't Hold Me to It

Commentators who think the Diplomatic Conference robbed civilian Peter to pay terrorist Paul are unimpressed with the several admirable provisions in Articles 43 and 44 that Ambassador Aldrich and other Protocol I proponents prefer to highlight. Notwithstanding the first sentence of Article 44(3), the skeptics see the new law as less kind to civilians and more generous to irregulars—guerrillas and terrorists—than the old law of the GPW. They note that the first sentence of Article 44(3) is less precise than the corresponding provisions in the GPW,[51] and in any event is merely hortatory; no rights or privileges hinge on adherence to it. In contrast, fulfillment by irregulars of the GPW's "openness" requirements is a condition of POW status thereunder. Moreover, the principle embodied in the first sentence of Article 44(3) is vitiated by the next sentence, which actually grants POW status to combatants who do not distinguish themselves from noncombatants during all military operations.

Under Protocol I, whatever protection noncombatants retain against the danger of combatants operating in civilian garb derives from this same hotly debated second sentence of Article 44(3). Failure to satisfy the "openness" obligation it sets forth is the only offense that would cause a combatant to forfeit his right to be a POW. Yet, as the commentators have remarked, several of the provision's pivotal terms—"deployment," for example—are undefined and subject to widely differing interpretation. Ambassador Aldrich outlined the problem in a 1981 law review article:

> [T] he term "deployment" is a critical one for guerrillas operating in occupied territory. The negotiating history reveals that there was no agreement on the meaning of that term. Some delegates asserted that any movement toward the place from which an attack was to be launched would be part of a "deployment." Certainly, the word is ambiguous . . ."[52]

For those who might wonder why such a "critical" term in so significant a provision was allowed to remain ambiguous, the Ambassador volunteers that "its ambiguity was probably essential to agreement at the conference to the text."[53] For those who might rudely query, "Who needs an agreement under such circumstances?" no answer is offered.[54]

In consequence of the ambiguity of "deployment," a state that captures in its territory a terrorist from one of the sanctioned NLMs and finds he is concealing a bomb would be required by Protocol I to grant him POW status unless it can establish that he was "engaged in a military deployment." Article 45 of Protocol I lays the burden of proof squarely on the state. If states targeted by terrorists were to adhere scrupulously to these provisions, it would be a boon for the terrorists. If, as is likelier, the states (even though parties to Protocol I) prosecute and punish the terrorists as mere terrorists (not "combatants"), it will show disdain for Protocol I, with inevitable collateral damage to other (and more estimable) treaties on the laws of war.

The Swiss representative offered a noteworthy condemnation of Article 44:

> [The] fundamental distinction [between combatants and civilians] was in danger of disappearing. Situations of armed conflict in which, because of the hostilities, the combatants were unable to distinguish themselves from the civilian population were not defined, but left to each party to appraise as it pleased and arbitrarily. The conditions added in sub-paragraphs (a) and (b) were without value. The Swiss delegation was therefore afraid that the article would only have the effect of doing away with the distinctions between

combatants and civilians. The consequence would be that the adverse party could take draconian measures against civilians suspected of being combatants.

Lastly, the explanations of vote by the delegations which had spoken on that article made it clearly apparent that no unity of view existed concerning it. Every one interpreted it as he thought fit. . . . Thus, [Article 44] was not a rule of law, since it lacked the precision of a legal standard. . . .[55]

Like the praiseworthy first sentence of Article 44(3), the provision in Article 43(1) stating that the armed forces of a Party to a conflict "shall be subject to an internal disciplinary system which . . . shall enforce compliance with the [laws of war]" lacks teeth. It states an obligation, but it does not state that a member of an otherwise-qualified armed forces forfeits his combatant status if those forces violate that obligation. The contention has been made that compliance with the laws of war is a "condition" for POW status for guerrillas,[56] but such an inference appears ill-grounded. Where the drafters wanted to make POW rights conditional—for example, in Article 44(3)—they did so expressly,[57] and the thrust of Articles 43 through 46 is to create an overwhelming presumption in favor of granting such rights in any doubtful case.

Where does this leave the contention—the chief justification offered by the U.S. delegation for their support of Articles 43 and 44—that dropping the broad "openness" requirements for irregulars desirous of combatant/POW status creates an incentive for irregulars to comply with the laws of war? Need irregulars comply with the law to obtain such status under Protocol I? Regarding compliance by individual members of irregular forces, the answer is an almost unqualified negative. As noted earlier, the only violation of the law that strips an individual combatant of "his right to be a prisoner of war" is nonfulfillment of the narrow and opaque "openness" requirements of Article 44(3)(a) and (b), and even in that case he "shall . . . be given protections equivalent in all respects to those accorded to prisoners of war by the [GPW] and by this Protocol." If there is an incentive here, it is pretty feeble, for it is hard to see the penalty for noncompliance.

Regarding compliance by armed forces collectively, even a policy of violating the laws of war would not, under the express provisions of Articles 43 and 44, deprive a member of his entitlement to combatant/POW status.[58] One could look for the elusive incentive in Article 96(3), which allows any so-called NLM to become, in effect, a party to the Protocol by filing a unilateral declaration in which it undertakes to apply the laws of war to its struggle. But once such a movement successfully files its declaration, no provision of Protocol I can deny its members POW status on the grounds of collective nonobservance of the rules. Hence, no incentive there either.

All in all, the humanitarian benefits of Articles 43 and 44, measured as a function of this putative incentive for irregulars to comply with the law, falls far short of the costs entailed in blurring (not to say erasing for all practical purposes) the distinction between combatants and noncombatants.

Over the centuries humanitarian law strove to mitigate war's harm to civilians through demanding discrimination between combatants and noncombatants. Then along comes the Diplomatic Conference and, in the name of "developing" humanitarian law, lays waste the legal and moral achievement of ages through a single subordinate clause. That clause, of course, is in Article 44(3): "Recognizing, however, that there are situations in armed conflicts where, owing to the nature of the hostilities an armed combatant *cannot* so distinguish himself . . ." The "cannot" is a masterstroke of amoral draftsmanship.

Notwithstanding the exegeses of Westerners straining to rationalize their complicity, the PLO representative (quoted above) correctly proclaimed the significance of this work of the Diplomatic Conference.[59] It amounted to an endorsement, in the politically potent form of a legal instrument, of both the rhetoric and the anticivilian practices of terrorist organizations that fly the banner of self-determination. One can find phrases and even whole sentences in Protocol I that repudiate bald terrorism and deprecate attacks on civilians, but they are not the gist of its operative provisions. They are a faint counterpoint to the booming "progressive," collectivist, ends-justify-the-means blare of the innovative elements of the document.

The Wages of Consensus-Mongering

There is much that is unconstructive in the goings-on of multilateral diplomatic forums around the world. But for truly malign perverseness, it would be hard to top the Diplomatic Conference. The Official Record tells a sinister and sad tale. What makes it sinister is the harm done to potential victims of war and terrorism through prostitution of the law. Beyond that, what makes it sad is the role played by the Westerners. The stakes were higher at the Diplomatic Conference than at the typical gathering of a UN political forum; the subject matter was no ordinary diplomatic resolution, but a treaty with actual potential for affecting the safety and well-being of war victims. The Westerners from the outset demonstrated appreciation of the stakes, astuteness in substantive analysis, and skill in pleading. But on issue after issue, when confronting the Socialist and "Third World" states' resolute attachment to patently harmful proposals, the Westerners backed down. They usually put up a good fight for a while, but then they either signed on or they slunk into the shadow of an abstention. At any of several junctures, they could have walked out and rendered the whole exercise academic (for without major

Western powers no humanitarian agreement would have much standing in the world). But they stayed. Representatives of tyrannies upheld their convictions—stood on their principles, as it were—while the representatives of states where law really governs exalted the necessity for flexibility and compromise above all other principles. Thus with nary a negative vote, the assembly issued up a proterrorist treaty masquerading as humanitarian law. O tempora! O mores!

Postscript

The United States signed Protocol I and Protocol II in December 1977. The decision on whether to submit either or both of the items to the Senate for advice and consent on ratification is currently under discussion within the Administration. It will hinge on whether the unacceptable elements are remediable through U.S. reservations and clarifications.

Notes

1. Protocol I Additional to the Geneva Conventions Relating to the Protection of Victims of International Armed Conflicts, *opened for signature* December 12, 1977, *reprinted in* 16 Int'l Legal Materials 1391 (1977); Protocol II Additional to the Geneva Conventions Relating to the Protection of Victims of Non-International Armed Conflicts, *opened for signature* December 12, 1977, *reprinted in* 16 Int'l Legal Materials 1442 (1977).

2. The four 1949 Geneva Conventions protect respectively "wounded and sick in armed forces in the field," *opened for signature* August 12, 1949, 6 UST 3114, TIAS 3362, 75 UNTS 31, "wounded, sick, and shipwrecked members of armed forces at sea," *opened for signature* August 12, 1949, 6 UST 3217, TIAS 3363, 75 UNTS 85, "prisoners of war," *opened for signature* August 12, 1949, 6 UST 3316, TIAS 3364, 75 UNTS 135, and "civilian persons," *opened for signature* August 12, 1949, 6 UST 3515, TIAS 3365, 75 UNTS 287.

3. Hague Convention No. III Relative to the Opening of Hostilities, *done* October 18, 1907, 36 Stat. 2259, TS 538, Bevans 619; Hague Convention No. IV Respecting the Laws and Customs of War on Land, *done* October 18, 1907, 36 Stat. 2227, TS 539, Bevans 631; Hague Convention No. V Respecting the Rights and Duties of Neutral Powers and Persons in Case of War on Land, *done* October 18, 1907, 36 Stat. 2310, TS 540, Bevans 654; Hague Convention No. IX Concerning Bombardment by Naval Forces in Time of War, *done* October 18, 1907, 36 Stat. 2351, TS 542, Bevans, 681.

4. Final Act of the Dip Conf, 1 Official Records of the Diplomatic Conference on the Reaffirmation and Development of International Humanitarian Law Applicable in Armed Conflicts, *Part One*, 6 (1978).

5. *Id.* at 5.

6. *Id.* at 7.

7. 1 H. Levie, *Protection of War Victims: Protocol I to the 1949 Geneva Conventions* 2-3 (1979) (hereinafter "Levie"). Levie's four volumes reproduced much of the Official Records of the Diplomatic Conference. Quotations herein cited to Levie are quotations from the Official Record, which is a summary account of the proceedings.

8. *Id.* at 6.

9. *Id.* at 4 (Yugoslavia).

10. *Id.* at 20 (Nigeria).

11. *See, e.g., id.* at 4 (Yugoslavia), 6 (Morocco).

12. *See, e.g., id.* at 9 (Madagascar), 17 (People's Republic of China).

13. *See, e.g., id.* at 13 (India).

14. *Id.* at 9.

15. *Id.* at 12.

16. *Id.* at 20.

17. *Id.* at 32.

18. *Done* June 26, 1945, 59 Stat. 1031, TS 9993, Bevans 1153; 1963 amendments, 16 UST 1134, TIAS 5857, 557 UNTS 143; 1965 amendment, 19 UST 5450, TIAS 6529; 1971 amendment, 24 UST 225, TIAS 7739.

19. *See generally* Moore, *A Theoretical Overview of the Laws of War in a Post-Charter World, with Emphasis on the Challenge of Civil Wars, Wars of National Liberation, Mixed Civil-International Wars, and Terrorism,* 31 American U.L.R. 841, 842 (1982) ("Just war is dead in international law. The United Nations Charter killed it, and rightly so. Under the Charter, the use of force is lawful in defense, but not as affirmative conduct to seek resolution of issues by force, however just the cause is perceived to be.").

20. 1 Levie 7 (paragraph numbers omitted).

21. *Id.* at 11; *see also id.* at 10 (Uruguay), 12 (Spain), 21 (Netherlands).

22. *Id.* at 16.

23. *Id.* at 74.

24. See note 6, *supra.*

25. 1 Levie 14.

26. *Id.* at 15-6; *see also id.* at 5 (Belgium), 19 (UK).

27. *Id.* at 25.

28. *Id.* at 65; *see also* Aldrich, *Guerrilla Combatants and Prisoner of War Status,* 31 American U.L.R. 871, 875 (1982) ("In the liberation war . . . identified as an international armed conflict . . . , the state allegedly suppressing the liberation movement is most unlikely to agree that the war is, in fact, a liberation war to which the Protocol applies. . . .").

29. *See, e.g.,* 1 Levie 8 (France).

30. The United Nations Charter provides that the Security Council has authority to make "decisions . . . in accordance with the present Charter" and that the other UN members are bound "to accept and carry out" such decisions. Article 25; *see generally* U.N. Charter Chapters VI, VII, VIII, and XII. In contrast, the General Assembly's functions and powers are explicitly nonlegislative: "The General Assembly may *discuss* any questions . . . [and] may make *recommendations.* . . ." Article 10 (emphasis added). In other words, the Security Council can make international law, but the General Assembly can make only nonbinding declarations.

31. The Friendly Relations Declaration is a UNGA resolution. G.A. Res. 2625 (XXV), 25 U.N. GAOR, Supp. (No. 28) 121, U.N. Doc. A/8028 (1971) *reprinted in* 9 I.L.M. 1292 (1970).

32. 1 Levie 73.

33. *See, e.g.,* 1 Levie 67 (Italy), 69 (France), 69-70 (Canada).

34. *Id.* at 68.

35. Department of Defense Law of War Working Group Review and Analysis of Protocols I and II adopted by the Diplomatic Conference on International Humanitarian Law (1977) at I-1-16a-17.

36. "[The combatants'] privilege provides immunity from application of municipal law prohibitions against homicides, wounding and maiming, or capturing persons and destruction of property, so long as these acts are done as acts of war and do not transgress the restraints of the rules of international law applicable in armed conflict." M. Bothe, K. Partsch, W. Solf, *New Rules for Victims of Armed Conflicts: Commentary on the Two 1977 Protocols Additional to the Geneva Conventions of 1949* 243 (1982) (hereinafter "Bothe").

37. The Chinese representative to the Diplomatic Conference theorized: "The heroic struggle of peoples against the colonial system . . . had not been foreseen in the 1949 Geneva Conventions. . . . [T]hat was already a grave oversight. . . ." 1 Levie 17.

38. *See* Paust, *Law in a Guerrilla Conflict: Myths, Norms and Human Rights,* 3 Israel Y.B. Human Rights 39 (1973); D. Hacker, *The Application of Prisoner-of-War Status to Guerrillas Under the First Protocol Additional to the Geneva Conventions of 1949,* 2 Boston C. Int'l & Comp. Law J. 131, 137 (1978) (hereinafter "Hacker").

39. Statement to ICRC Istanbul Conference, September 11, 1968.

40. Article 43 (in relevant part) provides:

1. The armed forces of a Party to a conflict consist of all organized armed forces, groups and units which are under a command responsible to that Party for the conduct of its subordinates even if that Party is represented by a government or an authority not recognized by an adverse Party. Such armed forces shall be subject to an internal disciplinary system which, *inter alia,* shall enforce compliance with the rules of international law applicable in armed conflict.

2. Members of the armed forces of a Party to a conflict . . . are combatants . . .

Article 44 (in relevant part) provides:

1. Any combatant, as defined in Article 43, who falls into the power of an adverse Party shall be a prisoner of war.

2. While all combatants are obliged to comply with the rules of international law applicable in armed conflict, violations of these rules shall not deprive a combatant of his right to be a combatant or if he falls into the power of an adverse Party, of his right to be a prisoner of war, except as provided in paragraphs 3 and 4.

3. In order to promote the protection of the civilian population from the effects of hostilities, combatants are obliged to distinguish themselves from the civilian population while they are engaged in an attack or in a military operation preparatory to an attack. Recognizing, however, that there are situations in armed conflicts where, owing to the nature of the hostilities an armed combatant cannot so distinguish himself, he shall retain his status as a combatant, provided that, in such situations, he carries his arms openly:

(a) during each military engagement, and

(b) during such time as he is visible to the adversary while he is engaged in a military deployment preceeding the launching of an attack in which he is to participate.

4. A combatant who falls into the power of an adverse Party while failing to meet the requirements set forth in the second sentence of paragraph 3 shall forfeit his right to be a prisoner of war, but he shall, nevertheless, be given protections equivalent in all respects to those accorded to prisoners of war by the [GPW] in the case where such a person is tried and punished for any offences he has committed.

5. Any combatant who falls into the power of an adverse Party while not engaged in an attack or in a military operation preparatory to an attack shall not forfeit his rights to be a combatant and a prisoner of war by virtue of his activities.

41. The April 1977 final vote in plenary on Article 44 was 66 in favor and 2 against (Brazil, Israel), with 18 abstentions (Argentina, Australia, Bolivia, Canada, Chile, Colombia, Denmark, Guatemala, Holy See, Ireland, Italy, Japan, New Zealand, Nicaragua, Spain, Thailand, United Kingdom, Uruguay). 2 Levie 486.

42. The exemption from the requirement for combatants to wear uniforms applies only to the irregulars. In this respect, Article 44 makes it easier for an irregular to obtain combatant/POW status than for a regular soldier to do so. *See* paragraphs (3) and (7) of Article 44.

43. Much perplexity has been generated by Article 44(4)'s requirement that a combatant who "has forfeit[ed] his right to be a prisoner of war . . . shall, nevertheless, be given protections equivalent in all respects to those accorded to prisoners of war by [the GPW] and by this Protocol." *See, e.g.,* 2 Levie 487 (United Kingdom).

44. 2 Levie 509.

45. *Id.* at 534.

46. *Id.* at 386.

47. *Id.* at 405.

48. *Id.* at 406.

49. *Id.* at 536.

50. *Id.*

51. The corresponding provisions in the GPW are subsections (b) and (c) of Article 4A(2), quoted *supra* at 15-16.

52. G. Aldrich, *New Life for the Laws of War,* 75 Am. J. Int'l L. 764, 774 (1981).

53. *Id.*

54. Another key undefined term in Article 44(3) is "visible." The PLO representative stated:

Contrary to the suggestions of certain delegations, his own delegation interpreted ["visible"] to mean visible to the naked eye, since any recourse to electronic devices would divest the article of its value and undermine its very purpose. 2 Levie 509 (paragraph numbers omitted).

55. *Id.* at 523.

56. See Hacker, *supra* note 37, at 147-8.

57. See Bothe, *supra* note 35, at 238 ("The structure of [Article 43(1)] . . . as well as the negotiating record and the provisions of Art. 44(2) strongly militate against any construction that this provision constitutes one of the conditions for qualification as an armed force."

58. Under the GPW, compliance with the laws of war was a condition for combatant status only for irregular forces. It was not made a condition for regular uniformed soldiers because, as it is standard propaganda practice to accuse one's enemies in a war of violating the applicable laws, such a condition would serve effectively as

an invitation for parties to deny combatant/POW status to all enemy soldiers. This in fact happened in the Vietnam War: North Vietnam deprived U.S. soldiers of POW privileges on the grounds of its allegation that the United States systematically violated the laws of war.

59. The hotly debated provisions of Protocol I are those treated in this chapter. There are other provisions of Protocol I, such as those dealing with persons missing in action and with protection of medical personnel and equipment, which are not controversial and could actually serve humanitarian interests. Even if Protocol I fails to win ratification in many states, its beneficial provisions could over time, through widespread voluntary observance, develop into customary international law.

Section H
Recommendations

18
Implications for American Policy

Robert L. Pfaltzgraff, Jr.

T he conflict map of the late twentieth century encompasses state and other actors armed with destructive potential of new dimensions available for utilization, and often actually employed, in support of disparate political goals. While deeply rooted divisiveness—both within existing states and at a broader level among states and nonstate entities—furnishes the political setting for violence, technology has provided an unprecedented spectrum of lethality in the hands of groups of various sizes, organizational structures, and ideological orientation. Weaponry is available to launch massive strikes against entire societies or to conduct limited attacks to compel large and small states or other groups to comply with the demands of would-be perpetrators. One state's possession of nuclear weapons has deterred other nuclear states from resorting to nuclear weapons or even conventional forces against it. In sharp contrast, the possessors of nuclear weapons have been the object of attack no less than nonnuclear entities by those who maintain the means for low-intensity warfare. In the resulting conflict-laden global security environment opportunities abound both below and beyond the nuclear threshold for the employment of force in a variety of unconventional modes.

There was general agreement among the contributors to this volume that the focus of concern and interest is the actual use of, or the threat to employ, unconventional forms of violence by individuals or groups against designated targets in order to achieve political objectives. "Low intensity" as a characteristic of conflict applies more to outside parties than to the intended or unintended victim of the attack—for whom the intensity is likely to be high indeed. Terrorism, as a form of low-intensity conflict, represents the application of violent action against an object wielding high political leverage. Terrorism may be committed by an individual acting with or without direct outside control. It may be utilized by small groups, or it may be sponsored by states in support of political goals.

However, as William Casey points out, state-supported terrorism has emerged to an unprecedented extent in the last fifteen years as a potent instrument of foreign policy, practiced by such states as Khomeini's Iran, Libya, Syria, and the Soviet Union. Terrorism provides such governments with a powerful means to pursue goals that they probably could not otherwise hope to achieve. By the same token, when backed with the resources of the state, terrorism acquires a lethality that otherwise would not exist. Its purpose is to produce the political and psychological basis for achieving desired objectives. Whereas low-intensity warfare has been mounted successfully in rural areas from Southeast Asia to Central America, terrorism per se appears to be most effective against technologically sophisticated targets in which the impact and casualties have a multiplier effect on their strategic value. However, terrorism is also practiced with effective results to destabilize Third World states. Terrorism and other low-intensity operations have offered the means, within a strategy of unconventional warfare, for the weaker eventually to overwhelm the stronger, as described by numerous past and present theorists and practitioners of such armed conflict. Although its acts may be sporadic, terrorism has become part of a seemingly permanent conflict without boundaries in the late twentieth century.

The study of the strategy of warfare—from the ancient world of Sun Tsu to Clausewitz, Lenin, and more recent theorists and practitioners of the use of force—reveals the integral conceptual relationship among the various levels of intensity in the use of force and the political objective sought. From such an analytic focus, it necessarily follows that the choice of the type of military power to be employed derives from strategic and tactical circumstances related to the political purpose for which it is to be utilized. Terrorism and other low-intensity operations represent uses of violence with as long a history as the strategic principles embodied in the literature of the art of warfare. In a detailed examination of the historic setting, Adda Bozeman traces the development of techniques for terrorism, irregular armed struggles, and insurgency from the remote time of the Byzantine Empire, which bequeathed a legacy to the Russian state and ultimately to the Soviet Union. This legacy is based upon the unsurpassed use of political warfare and the employment of surrogates and mercenaries in support of political objectives. The Byzantine tradition's lack of a clear juxtaposition between "peace" and "war"—in sharp contradistinction to Western political thought—has left its traces on the Soviet approach. This is demonstrated by the ease with which the Soviet Union, as opposed to the United States, is able to practice a form of statecraft that extends far beyond the political warfare practiced by Byzantium to encompass wars fought by Moscow for total subjugation, as in Afghanistan, and also the use of state-sponsored terrorism in support of Soviet global strategy. The Soviet Union employs a panoply of low-intensity warfare tactics not only for this purpose but also to transform states adjacent to the United States into Soviet clients.

Leninist strategy represents an amalgam of all forms of struggle, including low-intensity warfare, within a framework designed to achieve the goals of the Soviet state. Claire Sterling examines an emerging pattern of open identification by terrorist organizations, such as the Red Brigades, of their political interests with those of the Soviet Union, together with an increasing pattern of transnational links among groups of this kind. Such acts as attacks against, and the kidnapping of, NATO personnel and defense industrialists and the bombing of Alliance military installations have been carried out by organizations which have received massive arms shipments and training cadres from Libya and the PLO. Despite impressive evidence of Soviet complicity, there remains a perverse incapacity or unwillingness both in Western Europe and the United States to face the reality of what is known. Such perspectives, not unlike those that shape our activities toward mounting evidence of Soviet arms control treaty violations, were attributed to the desire to minimize obstacles to an improved relationship with Moscow. Such a Western mindset creates the paradoxical effect of encouraging further Soviet sponsorship of terrorism and other forms of surrogate operations without fear of evoking a strong Western riposte.

Low-intensity warfare has always represented an important dimension of the Soviet Union's strategy. Herbert Romerstein points to some of the numerous examples of such violence by the Bolsheviks, extending from the abortive Revolution of 1905, to the Comintern's assistance to revolutionary warfare in the interwar period, and to the international support apparatus currently functioning on behalf of the communist insurgency in El Salvador. According to John Dziak, the Soviet Union has refined the use of Special Operations forces to serve as the cutting edge of Soviet military intervention. In the early days of the Soviet state, such capabilities played a prominent role in quelling internal rebellion, as at Kronstadt, while special troop formations were employed to carry out the brutal collectivization campaign against the peasants in the 1920s. There exist stark comparisons between the use of such forces in Afghanistan today and within the Soviet Union itself in the period between the two World Wars. Given the prominence of the KGB in the Soviet political-military structure and the integral importance of special operations forces in Soviet military doctrine, SPETSNAZ units can be expected to become more significant in Soviet force structure deployed against NATO countries and elsewhere, with attendant implications for Western strategy. Surrogates such as Cuba are likely to acquire their own special operations forces in larger numbers for Third World contingencies.

The open society faces problems that do not confront its totalitarian counterparts, as a result of the pervasive impact of the electronic media with instantaneous communications capabilities that are utilized by the practitioners of low-intensity warfare. Sander Vanocur underscores the basic difference between the functions of government and the media in our society. The proliferation of broadcasting technologies, resulting in a large number of new television and radio networks and local programming, creates unprecedented opportunities for terrorist organizations to use such news organizations for their purposes. The growing sophistication of the electronic media is likely to be matched by comparable advances in the ability of terrorists to manipulate them.

A pervasive theme of this volume is the integral relationship between the political setting and the successful orchestration of terrorism and other low-intensity operations. Ideally, the perpetrator of such actions seeks to build broader popular support for the insurgency and, simultaneously, to deprive the adversary practicing counteroperations of comparable levels of public sympathy. Such a strategy, with its political, psychological, and military elements, has been utilized by the Soviet Union, especially in its escalating involvement in Third World conflicts from Vietnam to Central America. If its key military instruments, as Richard Shultz suggests, include arms transfers, the training of insurgent forces, and the deployment of Soviet or surrogate units, then its political-psychological dimension is based upon a variety of "active measures," such as overt propaganda, international front organizations, disinformation, and political activities within international organizations, notably the United Nations. The purpose is to condition opinion within pluralistic societies to view the insurgents as the legitimate representatives of the people and to portray their programs and activities (wars of national liberation) as just, while the government under attack is delegitimized as an allegedly corrupt puppet of the United States. In such a public conditioning process it becomes difficult, if not possible, for the United States to provide sustained support for elements resisting Soviet-sponsored rebellions, except at the risk of becoming "bogged down" in unpopular Third World conflicts. In its unremitting portrayal of the United States as the major cause of international conflict whose objectives are alleged to be opposed to those of Third World states, the Soviet Union has practiced a multidimensional and highly integrated strategy based upon the mobilization of propagandistic slogans escalated in direct proportion to the actual conduct of low-intensity military operations.

Among the specific purposes of such Soviet disinformation efforts is the masking of Moscow's resort to a variety of surrogates as part of an active and long-term strategy in the Third World. As Ernst Halperin maintains, Cuba has played a pivotal role in this strategy. Just as the Soviet Union has utilized Cuba as a surrogate for its power projection in this Hemisphere and elsewhere, Castro, supported from Moscow, has mounted low-intensity military operations in Central America. As part of a pattern of deepening Soviet–Cuban engagement in Central America, Sandinista Nicaragua, with its vastly increased military capabilities, is envisaged as the base for insurrection and revolution elsewhere in Central America. This has profoundly important implications for the global strategic position of the United States. In this sense, low-intensity warfare becomes for the Soviet Union and its proxies a low-cost, low-risk operation with the possibility of a huge payoff in the form of the diversion of vast American resources, attention, and energy from extended security commitments in Eurasia to our Hemispheric front yard. Such a pattern represents a now-classic utilization of low-intensity warfare.

What distinguishes present Soviet strategy is the greater willingness to utilize terrorism against external enemies, contrasted with a traditional propensity to employ such operations principally against domestic opponents. Because there is an integral relationship in Leninist thought between terrorism and other active measures, it follows that direct and indirect Soviet sponsorship of terrorist actions would increase along with other active measures. The Soviet leadership considers terrorism to be a useful tool in promoting the disintegration of the West. Although the Soviet Union provides specialized training, weapons, and other assistance to terrorist organizations, not all individual operations in support of Soviet interests are necessarily ordered by Moscow. In those cases in which the Soviet Union is actively involved, however, major operations have been approved at the highest level in Moscow. Since the 1970s, moreover, there has been evidence of increasing Soviet utilization of terrorist organizations to conduct assassinations, especially of defectors. The Soviet Union was said to benefit from the existence of a large number of leftist organizations that are "anti-imperialist," "anticapitalist," and "antidemocratic" in their ideological orientation and imbued with a belief in the necessity for armed struggle for victory.

Historically, the opportunities available to the perpetrators of low-intensity operations were limited by weaponry and by the targets themselves. Technology has produced the twofold effect of greatly increasing the means available for low-intensity operations and magnifying the impact of action against a specific target. Neil Livingstone points to the growing vulnerabilities of highly advanced societies to the operations of terrorists. Formerly, terrorism was limited with regard to the amount of damage that could be inflicted by the rudimentary nature of existing weaponry and the lack of high-consequence targets. The growing urbanization of societies and the heavy reliance on critical transportation, electricity, and communication nodes enhance the possibility for terrorists to attack our technological infrastructure with highly disruptive consequences. This condition is coexistent with weaponry of ever-increasing lethality based upon unprecedented accuracy and the widespread availability of a variety of systems. As a result, terrorist groups and other practitioners of low-intensity warfare have acquired access to weapons with a destructive potential previously available only to states themselves. While highly sophisticated, such weapons are simple to operate and do not require teams of trained soldiers, but merely individuals. Thus far such instruments have not included the weapons of mass destruction (nuclear and others) possessed by states, and the prospect that terrorist groups will actually construct a nuclear device is likely to remain remote. There are other equally lethal instruments, such as biological-chemical weapons, most of which could be purchased, stolen, or manufactured and employed in military operations by terrorists with comparative ease and devastating consequences.

As an instrument of statecraft and political coercion, terrorism and other low-intensity operations have been perfected and utilized more effectively and pervasively by totalitarian societies than by the open systems of the West. In fact, as Michael Ledeen suggests, the Soviet Union has been engaged in a systematic effort to destabilize and weaken the West. For many years the Soviet Union in an elaborate support and command network, has made extensive use of clandestine revolutionary organizations in a large number of countries. For example, terrorism in Italy has been part of a larger pattern of Soviet-supported low-intensity warfare. As a result of its links with the Soviet Union in the training of *fedayin,* the PLO represents, par excellence, a terrorist organization on which the USSR has bestowed special diplomatic status together with the benefits of easy movement throughout Eastern Europe. The Soviet Union also uses its own territory, as well as states such as Bulgaria, Czechoslovakia, and the German Democratic Republic, for the training of terrorists. Cuba and Nicaragua serve as staging bases for such operations in Central America. Indeed, there appears to be a two-way route in which European and other terrorists serve as advisers and instructors in Central America before an opportunity arises to send them back to such units operating secretly in Western Europe and elsewhere. Sandinista Nicaragua, for example, has provided a haven for some of Italy's most dangerous terrorists, and Sandinista cadres have been trained in Lebanon under PLO auspices.

Nothing more fully epitomizes the Soviet-sponsored international destabilization effort involving terrorism than the labyrinthine infrastructure established with Turkey as a target of immense historic and strategic importance to Moscow. Although a massive effort reached its zenith in the 1970s without achieving its immediate intended result, Turkey became a locus for a huge network of drug traffickers, arms transshipments, and international terrorist activities operated from Bulgaria and exposed by Ali Agca after his unsuccessful assassination attempt on Pope John Paul II. Soviet tactics have included leftist exploitation of rightist organizations and the use of the "Turkish Mafia" for narcotics operations, the profits of which have been used to purchase arms for additional Soviet-sponsored low-intensity warfare operations. A similar pattern, it was suggested, exists in the Western Hemisphere with Cuba as a key link in drug traffic extending from Colombia to the United States, and in which a close tactical working relationship has emerged between Soviet-sponsored international terrorism and organized crime, including the Mafia. As Paul Henze points out in considerable detail, international drug traffic has become an increasingly important part of Soviet strategy. In our open societies, drugs appear to represent, from Moscow's perspective, ideal weapons with which to weaken the social fabric of the United States and other target countries and simultaneously, as Charles C. Frost suggests, to earn the hard currencies needed to purchase weapons for the conduct of low-intensity warfare. Moreover, illicit drug traffic provides ready channels for the movement of explosives, weapons, and terrorists across international frontiers.

Although the closed society has advantages in its ability to control the printed and electronic media and to persist in various forms of low-intensity warfare far from its frontiers without domestic public scrutiny, its international support apparatus has certain vulnerabilities. As Uri Ra'anan suggests, the Soviet Union's extensive use of surrogates for the purposes of political destabilization has placed political strains upon such proxies themselves. Undoubtedly because he cannot be certain of the ultimate loyalty of his countrymen, Castro has availed himself of a Soviet-sponsored Praetorian Guard, together with other forms of military protection and a vast economic subsidy for Cuba's perennially faltering economy. Conceivably, the intensification of Soviet military operations in Afghanistan is directly related to the decision to exterminate Mujahedin freedom fighters and the population sympathetic to them in order to avoid a protracted conflict with rising Soviet casualties and domestic repercussions, however containable they might be in the closed society. Clearly, the analysis of such vulnerabilities represents a necessary prerequisite to the development of a U.S. strategy designed to heighten these costs so that the Soviet leadership would have to take into account the probability of painful penalties in the conduct of low-intensity warfare.

In pluralistic political systems, as Sam Sarkesian points out, there exist constraints and mindsets that create clear boundaries within which strategic thought, military operations, and political activities are delineated, even though open societies are most vulnerable to the various forms of low-intensity warfare. Indeed, the ideological and revolutionary goals for which terrorism is developed are alien to pluralistic societies. Moreover, the means employed to achieve such goals are in themselves antithetical to the values of pluralistic societies. The open system perceives the conflicts for which terrorism is utilized through conventional lenses, conditioned by an idea of the relationship between means and ends that is more in keeping with the values of our society than with those of revolutionary actors determined to replace an existing order by force if necessary. Therefore, it is difficult, if not impossible, for open societies to respond to terrorism in kind. Senator Malcolm Wallop emphasizes the need for moral clarity, for an objective standard with which to distinguish between friend and foe as the sine qua non of an effective strategy. Because open systems cannot adopt the tactics of the terrorist to combat low-intensity operations, they confront a fundamental dilemma in designing effective countermeasures, especially if such policies lie beyond the prevailing domestic consensus about what is permissable.

Yet, as B. Hugh Tovar suggests, the conditions of daily life in many parts of the world are scarcely distinguishable from warfare. Even assuming that the potential for large-scale conventional conflict directly involving the United States has diminished, the opportunities for the use of terrorism against advanced societies, including the United States, have scarcely been exploited. Although we clearly prefer, in keeping with our values, to counter the use of force with political means, we must give greater consideration to the relationship between political responses and forceful action. This is especially true if the adversary's answer to our political response is the use of additional force because our political response was interpreted as negotiations from a position of weakness. If violence is used by the terrorist because of its perceived efficacy, we must consider more fully the role of force either as a deterrent or in the termination of situations of low-intensity warfare on terms that do not encourage the attacker or potential imitators.

Low-intensity warfare and its practitioners have blurred the historic distinction, fundamental to Western legal thought, between war and peace, between civilians and armed combatants. As Douglas Feith points out, the traditional concepts embodied in the 1949 Geneva Convention Relating to the Protection of Victims of International Armed Conflicts have been modified in ways detrimental to the interests of the United States to give legal protection to the practitioners of "national liberation movements." In the 1974–77 Geneva Conference that negotiated two protocols to revise the 1949 Geneva Convention, the United States and other Western states succumbed to the political pressures of a Soviet–Third World radical coalition effectively defining such low-intensity conflicts as "international," rather than as the object of the municipal law of their respective states, and conferring upon the combatant members of such irregular forces, if captured, the international legal status of prisoners of war. Virtually ignored, as a result, are the rights of the potential victims of terrorism and war. Such prostitution of law supports the interests of those states and nonstate entities whose political goals contradict the rule of law as a protection for the rights of the individual against the coercive power of the self-appointed leadership.

A large number of the contributors to this volume addressed the policy options available to the United States in a world of low-intensity warfare. The United States has been placed in a variety of roles in such conflicts. These include: 1) assistance to other states in the form of military advice and hardware, as well as economic aid, designed to enable friendly states to combat low-intensity warfare; 2) military and economic aid to groups within states attempting to resist expansionist Soviet-supported communist and other extremist regimes; 3) direct U.S. military engagement in countries struggling to prevent the imposition of Soviet-style governments; and 4) American military intervention (Grenada) in support of a specified political objective, such as the rescue of American citizens or the liberation of the population from a regime dominated by the Soviet Union.

The contributors focused on a large number of existing or potential courses of action that were generally categorized either as passive or active measures to be undertaken by the United States alone or in concert with other governments sharing an interest in combating low-intensity warfare. There is general agreement that, however vital passive measures may be, they are not likely to be adequate in isolation from active steps. Taken together, passive and active moves should be seen as integral elements of a coherent strategy that must attract the sustained public support vitally important to its success. A series of passive measures can be found in this volume:

1. Appropriate protective barriers should be developed where they are needed to provide a security screen around critically important targets in order to raise the cost to those engaged in low-intensity warfare.

2. Existing international treaties, conventions, and other international agreements related to problems of countering terrorism should be systematically reviewed. Such measures include, for example, clarifying the definition of diplomatic privilege to prevent its abuse by states sponsoring terrorism or by entities aspiring to official recognition, strengthening measures to prevent terrorist acts against civil aviation, drafting agreements for the extradition of terrorists who seek (and receive) asylum in other countries.

3. The need for adequate intelligence remains vitally important. We must understand more fully the style, operating methods, and organizational structures of terrorist groups. Nevertheless, the absence of complete information, unlikely in any case to exist, should not furnish an excuse for inaction. The problems inherent in acquiring needed intelligence point up the difficulty in drawing a clearcut distinction between passive and active measures, especially if paramilitary and covert operations represent almost logical extensions of defensive counterintelligence efforts. In order to ascertain what an adversary seeks to do, how he proposes to accomplish his goals, and how successful his previous activities have been, it may be necessary to penetrate his political structure. Thus the effective utilization of intelligence in a defensive mode may require the pursuit of active steps embodied in counterintelligence.

4. Counterintelligence, as well as special operations in its support, should be directed from a single center at the highest levels of the National Command Authority with the intelligence component integrated at all levels. However, all intelligence collection and analysis should not be placed within a superagency. Instead, diversity and a multiplicity of collection

and analysis capabilities are vital ingredients in enhancing intelligence adequacy.

5. The development of transnational terrorist networks, in many cases operating from European NATO countries, increases the need for greater collaboration among these and other friendly countries in: a) developing an international intelligence collection capability; b) sharing information obtained by national intelligence authorities; and c) designing strategies and policies at a multilateral level. An international antiterrorist network based upon the exchange of intelligence, the ability to transmit alerts and warnings as rapidly as possible, and cooperation in advanced police training methods should be strengthened.

6. Concerted action by the United States, its allies, and other friendly countries must be undertaken to avert or reverse measures by international organizations and individual governments that elevate entities of an essentially terrorist nature to quasidiplomatic status, conferring immunity, recognition, and legitimation.

Although open societies, despite their inherent vulnerability to low-intensity warfare, face formidable problems in the development of necessary consensus, the need has increased greatly for the more effective utilization of active steps. These include:

1. The encouragement of insurgency operations in Soviet-supported states where resistance to the regime already exists, or where there is such potential. For too long Western democracies have accepted the irreversibility of the Brezhnev Doctrine, not disputing the belief that every regime that comes to power through Marxist–Leninist means remains forever inviolate.

2. An active policy against such states should include energetic diplomacy and other political initiatives, as well as military assistance to aid the resistance "on the ground." Although the United States has supported in a limited way fighters against Soviet oppression in Afghanistan as well as resistance to Sandinista rule in Nicaragua, there is little evidence that such efforts form part of a broader political-military strategy based on a clearly delineated concept and directed toward agreed-upon and understood political objectives. Military aid, whether overt or covert, cannot be a substitution for policy. Such aid is one of many instruments that should be configured in a way that permits the United States to achieve coherent objectives.

3. With regard to counterterrorism, there is evidence that the Reagan administration has begun to develop a policy that will include the use of

armed force for prevention, preemption, and even retaliation against terrorist attacks. The willingness to use force credibly is indispensable to efforts to combat terrorism, for otherwise the deterrent capacity of the United States will be ineffective.

4. Soviet sponsorship and support for terrorism in the form of training, and the provision of equipment, funds, and political backing has contributed greatly to the power of such groups. Therefore, the United States should: a) provide on a continuous basis public information about the extent of such Soviet involvement; b) encourage other interested parties to pursue their own investigations of Soviet complicity; c) develop intelligence gathering efforts as fully as possible to verify direct and indirect Soviet complicity or sponsorship; and d) bring diplomatic pressure to bear against the Soviet Union.

5. Because of Libya's role as a major instigator and supporter of terrorism, the United States and other interested parties should take steps designed to a) strengthen and unify opposition elements to Qadhafi, not only within Libya itself, but on a broader international scale, including the exiled Libyan community; b) support efforts to destabilize and, if possible, replace the present Libyan regime by means of a broad range of overt and covert operations; and c) respond with a commando strike, under appropriate conditions, against a Libyan facility, such as a port, if Libya is directly involved in a future major terrorist activity. Similar means should be considered to respond to the Islamic terrorism promoted by Iran.

6. The United States should be prepared to use small-scale commando raids and other special operation techniques in an appropriate manner against known terrorist installations, as well as against the bases and infrastructure of those who traffic in drugs with the support and assistance of communist states.

7. The United States should make clear that henceforth any action against a U.S. diplomat comparable to events in Teheran in 1979 will be treated as an act of war, requiring, for example, response against a major installation, such as (Iranian) oil production or export facility.

8. The United States should develop a comprehensive counterinsurgency doctrine that integrates both military and nonmilitary (economic, political, social, psychological) means. This doctrine should direct all appropriate elements of the U.S. national security apparatus to develop the required assets necessary to assist friendly governments threatened by insurgents sponsored by Moscow and its surrogates. Our approach to counterinsurgency should seek not to be defensive and reactive, responding only at that point when an ally is severely threatened. Our goal should be to avoid the stark options of either introducing troops or doing

nothing. Prevention requires foresight and an understanding of the indigenous causes of conflict in the Third World and how and where the USSR will seek to aggrevate these conflicts through the promotion of subversion, guerrilla action, terrorism, and related tactics.

The challenges facing the open society in combating low-intensity warfare in its various forms are likely to grow in the remaining years of this century as a result of the multiplicity of actors prepared to resort to such means, the numerous conflict issues, the increasing availability of sophisticated weapons technologies, and the consequent lethality of the threat. Such factors, together with the numerous international and transnational linkages among the perpetrators of low-intensity warfare, enhance the need for a strategy designed to prevent such operations at their source, to threaten credibly to punish those engaged in such activities, and otherwise to defend our societies from such attack. We have yet to integrate the necessary military and nonmilitary instruments of statecraft into a cohesive strategy for this purpose.

Part II
The Witnesses Speak

1
Documentation: A Plethora of Sources

I
n the Western traditions of scholarship, insistence on verification is a sine
qua non of any serious intellectual enterprise. The editors of the present
volume adhere to this tradition.

It was decided, therefore, to supplement the preceding chapters on international linkages between various groups involved in low-intensity warfare
with such relevant primary sources on this topic as could be obtained. The
evidence should enable the reader to judge the gravity of the threat posed by
surrogate warfare, particularly by state-sponsored terrorism.

The editors have been skeptical of assertions that the state-sponsored
international infrastructure for planning and conducting low-intensity operations, and particularly terrorism, is either impossible to expose or does not
exist at all. However, it did seem plausible that there might not be enough
primary documentation available to expose and delineate this international
support apparatus.

In fact, as the evidence presented in this part of the book makes abundantly clear, the opposite is the case. We were surprised by the plethora of
documentation explicitly addressing the topic of international linkages between terrorist organizations conducting low-intensity operations against
open societies and their state sponsors. This evidence reveals the specific dimensions and the degree, both quantitative and qualitative, to which those
carrying out such operations depend upon their international patrons in Moscow, Havana, Sofia, East Berlin, Tehran, Damascus, and in other capitals
hostile to the West.

In light of the wealth of extensive and reliable evidence discovered in our
research, it became apparent that the real issue was not whether convincing
primary sources existed. Rather, due to limited space requirements, the editors had to devote much time to rejecting testimony and documents of substance. Whenever a choice had to be made between two equally important
pieces of evidence priority was given to the more recent document. Prece-
dence was also given to documents dealing with high-level client-patron interaction over records of contacts between relatively lower-level officials.

The documentation that follows consists of two major categories of primary source material. First, we present testimony either by former members of the apparatus of states sponsoring terrorism or the actual practitioners who conducted operations "on the ground." Our "witnesses" include former high-ranking communist party officials and/or officers of various communist intelligence services, interviewed in the Oral History Project of Fletcher's International Security Studies Program. The readers will notice that each of them is not only a unique source of firsthand evidence about previous activities and operations in which he was directly involved, but all remain discerning observers and analysts of present-day developments. The witnesses were interviewed in an unprejudicial manner and great care was taken not to "lead" them toward any a priori assumptions.

Recollections of well-placed political actors are among the most valued forms of historical evidence. It is, therefore, significant to note that the testimonies of the witnesses complement each other. They are mutually reinforcing in establishing both the origins and expansion of the state-sponsored international infrastructure for low-intensity warfare. This is all the more surprising when one considers that they come from such culturally diverse and geographically distant countries as Nicaragua and Czechoslovakia.

In conjunction with these firsthand accounts, this section contains additional documentation in the form of arrangements and official agreements between terrorists and their state patrons, as well as textual records of high-level meetings by senior officials. It should be noted that this evidence consists both of previously available documents and a significant amount of material that until recently was either unavailable or unknown to the informed public.

The primary evidence—testimonies and documents—has been divided into several categories. It goes without saying that such division, no matter how well designed, is artificial and partially obscures the complexity of the relationship between terrorists and their state sponsors for the sake of functional "neatness." Real life, of course, is much more complicated and the evidence presented cuts across geographical areas and defies precise analytic boundaries. One need only mention the case of Ilyich Ramirez Sanches, a.k.a. Carlos the Jackal. Without going into details of his case, it is well known that the Jackal's footprints can be found in the Soviet Union, in neutral Vienna, Western Europe, socialist Cuba, the Middle East and at other locations in the shadowy network of linkages between those who carry out low intensity operations and those who provide the operational infrastructure of support and advice.

By its nature, the collection below deals with the recent past. Nevertheless, perhaps some relevant lessons may be drawn by open societies about the present and what can be expected, possibly in an escalated form, in the future. Viewed against the background of our evidence it seems quite possible that the next decade may test the ability of Western societies to survive as democracies—free, prosperous, secure, and as reliable allies. While much more could be said about the threat to open societies, the editors deliberately refrain from leading the reader from one conclusion to another. Rather, it was assumed that primary sources, in whatever form, speak best for themselves.

2
Surrogate Actors in the Caribbean: Central America

The following documents detail a wide range of Cuban–Soviet Bloc active measures in Latin America. Cuban–Soviet Bloc activities may be divided into two fundamental categories: operational support of insurgencies through arms transfers, intelligence sharing, and so forth; and political support through the creation of solidarity committees. The documents included in this section illustrate both types.

In Document 1, Miguel Bolaños Hunter, a former Sandinista counterintelligence agent in the Nicaraguan state security apparatus, gives a first hand account of the role of the various Soviet Bloc advisers in that organization. He also talks about the role of Cubans, Nicaraguans, and other foreign revolutionaries in the Salvadoran insurgency. Eden Pastora Gomez gives a unique inside view of the Nicaraguan Revolution in Document 2. Pastora also speaks about the role of various Soviet Bloc advisors and confirms Nicaraguan support of the Salvadoran insurgency. The major thrust of his account is that in their attempt to rid Nicaragua of Somoza, the major Latin American supporters of the FSLN (Costa Rica, Venezuela, and Panama) disregarded the essentially Marxist–Leninist nature of that movement. In Document 3 Tomas Borge, the Minister of the Interior of the Sandinista regime, admits that the Nicaraguan revolutionaries were granted Cuban economic aid as early as 1961 and describes Fidel Castro as the mentor of the Sandinista leadership.

The Cuban role in promoting the Salvadoran insurgency is emphasized in Documents 5, 6 and 7. Document 5 is a letter to Fidel Castro from the leaders of three of the Salvadoran guerrilla groups thanking him for his role in the unification of their organizations. Documents 6 and 7 are two letters to Manuel Pineiro from the DRU (the political-military coordinating body of the FMLN, the Salvadoran guerrilla alliance) announcing the formation of the FMLN. Soviet Bloc involvement in arms transfers to the Salvadoran rebels is graphically detailed in Document 4—Shafik Handal's personal notes summarizing his trip to the Soviet Union, East Europe, and Ethiopia.

The use of communist-led solidarity committees to gain international support for the rebels is detailed in Documents 8 through 10. Document 8 announces the formation of the World Front for Solidarity with the Salvadoran People (FMSPS) to gain international support for the FDR–FMLN alliance. Document 9 contains comments from a map detailing the international solidarity network of the FMSPS. Document 10 consists of excerpts from the personal notes of Farad Handal detailing his trip to the United States to meet with solidarity committees. These notes reveal a high degree of communist penetration of the U.S. solidarity movement. Finally, Document 11 shows Cuban involvement in promoting subversion on other fronts in a highly revealing passage from an account of the activities of the Venceremos Brigades.

For information about names and organizations, see the glossary for Part II at the end of the volume.

Document 1: Testimony of Miguel Bolaños Hunter

Miguel Bolaños Hunter is a former high-ranking counterintelligence officer in the counterespionage section of the Sandinista state security apparatus, the DGSE. In this position, Bolaños was responsible for overseeing Western embassies and the Western press. The role of the Soviet, Cuban, East German, and Bulgarian advisors in the Sandinista state security apparatus are clearly revealed in the following excerpts from the interview with Miguel Bolaños Hunter.

Source: Oral History Project, International Security Studies Program, Fletcher School of Law and Diplomacy.

The Nicaraguan state security apparatus (DGSE, or General Directorate of State Security) was created immediately after the triumph of the Revolution. In the following excerpt, Bolaños describes the basic structure of the DGSE and identifies its most important personalities. He notes that a Cuban occupies one of the most sensitive positions in the DGSE and acts as a conduit of Cuban influence.

"There are two major divisions of the DGSE, intelligence and counterintelligence. Intelligence for the outside; counterintelligence for the inside. There are many different sections for counterintelligence. It is organized along functional lines with each section designated by the letter F and a number, such as F1. One section for foreign embassies. One in charge of political parties, the church, and the independent labor unions. To the Sandinistas, the [traditional Catholic] Church is Enemy Number 1. There is no doubt about it. Additionally, there is a counterintelligence section in charge of private enterprises and the economy. One in charge of telephone tapping, microphones, surveillance, opening mail. An interrogation section. A section on information and analysis.

"Intelligence is organized along geographical lines.

"The head of everything officially and structurally is Luis Carrion. Carrion is Vice Minister of the Interior and thus under Tomas Borge structurally [Borge is Minister of the Interior], but Carrion is of the Proletarian faction and party agreements gave him a place in the National Directorate [the highest political authority in Nicaragua which consists of the Nine Commandantes]. So in a sense Carrion is also a co-equal of Tomas Borge. As the head of the DGSE, Carrion oversees both the intelligence and counterintelligence sections. The head of counterintelligence, my boss is Lenin Cerna. The head of intelligence is a Cuban named Barahona who goes by the nickname Renan Montero. Renan Montero knows Nicaragua better than I do and better than most Nicaraguans. He was the link between the FSLN and Cuba for many years. Now he is the intelligence link for Nicaragua from Fidel. That is why Fidel has him there. He is one of the main instruments for Cuban control of events in Nicaragua."

In the following excerpt, Bolaños tells of his progression up the career ladder in the DGSE to a post of the highest sensitivity in section F2 of counterintelligence.

"In my first post, I was assigned the section of state security that supervised the neighborhood bloc committees, the CDSs (Committees for the Defense of Sandinismo). In that section, Q4, we had a Cuban advisor who gave us two-hour daily training sessions for one month. That was in January 1980. In late February, I was transferred to one of the most sensitive areas of state security—Q2 [at that time the sections were designated by the letter Q], the section that controls espionage that comes from the outside. About two weeks later, in March 1980, I was sent to Cuba for four months of special training.

"My first posting was really a low status thing. The neighborhood that I was sent to was really poor and dusty. It was located on the outskirts of Managua and cars could not even enter it. I was sent there because the Cubans in charge of personnel for the DGSE did not trust me. You see, there were Cuban DGI men, personnel specialists, who were in charge of screening all of the applicants for state security. When I filled out the forms, one of the questions was 'Do you have any connections with Somoza?' Nicaragua is a very small country and it is impossible for anyone not to have any connections with a Somocista or the son of a Somocista. So I answered the question honestly and wrote down five or six names. I also mentioned that I had studied in the United States, that my mother was American, and that I was of bourgeois background. As a result, the Cubans did not want to let me enter. So I had to appeal directly to Walter Ferreti, then Chief of Security and a personal friend. Still, the Cubans did not trust me and thus posted me in a position of little importance.

"I got promoted to counterintelligence section Q2 because of my work in my first post. You see, there was a lot of corruption there. The Cuban adviser and the Nicaraguan chief of that section were having affairs with the secretaries and blackmailing some of the officers. So I made a report of the situation and sent it to Walter Ferreti. Ferreti did not know that I was there and told me that I would be promoted to a position of more importance. So I was promoted to section Q2, counterintelligence, dealing with foreign espionage, and sent to Cuba for training.

"I arrived in Cuba in March 1980 and stayed there for four months. We flew to Cuba on Cuban airlines as a group and they took us on a bus directly to the school, which is also a private museum run by the Minister of the Interior. It is located about four miles south of the airport, one and a half miles from the small town of Santiago Las Vegas, right outside of Havana. The school is called the Hermanos (Brothers) Martinez Tamayo, in honor of two Cubans who fought and died with Che in Bolivia. It is the farm where Che lived after the Revolution until he left Cuba. It still has Che's original furnishings—his bed, lamps, tables, everything. The school was built around that.

"We went to school along with other Cubans. There were about two hundred Cubans attending a two-year program, and we all graduated on the same day. There were also Grenadians and Angolans, but they attended a separate school about five kilometers away. Cuban instructors did all of the teaching. Important Soviet personnel, generals and colonels, would visit frequently, but only to observe. They did not teach.

"There were about fifteen students in each class, with one teacher for each subject. We studied four subjects—enemy activities, counterintelligence, operative psychology, and Marxism. We learned the basics of counterintelligence and more. This was a program for all sections. There were students there who were going to be assigned to deal with the church, the political parties, counterespionage, and the CDS's. So they had to give us one general program so that we could go back and work in each of these sections. But myself and another person coming from the counterespionage section received some special attention by a couple of teachers. For example, when I left Nicaragua to come to Cuba, my first assignment in the Q2 section was to start a program on how to control and deal with the foreign media. I had no idea of how to do this. A Cuban teacher gave me lectures on how to develop such a program when I returned to Nicaragua.

"Intelligence training in Nicaragua itself had been going on since December 1979. At that time, the courses were given inside the different sections. They had one teacher for each one. When I left for Cuba in March 1980, they fixed a place to become the central school so the teachers would not have to go around to the different sections anymore. When I left Nicaragua [May 1983], they were already building a school specifically for intelligence training.

"Nicaraguans were also sent to Bulgaria for training. In 1980, two groups were sent to Bulgaria for a six-month training period. There were about ninety people in each group. They were trained in counterintelligence also. Two colleagues who worked in my section were trained in Bulgaria. They were specialists in blackmail and things like that. Everytime they had a case, they would develop the possibilities for that case—sexual blackmail, money blackmail, and other things.

"Some Nicaraguans also studied in the Soviet Union. Two or three months before I left I was chosen to go to Moscow for a five-year program. The Soviets said that they had three different training programs—a one-year program; an intermediate program of three years; and an advanced program of five years. In the advanced program, you graduate not only as a specialist in some field of intelligence, but also with a related professional degree such as law or psychology."

Bolaños further describes the role of the various Soviet Bloc advisers in the state security apparatus. Also, he describes the role of Cuban advisers in DPEP, the Department of Propaganda and Political Education:

"The Cubans were the most open and public in their relations with state security. There was a Cuban general nicknamed Roberto who was the head of all the Cuban security workers in Nicaragua; in reality, he ran everything. Under him was a group of advisors who were the aides of the top officials in the DGSE, like Commandantes Carrion and Cerna. So you can see the control that this general exercised. Cuban control was one hundred percent; they designed the operations and we were like a typewriter or a pen. The Soviet advisors operated at the top levels but were very small in numbers; perhaps one percent.

"Cuban advisors also directed the propaganda campaigns when I was in Nicaragua. They had their own apparatus working on that and they would advise the Nicaraguan propaganda apparatus, which was a department of the party [DPEP, the Department of Propaganda and Political Education]. DPEP is in charge of propagating Marxist theories in the schools and in public life. DPEP also monitors the Nicaraguan people to know their feelings toward what is going on in order to know which propaganda themes to emphasize. DPEP is headed by Carlos Nuñez, a member of the National Directorate, but it is actually run by Cuban advisors. They decided the propaganda themes and DPEP implements them. The Cubans are analysts, experts in following circumstances and situations. They were the ones who advised the commandantes on what to do, what direction to pursue, what to emphasize.

"The Nicaraguans are not a bunch of zombies but the Cubans had the experience. They would say that this is a good way of doing things and the Nicaraguans would start doing it. The Cubans would work through security and the chief would call and say these are the points, move your agent in this direction, emphasize themes like the martyrs of the revolution and the legacy of Somoza.

"Cubans work in section F6 in surveillance and are specialists in kidnapping. There are also Cuban advisors in F1, interrogation. Nicaraguans do the actual interrogation while the Cubans stay in the back, in a hearing room, and listen. When the interrogator comes out, the Cuban might say 'You have to be stronger' or something like that. So the Cubans do not personally conduct the interrogations, but it is as if they were carrying it out. They use drugs in interrogations, but only in extreme circumstances, with strong personalities. Most of the time they break the individual—as they call it—without drugs. They also use mock executions. For example, they put Victor Francis before a mock execution squad before he decided to talk.

"There were two to three advisors in each section. Mostly Cuban DGI people, but also some Soviet KGB personnel. The Cuban advisors were mainly in counterintelligence. The Soviet advisors, on the other hand, were mainly in intelligence. There were not KGB people in all of the sections. The greatest number of KGB advisors was in our section, F2. There were two KGB operatives in our section, each with the rank of colonel.

"The KGB advisors were effective, but our relationship with them was terrible. For example, we were very privileged in our section because we were working on surveillance of the American Embassy. But the Soviets were very arrogant. They would come in and talk only with the head or chief of our section. They didn't care about anybody else. When a case came in from the Venezuelan Embassy that they were interested in, they went to the chief. The chief would call the officer, the officer would handle the file, but the Soviets did not want to talk to him.

"The relationship between the Soviets and the Cubans is also not without problems. The Cubans would tell us to be careful of the Soviets and at times would advise us not to give the Soviets certain pieces of information because the Soviets were interested in it for their own selfish reasons. The Cubans used to tell us stories about Soviet attempts to control them and how the resulting friction would almost explode into fighting. One Cuban DGI man explained it this way. He said that the Soviets are good people and try to help, but they are just too smart. They try to take advantage of everything.

"The relationship with the Cubans was much better. Because of this, the Cubans controlled operations much better than the Soviets.

"The East German advisors were mainly involved in electronic bugging and the tapping of microphones, in section F6. We had one East German advisor in my section, F2. He would come specifically to talk to the person in charge of the West German Embassy.

"The Bulgarians had a center for the analysis of information. We did not have a Bulgarian advisor in our section. We used to gather information for the Center of Information and Analysis and they would process it. They gave us advice through our chief. The chief was the only one who dealt directly with the Bulgarians. So the Bulgarians did analytical work for us, but the operation was more to their benefit."

The relationship between the Cuban advisors and the Nicaraguan agents in the DGSE was not without tension. Sometimes, Cuban attempts to influence operations became too blatant and led to problems. Bolaños gave the following example:

"There was a Cuban plot against the chief of my section, Alejandro Arguello. The Cuban advisor for our section, a major named Pancho, was also the aid to a Cuban General named Roberto, who had been a deputy chief of Cuban state security for ten years. General Roberto was the chief of all Cuban advisors working in Nicaraguan state security. The Cubans wanted to control our section because it is very important and sensitive. Also, they did not like my chief. So this major began to work on penetrating it, but his actions were clumsy. First, he tried to gain influence with the secretary of our section. He had an affair with her and they almost got married. But we knew exactly what was going on, and this Cuban major began to cause a lot of problems and troubles among us. Eventually, he was sent back to Cuba for creating problems. And General Roberto said, 'Can you believe that! Here is a Cuban advisor, who is supposed to maintain the best relations with Nicaragua, and he goes and makes all of that tension.' We all thought that was funny because we were almost sure that General Roberto had ordered the whole thing."

In the following excerpt, Bolaños tells of his impressions of the Cuban security services. He states that the Americas Department plays the dominant role in Cuban efforts at subversion. Also, he states that privilege, and not ideology, seemed to be the single most important motivating factor in the agents that he met.

"The DGSE is basically a copy of the Cuban DGI. The Cuban operation is larger, but structurally they are the same. Initially, the Cuban operation had a very simple structure, and it took eight years to develop into its present form. With Cuban help, we took only two years to achieve the same evolution. At the time of my defection, we had the same number of sections as the DGI, although they called them departments.

"Among the various branches of the Cuban security apparatus—the Americas Department, the DGI, and the DOE (Department of Special Operations)—the Americas Department is the most powerful. Americas Department personnel are very arrogant and consider themselves the elite. I know this because in my position I had personal dealings with some of them. We were interested in the same targets, like the CIA station, so they used to come talk to our Cuban advisor and discuss how the cases were developing. Sometimes, the Cuban advisor, who was a DGI man, would leave and the Americas Department people would talk to us. They talked of him sarcastically, saying that these counterintelligence people don't know anything. Americas Department personnel have more privileges than DGI personnel in Nicaragua, but they do not have any more power. I think in Cuba they have both more privilege and more power. In Cuba, everybody respects the job they do. The Communist Bloc respects them also—the Soviets used to remark on the good work that the Cubans do, based on the achievements of the Americas Department, not that of Cuban counterintelligence.

"In Nicaragua, the Americas Department personnel do not operate through the Cuban Embassy. They have their own station.

"The DOE is part of the Cuban Ministry of the Interior and has links with the DGI. The DOE moves are based on the information and advice they receive from the DGI. The DOE people are specialists in operations. In Nicaragua, the DOE is mainly involved in working with the Salvadoran guerrillas. For example, DOE personnel train the guerrillas in sabotage. The DOE has a separate command center to monitor and direct these operations.

"The three branches of the Cuban security apparatus remind me of the Christian Trinity doctrine: three different manifestations of the same thing.

"Cuban security people are ideologically motivated to a certain extent, but that is not the main motivation. What really matters are the privileges that accompany this sort of work. To understand what this means, you have to live in a communist country. The Cubans tried indirectly to make us understand the importance of privilege and the importance of protecting privilege.

"As to guarding against defections, we started, with Cuban encouragement, what we called Revolutionary Surveillance. We watched and listened to the colleague next door and reported anything that was wrong. We would discuss such problems at meetings of the Party Militants—these were very dedicated party members—and then we would decide whether an investigation was warranted and who would carry it out. So there was no special section within counterintelligence to carry out surveillance on DGSE agents. This function was carried out by the Party Militants. For example, once we had a problem with someone in our section; he was frequenting a whorehouse. So we had an investigation and put him back on track."

Bolaños also spoke at length on the role of the Palestine Liberation Organization (PLO) in Nicaragua and its relations with the FSLN.

"The PLO opened an office in Managua within a month of the Revolution, but PLO members had already been involved in the fighting. During the final offensive, there were three or four PLO members fighting as combatants with the International Brigade in northern Nicaragua. After the Sandinistas took power, the PLO's role was to assist in training for special operations such as kidnappings and murders. They also train Salvadoran guerrillas at three camps in Nicaragua. One is at Ostional in the southern province of Rivas. I heard this from a Chilean who is also an instructor there.

"FSLN–PLO relations have existed for quite a long time. They go back to the 1960s. The first links were arranged through Cuba. For example, Patrice Arguello first met with the PLO in Cuba. From Cuba he went to Europe and studied in Belgium, and then he went to train with the PLO. Later, he died on a mission. Yes, there were quite a few Sandinistas with PLO training. There was Enrique Smith, who died about four months ago. The Sandinistas say that the contras killed him, but that is a lie. In reality, the Sandinistas executed him. Then there was René Villas, a Vice Minister of the Interior and GPP man trained by the PLO."

Bolaños made the following comments concerning other Soviet Bloc advisers and revolutionary groups in Nicaragua: Libyans, Vietnamese, and North Koreans as well as members of M-19, ETA, Red Brigades, MIR, Tupamoros, and Montoneros.

"We also had Libyans, Vietnamese, and North Koreans. The Vietnamese were in the army. The Koreans were mainly in the infirmaries, the clinics, and the hospitals of the Minister of the Interior working as medical personnel. The Libyans were in the special operations team within the Fifth Directorate working on things like kidnappings and killings.

"We also had the Italian Red Brigades and the Spanish ETA. They set up offices in Managua. I really don't know about their specific activities.

"The first one that I heard about was the ETA, which came in about 1980 or 1981. They are very secretive, as are the Red Brigades and the M-19. These organizations are more secretive than the Chilean MIR (Movement of the Revolutionary Left), the Uruguayan Tupamaros, or the Argentine Montoneros. Inside the Sandinista apparatus, you find out a lot because these people have relations with the army girls. I had friends that were married to MIR people and Montoneros and they were fairly open, but the ETA, M-19, and Red Brigades were not.

"Contact with these groups is not maintained by security, as one would think, but through the DRI (Department of International Relations). Control is not strict; it is not surveillance."

In the following excerpt, Bolaños speaks of the functions of the Department of International Relations (DRI). His description suggests that the functioning of Nicaraguan foreign policy is rapidly evolving into the typical dual structure found within communist states, in which a foreign ministry handles affairs with noncommunist states while an international relations department of the party deals with sister communist states.

"The Department of International Relations in Nicaragua represents the party, the FSLN, particularly in its dealings with other communist states and revolutionary movements. It is a two-track policy of handling foreign relations. For example, the Nicaraguan Foreign Ministry has relations with the government of Colombia, as well as with the DRI.

"The DRI evolved from the Commission of the Exterior, which was set up in 1978 to seek international support for the FSLN. The connections were mainly with communist governments and revolutionary movements. Nora Astorga used to be in charge of the Commission of the Exterior, and later became the first chief of the DRI.

"The head of the DRI today is Julio Lopez. Renan Montero, the chief of the intelligence section of the DGSE, or what is known as the Fifth Directorate, coordinates on a daily basis with Julio Lopez on every important case that the DRI is handling. In fact, intelligence officers from the Fifth Directorate have been filling posts in the DRI.

"Eventually, the DRI will do the same kinds of things that the Cuban Americas Department does today. Changes were being made to do this when I left Nicaragua. In fact, the Cuban advisers in the DRI are Americas Department personnel. However, I never knew of any Soviet advisors in the DRI. They are also going to establish a separate Department of Protocol within the Party to handle official guests. Right now, the DRI does this. This would allow the DRI to concentrate more on political work, such as supporting foreign subversion.

"Right now, the responsibilities for maintaining liason with foreign groups in order to influence domestic politics in foreign countries are divided between the DRI and two or three other offices. There is CONIPAZ (The Nicaraguan Peace Committee), which is headed by a female commandante. The tour of a group from the Vietnam Veterans Against the War which came to Nicaragua was arranged by CONIPAZ. CONIPAZ set up the tour, and the DRI handled them when they arrived. CONIPAZ also arranges for tours of U.S. and Latin American groups which come to Nicaragua. CONIPAZ is also connected to the World Peace Council, a Soviet front group. There is another such group called the Nicaraguan Solidarity with the People, which handles mainly East European connections."

Bolaños made the following general comments about the Sandinista strategy for subversion of neighboring countries:

"El Salvador has been the main target for subversion, but the Sandinistas have not neglected other countries. They have been training Costa Ricans and providing them with weapons since 1980. Also, the Sandinistas have directed Costa Rican labor unions to pursue a hard line in negotiations with the government in order to create friction. They have also been working with the Hondurans and the Guatemalans. Right after Castro united the Salvadoran guerrilla groups, the Sandinistas did the same thing with the Guatemalans. They made them sign a unity pledge. Humberto Ortega was the main force behind this. Since then, they have aided the Guatemalans quite a bit.

"El Salvador is the test case. Subversion is a double-edged sword. If they are successful, the Sandinistas will remove some of the pressure on themselves by surrounding Nicaragua with allies. But exporting subversion can also attract attention and bring in the Americans. So the Sandinistas do their best to hide their involvement. For example, when a group of Chinchoneros (a Honduran revolutionary group) hijacked a plane from Tegucigalpa to Managua and asked for asylum, the Sandinistas refused to grant it. They sent the plane to Panama in order to avoid the appearance of having anything to do with the guerrillas.

"In Sandinista thinking, Guatemala is the next revolutionary situation. Very soon, Guatemala is going to blow up like El Salvador. One day, well-armed guerrillas are going to appear suddenly in large numbers. In Costa Rica, the situation is not so volatile. The Sandinistas are trying to destabilize Costa Rica by advising the unions to make unreasonable demands in their negotiations with the government. They are trying to force a confrontation between the government and the unions which would lead to repression. Repression would justify the creation of armed bands.

"In long-term strategy, Mexico is slated to be the last country to fall. The high-ranking Cuban intelligence officials that I talked with were very confident of their position in Mexico. They used to say that "we have everything under control.' They have a large number of agents in the unions and political parties. If they just snap their fingers, the situation will explode. They have also paid off and blackmailed the Mexican security forces, which would thus be paralyzed in a crisis.

"Ideologically, terror, as opposed to prolonged guerrilla warfare, is not a problem. The people in charge of subversion think only in operational terms—whether a particular action will be productive or counterproductive. They don't care about blowing up a busload of people if that action will have the desired effect."

In the following excerpt, Bolaños speaks of the training of the Nicaraguan Army by Cuban and Soviet advisers:

"Soviet military advisors came to Nicaragua right after the triumph. For example, Army Chief of Staff Joaquin Cuadra was advised by a group of five

Soviet generals and vice-generals as early as August 1979. This group of generals was the vanguard of Soviet personnel; they were sent to Nicaragua to advise on defense for both the short and long term. The Soviet made all of the crucial decisions on weapons and aid. For example, I saw one specific map of the Honduran–Nicaraguan border detailing the capabilities of each side. They were counting tanks on our side that we did not even have yet. I know this because as an assistant to Cuadra, I would have to clean up the room after the meetings.

"Training for the general staff began in 1979 and lasted nine months. Training was conducted in Havana at the Mateos Academy. Cubans did the actual training at the battalion level along with Chileans and other internationalists, but the Soviets supervised. To my knowledge, no one was sent to the Frunze Academy in Moscow."

Bolaños made the following comments about the training and direction of Salvadoran guerrillas noting that the Soviet advisers stay far away from this to avoid an East–West confrontation:

"Training the Salvadorans is handled by a mix of Cubans and Nicaraguans and other foreign revolutionaries—Chileans and Montoneros, for example. The Soviets are not involved in the actual training. We got the impression that the Soviets do not want to go into something if they can do it through a surrogate. Also, because of the possibility of an East–West confrontation, they had to be very careful. Even the Cuban DOE, which is in charge of the training, had to be very careful at first.

"Right after the triumph there was a lot of confusion. People were just going by themselves to help the Salvadorans, carrying weapons across the border. But it reached a point where it was getting risky for the FSLN, so the Army issued orders to shoot on sight anyone illegally crossing the border. I was still working with Joaquin Cuadra at the time and I remember him saying how crazy the situation was. They realized that they would fail unless they organized things better. The training camps in Nicaragua for the Salvadorans started then, about mid-1980.

"The Nicaraguans and the Cubans do not go into El Salvador itself, but the others do. For example, they sent in Chileans in groups of 10 and 15. As to the actual movement of personnel and equipment, the Nicaraguans took them up to the border and then the Salvadoran guerrillas took over. Because of large-scale infiltration of the Salvadoran Army by the insurgents, the Nicaraguan Army had good intelligence of where the Salvadoran Army would be.

"The Punta Huete airport is used for training in sabotage. The base is mainly controlled by Cubans; the head of the school is Cuban and so are most of the officers. Guatemalan and Salvadoran guerrillas are trained there. For example, the commando squad that destroyed Salvadoran Air Force planes at Ilopango in 1982 trained on models at Punta Huete.

"When I left Nicaragua, the Sandinistas had created two groups to handle the Salvadoran guerrillas—a Political Commission and a Military Commission. Bayardo Arce is in charge of the Political Commission, but his brother does most of the work. Humberto Ortega is in charge of the Military Commission, but Joaquin Cuadra runs it day to day."

Document 2: Testimony of Eden Pastora Gomez

E den Pastora Gomez first became involved in the struggle against the Somoza Dynasty in 1959. He gained international prominence when on 22 August 1978 he led a group of 25 Sandinistas in the seizure of the National Palace, taking more than 2,000 hostages. The raid was a tremendous blow to the Somoza regime. During the final offensive, Pastora commanded the southern front, which was the scene of the bitterest fighting of the war. After the Sandinista victory, he was appointed vice-minister of the Interior and was responsible for overseeing the Sandinista Popular Militias. He resigned quietly in 1981, and after ten months of silence surfaced in San Jose on 15 April 1982. He attributed his break with the Sandinista regime to "excessive foreign influence" on the revolution. Immediately afterward, he established the guerrilla group ARDE to challenge the Sandinista regime, which today he leads from Costa Rica. The following are excerpts from an interview with Eden Pastora.

Source: Oral History Project, International Security Studies Program, Fletcher School of Law and Diplomacy.

In 1976 the FSLN split into three factions, the Guerra Prolongada Popular (Prolonged Popular Warfare faction, GPP), the Proletarian faction, and the Tercerista (Third Tendency) faction, the first two of which were of communist inspiration. In this passage, Pastora describes his own faction, the Terceristas, and tells how the democrats lost in the struggle for power with the Marxists:

"It is well known to the people of Nicaragua that the FSLN was a Marxist–Leninist group that historically had contacts with communist governments.[1] In 1976 and 1977, there was a division within the FSLN. One of the factions, the insurrectional or "tercerista" tendency, severed these contacts and proposed a nationalist, democratic program. Part of this movement was the formation of the Group of Twelve, which also proposed a nationalist, democratic program.[2] We within the tercerista tendency didn't fear the three Marxists—Daniel Ortega, Humberto Ortega, and Victor Tirado Lopez—that were there. Daniel Ortega has mental limitations because he had been in jail for eight years. Victor Tirado Lopez was a Mexican and really just a hired worker. Humberto Ortega, even though the most dangerous of the three because of his skills of manipulation, was basically a coward. The attempt to maintain the independent, noncommunist tercerista tendency failed when the governments of Venezuela, Panama, and Costa Rica pressured us to unite with the other three tendencies. They sent some of the leaders of the three tendencies to Cuba to negotiate with Fidel Castro. Fidel told them that if they did not come together and unite, the social democrat in their midst, Eden Pastora, would eat them up alive. This caused them to come together and with that we, the democratic faction, lost the war. The decisive meeting must have occurred in April 1979."

In the following passage, Pastora reviews the history of relations between the FSLN and Cuba. Interestingly, he claims that the FSLN received no Cuban assistance from 1969 to 1978. This Cuban policy changed dramatically in 1978.

"It is well known that in the beginning the Cubans helped the FSLN. However, in 1969 the Cubans decided that revolution was not possible in Latin America and began to shift their interests to Africa. At that time, Cuba closed its training camps and suspended its economic aid to the revolutionaries in Latin America. Instead of promoting revolution, Cuba started a diplomatic offensive in Latin America. While this was happening, the revolutionary movements, including the FSLN, began to disintegrate. After making a careful analysis of the situation in 1976, we opted for a different type of revolution. We stopped trying to sell a Marxist–Leninist revolution and started trying to sell a democratic revolution.

"In the years 1976, 1977, and 1978 we received absolutely no military or economic assistance from Cuba. The GPP was being destroyed in the mountains.[3] The proletarian faction was stagnant.[4] It wasn't until October 1977 and the uprisings in Masaya, Rivas, and Granada that the FSLN again had the impulse to grow. After the takeover of the military barracks in Rivas, on January 2 and 3, 1978, Cuba began to reevaluate the situation in Nicaragua. That was the first time that the Cubans were interested in what was happening in Nicaragua in seven years, and they invited us to come to Cuba. The military action at Rivas was so successful and so extraordinary that even many of the U.S. military advisors said that it could only have taken place if there had been parachutists or Cuban commandos involved. Even the Cubans in Havana who were more or less knowledgeable of the situation could not understand how it was possible that thirty men could penetrate forty kilometers into a country and actually take over an area. After the attack on Rivas, Pepe Figueres opened up his warehouse and we received advanced weapons—machine guns, bazookas, and rocket launchers—that we never had before.

"We went to Cuba and talked to them, but ideologically and politically we were not on the same line. We talked to everyone from Fidel Castro to Ramiro Valdez, from Raul Castro to Manuel Pineiro.[5] They examined us closely, trying to figure out our political beliefs. They always insisted that we would be utilized by the bourgeoisie and other reactionary elements. Unhappy and without the assistance of the Cubans, we returned to our war in the south.

"The Nine, of course, had always maintained contacts with the Cubans, but there was still no military or economic assistance.[6] And the GPP and the Proletarians were much closer to the Cubans than were we, the Terceristas."

In this passage Pastora states that the bulk of the arms for the insurrection initially came from Costa Rica, Panama, and Venezuela. He describes the pivotal role played by Omar Torrijos in insulating the Sandinistas from Cuban influence. He also tells how the Cubans managed to overcome Torrijos' ploy and provide direct, massive assistance for the final offensive.

"The arms for the final offensive came from various Latin American countries.[7] Costa Rica gave us logistical support and their own territory as a backup, and then more help came from Venezuela. Panama also gave us logistical support. When the Costa Rican and Panamanian sources dried up, Venezuela provided us with assistance. Omar Torrijos made what I consider was a very intelligent manuever. He asked Fidel for arms for himself, which he then gave to us. Torrijos wanted to insulate us from Cuba, and to keep us from making a commitment to Cuba. In this way we began to receive thousands of rifles, machine guns, bazookas, and all other types of military equipment through Panama from Cuba while making no commitment to Cuba. While this was going on, the Costa Rican Minister of Security, Johnny Echevarria Brealy, went to Cuba to talk with Fidel. He said that it would be much better if the arms came directly to Costa Rica, but that Costa Rica would have to keep half of the arms for itself in case Nicaragua became angry and decided to attack Costa Rica. So Cuba was able to jump over the obstacle that had been erected by Panama. An airlift was started in June and July 1979 between Havana and Liberia, which is in the northwest of Costa Rica. Cuban help was now more obvious and the moral commitment to Cuba was now out in the open. The intervention by Echevarria angered Torrijos very much. Torrijos told me personally his view of what was taking place.

"At the time, nobody was particularly worried about the developing relationship with Cuba. Everyone concentrated on the overthrow of Somoza.

Pepe Figueres hated Somoza for historical reasons.[8] Carlos Andrez Perez had a personal grudge also, because of Somoza's aid to Perez Jimenez.[9] When Figueres personally asked him to assist in what was going on, Andres Perez became interested in the struggle against Somoza."

In the following passage, Pastora gives a detailed account of Cuban assistance during the final offensive. He also discounts Fidel Castro's role in promoting unity among the FSLN factions, claiming instead that unity was based on fear of the democratic elements within the FSLN, led by Pastora himself.

"Once the Cubans began to provide more support in 1979, they did not seem to favor the more Marxist–Leninist factions over the others. We received arms as a unified unit. They gave me the distribution orders and I distributed the arms as was necessary. No one was sent to Cuba for special training until mid–1978. Four or five months after the takeover of Rivas, fifteen or twenty men were sent to Cuba. Their training was so mediocre that they returned just as bad off as when they had gone. The Cubans were not really prepared to train them. All the schools had been torn down. Cuban intelligence assistance was also minimal. There was a person named Julian with three or four more Cubans with him.[10] They would go as far as Liberia, collect data, and send it back to Fidel. And a Colonel Alejandro with two or three other people came in the last few days. Their advice was not very good. For example, they suggested that we should put our command post about ten kilometers behind the firing line. And I said, well, then we should go ahead and put it all the way back in Liberia, Costa Rica. The area that we had taken was so small that that is what putting it ten kilometers behind the firing line would have amounted to.

"The Cubans were surprised by our success and were not prepared for it. Fidel has commented on that frequently. The intelligence element that appeared from the Cuban side was really there not so much to help us but to provide intelligence for Havana.

"During the preparation for the final offensive, the Cubans set up an operations center in San José under Julian Lopez Diaz. He was a sort of ambassador there, serving as a liason between the Cubans and the FSLN, making contacts and distributing arms. The operation was set up in May 1979. They operated right through the San José international airport. In fact, they unloaded the arms right in front of the OAS observers. They even had parties and dances with the girls from the OAS.

"When the meetings took place with the Cubans regarding unification, they did not demand unification as a precondition for sending arms. They were already giving help without the unification. The Cubans know what the North Americans do not know—in the dynamic of fighting, you get together.

In fact, the people were already united in their fight against Somoza. What was lacking was the formal unification of the leaders. The Cuban representative achieved this unity by saying, 'either unite or Eden Pastora will eat you up.' So the unity was based on Eden Pastora."

In the following passage, Pastora describes the military situation prior to Somoza's fall and tells of a dramatic secret meeting with a U.S. Embassy officer in which Pastora tried to convince the United States to pressure Somoza into allowing Pastora's forces to be the first to enter Managua. [His effort failed; in consequence, the communist-dominated insurgents were able to reach Managua first and eventually impose a regime in their own image.]

"I began to perceive that the revolution was being taken over by the communists two months before its triumph. In April 1979, when I saw a picture in the press of the National Directorate with everyone holding their fists in the air, I realized that we the democrats had lost the war. So I went and made contact with U.S. Embassy in San José. Secretly, so that the national directorate would not know about it, we had a meeting in the Europa hotel in San José. There I made a political analysis for this Embassy official and I explained to him that Somoza was losing the war. Politically speaking, Somoza was isolated from the Andean Pact, Panama, Costa Rica, and even Europe. The people in the United States had also given up on him. Militarily, he was being shot at from all directions. From Leon there was a noncommunist military force on the way whose leaders—Dora Maria Tellez and Paulo Rias—were communists. From the north there was a force coming down, another noncommunist force with communist leaders—Francisco Rivera, Bayardo Arce, and Ino Guerra. From Rama another noncommunist force with a communist leader—Commandante Guillen. And from Masaya yet another noncommunist force with communist leaders—Hilario Sanchez and Joaquin Cuadra. And I told this American official that the only noncommunist force with noncommunist commanders was in the south, my Benjamin Zeledon front. And I also told him that all of these groups were struggling to get to Managua and the first to reach it would get power. I made him see that all of these other forces had the path wide open to them, a clean path to get there. And I made him see that the only force that was blocked was the noncommunist force of the southern front, the Benjamin Zeledon front. I told him that Somoza had sent his best troops and his best commanders to the south. The narrowness of the isthmus by Rivas, which is only nineteen miles wide, didn't give us any room to maneuver and advance. So I asked this Embassy official to go to Washington and ask the people there to order Somoza to remove his troops from the south. And I said to this official that I was not asking him to help us to overthrow Somoza, but simply asking him to remove the blockage so that the democratic forces could be the first ones to get to Managua. I returned to the battle and much to my surprise, Pablo Emilio, the Somoza commander, had been reinforced with more and better troops. Somoza left on July 17 and we entered Masaya. On the morning of July 18 the force from Leon entered Managua and in the evening the force from Rama entered Managua. On the 19th we finally started to advance because the enemy began to retreat. It was not until the morning of the 20th that we finally entered Managua. By then power was already in the hands of the communists and there was nothing to do except submit and say, 'give me your orders.'

"Communists had come to lead noncommunist forces because in the alliance between the democratic and Marxist elements of the FSLN the democratic elements never received help from the democratic countries. The communist countries, on the other hand, certainly helped the communist elements within the FSLN. The help that they gave was economic, and economic power leads to political power. And as far as the leadership of the organization, we the democrats were gradually isolated and the communists took over.[11]

In the following passage, Pastora describes the development of Nicaraguan relations with Cuba and the Soviet Union. He describes the role of the Cuban, East German, and PLO advisors. Also, he tells of the conflict between himself and the other commandantes over the issue of obtaining Soviet tanks.

"Once Managua had fallen, Cuban intelligence and military advisors began to appear quickly. On the 20th, when I went to the command bunker, there was large group of Cubans whom I had never seen before. On the same day, the Havana–Managua airlift was started. The East German advisors who came are in charge of giving advice to the security police. They teach how to interrogate, how to use psychology, how to use fear. The Cuban who is in charge of the security policy was trained in East Germany; in fact, all of the Cubans in security were trained in East Germany. Cuban advisors are found at all levels of the Nicaraguan army. In most situations, they only advise. The first thing that the Cubans did when they arrived was to select who was to be sent for training in Cuba and other Soviet Bloc countries. They chose people for tanks, artillery, and aviation. Aviation instruction was in Bulgaria; tanks and artillery in Cuba. They were chosen on the basis of two criteria—ideological commitment and physical ability.

"The PLO is involved in the Air Force. But of all the advisors, I would say the Cubans are the best because of their facility with the language and their experience in Angola, and they are the same race of people.

"The Cubans operate within a strict military organization which places great emphasis on rank and discipline. They are commanded by two Cuban generals, Ochoa and Quintelan. They maintain direct contact with the National Directorate. The other groups are not so tightly organized. They maintain contact with the DRI, the Department of International Relations.

"Jihas Levin is in charge of military intelligence for the army. There are ten to fifteen Cubans in that section, but each military zone or region has its one military intelligence unit. And each one has its own Cuban advisors. External military intelligence is distinct and is headed by Alfonso Ramos.

"The international propaganda department, which is the biggest and most important department of the FSLN, is headed by Bayardo Arce. In the first two years of the Sandinista regime, they instructed officials to emphasize that they were a Sandinista revolution and not allow any mention that they were Marxist–Leninist. As you might have noticed, I never call them Sandinistas, because I know that is the most important thing that they are trying to do—maintain the mask that they have on.

"The Soviet–Nicaraguan relationship developed rapidly after the revolution's triumph. The first contact I know of occurred fifteen days after the triumph, when the Soviet ambassador to Mexico arrived at the Managua airport and Tomas Borge went out to meet him. He arrived drunk and spoke sort of nastily to Tomas. Tomas told him off and made him straighten up. Tomas told the Ambassador that he was going to report the incident to the USSR and Mexico. A note came asking pardon later. So a relationship was started but it was not very intense. For the most part, our relations were handled through Cuba. Later, when the Soviet embassy was established, a closer, more intimate relationship was started. Delegations of the Soviet ambassador and others began to visit the bunker. I noticed that the delegations were going to D'Escoto, Humberto Ortega, and some other people. The relationship was becoming closer.

"Discussions on obtaining Soviet Bloc arms began immediately after the triumph. They started to talk about obtaining Soviet tanks and airplanes and personnel. I was the only commandante among the national directorate who opposed obtaining these arms. It became such an issue that they prohibited me from talking about the tanks anymore. And to shut me up, they sent me to Moscow to sign the protocol agreement concerning the tanks. This trip, the first of two, was about eight to ten months after the triumph. I went with Joaquin Cuadra and we met with Defense Minister Ustinov and other top military commanders. We did not meet with any political people. The Soviets are very formal—in meetings, every one meets only with their counterparts—military men with military men, political men with political men, for example. There was not much discussion of the deal. They told me to sign, so I signed. It was already tied up as a package.

"The commandantes really believe that they need the arms. If you read all the speeches by Humberto Ortega, you will see that he is always talking about the Central American War. He says that if the United States invades

Nicaragua, then it will have to invade all of Central America. And there are plans to do so. Therefore, they need the tanks, the 122-mm howitzers, and other offensive weapons. Humberto talked about this in his very first speech.

"I know that it was Russian pressure to bring the tanks in. I'm convinced of that. Even Fidel and the Cubans were against bringing in the tanks. Moises Hassan was a member of the junta and participated in the meetings at which the topic was discussed. He was also against bringing in the tanks. He said that the Russians wanted to make us their soldiers. Because of his opposition, he was kicked out of the junta. He was vice-minister of transportation, but now he is way down, in a second or third tier position.

"The connections between the communists in the FSLN and Moscow were made through the International Department of the Communist Party of the Soviet Union. Doris Tijerino and Bayardo Arce are in charge of those matters. Their connection is direct, fraternal, and very close. However, it has not been without problems. For example, in March 1980, when Humberto Ortega went to Moscow, he had a meeting with the Russians and asked them what they were going to do if North American imperialism attacked Nicaragua. The question was apparently unexpected and the Russians did not answer. They started to vacillate. So Humberto told them, 'I have to know. Because we are willing to sacrifice the revolution in Nicaragua, but only if it is in order to save another revolution.' When Humberto told me this story, I could see that he meant it from his heart. As a nationalist, this episode really hurt me. I was repulsed. But I smiled and remained silent."

In this passage, Pastora confirms Nicaraguan operational involvement in El Salvador, promoting the Marxist–Leninist insurgency in that country.

"I was also opposed to our involvement in El Salvador, for many reasons. I said politically that the government of El Salvador was not as discredited as the Somoza government had been. And I said that while we were proposing a democratic project to the Nicaraguan people, the Salvadorans were proposing a Marxist–Leninist program, which is by its essence dictatorial. And while our program advocated a bringing together of the Nicaraguan family, the Salvadorans were proposing class struggle. Tomas Borge, in an effort to convince me, said that we were building a bargaining chip, such as the Cubans had when they brought in the missiles in 1962.

"They started really working on the Salvadoran situation about six or seven weeks after the triumph of the revolution. The Cubans do not actually participate in guerrilla activity in El Salvador. They are basically in charge of propaganda and information. There is training of Salvadoran guerrillas in Nicaragua. Hugo Torres is in charge of this. Joaquin Cuadra is in charge of logistical support.

"I have met, at various times, all of the political and military leaders of the Salvadoran insurgency—for example, the National Resistance Group.[10] They are less to the left, than, say Villalobos' groups.[11] They are experts in hand-to-hand combat, and have been in charge of all of those famous kidnappings. They are the ones that kidnapped the head of Phillips. They got thirty million dollars out of that kidnapping. Of that, they gave us half, fifteen million. However, two million was given as food. But the food was rotten and had bugs in it. After the triumph, external support was only given to the groups of Shafik Handal and Cayetano Carpio.[12] And the more moderate factions, the ones that had given us money, were pushed to one side. These were the ones that Torrijos wanted to help. The Cubans even had one of the more moderate leaders killed. They put a bomb in the airplane of Commandante Bolando, which exploded and killed him on a flight between Managua and Panama.[13]

"I couldn't say that the Soviet Union has authorized the arms shipments to El Salvador. Cuba, however, is totally committed to the Salvadoran Revolution. In fact, it was their idea. As far as what Managua gives the Salvadorans, what I can tell you is the following: I wish that the United States had given me half of what Managua is giving the Salvadorans. The FAL rifles that Castro gave us went to the Salvadorans. So did the M16s from Vietnam. Also, M1s, M60 machine guns, and light antitank rockets. While air is the most common route used, they also take the arms across the Gulf of Fonseca in small boats. Another route is by land through Honduras."

Pastora gave the following account of Fidel Castro's attitude toward the Sandinista Revolution. He confirms that Castro urged the Sandinistas to put a nationalist stamp on their regime, even to the point of questioning their request for more Cuban advisers. In Pastora's opinion, Castro's attitude reflected profound insecurity about the achievements of the Cuban Revolution.

"Fidel Castro's advice to the Sandinistas after the triumph was rather curious. He told them not to make a Cuban Revolution. He told them to make a Sandinista Revolution. He told them not to fight with the gringos. He told them not to bring the tanks in. And he was concerned about the many internationalists, the Cubans, coming in, even though we were asking for them. Once, when I was with Fidel, he asked me what I meant when I said that I was a Sandinista. And I told him it was sovereignty, it was nationalism, it was national dignity. He touched my shoulder and said, 'Always keep that position, keep it all of your life.' You try and figure out what that means from an international communist.

"I do not think that Fidel's advice was merely tactical. I think that Fidel is very intelligent and has seen his revolution fail. For example, the wife of Armando Hart, Haydee Santa Maria, committed suicide because, after twenty years of revolution, she could not stand to see Mariel. They are not stupid or foolish, they have seen the failure of their revolution. I talked to Fidel about fifteen times and it seemed to me that he was hoping for some way to get out of his own mess through the Sandinista Revolution. And I keep telling the Department of State that we need a successful Sandinista revolution so that Fidel can escape. A successful, nationalist Sandinista revolution, at peace with the United States, would give Fidel a powerful example to sell his own people. Fidel could do this if he wanted. If anyone opposes Fidel in Cuba, they cut off his head."

In the following passage, Pastora describes the Cuban role in Africa. He confirms that the Cubans receive economic compensation from the Soviet Union for services rendered in Angola.

"It was a learning experience. In armed struggle, you learn by your mistakes. The errors that they made in Angola were corrected in Nicaragua. Psychologically, they learned how the people respond to an occupying force. Also, perhaps they learned not to be so open in Nicaragua. The intervention in Nicaragua is more undercover.

"The international presence helps Castro to earn extra money. I know this for a fact. The Angolans, the Libyans, and Polisario members told me this. For example, when a Cuban worker, a military advisor, a nurse, or whatever, goes to another country, that country pays his salary in dollars to the Cuban government. The government, in turn, pays the family of the Cuban worker in pesos. In Angola, it works differently. I talked to an Angolan colonel at a celebration commemorating the fifth anniversary of the founding of the Polisario. Even though this colonel said that Angola did not owe anything to Cuba or the Soviet Union, he still bore those countries a certain amount of resentment, because the Cuban military is paid by the Soviet Union, and the Soviet Union is in turn paid by Angola in the form of coffee."

In this passage, Pastora describes Castro's attitude toward international drug trafficking and his current policy of full support for this traffic, at least in part to achieve the destabilization of American society. He recommended that the Sandinistas follow his example.

"What I know objectively is this. When Tomas Borge and other members of the National Directorate were in Cuba in 1982, Fidel Castro made some remarks concerning drugs and drug traffickers. He said that he was not going to be the policeman for imperialism anymore. Before, the Cubans captured drug traffickers and handed them over. Now, Fidel said, they can go and do whatever they want, so long as they leave us some money. Fidel said, 'We are going to make the people up there white, white with cocaine.' And Castro recommended that Tomas should do the same.

"Corn Island is already involved in drug traffic with Colombia.[14] I know that airplanes land there, and that drug traffickers have always brought drugs in exchange for arms.

"And also once I saw Humberto Ortega with bags of cocaine and LSD pills. He sent them to the airport. I don't know what exactly resulted."

Finally, Pastora made this comment about the role of China in promoting revolution in Central America:

"There was some contact with China in the mid-sixties. I think it was about 1965. After he went to Mexico with Carlos Fonseca Amador, Victor Tirado Lopez went to China. But the Chinese would not give him any money. And when he came back, some members of the FSLN said that he was a CIA agent because he went to get money and came back with nothing. After that, China was not involved."

Notes

1. The FSLN, the Sandinista National Liberation Front, was founded in 1963 through the fusion of a noncommunist group led by Colonel Santos Lopez, a former associate of the national hero Sandino, with a communist group led by Carlos Fonseca Amador, Tomas Borge, and Silvio Mayorga.

2. The Group of Twelve was a FSLN front group composed of respected businessmen and intellectuals who lobbied for international support for the revolutionaries. Members included Arturo Cruz Porras, Fernando Cardenal, and Sergio Mercado Ramirez.

3. Guerra Prolongada Popular, or the Prolonged Popular Warfare faction, was one of the three tendencies emerging from the 1976–1977 split within the FSLN. Its leaders were Tomas Borge and Henry Ruiz and it was heir to the FSLN rural organization.

4. The Proletarians were another of the three factions. This group, led by Jaime Wheelock, inherited the urban organization of the FSLN and was composed mainly of academics and intellectuals. It emphasized organizing and propagandizing the factories and poor neighborhoods.

5. Ramiro Valdez is the Cuban Minister of the Interior. Manuel Pineiro Losada is head of the Americas Department of the Cuban Communist Party and is in charge of coordinating subversive activities in Latin America.

6. "The Nine" refers to the nine commandantes who compose the National Directorate, the supreme political authority of the Sandinista regime.

7. The Final Offensive, which took place in June and July 1979, toppled the Somoza regime.

8. Somoza supported the enemies of Figueres during the events in 1948 and 1955, and granted asylum to the losers in the 1948 Costa Rican civil war.

9. Marcos Perez Jimenez was the dictator of Venezuela until he was ousted in 1958.

10. Pastora is referring to the Armed Forces of National Resistance (FARN).

11. Joaquin Villalobos is the head of the ERP (Popular Revolutionary Army) and is widely considered the most formidable guerrilla leader.

12. Cayetano Carpio was the head of the FPL (Popular Forces of Liberation). He committed suicide on 12 April 1983 in the aftermath of the murder of his principal lieutenant, Nelida Anaya Montes, one week earlier. Shafik Handal is the General Secretary of the Communist Party of El Salvador.

13. Pastora here is evidently referring to the death of FARN leader Ernesto Jovel on 17 September 1980.

14. The Corn Islands are on Nicaragua's Caribbean coast offshore from Bluefields.

Document 3: Interview with Tomas Borge

T he following document contains excerpts from an interview with the Sandinista Minister of the Interior Tomas Borge, published in a Colombian news magazine. It reveals that his group received economic assistance from Cuba as early as 1961.

Source: 3 January 1983 issue of the Colombian magazine *Cromos*. Translated from the Spanish.

Of his first visit to Cuba, Tomas Borge stated:

"From Costa Rica I went to Cuba. I participated in the Latin American Youth Congress. That was when I got to know Che Guevara. They took me to his office. I told him with great enthusiasm that I was bringing salutations from the youth of Nicaragua, since I had been appointed representative of the Nicaraguan University Center abroad, and Che said to me, 'Enough of these salutations.' But he listened to me patiently for about an hour, and at the end of our conversation he agreed to give us the economic assistance for which we had asked him. Then he embraced me and said to me 'I accept the salutation.' That was in 1961."

With the funds obtained in Havana, Borge and his friends Carlos Fonseca and Silvio Mayorga founded a new organization, which in 1963 merged with the noncommunist group led by Colonel Santos Lopez to form the Sandinista National Liberation Front (FSLN). After two guerrilla campaigns in 1963 and 1967, both of which failed, Borge returned to Cuba as the leader of a group of FSLN members sent there for military and political training.

He returned to Nicaragua to continue the struggle in 1969. After the Sandinista victory in July 1979, he again visited Cuba. His interview ends with the following glowing description of a meeting with Fidel Castro:

"Fidel is a great human being, a very sensitive, unusual person. We all hold him in a very special regard. I remember my first birthday after the victory. My birthday is on the same day as Fidel's, the 13th of August. In August 1979 I was in Cuba. That day Fidel invited me to a dinner in a small circle. There was Raul with other revolutionary leaders. There was Celia Sanchez, who was still alive. I brought as a present for Fidel, as a momento of the struggle, the map which had been used by Somoza. But at the hour of the toasts I told him that this was not my most important gift, because the main present that we brought him was the indestructible unity of the Sandinista front. That was just about what I said. I spoke for a few minutes, and my words stirred Fidel so much that his eyes filled with tears.

"It always moves me to remember this moment with Fidel. He is such a considerate person. He has never tried to impose his judgment on us. At the most, he has given us his advice while showing absolute respect for our decisions. He is a man of exquisite sensitivity, full of affection for the people. He has won the love of all his people and also our love. It moves me to think of him.

"Yes, I weep when I am moved. I am not moved by death. For instance, the death of a comrade does not move me especially. I am not moved by the sometimes unavoidable stench of combat. What moves me are the higher manifestations of humanity, men's self-denial, their ability to feel, and to sacrifice themselves for others. I am moved by their ability to express tenderness."

Document 4: Shafik Handal's Travel Notes

T he document below contains excerpts from a report by Shafik Handal, the General Secretary of the Communist Party of El Salvador. He describes his 1980 trip to Soviet surrogate countries in search of arms and other supplies for guerrillas in El Salvador.

Handal's account reveals the extensive network operated by the Soviet Union and its allies in their effort to destabilize the government of El Salvador. In this case, Handal arranged for weapons to be smuggled into El Salvador from such Soviet surrogates as Bulgaria, Vietnam, and Ethiopia.

The document also demonstrates that the Soviet Union and its allies are determined to cover up the traces of their support for the antigovernment forces in El Salvador. Moscow arranged for *U.S.-made* weapons to be provided to the Salvadorans from Ethiopian and Vietnamese stocks. Similarly, World War II vintage German-made submachine guns were to be shipped from Bulgaria, as were Czechoslovak arms generally available on the world market. Evidently, weapons actually manufactured in the USSR were not considered.

Source: This document was captured in El Salvador and has not been published previously in this form.

Trip to the Socialist Countries, Asia, and Africa

Vietnam, from 9 to 15 June. Received by Le Duan, secretary general of the Vietnamese CP; Xuan Thuy, member of the secretariat of the central committee and vice president of the National Assembly; and Tran Van Quang, lieutenant general, deputy minister of National Defense. Friendly and enthusiastic reception. They agreed to provide aid in weapons, the first shipment consisting of: 192 9-mm pistols; 1,620 AR-15 rifles; 162 M-30 medium machine guns; 36 M-60 heavy machine guns; 12 M-50 heavy machine guns (caliber 12.7mm); 36 6-mm mortars; 12 81-mm mortars; 12 DKZ-57 anti-tank rocket launchers. . . . Approximate weight of the entire shipment: 60 tons.

According to a message received at the embassy here on 24 July and read to the comrade, the above-mentioned materiel will be ready for shipment during the first five days of September. If sent by ship, it will be delivered in Ho Chi Minh City. It is recommended that it be packaged as commercial goods, stowed in dry holds at the bottom of the ship, and covered with real commercial goods.

The comrade requested air transport from the CPSU, but he left Moscow on 23 July without obtaining a reply. At the embassy here on 28 July he asked that a cable be sent urging a reply. Before he left here on 6 August there had been no reply. . . . It was decided that if a favorable reply to the request for air transport was received in time, we would take advantage of it, in which case we would need to coordinate with the Vietnamese. The reply of the CPSU will be received by Norma, the representative here.

Ethiopia, from 3 to 6 July. Received by Haile-Marian Mengistu. . . . [who] informed the comrade of the decision to contribute "several thousand weapons," which was confirmed by a cable from our embassy there on 3–4 August as follows: 150 Thompson submachine guns with 300 cartridge clips; 1,500 M-1 rifles, one thousand M-14 rifles. Ammunition: 90,000 rounds, caliber 45 mm, for the Thompson submachine guns; 360,000 rounds of M-1 ammunition and 240,000 rounds of M-14 ammunition with 2,000 cartridge clips. In addition, a supply of spare parts for these weapons.

Bulgaria, from 27 to 30 June. Received by Stanichiev, member of the secretariat of the central committee of the BCP and secretary for international relations of the BCP, with powers of decision. He informed the comrade of the donation of the following: 300 submachine guns of German manufacture (rebuilt, from World War II), Shpagin make, with 200,000 rounds. . . . He promised that the materiel would be sent here shortly by their own means or in coordination with the Germans or Czechs. . . .

Furthermore, he promised that the bureau of the party would approve other requests consisting of 10,000 uniforms according to the pattern which would be sent to him, and 2,000 individual medical kits for combatants. In fact, on 18 July Stanchiev met with the comrade in Moscow on the occasion of his attendance at the Olympic Games, and he informed him that these requests had been approved. . . . It was a very warm and fraternal reception; the conduct of the PCS was praised.

Czechoslovakia, from 24 to 27 June. Received by Bilak, second secretary of the central committee, member of the bureau and secretary for international relations. He informed the comrade of the decision already to send a quantity of weapons of Czech manufacture [similar to those circulated on the world market]. . . . He promised to coordinate with the GDR to transport this materiel here in German ships. . . . Warm, enthusiastic, and emotional reception by Bilak himself.

Hungary, from 30 June to 3 July. Received by Janos Kadar, secretary general of the Hungarian CP and "Gueisel," secretary for international relations and member of the Political bureau. Gueisel agreed to accept a request for two-way radios, although he did not specify the number (the comrade asked for 40 shortwave and 12 ultra-shortwave radios). . . . He offered medicines, field first aid kits and medical packs for soldiers. The offer was accepted. He offered to make 10 thousand uniforms according to the pattern and size sent to him. The comrades' decision about the pattern is still pending. Concerning weapons, he said that they didn't have any of Western, Chinese or Yugoslav origin and they would be willing to participate in a deal with Ethiopia or Angola. The comrade expressed his skepticism about the possibility of a trade and suggested other alternatives:

a) Ask friendly governments to purchase Western-made weapons.
b) Give money to the comrades so that they can buy the weapons.
c) Give Czech weapons of the type that are sold on the world market to the comrades.

He offered to study these possibilities and submit them to the Bureau for their decision. The welcome was fraternal and there was agreement in the points of view on the emphasis. Gueisel said that they would concern themselves with resolving the problems of weapons "since we want to be part of providing this aid". . . .

GDR, 19–24 June. Received by Axen, member of the BP and secretary of international relations. He said that a 1.9 ton shipment of medicines, 50 first-aid kits, 200 auxiliary kits, 2,000 combat kits, 10 megaphones with batteries, cameras and 16mm movie cameras had already been sent to Managua and he offered to respond to the other requests which were principally for weapons.

On 21 July the GDR Embassy in Moscow informed the comrade that Honecker had sent a cable which said that the BP had approved: a) authorization to the solidarity committee to provide resources, not directly military, to the DRU, valued at 2–3 million Marks in accordance with concrete requests from the Salvadoran side. For this reason, they ask us to send a comrade to Berlin with authorization to discuss these requests in detail b) contributing to the training of military cadres especially in covert operation and they expect concrete requests. c) Since they had no Western-made weapons, they decided to continue seeking a solution to this problem although no time frame was set for this. The welcome was warm and fraternal. They praised the PCS.

USSR. First meeting: 2 July with Mikhail Kudachkin, deputy chief of the Latin American Section of the Department of International Relations of the CC of the CPSU. He reported that . . . a decision had not yet been reached concerning the requests presented on 19 May. . . . He proposed the possibility of a high level meeting with Ponomariov, a member of the Central Committee and Secretary of International Relations. He suggested a trip to Vietnam since, in his opinion, the comrade is the right one to obtain the necessary assistance. He offered to finance the trip and did so. . . . The comrade presented a request that 30 communist youths, who were studying in the USSR and had asked to become part of the struggle, receive military training; he supported the requests presented by the Politico-Military Coordinator for weapons, explosives, ammunition, materials for making explosives, and money for the purchase of arms. And he drafted a written request for the meeting with Ponomariov which was to be held upon his return from Hanoi. The meeting could not be held then, and was changed to the return trip to the socialist countries of Europe and Ethiopia, which was not possible then either due to the jobs and commitments assumed by Ponomariov. On the eve of the departure from Moscow . . . the meeting was held with Brutents, head of the CC Latin American Section, and not with Ponomariov as was anticipated. Meanwhile, the comrade had presented a request to the CP to transport the weapons that the Vietnamese comrades provided. Brutents expressed CPSU solidarity and agreement with the ideas expressed by the comrade concerning the unity of the revolutionary forces and the struggle in the country, in view of the danger of foreign intervention and other aspects. . . .

a) In principle, there is opinion in favor of transporting the Vietnamese weapons but there has been no approval on the part of the leadership organs.

b) They do not have Western weapons and, closed as the possibilities of a trade with friendly governments appears, they do not see how to resolve this problem.

c) There is approval in principle for training the group of communist youths, though perhaps for lack of quotas, they would receive less than the 30.

The comrade again requested weapons and transportation of those that Vietnam provided, expressing the conviction that the CPSU is capable of resolving these problems, as well as insisting upon the training of the group of 30 comrades. After this meeting, the comrade made known through other channels his disagreement with the absence of the meeting at the proper level and lack of decision concerning the requests for assistance. On 29 July, he was notified by the Soviet Embassy here of a cable that had been received for him from Moscow, the content of which is as follows: (a) The CC of the CPSU wishes to receive the comrade for discussions in September or October; (b) and they agreed to train the group of 30. The Comrade asked to send a cable expressing appreciation for the message and requesting that the CPSU resolve within a short time the matter of the transportation of the Vietnam weapons and the decision to give them assistance in weapons.

He had not yet received any reply as of August 5. It was agreed that when the reply arrives, Comrade Norma is to be notified so that she can inform me. The comrade is expressing concern as to the effects that the lack of decision by the Soviets may have, not only regarding the assistance that they themselves can offer but also upon the inclination of the other parties of the European socialist camp to cooperate, and he requests that from the highest level.

Document 5: DRU Letter to Fidel Castro

T he following document is a letter addressed to Fidel Castro that announces the signing of a solidarity agreement between three of the Salvadoran guerrilla groups: FARN (Armed Forces of the National Resistance), CPES (Communist Party of El Salvador), and FPL (Peoples Liberation Forces). In recent years, Castro has demanded unity among the various national guerrilla groups as a precondition for Cuban aid. The unification of all of the Salvadoran guerrilla groups, finally achieved when ERP (Popular Revolutionary Army) entered the coalition in May 1980, represents the second use of this "unification" tactic. The first was the coalition of the three guerrilla factions listed above. This was finally achieved after negotiations between FSLN leaders and Fidel Castro in April 1979, and helped to ensure the final victory of the FSLN.

Source: This document was captured in El Salvador and has not been published previously in this form.

Havana, 16 December 1979

Comrade Fidel:

Our opening words bring to you the brotherly and revolutionary greetings of the heroic people of El Salvador. Comrade, brother and friend: the rich revolutionary practice, faithful to the proletarian internationalism of the Cuban people—headed by its Leninist vanguard, the Communist Party of Cuba, guided by your brilliant leadership as an unyielding and exemplary revolutionary—has been decisive for us, the representatives of El Salvador's revolutionary organizations, in understanding the urgent need for undertaking transcendental steps in the process of the unity of our people.

Today we can tell you, Fidel, that thanks to your help, to the help of your party comrades and to the inspired example of the revolutionary people of

Cuba, we have undertaken a transcendental step by signing an agreement which establishes very solid bases upon which we begin building the coordination and unity of our organizations: the unity and single direction so needed by our people in order to progress in its struggle to achieve popular freedom, democracy, peace and socialism.

This letter is accompanied by a copy of this agreement. It will allow you to appreciate its magnitude and scope and will surely bring you deserved satisfaction and renewed impulse in your indefatigable labors aimed at unity among the revolutionary ranks of our peoples who are oppressed by imperialism and dominant exploitative classes.

We shall honor the agreement we have signed just as we have proved our commitment to the heroic struggle of our people.

As we have remained faithful to the struggle of our people, so shall we prove worthy of the exalted internationalist and revolutionary example you embody, because the patient and wise work that Cuban solidarity has contributed to our success in taking another step toward unity is leaving its imprint on the accelerated pace that characterizes our people's march toward the ultimate success of its revolution.

For the Communist Party of El Salvador:

> /s/ *S. Handal*
> Secretary General of the Central
> Committee of the PCS

For the National Resistance:

> /s/ *D. Fuentes* (?)
> First Political-Military Officer

For the "People's Liberation Forces (FPL) Farabundo Marti":

> /s/ *Marcial*
> First Officer of the Central
> Command

Documents 6 and 7: DRU Letters to Manuel Pineiro

The following two letters provide the Cuban leadership with operational details concerning the Salvadoran insurgency. The letters are addressed to Manuel Pineiro, the head of the Americas Department of the Central Committee of the Cuban Communist Party, underlining the close cooperative relationship at the highest levels between Cuba and the Salvadoran revolutionaries. Pineiro is in charge of coordinating Cuban subversive activities in the Western Hemisphere.

Source: This document was captured in El Salvador and has not been published previously in this form.

Document 6

El Salvador, Central America 8 Oct. 1980

TO THE CENTRAL COMMITTEE OF THE
COMMUNIST PARTY OF CUBA
DEPARTMENT OF AMERICA

Comrade Manuel Pineiro:

In the name of the DRU of the FMLN, I have the honor to send you some documentation relative to the process of political, organic, and functional consolidation attained by the DRU in the last weeks.

Besides our growing relations with the "moderate" and progressive sector of the Army, which has been attained by taking advantage of the state of sharpening of contradictions within the breast of that reactionary organism, we are continuing to search for our proper part in the development of the revolution. . . .

Along these lines, now it is evident that the active but prudent line that the DRU followed in the days of the sharpening of the contradictions (the first fifteen days of September) was the most correct within the revolutionary framework and that conditions now justify the intensification of those contacts.

We want to thank you by this means for all the valuable ideas and suggestions that you gave us. . . .

We desire to show you that we feel very content and optimistic because the measures taken in the assigning of responsibilities within the framework of the Collective Direction will give the DRU the agility necessary for the appropriate political-military direction and that is a transcendant step in the Popular War. . . .

With revolutionary greetings,

"UNITED IN COMBAT UNTIL THE FINAL VICTORY"

UNITED REVOLUTIONARY DIRECTORATE POLITICAL-MILITARY OF THE FARABUNDO MARTI FRONT.

MARCIAL
Political-Military DRU (with functions of Coordinator-General)

Document 7

El Salvador, Central America 8 Oct. 1980

TO THE CENTRAL COMMITTEE
OF THE CUBAN COMMUNIST PARTY
AMERICA DEPARTMENT

Comrade Manuel Pineiro:

We salute you fraternally, desiring great success in your revolutionary work.

I have the pleasure to inform you about the decisions taken by the political-military bureau–DRU at recent meetings, concerning the assignation of individual responsibilities within the framework of the Collective Direction, as well as within the DRU and the Joint Commissions.

Also, concerning the naming of the FMLN, of which the DRU is the political-military bureau, and the symbols of the front.

Also, the naming of the fronts of the war.

I. The FFM

In the meeting of 21 September it was agreed:

1–That the group of political-military organizations that seek unity, whose political-military director is the DRU, is from now on called the Farabundo Marti Front for National Liberation, whose initials are FFM.
2–Whose symbol is the figure of Augustin Farabundo Marti, who will have two rifles crossed in front of him in a dynamic position as the official logo.
3–The flag of the FFM is the Red Flag with a white star with five points to his upper left; and in the center the name of the front.
4–Its theme is "United in Combat until the Final Victory" that will be complemented by another phrase that expresses the determination of our people to reach definitive victory.

At the same meeting the naming of the joint military fronts was approved; honoring the memory of revolutionary leaders of previous times:

II. Concerning the assigning of individual responsibilities in the framework of the Collective Directorate.

Front: Feliciano Ama (West)
Front: Modesto Ramirez (Central)
Front: Anastasio Aquino (Para-Central)
Front: Francisco Sanchez (East)

In the meeting of the DRU–PM of 29 September, it was agreed:

1–The approval of rules for the functioning of the DRU in the exterior; as well as that part of the DRU that will function in the exterior.
2–The naming of that part of the DRU that will be in the exterior that will have plenary powers, with an average appointment of 3 months, with headquarters in Lagos. . . .

Document 8: Formation of the FMSPS

T he following document announces the formation of the World Front for Solidarity with the Salvadoran People (FMSPS) in Mexico. As the propaganda arm of the FMLN, this organization would coordinate world-wide activity to support the Salvadoran Revolution. Note the presence of Sandy Pollack, a member of the Central Committee of the Communist Party of the United States and moving force behind CISPES (Committee in Solidarity with the People of El Salvador), on the Front's Permanent Bureau.

Source: This is the published manifesto of the FMSPS, translated from the Spanish.

The World Front for Solidarity with the Salvadoran People was founded in Mexico on March 26–28, 1982, with the following principles and objectives:

PRINCIPLES

Article 2: The World Front will be subject to the following principles:

a). It recognizes the FDR–FMLN alliance and its political leadership as the only legitimate representative of the Salvadoran people.

b). The unity that the World Front presents will be extensive, united and in step with the fight of the Salvadoran people.

c). The World Front will have an anti-interventionist character and will defend the inalienable right to liberty, sovereignty, and self-determination for all people.

d). The World Front will be an organization based on consensus and democratic norms of organization, resolution, and execution.

OBJECTIVES

a). To fight for the enforcement of human rights and for the respect of self-determination for the Salvadoran people.

b). To fight unconditionally at whatever the cost with the Salvadoran people to stop the intervention of the US government.

c). To denounce and combat the interventionist actions in El Salvador on the part of the regimes of Venezuela, Argentina, Chile, Guatemala, Honduras, Colombia, and the Zionist state of Israel, as well as any other pro-imperialist regime.

d). To develop and strengthen all potential solidarity with El Salvador that exists in the world.

e). To widen the context of solidarity to the rest of the Central American and Caribbean peoples, in order to support their legitimate fight for self-determination.

f). To fight to maintain the permanent character of the solidarity with the Salvadoran people in whatever form that is required: today, in the fight to defeat the dictatorship, tomorrow, for the task of national reconstruction.

The organizations, meeting in the International Forum of Solidarity with the Salvadoran People, resolved to name a Permanent Bureau and an Executive Secretariat, with the following members:

PERMANENT BUREAU

Executive Secretariat
Bill Zimmerman
President of the FMSPS
Andres Fabregas
Coordinator of the Executive
Secretariat
Lucia Pavletich
Heidi Terver
Willy Rozenbaum
Silvia Reyes
Enrique Colon

MEMBERS OF THE PERMANENT BUREAU

José Maria Mohedano
Father Mendez Arceo
Ahmad Zobeh
Julio Escalona
Josefina Finders
Massoun Kassawat
Jorge Gallardo
Jesus Escandel
Sandy Pollack
Antonio Silva

Document 9: Comments from FMSPS Map

The following document contains comments on movements against intervention in Central America. These comments are derived from a map detailing the international network of solidarity movements supporting the FDR–FMLN as a part of the World Front For Solidarity with the Salvadoran People (FMSPS). Comments on individual national movements, such as Australia's, suggest a high degree of central coordination. Other comments, for instance, those on Europe and Japan, reveal close coordination between the solidarity movements and the disarmament movement.

Source: This material is part of a Mexican publication, "Voces de Cuscatlan," October 1983, that describes itself as the official organ of the Salvadoran community in the United States. Translated from the Spanish.

SOLIDARITY
Forces Lobbying Against Intervention in Central America

In Canada the solidarity movement is on the rise. A national network with the Central American peoples consists of more than 15 committees.

The Solidarity movement in the United States gains more importance every day and is the principal force opposing intervention in Central America. More than 300 organizations say No! to the belligerent politics of Reagan. The solidarity movement appears bound to the national Black and Latin minorities and pacifist movements. On November 12 there will be a march against intervention.

Mexico is present in the solidarity movement yesterday, today, and always. More than 30 solidarity committees operate. The Mexican Committee of Solidarity with the Salvadoran People was the moving force behind the formation of the World Front.

Colombia: with the presence of more than 90 international organizations and 200 foreign nationals, Colombia has realized a great accomplishment in solidarity with the Central American and Caribbean peoples. The solidarity movement is growing and the Colombian movement is an important factor in widening and coordinating the movement in all of South America.

Evidence of adhesion to the World Front and of sympathy toward the cause of the Central American peoples is manifesting itself in the countries of the Southern Cone. In the next months we will see without a doubt that the people that defeat the dictatorships there will also take in their hands the cause of the Salvadoran people. For now, the advancement and deepening of their own struggle against dictatorship is the best method of solidarity.

In Puerto Rico, Jamaica, and the Dominican Republic the solidarity movement is making the people understand that the enemy of the Central American peoples is the same one that is exploiting them in the Caribbean. The small country of Grenada is present in the first line of solidarity with Central America.

In Norway, Sweden, Denmark, and Finland the Solidarity movement has also had great development. In February of this year the Third Nordic Encounter of Solidarity with El Salvador was celebrated in Denmark.

In Holland solidarity with the Salvadoran and Central American peoples has had great development. On January 22 they succeeded in mobilizing more than 10,000 people in Amsterdam. The first committee for the support of the Salvadoran people was formed in Holland.

In Europe the European Secretariat for Solidarity with the Salvadoran People, appointed by the World Front, coordinates solidarity in all of Europe. On June 11–12 the members met in Paris to evaluate and coordinate future actions.

In all Europe the solidarity movement has had great development in intimate relationship with the pacifist movement. Among the campaigns stands out the success of the one directed against the consumption of Salvadoran coffee that "is made with blood." The campaign has had great success all over Germany and Holland.

The Palestinian and Salvadoran peoples are conscious of the political solidarity that unites their two fights in the international context. Central America and the Middle East constitute today the most volatile zones of the globe. Even though there is not political unity in the Arab World due to the deteriorating relationship among various countries, the Arab world is engaged in the same struggle along general lines as the Salvadoran people, in that they are suffering an imperialist intervention. Israel has been converted into a guardian of US interests in Central America. Its arms sales to Latin American dictatorships are growing.

In Japan, the solidarity and the pacifist movements have understood that both fights are intimately related. The fight for peace and disarmament does not contradict solidarity with Central America. The fight against intervention is also the fight against the arms race. No more Hiroshimas and Nagasakis, No more Vietnams!

Vietnam, the major example for the Central American revolutionaries, shows what could happen if the US intervened in Central America. To avoid a new Vietnam in Central America is the work of millions of men everywhere. Since its foundation the Solidarity Movement of Vietnam has been incorporated in the work of the World Front.

In Australia, despite its distance, the solidarity movement widens day by day. Since March 1982, the solidarity movement has been in permanent contact and coordination with the World Front. Demonstrations are planned for October and January to repudiate the Reagan policy in Central America.

Document 10: Farad Handal's Travel Notes

T he following document is the personal report of Farad Handal, brother of Shafik Handal (General Secretary, Communist Party of El Salvador), detailing Farad's visit to solidarity committees in various major U.S. cities. For tactical reasons, Farad denied during this trip that he was a representative or member of the Communist Party of El Salvador. He apparently presented himself as a representative of the UDN (National Democratic Union), which is simply the Communist Party's legal front organization in El Salvador.

The notes establish that the Salvadoran Solidarity Movement in the United States is a target that the communist insurgents in Salvador aim to penetrate and influence. About half of the Solidarity groups that Farad met with are actually led by members of the CPUSA. Also prominent among the leadership are Salvadoran members of various guerrilla front groups—the BPR (Popular Revolutionary Bloc, the front of the FPL) and the UDN, for example.

The document details Farad's meeting with the Cuban Mission to the United Nations. Significantly, its members advised him to work with appropriate members of Congress to provide a useful cover. Also, Farad notes that the Cubans made contacts for him in Washington.

The document also details Farad's meeting with the Directorate of the CPUSA in New York. This included CPUSA Central Committee member Sandy Pollack, a member of the Permanent Bureau of the World Front for Solidarity with the Salvadoran People and moving force behind CISPES (Committee in Solidarity with the Salvadoran People).

The document further discloses that the members of the Washington Bureau of the CPUSA played a significant role in arranging a meeting with members of the U.S. Congress, to which Farad asribed great importance.

On the international front, Farad tells of a meeting with a PLO representative who offered training in arms usage. Also, he is told second-hand of the Mexican President's intention to help the Salvadoran struggle by moving troops to the Guatemalan border, tying down the Guatemalan Army and preventing their intervention in El Salvador.

Source: This document was captured in El Salvador and has not been published previously.

REPORT ON TRIP TO THE UNITED STATES

ROUTE:
San Jose–Mexico–New York–Chicago–San Francisco–Los Angeles–New York–Washington–New York–Mexico–San Jose.

Principal Objective: Establish a clear criteria about the character of the solidarity movement, its objectives and methods, taking into account the necessity to develop a broad movement to express a multitude of conditions. . . .

The visits to the different cities had the following results:

NEW YORK—three solidarity groups (already in existence)

1. Salvadorian Solidarity Front
2. Anastasio Aquino Solidarity Committee
3. Support Committee for the Struggle of the Salvadorian People—Farabundo Marti

Leadership:

Group	Name	Militancy	Nationality
1	Cecilia Vega	CPUSA	Salvadorian
1	David Mancia	Independent	Salvadorian
1	Daniel Flores	PAR	Salvadorian (nephew of MM)
1	Julio Valdez	UDN	Salvadorian (Sonsonate)
2	Hilda Millan	Independent	Salvadorian married to American
2	Gayls Riley	CPUSA	American married to Salvadorian
3	Bob Amstrong	Trotskyite	American—5 years in Peace Corps
3	German	Trotskyite	Salvadorian—Brother-in-law of Napoleon Duarte.

Efforts Applied: Two long meetings

First report (who I am, why I am here, who I represent and who I am commissioned by). . . .
Second meeting: With the participation of the leadership of the three groups, as agreed to by them; nonetheless a lot of the base membership came, more than in the previous meeting. The base was allowed voice, but not vote. . . .

Results: The creation of a Local Coordinating Committee

Identification of common tasks for the formation of favorable public opinion. . . .

WASHINGTON

Only one group (at the time of my visit)
1. Solidarity Bloc with the People of El Salvador
2. International Solidarity Committee with the People of El Salvador (organized during my visit)

Group	Name	Militancy	Nationality
1	Andrea	BPR	Salvadorian (sent)
1	Enrique	BPR	Salvadorian (sent)
2	Luis Miguel Vasquez	CPUSA	Ecuadorian
2	Arthur Griffiths	CPUSA	[illegible]

In addition, in Washington, there is a group that does very important private efforts. . . . This group has good relations with diverse international organizations, certain levels of government, and with multiple organizations of peace, solidarity, churches, Wola, etc.

Group 2 was organized with the help of the CPUSA after 3 talks with different groups backed by them, mostly within the youth movement of the CPUSA. . . .

With Group 2 I worked in the same way as in New York. They took the task of promoting an approach to Andrea and Enrique, who I introduced at the seminar at the Institute for Policy Studies. [In a section edited out of the document, Handal notes that this seminar was organized by Isabel Letelier]. Also, they proposed to undertake the work of creating favorable public opinion. . . .

Results: The creation of the International Committee of Solidarity with the People of El Salvador. (There are only two Salvadorians, the rest are from Chile, Uruguary, Ecuador, Bolivia, Cuba, Argentina, the Dominican Republic.)

CHICAGO: group—United Salvadorians of Chicago

Leadership:

Group	Name	Militancy	Nationality
1	Ricardo Melara	PAR	Salvadorian (Painter)
1	Dr. Hector Melara	PRAM	Salvadorian (Psychiatrist)

Efforts Applied: Two meetings

First meeting of information—A lot of uneasiness about participation in the first junta. A lot of questions about unity, they are uneasy about the image projected by a movement with many tenets. . . .

Second meeting: Work table at which the same topics as in the second meeting in New York.

LOS ANGELES, CALIFORNIA:

1. Broad Solidarity Movement
2. Central American Solidarity Committee
3. Solidarity Front

Leadership:

Group	Name	Militancy	Nationality
1	Isabel Cardenas	Independent	Salvadorian—daughter of Col. Pais
1	Juan Ramirius	CPUSA	Salvadorian
1	Ricardo Zelada	CPUSA	Salvadorian
1	Gloria Madriz	Independent	Salvadorian (sister of Ca.
2	Victor	PR (Maoist)	Salvadorian
3	Jovel	PAR	Salvadorian—San Miguel Inst. of Tadeo Ayala (?) (of the same style)

Efforts Applied: Two meetings.

First meeting. Great divisions within groups. They listen attentively to me. One of them wanted to see my credentials as a representative of the UDN or of the Coordinating Committee. In spite of the fact that I had never presented myself as a representative of the Coordinating Committee. Others demanded information about participation in the first junta. There were those who said that my talk was a scolding. Some of the participants took the attitude of great Marxist–Leninist philosophers. These philosophers accused as hypocrisy any attitude to not identify our revolution as socialist. There was heated discussion about the necessity to identify the solidarity movements as true Marxist–Leninist movements. They discussed whether this was what was of interest to the population of Los Angeles. . . .

The second meeting took place as a work table at which the same anxieties were solved as in New York, Chicago, San Francisco.

Results: Creation of a Local Coordinating Committee. Common work in the creation of favorable public opinion.

COMPLEMENTARY ACTIVITIES:

NEW YORK:

1–Interview with members of the Cuban Mission to the United Nations. This took place in the house of Alfredo Garcia Almeida. Their uneasinesses:
>   About participation in the government of the first junta.
>   About the framework of the tasks about to be undertaken in the USA.

I gave them ample information about participation in the first Junta. But I allowed myself to give them a review of the electoral process and its importance in the struggle. To explain our participation in the first Junta, I used the analysis that Sh. did about the recent happenings in October in which he fixed the position of the CPS (Communist Party of El Salvador). . . . After this information, they appeared to be very satisfied and said that in that manner everything was very clear.

With regard to my stay in the USA and the work which I would accomplish there, they recommended that I should carry out work of an informational nature about the situation in El Salvador with progressive Congressmen for the purpose of making the rest of my work appear more natural. And in that way to protect my visa. They offered to facilitate contacts in Washington. And they did that.

2–Interview with members of the Directorate of the CPUSA. At their invitation, in spite of the fact that I insisted that I did not represent the CPS, they insisted that they needed to meet with me, because they wanted information.

Attended: Secretary of Education of the CC of the CPUSA
>   Person Responsible for Press for the CC (Dominican from the CC of the CPD, Communist Party of the Dominican Republic)
>   Person Responsible for the U.S. Peace Council
>   Sandy Pollak, member of the CC of the CPUSA

The meeting took place . . . outside the offices of the CPUSA. This was because I was staying at the house of Cecilia, who is a member of the CC of the CPUSA.

Doubts expressed by the Secretary of Education:

1–He felt that the CPS had involved itself in an "adventure" (hazardous venture).

2–How I classified the party, the Salvadorian Revolution, at the present stage of the struggle. . . .

I asked them why they thought it was a "hazardous venture". They wanted to know if the party had identified where each of the different political forces were situated and they continued by beginning to tell me in great detail the manner in which they situated each of the political forces in the USA. But they did this in a manner which was contemptuous and not polite. (All of this man's statement was translated for me by two other comrades; the Dominican and Sandy Pollak). I answered that we and the CPS certainly did not have the capacity to accurately situate the political forces of the USA but we were able to situate and classify the political forces of El Salvador. . . . I responded in accord with what I had been informed as to what would be the program of the government. A Democratic, Popular, Anti-Oligarchical, Anti-Imperialist Revolution. After that they allowed me to speak and they began to behave more cordially and humanly; now they smiled and listened. . . . In the end they let me know that they did not have all of this information and that they would use it to inform the CC. And with them fix their position in regard to the solidarity movement in the USA. The meeting lasted several hours. . . .

WASHINGTON:

Summary:

Surprise encounter with Veronica (Chilean) of the CPUSA charged by the Directorate of the CPUSA of Washington with arranging a meeting. Meeting with Mouris [*sic*] president of the CPUSA in Washington who informed [him] that he had received instructions to give [me] any help that he might desire. He also asked for information about the movement in El Salvador, participation in the government of the first Junta, etc. etc. Pleasant meeting. The beginning of a valuable collaboration. They arranged three meetings with the youth group of the CPUSA.

They played an important role in the arrangements for the meeting with Congressman Ronal Dellums [*sic*], Congressman from the state of California. Black, but very progressive.

The comrades of the CP of Washington were the pioneers for the formation of the International Solidarity Committee that I took the advantage of forming in Washington.

The comrades of the Cuban Mission had recommended Juan Ferreira, from Uruguay. I contacted him at WOLA [Washington Office on Latin America]. He helped me at WOLA and the National Council of Churches. . . .

I contacted Isabel Letelier who had prepared a seminar at the Institute for Policy Studies of Washington. The seminar would be based on a talk by Napoleon Gonzales, which had already been announced. Gonzales was in Washington at the invitation of Amnesty International. Napoleon Gonzales had already spoken at WOLA, at which time he had mainly covered the situation of his newspaper and his person as objects of repression. Isabel Letelier informed me that at the last moment Napoleon had declined participation saying that he was leaving for Los Angeles. Because of this Isabel asked that I take over the talk. I accepted, of course. It took place Monday from 12:30 until 3:00 PM.

That same Monday at 4:00 PM the meeting with Congressman Dellums and his work team took place. At the beginning of the meeting which took place in the offices of the Congressman located in the Capitol building, his political counselor made known that my visit could not have arrived at a better moment. They were interested in better understanding the situation of El Salvador because they were ready to do battle against the Hawks who have today strengthened their position and influence in the Senate and Congress of the USA. My statement is transcribed in the attached summary. When the meeting was over they asked me to write it there in the offices of Dellums and they gave me a typewriter to use. They explained that they needed it to translate into English and make a report to all of the group of black congressmen. . . . They invited me to participate in that report. At that time we agreed that I would let them know my whereabouts so that they could advise me as to the date and time of the meeting and so that they could bring me back to Washington. . . . For this meeting I prepared a folder with the program of the Government of Coordination (photocopy of what was published in Prensa Grafica, I obtained it in Los Angeles). The English translation was done by the comrades of the CP of Washington. . . . All the arrangements and translations for the folders which we would give to the congressmen had to be done in Washington because it was there that we received information from WOLA. I received notice at the last moment while I was in Los Angeles and did not have time to prepare anything. I flew from Los Angeles to New York and the next day to Washington (Sunday). The meeting took place Monday at 3:00 PM.

Monday morning the offices of Congressman Dellums were turned into our offices. Everything was done there. The meeting with the Black Caucus took place in the liver of the monster itself, nothing less than in the meeting room of the commission of the exterior [House Foreign Affairs]. . . .

SAN FRANCISCO:

Summary:

Interview with the main leader of Amnesty International, Mrs. Janet. They asked for information about the first Junta, the Unity. They expressed doubts about groups not in accord with the solidarity movement. Need for a representative of the Coordinating Committee (coordinator body). Desire to collaborate, put forth the condition that they wanted to collaborate with the presentation of only one front, not just one group.

Meeting with representative of the National Council of Churches. Doubts about our participation in the government of the first Junta, desire to collaborate but with only one organism, public support if present a united front. . . .

SECOND VISIT TO NEW YORK:

Meeting with Sandy Pollak, Solidarity Coordinator for the US Peace Council. Sandy proposed a national conference under the auspices of the US Peace Council, the National Council of Churches, Amnesty International, WOLA, and various important unions of the US. The objective of the conference would be to establish a support mechanism for the solidarity committees in those states where it does not already exist.

The support that they proposed consisted in financing radio, TV and press programs, under its public patronage. They agreed to the idea of issuing a series of coupons worth one dollar that they would call Credit Bonds from the North American People to the Salvadorian People, as a counterpart to the credits given by the US Government to the Junta of El Salvador. But all of these propositions had the following as conditions:

1–That they would back the COORDINATOR [body] as they did not want to appear to be backing one organization in particular.

2–That the diverse images of the movement should be eliminated and that the image of a Broad Solidarity Movement should be presented, without a ideological label. For this they proposed that a representative from each of the organizations making up the Coordinator be present. Each of the representatives should have power to express a single [political] line. . . .

3–At this time they felt that it was indispensible that Monseigneur Romero be present. . . . I let them know that it would be very difficult to convince the Monseigneur to assume that role.

4–That it would be agreed to call for the conference in no less than 30 days. . . .

SECOND TRIP TO WASHINGTON:

Meeting with the group of Black Congressmen. . . . Conclusions from the meeting:

1–They would come out publicly against the credit. They did this two days later.

2–They proposed another meeting with Black Congressmen and, in addition, those congressmen who represented Latin minorities. With them, the group would number 32.

3–Maintain a close contact with us for information. They would be open to concrete petitions.

4–They were ready to undertake immediate tasks and establish a permanent climate in favor of the struggle in El Salvador.

It is good to point out that these people have influence and prestige. In reality, they are able to collaborate even in special promotions where their prestige could mean an effective support.

Meeting with a representative of the PLO. Through Rene Tensen, I was invited to a meeting with a PLO representative. He identified himself as a representative of one of the groups which make up the PLO. He said that it was one of the smallest groups but that it represented the authentic Marxist–Leninist Line. . . . At the end I told him that I did not have the authority for representations at the levels which corresponded to a conversation of this type. And that I would limit myself to carrying the news of their good intentions for helping us. He spoke about help in scholarships [training] for use of arms. He spoke of other types of help.

Document 11: Venceremos Brigades

T he following is an excerpt from an article by a Prensa Latina correspondent about the Venceremos Brigades. The Brigades were groups of youthful leftists who went to Cuba to help with the sugar harvest. It is important to remember that the Cuban DGI used the Venceremos Brigades as a recruitment pool for future members of the Weather Underground Organization (WUO). During the period of October 1969–September 1976 the WUO claimed responsibility for nearly forty terrorist bomb attacks in the United States. For further details see section 6, "Surrogate Warfare: The Threat Within."

Source: This document was published in "Direct From Cuba," a Prensa Latina publication.

VENCEREMOS BRIGADE IMPOSES ITS RHYTHM
By Joaquin Andrade
Special Correspondent of PRENSA LATINA

"Really learning"

They attend lectures, on Central-America (specifically on Guatemala) and on Argentina, Brazil, Uruguay and Chile. They know very little of what is happening south of the Rio Bravo. . . . And they ask questions constantly, with great eagerness: Susan wants to clear up some confused points of Marighela's "Mini-manual of urban guerrilla"; Bob would like to know how the Tupamaros function and organize themselves because "we could do the same in many cities of the United States"; a blond long-haired young man worries about "What actions could we carry out to cooperate with Latin American revolutionaries in their struggle against Yankee imperialism?"

3
Surrogate Actors in the Caribbean: Grenada

The documents that follow represent but a small fraction of the archives captured in Grenada during the October 1983 intervention by the United States and its eastern Caribbean allies. They illuminate the building of a totalitarian state and the transformation of Grenada into a surrogate of the Soviet Union, chiefly through Cuba. In effect, the documents reveal the steps taken to develop a surrogate of a surrogate. In other words, Grenada would function under the direction of Cuba. An analogous situation at present appears to exist in Nicaragua.

The first group of documents presented here—Documents 1 through 16—is primarily concerned with the quantity and variety of assistance received by Grenada from patrons such as the USSR, Cuba, Vietnam, North Korea, East Germany, and Czechoslovakia. While the extensive amount of Soviet arms found in Grenada is generally well known, the same is not the case when it comes to military hardware provided by North Korea, the military training offered by Vietnam, the party and propaganda instruction from Cuba, or the security equipment given by East Germany. The last four documents within this group (Documents 13 through 16) concern the intelligence support provided by Cuba to assist Grenada in its relations with communist parties worldwide and in its domestic religious situation.

Documents 17 and 18 are records of high-level Grenadian–Soviet meetings which underscore Grenada's surrogate status.

Documents 19 and 20 are selected excerpts from Grenada's Political Bureau and Party Central Committee meetings. They detail linkages not only with the Soviet Bloc, but also with groups such as the PLO and SWAPO,

---

Source: All of the documents presented here were captured in Grenada; some have been reproduced here with the courtesy of Paul Seabury and Walter A. McDougall for *The Grenada Papers* (San Francisco: Institute for Contemporary Studies, 1984), and Herb Romerstein and Michael Ledeen for *Grenada Documents: An Overview and Selection* (U.S. GPO, 1984). Permission to use material found only in Seabury and McDougall's work is gratefully acknowledged. Consequently, individual source references are not attached to the documents that follow.

which receive support from the network of Soviet proxies. Documents 21 through 24 pertain to the foreign relations of Grenada, and reveal Grenada's self-perception as an active participant in the Soviet network. Grenada's role as a Soviet "team player" is highlighted by documents 25 through 30, which detail Grenada's participation in world forums such as the Socialist International, which can be useful to Soviet objectives, and also in such outright fronts of the USSR as the World Peace Council.

Documents 1 and 2: The USSR Agrees to Arm Grenada

Together, these two documents indicate the degree to which the Soviet Union was underwriting the military buildup of the small island nation of Grenada. The agreements cover the years 1981 through 1985 and provide for the delivery of a total of 15 million rubles worth of military equipment. It would seem that Grenada was being armed far in excess of its legitimate defense needs. The U.S. Department of Defense has estimated that the equipment discovered in Grenada could have fully outfitted a force of 10,000 soldiers. The agreements reveal, further, that Soviet specialists were to be sent to Grenada, while Grenada would send soldiers to the USSR for training. The documents were classified "Top Secret".

Document 1

Top secret

AGREEMENT
between the Government of Grenada and the
Government of the Union of Soviet Socialist Republics on deliveries from
the Union of SSR to Grenada of special
and other equipment

The Government of Grenada and the Government of the Union of Soviet Socialist Republics,

guided by aspirations for developing and strengthening friendly relations between both countries on the principles of equality, mutual respect of sovereignty and non-interference into internal affairs,

proceeding from the desire to promote strengthening the independence of Grenada and in connection with the request of the Government of Grenada have agreed upon the following:

Article 1

The Government of the Union of Soviet Socialist Republics shall ensure in 1982–1985 free of charge the delivery to the Government of Grenada of special and civil equipment in nomenclature and quantity according to Annexes 1 and 2 to the present Agreement to the amount of 10.000.000 Roubles.

Article 2

The delivery of the equipment listed in Annexes 1 and 2 to the present Agreement shall be effected by the Soviet Party by sea, at the port of the Republic of Cuba.

The order of the further delivery of the above equipment from the Republic of Cuba shall be agreed upon between the Grenadian and Cuban Parties.

Article 3

The Government of the Union of SSR at the request of the Government of Grenada shall ensure rendering technical assistance in mastering of the equipment under delivery by receiving in the USSR Grenadian servicemen for training in the operation, use and maintenance of the special equipment as well as by sending Soviet specialists to Grenada for these purposes.

The Grenadian servicemen shall be sent to the USSR for training without their families.

The expenses connected with the Grenadian servicemen's training, upkeep, meals in the Soviet military educational establishments as well as with their travel fare from Grenada to the USSR and back shall be borne by the Soviet Party.

The Government of Grenada shall provide at its own expense the Soviet specialists and interpreters with comfortable furnished living accommodation with all the municipal utilities, medical service and transport facilities for the execution of their duties and shall ensure their having meals at reasonable prices at the places of their residense.

The Soviet specialists and interpreters shall not be imposed by any taxes and duties on entering or leaving Grenada and during their stay there. All other expenses connected with deputation of the Soviet specialists to Grenada shall be borne by the Soviet Party.

Article 4

The Soviet Party in periods to be agreed upon between the Parties shall depute a group of Soviet specialists to Grenada to determine expediency, opportunity and scope of rendering technical assistance in the creation of the stationary shop for repair of the special equipment and transport, commanding staff trainer school, training facilities for Armed Forces as well as the deliveries of missing building materials for construction of the storehouses and road.

The deputation of a group of Soviet specialists shall be effected on the terms and conditions of Article 3 of the present Agreement.

Article 5

The Government of the Union of SSR shall ensure free of charge the transfer to the Government of Grenada of necessary technical descriptions, instructions and manuals in standard composition on operation of the special equipment delivered under the present Agreement.

Article 6

The appropriate Grenadian and Soviet organizations shall conclude contracts in which there shall be stipulated the detailed terms and conditions of deputing Soviet specialists, receiving for training Grenadian servicemen and other services connected with the implementation of the present Agreement.

Article 7

The Government of Grenada shall not without the consent of the Government of the Union of Soviet Socialist Republics sell or transfer, formally or actually, the special equipment, delivered under the present Agreement, the relevant documentation and information or give permission to use the equipment and documentation by a third party or any physical or legal persons but the officials and specialists of the citizenship of Grenada being in the service with the Government of Grenada.

The Government of the Union of SSR and the Government of Grenada shall take all the necessary measures to ensure keeping in secret the terms and conditions of the deliveries, all the correspondence and information connected with the implementation of the present Agreement.

Article 8

The present Agreement comes into force on the date it is signed on.
Annexes 1 and 2 are an integral part of the present Agreement.

Done in Moscow on July "27", 1982 in two originals, each in the English and Russian languages, both texts being equally valid.

<table>
<tr><td>FOR AND ON BEHALF
OF THE GOVERNMENT OF
GRENADA</td><td>FOR AND ON BEHALF
OF THE GOVERNMENT
OF THE UNION OF
SOVIET SOCIALIST REPUBLICS</td></tr>
<tr><td>/s/ [illegible signature]</td><td>/s/ [illegible signature]</td></tr>
</table>

Part of Annex 1 follows to illustrate the type and quantity of equipment the USSR was providing Grenada.

Top secret

ANNEX 1

to Agreement of July "27," 1982

LIST

of special equipment to be delivered to the Army of Grenada from the Soviet Union in 1983–1985

Description	Unit of Measure	Quantity-Total	Years of Delivery		
			1983	1984	1985
Armour material					
BTR-152V1 armoured personnel carriers, used, repaired	piece	50	—	30	20
7,62-mm rifle cartridges without clips:					
with steel core bullet	thous. pieces	100,5	—	60,3	40,2
with B-32 armour-piercing-incendiary bullet and steel case	thous. pieces	37,5	—	22,5	15,0
with T-46 tracer bullet	thous. pieces	49,5	—	29,7	19,8
Artillery armament and ammunition					
76-mm ZIS-3 guns, used, repaired	piece	30	18	12	—
76-mm rounds:					
with fragmentation and high-explosive-fragmentation grenade	thous. pieces	9,3	5,6	3,7	—
with armour-piercing-tracer shell	piece	540	330	210	—
with sub-calibre armour-piercing shell	piece	450	270	180	—
with hollow charge shell	piece	540	330	210	—
57-mm ZIS-7 anti-tank guns, used, repaired	piece	30	18	12	—

Description	Unit of Measure	Quantity-Total	Years of Delivery		
			1983	1984	1985
57-mm rounds:					
with fragmentation grenade	thous. pieces	5,4	3,2	2,2	—
with armour-piercing-tracer shell	thous. pieces	4,0	2,4	1,6	—
with sub-calibre armour-piercing shell	thous. pieces	1,3	0,8	0,5	—
. . . .					
82-mm rounds for BM mortars:					
with fragmentation mine	thous. pieces	21,6	10,8	10.8	—
with inert charge mine	piece	200	100	100	—
Small arms					
RPG-7V light anti-tank grenade launchers	piece	50	—	20	30
Group sets of SPTA /1:9/ for RPG-7V grenade launchers	set	5	—	2	3
Repair sets of SPTA /1:01/ for RPG-7V grenade launchers	set	1	—	—	1
PG-7VM rounds for RPG-7V grenade launchers	thous. pieces	3,0	—	1,2	1,8
7,62-mm PKM machine guns	piece	60	20	20	20
Group set of SPTA /1:50/ for PKM machine guns	set	1	—	1	—
7,-62-mm PKMS machine guns	piece	30	—	10	20
Group set of SPTA /1:50/ for PKMS machine guns	set	1	—	—	1
. . . .					

Document 2

Top secret

PROTOCOL

to the Agreement between the Government of
Grenada and the Government of the USSR of
October 27, 1980 on deliveries from the USSR
to Grenada of special and other equipment

The Government of Grenada and the Government of the Union of Soviet
Socialist Republics have agreed upon the following:

Article 1

The Government of the Union of Soviet Socialist Republics shall ensure free of charge the delivery in 1981–1983 to the Government of Grenada of special and other equipment in nomenclature and quantity according to the Annex to the present Agreement to the amount of 5.000.000 Roubles.

Article 2

In all other respects the Parties will be guided by the provisions of the Agreement between the Government of Grenada and the Government of the USSR of October 27, 1980 on deliveries from the USSR to Grenada of special and other equipment.

Article 3

The present Protocol comes into force on the date of its signing.
The Annex is an integral part of the present Protocol.

Done in Havana on February "9", 1981 in two originals, each in the English and Russian languages, both texts being equally valid.

FOR AND ON BEHALF OF THE GOVERNMENT OF GRENADA	FOR AND ON BEHALF OF THE GOVERNMENT OF THE UNION OF SOVIET SOCIALIST REPUBLICS
/s/ [illegible signature]	/s/ [illegible signature]

Part of the Annex follows to illustrate the type and quantity of equipment the USSR was providing Grenada.

LIST

of special equipment and vehicles to be delivered to Grenada from the Union of Soviet Socialist Republics in 1981–1983

/free of charge/

Description	Unit of Measure	Total Quantity	Years of Delivery		
			1981	1982	1983
Armour					
ETR-60PB armoured personnel carriers	piece	8	8	—	—
BRDM-2 armoured reconnaissance and patrol vehicles	piece	2	2	—	—
14,5-mm cartridges:					
with B-32 bullet	thous. pieces	6,3	6,3	—	—
with BZT bullet	thous. pieces	6,3	6,3	—	—
7,62-mm rifle cartridges without clips:					
with steel core bullet	thous. pieces	30	30	—	—
with B-32 bullet and steel case	thous. pieces	5	5	—	—
with T-46 bullet	thous. pieces	15	15	—	—
GAZ-49B engines	piece	4	—	2	2
GAZ-41 engines	piece	2	—	2	—
Armament and munitions					
7,62-mm AK submachine guns, used, reconditioned	thous. pieces	1	1	—	—
7,62-mm cartridges of 1943 model without clips:					
with steel core bullet	thous. pieces	1000	1000	—	—
with T-45 tracer bullet	thous. pieces	300	300	—	—
9-mm PM pistols	piece	300	300	—	—
Group sets of spare parts /1:100/ to PM pistols	set	3	3	—	—
Repair set of spare parts /1:500/ to PM pistols	set	1	1	—	—
9-mm cartridges to PM pistols	thous. pieces	36	36	—	—
26-mm SPSh-2 signal pistols	piece	30	—	30	—
26-mm signal cartridges:					
red	thous. pieces	3	—	3	—
green	thous. pieces	3	—	3	—
yellow	thous. pieces	3	—	3	—
26-mm illuminating cartridges	thous. pieces	3	—	3	—
TZK-2 commander's periscopes	piece	5	2	3	—
B-8s/s binoculars	piece	100	100	—	—

· · · · · · · · · ·

Document 3: The Cuban Military Presence

Excerpts of a secret Cuban–Grenadian agreement providing for the establishment of a contingent of Cuban military specialists in Grenada for the purposes of training Grenadian soldiers. Cuba also agreed to grant military scholarships to Grenadian personnel, and both parties were to "take all measures to assure the secrecy" of the provisions of the agreement. General of the Armed Forces Hudson Austin signed the document for Grenada and Fidel Castro signed for Cuba.

"SECRET"
Copy No. _____

PROTOCOL
OF THE MILITARY COLLABORATION BETWEEN THE GOVERNMENT OF THE REPUBLIC OF CUBA AND THE PEOPLE'S REVOLUTIONARY GOVERNMENT OF GRENADA

The Government of the Republic of Cuba and People's Revolutionary Government of Grenada, in full exercise of their sovereign right as free and independent States, based on the fraternal relations existing between both countries with the aim of making a contribution to the strengthening of the defensive capacity of Grenada, have agreed upon the following:

ARTICLE I

The Government of the Republic of Cuba in agreement with the request formulated by the People's Revolutionary Government of Grenada, will maintain Cuban Military Specialists in that country in quantities and specialists established in Annex No. 1 of this document. (Protocol).

ARTICLE II

The Military specialists from Cuba in behalf of strengthening the military capacity of the Armed Forces will assist Grenadian military men on the questions of Organization of the Organic Structure, Organization of the Instruction and combative and campaign training of the troops and staffs in the preparation of cadres and minor specialists, and in the elaboration of the operative and mobilization plans for the defense of the country.

ARTICLE III

The Government of the Republic of Cuba will grant scholarships to military personnel of Grenada in the Military Training Centres of the Revolutionary Armed Forces with the quantities and specialist with the requirements that will be established in Annex No. 3 which will be elaborated afterwards.

ARTICLE IV

The Government of the Republic of Cuba has the pleasure of receiving during 1982 four delegations of the Armed Forces of up to three members each, of the following specialities:
—Engineering, (the fourth three-month period)
—Communication (the first three-month period)
—Logistics, (the first three-month period)
—Exploration, (the fourth three-month period)
The dates in which these delegations should travel to Cuba will be communicated to the Grenadian side, by the Cuban side twenty days in advance.

ARTICLE V

In order to lead the activities of the Cuban Military Specialists, the post of chief of the Cuban Military Specialists is established who will develop functions in the Ministry of Defense.

ARTICLE VI

The Cuban side according to the plans approved by its governments will carry out the systematic change of Cuban Military Specialists in the quantities foreseen in the present Protocol.

.   .   .   .

ARTICLE XV

The Present Protocol will be put into effect from the date of signature and it will be effective until Dicember [*sic*] 31ˢᵗ, 1984.

The Annexes No. 1, 2 and 3 are part of this Protocol.

Written up in two copies, original, in spanich [*sic*] and English, both texts are valid and signed in the City of _____
on the _____ days of _____ of 19 _____

/s/ *Castro*   /s/ *Austin*

Documents 4 and 5: Vietnam Offers to Teach Yankee Warfare

T he following two documents provide evidence of Vietnam's readiness to train Grenadian officials in American battle tactics and weaponry, defensive warfare, and population control and re-education. The first document is a letter from the Grenadian Ambassador in Cuba to his Vietnamese counterpart, and the second is a letter from Grenada's Embassy in Cuba, reporting on further offers of training from Vietnam.

Document 4

EMBAJADA DE GRANADA EN CUBA

23rd May, 1981

CONFIDENTIAL

Excellency,

The Embassy of Grenada in Cuba presents its compliments to the Embassy of Vietnam in Cuba, and has the honour to inform you that during his visit to Vietnam between June 2nd. and June 16th. 1981, General of the People's Revolutionary Army, Member of the Political Bureau and Minister of Defence and National Security, Comrade Hudson Austin accompanied by Major Bazil Cahagan and Captain Christopher Lowe wish to include the following items in their programme:

1. Techniques of defence against an occupying force.
2. Tour of appropriate trenches and exposure to the technique of trench warfare.
3. Tour of anti-air raid and artillery centres for defence.
4. Counter-intelligence techniques.

5. A study of captured U.S.A. military equipment.

6. An assessment of tactics used by U.S.A. imperialism in Vietnam.

7. Techniques of moving warfare.

8. How to counter the napalm weapon.

9. Techniques of dealing with counter-revolutionaries especially in the area of re-education.

10. Methods of dealing with lumpen elements.

As you are aware, Excellency, the delegation returns to Moscow from Mongolia on 1st June. We trust at that time that they will be able to collect their airline tickets from the Vietnamese Embassy in Moscow.

General Austin has asked me to convey to you his great pleasure in meeting and having discussions with you and he looks forward to a successful and rewarding mission to Vietnam.

The Embassy of Grenada in Cuba takes this opportunity to extend to the Embassy of Vietnam in Cuba the assurances of its highest consideration and esteem.

W. Richard Jacobs
Ambassador

Document 5

EMBAJADA DE GRANADA EN CUBA

Sta. Avenida No. 8409 Esq. 84	Telefonos
Miramir, C. Habana	29–5429
Cuba	29–3913

In accordance with the requests put forward at the 2nd Congress of the Communist Party of Cuba by the Prime Minister, the Vietnamese Ambassador has reported the following:

1. The Ministry of Defence and Interior is ready to receive from Grenada starting in April 1982 twenty appropriately qualified people to train in the following:
   (a) anti-chemical warfare
   (b) anti-radioactivity warfare
   (c) re-education of anti-social and counter-revolutionary elements
   (d) Yankee tactics and the weapons used in Vietnam

2. The Government of Vietnam is not in a position to send people to Grenada nor are they in a position to train pilots.

3. I enquired as to who will pay the passages for these people. The Ambassador promised to check on this question but pointed out that it was unlikely that Vietnam would be able to pay. He suggested that we approach a friendly country which has airline facilities.

/s/ [illegible signature]

18/2/82

Document 6: North Korea Adds to the Grenadian Arsenal

This document reveals the provisions of a secret agreement between Grenada and the Democratic People's Republic of Korea. North Korea was to have provided Grenada in 1983–1984 with 12 million dollars worth of military equipment, including 2 coast guard vessels, 1,000 gas masks, 6,000 uniforms, and 50 RPG-7 anti-armor grenade launchers. This agreement was signed for Grenada by Prime Minister Maurice Bishop.

AGREEMENT
between the People's Revolutionary Government of Grenada and the Government of the Democratic People's Republic of Korea on the free offer of military assistance to the People's Revolutionary Government of Grenada by the Democratic People's Republic of Korea.

For the purposes of further cementing and developing the friendship and solidarity between the peoples and armies of the two countries established in the common struggle to oppose against imperialism, consolidate the national sovereignty and safeguard independence, and strengthening the national defense power of Grenada, the People's Revolutionary Government of Grenada and the Government of the Democratic People's Republic of Korea have agreed as follows;

Article 1

The Government of the Democratic People's Republic of Korea shall give, in 1983–1984, the free military assistance subject to weapons and ammunitions covering US $12,000,000 indicated in Annex to this Agreement.

Article 2

The Grenadian side shall be responsible for the transport of weapons and ammunitions to be rendered to the People's Revolutionary Government of Grenada by the Democratic People's Republic of Korea.

Article 3

Both sides shall strictly keep the secrecy of the military assistance to be executed according to this Agreement and have an obligation not to hand over any matters of this Agreement to the third country.

Article 4

This Agreement shall come into force on the day of its signing.

This Agreement has been prepared in duplicate in the Korean and English languages and signed in Pyongyang on April 14, 1983, two originals equally authentic.

/s/ *Maurice Bishop*   /s/ [illegible signature]

By the authority of the   By the authority of the
People's Revolutionary   Government of the
Government of Grenada   Democratic People's
       Republic of Korea.

Part of the Annex follows to illustrate the type and quantity of arms promised.

ANNEX

of Agreement on the free offer of military assistance to the People's Revolutionary Government of Grenada by the Democratic People's Republic of Korea.

Hand flares	200	pcs
Ammunition for hand flares	4,000	rds
7.62mm automatic rifle	1,000	pcs
7.62mm light machine gun	50	pcs
Ammunition for 7.62mm automatic rifle	360,000	rds
7.62mm blanks	300,000	rds
7.62mm heavy machine gun	30	pcs

Ammunition for heavy machine gun	60,000	rds
RPG-7 launcher	50	pcs
RPG-7	500	rds
Hand grenade	200	rds
Instruction hand grenade	20	rds
Binoculars (8^x)	30	pcs
Anti-gas masks	1,000	pcs

. . . .

Documents 7 and 8: Arms from Czechoslovakia via Cuba

D ocument 7 is an undated letter from the Grenadian Embassy in Cuba, reporting that Czechoslovakia had agreed to provide Grenada with weapons. Automatic rifles, bazookas, ammunition and spare parts were to be furnished free of charge and shipped via Cuba. The letter also mentions another Warsaw Pact government, Bulgaria, as a source of military equipment.

Document 8 is a bill of lading for a shipment of rocket warheads, probably for RPG launchers, from Prague via Havana. The shipment appears to be 1,250 cases, totalling 32,500 warheads.

Document 7

EMBAJADA DE GRANADA EN CUBA

Sta. AVENIDA No. 8409 Esq. 84	Telefonos:
MIRAMAR, CIUDAD HABANA	29–5429
CUBA	29–3913

I have received the following note from the Checoslovacian Embassy:

Consequent upon a request from the Deputy Prime Minister Bernard Coard, presented during his visit to Checoslovacia in June of 1980, the Government of Checslovacia has agreed to provide to the Government of Grenada free of cost the following items listed below:

3,000—7.62mm automatic rifles type: 52/57

30 boxes of spare parts (SZY 1 KU 100) for automatic rifles type 52/57

1 million cartrages for 7.62 type 43

50 bazoocas P 27

5 boxes of spare parts (SZV II) for P 27

5,000 projectiles for bazooca P 27

These pieces of equipment will be sent to Cuba between the latter part of September and the early part of October and transhipped to Grenada. We are making the necessary arrangements through the Embassy with the Ministery of the Armed Forces.

As I understand it, you have already received information about the agreement of the Government of Bulgaria to provide other military equipment.

Typed by Richard Jacobs seen also by Otto Marero

Document 8

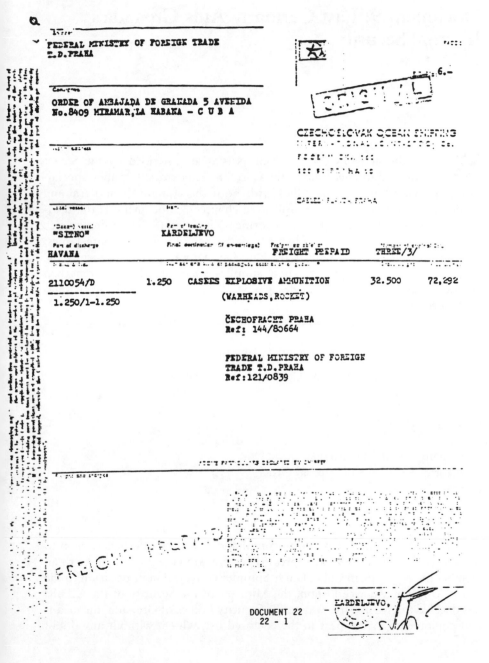

FEDERAL MINISTRY OF FOREIGN TRADE
T.D. PRAHA

ORDER OF AMBAJADA DE GRANADA 5 AVENIDA
No. 8409 MIRAMAR, LA HABANA - C U B A

CZECHOSLOVAK OCEAN SHIPPING

ORIGINAL

"SITNO"   KARDELJEVO

HAVANA   FREIGHT PREPAID   THREE/3/

| 2110054/D | 1.250 | CASSES EXPLOSIVE AMMUNITION | 32.500 | 72,292 |
| 1.250/1-1.250 | | (WARHEADS, ROCKET) | | |

ČECHOFRACHT PRAHA
Ref: 144/80664

FEDERAL MINISTRY OF FOREIGN
TRADE T.D. PRAHA
Ref: 121/0839

KARDELJEVO,

DOCUMENT 22
22 - 1

Document 9: East Germany Aids Grenada's Internal Security

W ithin the network of "fraternal assistance" provided by the Soviet Union and its client states, the German Democratic Republic specializes in providing its socialist allies with both the equipment and training needed for effective internal security (see chapter 2, document 1, the testimony of Miguel Bolaños Hunter, a former Nicaraguan counterintelligence officer). This letter from the Cuban Ministry of the Interior to Liam James, Grenada's security chief, reports on East Germany's agreement to provide Grenada with free equipment. These supplies were intended to strengthen Grenadian Security "in its struggle against . . . imperialism and the enemies of the people."

REPUBLICA DE CUBA

MINISTERIO DEL INTERIOR

Havana City

Lieutenant Colonel Liam James
Director of Security and Internal Order
Grenada

Dear Comrade:

I am pleased to inform you that in compliance with the offerings of help to the security of your country, expressed by the Ambassador of the German Democratic Republic in Cuba, Harry Splinder conveyed in its occasion to the Prime Minister Maurice Bishop, the Minister of the Security of the G.D.R. has decided to give in a free way to the Security Bodies of Granada, the means and equipments that appear in the enclosed list, which, without any doubt will help to strengthen the operative capacity of the Security Bodies of your country.

These materials, which we have at hand already, will be sent to your country as soon as there is an opportunity of transportation available.

Comrade James, we hope that this modest assistance will help to strengthen the operative capacity of the Granadian Security in its struggle against the imperialism and the enemies of the country.

We do not want to say good by without stating before, the interest shown by the Comrade Ambassador of the G.D.R. to realize this assistance.

Wishing you success in your work and in the important tasks assigned to you.

With revolucionarity greeting,

Colonel Luis Barreiro Carames
J'Estado Mayor Central

Document 10: Training Request to Andropov

In addition to delivering hardware for the military and security forces of Grenada, the Soviet Union and Cuba also provided selected Grenadian personnel with military, party, and intelligence training. The following is a letter from General Hudson Austin to Yuri Andropov, then chief of the KGB, requesting intelligence and counterintelligence training.

TO: Commander Andropov
     Chairman of the Committee of State Security
     Member of Politburo

FROM: General of the Army Hudson Austin

Dear Comrade,

Warmest revolutionary greetings to you, the Communist Party of Soviet Union and all Soviet people, from the Political Bureau of the New Jewel Movement, Government, Armed Forces and all the Grenadian people.

Let me first of all extend our deepest sympathies to your Party and people on the passing away of comrade Suslov, a true Bolshevik and hero of revolutionary people worldwide.

I write at this time to request assistance in the strengthening of our Ministry of Interior. This request stems from discussions held between Cde. Vladimir Klimentov, then attached to the Soviet Embassy in Jamaica, Comrade Maurice Bishop, Chairman of the Central Committee of our Party the New Jewel Movement, Prime Minister and Minister of Defence and Interior of the People's Revolutionary Government, Comrade Liam James, Member of the Central Committee of our Party and Head of the Ministry of Interior and myself. The People's Revolutionary Government formally requests the following training courses for four (4) of our comrades:

a) Basic course in Counter Intelligence for the period of one (1) year - three (3) comrades.

b) Basic course in Intelligence for a period of one (1) year - one (1) comrade.

We thank you once again for the tremendous assistance which our Armed Forces have received from your Party and Government in the past. We recognise the tremendous internationalist obligations of your people, yet we sincerely hope that these courses will be made available to our comrades in 1982, given the pressing needs in our Ministry and the continuing threat being posed to the Grenada Revolution by United States Imperialism.

I close by once again extending our greatest warmth and embrace to you and your Party - Sons and Daughters of the heroic Lenin. I look forward to hearing from you soon.

Yours fraternally,

> General Hudson Austin
> Member of the Political Bureau of NJM
> Secretary of Defence and Interior

Document 11: Grenadian Students in the USSR

T his report from Grenada's Embassy in Moscow indicates the variety of training support the Soviet Union was providing to Grenada.

Excerpts

EMBASSY OF GRENADA IN THE USSR

Dobryninskay Ulitsa 7
Apartment 221
Moscow
USSR

Telephone:
237–25–41
237–99–05

MEETING WITH THE MINISTRY OF DEFENCE

DATE: 24th November 1982

Present at the meeting were:

Colonel Petrov—Chief for preparing Students for Military High School; Colonel Germark—Responsible for Grenadian Military Students; Bernard Bourne—Minister-Counsellor.

There were two (2) points on the Agenda:

1. Grenadian Students in/expected in the Soviet Union;
2. Military Projects. . . .

Grenadian Students
At present there are fifteen (15) students pursuing courses in three cities of the Soviet Union:

a. Ten students are at the High School for Infantry in Odessa;

b. Two students are in Simferopoll; and

c. Three students are in Volsk.

Additionally, ten (10) students, including officers, are expected to come to the Soviet Union within the next seven months.

i. On December 1—two officers are expected to study in the city of Solnechnogorsky at the Vystrel Institute;

ii. On January 1—three more officers are expected to pursue studies at the same institute;

iii. On March 1—three comrades will arrive, one will study in the Political Academy and two will be trained as communication experts in Ulyanovsk;

iv. June 1—Two officers will arrive for studies. . . .

. . . Colonel Petrov mentioned that if we are thinking of increasing the number of students to pursue Military courses in the Soviet Union in 1983 then the Commander-in-Chief should send a letter to the Ministry of Defence on this matter not later than January 1, 1983. . . .

Document 12: Cuban–Grenadian Communist Party Agreement

This secret document reveals the high degree of collaboration that existed between the Communist Party of Cuba and Grenada's New Jewel Movement. The agreement details Cuban-sponsored party training, exchange of information, propaganda training, and interparty cooperation at international events. The document was signed for Grenada by Hudson Austin and for Cuba by Manuel Pineiro, head of the Americas Department of the CPC's Central Committee.

PARTIDO COMUNISTA-DE CUBA/COMITE CENTRAL

Secret

COOPERATION AND EXCHANGE PLAN BETWEEN THE COMMUNIST PARTY OF CUBA AND THE NEW JEWEL MOVEMENT OF GRENADA, FOR THE 1983 PERIOD.

INTRODUCTION

The Communist Party of Cuba and the New Jewel Movement, brotherly united by the same ideals of struggle in their respective countries, as well as of active solidarity in favor of the peoples that struggle for national liberation, and likewise, sharing the same convictions against imperialism, colonialsm, neo-colonialism, Zionism, and racism, became aware of the need to unite efforts and coordinate actions of cooperation in the different activities within their scope. Both parties . . . reach agreement on the following:

CHAPTER I

a) The CPC and the NJM will exchange delegations for the mutual study of the experiences in the different fields of Party work, according to agreements and needs that will be established between the parties. . . .

b) The CPC expresses its willingness to send, according to the requests formulated by the NJM in this sense, technical advisers [sic] for the organization of public meetings and propaganda of the Party in Grenada.

c) Regarding the political upgrading and professional assistance, the NJM and the CPC express their willingness to receive, at the "Ñico López" School, the NJM cadres that will be decided on mutual agreement.

d) The CPC and the NJM of Grenada will exchange information of mutual interest, both on the field of the development of the two revolutions and their experiences, as well as on the international situation. . . .

CHAPTER II

On political and mass organizations:

Both Parties agree on developing to the utmost the cooperation and assistance in the development and strengthening of the mass organizations of Cuba and Grenada.

These agreements on cooperation will include exchange of information, publications, and expertise built up by them.

Likewise, they will coordinate their positions at international events and conferences, by mutually advising each other on the common interests of both Parties.

CHAPTER III

On the exchange and cooperation between both Parties:

The CPC and the NJM of Grenada will approve, control, and ensure the fulfillment of the understandings and agreements of cooperation and exchange to be established at state level, for which they will create the mechanisms and controls that they consider relevant. Similarly, both Parties will periodically oversee the development of the cooperation and exchange between both governments, formulating the readjustments that become necessary for practical purposes. . . .

1983 PLAN

I. The Cuban Party will recieve [sic] in 1983:

a) Five comrades with secondary educational level to study at the "Ñico López" School, for one year.

b) Two technicians in drawing for . . . making billboards and posters.

c) Two comrades for specialization in sound equipment. . . .

d) A press photographer for training in Cuba.

e) Training of a technician in microfilm for the press.

f) A newspaper librarian, for training in Cuba.

g) Training of a press cartoonist.

h) Training of a technician in general graphic arts.

i) Two comrades linked to the work on religion for exchanging experiences and coordinating regional and international work.

j) Two comrades linked to the work on the Socialist International for exchanging experiences and criteria on this aspect.

k) A delegation made up of three comrades of the Ministry of Mobilization who have to do with the work of Foreign Affairs, fundamentally with the Caribbean, for exchanging experiences, criteria, and coordination in the region.

l) A delegation made up of a Member of the Political Bureau and two other persons for exchanging experience on the work of organization, internal education and propaganda of the Party.

II. The Grenadian party will recieve [sic] in 1983:

a) Two technicians in sound equipment for public meetings. . . .

b) Two technicians in billboards and posters. . . .

c) A delegation of two comrades from the Department of Organization for exchanging experience on the organization work of the Party.

d) A specialist in the work with the religious people for exchanging experiences in the work of the Party on this sector.

e) A specialist in internal education plans of the Party.

The Communist Party of Cuba and the New Jewel Movement of Grenada, satisfied by the discussed and agreed aspects, which fully correspond with the fraternal relations between both Parties, underwrite this document in the City of Havana, Cuba, June 29th, 1983.

/s/ *Pineiro*
The Communist Party of Cuba

/s/ *Austin*
The New Jewel Movement

Documents 13, 14, and 15: International Support Network

T he following three internal communications of the Cuban Party and Government pertain to Grenadian requests for information on and contacts with communist organizations throughout the world. The first is a memorandum on CPC letterhead to Manuel Pineiro, head of the Central Committee's Americas Department. The second is a memo to an Americas Department official from the analysis section of Cuban intelligence. The third document is a Cuban memo, classified "secret," giving the addresses of communist parties participating in a Conference of Solidarity with Grenada. Of particular interest are the references to the illegal communist parties of Chile, Brazil, and Turkey, which can be contacted through Cuban embassies in the USSR, Portugal, and East Germany, respectively.

Document 13

COMMUNIST PARTY OF CUBA/CENTRAL COMMITTEE

City of Havana
20 October 1981
"Year of the 20th Anniversary of Girón"
    RS/1899-1

Pineiro:

In accordance with your request on behalf of the New Jewel Movement of Grenada in relation to the addresses of Communist Parties in our area, here are the following:

Communist Party of Chile—Moscow, USSR—Secretary General Luis Corvalan. Through our embassy.

Communist Party of Peru—Gr. Lampa No. 774, Lima, Peru. Secretary General Jorge del Prado.

Communist Party of Brazil—This party is still underground in its country, but it is possible to communicate through its representative in Portugal, Colonel Enoir de Oliveira, who would be contacted by the Secretary General of the Portuguese Communist Party.

Greetings,

Hector Sanchez Gonzalez

Document 14

City of Havana,
19 October 1981
"Year of the 20th Anniversary of Girón"

To: Osvaldo Cardenas
     America Department

From: Analysis Section
       Department Gral. RR.EE.

We are continuing to send you the addresses of the communist parties of Europe and Asia, with the exception of the parties of socialist countries. . . .

Communist Party of Turkey
(This party is still clandestine and our communication with them is through our Embassy in the German Democratic Republic.)

Communist Party of Portugal
Rua Soeiro Gomes, Lisbon, Portugal.

Communist Party of Spain
Calle Santisima Trinidad No. 5, Madrid, Spain.

Communist Party of Sweden
Kungsgaten 84, Stockholm, Sweden.

Communist Party of Finland
Sturenkatu 4, Helsinki, Finland.

Communist Party of Denmark
Dr. Traergaden 3, 1302 Copenhagen, Denmark.

Communist Party of Belgium
Ave. Stalingrad 29, Brussells 1000, Belgium.

Communist Party of Italy
Via Della Bothege Oscuro 4, Rome, Italy.

Communist Party of Germany
Prinz-Georg Strasse 79, 4000 Dusseldorf, RFA.

Communist Party of San Marino
(Our communication is through our Embassy in Italy)

Communist Party of France
12, Cite (Place du Colonel Fabien), 75940, CEDEX, France.

Communist Party of Great Britain
16 King St., Covert Garden, London WC–2.

Communist Party of Ireland
43 East Essex St., Dublin, Ireland.

Communist Party of Austria
1206 Vienna, Hochestadplatz 3, Austria.

Communist Party of Norway
Gronlandsleiset 39, Oslo I, Norway.

Communist Party of Greece
Odos Kapodistriov 16, Athens 116, Greece.

Communist Party of Holland
Post Box 19563, 1000 GN, Amsterdam.

Communist Party of Luxembourg
B.P. 2106, Luxembourg Villa, G.D., Luxembourg.

This list also included the addresses of "Communist Parties of Socialist Countries of Asia" and "Communist Parties of Capitalist Countries of Asia." They are not included here.

Document 15

20.10.81   Very Urgent
1899–1   SECRET

From Comrade German

To Lino

Act. Response to the request for a list and addresses of the Communist
      Parties participating in the Conference of Solidarity with Grenada.

Comrade:

For the present time, we are sending you the Communist Parties that pertain to our area.

Argentina:

Communist Party of Argentina, (PCA)

Representative: Alberto Rodriguez.   Country: Cuba

Address: Building 602 of the microbrigade of communications, Calle Hidalgo corner of Colon, Apartment 2-I, 2nd floor, Plaza of the Revolution, Vedado, Havana.

Bolivia:

Communist Party of Bolivia (PCB)   Country: La Paz, Bolivia

Through the Cuban Embassy in Bolivia, to Comrade Hector Doran.

Uruguay:

Communist Party of Uruguay: PCU

Representative: Luis Hernandez   Country: Cuba

Address: Calle 25 #510, c/n H c I, Apartment 35, Vedado.

Paraguay:

Communist Party of Paraguay: PCP

Representative: Rogelio Gonzalez   Country: Cuba

Address: Radio Havana, Cuba.

Document 16: Cuban Report on Grenada's Churches

T he experiences of Communist revolutions in this century reveal that, in the words of Miguel Bolaños Hunter, the church is considered "internal enemy number one" (see the Hunter interview, chapter 2, document 1). The following are excerpts from a report on the religious situation in Grenada prepared by the Americas Department of the Central Committee of the Cuban Communist Party containing Cuban advice as to how Grenada should cultivate church support for its domestic and regional policies.

---

3. To promote contacts among clergymen and members of the laity from Nicaragua and other Latin American circles linked to the theology of liberation and, in general, to the idea of a church committed to the revolutionary positions, and the Christian sectors in Grenada through the Pope Paul Camp and maybe through talks with religious clergymen from [the] same order, particularly the Dominicans. These contacts should positively influence the Christian sectors of Grenada.

To consider the possibility of the Matanzas Evangelical Seminary inviting pastors from the Grenadian Protestant churches belonging to the Conference of Caribbean Churches (CCC), of which the Conference of Evangelical Churches of Cuba is a member, to short or annual courses. The language problem would be solved here. . . .

5. To promote the invitation of Grenadian members of the laity and clergymen, through the appropriate channels, to visit Cuba. In my opinion, it would be useful to immediately invite F. Cyril Lamontagne, Vicar of the Cathedral of St. George's (second figure in the diocese), who in our interview expressed his willingness to visit Cuba and was interested in knowing how he could be invited. Afterwards, I think arrangements should be made for a visit of F. Martin Simmonds, superior on the Order of the Dominicans in the British West Indies, in case the trip he told us he was planning to make to Havana from Jamaica early next October would not take place. In case he

would travel in October, we should be kept informed on his visit so as to organize activities that should help to positively influence his positions. F. Simmonds is the only clergyman who, in spite of his institutional responsibility, enjoys a positive reputation in the revolutionary circles of the Island. I think that after a new inquiry in Grenada we should assess the advisability of continuing this program of visits with other West Indian priests of the diocese.

6. The result of this visit ratifies an existing proposal in the sense of regularizing a reciprocal information link and an exchange of criteria on the strategy and tactics of the Church and the mechanisms of prevention and response. The action of the Church—particularly the Catholic one—has its origin in the policy of the Vatican towards Central America and the Caribbean, and therefore, entails the existence of mechanisms of combined action within the institution. The exchange on our part should comprise two levels: a regular one with a NJM–PCC bilateral character, and another one with a trilateral character in which the FSLN of Nicaragua would also participate.

Document 17: Bishop–Gromyko Meeting: Intended Use of Grenada's Airport

D ocument 17 consists of excerpts from a record of the meeting between Prime Minister Maurice Bishop of Grenada and former Soviet Minister of Foreign Affairs Andrei Gromyko in Moscow on 15 April 1983. Compiled from notes taken on Gromyko's presentation and from Bishop's outline of his own presentation, this document reveals the highest level of contact between officials of the People's Revolutionary Government of Grenada and the USSR. It further indicates both the high level of interest that the Soviet leadership had in Bishop's government and the degree to which the Grenadian Government saw itself as a Soviet client.

Bishop tells Gromyko of the strategic threat that the airport poses to NATO supply lines. Indeed, a line from the notebook of Liam James, Politboro and NJM Central Committee member, clearly reveals Grenada's intended use of the airport: "The Revo[lution] has been able to crush Counter-Revolution internationally, airport will be used for Cuban and Soviet military."

In the following excerpts, Gromyko describes Grenada as part of the regional progressive forces, which also include Cuba and Nicaragua. He indicates Grenada's important role in providing the USSR with information and analysis on the Caribbean and offers to strengthen Party ties in any way possible.

"Let me thank you for the very interesting and comprehensive information on your region. . . . Your information will be of great help to us in orienting ourselves in relation to the main questions that you touched upon. I will convey this information personally to Comrade Andropov who incidentally sends his warmest greetings, as well as to all my Comrades in the Soviet leadership.

"As regards the proposals that you put foreword, we shall study them very carefully and after that whatever we can see it possible to do we shall do it to meet your requests.

"What you said concerning the situation in your region and the general mood of the broad masses of the people in the Caribbean, the upsurge of the parties and groups, is on the whole in line with our own understanding made from afar. It is our opinion that this entire region is today boiling like a cauldron. There has been an amassing of anti-imperialist sentiments over the last centuries—and particularly in recent times, aimed at over throwing colonialism. They are seeking to change the old order. One cannot say that the situation in any one country is the carbon copy of another, yet, one can discern a certain commonality in the region as a whole in its striving for independence.

"We noted that you spoke with great warmth in relation to Nicaragua and Cuba. We believe that these countries are living examples for countries in that part of the world. Examples of people who wish to govern themselves in independence and freedom. What the U.S.A. is doing against Nicaragua and Cuba is an indication that they are on the right path. . . .

"In conclusion, I want to comment about regional support for Nicaragua. Our view is that the people of Latin America and the Caribbean should perhaps speak out louder and more strongly in condeming the U.S.A. acts against Nicaragua. People do condemn but it is not as loud and consistent as it should be. Your analysis will be very helpful to us.

"You were quite right to speak about countries or territories which are not independent and we appreciate the fact that you are working to improve the situation in these countries. It makes it incumbent on them to exercise great care and flexibility so as not to provoke the imperialist forces to smash the progressive forces. Of course there is no force in the world that can crush the class struggle. But you have to be flexible so that imperialism is not agitated to attack you.

"We are very interested in what you have to say about the seminars that you held with the progressive forces in the Caribbean. It has a very scientific and scholarly form. The imperialists will be hard-pressed to accuse you of conspirators who need to be crushed by armed force. That is the sign of flexibility that you are showing in organizing such meetings. You seem to have chosen the right form and structure. . . . Whatever we can do to strengthen the ties with your party—we will do."

Maurice Bishop's presentation emphasizes Grenada's special geographical position and his government's desire to promote communism in the region. Bishop's introduction on "Recent International Developments" proclaims the following:

"Recent Soviet initiatives have caught the imagination of the world.
"World peace forces are on the offensive.

"We are interested in your view as to how Grenada can help in the peace campaign. . . ."

Bishop explains that, happily, the regional trend is that the best left-progressive parties are increasingly on Marxist–Leninist trend.

"Of course, it is part of our internationalist duty to assist these developments to the extent of our capacity. We hold organisational/ideological seminars twice yearly. Even this limited assistance (i.e. airline tickets, subsistence etc. *plus* direct financial grants to left parties) amounts to well over EC$500,000.00 so far. This is in fact already beyond our abilities and it will grow in quantity as these organisations develop. The USSR needs to get involved in providing some material support—through the most appropriate channel, to ensure the survival and development of these progressive organisations."

Bishop then thanks Gromyko for the USSR's "generous assistance/especially given your heavy and increasing internationalist responsibilities."

"Soviet assistance has been prompt, all-rounded, and high quality [in] Party to Party, Mass organisations to Mass organisations, Trade Union, Military, Technical, Trade [areas.]"

Bishop concludes with the issue of Grenada's international airport which, though 75 percent complete, is faced with serious financial difficulties. He points out the strategic importance of the airport.

"Grenada's airport is [a] direct threat to the security interests of the USA [by its possible use in] interdicting NATO supply lines."

Document 18: Bishop's Meeting with Soviet Ambassador

This document consists of excerpts from typewritten notes, in shorthand form, which summarize a meeting between Prime Minister Bishop of Grenada and the Soviet Ambassador to Grenada. These notes indicate the role of the Soviet Union in regional Communist Party activities and Moscow's liaison with regional CPs. The document also details the planned delivery of additional equipment and supplies, primarily of a military nature, from the USSR to Grenada, via Cuba. In addition, the notes also show that Soviet interest in Grenada was mainly for intelligence and propaganda activities.

[The Soviet Ambassador] explained that he had spoken with the General Secretary of the Venezuelan Communist Party and among other things, had raised the question of the level of counter-revolutionary activities in Venezuela. The General Secretary explained that there was, he thought, contact between the Venezuelan Government and the counter-revolutionaries and thought, but wasn't sure, that the President knew of it. The Ambassador asked him to work on it and send him more precise information.

The Ambassador reported that special equipment, [including] 2 Coast Guard patrol boats and foodstuff were being sent directly to Grenada. . . . The Ambassador indicated that the supply of the vehicles [military trucks, jeeps, pickups] and the fire-engines was based on the intergovernmental protocol of 11th July, 1980. The conditions were:

1) 15% within 1 year of date of delivery;

2) 85% over 10 years from date of delivery. . . .

3) 4% interest rate.

This, the Ambassador said are the most favourable conditions given to any body by the Foreign Trade Division of the U.S.S.R.

Ambassador informed that General Chief of Staff, Ogarkov, will like appointment with Cde. Hudson Austin. He reported that 12,000 roubles supply of

14.5 shells for armoured carriers delivered to Cuba in January 1983. Another 30,000 will be supplied this year through Havana. 35,000 roubles in spare parts can be delivered in the 3rd quarter of 1983 after letter of credit comes from Grenada. Soviet trade representative now in Grenada, can discuss this. The P.M. promised to have someone contact him. . . .

Aircraft to be supplied to Grenada will be delivered to Cuba. Can seat 39 paratroopers and hold 6 tons of cargo. Has 4,000 flight hours capacity and 4,000 landings. . . . Can be assempled [*sic*] in 90 days and will be done in Cuba. . . . P.M. explained that plane can be used for a dual purpose with the other being a Grenada/Cuba weekly run. . . . He also pointed out that the kind of plane, a military make, can pose problems landing in the more reactionary countries in the region as civilian make craft will not have those conditions.

Fifteen specialist will travel from Moscow to Havana to work on the aircrafts. The Ambassador said that they will prefer Cubans pilot to use it. Grenada must indicate what colours, emblems, service number are to be put on the plane.

The Ambassador pointed out that technicians can be sent to help develop the socioeconomic plan for 1983–85. He reported that equipment had been sent to G.I.S. [Grenada Information Service?] from TASS Agency. . . .

The Ambassador thus pointed out that the state section was strengthening; he was concerned about the newspaper not being published for three weeks and about the level of propaganda and ideological activity by the mass media.

He offered to consider assistance to the media and requested an outline of what the problems were and what assistance was required.

The P.M. asked the Ambassador to express his greetings to Cdes. Andropov, Tichonov, Tronyks and the C.C. of the C.P.S.U. and to indicate his satisfaction on the progress in the development of the relation[s] and anticipation for even more deepened relations.

Document 19: Minutes of Political Bureau Meetings

The following are excerpts of the minutes of selected meetings of the People's Revolutionary Government of Grenada (PRG). They show the significant number and diverse character of the lines of coordination the PRG maintained or pursued with the Soviet Union, Cuba, and other Soviet client states or groups otherwise connected with the Bloc: Libya, the PLO, SWAPO, and so on. These linkages deal with financial, military, training, propaganda, and construction assistance for Grenada. The minutes also indicate the support the PRG wished to provide in return, thereby increasing the prestige and emphasizing the progressive role of the New Jewel Movement in the fight against imperialism. Several points are noteworthy: Grenada's desire for close ties with Libya, including a loan request for $75 million; the PRG's promise of $50,000 to SWAPO; the CPSU's providing Grenada with various types of equipment, including four guillotines; the employment of PLO personnel displaced by the events in Lebanon; propaganda support for North Korean policy; and a VIP plane to be delivered by the USSR—an Antonov–26 paratroop transport. Grenada's full participation in the world network of Soviet client states and aligned groups appears to be the objective of the New Jewel Movement.

---

6 May 1981
These following people are to attend Cabinet meeting this afternoon to discuss offer from the GDR for our telephone system: [names]
Requests are to go by two telexes, through our appropriate embassies to Lybia and Iraq, requesting that discussions be held between our two countries to discuss "matters of great concern to Grenada". These talks should take place at the highest possible level. The visit to Lybia will be from 24th–26th May with a request to them for $75M (US). Iraq should be visited if the request to Lybia has not been met. . . .
MONGOLIAN PARTY CONGRESS— . . . Comrade Austin will attend. . . .
He will carry Comrade Fraser with him to help seek military and other

assistance in the countries including the U.S.S.R. and Vietnam. . . .
Among the projects to be discussed on the trip are the International
Airport and the Party's headquarters. . . .

3 June 1981

[Regarding the damage done by an unfavorable CBS program, Bishop suggested] that an "independent" person goes to New York to address a
rally . . . names . . . were suggested for the "independent" type.

The Libyan/USSR Ambassador—It was noted that both ambassadors are urgently needed . . . Cde. Coard has said that the Libyan Ambassador is
more key [*sic*] than the one for Iraq.

Cde. Jacobs raised the issue of Cde. Leader's [Bishop's] visit to the U.S.S.R.
in his letter. He said that the visit is not sure and the best way to "get
to" the Soviet Union is through Bulgaria and or the G.D.R. He suggested that Cde. Bishop first pay a visit to these countries. He pointed
out that Cde. Ortega has been to Moscow on four occasions, but has
not seen Cde. Brezhnev . . . there are plans to have one Ambassador
to Grenada representing all the socialist countries. . . . We have also
received offers from Bulgaria to send 24 Comrades to their Party
school. . . .

Ambassador Jacobs said that the S.U. [Soviet Union] is willing to give us
cement and other construction materials worth $150,000 (US) [for
NJM Party Headquarters].

LIBYAN DELEGATION—two Libyans will be arriving here this week.

Has Comrade Louison checked out the ten university scholarships to the
GDR? . . .

.   .   .   .

11 November 1981

. . . Cde. Strachan received a proposal that we purchase our own PA system. . . . from Hungary. The Cubans have agreed to train the persons
to use it.

The rally in solidarity with Angola is to be held tonight . . . The programme
will include the Angola representative, the SWAPO representative and
one comrade from the Party.

9 December 1981

SWAPO—Cde. Coard is to arrange to get the $50,000 promised to SWAPO
sent to their representative at the United Nations.

28 December 1981

NICARAGUA—Cde. Bishop reported that he had a meeting . . . re. the literary programme in Nicaragua. They came up with a list [of people]
to be sent there as tutors/trainers to help in the programme. . . . The
sending of the volunteers is to be co-ordinated with the Nicaraguan
Ambassador in Cuba.

15 September 1982

SOVIET UNION PARTY AGREEMENT— . . . the draft agreement and
work programme between the two parties as brought by us and
agreed,

a.   The Soviets to items for Party Headquarters.

b.   A number of schlarships [*sic*] for Party School—15 NJM comrades can
come from October . . . three, six or twelve months.

c.   The CPSU offered to host 5 NJM comrades for rest and recreation; 5 for
a familiarisation visit.

The following will also be given to us by the CPSU:

a.   2 autobuses (25-seater)

b.   2 Niva cars

c.   3 P.A. amplifiers

d.   12 loudspeakers

e.   6 16mm projectors

f.   12 tape recorders

g.   150 cassettes

h.   1 photocopying machine

i.   7 duplicating machines

j.   6 English typewriters

k.   4 Guillotines

m.   2000 folding chairs

27 October 1982

Letter from Libyan People's Bureau—They are requesting our assistance in
contacting seven of the regional Parties to come here for follow up
discussions held in Libya. . . . This was agreed to by the PB

Letter from Islamic Foundation—They are requesting that the main route to
the International Airport be called "Palestine Drive." Reply to be
sent—a committee will look at the entire naming of the area. Comrade
Strachan to follow up on this.

Communication from Richard Jacobs—Request re provision of jobs for a few
displaced PLO persons. PB's response—should accept between 5–10;
Comrade Louison to follow up on this.

15 Comrades for Soviet Union—15 Party comrades will leave for the Soviet
Union on a one year political training. . . .

3 November 1982

Memorandum from the DPRK [Democratic People's Republic of Korea]: requesting our co-operation in giving support to them on the issue of

South Korea and the way it is being used by the US imperialism. Response: decide to give "wide publicity" . . . Cde. Strahan [sic] to follow up on decision re giving wide publicity to the South/North Korea issue and the aggression of the US

17 November 1982
Report from Cde. Austin on visit to Cuba:
    —visit to Cuba was to discuss:—i) Airport ii)Statellite [sic] Dish
                          iii) Party Headquarters
on the Airport:—
    —the runway will be finished by 1983
    —Cuba has agreed to send 100 men to help finish most aspects of the Airport in 1983 and they will then help with other construction projects
on the Statelitte [sic] Dish:—
    —Cuba will send an expert next month to look at whether the Statellite [sic] Dish will be able to carry out the role/function of Cable and wireless or whether we will need to keep them
    —the Soviets will be giving us the Dish with experts from Cuba giving us assistance
Other matters:—
    —spoke with the Minister of Transport re the AN26 [Antonov–26] for the leadership
    —the parts will come from the Soviet Union and Cuban experts will assemble it in Cuba
    —Cuba say that we should get the S.U. to train our pilots; Cuba only upgrade pilots
    —Cuba will give us the technicians for the plane
    —the possibility of using the plane on a commercial basis between here and Cuba was also discussed

29 December 1982
Message from M–19, Colombia: The 8th National Conference of the M–19 of Colombia sent greetings to the NJM and stated their desire to develop best possible links with our Party. . . .

5 January 1983
Visits in 1983: The following countries were looked at for possible visits during this year both by the Comrade Leader (in some instances) and the Foreign Minister alone (in other cases):—
    i. Iran, Iraq, Algeria
   ii. Yugloslavia [sic], Korea
  iii. Romania
   iv. Angola, Tanzania, Zambia
    v. Kuwait, Suadi [sic] Arabia

    iv. Hungary, Czeckoslovakia [*sic*]
    vii. Sweden
   viii. Argentina, Brazil, Columbia
    ix. Austria, Switzerland

Cde. Whiteman stated that the Government of Kampuchea has invited Comrades Bishop and Whiteman to visit their country. . . . It was noted that if agreed to, Vietnam and Laos can be visited around the same time. The visit to Kampuchea was agreed to by the PB.

Don Rojas' Trip to Angola: This comrade is going to Angola as the Caribbean IOJ representative; he is to carry with him a letter to Santos from the Comrade Leader inviting him to come to Grenada.

re Non-Aligned meeting in Grenada . . . the Cubans will help with the financing.

Document 20: Minutes of Central Committee Meetings

A lthough Grenada's Central Committee meetings dealt mainly with internal and Party affairs, the following excerpts reveal Cuban involvement in the country. The criticism by two high-ranking Cuban officials indicates that Cuba considered Grenada to be a clear subordinate in the socialist chain of command.

---

26 August 1983
Comrade Cornwall . . . had been told by a Comrade from the G.D.R. that the state of work is bad. Similar allegations were made by Cuban Comrades Carlos Diaz and Pinero [Pineiro—head of Cuba's Americas Department].

25 September 1983
Cde. Cornwall [Grenada's Ambassador to Cuba] [said] basic information that any ambassador should know was not being provided to him. He sited [*sic*] the continuous failure for the newspapers to be sent to the embassy and the fact that other embassies were providing him with their newspapers and always asking him for copies of Grenada's. This became a source of personal embarrassment. Also he was not informed except one hour before the plane landed in Cuba when Cde. Bishop was coming to Cuba in March on his way to New Delhi and this information was given to him not by Grenada but by the Cuban Comrades. This he said is unheard of. Also on several occasion [*sic*] when other leaders of the revolution travel to Cuba the same occured [*sic*]. . . . He also sited [*sic*] an example of when he was asked by Grenada to pass on some information to Cuba and was experiencing difficulties to get that meeting but instead a Cuban Comrade—not a member of the CC of the Cuban Communist Party was able to fly in to Grenada and immediately get a meeting with four members of our Political Bureau including Cde. Bishop and deal with the same matter he was supposed to deal with. . . .

Document 21: Bishop–Assad Letter

T he following letter from Maurice Bishop to Hafez El Assad of Syria
clearly states Grenada's support for Syrian leadership in "social progress" in the Middle East. Of particular interest is paragraph seven, wherein
Bishop promises Grenada's "continued support . . . to the just cause of the
Palestinians under the leadership of the P.L.O."

4th October, 1979.

H.E. Hafez El Assad,
President of the Arab Republic of Syria,
Arab Republic of Syria,
C/O The U.N. Ambassador from Syria,
Syrian Embassy,
New York,
U.S.A.

I am very happy to take this opportunity to write to you concerning the
discussions we recently had in Havana during the Non-Aligned Conference.

You will recall that during our discussions, we agreed on the need for
our countries to establish diplomatic relations at the earliest opportunity and
thereafter for your country to accredit your Ambassador to Havana to
Grenada.

We also agreed that a Technical Co-operation Team from your country
should visit Grenada at an early opportunity with a view to assessing areas
of possible technical and economic co-operation and assistance between our
countries. Needless to say, I am very anxious for further discussion on these
areas of possible co-operation and as such, on behalf of the People's Revolutionary Government of Grenada and the people of Grenada, I am inviting
you to send such a team to Grenada as soon as possible.

I want you to know that it was a real pleasure for me to have had the opportunity to discuss so many matters of mutual concern to our countries with you. I sincerely hope that you will be able to come to our country on a state visit at a mutually convenient date in the future. At the same time, until that visit, I am asking you to assist our people in Grenada to learn more about The Republic of Syria and as such we would very much appreciate receiving, if possible, copies of any radio tapes, television video tapes, 16mm or 35mm films or printed matter that your government may have on your country and your struggle for true independence.

We would also welcome a visit to our country by any cultural group from your country that might happen to be coming to this region.

You can rest assured of the continued support of our government and party to the just cause of the Palestinians under the leadership of the P.L.O., our commitment to continue resisting the manoeuvrings [*sic*] of imperialism and the Israeli Zionists and our continued opposition to the treacherous Camp David Agreement.

On behalf of my government, party and people I send warmest fraternal regards to you, your government and people.

Long live the just struggle of the Arab Republic of Syria for social progress, genuine independence and peace with justice in the Middle East!

Yours fraternally

MAURICE BISHOP,
PRIME MINISTER.

Document 22: Embassy Report from Moscow

T his is a letter from Bernard Bourne (Minister-Counsellor in the Grenadian Embassy in Moscow) to Maurice Bishop, dated 30 June 1982, reporting on the Embassy's Party political work. The section of the letter that describes meetings with CPSU officials is of particular interest, and is excerpted below. The New Jewel Movement's desire to be taken seriously by the USSR as a Communist Party of regional significance is explicitly stated. Apparently, Moscow saw the possibility of Grenada serving as a base from which to assist nonruling parties and movements in the Caribbean. As the letter notes, "Upcoming State and Party Visit[s]" by Maurice Bishop are to be held with Boris Ponomarev, the head of the International Department of the CPSU's Central Committee.

---

1. MEETING WITH CPSU

During the last two months comrade Ambassador and myself held three meetings with representatives of the CPSU responsible for our area. The meetings were held on April 22, May 7 and June 9. In the meetings we discussed a wide range of issues, some of which are included in this report. . . .

With reference to an existing agreement between the CPSU and NJM . . . in our assessment, our Embassy will also serve as a bridge between the CPSU and LEFT PARTIES in the English-Speaking Caribbean. We will be decisive in their work by being able to give details of the situation in each of these countries. In that way, we are certain to develop good working relations and become a trustworthy ally of the CPSU. It goes without saying, therefore, that we will have to be supplied with details of analyses and assessments by the CC NJM and information on developments at home and in the region.

On the question of attending the CPSU Party School, we were informed that ten (10) of our cadres can attend the school; they are waiting on us. The system is such that if students begin classes in September, the course will be for 9 months. Also, there are three and six months courses which begin in January and it depends on us to decide how we are to utilize the scholarships.

The comrades are pressing us to take up the scholarships. At our last meeting I promised the comrades that as of this September we will take up the offers.

(NOTE: It is my opinion and also that of other comrades that in order for the CPSU to have greater confidence, trust and reassurance in our Party and our process it is absolutely necessary that we should take up these offers and attend the Party School courses. It is important for the image of our Party, the NEW JEWEL MOVEMENT.)

2. UPCOMING STATE AND PARTY VISIT

On this subject the document on the proposed agenda for meeting with the CPSU during the visit was handed over to the Chief of the Department for North America and the English-Speaking Caribbean, Comrade Nikolai. With reference to Party-to-Party collaboration we would have to prepare beforehand written documents and hand over to the CPSU.

Additionally, we conveyed your desire to meet with the General Secretary, Comrade Brezhnev and asked for confirmation of all three occasions. Up to now there is no final word on that score. However, we were told that Comrade Boris Ponomarev will be present during the Party-to-Party discussions.

Document 23: Foreign Relations Report to the Central Committee

T his document reflects Grenada's foreign relations in late 1982–early 1983. Submitted to the Central Committee of the New Jewel Movement, the report highlights Grenada's desire for solidarity with the socialist world and fraternal relations with Soviet Bloc and surrogate countries. The report also makes clear Grenada's support for "national liberation movements" such as the FDR in El Salvador, SWAPO in southern Africa, and the PLO in the Middle East.

GRENADA AND THE AMERICAS

On the El Salvador question Grenada's position is clear and irrevocable: the Junta in El Salvador is a genocidal regime backed solely by U.S. . . . The true and authentic representative of the Salvadorean people is the Frente Democratico Revolucionerio (FDR).

Grenada has excellent relations with the Revolutionary Governments, people and countries of Nicaragua and Cuba. . . . Grenada has several agreements with Cuba and receives tremendous and invaluable assistance from Cuba in numerous areas—the New International Airport, Fisheries, Education, Military, Agriculture, Health. . . .

Nicaragua has also supported Grenada internationally and Grenada has received technical assistance. . . . Grenada in return has supported and defended Nicaragua internationally. . . .

EASTERN EUROPE

Grenada perceives the key role the Socialist Community has played in defending the developing countries and in consolidating the hard won independence of these countries. Also, the support National Liberation Movement have had from the Socialist Community has been tremendous and often decisive. Thus, for Grenada the Eastern European Countries can be a real source of political and diplomatic support apart from the vast potential they have for technical and economic assistance. For those two reasons Grenada must continue intensifying its relations with Eastern Europe. Therefore, the possibility of establishing an Embassy in Moscow must be seriously and positively explored.

THE MIDDLE EAST

Grenada's foreign relations with the Middle East [have] been guided by the recognition as well as by Grenada's principles of anti-zionism and anti-imperialism. Grenada has developed close relations. . . . [and] has technical assistance arrangements with Libya, Algeria, Syria and Iraq and has received substantial assistance from these countries. . . .

Grenada's Middle East policy is also geared to develop close relations with the anti-imperialist, anti-zionist forces in the region and to support the Just Struggle of the Palestinian people. Thus, Grenada has recognized the PLO [and] . . . has taken a position irreconcilably opposed to the Camp David Agreement.

WESTERN EUROPE

Grenada has also sought through the Socialist International to develop strong relations with the Social Democratic Parties of Western Europe some of which are in power in their countries. This is a policy which has tremendous potential for realising material assistance for Grenada. Also, through the Socialist International Grenada can make its contribution to detente disarmament and peace in Europe.

FAR EAST

Grenada has been critical of the South Korean fascists and has developed healthy relations with the Democratic People's Republic of Korea (DPRK) (North Korea). . . . A technical and economic cooperation agreement between Grenada and the DPRK has been discussed and negotiated. A Grenada delegation is scheduled to visit Mongolia and Vietnam very shortly. . . .

AFRICA

As a concrete manifestation of its commitment to the liberation struggle in South Africa Grenada in February 1981 gave EC$50,000 to the Namibian Liberation Fund set up by the Organisation of African Unity (OAU). Grenada has recognised and has established diplomatic relations with the Saharan Arab Democratic Republic showing once again its support of just liberation struggles.

THE MOVEMENT OF NON-ALIGNED COUNTRIES

This international organisation is key to Grenada's foreign policy. Grenada joined the Movement in 1979 and was immediately made a member of the Coordinating Bureau. In the Movement Grenada has expressed organised support for the liberation struggles the world over and has reinforced its anti-imperialist, anti-colonialist character.

SOCIALIST INTERNATIONAL

In the Socialist International [SI] Grenada has been able to show organized support for peace, peaceful co-existence, disarmament detente, cooperation between nations and for the national liberation struggles. Grenada's relations with the SI, developed through the attendance of its meetings by Cde. Unison Whiteman, has earned for Grenada statements of solidarity with the Grenada Revolution. . . .

Membership in the SI has also permitted Grenada to develop relations with progressive parties and sectors of Western Europe. Cde. Maurice Bishop's recent attendance of the SI Meeting in Holland served to make good contact with the leading personalities and parties of the SI.

Document 24: Relations with the Soviet Union

T his report by the Grenadian Ambassador to the USSR summarizes Grenada's understanding of its relations with the Soviet Union as of July, 1983. The excerpts below imply that Grenada's surrogate role is expected in order to ensure continued USSR assistance; the need to support Moscow's global objectives and interests is stressed. Grenada appears to have believed that its relations with the USSR would be enhanced by an active role in regional affairs—especially regarding the English-speaking Caribbean countries. The aim was to bring these states into the "progressive fold." Cuba's leadership in the Latin/Central American progressive movement is also emphasized.

Ideological Orientation of NJM

Grenada is regarded as being on the path of Socialist orientation. There is a general acceptance among Soviet authorities that we are at the national democratic, anti-imperialist stage of socialist orientation. The USSR assigns a special place to these types of countries in its foreign policy. . . . Therefore, whatever the internal debate, it is important that we continue to maintain our public assessment of our stage of development as the national democratic, anti-imperialist stage of socialist orientation. After all, the PM himself made that assessment when he was here in Moscow as well as during his visit to Berlin. . . . So it seems absolutely necessary that we maintain this line. This is made all the more important by the very high priority that is placed on consistency of analysis here. . . .

Basis for Soviet Support for Grenada

The Soviets have been burnt quite often in the past by giving support to Governments which have either squandered that support, or turned around and become agents of imperialism, or lost power. One is reminded of Egypt, Somalia, Ghana and Peru. They are therefore very careful and for us sometimes maddingly slow, in making up their minds about who to support. They have decided to support us for two main reasons: 1. Cuba has strongly championed our cause. 2. They are genuinely impressed with our management of the economy and state affairs in general.

Grenada's Role in Regional Affairs

By itself, Grenada's distance from the USSR, and its small size, would mean that we would figure in a very minute way in the USSR's global relationships. . . . For Grenada to assume a position of increasingly greater importance, we have to be seen as influencing at least regional events. We have to establish ourselves as the authority on events in at least the English-speaking Caribbean, and be the sponsor of revolutionary activity and progressive developments in this region at least. . . . The twice per year meetings with the progressive and revolutionary parties in the region is [sic] therefore critical to the development of closer relations with the USSR. In order to keep both the Embassy and the Soviets informed of the outcome of such meetings, perhaps a good model would be for a member of the CC to pay a visit to the USSR after each such meeting. The mission of such a person could without difficulty be mixed with other activities. We must ensure though that we become the principal point of access to the USSR for all these groups even to the point of having our Embassy serve as their representative while in the USSR. . . .

Of all the regional possibilities, the most likely candidate for special attention is Surinam. If we can be an overwhelming influence on Surinam's international behaviour, then our importance in the Soviet scheme of things will be greatly enhanced . . . another candidate is Belise.

Relations with other Members of the Socialist Community

It is well to remember that there is a constant and very detailed consultation process that takes place between members of the socialist community. For example, on my recent mission to the GDR (June 1983) they made it very clear to me that they had been briefed on the PM's discussions with Gromyko, and this is to be expected. As a result, our performance in various aspects of our relations with members of the socialist community directly affects our relations with the USSR—not to mention the fact that it directly determines the relationship between Grenada and the country involved. . . .

Linkage of Grenada's International Activities to Relations with the USSR

From the point of view of our relations with the USSR, our international activity is important from the following perspectives:

1. The consistency of our political line.

2. The influence of Grenada in the international community.
3. The degree of support offered to the positions taken by the USSR.

Our performance is assessed at the following levels:

1. The United Nations and its agencies—UNESCO, UNCTAD, etc.
2. Organization of American States
3. Non-aligned Movement
4. Missions in various countries (Embassies).

It is very difficult for me to assess their view of our performance in the UN, its agencies and the OAS. . . . But during the period of the threats, etc., in March 1983, they advised us to play a more active role in the UN especially at the Security Council and spoke approvingly of Nicaragua's performance at the Security Council. But I suspect that we need a bigger staff at the UN to do the kind of job that would impress internationally. . . .

At the non-aligned movement, they have a high valuation of our role. You will recall that before the New Delhi Conference they gave me a detailed briefing on their positions and when Comrade Whiteman visited afterwards, they expressed admiration for our performance. . . .

On the whole, I have formed the view that the USSR is satisfied with the degree of support that they received from Grenada. . . . Considering the risks that we have taken on this and other matters, it might be fair to say that their support for us is actually below our support for them. We must therefore work to establish a balance of interests. This might best be done by gentle reminders at critical stages by members of our leadership. . . .

Documents 25, 26, and 27: Grenada, the Socialist International and Cuban Infiltration

T he following three documents demonstrate the surrogate role played by Grenada on behalf of the USSR and Cuba in the Socialist International (SI), and confirm Havana's attempt to influence that organization. Document 25 is a Grenadian statement of its role and objectives as a member of the SI. This seemed to spring not from an ideological commitment to the goals and ideals of the SI, but rather is an affiliation that would be used to conduct "active measures" on behalf of their patrons. For example, though there are "fundamental contradictions" between the program of democratic socialism advocated by the SI and the NJM's promotion of revolutionary socialism, the Grenadians recognized the benefits of a "working relationship" with the SI, particularly with regard to its support for regional "progressive" movements such as the FDR in El Salvador and the FSLN of Nicaragua. Excerpts from a Grenadian report on the SI's 15th Congress (Document 26) confirm this attempted tactical use of the SI in promoting "progressive and revolutionary forces" in the region while criticizing the United States. Finally, Document 27 reveals that a "Secret Regional Caucus" of these "progressive forces" of Latin America and the Caribbean had been formed and operated in cooperation with the Cuban Communist Party (PCC). The inclusion of the PCC in the list of participants at a meeting of this Secret Caucus is significant, since it is barred from SI membership. Nevertheless, it seems apparent that Cuba was operationally involved in an attempt secretly to influence the SI.

Document 25

N.J.M. AND THE SI.

The NEW JEWEL Movement became a full member party of the SI at the last Congress of the SI in Madrid, Spain. . . . The question of whether the N.J.M.–Grenada ought to be a member of SI has arisen. . . . Now it has been established beyond dispute that the Grenada Revolution of March 13th faces grave threats from imperialism, mercenaries and external reaction.

Given this, one of the ongoing objectives of Grenada's Foreign Policy has to be: to harness moral, political, economic and other support from the international community so as to stave off and combat external aggression and subversion.

One of the means of achieving this objective is through forging broad alliances internationally. . . . The SI is such an organization: thus, Grenada–N.J.M. is correctly a member. . . . Another objective of the [Grenadian] foreign policy is: to support the struggles of oppressed people.

Through membership in the SI Grenada can express organized support for the progressive struggles; in Southern Africa, the Western Sahara, Palestine, El Salvador, Nicaragua and other parts of Latin America, etc. . . .

Some would argue, yes, these are your objectives, yes, they are realized through membership in SI. But what about principles? The ideology of the SI is Democratic Socialism. The Grenadian revolution aspires to advance beyond democratic socialism. Thus, there are differences between the N.J.M. (Grenada) and the SI.

Of course there are differences. There exist fundamental contradictions between revolutionary socialists and democratic socialists. But this does not mean that the two cannot strike a working relationship under certain conditions when the objectives are sufficiently [broad]. . . .

The SI fully supports the struggle in Southern Africa, condemns strongly apartheid and racism, is in firm solidarity with the FDR in El Salvador, the FDCR in Guatemala, the FSLN in Nicaragua and generally takes a very progressive position in Latin American issues. Those views and positions are identical to Grenada's. Thus, a working relationship, membership, is quite in order.

On issues where there exist a difference of views—Afghanistan, the two Superpowers, two imperialisms thesis, Kampuchea, the structure of the SI is sufficiently flexible to permit dissension. Thus, Grenada's sovereignty and principles are not compromised by being in the SI. . . .

In sum then Grenada's membership in the SI is quite consistent with its principles and objectives. . . . The SI can be a useful element.

Document 26: From the Grenadian Report on the 15th Congress of the SI

The sector of progressive and revolutionary forces, made up by the Salvadoran representatives (DRU, FDR and MNR), Commander Bayardo Arce of the FSLN, Jamaica's PNP, the NEW JEWEL of Grenada, and others. The positive role played by Manuel Ungo and Hector Oqueli of the MNR should be stressed, as well as the work done by Commander Bayardo Arce. The main objective of these forces was to thwart the maneuvers of the center right, strongly stimulated by the Panamanians, and avoid a set-back of S.I. positions on Latin America and the Caribbean. . . .

Contacts and meetings took place before the holding of the Congress among State Department officials and Social Democracy leaders. The main interest for the US government remained unchanged: to avoid the S.I.'s condemnation of the Junta in El Salvador and actually to promote its support, and to prevent criticisms on the policy of the United States toward Latin America and the Caribbean. . . .

In making a comparative analysis of this Congress' section on Latin America and the Caribbean with the previous Congress, one clearly observes important progress. The formulations adopted relate to the most important issues of the region's political life at present and to a large extent meet the objectives that the progressive and revolutionary forces aspired to have reflected in the document. . . .

The way the Congress dealt with Nicaragua is truly illustrative. The Nicaraguan Revolution is, without doubt, a trial test for the S.I. policy toward Latin America. The establishment of an International Committee for the Defense of the Nicaraguan Revolution and the support of the S.I. to the Sandinista Front, is an unmistakable proof of its interest to continue making efforts to influence this process, which is decisive for their influence work in the area and specially in Central America.

Document 27

REPORT ON MEETING OF SECRET REGIONAL CAUCUS OF
[word missing] HELD IN MANAGUA FROM
6TH–7TH JANUARY, 1983

The following Organizations were represented:

F.S.L.N.	Nicaragua	Antonio Marguin [Jarquin]
M.N.R.	El Salvador	Hector Oqueli
R.P.	Chile	Freda
P.N.P.	Jamaica	Paul Miller
P.C.C.	Cuba	Silva
N.J.M.	Grenada	Chris DeRiggs

I. ANALYSIS

i) Regional Situation—the progressive forces are in control.

   a) There are fourteen members of the S.I. Committee for Latin America and the Caribbean. Of these fourteen, there are seven parties that are generally progressive and some within a Marxist–Lennist [*sic*] trend. There are three (3) new parties that have recently gained consultative observer status in S.I. They are: (I) Puerto Rico (II) WPA–Guyana (III) PLP–St. Lucia

   The presence of these parties will help to strengthen the influence of the progressive forces within the Regional Committee. These parties can, in effect, function like full members of the organization. We must always consult with them and keep them informed.

2. EUROPE IN RELATION TO LATIN AMERICA

a) There are sharp divisions among the European parties in their outlook on Latin America.

b) Our friends in this area are prepared to accept the Latin American Revolutionary process as being palatable if restricted to the Latin American context. . . .

d) Many of the European S.I. parties expect us to understand the concept of "the Soviet Menace". . .

g) Our strongest allies in Europe are the Nordic S.I. parties and that of Holland. There is also good potential with the U.D.P. of Canada.

h) Our principal enemies are to be found among the parties of Soares and Horgo in Portugal and Italy respectively—the Social Democrats of the U.S.A. are also our sworn enemies. . . .

. . . .

DECISIONS

1. Michael Manley of P.N.P. and Anselmo Sule of P.R. will coordinate with B. Carlson of the S.I. Secretariat on the next meeting of the Broad Latin America Region S.I. Committee. . . . Member parties will be informed accordingly.

2. A broad resolution on the Latin American and Caribbean situation will be passed at the meeting of the Regional Committee. . . .

3. Hector Oqueli of M.N.R. of El Salvador will draft a Resolution on Latin America and the Caribbean by 31st January, 1983. This Resolution will be specifically for the Sydney Congress and will address only the most major issues.

The following guidelines will be the basis for the Resolution:

(a) The Basle Resolution—including such themes like Peace and Non-Intervention, Anti-Militarisation in the Region, Anti-dictatorship, the settlement of disputes, etc.

(b) Solidarity with Nicaragua, Grenada and the F.D.R., F.M.L.N. and M.N.R. of El Salvador. . . .

(d) The creation of a platform and frame of reference in S.I., the approach on the Latin America and Caribbean Region until the next Congress in Belgium (in the subsequent 2 years).

4. Subject to the approval of N.J.M., the next meeting of the Secret Regional Caucus of progressive S.I. parties will be in Grenada around the 13th and 14th March. This meeting will have strategic value in that it will provide the opportunity to:

   i) Assess the results of the tour of Europe by the selected parties, and

   ii) Conduct a final assessment on issues related to the Sydney Congress— questions of tactics and levels of co-ordination can also be discussed.

Submitted by,
CDE. CHRIS DE RIGGS.

Document 28: The "World Center" and Cuban Influence

T his document provides additional evidence of Cuban leadership in front group activities. This report by the NJM delegate to the General Congress of the World Center for the Resistance of [*sic*] Imperialism, Zionism, Racism and Reaction discloses an attempt by Libya to influence the organization. It is clear that Grenada wished to follow the Cuban lead, especially after consultations with Manuel Pineiro (here referred to as Cde Phinera), the head of Cuba's Americas Department.

REPORT ON THE GENERAL CONGRESS
OF THE WORLD CENTER FOR THE
RESISTANCE OF IMPERIALISM, ZIONISM, RACISM AND REACTION

FROM: The N.J.M. Delegate
TO: The Central Committee of the N.J.M.
DATE: June 26th, 1982.

Comrades, I left Grenada on June 11th to attend what I was informed to be a Conference in Solidarity with El Salvador. It was only on my arrival in Cuba, together with delegates from other Caribbean Revolutionary and Democratic parties and Organizations that I learnt the true character of the Conference in Libya.

On Saturday June 12th the Caribbean Delegates met with Cde Phinera [Pineiro], a member of the Central Committee of the P.C.C. in charge of American Affairs. He explained to us the nature of the Conference and put forward key guidelines for our approach to the major issues of the meeting.

(1) That we should avoid giving support for the idea of Libya being the center of the World anti-imperialist struggle and its military implications of a rapid Deployment force against imperialism.

(2) That we should only give solidarity expressions for the proposed World Center.

(3) That the Secretariat of the World Center should include Latin American and Caribbean Revolutionary Forces, he also said that Cuba will be participating . . . in the Congress. . . .

After the meeting with Cde Phinera the Caribbean Delegates continued to meet to analyse the new information and to take some common positions. The full implications of Cuba's participation in the Congress (but) not as the PCC suddenly dawned on us and was a source of great concern but this did not prevent us from taking common decisions. . . .

N.J.M. agreed to speak on behalf of the Caribbean but pointed out its concern over the level of Cuba's participation in the conference. The fact that they were not attending as the PCC indicates the low profile being taken by the Cubans and that it is of concern to us since Cuba is the leader of the Revolutionary Movement in this part of the World. We should therefore express our concern about this. . . .

There were expressions from several delegations of the fact that they were invited to Libya to attend a Conference in Solidarity with El Salvador and now being confronted with the real nature of the Conference, they cannot concretely commit themselves to the center because they have no mandate from their organizations to do so. They suggested bringing back the documents home so that their organizations can study them. . . .

There was a line that Cuba was using Grenada to influence the other Caribbean parties and organizations. The reason I believed that this line developed was the fact that Cuba was always keeping in touch with Grenada. Cuba always contacted Grenada to invite the Caribbean to the Latin American and Caribbean meeting, and generally made Grenada aware of the behind the scenes issues involved in the Congress and what is their position and general guidelines for us to follow.

Document 29: Havana Conference Agenda

T he following document is a letter inviting the New Jewel Movement to attend a conference in Havana with the Latin American Communist Parties and revolutionary movements on the "General and Particular Characteristics of the Revolutionary Processes in Latin America and the Caribbean" on 26–28 April 1982. It underscores the close links between the New Jewel Movement and the Latin American communist parties. A reading of the excerpts from the accompanying agenda reveals the conference's main goal to be the facilitation of the revolutionary struggle in Latin America and the Caribbean. In addition to the usual points addressed by such gatherings, there is point III.4, which emphasizes the "importance of the unity between marxists and Christians in the revolution." Indeed, the Christian-Marxist alliance and the whole question of "liberation theology" has been one of the most dramatic developments in Latin America in the last decade.

COMMUNIST PARTY OF CUBA/CENTRAL COMMITTEE

City of Havana, 14 January 1982
"Year 24 of the Revolution"

New Jewel Movement
of Grenada

Esteemed Comrade:

The International Magazine and the Communist Party of Cuba will celebrate in the City of Havana, during the 26th through the 28th of April of this year, the International Theoretic Conference "General and Particular Characteristics of the Revolutionary Processes in Latin America and the Caribbean."

This event will be attended by delegations of the Communist Parties and other revolutionary organizations of Latin America and the Caribbean.

At the present we extend the invitation to attend this Theoretic Conference, enclosing in addition the agenda of the problems that will be the object of examination and discussion. . . . The questions selected are of the greatest importance . . .

It would be highly useful for the development of the event if you can contribute upon the imperialist dominion in Latin America and its influence on the fight for national liberation, the role of different classes and social groups, etc.

With revolutionary greetings,

Antonio Diaz Ruiz
Department of Internal Education
Central Committee of the Cuban
Communist Party

AGENDA FOR THE THEORETICAL CONFERENCE ON THE GENERAL AND PARTICULAR CHARACTERISTICS OF THE REVOLUTIONARY PROCESSES IN LATIN AMERICA AND THE CARIBBEAN

The development of Latin American and Caribbean revolutionary movements includes valuable experiences of military struggle that illustrate not only the national peculiarities of where they occurred, but also the general characteristics of revolutionary transformation of the present day.

The purpose of this event is to promote the analysis and debate among the participants of the experiences of the revolutionary campaigns in Latin America and the Caribbean with a predominantly political perspective, such that the conclusions that are reached serve, in actual conditions, as an interpretive instrument to armed revolutionaries in our continent.

The proposed agenda does not pretend to cover all the subjects that could be treated . . .

I.   Character of the Revolution
     1. The premises for revolutionary triumph.
     2. The strategic objective of the revolution.
     3. The phases of the revolution and the principal tasks in each one of them.

II. The vanguard of the social revolution in Latin America.

1. Creation of the revolutionary vanguard from the organizational and class point of view. Experiences.

2. The vanguard and its binding to the masses.

3. The vanguard, its composition and objectives according to the different stages of revolutionary struggle.

III. Regarding tactics and strategy.

1. The ways of seizing political power.

2. The dialectics of various forms of struggle.

3. The politics of alliance, in both the national and international arenas.

4. Importance of unity between the marxists and Christians in the revolution.

5. The program of the revolution, in stages.

Document 30: Grenada and World Peace

D ocument 30 consists of excerpts from a report by Bernard Bourne, Minister-Counsellor at the Grenadian Embassy in Moscow, to the Grenada Peace Council. The report, dated 6 November 1982, is titled "Report on Peace Meetings in Lisbon," and details the surrogate role of Grenada within the World Peace Council, a well-known Soviet front organization. Bourne also has specific recommendations to increase the influence of the Grenada Peace Council (GPC). Of note is the support expected from East Germany, Cuba, and the Soviet Union.

OBSERVATIONS

A very important development—in my view—in the World Peace Council and Movement at the present international situation is the great urge to build the strength and unity of the world's peace forces, regardless of political, ideological or religious persuasions, on the question of the need to avert a thermo-nuclear catastrophe. The Leadership of the WPC puts it this way: "the only qualification for joining the Peace Movement is the support of the struggle to prevent a nuclear war".

Furthermore, a very significant focus of the World Peace movement and its leadership is the inextricable link between the struggle for World Peace and the struggle for national liberation, independence, democracy and social progress. This link is profoundly proclaimed at every opportunity.

For this last reason, it is my genuine recommendation for us to develop our Grenada Peace Council to a very high and prominent level. . . .

RESULTS

1. The Latin American Commission at the meeting agreed to coordinate these activities in 1983: a. The bicentenary of Simon Bolivar; b. The 10th anniversary of the fascist coup in Chile and c. Support for Nicaragua in United Nations Security Council.

2. A resolution was unanimously adopted which gives support to progressive forces in the region, including the Grenada Revolution.

3. A press conference was held by all representatives of the region, the focus being the situation around Nicaragua, fully expounded by the Nicaragua delegation. A renounciation [*sic*] of the aggressive activities against Nicaragua was signed by participants of peace movements from Latin America and the Caribbean.

4. The WPC decided to make the first week in December 1982 "a week in Solidarity with Nicaragua" in view of the dangerous scheme planned by the Reagan Administration in collusion with the reactionary Honduran Government in Central America, for the beginning of December.

INITIATIVES BY GRENADA

[One of the suggestions put forward was that] the WPC should send films of the Peace Movement to the GPC.

On this suggestion I was advised that the WPC does not make films, and that we should approach the GDR Peace Movement because they have good films of the Peace Movements. I spoke with a German on the subject and asked that he raise it for the GPC with the GDR Peace Committee. . . .

Additionally, the WPC is leaning and depending on the Grenada Peace Council in order that the WPC could develop wider and deeper relations with the Peace movements in Guyana, the Eastern Caribbean, French Caribbean, Cayenne, Barbados and Trinidad and Tobago. This was mentioned to me by Comrade Hill Arboleda.

Finally, on the question of participation in WPC activities, the one drawback of the WPC is finance to buy tickets. I was told that the Soviet Peace Fund, through Aeroflot, Soviet Airlines and Cubans make some contributions; plus the various Peace committees around the world. For example, at previous meetings the Latin American Peace Committees assisted the WPC by paying 80 000 US dollars for tickets.

Concretely, as far as the GPC is concerned, it would be invited to participate in WPC activities, but would be called upon to pay for its participants for part of the flight, namely, from Grenada to Havana where the future delegates would collect Aeroflot and get a free ticket. If the GPC could raise sufficient funds and pay up to Havana, it could send up to six (6) delegates to the Prague Assembly from June 14 to 19, 1983.

My last recommendation to the GPC is that it should send all information to the World Peace Council via the Embassy of Grenada in the USSR.

4

Surrogate Actors: Nark-Intern (Narcotics International)

> Before, the Cubans captured drug traffickers and handed them over. Now, Fidel said, they can go and do whatever they want, so long as they leave us some money. Fidel said, "We are going to make the people up there [the United States] white, white with cocaine."
>
> Eden Pastora Gomez
> (See chapter 2, Document 2)

It seems ironic that, a century and a quarter after Karl Marx condemned religion with the epithet "opiate of the masses", some of his self-proclaimed heirs now appear to be in the business of dealing in real opiates: marijuana, cocaine, and heroin. The support of this flow of narcotics aims at not only the possible destabilization of Western society, but also the more immediate goal of obtaining hard Western currency with which to finance some of the operations that are the subject of this book. Involvement in drug trafficking also allows for the exploitation of organized crime channels for the movement of explosives, weapons, and men across international frontiers.

For the past two decades evidence has been accumulating that points to the conclusions that client states of the Soviet Union actively support and participate in drug trafficking. The editors use the term "Nark-Intern", or Narcotics International, because the ultimate effects of these operations might replicate the aims of the pre–World War II Communist International, that is, the eventual destabilization of Western society.

Nark-Intern profits are instrumental in funding terrorist groups in widely scattered portions of the globe, such as the M–19 organization in Colombia or the PLO which, although not an integral part of the Soviet system, pursue aims which, as shown elsewhere, often run parallel to and are coordinated with the policies of the USSR and its surrogates. The risk to these surrogates resulting from involvement in the narcotics traffic has proved to be small; the current dearth of media coverage, public awareness and concern, and serious official protest on this issue indicate a positive payoff on this particular gamble. Only occasional flickers of interest have resulted from articles in newspapers such as the *Miami Herald,* the *Washington Times,* and the *Washington Post,* and by the open, previous publication of documents such as the

Senate testimonies presented here. Document 1 contains excerpts from an interview with Carlos Lehder Rivaz, reportedly the most important Columbian drug trafficker. In Documents 2 and 3, former Cuban intelligence (D.G.I.) agent Mario Estevez Gonzales reports on Castro's personal involvement in supporting the drug trade, the number of Cuban agents who had infiltrated the United States during the 1980 Mariel boatlift, and the profitability of Cuba's drug business.

Also presented are testimonies by former drug smugglers Johnny Crump and David Lorenzo Perez, Jr. (Documents 4 and 5). These men were involved in the 1981 Jaime Guillot Lara case, an operation in which Cuba provided support for the trafficking of drugs from Colombia in exchange both for cash and Guillot's services in running arms back to the M–19 terrorists in Colombia. This case resulted in the 1982 indictment by a Federal grand jury of fourteen persons, including the following high-ranking Cuban officials: Fernando Ravelo Renada, Cuban Ambassador to Colombia; his first secretary Gonzalo Bassols; Rene Rodriguez Cruz, president of the Cuban Institute of Friendship to the People (ICAP) and a member of the Central Committee of the Cuban Communist Party; and Aldo Santamaria Cuadrado, Vice Admiral of the Cuban Navy. These names appear in the testimonies published here.

Document 6 contains the testimony of Antonio Farach, a former Nicaraguan diplomat, who provides evidence of the high-level participation of Sandinista officials in drug trafficking. In document 7, Mr. Clyde Taylor of the U.S. State Department's Bureau of International Narcotic Matters presents a statement on Managua's involvement in drug trafficking.

The involvement of the Bulgarian government for over a decade in this Nark-Intern has been documented by writers such as Clare Sterling, Paul Henze, and Nathan Adams. Included here as Document 8 is a comprehensive overview of the Bulgarian situation prepared by the U.S. Drug Enforcement Administration.

Document 1: Interview with Carlos Lehder Rivas, Reputed Colombian Drug Trafficker

This document contains excerpts from the transcript of an interview with Carlos Lehder Rivas, aired on Colombian television in March 1985. Lehder is reported to be the biggest drug dealer and exporter in Colombia. He is also the founder and leader of a political party called the Latin National Movement (Movimiento Latino Nacional), the majority party in Lehder's native territory, the department of Quindia. Kidnapped by the Cuban-supported M–19 terrorist organization when relations between the radical left and the drug "Mafia" were hostile, he managed to escape and now advocates a "national dialogue" with the M–19 and—as will be seen in the interview that follows—co-operation between the drug industry and the "Latin American revolutionary movements" in the "struggle against imperialism." Other evidence in this chapter demonstrates that this alliance has in fact been established.

Lehder has been in hiding for nearly two years because there is a warrant out for his arrest. The United States has demanded his extradition. The interview was conducted on a riverboat "somewhere in the Colombian jungle" by the Central American correspondent of Spanish television, Cristina Navarra. Her first question concerns the assassination of the Colombian Minister of Justice, Rodrigo Lara Bonilla, in May 1984.

Cristina Navarra (henceforth CN): Carlos Lehder, who killed the Minister Lara Bonilla?

Carlos Lehder (henceforth CL): The Minister Lara Bonilla was executed by the Colombian people, and I am certain that the Colombian people are ready to execute anyone who is about to trade it. . . .

CN: Does that mean that you are justifying the assassination of our Minister Lara Bonilla?

CL: Affirmative. I justify the execution of any one of the traitors.

CN: Would you, in the name of this populism, support a military government in Colombia?

CL: Affirmative. Affirmative. I would support a military government in Colombia. Of course I would support it only if the army were a popular army. . . .

CN: Are you speaking as the representative of a group of persons whom they call the "Mafia" of this country, a group of drug dealers or is this your individual opinion?

CL: Yes, I accept responsibility for my actions and for the actions of Latino Nacional. I do not belong to any Mafia . . . the oligarchs of course lie about us; I do not belong to any drug business and have never in my life been mixed up with any kind of drugs. . . .

CN: But isn't it certain that you owned an island in the Bahamas which was used for the refueling of the airplanes carrying cocaine that then went on to the United States, that you had this island in order to provide a series of services to the drug dealers?

CL: That is what the government of United States claim, and for that is has demanded my extradition [*sic*], yes, and the territory of the Bahamas is under the jurisdiction of the government of the Bahamas, and not of the government of Colombia or of the government of the United States.

CN: But it is known that you bribed officials of the Bahamas so that they sold you this land and left it to you. . . .

CL: No, this land in the Bahamas was rented, was bought, yes, and developed for tourism. . . . The question today no longer is whether there is drug dealing or no, whether this produces a bonanza or no, or who profits from this bonanza. This bonanza is a revolutionary means of struggle against imperialism and against the monarchical oligarchy, and I would prefer to see the Colombian revolutionary movement, yes, sharing this bonanza rather than to see them kidnapping, yes, and blackmailing, and squeezing the ranches, the coffee planters and the industrialists of the country.

CN: When you speak of a bonanza, do you mean the cocaine bonanza?

CL: That is the only bonanza that has occurred.

CN: Carlos Lehder, tell me about your political ideology.

CL: I believe in a totally popular government. . . .

CN: You also believe in the ideas of Adolf Hitler.

CL: Yes. I believe in Adolf as a warrior, I admire him because for me he is the greatest warrior of all time. . . . He eliminated ten million Allies who tried to invade him, yes, and finally, yes, he eradicated the Jews. . . .

CN: And they were eliminated. . . .

CL: . . . They had attempted to kill him. But in Germany there never lived more than a million Jews, which means that the Jews died because they worked in the fields and the factories and at the end of the war there was nothing left to feed them.

CN: Carlos Lehder, why have you come back to Colombia where you intend to stay in the coming years, if they are looking for you?

CL: When I learned that they extradited [to the United States] four fellow-Colombians, I immediately returned. I have returned in order to engage in a dialogue with the commanders of the Colombian Army, with Commander Mariano Ospina of the Movement of the 19th of April [M–19], who is a Nationalist and Revolutionary. I have returned in order to speak with my Movement, the Movimiento Latino, and I have returned to participate in the great national dialogue which is about to take place either in the public square or in secret.

CN: Do you feel responsible for the massive consumption of cocaine in the world?

CL: Negative. . . .

CN: . . . why do you specifically deal with cocaine in the United States?

CL: Because cocaine is the Latin American Atom Bomb.

CN: What does that mean?

CL: That means that with the mild stimulants, because coca and marijuana are mild stimulants, and with the merchandize [*sic*] that apparently the North Americans need in order to function, yes, the Latin American revolutionary movements are being financed, and we prefer to see the Latin American revolutionaries, yes, benfiting from the bonanza or benefiting from the production of stimulants, benefiting because it is a double struggle; it is a struggle against imperialism that has come in order to poison us, to corrupt us, and it is a struggle for the dollars needed by the peoples of Latin America in order to liberate themselves and shake off the imperialist yoke forever.

Document 2: Testimony (I) of Mario Estevez Gonzales, Former Cuban DGI Agent

M ario Estevez Gonzales is a former agent of Cuban Intelligence (DGI) who infiltrated the United States during the Mariel boatlift of 1980. After he successfully penetrated and committed sabotage against an anti-Castro group, the DGI assigned Estevez to traffic in drugs. He was also involved in the Guillot case (see Document 3). In this Senate testimony, Estevez gives details of the smuggling operation and Cuba's support of this trade.

Source: This testimony of Mario Estevez is taken from the Joint Hearings before the Subcommittee on Security and Terrorism of the Committee on the Judiciary and the Subcommittee on Western Hemisphere Affairs of the Foreign Relations Committee and the Senate Drug Enforcement Caucus, *The Cuban Government's Involvement in Facilitating International Drug Traffic,* 30 April 1983.

TESTIMONY OF MARIO ESTEVEZ GONZALEZ

Ladies and gentlemen, my name is Mario Estevez Gonzalez. I was born on January 1, 1950, in the city of Havana, Republic of Cuba. . . .

From an early age, I belonged to the Communist Youth in Cuba and did my preuniversity studies. I participated in various Communist programs in which I was selected because of my dedication to Cuban communism and to the revolution of Fidel Castro. Because of my efforts in the Communist Party, I was selected to work in the Ministry of the Interior, in the BEM section, known as the Official Bureau of the Ministry. My function in the BEM was to act as a spy on others working within the system. Because of my merits, I was made a sergeant. From sergeant, I was selected to act as a spy and to sabotage anti-Castro organizations in the United States.

During the Mariel exodus, which was in 1980, I came to the United States and was able to infiltrate myself in Alpha 66, an anti-Castro organization. I was in Alpha 66 about 2½ months. My function was to sabotage equipment of the organization, and in that period of time, I was able to sink two boats which costs thousands and thousands of dollars.

After I finished my mission, I was ordered to return to Cuba. For me and for many others, who have infiltrated, it is very easy to come and go to Cuba.

The first thing that I would do would be to send a telegram to my immediate supervisors. . . . They are members of the DGI assigned to the ICAP whose head is Rene Rodriguez Cruz. After the telegram was sent. . . . I would go to Havana where my supervisors would interrogate me on my contacts, my actions and my knowledge acquired in Miami. . . . At that time [I received] instructions to make contact with drug traffickers in the United States and Bimini. My supervisors gave me $5,000 for my expenses to infiltrate.

Based on my contacts with the drug traffickers, I began to traffic in drugs about August 1980 until I was arrested on November 29, 1981, for trafficking in marihuana.

During my period as a drug trafficker, I imported to the United States more than 270 kilograms of cocaine coming from Cuba. The cocaine I would sell to individuals in Miami, Chicago, Ohio, New Jersey, New York, and other cities in the United States. The money they would pay to me for the sale of the cocaine. I had to take to Cuba and deliver it to the Cuban Government. On other occasions, I was ordered that it was "important to load up the United States with drugs."

My supervisors ordered me to return to Bimini and meet another agent of ours, who was called Frank Bonilla. When I arrived in Bimini, coming from Cuba, I found a friend of mine called Papito. Papito showed me where Frank Bonilla was. Bonilla came and greeted me, and we went to his boat, which was called the *Lazy Lady*. . . .

When we arrived in Cuba, we went directly to Paredon Grande. There we found the *Viviana,* which belongs to Jaime Guillot Lara, escorted by other armed vessels from the Cuban Navy. The *Viviana* had aboard about 8 million quaaludes.

While we were in Paredon Grande, we were interviewed by the chief of the Cuban Navy, Aldo Santamaria Cuadrado, and by Rene Rodriquez Cruz. Santamaria Cuadrado told me that his name was Rene Rodriquez Baeza or Rene Rodriquez, but I had met him previously because I had worked for him at an earlier time. *As far as Rene Rodriguez Cruz goes, there was a moment when he put his arm on my shoulder and said, we are finally going to have a drugstore in the United States. . .* [Emphasis added]

When we left Cuba, the *Viviana* towed the *Lazy Lady* to Andros in the Bahamas. There we offloaded the quaaludes from the *Viviana* and put them on the *Lazy Lady*. After we finished the quaaludes mission, I returned to Guincho Key with another boat. . . .

On Guincho Key we picked up 23,000 pounds of marihuana which had come from Cuba. The marihuana had come in one of Guillot's boats that was commanded by the very same captain of the *Viviana*.

We picked up 12,000 pounds of the 23,000 pounds of marihuana and went to Bimini, while the other boat returned to Cuba. Two or three days later, we received instructions to return to Guincho Key to pick up more marihuana. When we go there, there was another Colombian boat there, also belonging to Guillot, which had about 3 or 4 million tablets and about 11,000 pounds of marihuana on board.

The tablets were carried to other people or, rather, the tablets were taken off by other people whereas we took off the marihuana which finally reached Miami except one speedboat which was seized by the American authorities.

Ladies and gentlemen, I am glad to be able to answer any questions you may have.

Senator Hawkins: Thank you. Mr. Estevez, you arrived in Florda in the Mariel boat lift?

Estevez: Yes.

Hawkins: How were you chosen to go to Florida?

Estevez: When I was in the city of Las Villas in 1978, I was ordered to report to the city of Havana at the head office of the Ministry of the Interior.

Colonel Blanco met me there, told me that I had been selected for a special training school by the Ministry of the Interior. . . .

I was trained there for about a month and a half with guerrillas who were coming from other countries. There were men there from Peru. There were Chileans and Colombians, too.

. . . .

I was ordered to make contact with my brothers in Miami. It was a little hard for me to do that because I have been out of touch with them for years. It was not easy.

I made contact with them, though, and told them that I was sorry that I had been a Communist, and that I wanted to come to the United States and needed their help. I was supposed to go via Spain. At the end of 1979, I was told to get ready and I went to the Province of Havana.

I was in Artensia there and then, in February, I was getting ready. I was studying the codes and so on and signaling systems that I would use when I was here, in Miami. Then, at the beginning of 1980, when the Peruvian Embassy situation, I was told to get ready and then, after that, is when the Mariel operation began.

. . . .

In the school of the DGI that I was in in Soroa, all of them were pretty young fellows. All of those terrorists that Fidel Castro trains are young fellows, about 27, 28 years old . . . there were 1,500 of them there.

Hawkins: Was it thought that all of them were going to go to Florida?

Estevez: The DGI had a very broad plan for them.

Hawkins: What does that mean, they go to more countries than the United States?

Estevez: Yes. If I had not been arrested back in November, I would be in Europe or Central America right now.

Hawkins: Mr. Estevez, can you give me an estimate of how many trained agents are in the United States?

Estevez: It is hard to give an idea. There are DGI agents here in the United States. Some come with Cuban papers and a lot of them with Puerto Rican papers. The arrangements that Fidel Castro made with the ordinary, common criminals or political prisoners who were released were not the same arrangements that he was making with agents such as myself that were being trained by the Government.

Hawkins: When you got to Miami, could you tell us what sequence of events happened?
Did someone check you off the boat?

Estevez: No, it wasn't like that. It was a sort of a difficult situation. I didn't make any contact with anybody when I arrived here.

Hawkins: You just got off the boat and walked down the street, Biscayne Boulevard?

Estevez: No. No. No. No. When I got off the boat, I went on to Arkansas. In Arkansas, there were plenty of other guys that had been trained like me. I saw them there. . . .

Hawkins: This was the camp that was set up for the Marielitos in Arkansas?

Hawkins: Did the officials, U.S. officials, ask you your background?

Estevez: Sure, they asked me, but those questions are so easy that anybody can infiltrate. . . .

Hawkins: Have you ever gotten any money from the American Government as a Marielito who is eligible for Federal help?

Estevez: No, I never received any aid from the Government. I always had money from the time I arrived.

Hawkins: Where did you get it?

Estevez: Money from the Cuban Government.

Hawkins: Did they mail it to you at the post office box or____

Estevez: Fourteen days after I arrived here, I was back in Cuba. . . . I went back in a boat. . . . The boat belonged to the Alpha 66 [anti-Castro group], and since I had the boat. . . . I just went.

Hawkins: How did you get back to America?

Estevez: Easy, just the same way I went to Cuba. . . . I brought drugs over in October and in January 1981.

Hawkins: Oh. So, 14 days after you arrived in the United States, you were back in Cuba?

Estevez: Sure.

Hawkins: How many times had you gone back and forth?

Estevez: I would go every month, two or three times.

Hawkins: And when you would come back to the United States, did anybody check any of your documents or ask for any identification?

Estevez: This is a very free country. They don't ask you for anything here.

Hawkins: I am beginning to see why we have so many problems.

Estevez: That is right.

Hawkins: So, you get your money, I know——you say you always have Cuban money?

Estevez: Yes, I always had money.

Hawkins: And you get it from Cuba?

Estevez: Sure . . . I had to go to Cuba in my case to report on my espionage activities. My situation wasn't the same as that of other agents who were here.
    They get checks from the Cuban Government that come to them through businesses that are established here, that are controlled by the Cuban Government.

Hawkins: In the United States?

Estevez: Sure.

Hawkins: How much money did they pay, Mr. Estevez?

Estevez: Every time I went, I would get $5,000 or $7,000 more or less.

    .   .   .   .

Hawkins: We have received considerable testimony that drugs produced in South America are being smuggled through Cuba to the United States. To your knowledge, could Cuba produce drugs which they later sent to the United States?

Estevez: Yes, Cuba does produce drugs, not cocaine, but they produce marihuana.

Hawkins: Have you seen the fields?

Estevez: Sure.

Hawkins: Could you show us on the map where the marihuana fields are?

Estevez: Sure, I can.

Hawkins: Would the marshal lead you over? [The witness indicated on the map.]

Senator DeConcini: Can you identify this area?

Estevez: Manzanillo area.

DeConcini: Is Manzanillo the only area?

Estevez: That is the only area that I know about, that I saw.

DeConcini: How big is that area?

Estevez: It is a very extensive area and the marihuana is as good as the Hawaiian variety. . . .

DeConcini: Does the government operate cultivation and protection of the product?

Estevez: Yes, the DGI has that in its charge.

DeConcini: Does the DGI have any other areas in Cuba?

Estevez: Yes. When I was working in the Ministry of the Interior in Villa Clara Province, I heard them talk about marihuana plantations in the Escambrai Mountain area.

DeConcini: Where is the Escambrai Mountain area? [The witness indicated on the map.]

DeConcini: How long has the DGI been involved in this sort of activity?

Estevez: I was working there in 1975, 1976, and 1977. I was chief of information there and I was chief of recruitment and information in the BEM department, and then, when they transferred me back to Havana, I was told not to be concerned any further with that matter, that that was under the DGI.

DeConcini: Do you know whether the DGI had been in the production of marihuana for a long period of time before 1976?

Estevez: Fidel has been planning on this for a long time. The Soviet Union has been involved. This goes back to Vietnam days.

DeConcini: Do you have any dollar value estimate of the export of the marihuana?

Estevez: About $200 million.

DeConcini: A year?

Estevez: No, I don't know whether that would be each year, but they get a lot of marihuana that they seize from others in Cuba.

The guerrillas pay in cocaine for their training. The Colombian guerrillas, the El Salvadoran guerrillas, and the cocaine that they seize from ships that they get, all of that comes up here to the United States. [Emphasis added]

DeConcini: Do they export to any place other than to the United States?

Estevez: Yes, to Canada.

DeConcini: And other countries?

Estevez: Other countries, I don't know, but I know about Canada. I was in Canada.

. . . .

Senator Denton: I would like to ask you what reasons were given you by the DGI for the Cuban Government's interest in the drug traffic? Was it principally for profit for the Cuban Government or was it principally for what you might call destabilization within the United States or other countries or a mixture?

Estevez: In all of this, the Soviet Union is involved. Since Fidel Castro took over the chairmanship of the nonaligned countries, they have tried, through the Soviet Union, to undermine the United States in the eyes of the world, just like the Soviets did in Vietnam where they undermined the prestige of the United States and another one of their operations there was the heroin for the United States forces.

After that, Fidel Castro took advantage of that Peruvian Embassy situation and the Mariel exodus situation. That had been planned for years. You can be sure that that did not just happen. A lot of people seem to think that Fidel made a slipup with that Peruvian Embassy situation. If Fidel Castro wanted, you would not have found four people inside that embassy.

This business of the narcotics traffic to the United States is a top secret one in Cuba. The only ones who know about it are the DGI agents and Fidel Castro, in particular.

I can tell you one thing, that no Cuban soldier would allow Fidel Castro to traffic in drugs because one thing I can tell you about our country is that Cubans hate drugs.

One of the reasons for this drug traffic with the United States is to throw the United States off in Central America and this big operation of drugs coming up to Miami is part of that. They are trying to create an atmosphere of crisis in the Southern United States and then throw you off and work up in the northern areas bringing equipment and medical equipment and supplies and other stuff through Panama and electronic equipment through Panama.

Lots of those arms that are sent to El Salvador and other places are American arms.

Denton: Yes. Mostly captured in Vietnam.

Estevez: Yes.

Denton: And some of the arms there are 23 millimeter, very modern Soviet arms in Nicaragua.

Estevez: Yes, I can tell you something about Nicaragua because I have relatives there, and I met lots of Nicaraguans who were training in my country, although during our training, we were forbidden to speak to each other about our training and missions. We had to talk about the weather and just topics in general to each other.

They received stricter training than we did, and they were trained by Russians. . . .

We receive a lot of political information and political orientation training. That is why when we are sent on foreign missions, we go in blind obedience.

We do what we are told, and it doesn't matter what the means. If we have to kill a member of our own family to accomplish the mission, we do it. . . .

Denton: I am most interested to learn that the drug traffic activity destabilization which they tried to bring about by this drug introduction began and goes back to Vietnam and the Soviet efforts to get heroin introduced into the United States via our troops. I am interested to hear you say that this is a secret action which is known only by the DGI members, and that even Cuban Communist soldiers would oppose that.

Do I have that correct?

Estevez: Yes.

Denton: What was your own personal interest over the past few years, personal profit or service to the DGI in terms of its infiltration and espionage regarding counterespionage, counterintelligence activities; about 50–50?

Estevez: No. No. No. I was born under the revolution. Since I have been 11, I have been familiar with guns.

.   .   .   .

You are relating to this matter of the terrorism which you have mentioned. When, in my country, the people seem to be getting a little upset or excited with events, such as in 1978, they burned a children's training institution. The Cuban Government itself rigged that and then, the government comes out and Fidel Castro says, that is the imperialists and the Americans who came in here and burned down our children's training school. But until 1981, I was a good Communist and a good revolutionary.

.   .   .   .

DeConcini: What is your estimate as to how many Cuban agents came over to this country during the period of time when there was the great exportation? Even though it may be an estimate, can you give us some idea?

Estevez: Yes. I could give you a more or less good idea because I was the head of the information and recruitment for the BEM, and I would receive reports on this. Besides that, I was in those three training schools at Soroa and . . . near Havana, and the other in Matanzas.

Here, in the United States, you have different kinds of spies, propaganda spies, you have economic spies, terrorist spies, and spies that are being trained for operations in Europe. Now, I am speaking of these as these are sort of special categories, not just those that are in the armed forces; but those that are in the Ministry of the Interior.

I think there has got to be something around 3,000 or over 3,000, and among those political prisoners, also there are spies. Then, you also have those common criminals and there were also lots of them who had been in Angola previously, and they were sent over here in groups of 20 and 40. Their mission would be that if there were ever any kind of trouble with Cuba or war with Cuba to create chaos here, in the United States.

DeConcini: That estimation is well in excess of 3,000 in the various categories.

Estevez: I think about 7,000.

DeConcini: To your knowledge, do those agents report periodically and under a certain agenda back to the mother country?

Estevez: I don't know how that is now.

There are certainly quite a few just like me here, who report every so often. They work this way: sometimes you have those that are going back north to Cuba, and each one of them is in charge of, say, 10 or 12 others. . . . There is one overall head or chief operative but the others don't know each other. They are all interconnected without knowing who the others are.

DeConcini: Did you have a group? Were you the chief of a group?

Estevez: No. When I started out in the drug traffic, I did meet some others that I thought were like that, but at that time, I only had a couple who were working directly for me. One of them even met my supervisor in October 1981.

DeConcini: You mentioned that the soldiers in the military in Cuba would not accept their government's involvement in the drug production or trafficking or export. Is that true of the general public? I assume it is.

Estevez: That is so very true. . . .

DeConcini: Do the military and the general public know of the Government's involvement in marihuana and other drug trafficking?

Estevez: The Cuban people cannot believe the involvement of the Government.

DeConcini: The Cuban military and the people?

Estevez: Both the military and the Cuban people.

DeConcini: Is it kept quiet through censure and nondisclosure?

Estevez: You never hear anything about it there. If a radio station from the United States could get through to Cuba with that information, I don't think that the Castro government would last a year. That, I can tell you for sure.

I was told that if any type of radio transmitter station such as Radio Marti was set up here, that it would have to be urgently destroyed.

DeConcini: In your opinion, would another revolution occur if the Cuban people, even the military people, many of whom are members of the Communist Party, knew that their government is involved in the massive drug production and exportation?

Estevez: Certainly, there would be another revolution. Both the Cuban people and the military forces in Cuba, which are part of the Ministry of the Interior, just as in the case of me, personally, I used to have under my supervision members of the armed forces and members of the party, too, everyone is being checked and watched.

.   .   .   .

Mr. Manion: In your testimony about drugs going from Cuba to the United States, you mentioned drugs seized by Cuba that went into that supply that Cuba then sent northward. From whom were these drugs seized?

Estevez: The ones that don't have the contacts made with the government. The ones that are not doing it with Fidel.

Manion: A recent visit to Cuba by a colleague of mine on the staff of the Foreign Relations Committee included a lunch with a high official of the Cuban Government. That high official said that Cuba was very hard on drug smugglers, and that there were Americans in Cuban jails to prove that.

From your experience, would you say that that high official was telling the truth?

Estevez: Yes, I think I can say that there are cases when Americans do go with drugs to Cuba. There are others, of course, who do not.

Manion: So, your point is that if they don't cooperate with Castro's operation, Castro will be very hard on drug smugglers?

Estevez: Castro, of course, seizes the drugs and arrests them, too. The ones that they are dealing with, though, don't have any problem at all.

Manion: You testified, earlier, that you had taken cocaine to the United States and had taken cash back to Cuba—or, rather, had taken money back to Cuba.

Was that in cash or was that in negotiable instruments?

Estevez: I would carry cash and also I would take back armaments and equipment of various kinds.

Manion: I see. Does some of the Cuban drug money stay here, in the United States, perhaps, to finance the DGI network of thousands of agents that you have described?

Estevez: To finance all of the DGI agents here, in the United States, is no problem at all. They have all kinds of businesses operating here. They even have banks.

Manion: To your knowledge, were any Cuban DGI agents trained to aid the guerrilla effort in El Salvador?

Estevez: Well, Colonel Blanco is one of them.

Manion: Was he trained and sent to El Salvador?

Estevez: No, it is that—Colonel Blanco is in charge of training of agents and of guerrillas, and then, they send them to El Salvador. . . .

For more on Cuban training of Salvadorian "rebels," see the interview with Miguel Bolaños Hunter, former Sandinista counter-intelligence officer, chapter 2, Document 2.

Document 3: Testimony (II) of Mario Estevez Gonzales, Former Cuban DGI Agent

I n this Senate testimony Estevez confirms that Cuban Intelligence (DGI) agents infiltrated the United States during the 1980 Mariel boatlift; he provides the number of DGI agents and details how many of these were specifically assigned to the drug trade. Estevez also gives evidence of the profitability of Cuba's involvement in this trade through his estimation of the cash flow for which he was personally responsible.

Source: This testimony of Mario Estevez Gonzales is from Hearings by the Senate Select Committee on Crime, *Narcotics Production and Trafficking by the Cuban Intelligence Service (D.G.I.)*, 14 April 1983.

Senator D'Amato: In 1980, Fidel Castro sent over 125,000 Cubans to the U.S. Most of these Cubans were good, decent people who merely wished to escape the tyranny. However, as many as 25,000 to 30,000 Cubans, who are known as "Marielitos," were hardened criminals. They were dumped out of Cuba by Castro, out of the prison system; and among these 25,000 to 35,000 there were up to 3,000 agents. It has been said by some that they make our criminals and our thugs on the streets look like Sunday school students.

Even more shocking is the recent disclosure that the network in this country is a very comprehensive network with the 3,000 agents who are facilitating the trafficking of drugs. We have as our first witness this morning an individual who has testified to the Cuban connection in U.S. drug traffic. Further, the U.S. Attorney's Office in southern Florida has indicated that the testimony we are about to hear has been independently corroborated by other sources. . . .

How many other agents were you aware of [assigned to the drug trade]?

Mr. Estevez: While I was training there were specific orders that no one was to engage in any conversation as far as mission being trained. However, there were people being trained. As far as agents of the Cuban government right now, working in the United States with the drug trafficking, I have informed the drug enforcement agency of the United States of approximately

400 agents specifically in drugs. I also have provided to the United States Government the names of a lot of those agents. At the same time, as far as agents going back and forth to Cuba and bringing drugs in to this country, very specifically one or two at a time. For example, last week, an agent friend of mine got ordered to return to Cuba; and at this time he is in Cuba receiving new orders for a new shipment into the States. That information has been passed onto the U.S. Government.

D'Amato: Did there come a time when you were finally able to successfully get drugs into this country and what, if anything, did you do with the proceeds? How much did you derive? And what did you do with the funds?

Estevez: On February 1, I received orders to go to Cayo Coco, which is the northern part of Varadero Beach close to Havana, Cuba. Here I met the Cuban official, I was transported to Havana. At that time, I arranged to receive 75 kilos of cocaine. I delivered the 75 kilos of cocaine to Miami. I received $1,250,000 American money, and that money was returned to Cuba.

D'Amato: In other words, upon the consummation of the sale you received $1,250,000. You then took that money and brought it back to Cuba. How long between the sale and your going back to Cuba with the money did you take?

Estevez: The whole transaction took approximately 30 days, by the time I came to the shores of the United States, made delivery, the money handed down and returned back.

D'Amato: How much money did you, and over what period of time, raise by sale of drugs—cocaine, Quaaludes, marijuana—and how much did you turn back to the Cuban government?

Estevez: From the period of '81 to '82, I feel that I was approximately responsible for $7 million from drugs returning to the Cuban government by trafficking back and forth.

D'Amato: You turned over $7 million in money to the Cuban government?

Estevez: Right . . . I was equipped with a special boat. I think we call them Cigarette Boats, speed boats. They usually have a V-8 automobile engine in them, and they are racing boats. The boats are made out of fiberglass. Some of them carry two engines. For example, my boat had two 427 cubic inch engines. They're made out of specific material in the bottom, where two pipes are formed at the time you make the boat; and each of these pipes has a cap at the end which is threaded with a cap and seal. That is where the cocaine is deposited at the bottom of the boat. The boat has a capacity of 285 gallons of fuel. It will take approximately——at the speed of 70 to 75 miles per hour, approximately two hours from Paredon Grande, which is the northern part of Varadero, to the Keys in the U.S. So basically——most of the time, that is the way I went back and forth to Cuba, using the speedboat. . . . I estimate that during the period '81–'82 I traveled two to three times a month back and forth to Cuba from the Miami area. The money was turned to a code name Lieutenant Colonel Carlos, who was a subordinate of the chief of ICAP, which is an agency, an internal agency such as HUD in the United States, Urban Development, and the name of the person who was in charge of this thing was Rene Rodriguez-Cruz, who was the chief of operations for this whole connection, if you want to call it that.

D'Amato: What was Mr. Cruz' official position?

Estevez: He was probably equal to Minister of ICAP. . . .

.   .   .   .

Senator Bernstein: Who in the Cuban government set the price at which drugs were to be sold per kilo?

Estevez: It doesn't matter what moves in Cuba or takes place in Cuba, nothing gets done in Cuba unless it has the blessings and the price set by Fidel Castro himself. . . .

For example, the kilo of cocaine was set to be sold $38,000 minimum, $40,000 maximum per kilo. Now, I would sell that one in Miami for $47,000 a kilo. The $7,000 difference between $40,000 and $47,000 my pocket money.

D'Amato: The only thing we can specify—because I think that begins to get speculative—is the fact, though, that this one agent in a period of a year accounted for $7 million in cash that he personally turned over to the Interior Minister and/or his—or the Minister of Housing and/or his deputies in direct line of responsibility. In addition, when one considers the fact that he estimates that 300 to 400 agents—and I think he is very responsible in not attempting to inflate that number—300 to 400 of the 3,000 agents were assigned to the task of smuggling in drugs and were similarly turning in their proceeds to the Cuban government, then we see a pervasive, systematic movement brought about by the Cuban government to destabilize, to raise funds, to create mayhem in our cities throughout this nation; and they have been quite successful in undertaking this. The fact of the matter is that here's not a person who's selling drugs for profit but that he had spent two years infiltrating groups, bringing about terrorists attacks, infiltrating Alpha 66. We're hearing from a person who's turned state's evidence to save himself who was an actual operative agent of the Cuban government.

Now, you have indicated before, this testimony has been corroborated by independent sources; that is not his own testimony. We find him an absolutely creditable witness, and someone who we owe a great deal of gratitude to. Now, I don't know how successful the other agents were; but given the fact that there were 400 agents and if they approached anywheres near his success, we are talking about $2,800,000,000 that would have flowed to Cuba. That is an incredible thing. . . .

Documents 4 and 5: Testimonies of Former Smugglers Crump and Perez

J ohnny Crump and David Perez are former drug smugglers who were involved in the Jaime Guillot Lara case, in which Cuba supported Guillot's operation in exchange for both a fee and Guillot's services in running arms back to the M–19 terrorist group in Colombia.

Source: Both testimonies are from the Joint Congressional Hearings, *The Cuban Government's Involvement in Facilitating International Drug Traffic,* 30 April 1983.

Document 4

TESTIMONY OF JOHNNY CRUMP

Mr. Crump: . . . In the end of 1975, after Colombia beginning again diplomatic relations with Cuba, I met the Cuban Diplomatic Fernando Ravelo Renedo, Ambassador, and his First Secretary, Gonzalo Bassols Suarez.

In 1979, when I move with my family from Barranquilla to the capital, Bogotá, our relationship was more closely. At this time, they know that I was involved in the narco traffic, but was in the eighties when we talk about use Cuba like an overstop for the drugs to the United States. In this meeting was Jaime Guillot Lara, which they know that day between me.

Between the paying $700,000, the dream of any narco traffickers to have a point at 90 miles from Florida will be true. In August of that year, . . . we send the first boat.

One week later, I flew to Cuba with Ravelo. . . .

During this time, Ravelo and Norberto de la Osa, former Cuban Ambassador in Venezuela, which I met in this time, they confirm me that the *Viviana,* the boat, had the security of the Cuban Navy all the time that was necessary. When we was again in Colombia, Jaime beginning to fix another boat that was sent in the end of the 1980, November, October. The boat was seized by the Cuban Navy and taken to Havana. Then they asked between telex to Ravelo if the boat was in the deal that we made. Then, as soon as

Ravelo give the green light, they full up the boat with fuel and food and the Navy, the Cuban Navy, go to the boat to the point where they was supposed to meet with me—Jaime's friend to pick up the marihuana. In this time was 30,000 pounds of marihuana.

Later, that Ravelo and the commander, Rodriguez Cruz, which I meet in the beginning of the 1980, and I meet again in Cuba when I was in Cuba, they talk to me the possibility of buy and send to Chile between Panama weapons for some people that was against General Pinochet.

A week later, one of the supposedly Chileans that his name was Dr. Galvan give to me a microfilm in a cigarette that contained a list of weapons, food, and ammunition for 300 men. In way to buy the weapons and fix boats and everything to send that merchandise to Chile, I flew to Miami to try to collect some money for my business, drug business, and, according to Jaime to try to collect the money his connection owed to him.

In the beginning of 1981, when I was in Miami, the Colombian Army detect and destroy a group of guerrillos or guerrilleros that tried to go into Colombia in the south of the country through the Pacific coast. Casually, the same area where the Comandante Rodriguez Cruz asked me to go with him in a boat in the end of the 1980.

The commander of this group of guerrilleros was the Dr. Toledo Plata, one of the leaders of the M–19, and Rosenberg Pabon Pabon, commander one of the group that took the Dominican Embassy in Bogotá and after that flew to Cuba.

At the same time, in the same Pacific coast, but at the north of the country, the army find another guerrilla, group of guerrilleros at the commander of Carmenea Cardona Lachiqui that was the guerrilla dealing from the M–19 group during the 2 months that take the Dominican Embassy affair that supposedly was in Cuba and——not supposedly, he flew to Cuba with Ravelo, the diplomatic and the M–19 people.

One of the guerrilleros give the testimony that he was in Cuba all this time, and after that, they fly to Panama and from Panama they took the boat named *Freddie* to Colombia. Colombia broke the diplomatic relations with Cuba, and then, from Panama, after the broke of the diplomatic relations, Bassols, with Jaime call me to Miami.

Then, again, the Chilean, Dr. Galvan, ask me about if I remember the microfilm. At this time, the Dr. Galvan, name was Mariano, they asked me to try to find——to buy the weapons here, in the United States and send it in planes that will be in Colombia to take drugs from Colombia, but at the same time, Jaime, with some money that the M–19 give to him, send a boat with 40,000 pounds of marihuana. The boat, again, named *Viviana,* was sent to Cuba for some people in New York. The people asked to Jaime that make an appointment in a point between Cuba and New York, but when the boat was in front of North Carolina was taken for the American Coast Guard and taken to Charlotte. . . .

. . . .

In 1981 and 1982 I was arresting with the charge of narco traffic. From the FCI, they send me to the North Detention Center. The newspaper talk to me first about my relation with Cuba and Jaime Guillot, and, later, when I made a decision to collaborate with the North American Government, again the paper talk this, about my decision.

Then, when I was in this jail, a Cuban named Mario Estevez talked with me in the jail and said that he was a sergeant from the DGI, Cuban Secret Police, but that he was interested in deserting. Estevez was present in two or three boats that Jaime sent with marihuana and quaaludes to Cuba. He was one of the in-charge with David Perez . . . Jaime's connection in Maimi to bring the drug from Cuba to the United States. . . .

Senator Hawkins: Mr. Crump, we have a collection of photos that we are going to show on the screen, and we would like you to identify them, please, as we project them.

Crump: The person in the middle is myself. Then on my left is Fernando Ravelo Renedo, the Cuban Ambassador, and on my right is Gonzalo Bassols, his first secretary————

Senator Denton: Madam Chairman, may I clarify?
Was that the witness with the two aforementioned high-ranking Cuban officials?

Hawkins: Yes. . . .

Crump: On your right is Jaime Guillot Lara. I don't know the person on the left.
[The photographs on the screen were changed.]

Crump: That is two pictures taken at the baptism of my daughter. Viviana. In the center of the picture, on my left, is Ambassador Fernando Ravelo Renedo and his wife.

Denton: May I ask a question, Madam Chairman?

Hawkins: Yes.

Denton: Is that the Cuban Ambassador to Colombia?

Crump: Right.
[The photograph on the screen was changed.]

Crump: That is the commmander, Rene Rodriguez Cruz, president of the ICAP. . . .

Hawkins: Thank you. Those are all the photos we have. You may be seated again, Mr. Crump.

You stated the name of the four Cuban officials that were indicted during the *Jaime Guillot* case and your relationship with them. In your opinion, were their actions isolated acts by individual corrupt Cuban officials, or do you feel that there could have been or that it was the action of the Cuban Government?

Crump: For sure that was action of the Cuban Government. . . . I meet Ravelo for 5 years before, and he was doing that because it was his ideology. In his way, he was an honest——he is an honest man in his way, I believe, and I am sure that he never do something to or for his own benefit, first, and, second, it is impossible in a country like Cuba that you can do all these things. . . .

That means that the Cuban Government was involved in the thing. That was not a personal——was not Ravelo or Bassols or somebody personal that was involved in the business. That was the Cuban Government that was involved.

Hawkins: What was the goal of the Government of Cuba in promoting drug trafficking to the United States?

Crump: I believe—I don't believe that was make money. I believe that was try to hurt in any way the United States.

Hawkins: Who told you that?

Crump: In the beginning, when we beginning to talk, Jaime said that he wants to leave clear that if the business will be OK, we pay the amount of $700,000, but if we lose the merchandise, then we cannot pay the amount. Then they say, Ravelo and Bassols, that, don't worry, that they can wait, and they don't care about the money——OK?——that——because his goal was hurt the United States full with drugs. . . .

. . . .

Denton: As I understand it, Mr. Crump, it was in November 1979, in a joking fashion that the question first came up about Cuba being used as a stopover for narcotics shipment to the United States.

Crump: Yes, sir.

Denton: It was then later, in July 1980, that you were in Bogota and you asked your friend, Ravelo, the Cuban Ambassador to Colombia about this matter again, and Ravelo sent a telex to Havana requesting——well, you asked him for information about the release of a man named Masters, who had been incarcerated by the Cubans for drug trafficking, and Ravelo sent a telex to Havana requesting information about that gentleman and received, in return, a complete list of United States and Colombian citizens in jail in Cuba on narcotics charges. Also, on that list was the name of the boat *El Bravo* and Ravelo showed you the whole list and asked if you knew anyone on it.

Ravelo told you that for a price, certain individuals might be freed by the Cuban Government.

May I ask, was that telex which was used for that communication and others later, was that telex the official telex in the Cuban Embassy in Colombia?

Crump: Yes, sir. All the times that we talk about this business was in my home or in Bassols' apartment, Ravelo's apartment, and the communication that they made was from the Cuban Embassy in Bogotá.

Denton: Thank you, sir.

You, then, have indicated that, in the meantime, Jaime Guillot Lara arrived in Bogotá and that Ravelo told Guillot and yourself that Ravelo remembered the conversation about Cuba being used possibly as a stopover point for the drug trade, and he said, Ravelo did, that if you all were serious about this issue, he would have to get permission from his superiors by telex before he could answer. Then Ravelo used the same telex, I presume, and I see you nodding in the affirmative, and he got an answer from Havana which was in the affirmative. You have also indicated that you think that Ravelo was such a man that he would not fake such an incident, that he, indeed, would have, according to your knowledge of his nature, been telling the truth when he said that he sent the telex to Havana and got the response.

Would you give the approximate date of that?

I am interested in the date, if you can recall it, when Ravelo sent and received the information which more or less officially made or gave the assent for Cuba being the stopover point.

What is the date of that telex?

Crump: That is impossible to remember, sir, but anyway, it was between March to July 1980, but the exact day right now, for me, is impossible to remember.

. . . .

Senator Helms: . . . When did you get into the drug business?

Crump: 1975, 1976.

Helms: You don't recall precisely, 1975 or 1976? All right. What drugs did you deal in, primarily?

Crump: Marihuana.

Helms: Marihuana?

Crump: Right.

Helms: Anything else?

Crump: I believe that one or two times quaaludes, methaqualone, quaa-ludes————

Hawkins: Quaaludes.

Helms: No cocaine?

Crump: Yes, sir, but not directly, myself. I mean, I help to make one business of cocaine, but I was not directly involved like in the marihuana business. That means that the marihuana, I go to the field, buy the marihuana and do all the things. . . .

The thing is that, like I say in my statement, . . . [to have] a point, like Cuba, 90 miles from Florida, as a secure point, that means that a complete government is behind you, is a dream. I mean, it is something that you cannot find in any country, even in Bahamas. . . .

Helms: But it is your impression that Cuban embassies are used, I am asking only for your own knowledge, based on your experience, would lead you to believe that they are using the embassies for that function?

Crump: Yes, sir.

Helms: And you have no doubt about Cuban agents in the region participating?

Crump: No, sir, I am sure. . . .

Senator DeConcini: When you bought your marihuana, did you take it upon yourself to see that it was shipped out of the country?

Crump: Sometimes I was present.

DeConcini: How did you generally ship it?

Crump: Ninety percent I send it in planes.

DeConcini: In planes, and those planes were destined for where? Did you know where they were going to go?

Crump: To here.

DeConcini: What parts of the United States?

Crump: Florida.

DeConcini: To Florida, primarily?

Crump: Yes.

DeConcini: Were those planes operated by Colombian pilots, American pilots, or a combination, or do you recall?

Crump: No; American pilots.

DeConcini: American pilots. Were they American airplanes?

Crump: Yes; American airplanes. . . .

. . . .

Hawkins: Mr. Crump, do you see the map on the wall over there? If you would, stand by it. The marshall will help you over there.

Would you show us the routes that you used, the ports you used while you were in this business?

Crump: Normally, we dealing in this part of Colombia [indicating], which is Guajira, here, in about, I would say, 100 fields that can take it from Aero Commander to DC–6 planes. That means from 1,000 meters to 2,000 or 3,000 meters long, the field.

The planes normally fly to Florida. They could not fly over Cuba, but one time when we began the conversation with the Cuban Ambassador, he agreed with me that we can use Camaguey to landing and refuel the plane and that way can go into the United States, not Florida, but we never use it. Was only a conversation. We never do that.

Normally, the plane flying this way [indicating] or this way [indicating] to Florida.

In the boat, the boat coming to this part [indicating Yucatan Straits] of——between Mexico and Cuba from 2 years, 3 years ago, they have to change it because the Coast Guard, the American Coast Guard block this——

Hawkins: The Coast Guard blocked it?

Crump: The North American Coast Guard blocked——

Hawkins: The American Coast Guard blocked it.

Crump: The Yucatan Straits, I believe. Then they go this way [indicating] or this way [indicating]. Now, this way [indicating] is again blocked by the North American Coast Guard, OK? The boat that we sent it through Cuba go to here, Sagua la Grande [indicating] and Cayo Paredon Grande [indicating] and then, I believe that you have to here [indicating]. Then, from there the people from Miami that were supposed to pick up the drug in Paredon Grande, they stay in Cayo Guincho in the Bahamas and from there they coming here, to Florida.

Hawkins: It goes from Cuba to the——

Crump: Bahamas——

Hawkins: [continuing] Bahamas——

Crump: [continuing] And from there——

Hawkins: [continuing] Into Florida?

Crump: Florida.

Hawkins: Thank you very much, Mr. Crump.

Document 5

TESTIMONY OF DAVID LORENZO PEREZ, JR.

Mr. Perez: In or about July 1980, Jaime Guillot Lara, a Colombian national, make contact . . . at my home. At this time, I spoke briefly to Jaime Guillot Lara. He was interested in whether or not I could supply him with an airplane to be picked up so that I could pick him up from Nassau and bring him into Miami. I told him that I had a pilot, a black pilot, in Nassau, with a Cessna 414, that if he could find it, he would be able to bring it. . . .

Soon thereafter, Jaime Guillot Lara did come to Miami, where I met him. . . . At this time, Jaime Guillot Lara told me that he could get drugs into Cuba easily because he was paying money to the Cuban Government for their protection. He even mentioned Paredon Grande, which lies in Cuban territory.

At another meeting within a short period, Alberto Cortez was brought into the plan by myself because Cortez had the ability to locate a reliable boat captain. Cortez, in turn, brought in Jose Luis Martinez . . . [who] was to be paid $150,000 for acting as boat captain.

Since Jaime did not have the money to finance the planned conspiracy, I went to Carlos for funding: approximately $40,000 to $50,000 for the purchase of necessary vessels.

Soon after the second meeting, Jaime Guillot Lara returned to Colombia and left the code words "the family has left" in order to give rise to the conspiracy.

Once Jose Luis Martinez became aware of the Cuban Government's involvement, due to his navigational experience, he indicated that the best route to take for this conspiracy was for the vessels to travel from Miami to Bimini to Williams Key to Andros Island and into Guincho Key, right across Cuban waters. . . .

In order to properly signal the Cuban Government, Jaime Guillot Lara had told me to lower the American flag aboard the ship and to fly a white flag with the Cuban flag. I was led into Paredon Grande by a Cuban boat and a Cuban gun boat.

After a lengthy period of time, two Cuban officials, Aldo Santamaria Cuadrado and another, came looking for David Perez by name. I was escorted to a large Cuban ship where I met Rene Cruz. . . .

Rene Cruz asked if we needed anything on board, as he knew what we were waiting for. Rene Cruz provided us with a mechanic to look at our boat engine even though they were not accustomed to working on American engines. Rene Cruz became quite taken by American outboard motors and asked me if I could possibly obtain 50 to 75 motors for the Cuban Government, preferably Johnsons or Mercury, and also batteries for automobiles and boats. . . .

. . . .

The quaaludes were loaded from one boat to the other. . . . There were 426 boxes, each holding 25,000 to 30,000 tablets, as a cost of 10 cents apiece. There was no money exchanged at this point.

I did not leave with the quaaludes but stayed in the area because Jaime Guillot Lara made radio contact with me and told me a marihuana load was en route with an approximate value of $5 million.

Due to a Coast Guard sighting, the crew of the *Lazy Lady* dumped the quaaludes in the open sea and met with another ship loaded with marihuana and arranged for the marihuana to be taken to a farm in Homestead, Fla., where it was to be safeguarded by Richard DeLeon.

Soon thereafter, Jaime Guillot Lara made contact with me and told me that Cuban friends wanted their share of the money even though they had been lost.

When I told Jaime Guillot Lara that he could not obtain any funds to pay the Cubans other than piecemeal through the sale of marihuana, Jaime Guillot Lara told me that they could work off the owed money by carrying guns to South America's rebels and that the Cuban friends wanted me to act as their courier. . . .

In order to sweeten the take, Jaime Guillot Lara told me that I could always go to live either in Cuba or in Brazil, and that if matters ever really got hot, that Jaime Guillot Lara would be set up in Barradero Beach in Cuba.

The Cuban Government was also to receive one-third of the profit of the marihuana sale. However, there was no profit, and, to date, the Cuban Government has not been paid even though Jaime Guillot Lara did receive $450,000, which he was to use for payment to the Cuban Government. . . .

Senator Hawkins: . . . Mr. Perez, it is my understanding that your role in the Cuban connection is probably to smuggle drugs into the United States.

What Cuban ports did you use and what routes did you take, would you show us or tell us? . . .

Mr. Perez: OK. We would leave from Miami into Bimini, from Bimini we would come here, to Williams Key, right around this area. Then we would take this course over here . . . to Guincho Key and to Paredon Grande. . . .

Paredon Grande is a port in Cuba. . . .

Hawkins: You may come back to the table.

What Cuban officials did you meet with while you were on Paredon Grande?

Perez: Rene Cruz, ma'am, and Aldo Santamaria Cuadrado.

Hawkins: What did they tell you?

Perez: We talked for a long time. Rene Cruz, especially, was really actually doing most of the talking, and he told me I could have anything I wanted. It was——the impression was they knew my name when I got there. They were expecting me, and he told me so, that they were expecting me.

The Colombian boat, which was the *Viviana,* that was already there when I arrived in Cuba, he told me that——if that boat was what I was looking for, and I told him, yes, the boat was what I was looking for, and we discussed the thing that what I could have was, like mechanics, if I needed mechanics. He put a mechanic aboard the *Lazy Lady* to try to fix one of the engines and give us food, and he was going to give us some fuel. . . .

. . . .

One of the things he specifically said during our conversations was if they could take over Florida, that the Cuban Government was happy that we were bringing all the drugs into the United States.

Hawkins: It is my understanding that while there, there were two . . . gun boats present while you were at Cayo Paredon Grande. . . .

Perez: As we were going in, into Cayo Paredon Grande, the boats came to our side and escorted us into the bay. . . .

Hawkins: . . . Are you aware of others that are in that business who use the Cuban connection to smuggle drugs into the United States?

Perez: After I came back, ma'am, I told another one of Jaime's connections about where I had been, and what had happened, and he told me that he had been approached, and that he was in a meeting with Cuban officials here, in Miami, but that he refused to do it because, I guess, that, he told me if they approached him with the weapon situation at first, which I never knew until later on that I was to be carrying weapons down to Cuba for the leftists in Central and South America. . . .

. . . .

Senator Denton: According to your testimony, Jaime Guillot Lara told you that he could get drugs into Cuba easily because "he was paying money to the Cuban Government for their protection."

Perez: Yes, sir. As a matter of fact, we had several meetings about it because I was kind of reluctant, at first, since I am of Cuban nationality, and I left Cuba even though I was young, but my father was against the Communists and I was kind of reluctant about it, about going into Cuba or doing any kind of deals with the Cubans and he told me there was nothing to it, not to worry about it, that the Cubans would take care of us, and there was no problem on political things or anything like that which the reason he did not tell me the whole story was because, I guess, he knew I was going to back out of it once I learned about the weapons' trade and the whole situation became clear. . . .

Denton: Do you have any doubt, considering the scope, location, and nature of these maritime illegal drug activites on the northern coast of Cuba, that they could have taken place without the knowledge of the highest level of the Cuban Government?

Perez: There is no doubt in my mind, sir, that the whole Cuban Government is very aware of what they are doing because during our conversation, one statement that Rene Cruz made to myself was, Fidel Castro himself was out in Central and South America doing all the kind of work related to what we were doing there, and that they were happy that we were bringing the drugs into the country and one specific statement that he made, and he was pretty serious about it, was that they could take Florida at any time that they felt.

Hawkins: "They" is who?

Perez: The Cuban Government.

Hawkins: The Cuban Government could take Florida at any time?

Perez: Yes, ma'am.

Denton: Could you elaborate on what you mean by "Castro was conducting other operations like this in the Americas"?
What was that context? What was that conversation like?

Perez: We were discussing the fact that they——he told me that they were financing this operation because Jaime Guillot Lara did not have the money to buy the drugs in Colombia.
Now, when we kept on discussing, I guess he had the feeling or the impression that I knew about these guns which Jaime never told me about the guns at first. Later on, the guns became clear to myself, but he said that——the statements made by himself to myself was that Fidel Castro did know about it, and that he was doing other things related.

Denton: I see. So, you are not only referring to the drug operation, but you are referring to your testimony relating to the guns put aboard for the return trip to Colombia, which were intended for the M–19 terrorists in Colombia; is that correct, and in that context, he was referring to Fidel Castro's operations in other parts of the Americas?

Perez: Yes, sir.

Denton: Thank you, Madam Chairman.

Hawkins: Did you tell us the amount of money major drug operators like yourself would be talking about? . . .

Perez: If I would have remained on that level, dealing with Jaime Guillot and the Cuban Government, I would say we would have gone onto really high levels, higher than anybody could have expected because of the Cuban Government's backing. . . .

There was a discussion between Jaime Guillot and myself about the Cuban Government was going to purchase 500 kilos of cocaine a month, so, very simply, just mutliply 500 by 50,000. Each kilo of cocaine was worth, like $50,000 here, in the U.S. wholesale price at that time, so that it is an awful lot of millions of dollars, ma'am.

They were to pay me $2½ million for each time I carried that amount of load in.

Hawkins: They paid you $2½ million for every load you took in?

Perez: Of this cocaine, ma'am, although I never got to do it, but that was the offer. . . .

·   ·   ·   ·   ·   ·   ·   ·   ·   ·   ·

For these marihuana loads and the methaqualone load, the Cuban Government was not going to pay me nothing.

Senator DeConcini: They weren't?

Perez: I was bringing the load in. I would sell it, distribute it, collect the money.

DeConcini: Do you mean, you were bringing it into the United States?

Perez: Into the United States. I would sell it, collect the money, like for the methaqualone pills. . . . it was going to be a profit of approximately $5 million.

Then, I was to get one-third of that. Jaime Guillot Lara was to get one-third and the Cuban Government was to get another third.

DeConcini: Who was to pay the Cuban Government?

Perez: Jaime Guillot Lara.

DeConcini: Did he work for the Cuban Government? Do you know what his relationship was to the Cuban Government?

Perez: My understanding, his relationship to them was pretty close. I don't think he worked . . . for them. I think he worked with them. . . .

. . . .

DeConcini: You don't know, from your trade and business, whether or not Cuba is a producer?

Perez: No, sir. One thing they did, though, was, out of the methaqualone pills, they kept a box.

DeConcini: They kept a box?

Perez: Yes, sir, Rene Cruz told me, himself, that he was keeping a box.

DeConcini: Did he say for what purpose?

Perez: He didn't explain to me. I didn't really want to ask him. . . .

. . . .

Senator Helms: . . . There was an indication earlier that the Cuban Government is, in fact, underwriting some of this stuff. You have no knowledge of that?

Perez: I don't quite understand your question, sir.

Helms: Well, the indication that I had earlier was that the Cuban Government or officials thereof, if not providing the capital themselves, were assuring those who do invest that they will take care of any losses that you have in the event of seizure, in the event of interdiction. You have no knowledge of that?

Perez: One thing I do have knowledge of was that Rene Cruz told me, himself, they had financed that first operation as far as it goes in Colombia.

See, in Colombia, in order for that merchandise to leave Colombia, it is a lot of corruption in Colombia, officials which I don't really know who they are, but I know for a fact that they have to pay like some of the Coast Guard and some of the officials over there so they will be in another place so the boat can leave with the merchandise safe out of Colombia, so they do have to pay money up front before they leave Colombia. . . .

Documents 6 and 7: Sandinista Drug Trafficking and Support: Testimony and Statement by Antonio Farach, Former Sandinista Diplomat; Statement by Clyde Taylor of the U.S. State Department

I n Document 6, Antonio Farach, formerly a diplomat of the Sandinista government, who defected from Nicaragua in 1983, testifies that [in the drug trade] "the Government of Nicaragua was involved . . . at the highest level," including granting traffickers permission to use the international airport at Managua and the issuing of Nicaraguan passports to smugglers. Mr. Farach also states that Nicaragua, through its diplomatic officials, provides "support and cover" to terrorist organizations such as M–19, FARC, and the PLO. These points are confirmed in the testimony of Miguel Bolaños Hunter, chapter 2, Document 2.

In Document 7, Mr. Clyde Taylor, the U.S. Deputy Assistant Secretary of State for International Narcotic Matters, provides a brief overview of Sandinista drug trafficking and support thereof, including the use of troops to load cocaine onto planes in Managua.

Source: This material is from the Hearing before the Subcommittee on Alcoholism and Drug Abuse of the Committee on Labor and Human Resources, United States Senate, *Drugs and Terrorism, 1984,* 2 August 1984.

Document 6: Testimony and Statement by Antonio Farach

Senator Hawkins: Our next witness will be Antonio Farach, the former Minister Counselor of the Nicaraguan Embassies in Venezuela and Honduras. He will provide this committee with first-hand information regarding Nicaraguan support for terrorism and drug trafficking.

His translator will be Frank Gomez.

We would like the hearing room to be quiet, please. Mr. Farach has decided he would not wear the mask to keep his identity a secret, and he is a very brave man to participate with us today.

Mr. Farach will read his statement at this time in Spanish, and we will have it translated. Proceed, Mr. Farach.

Mr. Farach: [translated by Mr. Frank Gomez] Thank you very much for the opportunity to be here today. My name is Antonio Farach. I came to the United States in September of 1983 to request political asylum. I came from Caracus where I left my post in the diplomatic service of Nicaragua.

I wish to point out two things before completing my statement. First of all, my testimony this morning comes from my experience as an official of the Nicaraguan Government, and the information comes from sources, friends of mine who were and are officials of the Nicaraguan Government. Therefore, it is not a matter of testimony from a firsthand witness, but rather testimony based on my knowledge through conversations with ranking officials who were in sensitive positions which enabled them to have information about this subject.

The second point I wish to clarify is that I cannot reveal the names of my sources. They are still government officials in Nicaragua, and despite our ideological differences, moral reasons and humane reasons, prevent me from endangering their personal safety and their lives.

Information and my knowledge covers two aspects. First, drug use on the part of high-ranking government officials in Nicaragua. This drug use was often occasional, but in other instances, it was a matter of addiction. The official government apparatus in Nicaragua in which drugs were most commonly used was the DRI, the Department of International Relations of the FSLN. That is an organization which parallels the American department in Cuba, and it is the real decisionmaking center for Nicaraguan foreign policy.

The two highest ranking officials of that office were people who were visibly addicted to drugs. . . .

The second aspect of the information which came to me was the involvement of high level Nicaraguan officials in international drug trafficking, trafficking through the so-called Colombian and Bolivian connection in order to move drugs into the United States.

The first time that I had information about these events was something that happened in September of 1981 during a visit of the Minister of Defense of Cuba to Managua. When I tried to find out what the purposes of that visit were, I was told that it was the beginning of a new and special business for the Nicaraguan revolution.

I was able to understand, and I was able to deduce from the words of my source that the Cubans had references and connections with international traffickers which could guarantee in a reasonable and safe way the entry of the Nicaraguan Government, the Sandinista government, in this trafficking.

With respect to this point I want to mention that deducing from information which reached me during a year and a half, I cannot affirm here that the Government of Nicaragua was involved as a government. They were government officials at the highest level in their private or individual capacity.

I understand that the person who was directly involved in the trafficking was the Minister of Defense of Nicaragua. I also understand, and this was confirmed by my sources, that the international traffickers besides landing strips and facilities that were offered to them, they also obtained international travel documentation which was granted or issued fraudulently by the office of immigration of Nicaragua.

I want to open a brief parentheses here to point out that this illegal practice of granting false travel documents had been a practice of the Sandinista government, a practice in which I was personally involved during my years of service in Honduras and in Caracus. On many occasions I was instructed to give Nicaraguan passports to non-Nicaraguan individuals, of obvious South American origin and some citizens who had clearly come from the Middle East.

I do not think that the international drug traffickers are using clandestine airport facilities or landing strips in Nicaragua. They did not need to do that. In a totalitarian police state such as Nicaragua, at the time which they reach agreement not with the Minister of Defense of that country, but rather with the owner of the country, they had a perfect right to use the international airport in Managua. . . .

The drugs were destined for the United States. Our youth would not be harmed, but rather the youth of the United States, the youth of our enemies. Therefore, the drugs were used as a political weapon because in that way we were delivering a blow to our principal enemy. . . .

. . . the high-ranking officials involved in drug trafficking . . . said that in addition to a political weapon against the United States, the drug trafficking produced a very good economic benefit which we needed for our revolution. Again, in a few words, we wanted to provide food to our people with the suffering and death of the youth of the United States.

The following relates part of the questioning of Antonio Farach by the committee:

Hawkins: . . . You testified [that] Raul Castro, who is the Minister of Defense and also the brother of the Cuban dictator, Fidel Castro, visited Nicaragua in September of 1981. I believe you said he met with Umberto Ortega who is the Minister of Defense and who happens to be the brother of Daniel Ortega, who is running for President; is that correct?

Farach: Yes; that is correct.

Hawkins: Did Raul Castro, to your knowledge, suggest the Nicaraguan Government engage in narcotics trafficking, or did he order the Nicaraguan involvement?

Farach: The precise terms used or probably used by Mr. Castro in his conversations with Mr. Ortega, whether they were suggestion or an order, I cannot say, but I can affirm that never in my experiences with Cuban officials during 4 years of service in the Government, the relationship was never one of respect between Cubans and Nicaraguans. The Cubans always spoke as if they were the bosses. They were always very arrogant and demanding. They do not suggest in Nicaragua. They order in Nicaragua.

Hawkins: Cuba and Nicaragua are not equals in the minds of the Cubans?

Farach: Evidently that is the case, just as Cuba and the Soviet Union are not equal.

Hawkins: Does the Nicaraguan Government recognize terrorist organizations, such as the M–19 or the FARC, PLO?

Farach: The Government of Nicaragua not only recognizes those organization, but it instructs its diplomatic officials, such as in my own case, to provide every support and cover when those men from international terrorist organizations are traveling in countries where Nicaraguan diplomatic officials reside.

Hawkins: Did you ever provide passports to terrorists?

Farach: With absolute certainty, I could not point out any terrorist in particular, but I can tell you with certainty that on many occasions I handed over Nicaraguan passports in a clandestine and illegal way to persons who were not Nicaraguan citizens. The purpose for those actions was never explained to me in a thorough way.

Hawkins: Did you know who they were given to?

Farach: On some occasions the persons who received those documents were clearly from South America, and in two or three occasions, I was certain that they were persons of Arab origin.

Hawkins: How did the phoney passports help the terrorists?

Farach: In the language of the international Left, there is a term which is to "clean a person." The manner of using a passport to travel to a given country, to change a passport or exchange passports in that country, and to continue to the point of destination. Let me tell you in more graphic terms.

A person leaving Nicaragua trying to get into Canada can go very easily from Managua to Amsterdam, Paris, Madrid, Mexico, and in Mexico change a passport and continue on to Canada. Even today, despite the recent events, a Nicaraguan passport is still a little safer than a Libyan passport, perhaps.

Hawkins: How extensive is document counterfeiting in Nicaraguan, whether it be passports or others? You call it to "clean a person." We call it "laundering." Is there wide abuse there?

Farach: The Office of Immigration and Naturalization is absolutely controlled by Cuban government officials, and this is not———

Hawkins: Cuban Government?

Farach: Cuban government officials, and this is not secondhand testimony. This is my personal testimony. In this case, I can assure you as an eyewitness that they were Cuban officials who directly controlled the immigration office.

Hawkins: We thank you very much for coming here today. I know we were supposed to disguise your appearance. I appreciate your bravery in letting us see you. I know that you are the highest ranking official from Nicaragua to ever testify, and we appreciate that very much.

The Nicaraguan Government has criticized you for talking publicly. Why do you think that they would go to such lengths to try to discredit your testimony?

Farach: I understand that the accusations of the Government of Nicaragua are attempts to discredit me, such as accusing me of stealing government funds and accusing me also of homosexual practices. In the second case, an accusation of that kind reveals how repressive the mentality of the Sandinistas may be because, after all, and I am not a homosecual, but if I were, that would have no affect on the validity of my statements.

With respect to my own integrity, I want to point out that I left my post in September 1983, and it is strange that those accusations have not surfaced until now. The Government of Nicaragua must be more concerned about presenting incontrovertable evidence beyond any doubt about its involvement in international drug trafficking, about its connections with international terrorists, and its humiliating obedience to Cuba and to the Soviet Union than my personal integrity. The people in Nicaragua hope for clarification. The international community awaits a clarification not as a function of my personal role, but rather, in their role as a government.

Although I possess information about a doubtful moral past, about at least seven of the nine members of the Sandinista junta, I have never made any accusations in public. I cannot conceive of a debate about Nicaragua being reduced to personal terms. After all, the attempts to discredit those persons who leave Communist governments were not invented by the Sandinistas. They have a good past with Stalin as an example.

Hawkins: We thank you very much for participating with us and welcome you to our country. We will excuse you at this time.

Document 7: Statement by Clyde Taylor

Within the past year, two officials of the Nicaraguan Government of National Reconstruction (GRN) have been charged with involvement in cocaine trafficking. The evidence in both cases appears credible. There are indications that high GRN officials were involved in this trafficking.

In late July 1983, Canadian authorities arrested Rodolfo Palacios Talavera, a First Secretary of the GRN's Embassy in Ottawa for possession of cocaine with an estimated value of $10,000. According to an unconfirmed report from a police informant, the Nicaraguan diplomat was part of a major drug trafficking ring which included Interior Minister Tomas Borge and other senior Sandinistas. Following judicial wrangling over his diplomatic status, Palacios was declared *persona non grata* in February 1984 and departed Canada, presumably for Nicaragua.

In mid-July 1984, a federal grand jury in Miami, Flordia, indicted 11 persons including an aide to Interior Minister Borge on cocaine smuggling charges. According to the indictment, Frederico Vaughan actively assisted Colombian smugglers in their efforts to ship 1,500 kilos of cocaine to the United States. The indictment, which is based in large part on the testimony of a U.S. Government informant in direct contact with Vaughan, further alleges that Vaughan had a standing arrangement with the Colombians to assist cocaine trafficking using GRN facilities.

The fact that, according to the complaint, GRN troops assisted in loading the cocaine onto the plane, and that the plane was allowed to park at the military part of the Managua airfield, suggests approval and participation by additional GRN officials.

Document 8: DEA Report on Bulgarian Involvement in Drug Trafficking

E xcerpts from a report by the U.S. Drug Enforcement Administration give
a detailed overview of this activity, and are published below.

Source: The DEA report is from the Senate Hearings of 2 August 1984, *Drugs and Terrorism, 1984.*

DRUG ENFORCEMENT ADMINISTRATION REPORT ON

THE INVOLVEMENT OF THE PEOPLE'S REPUBLIC OF BULGARIA IN
INTERNATIONAL NARCOTICS TRAFFICKING

INTRODUCTION

Information accumulated by the Drug Enforcement Administration (DEA) and its predecessor agencies over the past 14 years indicates the Government of Bulgaria (GOB) appears to have established a policy of encouraging and facilitating the trafficking of narcotics under the corporate veil of KINTEX. KINTEX is the official import/export agency of the GOB, overseeing the international trade of such legitimate commodities as arms, textiles, appliances, and cigarettes. Since 1970 and continuing to the present, DEA has received statements from several different sources delineating Bulgaria's involvement in illicit trafficking activities. Descriptions of Bulgaria's motives and methods of operations, the involvement of government officials, government agencies, and selected arms and narcotics traffickers, have remained consistent over the years. The reliability of this information coupled with disappointing responses from the GOB when confronted with these allegations led the United States, in the fall of 1981, to suspend working relations with the GOB in the area of law enforcement.

Background

Press coverage of Bulgaria's involvement in illicit activities began as early as 1972 when the syndicated columnist Jack Anderson quoted portions of a classified CIA document which called Bulgaria "the new center for directing narcotics and arms trafficking between Western Europe and the Near East." In 1973, the Long Island newspaper *Newsday* began a 40-part series, "The Heroin Trail." An installment entitled "The Bulgaria Connection: A Throughway for Drugs" cited the use of KINTEX by the Bulgarian government to smuggle arms and drugs. It was alleged that arrangements were made by KINTEX with selected Turkish traffickers, allowing morphine base to move through Bulgaria in exchange for the transport and delivery of guns and ammunition to left-wing terrorist groups in Turkey. More recently, "The Plot to Murder the Pope" and *The Time of the Assassins* by Clare Sterling; "The Plot to Kill the Pope: The Bulgarian Connection—Was the KGB Behind It?" by Paul Henze; and "Drugs for Guns: The Bulgarian Connection?" by Nathan Adams have been published. These authors contended the existence of a complex and well-calculated Warsaw Pact conspiracy which is planned and directed at undermining and destabilizing Western societies.

In the latter article, "Drugs for Guns: The Bulgarian Connection," appearing in the November 1983 issue of *Reader's Digest,* Nathan Adams interviewed an ex-Bulgarian State Security officer who stated that, in 1967, the heads of the Warsaw Pact Security Services met in Moscow, U.S.S.R. to "exploit and hasten the inherent 'corruption' of Western society." According to the source, a subsequent meeting of Bulgarian State Security officers was held in Sofia, Bulgaria to devise a three-year implementation of this strategy. The article further stated that a Bulgarian State Security directive was issued in July 1970, the subject of which was "the destabilization of Western society through, among other tools, the narcotics trade." The vehicle chosen to operationally execute this strategy was KINTEX. . . .

In 1970, a source alleged that KINTEX was formed in 1968 as the result of the merging of three commercial import/export firms. According to the source, the directors of KINTEX were top ranking members of the Bulgarian intelligence service. As a source of income, the Bulgarians, through KINTEX, were active in assisting the flow of illicit arms and ammunition throughout Europe to the Middle East and had recently begun to sell seized heroin and morphine base to European traffickers. The source further disclosed an alleged plan by the directors of KINTEX to licitly import large amounts of opium into Bulgaria for conversion into morphine base and heroin by selected Turkish traffickers in Sofia. Prior to the disclosure of this plan for the manufacturing of narcotics in Sofia, West German authorities, in December

1969, seized 200 kilograms of morphine base at Frankfrut. Chemical analysis performed by German chemists indicated that the morphine base was produced in Sofia. This conclusion was due to the presence of chemicals found in the base used only in that area. A Turkish national and two Syrians were arrested at the time of the seizure; subsequent investigation revealed the source of supply to be a Turkish national based in Sofia. . . .

.   .   .   .

Political Motivations

While an ultimate goal of using drugs as a political weapon to destabilize Western societies may be inferred, more immediate motives for Bulgaria's encouragement and support of both narcotics and arms smuggling activities may be categorized as follows:

1. An attempt by the GOB to obtain hard (Western) currency which is in short supply in Bulgaria;

2. An attempt to supply and support several dissident groups in the Middle East with Western arms and ammunition, in support of communist revolutionary arms. Payments for arms at times are made by these revolutionary groups with narcotics, which then are smuggled to Western democracies and sold at a considerable profit; and

3. Intelligence gathering requirements which the Bulgarians are able to levy on the various traffickers in both the Middle East and in Western Europe by allowing and supporting such traffic.

Key Trafficking Figures

In virtually every report available to DEA since 1970 containing information on trafficking in and through Bulgaria, the state trading organization KINTEX is mentioned as a facilitator of transactions. In turn, sources consistently state that top-ranking members of the Bulgarian intelligence service and/or former heads of Bulgarian ministries comprise the directorate of KINTEX. The Bulgarian State Security Service is the most closely aligned to the Soviet Union of all Soviet Bloc nations.

Certain smugglers are permitted to conduct their activities within and through Bulgaria. In effect, Bulgarian officials, through KINTEX, designate "representatives" to operate as brokers who establish exclusive arrangements with smugglers for bartered contraband for a fee. These representatives and smugglers are non-Bulgarians, primarily composed of Turkish nationals of Kurdish ethnicity. Selected smugglers, however, also include Syrian, Iranian, Jordanian, Lebanese and European nationals. KINTEX has in the past denied any knowledge of or association with these representatives. Bulgarian officials, in defense of trafficking allegations, claim the presence of foreign nationals on their soil constitutes no crime. They further emphasize the fact that no Bulgarian nationals have been implicated in large-scale drug smuggling activities either inside or outside Bulgarian territory. . . .

Incidental to drug-related investigations overseas, a limited amount of terrorist-related activity has been made known to DEA. In its quest for hard currency, KINTEX assists the flow of illicit arms and ammunition primarily to left-wing insurgency groups, although it has been known to supply terrorist groups regardless of political affiliation. According to press releases, prior to the civil war in Lebanon, in 1974 and 1975 Bulgaria sold several shiploads of arms to right-wing Christian militias until the local communist party in Lebanon protested that the weapons would be used against its members and their left-wing and Palestinian allies. DEA reporting indicates that KINTEX chiefly has supplied weapons through Turkish traffickers to leftist terrorist groups in Lebanon and Turkey. Some Turkish and Iranian traffickers, who are known representatives of KINTEX in Bulgaria, have also been named as associates of members of the right-wing "Baskurtlar" or "Gray Wolves" in Istanbul and Frankfurt, West Germany. . . .

On June 30, 1983, A DEA representative from Austria met with a high-level Bulgarian customs official in Sofia. This official responded to a question on Bulgarian arms smuggling by stating that the United States was "also" a major supplier of arms. By inference, this was an admission that Bulgaria dealt in arms.

When countered with the distinction between U.S. weapons sales to established governments and illegal Bulgarian sales, he replied that Bulgaria sells arms to organizations representing "freedom fighters" whom it considers as legitimate as established governments.

KINTEX Structure and Methods of Operation

KINTEX is structured as an umbrella organization which orchestrates the trafficking of contraband through Bulgaria. KINTEX has been identified as the principal narcotics and weapons shipping agency; other government agencies have been identified as operating in conjunction with KINTEX, primarily as distribution outlets. Each of these agencies reportedly is headed by Bulgarian State Security officials. Additionally, Bulgarian customs officials have been implicated in assisting traffickers and their vehicles from or through Bulgaria.

A scenario typical of a KINTEX operation is as follows: A European arms dealer, a sanctioned customer of KINTEX, purchases weapons from Western or Eastern European countries through licit or illicit channels. The arms dealer sells these weapons to KINTEX through a representative in Sofia. These weapons, in turn, are resold to a Middle Eastern trafficking group, which then supplies an insurgency group. Payment to KINTEX from the Middle Eastern group may take the form of heroin in selected cases. The heroin is then sold through KINTEX to selected Western European trafficking groups.

Transportation Methods

While contraband transiting Bulgaria at times is transported via vessel to customers in Western Europe or the Middle East, the majority is carried overland by truck. As early as 1972, information available to DEA cites the use of Iranian, Turkish, and Bulgarian TIR trucks to smuggle illicit goods through Bulgaria. A number of Turkish patrons of KINTEX are owners of TIR trucks.

The Customs Convention on the International Transport of Goods under the cover of TIR (Transport International Routier) Carnets is a multilateral treaty under the auspices of the United Nations. It is a worldwide instrument which provides for a customs transit system to facilitate the international transport of goods by eliminating, to the extent possible, the necessity for customs examination of road vehicles as well as containers carried on road vehicles at each international border. . . .

Road vehicles and containers which have been previously approved for the transport of goods under customs seal are sealed after normal customs formalities at the beginning of the journey and are not inspected again until the end of the journey. . . .

The United States, all major European countries including Bulgaria, and the Southwest Asian countries of Afghanistan, Iran, and Turkey are participants in this international agreement. It is estimated that at least 50,000 trucks per year transit Bulgaria and Yugoslavia either to or from the Middle East and Europe. Approximately half of these vehicles are TIR trucks.

A preferred method of smuggling narcotics aboard TIR trucks is within "traps" built into the vehicle itself; "traps" built into the gas tanks are the most reported method. To a lesser extent, narcotics from Southwest Asia source countries are concealed within legitimate cargo, undergoing only cursory examination at the source with the knowledge and complicity of a customs official. Because of their exemption from customs examination and the volume of traffic, TIR trucks are rarely searched enroute to their destination unless specific intelligence information is transmitted to appropriate customs officials.

Status in International Affairs

Although the reporting of Bulgarian involvement in narcotics trafficking continues to date, the amount of heroin and morphine base transiting Bulgaria is not as significant as in the past. During the "French Connection" era, several traffickers operating from Bulgaria were identifed as key suppliers of morphine base to laboratories in France and Italy. The situation in Bulgaria has been overshadowed in the past few years by the enormous availability of processed heroin trafficked directly from Southwest Asian countries to consumer markets in Western Europe and the United States. In light of the increased reporting of heroin laboratory activity in eastern Turkey, which had remained dormant during Turkish military rule from 1980 until 1983, the trafficking activity through Bulgaria may escalate. . . .

5
Surrogate Actors in the Middle East

O ver the last two decades state-sponsored or supported terrorism and other forms of surrogate combat in the Middle East have emerged as potent instruments of foreign policy practiced by a number of states, including Khomeini's Iran, Libya, Syria, and members of the Soviet Bloc. Since the mid-1970s, the nature and extent of this assistance to various terrorist and insurgent groups has escalated considerably. The documents in this section bear testimony to many of the facets of this complex, widespread, and often covert network of state support. This includes the transfer of arms, paramilitary training and tactical advice, intelligence support, as well as collaboration and coordination in fashioning political-psychological warfare strategies to legitimize terrorist groups in the international arena. Moreover, significant documentation reveals the existence of linkages between various terrorist and insurgent entities spanning continents.

Document 1 is indicative of this pattern of events in the Middle East. It contains the minutes of a top-secret meeting of the Iranian leadership on May 26, 1984, that made operational decisions concerning the creation of a brigade-size unit "for carrying out unconventional warfare in enemy territory." The primary targets include the more-conservative Arab regimes and Western states. This is followed by the operational charter of Hizballah, the Shiite terrorist group, openly avowing that it is directly linked to Iran and admitting its responsibility for the massacre of U.S. Marines south of Beirut (Document 2).

During the period under examination, the Palestinian Liberation Organization (PLO) emerged on the Middle Eastern and international scenes as a—if not *the*—predominant practitioner of the art of protracted warfare. Within the network of state-sponsored and supported international terrorism, the PLO has been both a recipient and supplier of the types of assistance already described. Documents presented in this section reveal the complex nature of these linkages between the PLO and a number of states, as well as with other international terrorist and guerrilla organizations.

The primary evidences published in this chapter, indicate that since the end of the 1960s, the PLO–Soviet connection has become increasingly intimate, with steady intensification of cooperation and coordination between them. The high level at which such coordination of policies and actions between the USSR and the PLO takes place is disclosed in the documents. Thus, Document 3 contains the minutes of a November 23, 1983 meeting between Soviet Foreign Minister and Politburo member Andrei Gromyko and leading PLO officials, headed by "Foreign Minister" Farouk Kaddoumi. The account embodied in this record indicates the degree of Soviet involvement with its surrogate, including Gromyko's "advice" that the PLO subordinate itself to Syria, Moscow's principal ally in the region. Document 4 contains excerpts from the record of an analogous but earlier meeting, a 1979 meeting in Moscow between Yasser Arafat, Gromyko and Boris Ponomarev, head of the International Department (ID) of the CPSU's Central Committee. As with the Gromyko–Kaddoumi encounter, the text of the document reveals both the high level and degree of intimacy in this patron–client relationship between the Soviet Union and the PLO.

Further evidence of this intimacy is found in Document 5, excerpts from testimony given by V.N. Sakharov, a former senior USSR official in the region. Drawing on his operational experience in the Middle East from 1967 to 1971, he describes the initial establishment and growth of the Soviet–PLO connection. A report to Arafat from a PLO delegation at a Soviet training camp for terrorists provides additional corroborative evidence of this relationship (Document 6). The PLO openly acknowledges its close relationship with the USSR in Document 7, while a letter from one Iranian official to another in Document 8 attests to the Soviet penetration of the PLO—the writer identifies a member of the PLO delegation as an undercover agent of the KGB.

Although political-psychological warfare occupies a very prominent place on the PLO–USSR agenda, the PLO leadership appears to have closed the door to the organization becoming a genuinely political entity by adding a new paragraph to its Covenant (Document 9) which stresses that the use of violence is a *strategy* in itself, not a mere means of achieving political aims. Indeed, Document 10 reveals the use of PLO headquarters in East Berlin as a terrorist base.

This emphasis on terrorist tactics also brought the PLO into contact with other terrorist and insurgent groups. Document 11 identifies a number of such groups that received paramilitary training by the PLO in Lebanon (also see Documents 12–14 for related information), while Document 15 reveals the PLO's cooperation with the West German Neo-Nazi group headed by Karl-Heinz Hoffman.

The documentation in this chapter discloses aid for the PLO coming not only directly from the USSR, but also from its various surrogates in Eastern Europe (Documents 16–20), the Caribbean (Document 21), Central America

(Document 22), and Asia (Documents 23–26). This includes such hardware as tanks, military vessels, Katyushas, small arms, and ammunition, as well as training in such locations as Simferopol in the Crimea (see Document 27). Furthermore, the Soviet Union and its surrogates provide political training at such institutions as Patrice Lumumba University (see Document 5), and political support through international front organizations, including the Afro-Asian People's Solidarity Organization.

The PLO receives assistance from Arab, Islamic, and other Third World governments. This includes Syria (Documents 28–29) and Saudi Arabia, which apparently has violated U.S. law by providing American-manufactured arms to the PLO (see Documents 30–31). Aside from weapons, Arab states also have provided military training and financial support. Lastly, support is revealed from the UN Interim Force in Lebanon, which apparently ignores the establishment of a PLO base and the presence of armed PLO men within the UNIFIL zone (Document 32).

The PLO is a supplier and not just a recipient of aid. It acts often as a middleman, and is at the center of an international support system for terrorism and insurgency. The global extent of this support is shown in many of these documents. PLO involvement in almost all continents is demonstrated. Cooperation between the PLO and the Italian Red Brigades caused the High Court of Venice, in September, 1984, to issue an arrest warrant against PLO leader Yasser Arafat and his deputy, Abu Iyad (see Chapter 6, Document 4). Documents 22 and 33–35 reveal a PLO presence in Central American and West Africa. The long-term relationship between the PLO and Latin American insurgents is particularly clear.

Document 1: Formation of Iranian Terrorist Unit

The document below contains the top secret minutes of a meeting between Iranian government leaders in which they decided upon the creation of a brigade-sized terrorist unit to attack targets throughout the Middle East. Shiite terrorist groups have claimed responsibility for a number of incidents in recent years, including the bombing of American embassies in Kuwait and Beirut, several airline hijackings, and the destruction of the Marine Corps barracks in Lebanon. While many allegations have been made concerning possible state support for such acts of violence, this document provides conclusive evidence, for the first time to the editors' knowledge, of Iran's sponsorship of shiite terrorist groups.

The first section is a memorandum sent by Iran's Minister of National Guidance, Seyed Mohammed Khatami, requesting the attendance of the highest-ranking Iranian military and civilian officials at a meeting on May 26, 1984. (The date on the memorandum, 5/3/1363, refers to the Iranian calendar, which differs from the Arab Moslem calendar.) The second section consists of minutes of the meeting, including the text of Ayatollah Khomeini's exhortations.

The head of the "Islamic World Organization," referred to only as "Mirhashem," describes the requirements for a new brigade-sized terrorist unit, including capabilities to operate on land, sea, or in the air. The intelligence needs of the new brigade also receive attention, including such measures as the use of former SAVAK agents and the future benefits to be received from the penetration of the Israeli Army by five Palestinians.

Source: This document was smuggled out of Iran to Britain and was made available to the editors, who have included it as received.

TOP SECRET

Subject: CREATION OF AN INDEPENDENT BRIGADE FOR CARRYING OUT UNCONVENTIONAL WARFARE IN ENEMY TERRITORY

In the process of obeying the orders of His Eminence . . . Ayatollah Imam Khomeini . . . , the great leader of our revolution, and the founder of the Islamic Republic, which were given in handwriting, I would be pleased if you attended a meeting at the building of the Ministry of Islamic Guidance on 5/3/1363 at 1600 hours. Should Your Excellencies' presence for some reason not be possible, then one of your deputies or, otherwise, one of your senior responsible staff with full powers of authority on your behalf should attend the meeting, and his name, qualifications and title should be relayed 48 hours before the meeting.

Signed on behalf of the Minister of National Guidance

Seyed Mohammed Khatami

List of recipients of the memorandum

—Chief of the Joint Staff of the Islamic Republic Armed Forces
—Representative of the Imam in the Supreme Defence Council
—Commander of the Revolutionary Guards of the Islamic Republic
—Commander of the Ground Forces of the Islamic Republic
—Commander of the Air Force of the Islamic Republic
—Commander of the Navy of the Islamic Republic
—Chief of the G2 Section of the Joint Chiefs of Staff
—Chiefs of the Political-Ideological Offices of the various forces
—Chiefs of the Islamic Committees (Head of the combattant clergy organisation)
—The Representative of the Imam in Haj
—Minister for Foreign Affairs of the Islamic Republic
—Hojat-Ol-Islam, Mohammed Baquir Hakim (Islamic Revolution of our brother country, Iraq)

TOP SECRET

Official proceedings concerning the creation of an independent brigade for carrying out unconventional warfare in enemy territory

The meeting commenced with the speech of His Eminence, Ayatollah Khatami, the Minister of Islamic Guidance, who said the following:

"In the name of God, the Merciful, the Compassionate, dear Brothers, I wish to welcome you on behalf of the International Islamic Movements Organisation, and to explain in brief why this meeting has been called. On 24th of "Ordibehesht," I, accompanied by the Head of this movement [Islamic World Organisation] were received by our beloved leader to whom we presented our progress report. His Eminence, the Imam, expressed dissatisfaction with the behaviour of the leaders of the sheikdoms of the Persian Gulf and of the Saudi regime. Of course, he was not pleased either with others who pretend to be leaders of Islamic nations. After moments of silence which were evidence of his deepfelt anxiety and dissatisfaction, His Eminence in his usual style of firmness concerning all living matters made certain comments which are as follows:

"From the beginning of the revolution, we have had many enemies, but our expectations from Muslims was something else. Unfortunately, all the rulers of Islamic countries are servants of foreigners and instead of learning from our advice and being in step with us in the direction of Islam and the Islamic "Ummah", they have chosen the path of hostility and have acted in the same fashion they acted with the prophet [Mohammed] at the dawn of the Islamic period, and have consequently stepped on all the laws and traditions of the Koran and have left the entire Islamic heritage in the hands of the foreigners—first of all Sadam [Hussein, President of the Iraqui Republic] began to fight against Islam. Although his situation is near termination, these poor people are also sinking in the well with him; by this I mean the reactionary rulers of Arabia who also consider themselves the guardians of the Holy Shrines, and others, Kuwait, etc. These people think that because their bosses are Russians or Americans that they can by strong guns and tanks face the Iranian Ummah which has given so many martyrs. The destiny of the Shah, Sadam and their bosses, America, has not been a lesson to them. Now, it is up to them. We have a heavy responsibility in the face of the Koran, His Holiness, the Great Mohammed [the Prophet] and Islam. We have to spread Islam everywhere, and in this path we have given a great deal of blood, and we will give more until, with the help of God, Islam becomes victorious. You should act according to your religious duties. Whatever is necessary to destroy them must be carried out. There is no longer any time for talk and advice. That's it." [end of Khomeini's comments].

The Minister for National Guidance continued:

"Our brothers are aware that for four full years we have been at war with Sadam, and we have borne a lot of suffering, and until such time as we have destroyed him and liberated our brother Iraqi nation, we cannot stop. On the other hand, all the forces of world oppression have united against this righteousness and have begun to pull the strings of their puppets everywhere to damage our glorious revolution. Inside, groups which have sold themselves, and outside, countries like Iraq. Therefore, based on what has been said, we are encircled by such an enormous satanic force and we must accept this truth, that apart from fighting this imposed war we face thousands of other internal and external problems. Apart from this, as indicated by our beloved leader, we have a heavy duty towards Islam and as such we must prepare ourselves to face the challenges of any enemy until such time as we have carried out the wishes of our leader and our 'martyr-raising' Ummah, and we have liberated all Islamic countries from the yoke of corrupt and reactionary rulers. Therefore, because of the present difficulties which have been mentioned, it is not possible for us to directly confront this enormous force that is supported by the super powers, based on a plan that has been prepared in almost 200 pages and on which you will be subsequently informed, it has been decided that the strikeforce which at present is composed of a few groups of 10–20 people each, who are currently serving in the Lebanon, [*sic*] should be increased to the size of a brigade. This force, for security reasons, and for the purposes of making sure that legal impediments do not delay its formation, will be formed under the aegis of either the Revolutionary Guards or the Armed Forces. Of course, the decision in this respect will rest with His Eminence, the Leader. At this time, we are concerned with its creation. This force will act independently and will present all its reports directly to the Commander in Chief. Because the carrying out of this plan required the assistance of all revolutionary organs, the matter was presented to His Eminence in that initial meeting, and he accepted the proposal. What has been said has been a brief introduction, and now we will enter the main substance and I shall pass the platform to Brother 'Mirhashem', who is responsible for this organisation. Of course, all present here are fully familiar with his [Mirhashem's] features; however, please allow for prudence-sake that we refer to him as 'Mirhashem'."

Brother Mirhashem thanked His Eminence, Ayatollah Khatami and all respected people present.

"From what was said at the beginning, there was some reference made to the creation of a brigade. For the information of all present, I must say that we have at present a number of dedicated groups who are ready for action and who have, to the outside world become known as suicide groups. These groups have already performed certain actions. But since regional reactionary forces out of fear from the Islamic Revolution and the hard blows of the fighters of Islam, with each passing day under different pretexts are preparing themselves more and more, and this in itself is a big threat for the continuation of the revolution, these groups that we have are by themselves inadequate. Also, the personnel in these groups are commited only because of their beliefs for which they are ready to do anything, but they lack warfare experience. Therefore, the personnel of this brigade must from the point of view of military combat experience be of a very high echelon. If we wish to commence this task from the beginning, that is from the training stages, by the time that we can prepare such people for utilisation at least one year will have elapsed, and this is something that will create an interlude in our activities and will award our enemies more time. Therefore, it has been decided to select dedicated religious and fully commited candidates from all combat [Nahad] organisations so as to prevent any interlude in the continuation of our operational activities.

"For the purposes of dealing with the main substance, I will list our requirements for you so that all brothers present will be informed of the boundaries of their duties and contributions towards the creation of this brigade. It is pertinent here that I should remind all that as indicated in the invitation memo the name of this brigade is for carrying out unconventional warfare in enemy territory. To commence operations and confrontations we must have excuses. Therefore, we must begin by propaganda—and here this is the responsibility of the combattant clergy organisation and the Friday Mosque prayer leaders [throughout the country] who must in the course of their political-religious sermons propose the plan that the administration of the Holy Shrines belongs to all Muslims in the world and must be controlled through a trusteeship consisting of all Islamic countries, and also the question of renovating other religious shrines and buildings of which I have no specific knowledge. I refer only to the heading which is in line with the wishes of His Eminence, the Imam, and the Friday prayer leaders are more than capable of dealing with the substance of these headings.

"Second, propaganda and operations during the month of the Holy Pilgrimage which Hojat-Ol-Islam Moussavi Khoiniha, who is himself both a contributor to the original plan and an operator as well. If necessary, he can say a few words concerning the operational plan for Haj.

"Third, the combat structure of the brigade which must be ready for operation in the waters, airspace and territory of the enemy.

"A. At this time, we request the commanders of the various forces [Revolutionary Guards and the three regular forces] to introduce dedicated and religiously commited qualified candidates to the temporary staff of this brigade. These people must have obtained a high school diploma and must have participated in the four years war [with Iraq]. They must not be more than 30 years old, preferably bachelors. Their candidature must be approved by the political-ideological offices and these people must be introduced no later than the end of the month of "Tir". I underline that these people must in the course of their total commitment to the path of Islam place no value on their life, and must be totally commited to martyrdom.

"B. To train these personnel, it is necessary to have the services of officers and non-commissioned officers specialising in partisan warfare [ground forces]. His Eminence, our leader, has agreed that should we at present be faced with a shortage of such people, we can invite former officers and NCOs with these qualification to return to work. In this respect, if necessary, our military attaches in foreign countries can prepare such invitations for military people who are, for whatever reason, living abroad, and they can give them whatever assurances that are necessary. The only point concerning personnel living abroad is that care must be taken that no recommendation be made of people who have acted in a hostile way towards the Islamic regime. Unlike combat personnel, there is no age criterial for these specialised trainers.

"C. Specialised officers and NCOs for training people for naval activities—according to the information given by the Navy in the past and at present—were in possession of a strikeforce which might still exist, personnel from this structure are also required by the brigade. If faced with a shortage of such personnel, the above instructions are also applicable in this case.

"D. For training in the art of piloting light aircraft, it is essential that we introduce certain candidates to the Airforce. It would be better if the Airforce could create a training centre outside its present bases for it would be more secure. In this regard, more will be said later.

"Another thing which is required is combat information, that is airforce intelligence, naval intelligence and ground force intelligence. For this, whatever information which at present is available concerning enemy territory within the various intelligence units of the forces must be made available to the temporary intelligence, and more intelligence officers should be sent to the countries under consideration, under the umbrella of the military attache's office. In this respect, I repeat once again the same procedures as those applicable to specialised officers and NCOs are to be followed, and in this regard, utilisation can be made of former Savak agents and the counter intelligence files of Savak. Here, I have a very important and secret matter to divulge, and that is that so far our organisation has been assisted by five Muslim brothers of occupied Palestine who, for many years have served in "the Army of the occupiers of Qods" [Israeli Army], and in the future they will be making all their knowledge available to us.

"The target countries are as follows. The first tier is Saudia Arabia, Kuwait, United Arab Emirates and Bahrain. The second tier is Hashamite Jordan. The third tier is as needs be, France and other countries who will try and confront the Islamic Republic.

"Our brothers are informed and as stated, know that the reactionary forces of the region with each passing day, either out of fear or for reasons of dependence on the super powers, are arming themselves to the teeth, which is not to the advantage of the Islamic Republic of Iran, and there is no way that we can bring them to their knees unless we are able to inflict relentless blows on them from within. That is, to neutralise them at every step. Here it is necessary that I give a word of caution, that to obtain information from enemy territory you should select and introduce officers who once they have completed their observations and have submitted their reports, do not omit the slightest bit of information which might be of intelligence value.

"With regard to Iraq, with the assistance of the 12th Imam, the Sadam regime is gasping its final breath, for operations inside Iraq the political organisation which has been through the tireless efforts of the son of Ayatollah Hakim and other brothers is capable of exercising great strength, and in the not too distant future they will enter into operation.

"The final request of this organisation is that the Ministry of Foreign Affairs ensure that the fullest cooperation is given to all personnel who are to sent by the organisation abroad [to ensure that they can proceed without delay etc.].

"And finally, before I end, I wish to remind you that all specialised and intelligence personnel unlike ordinary personnel must be introduced no later than the 10th day of "Tir" so that there is no interlude in our activities.

"Concerning the number of personnel to be introduced, outside the meeting certain questions were asked to which I must respond in this fashion, that apart from the command and HQ staff, the ordinary personnel introduced must number between 1500 and 2000, so that proper selection [taking into consideration ideological, combat and other credentials] can be made. There is no objection if the number of candidates exceeds the allocated amount. The other matter is that for forthcoming meetings either for exchange of opinion or for analysing the plan between the various organisations present in this meeting, without resorting to writing, each organisation must introduce a responsible person no later than the 10th day of "Khordad".

"I have nothing else to say."

Closing remarks by Ayatollah Khatami.

"With repeated thanks to all those present, I request that should any proposals for the further strengthening of this brigade come to anyone's mind, they be submitted in writing by the chosen candidate who will deliver it by hand so that they can be utilised.

"Also, since the above proceedings will appear on paper from a cassette disk, I would be grateful if it was accepted that all irrelevant discussions be omitted. If there are no more comments in this regard, we can end the meeting."

The meeting ended at 2400 hours, and this record of the proceedings, after the omission of unnecessary items from the tape was prepared and is certified by all of us.

The Secretary [signature]

The Head of the International Islamic Movement's organisation— "Mirhashem"

Document 2: Hizballah Manifesto

T he document that follows contains excerpts from the "Open Letter" of Hizballah or "Party of God," a Shiite terrorist group operating in the Middle East, primarily in Lebanon. In effect, this constitutes the operational charter of Hizballah, outlining its purpose, goals, and methods.

Hizaballah emphatically states that it is directly linked to and receives guidance from Khomeini's Iran. In this document there is no attempt to conceal its activities; rather, Hizballah openly proclaims responsibility for such acts of terrorism as the bombing of the Marine Corps barracks in Lebanon.

Hizballah outlines its list of enemies, including the United States, NATO, and France. Israel, however, is the object of its most vituperative statements. The use of biological terms such as "ulcerous growth" and "cancerous germ" is strongly reminiscent of the Nazi lexicon, but even Hitler at least used the euphemism "Final Solution" while Hizballah openly calls for the "obliteration" of Israel.

The description of certain Arab states as "reactionary" and "defeatist" closely parallels the typology evident in other, particularly Soviet, documents. For example, Document 3 reveals [then] Soviet Foreign Minister Gromyko using similar terms in a discussion with Farouk Kaddoumi of the PLO.

Source: Joint Publications Research Service, *Near East/South Asia Report,* 19 April 1985.

The statement opens with a dedication:

To the pioneer who was faithful to his kinsmen, who offered them the model for jihad and who did not spare his own life until he died a martyr in supporting them and a witness to the injustice of world arrogance and its insolence. . . .

To him who scattered America's dreams in Lebanon and who resisted the Israeli occupation, carrying the banner of action under the patronage of Abdallah Khomeyni, the leader jurisprudent whom he always liked to describe as the amir [prince] of the Muslims. . . .

It continues by describing Hizballah's relationship with Iran:

Hizballah

In the name of God, the compassionate and the merciful:

Say, "the truth is from your Lord"; let him who will, believe and let him who will, reject [it]; for the wrongdoers we have prepared a fire whose [smoke and flames], like the walls and roof of a tent, will hem them in; if they implore relief, they will be granted water like melted brass, that will scald their faces. How dreadful the drink! How uncomfortable a couch to recline on! . . .

We, the sons of Hizballah's nation, whose vanguard God has given victory in Iran and which has established the nucleus of the world's central Islamic state, abide by the orders of a single wise and just command currently embodied in the supreme Ayatollah Ruhollah al-Musavi al-Khomeyni, the rightly-guided imam who combines all the qualities of the total imam, who has detonated the Muslims' revolution and who is bringing about the glorious Islamic renaissance. . . .

After reviewing the situation in Lebanon, the statement outlines the aims and methods of the organization:

Our people could not withstand all this treason and decided to confront the imams of infidelity of America, France and Israel. The first punishment against these forces was carried out on 18 April and the second on 29 October 1983. By that time, a real war had started against the Israeli occupation forces, rising to the level of destroying two main centers of the enemy's military rulers. Our people also escalated their popular and military Islamic resistance to the point where they forced the enemy to make its decision on phased withdrawal—a decision which Israel was compelled to adopt for the first time in the history of the so-called Arab–Israeli conflict.

For the sake of the truth, we declare that the sons of Hizballah's nation have come to know well their basic enemies in the area: Israel, America, France and the Phalange.

Our sons are now in a state of ever-escalating confrontation against these enemies until the following objectives are achieved:

Israel's final departure from Lebanon as a prelude to its *final obliteration from existence* and the liberation of venerable Jerusalem from the talons of occupation. [emphasis added]

The final departure of America, France and their allies from Lebanon and the termination of the influence of any imperialist power in the country. . . .

In Lebanon and in the Palestine area, we are mainly concerned with confronting America because it is the party with the greatest influence among the countries of world arrogance, and also with confronting Israel, the ulcerous growth of world Zionism. Therefore, we are concerned with confronting America's allies in NATO who have gotten embroiled in helping America against the area's peoples. We warn the countries that have not gotten involved yet against being dragged into serving American interests at the expense of our nation's freedom and interests. . . .

As to our military power, nobody can imagine its dimensions because we do not have a military agency separate from the other parts of our body. Each of us is a combat soldier when the call of jihad demands it and each of us undertakes his task in the battle in accordance with his lawful assignment within the framework of action under the guardianship of the leader jurisprudent. God is behind us, supporting us with His care, putting fear in our enemies' hearts and giving us His dear and resounding victory against them. . . .

We are moving in the direction of fighting the roots of vice and the first root of vice is America. All the endeavors to drag us into marginal action will be futile when compared with the confrontation against the United States.

Imam Khomeyni, the leader, has repeatedly stressed that America is the reason for all our catastrophes and the source of all malice. By fighting it, we are only exercising our legitimate right to defend our Islam and the dignity of our nation. . . .

Thus, we have seen that aggression can be repelled only with sacrifices and dignity gained only with the sacrifice of blood and that freedom is not given but regained with the sacrifice of both heart and soul. . . .

As for Israel, we consider it the American spearhead in our Islamic world. . . .

Therefore, *our confrontation of this entity must end with its obliteration from existence.* This is why we do not recognize any cease-fire agreement, any truce or any separate or non-separate peace treaty with it. [emphasis added]

We condemn strongly all the plans for mediation between us and Israel and we consider the mediators a hostile party because their mediation will only serve to acknowledge the legitimacy of the Zionist occupation of Palestine. . . .

Islamic resistance must continue, grow and escalate, with God's help, and must receive from all Muslims in all parts of the world utter support, aid, backing and participation so that we may be able to uproot this cancerous germ and obliterate it from existence. . . .

Hizballah continues with a warning for certain Arab regimes:

We have great hope in the Muslim peoples that clearly have begun to complain in most of the Islamic countries and have been able to infiltrate into the world of revolutions to learn from its experiences, especially from the triumphant Islamic revolution. The day will come when all these brittle regimes will collapse under the blows of the oppressed, as the throne of the tyrant in Iran has already collapsed. . . .

We also warn these regimes against getting involved in new capitulationist plans and in aggressive schemes aimed against the young Islamic revolution because such involvement will lead the leaders of these regimes to the same fate faced by Anwar al-Sadat and by Nuri al-Saʿid [last Iraqi prime minister under monarchy] and others before them. . . .

The document closes with a call to action:

We strongly urge on all the oppressed of the world the need to *form an international front* that encompasses all their liberation movements so that they may establish full and comprehensive coordination among these movements in order to achieve effectiveness in their activity and to focus on their enemies' weak points. . . . [emphasis added]

It is time for us to realize that all the Western ideas concerning man's origin nature [sic] cannot respond to man's aspirations or rescue him from the darkness of misguidedness and ignorance. Only Islam can bring about man's renaissance, progress and creativity because "he lights with the oil of an olive tree that is neither eastern nor western, a tree whose oil burns, even if not touched by fire, to light the path. God leads to His light whomever He wishes." . . .

These are our visualizations and objectives and these are the rules that govern our course. . . .

God's peace, mercy and blessings be upon you.

Hizballah

Document 3: Gromyko–Kaddoumi Meeting

T he document below contains the minutes of a meeting held on 23 November, 1983 between Soviet Foreign Minister Gromyko and a PLO delegation led by PLO "Foreign Minister" Farouk Kaddoumi, who goes by the code name Abu Lutf. The personal involvment of Gromyko at this meeting clearly demonstrates the extent and the level of Soviet relations with the PLO. The close coordination of PLO policies with the Soviet leadership indicates the depth of Kremlin interaction with its surrogates, including political tactics.

The account describes one manifestation of surrogate-to-surrogate diplomacy, whereby Cuba sought to influence Syria on behalf of the PLO. Gromyko mentions Soviet contacts with Assad and strongly intimates that the PLO should subordinate itself to Syria, the principal Soviet ally in the region, for the pursuit of the greater long-term goal of reducing American influence in the Middle East.

Source: Al Khalij, United Arab Emirates, 18 December 1983. Translation courtesy of Dr. Raphael Israeli.

The Palestinian Delegation included: Faruq Quaddumi [Abu Lutf], Ahmad al-yamani, Yasser abd Rabbih, Mahmud Abbas, Issam Kamil and Rami Sha'ir.

The Soviet delegation was composed of: the Foreign Minister, the Director of the Middle East Dpt. and three other officials from the Ministry.

Abu Lutf: The Soviet Union is a great friend to us; we share with her, in all honesty, our concerns. . . . A few months ago we had visited you and presented to you our problems. Since then, some developments have occurred in the middle East, such as the increasing troop concentrations in the area by the Americans and the Israelis, and the mounting danger of war. This has prompted us to call for Arab unity to face this threat. . . . There is no doubt that Syria, the PLO and the Lebanese National Forces are at the forefront facing these hostile concentrations. . . .

Unfortunately, as you know, we have also been facing internal problems within the Resistance Movement, which have reflected on the relations between us and Syria. We had discussed at length these relationships in our previous visit. Thereafter, we made great efforts to arrest the state of deterioration in these relationships. As Gromyko would recall, a Cuban mediation has taken place, to bring about a meeting in order to resolve the problems between us and Syria and to reconcile the internal differences within the Resistance, but no positive development can unfortunately be reported. . . .

Following contacts between Saudi Arabia and Syria, our two parties agreed that a member of the PLO Executive should go to Damascus to contact the Syrians. In fact, Khaled al-Hassan went to Damascus and met with President Assad. He stayed there for ten days to pursue his efforts, but Assad insisted that he was neutral in the internal strife among the Palestinians, although he was prepared to act as a go-between [for] them. . . .

Then we turned to the Non-aligned world. We explained our problems to the Committee of Eight which convened in Delhi, repeating our desires to resolve our problems with Syria. That committee formed a Committee of Four, consisting of the foreign Ministers of India, Cuba, Algeria and Senegal in order to obtain a cease-fire and give the PLO a chance to resolve its internal problems without foreign intervention. . . . The Committee of Eight reiterated its support for the PLO as the only legitimate representative of the Palestinian people. . . . These were our efforts, in addition to those made by the USSR, in this regard. The ramification of this battle would amount to weakening the international stature of the PLO and to turning the PLO attention to its internal problems. It will also weaken Syria's position in the world and blemish its reputation. As a result, a blow will be dealt to Soviet prestige due to the conflict between two of its allies. This conflict will also open the way to American schemes in the Middle East, and especially to the Reagan Plan vis-a-vis Jordan. All this is bound to hurt the PLO psychologically. . . .

Gromyko: Do you have problems inside Syria?

Lutf: Yes, our offices were occupied in Damascus. We asked them in this respect and they said that it was due to our internal problems, while they were neutral. . . . But we regard their encouragment of the PLO to participate in the battle as an intervention in our internal affairs. . . .

We must say, in fact, that this battle could only advance the American–Imperialist plans in the area. . . . We regret profoundly that Syria did not respond to all the mediation efforts to stop the fighting, and we sense that our Soviet friends could play a role in this regard. We appreciate the Soviet role and we understand the embarrassing situation where you find yourself, but we feel that you can intervene with the Syrians to stop the fighting, by sending a high-level official to act on this behalf. . . .

. . . the opportunity must be given to the PLO forces to continue to play their positive role in Lebanon.

.   .   .   .

We want to resolve the problem and we are committed to negotiate and deal with Syria, because it is only natural that we should maintain our alliance with Syria in order to face the American schemes. . . . Thus, we are presenting the problems to you so that you help us gain a knowledge of the Syrian position and intents. . . .

Gromyko: I wish to pose a few questions and clarifications, but I beg you to keep your answers brief: What is the basic demand that the Syrian leadership submitted to you and what are their chief grievances against you?

Lutf: The Syrians say that although they basically have no quarrel with us, they sometimes claim that Arafat is prepared to accept the Reagan Plan and the Jordanian option. We had repeatedly rejected the Reagan Plan and refused contacts with Jordan on this basis, but they continue to shun cooperation with Arafat.

Gromyko: How do you explain that in this bad situation . . . the Arab countries are sitting by, their arms crossed, as if they were watching a movie? We condemn their inaction. . . .

Lutf: . . . Some reactionary regimes enjoy the conflict between the PLO and Syria, for the latter has a bad relationship with Iraq, Jordan and others, and it is friendly to the USSR, while they are aligned with the U.S. and it would be in their interest to hamper the Syrians. Therefore, some of them exerted financial pressure on Syria, but we begged them to exert political pressure only and to pursue the economic aid which would allow Syria to face the plots against her.

Gromyko: How do you explain the prevailing silence in the face of what Israel and America are doing in Lebanon, their attempts to partition it, and the American aggression against Lebanon, including their troop concentrations along its shores; nevertheless, no international forum has discussed this situation and some countries have only issued statements on this question?

Lutf: The USA and Israel are acting to increase their presence in the area. They combined their forces against the PLO in Lebanon. . . . President Gemayel said that the USA alone could resolve the Lebanese problem and therefore he did not ask anyone else to interfere. . . . Then he began direct negotiations with Israel without consulting with the Arabs and he signed an

American-sponsored agreement with Israel. Thus, we regard the Lebanese authorities as agents of the USA. . . .

. . . .

Gromyko: While the Lebanese government is opposed to discussing its affairs with the Arabs, it at the same time let the U.S. and Europe intervene, and this has an impact on the Arabs. This in itself gives the Arabs the right to interfere, because the matter touches upon their interests. So, why didn't they impose their intervention on Lebanon?

Lutf: . . . Only the Palestine Revolution, Syria, Democratic Yemen and the Lebanese National Forces recognize these dangers, but the others ignore them. . . .

Gromyko: The Lebanese President was to go to the U.S. to discuss the Geneva talks, but Reagan refused to see him. . . . Why didn't the participants in Geneva address the American refusal to meet the Lebanese President. This must be regarded as an act of contempt to all! One must condemn this conduct of the American President. . . .

Lutf: . . . Syria and the Palestinians being at odds, they do not deal with the other problems. . . . When the balance of power is in the Arabs' favour, they are able to do something: they were to continue to fight in the Mountain area in order to pin down the Lebanese fascist forces there, and *to pursue the fighting against the American Marines in Beirut,* in order to facilitate the return of the Palestinians to Beirut and *create more problems for the Marines there.* But, unfortunately, what has happened has hampered all this. . . . [emphasis added]

Gromyko: We wish to present our opinions and assessments only in part and without any connection to your own considerations; what we have in mind are the developments in the area only. The situation has deteriorated compared to 2–3 years ago. The important fact is that the U.S. is now militarily present in the Middle East. In the past, it was Israel who had contributed to the deterioration of the situation; but now, in addition to the Israeli factor, there are American forces in Lebanon and naval fleets are surrounding the Lebanese capital. The Capital and the Mountain have become targets for shelling, making the American hostile designs quite evident. Imperialism has again evinced its greedy designs. The other factor which intimidates the Arabs, the anti-imperialists and their friends is that the Arab region is undergoing a process of fragmentation unparalleled in history. There is no sign of unity these days. . . . , the infighting within the Palestinian camp is a source of anxiety to us, inasmuch as it puts a question mark on the future of the PLO. . . . We are supporting Syria and the PLO and we are not intimidated, neither in theory nor in practice. We are just asking ourselves how did all this come about and how did Syria and the PLO allow this grave situation to develop. No one can imagine to what extent have the U.S. and Israel rejoiced these developments, which are beneficial to our rivals. There is no point in simply describing the situation, but we must also so act as to reverse the trends in order to overcome the rift between Syria and the PLO. We have suggested this matter to Minister Khaddam during his visit here, when we surveyed this issue thoroughly. These are our same objectives during our meeting with you now. . . . Khaddam has pledged to try to settle the matter peacefully, and we shall live and see what happens. Andropov has shared with Assad on several occasions his views with regard to the relations between Syria and the PLO, and the necessity for Syria to bring its influence to bear and find common grounds with the PLO. . . . We have been maintaining contacts with the Syrians in accordance with what Comrade Arafat has asked us, and we reported to him all the reactions that we had received. . . . We shall continue to strive in the same direction and we want to assure you that we shall leave no stone unturned to deal with this issue. . . .

We do support the common case of the Arabs against America and Israel and we support the Palestinian Revolution and the right to an independent state, and the full withdrawal from all occupied territories. This is the basis of our stand towards the Arab question, including our position towards the present situation in Lebanon. As you can see, our position is one of principle and has nothing to do with our egotistic interests or sentiments. At the same time, we like to present to you our honest views. We think that you should analyze the situation and make sure that you did all you can to resolve the internal rift in the Fatah and with Syria. You may find some ways and means that you have not explored so far. How can the Arabs find a common way to face the common enemy which wants to reduce the Arabs to slavery? We have heard some rumours that we cannot confirm, because we had to rely on the official communiques of the PLO, according to which the PLO and the Fatah leadership take lightly the American schemes instead of taking a firm resolution towards the Reagan Plan. We heard that when discussions were held between King Hussein and the leadership of the PLO, the latter suggested that the solution should be based on self-rule (for the Palestinians) and they no longer insisted on an independent Palestinian state. When we inquired about these rumours, we were told that in the framework of such an arrangement, security and foreign affairs of the Palestinians would be within the jurisdiction of Jordan. If that is true, that means the abandonment of the idea of an independent Palestinian state. These new thoughts among the Palestinians may be part of the reason for the deterioration of the relations between Syria and the PLO. If we understand the present situation, there is no contact there now between the leaderships of Syria and the Palestinians. Arafat may think that as long as the Syrian President does not take the initiative to resolve the situation, he too is absolved from doing so. If the two leaders persist in their positions, a major obstacle would have been erected in the way of improving the relations between them, a solution would become impossible, and the only communication between them would take place via condemnations in newspapers and broadcasts. It would be useful if Arafat took an initiative in order to show that bridges to Syria are still open, and so he will be able to resolve his own problems. This is not an official proposal, but when we discuss these problems in our leadership, we think about all these possibilities, which evince our goodwill towards you and towards Syria. For we are friends to both Syria and the PLO, and any rift between them is bound to embarrass us, who are friends of both.

You have correctly discussed some Arab countries which are friendly to the U.S. and therefore can play no part in the resolution of your rift or in condemning the U.S. and Israel. We agree to this assessment but we also understand your position and your constraint to maintain relations with countries of this sort. The question is: does your relationship with those countries, from which you get financial support, ultimately constitute a harm to your relations with the other Arab countries, and a further liability to the political position of the PLO? You do get some support now, but you will lose politically, if we balanced between the two. You may find it difficult to cut yourself off from the countries that support America, but you should revise your position, reassess your policy and correct your course. There is no doubt that the first and foremost element facing Israel militarily is Syria. If anything should happen to Syria, the entire structure of the struggle against the American and Israeli aggressors would totally collapse. . . .

Another question poses itself with regard to the Front of Resilience, since we have heard nothing about it. If it is difficult to rally all Arab countries, why don't some of them, who participate in the Front, get together on a limited basis, for any activity where two states are bound to be better than one when striving for the same goal, three are better than two, etc. . . .

These are our views as we found necessary to present to you, hoping that you would find them useful. We have listened to what you had to say and we shall report it to the Soviet leadership and to Comrade Andropov personally. It has certainly contributed to our understanding of the area. . . .

Lutf: Thanks for your candid remarks. We shall now answer your questions.

1. Regarding the Reagan Plan, our National Council has rejected it . . . and the PLO has announced that it was a new phase of Camp David. We are prepared to issue a joint communique with Syria rejecting the Plan. It is true that the Baath Party has refuted the Plan, but the Syrian Government has yet to announce its own rejection of it.

2. With regard to the slogan of an independent Palestinian State, we are committed to it and we have never agreed to mere self-rule. The major reason why our negotiations with Jordan have failed is because they insisted on accepting the Reagan Plan. If we had accepted the Plan as a base for negotiations, these would have been successfully completed. . . . We did not reach any agreement with Jordan regarding our self-rule, where foreign and security matters would be left to Jordan. Already in the beginning of the 1970s we had rejected the idea of the United Arab Kingdom. . . .

3. Concerning our warm contacts with reactionary Arab regimes: we do maintain them, even though we realize their relationship with the U.S. But we do not permit them to dictate the political line adopted by our National Council. We are a landless people and our people are dispersed in the entire Arab world. One third live in Jordan, ¼ million in Saudi Arabia and the Gulf. . . . Thus, we are compelled to cooperate with those countries. . . . When the Fahd Plan was advanced in 1981, we were the ones who refuted it and brought about its abortion, thus raising the wrath of Saudi Arabia.

4. As regards the Front of Resilience, the idea had originated from the Palestinians and we pressured countries like Iraq to join such a Front. . . , but the Lybian–Algerian rift in particular has hampered those efforts. Our National Council has taken a resolution to reactivate the Front. . . .

5. As concerns the improvement of our relations with Syria, we have established contacts with them at the highest level. . . . But we were surprised when Arafat was expelled from Syria and prohibited from returning there. . . . We were prepared to send a delegation, and Arafat is prepared to go to Syria to meet with Assad, if they are prepared for it. . . . All this emanates from our recognition that Syria is the pillar of confrontation with the American schemes. . . . We do not want to escalate our rift with Syria, because we realize that only the enemy stands to gain from that. We do not want to weaken Syria in its confrontation with American imperialism and its stooges in the area. We have been trying to mend the fences between Iraq and Syria in order to provide depth for Syria's confrontation with the enemy. . . . After 1973 we played an important role to bring about Syrian–Iraqi unity. . . . In Fez, we took a unified stand with Syria against the Reagan Plan. . . . We shall continue to strive for the solution of our problems with Syria, and we hope that our efforts to extend the ceasefire will succeed. . . .

Gromyko: It is imperative to continue to strive to attain this goal. We have already expressed our views in this regard and we shall continue to follow the same course. . . .

Document 4: Arafat Meeting with Gromyko and Ponomarev

T he document below contains the excerpts from minutes of a 1979 meeting in Moscow between Soviet Foreign Minister Gromyko, International Department Chief Boris Ponomarev, and a PLO delegation led by Yasser Arafat. The participation of such senior Kremlin figures as Ponomarev and Gromyko demonstrates the importance the Soviet leadership places on support and guidance of the PLO. The document reveals Soviet–PLO operational coordination on issues ranging from strategy in the United Nations to thwarting U.S. diplomatic initiatives in the Middle East.

The meeting also covered a number of PLO contacts with Cuba, Syria, the Polisario, and Iran during the American hostage crisis. Soviet strategic *and* tactical guidance on the issues discussed illustrates the degree to which the PLO functions as a Soviet surrogate in global political operations.

Source: Raphael Israeli, *PLO in Lebanon*, Document 7 (Weidenfeld and Nicolson, 1983). All documents from this source were captured in Lebanon.

SOVIET DELEGATION
Foreign Minister Gromyko
Ponomarev, Gromyko's Deputy[1]
Grinevsky, Head of Middle East Department of Foreign Office

PLO DELEGATION
Abu 'Ammar (Yasser Arafat)
Abed al-Muhsin Abu Meizer (Member of PLO Executive Committee)
Talal Naji (Jibril Front, Member of PLO Executive Committee)
'Issam al-Quadi (Sa'iqa)
Yasser 'Abd Rabih (Democratic Front, Member of PLO Executive Committee)
Habib Kahwaji (Sa'iqa, Member of PLO Executive Committee)
Taysir Qub'a (Popular Front/Habash)

Muhamed al-Sha'er (PLO representative in the USSR)
'Abd al-Rahim Ahmed (Arab Liberation Front) . . .

. . . .

Abu 'Ammar:　We have not talked together for a long time. Before the Baghdad Conference[2] I told you that it would be among the most important summits and its results were in fact important as I expected. This was so since the Baghdad Summit put the Arab nation as a whole against the "Camp David combination," except for two states. . . .

The importance of Baghdad is that the Arabs met without Sadat, who had declared that the Arabs could not have a summit without him, and passed resolutions condemning the Camp David Accords.

The foreign and economic ministers' meeting was more important because its resolutions involved the implementation of the decisions taken at the political summit [in Baghdad]. . . .

And as you know, Brzezinski carried out a visit in the region, and announced that the purpose of his visit was to prevent the implementation of the decisions of the Baghdad Conference.

Gromyko:　Do you refer to his last trip?

Abu 'Ammar:　The trip which preceded the meeting of the Arab foreign and economic ministers. The importance of the second Baghdad Summit[3] of Arab foreign and economic ministers——was in the coordination which found expression in a tripartite axis of Iraq, Syria and Palestine. This axis led the Steadfastness Front, and later directed the course of the entire conference.

These decisions were taken and I regard them as economic decisions—— which are more important than the political decisions. And we can say that the Palestinian delegation played in important role in making these decisions.

. . . .

Gromyko:　Comrade Arafat, forgive me for interrupting you but I ask you to express your opinion about the extent to which the decisions taken at the Baghdad Conference were implemented.

Abu 'Ammar:　That is precisely what I am about to talk about. Some of the Arabs wanted to provide us with a political decision and [then] manipulate the economic decisions [in their own interests]. The Palestinian delegation submitted a clear economic [working] paper, which was supported by the delegations of Syria and Iraq. . . .

As regards the economic decisions, it is fair to say that against Egypt about 90 percent were implemented. I say 90 percent since 10 percent of the deposits have still not been withdrawn [from Egyptian banks]. . . .

. . . We demanded, in our Palestinian working paper, to punish America economically and we know it is not easy to implement this demand. But our purpose was to put this on the record, and thus stimulate a debate on the subject.

The Palestinian delegation even entered a reservation [in the protocol of the conference] after the debate [on sanctions against the United States], since the Arab punishments do not really harm the US.

What is important is that we made these resolutions and that 90 percent of them were carried out. This is a big success relative [to what is known] in the region of the Arab world. As regards the support of the Steadfastness Front from the financial point of view, all Arab states paid their dues.

Gromyko: Are you talking about a deficit caused to the PLO?

Abu 'Ammar: The deficit affected everyone [all the states which were to receive payments from the Baghdad fund, like Jordan and Syria]. . . .

Later we went to the Organization for African Unity Congress in Monrovia. Sadat achieved a significant political victory in the congress for several reasons. One was the behaviour of the Liberian government towards the Palestinian delegation. This government denied the Palestinian delegation the right to speak and this forced the delegation to leave. The behaviour [of the Liberian government] towards the secretary-general of the Arab League, who was forced off the speaker's rostrum, compelled him, too, to leave [the conference]. Another reason for Sadat's success at the conference is that the bloc of forces that were opposed to Camp David was not represented at the conference at all, or rather, was not present at all. All these factors left the arena open for Sadat, and provided him with the decisions he was interested in. I record this in order to state that when we left for the Havana Conference,[4] 49 African states were equipped with the decisions of the Monrovia Conference. Despite all this, we managed to pass [in the Havana Conference] decisions sharply condemning the Camp David Accords and we managed to change African public opinion.

Gromyko: This was a blow to the Monrovia Conference and its decisions.

Abu 'Ammar: Yes, Yugoslavia and India were against an anti-Egyptian decision. Our Cuban comrades told us when we arrived in Havana that it would be difficult to achieve an anti-Camp David stand and I suppose this was your estimate, too. Now I have no choice but to mention the fact that prior to the Havana Conference there had been a sharp disagreement between Syria and Iraq. But the Palestinian delegation played an important role in coordinating the tripartite position, as we had done at the Baghdad Conference. The two presidents, Saddam Hussein and Assad, played an important and central role in the anti-Camp David decision-making in Havana. Through this magnificent tripartite coordination and due to the role comrade Castro played——whom we shall not forget——we succeeded in constructing a massive lobby by which we achieved those well-known decisions.

Ponomarev: The Cuban comrades played an enormous role.

Abu 'Ammar: Castro's wisdom played an important role in reaching the results. One should also mention here the role of the many progressive countries that were of considerable help to us. I will proceed to talk about the Lisbon Congress, which is no less important than the Havana Congress. The latter was a congress of governments, while the former was a popular congress. It was one of those wonderful popular congresses and it was the first to be held in a European country. The Portugese Communist Party played an important role in ensuring its success and so did your solidarity committee.

Ponomarev: We sent the head of the solidarity committee and Comrade Brezhnev sent a message to the congress.

Abu 'Ammar: Right. There were many letters from kings and presidents, first and foremost that of Comrade Brezhnev. Lisbon was a turning-point in the PLO's favour in the Western world. . . .

. . . [the Israelis] have concentrated on us [militarily], a concentration that is close to hell in southern Lebanon. . . .

We fought alone, and still do so, and we do not receive any single bullet except from the Iraqi and Syrian brothers who clashed twice with the Israeli air force.

Gromyko: How do you evaluate the results of the Syrian–Israeli air combat?

Abu 'Ammar: I'm no aviation expert. What interests me are the political decisions. What matters to me is that our fighter should not feel he is alone.

Ponomarev: What is important is that they have not succeeded in breaking your steadfastness and your [ability] to endure.

Abu 'Ammar: What happened was a war. . . .

There is now a let-up in this hell in the south, due to an American working paper submitted by Philip Habib.[5] I will give you a copy of it so we will not waste time. The most dangerous of the statements in the paper is that they speak about convening all the parties, and they also state that this relates to Israel, Lebanon, Syria, Jordan and the PLO under the supervision of the USA. Why Jordan?

Ponomarev: Without Egypt?

Abu 'Ammar: Without Egypt. . . .

. . . [The Americans] encourage the Egyptian regime to supply arms and ammunition——and possibly forces too——to the King of Morocco. This means the return of the king to the Camp David group by exploiting the defeats he suffered in the desert.[6] Therefore we went about a month ago to Morocco and Algeria and achieved good results. We received from King Hassan, after a three-and-a-half-hour meeting, his consent for a referendum. This is an important political achievement that we gained in North Africa. I returned later to Algeria, and informed President Chadli about the matter. A few days ago I informed the Polisario leaders about it and we await their reply.

Ponomarev: What do you mean by a referendum? A disengagement of forces?

Abu 'Ammar: Self-determination for the inhabitants of the desert.

Gromyko: Do both sides agree to a referendum?

Abu 'Ammar: The King of Morocco agreed and I await the reply of the Algerians and of the Polisario leaders. . . .

. . . We have made major political moves, for example: our missions to Asia, Africa and Latin America are still intact. When Nyerere decided to turn the PLO office into an embassy,[7] he said he discovered the organization at Havana. We received 189 delegations during six months from all over the world.

Gromyko: Most of whom were representatives of popular organizations?

Abu 'Ammar: Yes, all. I am not speaking about the official delegations. We maintain coordination with the Afro–Asian Solidarity Committee, with the World Peace Council and other international institutions, such as the Democratic Lawyers Association, which some time ago held a symposium in Paris and condemned Camp David from the judicial point of view. We made diplomatic moves in the countries we visited: Vienna, Ankara, Madrid, Lisbon and lately the meeting I had with Marchais[8] in order to obtain an invitation for a visit to France. All this in addition to other activities which we conduct, aware as we are of the fact that such activities have an influence only up to a certain limit. We have no illusions about them.

We have rejected the old idea of avoiding places where the Israelis appear. We have to challenge them at conferences, as was the case at the conference of the Association of Political Science Lecturers,[9] where Comrade Ponomarev participated, since our case is stronger. That happened in the Rome symposium too.

Now let us talk about an urgent subject. We are afraid of what might happen in Iran. The Americans contacted us through some Arab states and others and our answer was clear: we are not intermediaries, we stand by the Iranian revolution.[10]

Gromyko: Did the Americans contact you on their own initiative?

Abu 'Ammar: Not us [directly but through] Ramsey Clark, who is one of our sympathizers. We do not mediate, we support the Iranian revolution in its joy and in its sorrow. Khomeini's position is good and he shows understanding towards this position of ours. We sent the director of military operations to Iran, since the military option is possible. . . .

. . . .

Ponomarev: There are two questions: Comrade Arafat, with the unprecedented relationship with Austria, did you present your assessment of these achievements in your meetings with Kreisky and Brandt?

The second question concerns the Syrian troops present on Lebanese territory: do they supply you with arms? Do they participate with you in stopping the aggression?

Abu 'Ammar: . . . there were two air clashes between Israel and Syria. The Syrians also decided to send some air defence units in order to protect the [refugee] camps in their areas from Israeli air raids. This, especially after Israel announced it will strike at these camps. . . .

As regards your first question, about the horizons of political activity, what is important to us in this context is to explain our problem to world public opinion, as, for example, to the non-aligned states.

I recall participating in a conference in Algeria in 1973 and, despite the fact that the conference took place in Algeria, we did not achieve there what we tried to achieve. But during the past six years our activities among the non-aligned states produced results at Havana. Our activity in Europe is based on Europe's need for Arab oil. Oil has not yet been introduced as a factor in the battle, but there is apprehension of that there. Some of the Arab states help us in this respect.

Ponomarev: Kreisky became a friend of the Arabs?

Abu 'Ammar: Nobody says so. But we have to profit from it.

Ponomarev: It was an achievement, at least, that after your meeting with him cracks appeared within the Zionist camp. This is because he was previously among Israel's advocates.

Gromyko: Good. Thank you for the news you brought about some of the international problems and the assessment of the present situation.

First of all I will speak of the main problems of international politics, and about our position concerning these problems, although this position is known and I can discuss it in brief.

The USSR continues its principled policy regarding the Middle East as it did in the past. We are in favour of Israel's withdrawal from the occupied territories and in favour of granting the Palestinians their legitimate rights and the establishment of their independent state, together with the right of all states in the region to be sovereign. This is the essence of our position regarding problems of the Middle East.

We favour a comprehensive settlement, on condition that it be a just one. Leaders in the Arab world concentrate on a just solution and we share this view.

Sadat and the Americans speak of a just solution but their solution is unjust. Now too, as in the past, we sharply condemn separate agreements with the aggressors including the Camp David Accords.

The external form which is used to present these accords is irrelevant. Their essence did not change. They are accords of treason for the Arabs and their interests.[11] The whole world knows our position and our view regarding the Camp David Accords. In our talks with the Americans we do not use gentle language. In our meeting with Carter in Vienna, Comrade Brezhnev presented the steady Soviet position regarding the various problems. We want our Arab friends to know about this steady principled position of ours.

We attach special importance to the problem of unity in the Arab world. The more the Arab world is united, the more Egypt's situation and the situation of its leadership deteriorate. We identify with your views regarding the two Baghdad conferences. We observed the unity of the Arab peoples expressed in these two conferences where it was decided to take a correct posture towards the policy of imperialism, Israel and the Egyptian leadership. We were very satisfied with the success of the two conferences and the unity of the Arab peoples achieved there. We sincerely appreciate——and this is the clear-cut opinion of the Soviet leadership——the role of the PLO leadership and the role you, Comrade Arafat, played personally in these two conferences.

Some of the participants of the conferences would have been ready to "bend" to the aggressor were it not for the role you played. There were differences of opinion in the conference, but the result was favourable and it was expressed in the successful resolutions.

The Soviet leadership is interested that there be no retreat from these successes and achievements. They must be the basis for the next action. You can play a role in this matter. Your role will be of great importance in the future.

We attached importance to my conversation with King Hussein, the sub-stance of which was to adhere to the need to establish an independent state, if the Palestinians so wish. We notified Khaddam[12] about this Jordanian po-sition and he said, "I respect this declaration but I have my doubts regarding the king's sincerity and the seriousness of his declaration." It serves our com-mon interests that the king should not retreat from his declaration. You em-phasized the importance of cooperative action between you, Syria and Iraq in the struggle against Camp David. We attribute great importance to this. You can play a positive role in overcoming the differences between Syria and Iraq. You have not exhausted your possibilities in this regard yet.

There is another matter which you did not mention because of lack of time, which is the Saudi Arabian position in the last conferences——a position which was much more positive than we expected. Possibly it was influenced by the atmosphere prevailing at these conferences. The Syrians believe that there are several weak points in Saudi Arabian policy, expressed in the feel-ings of some members of the royal family who think that their defence and support can come only from the Americans.

It seems that the Steadfastness Front states have already gained some expe-rience in handling Saudi Arabia and in applying pressure on it.

Abu 'Ammar: Not all of them. Democratic Yemen [South Yemen] is differ-ent in this regard, especially after the treaty it signed with you.

Gromyko: Not decisively. The idea is the influence of the PLO and of other Arab elements. We think you should exploit this experience, because of the importance of Saudi Arabia's role in the Middle East problem. As for Dem-ocratic Yemen, its situation is delicate and difficult. But it goes along with the general policy stream of the Steadfastness Front. Saudi apprehensions about our friendship treaty with South Yemen have no basis; we do not in-terfere in the internal affairs of any country. The position of the Moroccan king is not based on principle; we should prevent these differences of opinion from removing King Hassan II from the Arab consensus.

Your evaluation of the Israeli–Egyptian–American steps concerning the West Bank was correct. We are witnessing an imperialist–Israeli–Sadat conspiracy. We could make some sharp statements on this matter, but the important thing is that we agree with your evaluation. You mentioned the American counter-attack. The Arabs are capable of responding to it if they unite in a struggle against it.

What is happening in southern Lebanon is part of the conspiracy and the spearhead of this conspiracy, and is directed against the Palestinian resistance, against Syria, and against Lebanon as a sovereign state. When we analyze this situation, we discover that the alliance between Syria and the Palestinian resistance in southern Lebanon plays a decisive role in the struggle against the American offensive. You mentioned the difficulties facing you in southern Lebanon. Desite the physical distance between us, we appreciate the extent of these difficulties and the efforts of the Palestinian resistance and Syria to thwart the American attack.

As for the Tunis Conference, there are differences of opinion regarding the success or failure of this conference. There are reports that Saudi Arabia will not play an honourable role concerning southern Lebanon. But the five Steadfastness Front states can play a role in blocking the imperialist assault, bearing in mind that such a role is the core for national action, the purpose of which is to bring about the success of the summit.

The way you described Philip Habib's proposals was to the point and accurate. These are imperialistic proposals and are hostile to the Arabs. We hope the evaluation of the Arab states with regard to these proposals will be similar.

We also agree with you as far as the internationalization of the Lebanese crisis is concerned. If this dangerous conspiracy succeeds, then it will pave the way for America to influence her friends in Europe to cause the internationalization of the Lebanese crisis. It will have a negative impact on Arab interests and, consequently, it will improve the ability of Sadat and Israel to extend their influence. I wish to emphasize that the Soviet position regarding these conspiracies——like the autonomy conspiracy and the conspiracy to internationalize the Lebanese crisis which Philip Habib brought——is no different than the position of the Arabs who adhere to their principles. Furthermore, we know that our socialist comrades share the same view.

We heard with satisfaction your statement that 90 percent of the Baghdad resolutions were implemented. This is a success for the Arabs. It is the first time I have heard such a clear and accurate assessment.

Now I wish to move on to some international problems.

Iran: I refer to the recent events concerning the occupation of the American embassy in Teheran and the American activity connected with it.

The Americans contacted us a few days ago requesting that we play a role in the affair through the senior foreign diplomat in Teheran, the Czech ambassador, for the purpose of freeing the American diplomats.

We informed the Americans that we adhere to international agreements and that our position results from the contents of these agreements [relating to diplomatic immunity].

If we look at this problem from the point of view of international agreements, then we must show understanding to the Americans and there is no justification for Iran to criticize us.

If we don't consider it within this framework, but rather from the point of view of American–Iranian relations, then we do not wish to protect American interests, despite their request that we do so. Therefore, we will not get involved in a complicated discussion on the subject and in no way are we going to protect the Americans in this matter. We think there are no differences of opinion between us in this matter, despite the difference in status between us——we as a state and you as a national liberation movement. This is quite satisfactory.

So far we have not received the American reaction to our response.

Abu 'Ammar: The Iranians understood from your delegate that he accepted the American request.

Gromyko: Our representative did not object to the announcement of the Security Council chairman, since this is a brief declaration concerning international agreements regarding the diplomatic corps.

Abu 'Ammar: Let us not forget that the declaration includes some threats of the use of force.

Gromyko: We read this declaration and found in it no more than the formulation of international agreements regarding diplomatic representation, and this formulation is balanced. There was a sharp dispute on the subject relating to hints about using force. Our position, which rejects and condemns such actions, is clear.

When the Iranian revolution broke out, there were talks then about the use of force. We opposed this logic and our position remains as it was.

We are now just prior to the presentation of the Palestinian issue in the UN. This matter is very important to us and to yourselves. The question is: what do you expect from the discussion? What is your minimum demand of this discussion? Did you think carefully about the form in which the subject will be presented and how it can be achieved? I ask you to answer this after I finish my words in a short while.

We will no doubt support and assist the Palestinian and Arab position, and we will back every proposal and every plan which you submit to the UN. This support also applies to our socialist comrades. The last question is, and it is only a question: it is known that America——when it talks with us about the Palestinian problem——its delegates tell us: How is it possible for us to recognize the PLO and the establishment of an independent Palestinian state when the PLO does not recognize Israel and the well-known UN resolutions?

We heard the very convincing agrument from your side regarding the motives for your refusal to accept those resolutions, since they deal with refugees and make no mention of the "Palestinian people." These reasons are known. But in our talks with the Americans, we always confront this obstacle and this limitation which cannot be overcome.

Here I wish to ask you a question: Are you considering certain tactical[13] concessions in return for getting recognition from the hostile camp? Are you considering recognizing these international resolutions? And are you also considering recognizing Israel's right to exist as an independent sovereign state? I remember my conversation with Yigal Allon[14] who asked me, "How can we talk with the PLO when they do not recognize Israel's right to exist as an independent state, and when the PLO does not even recognize the UN resolutions?" He also told me that if the PLO recognized Israel and the UN resolutions, the situation would be different, and in that case we [Israel] would have dealt with it in a different manner.

My question to Allon was: Which side will make the first step, the PLO or Israel? Allon replied, "If Israel would have initiated a declaration in that direction, the PLO would not have agreed to issue a similar declaration on its behalf, based on the recognition of Israel and the UN resolutions." Now the government [in Israel] has changed,[15] and I do not know what your [PLO] position is now.

I would also like to ask you, is your position to reject all concessions on this problem, even those not involving principles? What matters to you is the establishment of a Palestinian state, and, notwithstanding the differences that may exist [among yourselves], the establishment of a Palestinian state is the foundation and contains all the other things.

During the discussions with the Americans we felt we were at a dead end. Here I would like to know what your opinion is and please regard it as a question only. . . .

Ponomarev: You spoke alone, whereas both of us spoke: Gromyko presented to you in detail the general direction of the Soviet leadership towards the Middle East and the Palestinian problem. We know, from reports we have received and from reports you have, that the PLO marches onward, and you have outgrown the framework of an Arab liberation movement. The facts are known to us and the recognition by many states is known. We are very satisfied.

We have assisted and will continue to assist in the future [concerning recognition].

We think that the greetings Comrade Brezhnev conveyed to you congratulating you on your birthday help in this matter, as did the message Comrade Brezhnev sent to Barcelona. This will help you from the Arab and international points of view, to enable the world and the Arabs to understand the principles of Soviet policy towards you.

You now face two major events:

1. The Tunis Conference.
2. The UN debate on the [Palestinian] problem.

You raised the subject of consultations on this matter [of the UN debate]. We always asked you to consult us on this subject. It is very important that we know in advance the steps of the adversaries in the UN so that we can exploit the UN stage by exposing aggressive actions which Israel conducts in southern Lebanon.[16] It cannot be condemned inside Israel,[16] but Israel has friends in the US and it is useful to campaign to expose Israel's actions against elderly people and children, using all propaganda means.

As regards the Tunis Conference, you know more than we do. We agree with your opinion that it is not worth devoting the whole conference to discussing the subject of southern Lebanon and to avoid a debate on the overall problem, the Middle East problem. It is very important that you mobilize all your resources for this purpose and that your Arab friends are active so that the conference will make the right decisions.

It is important that we devote special attention to Algeria. Lately we have had strong ties with Algeria. We received a party delegation [from Algeria] and sent a comrade, Brezhnev's deputy, to participate in the ceremonies in Algeria. They told us that President Ali Chadli Ben Jedid and Party Leader Salah Yachiawi are determined to continue Boumedienne's policy. The Algerians said the same things to our delegation chief who attended their ceremonies. Algeria's word has considerable weight now.

Lately we had contacts with the National Movement in Lebanon, especially with the Communists and Jumblatt. All of them stressed that their relations with the Palestinians are good and that they are participating in the fight against the Israelis and against the reactionary leadership in the country [Lebanon].[17]

Abu 'Ammar: There is a joint command which I head.

Ponomarev: For this reason it is very important that the relationships be good, not only with the anti-imperialist organizations in Lebanon, but also with the other forces, like Franjieh[18] for instance. We must have influence with the leadership of the Lebanese state. It is necessary that the Syrians play a role in the contacts with Lebanon. Of course, you, because of your presence in Lebanon, must take care that your relations with the Lebanese state should not worsen because then your situation would be difficult.

Abu 'Ammar: Our relations with Al-Hus [Lebanon's prime minister] are good, with President Sarkis——not bad. The relations with the Islamic Council, with the National Front and with President Franjieh——good. This year we spent 19 million Lebanese pounds on reparations for the south and nine million pounds on treating civilians.

Ponomarev: This is your message and it is good. You have to present it in the UN and in Tunis. To conclude I would like to stress that in all our talks with the Arabs, especially with President Assad, we stressed a just and comprehensive solution to the Palestinian problem. We declared this position in formal talks, through the party and the various popular organizations.

Lately we established a committee for friendship and solidarity with the Palestinian people. When the Vietnamese people struggled with the USA, we established a similar solidarity committee. Vietnam, as we know, later won and we hope that this time victory will be achieved too. The committee has been established and we wish you every success.

Abu 'Ammar: For our part we set up a committee for solidarity with you. As for Comrade Gromyko's question, we are ready to reply to it, if it will lead to any results, since it indeed deserves an effort on our part. . . . I say that I agree to the Soviet–American communique, and accept what you agreed upon with the Americans.

Gromyko: The Soviet–American communique mentions the Geneva Convention and Palestinian rights. This communique, which you asked about, did not have results in the field. If it were implemented, the circumstances would have been more favourable. I do not wish to put pressure on you to reply on this subject.

If there is a change in your position. I ask you to notify us, since one cannot escape this issue. In every statement, the Americans say: How can we recognize an organization while they are not ready to recognize anything? This is demagoguery, but we have to know how to deal with it. I ask you to think about it and to make your comments.

Abu 'Ammar: The USA itself cancelled the Soviet–American communique; it pushed Sadat to go to Jerusalem. We were told: if you recognize 242 after you add your reservations——we will recognize you, open the dialogue with you and take the commitment to establish a state. This was in 1977.

Later the USA withdrew from this. Through Rashad Faron they told us, "The train of settlement is moving along. If you want, join it——if not, you may do whatever you wish." Later they offered us a formula relating to 242——

that we should announce our consent to it——and this was for the sole purpose of starting the dialogue with us.

Ponomarev: They conspired with the Egyptians and fortified their positions.

Abu 'Ammar: This strengthens our and your view. . . .

. . . .

Gromyko: I thank you for the useful discussion. We think that we march with you on the same path concerning the Middle East problem. The Soviet Union is a friend of the Arabs and does not tend to change its friends. We hope that the Arabs and the PLO feel the same way.

Abu 'Ammar: The PLO has no doubts.

Gromyko: If there is any point in publishing a joint communique, we have a draft we ask you to look at.

Notes

1. Boris Ponomarev, in fact, is not "Gromyko's Deputy," but head of the International Department of the Central Committee of the CPSU.
2. The conference of the Rejectionist Front, which immediately followed the signing of the Camp David Accords in September 1978. This conference, in which almost all Arab countries participated, was an attempt to lure Egypt back into the Arab fold, although Egypt itself was excluded.
3. The second Baghdad Summit was held following the signing of the peace treaty between Israel and Egypt in March 1979.
4. The Havana Conference was the tri-annual gathering of non-aligned states, held in the summer of 1979. The previous conference had been held in Colombo, Sri-Lanka, in 1976, and the forthcoming one is scheduled to convene in Baghdad in September 1982.
5. Habib, then a senior State Department official, had been assigned trouble-shooting duties under the Carter administration. President Reagan recalled him from retirement in the summer of 1981 as a negotiator in the Lebanese crisis.
6. This refers to Morocco's protracted war in the Sahara against the Algerian-supported Polisario.
7. President Nyerere of Tanzania, who befriended the PLO delegations at the Non-aligned Conference in Havana, raised the PLO office in Dar-al-Salam to the rank of embassy.
8. Georges Marchais, the leader of the French Communist Party.
9. The International Conference of Political Scientists held in Moscow in the summer of 1979, to which an Israeli delegation was accepted after many delays on the part of the Soviets.
10. Commitment to the revolution, any "people's revolution," seems to be the PLO's guideline.

11. This is an attempt by the Soviet foreign minister to assume a role in the Middle East peace process by dismissing the Camp David Accords as an "American–Egyptian treason" of the Arab camp. He does not hide his hostility toward Sadat and toward American Middle East policy.

12. 'Abd-al-Halim Khaddam, Foreign Minister of Syria.

13. Very significantly, Gromyko does not ask the PLO to make any substantive concessions with regard to recognizing Israel, but only to make tactical changes in its rhetoric, in order to lure the "hostile" West into recognizing the PLO.

14. A former Israeli foreign minister. He met with his Soviet counterpart in 1975 during the UN General Assembly session in New York.

15. In May 1977, the Labour Party, of which Allon was a leader, lost the elections and the Likud government took power.

16. This refers to Israel's peace movement, which criticized the government for its preventive raids against PLO positions in Lebanon.

17. This attests to Soviet collusion with the pro-PLO forces in Lebanon (Jumblatt's Socialists) and its subversion of the pro-Western ("reactionary") forces there.

18. Suleiman Franjieh was president of Lebanon from 1970 to 1976. He comes from the northern township of Zagharta and leads a pro-Syrian group among the Maronite Christians of Lebanon.

Document 5: Testimony of Vladimir Sakharov

Vladimir Nikolaevich Sakharov is the pseudonym of a former Soviet Ministry of Foreign Affairs official who worked clandestinely in cooperation with the KGB from 1967 to 1971. During his service in North Yemen, Egypt, and Kuwait, Sakharov was personally involved in a variety of Soviet operations.

In the following excerpt, Sakharov draws on his extensive operational experience in the Middle East to bear witness to the early years of Soviet–PLO relations. He details the increase in Soviet support for "National Liberation Movements" after the 1967 war and how this affected links with the PLO. Sakharov reveals the nature of Soviet support, such as the training programs conducted by the KGB and GRU, and shows that the PLO was merely one instrument of Soviet Middle Eastern strategy.

Sakharov also describes Soviet coordination of various aspects of the political campaign waged primarily through the network of front organizations run by the International Department of the CPSU's Central Committee.

Source: This excerpt is taken from an interview conducted in 1985 by the Oral History Project of the International Security Studies Program at The Fletcher School of Law and Diplomacy.

Q: I'd like to go into the educational process for a moment. Those who were sent into the Soviet Union for training—from national front organizations, terrorist groups, and so forth—they weren't interested in learning about Russian history. These people were then, were they not, for special military and intelligence preparation?

A: Yes, of course. The KGB and GRU each had quotas to fulfill in sending people to the training centers. Nor were these people just Egyptians. Many of them were either Palestinians or Jordanians. It really didn't matter too much who exactly was chosen to go. I knew in Kuwait, for example, that it came to be simply a matter of filling quotas for both the KGB and GRU.

Q: Who had the responsibility for determining which of the Egyptians or Palestinians would be sent for that training? Was this primarily a GRU responsibility?

A: No. The GRU people were the military attaches, and so forth. They would evaluate lists presented to them by the Egyptian military commanders. These lists were drawn up for the consideration of Soviet military advisers in the country. They would sit around at a meeting and the Egyptians would give them these lists of people they wanted to have the training.

With other groups, though, there really was no set procedure. There were some criteria. Number one among these was sympathy to the policy of the Soviet Union in the Middle East. Anti-Americanism was assumed for all the Arabs. By itself, however, it wasn't enough. There also had to be a degree of sympathy for the Soviet line. Nor was there a particularly thorough screening process. Political reliability was not evaluated until after these individuals arrived in the Soviet Union. Many of them went to Patrice Lumumba University—ostensibly to study "agriculture"—and others went to the Academy of Social Sciences in Moscow. Of course, most of these people have no knowledge of the Russian language when they come, so language instruction is given to them. This gives more time for evaluation. After this assessment, they are sent on to other schools if they seem promising.

Q: The years you spent in Yemen, Egypt, and Kuwait during the late 1960s and early 1970s are a very important period for Soviet policy toward the third world. After the fall of Khrushchev, Soviet support for so-called "national liberation movements" grew significantly. Could you discuss just in general terms what you found first in Yemen, and then later in Egypt, with regard to changes in Soviet doctrine or policy toward the Third World?

A: My first experience with a national liberation movement was Kowi Makowi's organization in South Yemen. At that time, Soviet policy was to support Makowi and to make sure that he didn't fall into the hands of the Chinese. He was working directly with the KGB resident—it was no secret to any of the Embassy personnel that we were supporting him, and that the primary target was to use him as a main figure in the liberation movement in the British colonies. The supply of arms from the Soviet Union, however, was zero. The Soviets were trying to make a deal with the Egyptians, so that the Egyptians would supply Makowi with certain items—you see, the Egyptians were to be used as a conduit.

This was before the 1967 war. At that time, there wasn't a strong commitment to any sort of strategy on how to deal with Arab nationalism. Makowi was not by any means a communist or even ideologically sympathetic to the Soviets. So, at this time, there was the historic commitment to support national liberation—since Khrushchev's time—but there was no real experience in the way of dealing with Arab nationalist movements, or national liberation governments. They were leery of making another mistake like Israel, as far as dealing with Britain. Here the Soviets had pushed hard to get Britain out of Israel in 1946 and 1974, and then they ended up with a problem on their hands.

I even saw evidence of this when I was at the Academy of Social Sciences. The Soviets had tremendous numbers of Algerians, Iranians, and other Arabs in Moscow. There were Moroccans, there were Egyptians—you name it. They were being united in the science of revolution, the subject that was taught for one year as a sort of engineering science. This course was based on the Soviet experience, and the works of Lenin on how to take control of the state. How to destabilize the state; how to control communications; how to control the press; all these stages of revolution were part of the curriculum.

The PLO was not really in the cards at that time, because it was conceived as essentially an Algerian organization. Arafat was originally very close to the Algerians, and the Soviets didn't have much faith in him. After 1967, however, I believe we came to a whole new stage in the Soviet assessment of the Middle East.

Q: On what basis? Why do you say that?

A: The Soviets were pushed very hard after the war. On the local level, I can tell you that there were demonstrations in the streets against the Soviets and all their input. Some Soviet diplomats were killed. In Yemen, the Soviet Ambassador sort of gave us the new assessment. We were to express total commitment to the Arab cause—without any reservations. That seemed like a steady line for 10 days. After the war happened, we really had to go out to the masses. I'm sure this was done at higher levels also.

Q: So after the 1967 war there was more of a commitment to the Arab cause. What did this mean in terms of the liberation movements?

A: Well, right after '67 the Soviets had a number of survey teams which came from the Ministry of Foreign Affairs, the KGB, and the International Department (ID). I think there was a great deal of dissatisfaction with the nature of Soviet embassy reporting before the war. When I arrived in Alexandria, I saw a great deal of reshuffling. There were many new cadres sent. Three ambassadors were kicked out.

And that year, from '67 to '68, was the year of the formation of a relationship between the PLO and the Soviet Union. It was a very strong commitment especially in terms of, as I mentioned, the establishment of quotas of PLO members to be trained in the Soviet Union. There were rallies organized by the Soviet cultural centers, which focused on "Solidarity with the people of Palestine," and the support of Resolution 242.

Q: This support came through the Soviet Cultural Center?

A: Through the Cultural Center, the Embassies, and so forth. The ID was involved with political support of the PLO, but not directly—I don't recall any instance of them communicating directly. But the KGB and GRU had extensive contacts with them. As far as their personal contacts were concerned, I know there was an operative in Cairo who handled PLO problems. There were two other operatives who worked out of the Cairo Embassy that shuttled to Beirut and Cairo all the time. They were in charge of liaison, setting up PLO organizations in Beirut. These two looked very military, but they were KGB.

Q: Was there any distinction made between the various splinter movements within the PLO?

A: The distinction came a little later. Originally it was a commitment to the PLO as a political force that would be able to take over occupied lands. It was rather like a big campaign to build up the PLO and the Palestinians in the Middle East as a great political force. It was thought that the PLO would be a very good vehicle to establish Soviet popularity among the Arabs.

So it was simultaneously a political operation and a military operation. The military support, however, was on a far more clandestine level. At this time tremendous numbers of PLO were being sent to the Soviet Union for training. Most of them weren't going through Egypt, however. The Soviets had to treat Nasser with caution, because Nasser wanted to be number one— he was leery of the PLO and leery of the Soviet's connections with the PLO. He didn't want to see Soviet support diffused among various nations. Therefore, the Soviets were very cautious to hide their PLO support from Nasser, and also from Kuwait. Most of the PLO trainees were sent from Beirut or Latakia. I also had a classmate in Algeria who was doing something with the PLO in Algiers.

There was, of course, a contradiction between the Soviet line on the Middle East and the line we were giving the PLO. We tried to basically muffle the issue in discussions with PLO members.

Q: Let's go on to the early '70s. Did you see any shift in policy regarding the PLO?

A: As I've said, Egypt was a hostile territory to the PLO. Direct supplies and arms were conducted by the Soviets through Syria. That started to occur without any reservations by the early '70s. The Egyptians I came in contact with considered the Palestinians as second-rate citizens. But in Syria and in Beirut, the Soviets developed a very strong organization. There was a continuous increase of PLO members going to the Soviet Union and to Moscow for all kinds of things. I saw people going to the Medical School, to the Land Grant University, to Patrice Lumumba, and so forth.

Q: After September of '70, what sort of political action was taking place in

Egypt? Were any of the political fronts more active, particularly the Afro–Asian People's Solidarity Organization (AAPSO)?

A: Egypt became a center of rallies. It became the center of the joint Soviet–Arab fight to liberate Palestine, and to push Israel back to where she was before the '67 war—by Soviet standards. This became one of the central themes for the front apparatus.

Q: Let's talk about the fronts for a minute. Who was in charge of their operations—KGB? ID?

A: You see, they came under the auspices of the Cultural Center. Their contacts through the Cultural Center were on a permanent basis, and the campaigns were put on by the International Department. Therefore, the KGB was in permanent contact with the administration of both organizations.

Q: Give us an idea of what these organizations would do in a year in Egypt.

A: Well, there were many sorts of rallies—there was one a month—on many themes. There was a meeting about the Chinese border claims. We would rally them against the Chinese, to make sure the organization was not likely to become Chinese-influenced. That was the Soviet goal. Before I got there, they had a row over the Dominican issue. The World Peace Council was there, too. They had some members in Egypt. They had meetings organized, not specifically on the subject of "hands off Vietnam, Americans go home," but on the subject of Soviet support for those who were fighting imperialism in the world. We had the movie *War and Peace*. We had a showing of this movie, and everybody who was a spy was there. The outcome of the meeting was how the Soviet Union was fighting imperialism. So this was all part of a wider effort, it was all tied in to what was happening in the military support activities, and so forth.

Q: Around this time—1970, 1971—was there any shift in the line toward the PLO?

A: Around the end of the month of February 1971, a cable came from Moscow, a very short cable. It said that, from now on, official contacts with the PLO would be conducted through the Afro–Asian People's Solidarity Organization (AAPSO). The diplomats would refrain from any official contacts; there was the Solidarity Organization and civil friendship societies through which we were to contact the PLO. I interpreted this as a shift toward a higher degree of clandestinity in our relations with the PLO. Whether or not this was caused by the Black September movement I don't know, but it was a major shift at the time.

Document 6: Report of PLO Mission to the USSR

This document contains excerpts of a report addressed to Arafat from the PLO delegation at Simferopol, the Soviet Union's terrorist training camp in the Crimea. This is another example of direct Soviet assistance to the PLO. Most factions of the PLO are represented. In addition to its terrorist training, the PLO was being trained to fight a conventional war with Israel and, probably, to subvert any strengthening of Lebanese sovereignty. A further important factor in this report is the *propaganda* role that the Commander of the delegation envisions for the Palestinian trainees.

Source: Raphael Israeli, *PLO in Lebanon*, Document 27.

The brother, head of the PLO Executive Committee, the General Commander of the Palestinian Revolutionary Forces, the brother Yasser Arafat, may Allah protect him!

Subject: Report on the Palestinian delegation to the Soviet Union
Date of Report: 22 January 1981

On 1 September 1980 the delegation arrived in Simferopol in the Soviet Union, where it had been decided to hold the courses. The delegation numbered 194 officers and NCO's. Courses were given for the following posts:

1. Tank battalion commander
2. Tank company commander
3. Infantry company commander
4. Reconnaissance company commander
5. Infantry platoon commander
7. Anti-tank platoon commander
8. Sagger missile platoon commander
9. Anti-aircraft platoon commander

Factions of the Resistance (movement) as follows:

1. The Palestinian National Liberation Movement—Fatah
2. The Palestine Liberation Army
3. The Armed Struggle
4. The Popular Front
5. The Democratic Front
6. The General Command
7. Sa'iqa
8. The Arab Front
9. The Popular Struggle Front
10. The Palestine Liberation Front

Studies began in all the courses in a regular fashion, according to the programme which had been prepared. The delegation command studied the programme for each course and made comments, which were taken into account by the heads of the college and implemented in the study programme as far as possible, especially in connection with theoretical issues which suit our conditions and combat procedures in towns, mountains, and coastal plain defence.

After classroom studies were completed in the various courses attended by the delegation, the time arrived for final manoeuvres, [*sic*] in which all members of the delegation participated. The exercise included:

1. Command and staff exercise (work on maps).
2. Tactical exercise.

When discussing the exercise, the delegation command proposed that the command and staff exercise involve the entire delegation, in accordance with the specialization in each course and its role in the battle; the tactical exercise would then follow. However, the college commanders pointed out that the method which the delegation command wanted to use was not feasible, due to its heavy demand on resources which the college was unable to provide under the circumstances. In the end, the delegation command accepted the college's opinion, and the exercise was carried out in the following way:

1. Command and staff exercise at brigade level:

    The battalion commander students comprised the brigade command in the exercise. The brigade staff was made up of students from other courses. Altogether 17 officers participated. Work on the map lasted for three consecutive days. The result was excellent according to the officers who supervised on behalf of the college. The work was done under the daily and personal supervision of the college commander. The command and staff exercise included the following stages:

a) Advance when expecting an encounter battle; carrying out an encounter battle
b) Attack in direct contact
c) Defence

2. On the fourth day of manoeuvres, the tactical exercise was begun by members of the delegation—an infantry company reinforced by a tank company in a direct contact attack. All types of organic and attached weapons were used in the exercise imitating a real battle. The exercise was carried out in earnest by the Palestinian combatant, despite the difficult weather conditions. The exercise was a success; it earned the praise of teachers, observers, and other delegations at the college.

Achievements of the delegation:

1. In instruction
   a) The subject matter was picked up very well. The teachers saw that the Palestinian delegation was the best in rapid learning, compared with the other delegations.
   b) The anti-tank course teachers noticed that trainees prepared their guns and took up firing positions in less than the required time.
   c) Teachers who accompanied anti-aircraft course trainees on their trip to the firing range reported that they performed very well.
   d) The delegation did well in discussions on political topics in the framework of the political lessons; the Soviet comrades deem such lessons very important and concentrate on them.

2. Ties [between nationalities at the school]
   a) Creation of good ties with instructors and workers at the college.
   b) Familiarization with the customs and traditions of the peoples of the host country.
   c) Explanation of the Palestinian cause, the role of the PLO as the only legitimate representative of the Palestinian people, and the Palestinian revolution until the realization of victory and the establishment of an independent state.
   d) Getting to know the other delegations and liberation movements, and establishing good ties while explaining our case, whether during personal meetings or in the framework of official meetings.

. . . .

The commander of the delegation from South Africa showed full understanding for our revolution and cause, so much so, that during the closing ceremony for his delegation, he spoke in front of all the delegations and the Soviet comrades about the Palestinian revolution and Yasser Arafat more than about himself and the host country.

Negative aspects of the mission: . . .

2. From the point of view of the delegation

    a) The participants in the courses did not correctly understand the political aspects of sending military delegations abroad. As a result, the upper echelon of the delegation, namely the participants in the battalion officer course, refused to study and asked to return, using all sorts of illogical excuses. If this is considered according to the correct military criterion, and despite the possibility of overcoming these difficulties very simply—if each one of them had remembered the orders he received during his meeting with the commander of the struggle before the trip, the situation would have been entirely different. This was noted by the delegation command in the report which was sent to Your Excellency through the representative of the organization in Moscow, Colonel al-Sha'ar, on 22 September 1980.

    b) Those responsible in most of the organizations were not careful in choosing candidates for the course and the delegation command was forced to send a few of them home. . . .

Names of individuals concerned are given in the document, but have been deleted here for reasons of space.

.   .   .   .

Following are the proposals: . . .

   3. The subordination of the officers to the course command so that their personal ability as commanders can be checked without taking into account the considerations of organizations or preferences according to former opinions. . . .

   9. The military delegations in foreign countries must be equipped with a large number of books in foreign languages, especially in the language of the host country—in political, historical and cultural subjects. They should also have PLO stickers and slogans in booklets and publications, etc.

10. Similar material should also be sent by post.

Sir, the Supreme Commander, may God protect him, I am sending this report on behalf of the PLO delegation to the Soviet Union, and pledge our adherence to wise behaviour which will guide us to victory and the establishment of our independent state; long live the PLO under your leadership, the sole legal representative of the Palestinian people.

/s/ *Colonel Rashad Ahmed*, Commander of the Delegation.

Document 7: PLO Statements on Relations with the USSR

T he following statements reveal the services with which the PLO repaid the USSR for weapons, military training, and so forth.

Source: Israel Defence Forces Spokesman, *PLO Ties with the USSR and Other Eastern Bloc Countries, September 1981.*

"Relations between the PLO and Moscow couldn't be better, with both parties maintaining close political ties. The PLO has a coordination agreement with the Soviet Union—signed last year during Arafat's visit to Moscow—according to which, when a problem arises, a high-level Palestinian delegation embarks for Moscow to coordinate a joint stand with the Soviets.

"Hundreds of Palestinian officers holding the rank of brigade commander have already been accredited by Soviet military academies, and members of the PLO use arms of Soviet and East European manufacture in their guerrilla warfare against Israel. Today some 2,000 Palestinians are enrolled in Soviet institutions of learning, and 200 scholarships are granted annually to PLO members, mostly in the field of science and technology.

"The PLO enjoys special diplomatic status in the Soviet Union: the PLO representative is free to travel throughout the country, unlike the other diplomatic representatives."

> Muhammad ash-Sha'er, PLO representative in Moscow, in a lecture in Beirut, *Radio Monte Carlo*, 17 February 1981.

"I call upon you to adopt the most violent means against the US and its interests in the region."

> Yasser Arafat, *The Voice of Palestine*, Beirut, 27 April 1979.

"We emphasize a firm and clear stand against imperialism and its interests in the region and affirm that imperialism—primarily American imperialism—is our principal enemy. Therefore the interests of the US in the area should be crushed, and any thought that that country could be neutral in our conflict with the Zionist enemy should be abolished and rejected."

> George Habash, *Al-Dustur,* London, 30 April 1979.

"The Iranian revolution is an example of damaging American interests.

"The loss of American installations in Iran is an example of a determined Islamic decision to attack American interests throughout the world."

> Yasser Arafat, *Tages Anzeiger,* Switzerland, 14 May 1979.

"American interests in the Middle East and elsewhere in the world are well known to us, and we will hit them because we realize the enormity of the animosity that the Americans harbour for us, Palestinians. . . .

"We Palestinians will perpetuate the war of attrition against Israel until our rights are completely regained. And I am prepared to extend a hand of friendship and alliance to any power, even the devil, to crush Israel and undermine American machinations."

> Arafat's deputy Abu Ayad, *AP,* Qatar, 15 May 1979.

"We shall set petroleum ablaze if the American forces try to approach it. We shall set it alight in defence of Arab petroleum."

> Yasser Arafat, *Reuters,* Beirut, 6 April 1980.

"The Russians have helped progressive forces in Afghanistan to foil efforts by pro-American elements to take control of the country's institutions.

"The Americans have backed opponents of the Afghan government in an attempt to counter blows to the US in neighbouring Iran, where militant students have 49 American hostages in the US Embassy in Teheran since 4 November.

"Western hypocrisy was underlined by the fact that the US and its Western friends were bitterly opposed to the Islamic forces in Afghanistan."

> Bassam Abu Sherif, Spokesman of the PFLP wing of the PLO, *Reuters,* 8 January 1980.

"The Russian involvement in Afghanistan is an important asset to all revolutionary forces which oppose the expansion of the American presence in the Middle East."

> Yasser Abd Rabhi, head of the PLO "Department of Information and Culture," *Radio Monte Carlo*, 8 January 1980.

Document 8: KGB Agent in the PLO

T his document demonstrates the USSR's utilization of the PLO for Soviet purposes. The following letter by an Iranian official informs his superiors that a Fatah official is an agent of the KGB. Further, the Iranian official complains that in this capacity the Fatah representative has worked against the "interests of the Islamic revolution."

Source: Raphael Israeli, *PLO in Lebanon,* Document 54.

Top Secret

From: Iranian Embassy in Beirut

To: Foreign Ministry, Director General of Asian-African Affairs, Mr. Louasani

cc: Political Director-General, Mr. Sheikh al-Salam

It has come to my attention, that in the future you may appoint Mr. Ahmed Mawahdi to a position at one of our embassies. I thus feel myself obligated to convey to you the following information. I assure you, no personal grudge is involved.

1.   The man is an indirect spy for the KGB who worked through Fatah.

2.   During his service in Beirut, he totally ignored the interests of the Islamic revolution, and acted as an agent.

3.   As a result of his mistaken policy, he misled about 60 percent of the workers due to his improper conduct.

4.   During his period of service, he caused consternation among the Shi'ites who were faithful to the Islamic revolution.

5.   I have attached photocopies of his reports.

Once again I note that I do not expect that you either accept or reject this information, but it is, I repeat, for the sake of God.

/s/ *Syed Mehsan Musawi*, Temporary Chargé D'Affaires

Document 9: Palestine National Covenant, Article 9: "Armed Struggle" as a "Strategy"

In 1968, the PLO's Palestine National Covenant was amended. Its new Article 9 addressed the role of violence in the Palestinian struggle, stating that "armed struggle" is to be a *strategy* and not a means to an end: "armed struggle" is an end in itself. There can be no permanent political solution, short of the replacement of all of Israel by a Palestinian state. There will be no political deal for other than *tactical purposes;* as a result such a deal will not last. Since this article has neither been amended nor deleted, it is still the basis of the PLO's strategy.

Source: Palestine National Covenant, Article 9, 1968.

Article 9: Armed struggle is the only way to liberate Palestine and is therefore a strategy and not tactics. The Palestinian Arab people affirms its absolute resolution and abiding determination to pursue the armed struggle and to march forward towards the armed popular revolution, to liberate its homeland and return to it [to maintain] its right to a natural life in it, and to exercise its right of self-determination in it and sovereignty over it.

Document 10: PLO Diplomatic Missions: Terrorist Headquarters

T his document contains excerpts of testimony by Hamed Ahmed Muhammed 'Isa, a Palestinian from Lebanon. His testimony reveals that Palestinian offices in East Berlin were being used as bases for terrorist acts against the West.

Source: Raphael Israeli, *PLO in Lebanon*, Document 79.

This interview was broadcast on Israel Television on 23 July 1982 (translated from Arabic).

One day, Ahmed took us to the offices of the organization [PLO] in East Berlin and the man in charge was at home. . . . Ahmed came to report that we were entrusted with a mission. We asked what it was and he said, "some kind of bombing." 'We said, "We came here to have a good time; if we are caught we'll be in trouble." He said, "Don't worry." We insisted that we did not want to do it. He said, "OK, leave the task to me," and we went on roaming around the city with him. . . .

Then, I went to order my return ticket to Lebanon since my vacation was over. I went home and saw Ahmed again. He said, "We are going out for our mission." I said that I refused to go because I was going back to Lebanon. He said, "OK leave it to me," and he went downstairs. Downstairs a dark-skinned boy was waiting for him, holding a briefcase, which he handed over to Ahmed. I asked what it was but he said, "Don't worry . . ."

There were Germans who collaborated with our organization, such as Wolfgang Iwot [and] Tatlev Mercury. . . . Another was called Hiblmar Krist and another was Karl Kamele. . . . They are Communists. . . . They published articles for us in the newspapers because they knew German better than us. . . . They also organized political gatherings. . . .

At 21:00 that night a bomb exploded in a restaurant, wounding 25 people,

8 of them seriously; a one-year-old baby is still in critical condition. The bomb was so powerful that all the traffic was blocked, the bomb had been hidden in the briefcase, and a woman was seen leaving the restaurant briefly prior to the explosion. . . .

Q: Why would they want to blow up an Italian restaurant in West Berlin?

A: According to Ahmed, that restaurant was frequented by foreigners: Americans, Pakistanis; that is, foreigners. Therefore, they decided to blow it up.

Document 11: PLO Training of Other "National Liberation Movements"

This document shows PLO support for many insurgent groups. Printed below are excerpts of an office diary which includes the dates for training of Salvadorians, Haitians, South Africans, Turks, and Malawese. The diary was captured in Tyre, June, 1982.

Source: Raphael Israeli, *PLO in Lebanon,* Document 55.

Translations of diary entries follow.

February 26: Final exams for the Salvadorian course
April 6: The course for the comrades from Haiti began today
April 29: Abu Hamid, Damascus, 446608
May 16: The comrades from South Africa left today
June 4: A group of five persons arrived from Turkey
June 8: The course started for the comrades from Turkey
June 11: A group arrived from Africa, 10 people from Malawi
June 23: The training started for the comrades from Malawi
July 4: The course of the comrades from Turkey was completed
July 6: The Turkish group left

The diary entries are reproduced on the following page.

Document 12: The Japanese Red Army Explains Its Relations with the PLO

E xcerpts from a pamphlet published on the seventh anniversary of the Lod (Lydda) massacre, explain the Japanese Red Army's connection with the PLO. The relationship has resulted from mutual devotion to "simultaneous world revolution." Leadership can only be found through violence. "Comrade Okamoto," who was captured at Lod and recently released, is used as a symbol of the Japanese Red Army's call for developing international linkages between terrorist organizations.

Source: Let's Consolidate Our Standpoint of Internationalism and Self-Reliance!, a publication by The Japanese Red Army, 30 May 1979.

And it is required that all Arab national forces determine the future direction of national struggle; either they must stand on the side of the Palestinian Arab people in order to realize the national liberation, or to be hostile to people as an imperialism's ally, the puppet of the foreign forces.

We in the Japanese Red Army, too, shall represent the Japanese people's will and carry out the same task with the internationalist mission. For the encirclement of the Palestinian Arab people is also the encirclement of the Japanese people, who have the same enemy and class interests. The Palestinian Arab people's advance is an assurance of the advance of the Japanese people.

Japanese imperialist connection with the [Israeli–Egyptian Peace] treaty can be pointed out as follows;

1) The treaty has increased the Japanese imperialist role in Asia in the US–headed imperialist reorganization of the world strategy. The treaty has the same character as the Japan–US security treaty, which is central in the anti-communist military alliances in Asia, and aims at forming an anti-people system throughout Asia and the Middle East, closely linked with each other.

. . . .

Exactly because we in the Japanese Red Army represent the Japanese people's struggles and regard the Palestinian Arab people as a strategic friend, we, uniting with all the revolutionary and progressive forces which aim to liberate Palestine on the basis of an anti-imperialist position, confronting the common enemy, again promise to you to continue to fight as we have done so far, no, even more.

.   .   .   .

Because of the lack of understanding of the people's power as the very mainspring of revolution and because we couldn't find the vanguard leadership in any other field than violence, we have had a view of the direct formation of the International Party. We have simply hoisted, what we called, internationalism. . . .

Concerning the concept of the 'Simultaneous World Revolution', we redefined it as the conscious effort to prepare the homogeneity of revolutions in every country, and not to mean simultaneousity in time. We can now say that the question is how to create such homogeneity in the Japanese revolutionary movement.

We in the Japanese Red Army confirm our strong will to relentlessly follow up the Lydda Operation and to have a showdown with 'Israel' and the Zionists, with heart-felt anger. We will continue our struggle to liberate and recover Comrade Okamoto along with numbers of Palestinian comrades. . . .

Document 13: Fatah Political Platform

T his document consists of excerpts from the political platform adopted by the fourth Fatah Conference in May 1980. Here, the PLO is proclaimed to be an integral part of the Soviet-sponsored "World Liberation Movement." In the discussion of the PLO's goals on the international scene, it is stated that a strategic (not tactical) alliance must be formed with the socialist countries for the sake of the Palestinians and of other "liberation" movements. This underlines the lasting nature of the PLO's relations with the Soviet Bloc.

Source: Raphael Israeli: *PLO in Lebanon,* Document 2.

THE INTERNATIONAL DOMAIN
Since the Palestinian problem has been the major issue affecting the Arab nation in its just struggle against the Zionist and imperialist enemy, and since the Middle East has a great strategic importance, the Palestinian problem has had a great international significance beyond its own inherent aspects. . . . *Out movement is part of the world liberation movement* and the struggle against imperialism, Zionism, racism and their agents. We commit ourselves to alliances on the international scene in accordance with our principles and the Palestinian National Convenant. [emphasis added]

· · · · · · · · · · ·

B. On the level of our friends:
1. To strengthen our strategic alliance with socialist countries, foremost of them the USSR, inasmuch as this alliance will help to frustrate effectively all American and Zionist plots against the Palestinian problem and against all issues of liberation in the world. . . .

Document 14: The PLO Defines Its Role in the World Revolution

I n this document the PLO describes itself as "an organic part of the forces of world revolution" and denounces the "Arab ruling classes" as being "allied with imperialism."

Source: The Palestine Resistance a National Liberation Movement, a publication by the Political Department, Palestine Liberation Organization (no publication date).

The Palestinian resistance movement which leads the struggle of the Palestinian people is an organic part of the forces of world revolution: the socialist countries, the international liberation movement, and the working class parties in the capitalist countries. . . .

Israeli leaders insist that any solution for the Arab–Israeli conflict must include normal relations (economic-commercial-diplomatic-cultural) between Israel and the Arab countries. Any such relations would be of dependency to Israel's advantage, as the case is between imperialist countries and the "third world" countries. . . .

Israeli aggression also contributes to the power of the Arab ruling classes which are allied with imperialism, since some forces believe that the major contradiction is with Israel and not with imperialism and that "neutralizing" imperialism is the best way to defeat Israel. Another political position which contributes to the strength of the Arab ruling classes is that which states that Arab solidarity is the best way of facing Israel's threat. Such a position diverts attention from the true character of Arab regimes which are antagonistic to progress, and diverts attention away from imperialist interests in the area.

The justice of the Palestinian struggle calls upon all revolutionary, anti-imperialist, socialist, democratic and peace-loving forces in the world to support this struggle with all its capabilities. This is a duty necessitated by international solidarity and by the need for alliance between the socialist countries, the national liberation movements and working class parties in the capitalist countries. . . .

. . . all of this shows the necessity for the revolution and the P.L.O. to strengthen and enhance its alliance with these forces—an alliance of strategic nature. The Palestinian revolution is an integral part of the three forces of international revolution, and its victory is dependent upon the victory of these forces, and its victory represents a definite support for these forces in their struggle against imperialism and its local tools. . . .

Document 15: The PLO Aids Neo-Nazis

T his interview with Abu Iyad demonstrates the PLO's willingness to establish connections with such groups as the West German neo-Nazis led by Karl-Heinz Hoffman. Iyad justifies this by stating that the PLO will work with any organization that will aid in the achievement of tactical goals, even if there are strategic differences. He admits that the PLO has connections with several groups in Europe.

Source: "They said our Boss's name is Hoffman," *Der Spiegel,* 13 July 1981, pp. 76–77.

Spiegel: Do you know a Karl-Heinz Hoffmann?

Abu Iyad: I have never met him. He has constantly tried to meet me, though.

Spiegel: The PLO is being accused of having accommodated and protected members of his "Military Sports Groups." Do you concede that?

Abu Iyad: Yes.

Spiegel: Why is that? While considering yourselves a leftist liberation movement, you shelter neo-Nazis.

Abu Iyad: Let me explain something: there is an enormous distance between us and the fascist ideologies of the Nazis. I will tell you one thing: even if the Nazis were to tell us today, "We are going to liberate Palestine for you," we would say, "We would then give that Palestine to the Russians."

Spiegel: All the more reason to ask why you have cooperated with such people.

Abu Iyad: He told us he was no such thing as a neofascist. While his group was a national movement that wanted to reunite Germany, it was more of a sports association, a kind of scouts organization. If we should have any fascist ideas, he said, we stand ready to be convinced by you. . . .

. . . We told him about other European groupings that also were patriots, progressive forces cooperating with us here. . . .

Spiegel: . . . From what countries?

Abu Iyad: From Norway, Sweden, Denmark and so on and so forth, a kind of association of Palestinians and forces supporting us. On that level, we explained to Hoffmann, we could also cooperate, if he was interested.

Spiegel: How did you get in touch with him?

Abu Iyad: Last May we arrested some West Germans who admitted having been trained with the Falangists [*sic*]. They refused to make any further statements, saying, "We have a boss who will talk to you about this, his name is Hoffmann." After a month, he actually came to see us, accompanied by another four men. He said we should release his men. . . .

Spiegel: How many Hoffmann people were there in fact?

Abu Iyad: Altogether 12 at one time.

. . . .

Spiegel: Are the Germans still in this country?

Abu Iyad: No, they are all gone—we don't care where. After the Munich bomb attack I said, "No matter whether they are supporters or not, they have to leave."

Spiegel: But that was 9 months ago, and in mid-June some were still with you.

Abu Iyad: First of all, we wanted to part peaceably. But Hoffmann shamelessly took advantage of that. He constantly embarrassed us. "I must first look for a new hiding place," he said. And then again: "You must help me; let them stay till I have found something. He constantly asked for a respite—for example in January, when he said: "I must find an asylum for them; they are being persecuted in Germany." And then he was gone again for a month. We didn't know just what would happen with that fellow. . . .

Document 16: Report of PLO Delegation to East Germany

This report is an example of the ongoing high-level relationship between the PLO and a Soviet surrogate. In this April 1982 meeting between the Palestinians and various top East Germans (the Chief of Staff and a Deputy Defense Minister), military assistance and training are both discussed. Equipment provided by East Germany includes a small ship, which would seem to serve no other purpose than for launching raids on Israel.

Source: Raphael Israeli, *PLO in Lebanon*, Document 28.

The delegation arrived at the East Berlin airport at 13:00 and was met by the Deputy Defence Minister, General Fleissner; the Chief of Staff, General Helmuth Borowke; Colonel Karl Keides; and the interpreter, Captain Roland Kuchbuch.

After a brief rest in the VIP room at the airport, General Fleissner handed us our visit schedule:

14 April—no formal talks.

15 April—talks about training with General Borowke and Colonel Bonowke, the man in charge of recruitment and training in the military training centre. In the afternoon, a colonel from General Fleissner's office will survey the military assistance to be delivered to us, and will determine with us the time and location of delivery. Once agreed, a final protocol will be prepared for signature.

16 April—Visit to the recruitment and training centre of the ground forces to review the training programme, training aids, ranges, naval equipment, training in grenade launching and anti-aircraft training. Later on, discussions will be held with air defence and coastal defence experts to determine our needs.

17 April—Talks with the Department of Foreign Trade and sightseeing.

18 April—Visit to Berlin.

19 April—Signature of the protocols, official banquet, special tour of the city and then departure to Hungary.

The Visit:

On 15 April we held discussions on training; General Borowke, accompanied by Colonel Bonowke, Karl Keides and Captain Roland came in. The Palestinian delegation included Captain 'Abd al-Na'im.

General Borowke: In view of the talks held last October between General Fleissner and the deputy commander of the PLO, we had agreed to accept PLO trainees into our military, and absorb them in our military schools. I wish to point out that in training our officers, we stress the following:

1. Political indoctrination: a general survey of sociology and politics and clarification of the general purpose of training. All this is done under the supervision of an army officer.
2. Technical and tactical training.
3. Physical fitness.

We also teach mathematics, physics and the German language. The Marxist–Leninist theory is the foundation of our training. Do you object to that?

Answer: Not at all!

Our query: Will our trainees be trained separately or together with German officers? We would like them to be mixed with the Germans and to undertake the same pattern of training.

Answer: There is no special training camp for the Palestinians. Therefore, they will train with German officers, although as a separate group, because of their limited knowledge of German and because the Germans also study Russian.

Our delegation stressed once more our request that the training be mixed with German officers.

General Borowke: We have another problem. We have explained to the deputy commander of the PLO that our training period is three years. In our artillery course we train in fast and comprehensive deployment. The deputy commander has asked us to speed up the training and we agreed to concur down to the battery level.

Our delegation asked about the numbers of our candidates and their skills.

Answer: In our previous talks we agreed about the numbers, and agreed that they would be trained to operate Soviet weapons.

Our delegation asked that the numbers be increased and that relations be further strengthened between Palestinians and the German army and people.

Answer: In principle, we will maintain the number of trainees we agreed upon and we will determine the programme of training accordingly. We will inform you of all details through the embassy* as regards any increase in the number of trainees and we will specify that in the protocol.

Our delegation: How about altering the specialization of trainees already agreed upon in the protocol?

Answer: If we distribute them in various units, this would increase expenditures. However, with regard to certain specializations, we will dispatch the trainees to the Soviet Union.

Our delegation: If you approve an increase in numbers, we would like the following specializations: 10 trainees in armour and 10 in engineering.

Answer: We agree, and we will let you know via the embassy before May 30.

The protocol was approved.

Our delegation expressed its gratitude about the understanding shown for our needs and the response to our requests. We submitted an invitation to the minister of defence on the part of the deputy commander of the PLO to visit us. General Fleissner had suggested that we invite him during our rest at the airport, and asked us to inform the deputy commander of the PLO that the minister would visit Syria in September, and would like to meet the commander general of the PLO and his deputy in Damascus. Our delegation also asked to meet with the defence minister in order to deliver to him personally the greetings and the invitation of the commander and his deputy.

Thursday afternoon
Colonel Karl Keides from the Ministry of Defence declared that he was authorized by General Fleissner to discuss military assistance. Before he began, he apologized that the minister would be unable to meet us; our delegation showed understanding.

18 April 1982, 10:00
The foreign trade official brought along the prices of the items we want to purchase:
(1) A light coastguard vessel, armed with a missile—$118,000.
[In the original, a variety of ammunition and guns—27mm, 57mm, 100mm, 122mm, 130mm—are listed with their prices.]

---

*In the Soviet bloc, the Palestinian envoys are accredited as full ambassadors and their legations enjoy the rank of embassies.

Delivery
Some items can be delivered immediately, and others within four weeks of payment in bank. The above prices include loading aboard ships in Rostock, Germany. The prices will be increased by 10 percent if the deliveries are brought to Tartus.

Monday, 11:00
Signature of the protocol and its annexes in the presence of General Fleissner. Then an official banquet and exchange of presents.

Monday, 19:00
Dinner at the residence of the Palestinian ambassador with General Fleissner attending, along with the deputy defence minister and Chief of Staff General Borowke. The general delivered a speech expressing his admiration for the quality of our delegation, its courtesy, andd its military, political and professional skill.

Documents 17–20: The PLO and Soviet Surrogates—Eastern Europe

T hese four documents give evidence of East European Communist support for the PLO. They are selected from captured certificates and letters dealing with PLO training courses organized by the USSR, Hungary, and East Germany.

The time and type of training appears to coincide with the PLO's attempt to change tactics to be able to confront Israel at the conventional level of conflict. Except for one certificate from 1976, all the certificates are dated 1980 or later. The training was for NCOs and officers in infantry, reconnaissance, armour, air defense, engineering, and staff courses. This training occurred at several levels—platoon, company, and battalion. A Yugoslav chemical warfare handbook was also discovered.

When the Israelis moved into Lebanon, they discovered that the PLO had planned to build up a quite sizable conventional force. The PLO was in the process of receiving training in this type (conventional) of conflict from the same source as the arms—the USSR and its surrogates.

Document 17 is a cable from the PLO to its forces about a training course in East Germany. Documents 18–20 are reproductions of one Hungarian and two Soviet diplomas attesting to the completion of training programs.

Source: Raphael Israeli, *PLO in Lebanon,* Documents 8–16, 18, 19, 21, 23, 29, 30, 33, and 35.

Document 17

The PLO, Fatah, Division of Training and Operations

To all forces and units—11 Jan. 1982

We wish to inform you that a three-year military engineering course will take place in the Democratic Republic of Germany. The Requirement[s:] good health, no older than 23 and graduation from high school or its equivalent. At the end of the course the grade of Lieutenant will be awarded. Please ask the candidates who meet the requirement to [go to] the Division of Training and Operations tomorrow, due to the urgency of the matter.

Document 18

Soviet diploma awarded to Captain 'Abd-al-'Aziz Mahmud Abu Fedda in March 1976, upon completion of a course for infantry battalion commanders.

Document 19

Soviet diploma awarded by the Ministry of Defense to Muhammad Mabry Hussain upon completing a course for electrical technicians at the Odessa Military School in June 1980.

МИНИСТЕРСТВО ОБОРОНЫ СССР

СВИДЕТЕЛЬСТВО

АН № 35064

Настоящее свидетельство выдано ....
.....Мухаммед Мабри Хусейн.....

в том, что он ...Декабре 1978 г. поступил ....
и в ...июне... 1980 г. окончил курсы при
Одесском объединенном
военном училище
по специальности ...техник по...
системе электропитания

Настоящее свидетельство дает право на
самостоятельное выполнение работ, связан-
ных с полученной специальностью.

Начальник
генерал-майор /С.Пелех/
« 12 » июня 1980 г.
Регистрационный №

THE MINISTRY OF DEFENCE, USSR

CERTIFICATE

АН № 35064

This is to certify that ....
........MOHAMED MABRY HUSSAIN......

entered in DECEMBER 1978 and graduated
from COURSES AT ODESSA COMBINED
MILITARY SCHOOL
in JUNE 1980
majoring in TECHNICIAN OF ELECTRIC
POWER-SUPPLY SYSTEM

The bearer of the Present Certificate enjoys
the privilege for independent activity associated
with the Major Subject.

Commanding Officer
MAJOR-GENERAL S. PELEH
« 12 » JUNE 1980
Registration No.

Document 20

Hungarian diploma awarded to Muhammad Farlin Kador by the Hungarian Military Academy upon completion of a course for T-34 tank drivers, in February 1981.

Document 21: PLO Representative in Cuba

The following is an excerpt of a letter of gratitude issued by the PLO Permanent Mission in Havana to the Cuban government. It discloses the linkages between the PLO, a key Soviet surrogate, and other anti-Western states and regional organizations.

Source: Raphael Israeli, *PLO in Lebanon,* Document 36.

Dear Comrades,

I should like to take this opportunity to express once more our gratitude to the Cuban Communist Party, and to all of you, for your solidarity with our revolution, and the gratitude of the Palestinian fighters under the leadership of Yasser Arafat. . . .

Our victories, which we have won, thanks to the assistance of the socialist countries, the Organization for African Unity and the Islamic countries, constituted the decisive factor in defeating the aggressive forces of imperialism. We are in the same boat with all the anti-imperialist forces.

We take this opportunity to express our respect and admiration for revolutionary Cuba, led by Fidel Castro, and for your goals. We will follow a road similar to yours until we reach our common path. . . .

The success of the popular revolution in Iran, under the leadership of Khomeini, has had a great impact through its support of the Palestinian revolution under the leadership of Arafat, the supreme commander of the Palestinians. Iran will directly oppose Israel and imperialism to enable our people to achieve its objective of establishing its own independent homeland. . . .

We wish; to ask for your help in our war against the imperialist-Zionist plot, which is attempting to liquidate our people and all forces of liberation in the world.

The victories in Vietnam, Laos, Cambodia, Africa and Latin America are our own, for we stand beside all peoples who fight for their liberty everywhere in the world. We support the Vietnamese and Nicaraguan people. The pursuit of our armed struggle is our way to freedom. We are all united until we topple imperialism and Zionism, until we liquidate the Camp David treason.

Long live the PLO, the only representative of the Palestinian people!
Long live the Cuban Revolution!
Long live Yasser Arafat!
Long live Fidel!
Revolution until victory!

[PLO, Permanent Mission, in Havana]

Document 22: The PLO and the Sandinistas

J orge Mandi, a Sandinista spokesman, affirms the continuing relationship
between the PLO and the Sandinistas in excerpts from an interview with
the Kuwait newspaper *Al Watan*. He recalls past Sandinista cooperation
with the PLO in the multiple hijacking of four aircraft in 1970. One Sandinista, Patrick Arguello, was killed during this operation (see testimony of
Miguel Bolaños Hunter, chapter 2, Document 1).

Source: Al Watan, August 7, 1979.

"There is a long standing blood unity between us and the Palestinian revolution. . . . Many of the units belonging to the Sandinista movement were at
Palestinian revolutionary bases in Jordan. In the early 1970s, Nicaraguan and
Palestinian blood was spilled together in Amman and in other places during
the 'Black September battles'. . . .

"A number of Sandinistas took part in the operations to divert four aircraft
which the PFLP seized and landed at a desert airfield in Jordan. One of our
comrades was also wounded in another hijack operation in which Leila
Khaled was involved. She was in command of the operation and our comrades helped her carry it out. It is natural, therefore, that in our war against
Somoza we received Palestinian aid for our revolution in various forms. . . ."

Documents 23–25: Communist Support for the PLO—Asia

T hese documents show that the PLO receives military support from the three major communist Asian powers—Vietnam, North Korea, and China. The courses included air defense and one for commanders. Again these certificates are from 1980 or after, coinciding with the PLO's change in tactics. From these documents it appears that the PLO's international support system is truly global. A Chinese communist instruction booklet for the use of explosives was discovered, but is not reproduced here.

Document 16 consists of a copy of a Vietnamese diploma, Documents 17 and 18 are letters concerning training in Vietnam and North Korea.

Source: Raphael Israeli, *PLO in Lebanon,* Documents 14, 17, 20, 23, and 34.

Document 23

Vietnamese diploma awarded to Mahmud 'Abdul-Fattan Zeidan in May 1980, upon completion of a course in Vietnam.

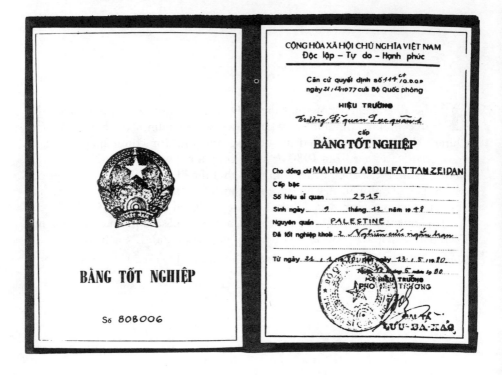

Document 24

13 Dec. 1981

The Palestinian National Movement of Liberation
Fatah
General HQ of the Asifah Forces

To: the Commanders of the Yarmuk, Karameh, Kastel, Ajnadayn, militia and No 17 Forces, the Air Defence unit, the Palestine Liberation Army and The Armed Struggle

Greetings of the Revolution !

1. It has been decided to send several officers to the Socialist Republic of Vietnam to study the air-defence system there, for a period of 45 days.
2. We request that you dispatch your candidates, with their travel papers, so that the delegation can reach Vietnam on . . . Dec. 1981.

Revolution until Victory !

General HQ of the Asifah Forces
Abu al-Walid

Document 25

Fatah, 21 Jan. 1980

To: Air defence units

Re: *the Korean course*

Greetings of the Revolution !

In Annex I is a list of those who have successfully completed the course in Korea from March 1, 1979 until Oct. 10, 1979.

Please note and act accordingly.

Revolution until victory
Colonel (_) Director of Central Operations
Abu al-Walid

[Annex I—21 names and their units.]

Document 26: PLO Officers Training in South Asia

T his document—a letter concerning courses for Fatah officers in India— shows that the international support system for the PLO extends beyond the Middle East and the communist countries to South Asian states.

Source: Raphael Israeli, *PLO in Lebanon*, Document 52.

---

27 March, 1981

Fatah
HQ of the Asifa Forces
Karameh units

To the Commanders of the Galilee, Carmel Battalions, the Arqub Eagles, the Motorized forces, the First Engineering Unit

Re: courses abroad

Revolutionary greetings,

1. Each of you has been allocated one seat in the following courses : which will take place in India: platoon commanders, political course for officers, basic engineering for officers.
2. We ask you to appoint your candidates and notify us of the names by 1 May, 1981.
3. Candidates have to meet the following requirements : health, a knowledge of English, be no older than 30 and of the rank of Second Leutenant.

Revolution until victory !

Colonel Abu Hajez
Commander of the Karameh Forces

Document 27: The Global Extent of Military Support for the PLO

T he following list of courses taken by officers and NCOs of the September Martyrs Battalion, Qastel Brigade, Fatah, was captured at Sidon in 1982. It reveals the extent of the international support system for the PLO, geographically and ideologically. Among the countries included are many East European and most Arab states, Pakistan, Cuba, and China. Courses covered political education and military tactics at both the low-intensity level (frogmen) and the conventional level (armored warfare).

Most of the early training was in Arab and Islamic countries, but since the mid-1970s training in communist countries has increased greatly. There was also a growth in the conventional type of training, such as armored warfare. This coincides with the PLO's change in tactics and the use of Lebanon as an armed camp. For the USSR this military relationship was probably seen as a way to reestablish its influence in the region since it had been declining.

Source: Raphael Israeli, *PLO in Lebanon*, Document 26.

Excerpts from a list of courses follow.

No.	Military ID. No.	Name	Rank	Date Rank Received	Course	Place	Date
1.	31487	Faisal Muhammad al-Sheikh Yussuf	Major, staff officer	—	1. Sa'iqa 2. Cadre 3. Military Academy 4. Battalion Commander 5. Staff Officers	Syria Syria China Moscow Pakistan	1968 1968 — — 1979
2.	44552	Jamal Ya'kub Zaidan	Captain	1 February 1976	1. Basic 2. Frogmen 3. Fedayin Commanders 4. Armour 5. Armour	Jordan Syria Moscow Syria Hungary	1968 1969 1972 1978 1980
3.	41054	Fadl Muhammad 'Uthman	First Lieutenant	1975	1. Sa'iqa 2. Platoon Commanders 3. Company Commanders	Baghdad Moscow Vietnam	1968 1975–76 1977–78
4.	44818	Muhammad Abd-Allah Salamah	First Lieutenant	1 January 1976	1. Sa'iqa Instructor 2. Platoon Commanders 3. Company Commanders 4. Armour 5. Armour 6. Armour Company Commanders	Baghdad China Syria Lebanon	1967 1977 1978
5.	32242	Jawad Ahmad 'Abd al-Ghani	Captain	1 January 1976	1. Military College 2. Mortar 3. Armour 4. Political Cadres 5. Political Cadres	Algeria Syria China Bulgaria	1969 1970 1978 1978–79 1979–80

No.	ID	Rank	Name	Date	Training	Location	Year
7.	31492	Second Lieutenant	Ratib Musa Mahmud Abu-Samarah	1975	1. Sa'iqa	Baghdad	1968
					2. Explosive Engineering	Baghdad	1968
					3. Cadre	Syria	1969
					4. Military Academy	Fatah	1974–75
					5. Infantry Company Commanders	Moscow	1977
					6. Armour	Syria	1978
					7. Armour	Hungary	1979
8.	71281	Second Lieutenant	Yasin Khadr Muhammad	1 September 1976	1. Fighter	Syria	1968
					2. Fighter	Syria	1974
					3. Military Academy	Fatah	1976
					4. Armour	Syria	1978
					5. Armour	Hungary	1980
					6. Armour Company Commanders	Moscow	
12.	46897	Second Lieutenant	Khaled 'Isa 'Abd Hassan	1 June 1977	1. Military Academy	Algeria	1975–76
					2. Political Education	Beirut	1978
					3. Basic Course in Armour	Pakistan	1979
					4. Armour	Hungary	1980
					5. Armour Company Commanders		
18.	15361	Second Lieutenant	Mustafa Hasan Mustafa Qindil	27 April 1978	1. Military College, Fatah	Syria	1978
					2. Armour		1978
					3. Political Education		1979
					4. Social Sciences	Bulgaria	1979
					5. Armour	Hungary	1980

No.	Military ID. No.	Rank	Name	Date Rank Received	Course	Place	Date
22.	73937	Second Lieutenant	Ahmad Muhammad Ahmad Mar'i al-Sharqawi	27 April 1978	1. Military Academy · 2. Fatah · 3. Anti-aircraft Company Commanders ·	Egypt Moscow	1978
2.	53477	Seargent-Major	Abd al-Rahman Ahmad Hussein a-Sharif	6 April 1977	1. Light Weaponry · 2. Communications · 3. Armour · 4. Military Academy (did not graduate, stayed for six months) ·	Hungary Cuba	1980 1979

Document 28: PLO Military Council Meeting

T he excerpts from the protocol of a PLO military council meeting show that both Syria and Saudi Arabia have promised the PLO military assistance.

Source: Raphael Israeli, *PLO in Lebanon,* Document 41.

THE PALESTINE NATIONAL LIBERATION MOVEMENT
FATAH
'ASIFA FORCES GENERAL COMMAND

Date: 25.7.81

Protocol of the 6th meeting of the military council dated 25.7.81.

Present:
Commander-in-Chief:
     Abu 'Ammar (Arafat)
     Abu Jihad
     Abu al-Walid, et al.

. . . .

In addition, the military committee was informed about the dispatch of three anti-aircraft batteries by Syria, following the visit of Abu al-Walid and his meeting with Hekmat al-Shehabi. [The Syrian Chief of Staff]

. . . .

Saudi Arabia promised to fulfil all our requests for the supply of arms and ammunition.

Document 29: Sa'iqa, East Germany, and Syria

This letter is from the Syrian backed Sa'iqa faction of the PLO. Sa'iqa has appointed a new head of its organization in East Germany and is requesting an exit visa for him from Syria. The Syrians control the movements of Sa'iqa members. This reveals the triangular relationship between Syria, East Germany, and a PLO faction.

Source: Raphael Israeli, *PLO in Lebanon,* Document 31.

General HQ, Sa'iqa Forces

To Comrade Foreign Minister

Arab Greetings !

We ask that Comrade Muhammad Amin al-Askari be granted a laissez-passer and an exit visa for six months. The said comrade has been holding the position of Head of the Branch of our Organization in Democratic Germany. Our request is related to his functions.

Long Live the Struggle !

Documents 30 and 31: Saudi Arabian Military Assistance to the PLO

These labels and arms crates captured in PLO arms dumps in Lebanon disclose Saudi Arabian military support for the PLO. This transfer of arms and ammunition to the PLO is probably in violation of U.S. law. Recipients of U.S. weapons have to agree that they will not transfer arms obtained from the United States to a third party without permission.

Source: Raphael Israeli, *PLO in Lebanon*, Documents 42 and 43.

Document 30

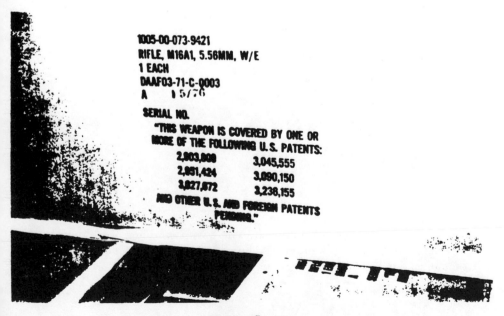

M-16 rifle crates

Document 31

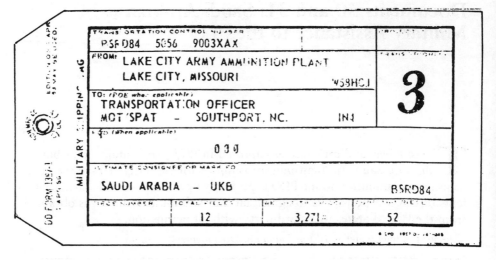

Ammunition shipping tag: Missouri–Saudi Arabia

Document 32: PLO Base in UNIFIL Zone

T he following excerpt from an interview with a PLO guerrilla provides clear evidence of support for the PLO through inaction by UNIFIL (United Nations Interim Force in Lebanon). No attempt is made to disarm PLO terrorists in the UNIFIL zone. Fatah has even been able to set up a base in the zone.

Source: Interview with Abu al-Ra'id on *Israel Television,* 20 April 1979.

Q: What is the name of the organization to which you belong?

A: Fatah.

Q: What is your name?

A: Abu al-Ra'id.

Q: Where do you conduct your patrols?

A: We used to patrol in the southern sector, and once we even entered the UNIFIL zone of the United Nations—where Fatah has a base—and patrolled there.

Q: Do you cross the lines of the international forces?

A: Yes. They see that we are armed, but say nothing to us.

Document 33: The PLO in Central America and West Africa

T he following excerpt from a speech by Arafat reveals a PLO military presence in Central America and West Africa.

Source: FBIS—Inter-Arab Affairs 5(998) 13 January 1982, p. Al.

'ARAFAT: PLO REVOLUTIONARIES IN CENTRAL AMERICA

NC121349 (Clandestine) Voice of Palestine in Arabic 1135 GMT 12 Jan 82

[Speech by Yasir 'Arafat—indentified as Abu 'Ammar—delivered 11 January at the poetry recital held by the Palestinian writers and journalists permanent secretariat in Jamal 'Abd an-Nasir Hall at Beirut Arab University—recorded.]

[Haig] said: I can stomach that there might be Soviet pilots in Nicaragua and possibly Cuban, but Palestinian pilots? I tell him: There are Palestinian pilots in Nicaragua! There are Palestinian revolutionaries with the revolutionaries in El Salvador, Angola and everywhere in the world there are revolutionaries. [applause] The Palestinian revolution reflects the march of free and honest men in the world. . . .

Document 34: Libyan Officer in Charge of PLO Air Defense

T his document consists of an administrative order appointing a Libyan officer to direct the PLO's air defense. This reveals Libyan backing of the PLO. Qadhafi's support of the PLO had always been substantial. For example, he has been known to make payments to the families of terrorists who have been injured or killed.

Source: Raphael Israeli, *PLO in Lebanon*, Document 39.

Popular Front for the Liberation of Palestine
General Command
No. 4128/ZA'AH
Date: 26 April 1982

Administrative Order

1. Capt. Hamduni, attached from the Libyan armed forces, was appointed assistant to the commander of Al-Na'ama stronghold for air defence matters, valid as of today.

2. Capt. Hamduni continues to supervise the air defence forces in all military districts. He was assigned the following by the secretary-general:
   a) To train the air defence units of the Front in all strongholds.
   b) To raise the level of training and tactics.
   c) To guarantee their needs in weapons, ammunition and equipment in coordination with the air defence headquarters of the armed forces in Tripoli.

3. Capt. Hamduni will supervise the air defence forces attached to Fatah.

4. Capt. Hamduni will conduct a comprehensive and documented survey of the following items in the air defence forces:
   a) Arms and equipment.
   b) Military installations and instruments.

c) Vehicles and technical equipment.

The reports will be submitted according to regulations to the secretary-general within 15 days.

5. It is the task of the commander of the Al-Na'ama stronghold to:
   a) Guarantee Capt. Hamduni a place to stay and properly attach him to the stronghold.
   b) Guarantee residence for Capt. Hamduni's men inside the stronghold.
   c) The assignment of Capt. Hamduni will be fully integrated with the table of organization of Al-Na'ama stronghold in everything relating to personnel, military finance, administration and the munitions centre.
   d) Capt. Hamduni will be put in charge of air defence in the stronghold and will set down a full programme for approval by the stronghold commander, with a copy to the central military officer.
   e) All air defence equipment and personnel in the stronghold will be subordinate to Capt. Hamduni. Daily activity will be his responsibility.
   f) It is necessary to ensure that Nakib Hamduni has a fire control position in the stronghold at times of enemy attacks.

6. During visits of Capt. Hamduni in other strongholds, which have air defence systems in the front, it will be his responsibility:
   a) To ensure that the air defence equipment is in operational order.
   b) To ensure that such equipment is properly and effectively deployed.
   c) This will be done in cooperation with the stronghold commander and the soldier responsible for air defence in the stronghold.
   d) Once every month Capt. Hamduni will submit a periodical report about the air defence situation in the strongholds, along with his proposals.
   e) Capt. Hamduni is not permitted to transfer personnel or weapons from one stronghold to another, but will submit his proposal to the officer responsible in the front, and if required, an order concerning the matter will be issued by the secretary-general.

/s/ *Secretary-General*

Copies:

File
Fara military hq
Front positions
Colonel Zallah

Document 35: PLO Links to Insurgents in Niger and Mali

I n this PFLP report one sees how, after a failed coup in Niger, rebels escaped to Libya with help from Polisario. After this the rebels set up the Front for the Liberation of the Central Arab Desert with the aid of the Libyans and the Algerians. Just as in many other regions of the world, North Africa is covered by a network of linkages between guerrillas, terrorists, and those states that support them. This document reveals PLO links to insurgents as far away as Niger and Mali.

Source: Raphael Israeli, *PLO in Lebanon*, Document 58.

POPULAR FRONT FOR THE LIBERATION OF PALESTINE
GENERAL HEADQUARTERS
MILITARY HEADQUARTERS

When the plot was uncovered, a battle broke out on the night of 15 May. 300 soldiers were killed. Three officers from the Niger forces seized Sgt. Sidi Muhammad, the two officers and the soldiers who launched the coup. But the Imam, who is secretary-general of the Front, succeeded in escaping via the desert to Mauritania. There, together with his deputy, Muhammad Musa, he met up with the Polisario fighters, and then reached Libya where they remained.

The current activity of the revolutionaries is continuing deep inside Mali. The revolution has organized a widespread underground movement based on mobilizing the masses, ideological indoctrination and a financial fund, which was set up in order to raise 10 million francs to release the leader, Zaya ben Tehir, who had sought refuge in Algeria. Ben Bella extradited him to Mali where he was imprisoned from 1963 until 1979. Now he lives under supervision in Mali. The revolution is pursuing underground mobilization. Each new recruit takes an oath on the Qur'an to keep allegiance to the revolution and never to uncover its secret.

The founding conference of the Front took place in 1979 with the participation of all its leaders. There the Front's organizational framework was laid out, and camps and offices were opened in Libya in coordination with Algeria.

The goals of the Front for the Liberation of the Central Arab Desert are:

1. Liberation of the Central Arab Desert from the colonialism of Mali and Niger, and its reunification.
2. Annexation of the Desert to the Arab homeland and unification with any Arab country so willing.
3. Making Arabic the official language of the Desert.
4. Establishing a free, democratic state, its slogan being "Freedom, Islamic Socialism and Unity."
5. War against colonialism, imperialism, Zionism and racial discrimination.
6. Liberation of the citizens of the Desert from all their shackles.
7. Liberation of the national economy from foreign domination.
8. Evacuation of foreign bases from the north.

6
Surrogate Actors in Europe

T he linkages between various facets of terrorist operations in widely separated portions of the globe are brought out particularly clearly in this section, which shows surrogates in Eastern Europe working with terrorist and insurgent groups in Latin America and the Middle East, while a Middle Eastern surrogate, the PLO, helps to equip European terrorists, in this case the Italian Red Brigades.

Two former very highly placed Czechoslovak officers, from the military and intelligence sectors, who played significant roles with regard to surrogate operations (both of a combat and of a psychological warfare nature), present their testimonies in Documents 1 and 2. The evidence provided by them is detailed and reveals both the varieties of significant assistance given to terrorist and insurgent groups and the very high level at which such decisions were taken. One of the officers in question, General Jan Sejna, offers testimony of the deep involvement of the Soviet Union in all the more important phases of this process. His revelations (Document 1) are corroborated by those of Dr. Ladislav Bittman (Document 2), and, with regard to the intimacy between Soviet intelligence and the services of the East European client states, by a former senior Bulgarian official, Vladimir Kostov (Document 3). Both the level at which all three witnesses operated, and the nature their duties, allow us to view them as primary sources of the most valuable kind, and their mutual corroboration underlines their reliability. It is significant that operations not merely in the Third World, or even in Western Europe, are mentioned, but even support for terrorists inside the United States.

An arrest warrant by the High Court of Venice against PLO leaders Arafat and Abu Iyad contains detailed evidence of weapons supplied by the PLO to the Italian Red Brigades. Although the warrant itself was not upheld by the Supreme Court of the Republic of Italy, for technical reasons, the evidence concerning the weapons transfers themselves remains valid.

Document 1: Testimony of General Jan Sejna—A View from the Top

Major General Jan Sejna is one of the highest ranking Communist officials ever to seek asylum in the West. For more than a decade before fleeing to the West Sejna had served in a number of positions at the apex of the Czechoslovak government, including personal staff chief to the Minister of Defense, member of the Presidium of Parliament and the Presidium Party group, and First Secretary of the Party Committee at the Ministry of Defense. Most importantly, Sejna served as Secretary of the Czechoslovak Defense Council, which he describes as the supreme national security decision-making body in Czechoslovakia. Thus, he is eminently qualified to describe and analyze Communist state support of international terrorism as well as other aspects of low-intensity warfare.

The following is an excerpt from an interview with General Jan Sejna conducted by the editors on 21 June 1985, as part of the Oral History Project of the Fletcher School's International Security Studies Program.

Q: In the following discussion we want to focus on such aspects of low-intensity warfare as terrorism, active measures, disinformation, technology and arms transfers, and the role of drug pushing. . . . We are interviewing General Jan Sejna.

What interests us primarily is the operational aspect. Let us look first of all at the Soviet Union. How was the decision-making process regarding low-intensity warfare structured? And how did Moscow assign individual responsibilities to its [clients]?

A: As you know, in the communist system planning is everything—everything must be covered by a plan. In this area, the Soviet chief of General Staff is ordered to discuss with the GRU [the Soviet military intelligence], which is under his command, what assignment would be Czechoslovakia's under the current plan. There are, of course, many different plans. There is the long term plan which covers from ten to twenty years, there is a five-year plan, a one-year plan, an alternate plan for each action, and so on.

Let me give you an example. In October 1964, all satellite intelligence services, except for Romania, attended a conference in Moscow. Previously, all had been done without any legal records. This was the first time the Soviets had decided to put it on a legal base.

Q: All the Soviet Bloc countries, minus Romania, were represented by their chiefs of general staff?

A: And the chiefs of their military intelligence.

Q: Who represented Czechoslovkia?

A: On the Czech side it was General Rytir and Colonel Burda, Oldrich Burda. He was the head of military intelligence.

Q: Is it the ZS?

A: Yes, it's the ZS, *Zpravodajska sprava.*

Q: Who represented the Czech intelligence service, the StB?

A: The StB was represented by the first deputy minister of interior.

Q: Did you participate at the conference?

A: No, I only participated at the discussions in the Defense Council which took place after the Czech delegation had returned. They presented the plan and the protocol which they had signed in Moscow. Otherwise, I wasn't there.

Q: But you talked directly to those who had attended the conference?

A: Sure. At that time Czechoslovakia was perhaps the most important country of all Soviet satellites. The Soviets said repeatedly they trusted Czechoslovakia above anybody else. And that's why Moscow used Czechoslovakia to operate in the whole world while Bulgaria, for instance, operated only against Turkey. The Czech area of operations covered Latin America as well as Africa.

Q: So at the 1964 Moscow conference terrorism and other aspects of low-intensity warfare were . . . discussed?

A: Sure, terrorism, production of special equipment, training of foreign agents in sabotage and terrorism. Regular intelligence and coordination of all intelligence operations were also discussed.

Q: And each [client] was given its assignment?

A: Each satellite was given its area of responsibility and a list of projects. That's how the Soviets operate: they attempt to assign responsibility in areas in which their satellites are best qualified. That doesn't mean that you would be passive elsewhere. The Czechs were ordered to focus their operations on

Latin America, Austria, West Germany. Czechoslovakia was also heavily involved in Egypt. One hundred and ten Czech army and intelligence officers were in Egypt at least since 1956. And even Ethiopia and Afghanistan came under the Czech area of responsibility. For example, when Haile Selassie visited Prague and Moscow we had already been working to remove him from office.

Q: Are you now talking about the early '60s?

A: Sure. . . .

Q: On the division of labor at the October 1964 conference, was it simply geographical, or was it also functional?

A: It was both.

Q: When you give us a list of all the countries that Czechoslovakia was "given," was the understanding that you were supposed to destabilize them?

A: To destabilize them, to establish what the Soviets call "second power." The first power is the government that is in office but the Soviets and we were working with different parties, mass organizations, and individuals. We were working to prepare groups of people that could take over a country when the revolutionary situation would be correct. The Soviets called these people "bullets"—*patron*. Such people, you know, were secretly trained and prepared and we could then "shoot" from them when we needed it.

Q: The policy was . . . . to insert such agents into positions of responsibility?

A: Yes, you try to direct them into important positions. Czechoslovakia was very active in . . . . the social democratic international in Europe and worked against social democrats in general.

Q: Can you tell us something about the methods that were applied in such operations?

A: First of all you've got to recruit future agents. Some of those recruited are then taken to Czechoslovakia for education and training. The recruitment goes through communist parties and through the resident agent. The selected are then taken to Czechoslovakia through Vietnam, Stockholm, or Vienna. There they are given Czech passports and they travel to Prague as Czechoslovak citizens.

Q: Now, what kind of people are they? . . .

A: These people could be either direct members of the party or they are sympathizers. There are several different categories into which they have been divided by the time they reach Czechoslovakia. Some have been selected to assume high military positions when the revolution succeeds and they are educated not only in Czechoslovakia but also in the Soviet Union, in the Frunze Academy. But most do travel first through Prague. It's like a transit station where they are given medical checkups and may be then flown to Moscow.

Q: Okay. So when these people are smuggled into Czechoslovakia, what happens next? Where does the training take place?

A: It depends on what they are to be trained for. For example, if they are to be trained as a group for terrorist operations they go to Doupov, near Karlovy Vary. At the time when I was in Czechoslovakia there was also a training camp in Boletice, near Krumlov. In addition, there was also a full military intelligence brigade in Prostejov. This brigade consisted of diversionary units and had some 1,500 soldiers all together. This brigade operates as part of the Czech military intelligence's plans.

Q: Can we come back to the nature of training . . . selected Latin Americans were put through in Doupov?

A: Those who are to penetrate military organizations in their home countries are often trained in groups. Intelligence officers, of course, are trained individually because they don't like for anybody else to know who they are. If it's a short course it often takes place in special villas in Prague. The counterintelligence has one such place in Pohorelec. Still others are trained to become members of the SPETSNAZ counterintelligence battalion. Their task is not just to watch people but to execute them in peace and in war.

Q: So these are really "wet" operations experts.

A: Yes and such agents are trained all over the country.

Q: And how are the terrorists disguised during their training? I can't picture them walking around the Doupov base. Wouldn't they look conspicuous?

A: If they are in Doupov or in the brigade you never see them in the city. They stay in the barracks until the training is finished. The whole course often lasts between three to six months.

Q: What does it consist of?

A: If they are trained for sabotage, the first thing they have to undergo is political education and a rigorous course in Marxism–Leninism. The political part of their training takes about four hours a week. In addition they undergo practical training in leadership and sabotage. Leadership is especially important since after they return home they must organize their own cells and train their own subordinates. They become experts in establishing such networks, in operating secretly; they receive training in how to use most explosives as well as chemical materials.

Q: Oh, chemical weapons are also included! Who are the instructors?

A: Well, most of them are from the ZS, the Czech military intelligence. They are highly educated and experienced intelligence officers whose cover has been blown and consequently they can no longer operate abroad. For example, Colonel Pribyl who had been kicked out of Britain. Other instructors are intelligence officers too old to work in the field.

Demolition and sabotage are usually taught by former chemical troops and engineering officers. I can tell you, for instance, that Colonel Kaspirek was one of them. I had known him quite well because I myself started with engineering troops. All the instructors are carefully selected from the security point of view; they also undergo intelligence training and, finally, they are of course professionals and experts in their respective fields.

Q: What's the language of instruction, how do the instructors communicate with the terrorists?

A: Well, the intelligence officers speak foreign languages. Don't forget that the Czech intelligence school which used to be in Prague takes two years. Further, even simple intelligence agents after 1965 are graduates of the military academy in Brno, which takes four years. After that they must attend the intelligence academy in Chotkovy Sady, Prague. Now, if you are to be trained for sabotage and strategic intelligence you must undergo a one-year-long training [program] in the Soviet Union. Every agent must speak of course Czech and Russian and at least two other languages. So you can see that they are very well prepared. The instructors are among the best educated people in the country.

The pressure to learn languages intensified in the 1960s. I didn't know one guy there who wouldn't speak several foreign languages.

Q: Were there any Soviets in the Doupov base?

A: The largest KGB station is in Karlovy Vary and they control everything there. On the other hand the Doupov base is controlled by the Soviet GRU. When I left Czechoslovakia there were eighteen Soviet advisors in the Ministry of Defense of whom twelve were intelligence officers. They controlled absolutely everything.

For instance, we all had to attend briefings at the ZS. The Soviet advisor always sat next to the Czech chief of the ZS.

Q: Were Soviet advisors actually present at the training centers in Czechoslovakia?

A: Absolutely. They could go anywhere they wanted.

Q: What about the Irish Republican Army? Were you aware of any effort on the part of the Soviets to exploit the situation in Ireland?

A: I think that Czechoslovakia had extensive contacts there, especially with anarchist and communist groups. Incidentally, it wasn't even too secret. We supplied them with explosives, some radio stations, and also some money. These connections had been established already in 1963.

The material and financial aspect of Czechoslovakia's support of foreign terrorist groups was taken care of by the Department for Foreign Technical Assistance, *Oddeleni zahranicne technicke pomoci.* For instance, in 1967 the Czech Defense Council provided the Palestinian Liberation Organization with 10,000,000 crowns for training, education, and material assistance. This was for just one year. If you put it in dollars it doesn't seem much. But, you know, a machine gun in Czechoslovakia doesn't cost $5,000 like here, but maybe $200. It's a lot of money.

Q: Who controls this Department?

A: The Chief of General Staff. When I was in Czechoslovakia the head of the Department was Colonel Fort. He was a very experienced man. It was his responsibility to supply terrorist groups or revolutionary forces with material assistance.

Q: What about the Material and Technical Plan?

A: Well, this plan also includes provisions for sabotage abroad and support of guerrillas. Of course, those who work on the plan don't know exactly what goes where. Only the appropriate military intelligence officer of the ZS knows that. You know how it works in communism, you better not ask. You ask and you are in trouble.

Q: Let me take you back again to the structure of decision making regarding low-level violence. How does Moscow communicate with the Czechs?

A: First, the Soviet Defense Council must approve all assignments for the individual satellites. This plan was prepared by the Soviet KGB and GRU and approved by the Party. When it's ready the Czech chief of general staff and the military and civilian chiefs are called to Moscow. Simultaneously, Moscow invites the chief of the administrative department of the Central Committee. He is given the strict Party line. You must understand that in the Soviet Union nobody is trusted. The Party wants to insure that the intelligence people are not playing behind its back.

When the chief of general staff with his colleagues from intelligence come home they start working on the Czech version of the plan. This work begins around July and August. Naturally, Soviet advisors are constantly around, observing everything, making sure that everything is done according to Soviet instructions. When the advisors think the plan is ready it's sent to the Soviet Union again. There it goes before the Soviet chief of staff, GRU, KGB, and the Party.

Q: And all that takes place before the plan is presented to the Czech Defense Council?

A: Yes, even before it goes to the Defense Council. . . . Before the Czech Defense Council can start analyzing the plan, there must already be a formal statement on it to the effect that it has been sent to Moscow and that Soviet comrades approve of it. Of course, all this makes it a lengthy process. The Soviets are lazy and it usually takes them two months before they call the Czech chief of general staff back to Moscow for further discussions. If there are no problems he doesn't have to go there and only the chief of the ZS flies there to pick it up.

When the plan is safely back in Prague with the Soviet approval a copy is made for every member of the Defense Council. However, no one receives his copy in advance. They are given the plan only at the meeting itself. At that point, the secretary general calls for a one hour coffee break during which the plan is studied. Afterwards, there comes the discussion.

I attended many such sessions, took notes and wrote reports. When the report was approved I would burn immediately all the copies that had been made for members of the Defense Council. These meetings when I was in Czechoslovakia took place in the building of the Central Committee.

It was my duty to deliver orders embodied in the approved plan to the responsible authorities. They had to report periodically on how the operations for which they were responsible were proceeding. If it was just an average operation the Minister of Defense would report twice a year to the Defense Council on the progress they had achieved. Of course, the general secretary of the party had a report on his desk every morning from both intelligence services on what had happened yesterday.

Q: You served in Czechoslovakia both under Khrushchev and Brezhnev. Was there any major difference in their respective attitudes toward low-level warfare?

A: Khrushchev at the beginning tried to prove that he was different, that communism under him was different. He initiated a major deception campaign called the policy of peaceful coexistence. I met Khrushchev for the first time in 1954 when I was elected to the Central Committee. I attended a party during which Khrushchev said: "Comrades, if we want to move communism farther we must change the image of the Soviet Union and communism." Khrushchev attempted in some cases not to proceed too aggressively, he relied on political deception.

During the Brezhnev years we were told that Khrushchev's policy was not realistic because capitalism and imperialism had remained unchanged. Consequently, Moscow decided to put througoh the so-called strategic initiative relying heavily on sabotage, espionage, disinformation, and theft of high technology. . . . That doesn't mean of course that the intelligence services under Khrushchev were not active. Absolutely not. But the aggressiveness in the area of terrorism, sabotage, and other low-level violence operations, active measures, it came under Brezhnev.

Q: So Brezhnev made the decision to proceed more aggressively toward destabilization of open societies than Khrushchev.

A: Yes, the decision was made by the Soviet Defense Council. Previously, Khrushchev had argued that he had no need for agents walking around U.S. military bases in West Germany and collecting information on how many tanks had passed through the gate. I need an agent, said Khrushchev, who is in the Pentagon, a man who can tell me whether Kennedy is going to push the button and start the war. Thus, Khrushchev focused more on strategic intelligence than everyday spying. Brezhnev, of course, retained strategic intelligence but added active measures, sabotage, and low-level operations.

Let me give you an example. Look at the plans we had for Great Britain. The Soviets believe that Great Britain is very important because it would remain a U.S. ally even after NATO would be destroyed. Of course, Soviet leaders are more intelligent than Hitler who had bombed the British Parliament. Instead, our plan stipulated that networks of agents should be established by 1972. I remember the Czech minister of interior, Rudolf Barak, who told us that the easiest way to ship explosive material to Britain is via India since ships from the British Commonwealth are much less vigorously searched than ships from a communist country. All other plans were equally indirect. Instead of destroying the Houses of Parliament our plan called for the poisoning of the water supply system, especially in districts inhabited by the bourgeoisie.

Q: Would this be done by a network of illegals in place or would it be done by special warfare teams infiltrated to Britain just prior to the action?

A: Some British participate in this. They have been mostly selected by the British Communist Party. I would say that most don't know what they have been selected for. You must never be specific. The British Party is simply told to supply a certain number of people. They are however completely controlled by Czech agents.

But you never asked me about the communist involvement in the international drug trade!

Q: I was just going to mention that.

A: Mao Zedong [Mao Tse-tung] decided already during the Korean War to make drugs available to U.S. troops. But the Soviets picked up the idea very quickly because it was so smart. They not only collect money but the product they sell also helps to destroy Western societies. In 1963 Moscow decided to increase its involvement in international narcotics trade. It had become clear that drugs were very important for the demoralization of troops. The Vietnam situation later confirmed that analysis.

Moscow often acts through satellites. For instance, Bulgaria has been quite successful with narcotics because it's so close to Turkey. Czechoslovakia operates in Latin America and so do the East Germans. It's interesting to note that until 1965, East Germany had not been permitted to conduct high-level strategic operations together with the Soviet Union and other allies.

Q: The East Germans were not trusted by the Soviets. . . .

A: In 1965 Moscow decided that there were simply too many former Nazis in South Africa and Latin America and that it would be better and easier to allow East Germany to exploit them.

Q: So in 1965 East Germany joined the family.

A: They joined as an equal member of the family.

I know of one occasion when Soviet analysts of the United States, who are generally excellent, were dead wrong. In the early '60s a Vietnamese delegation told us in Moscow that Vietnam was going to destroy the United States economically and politically and to achieve a military victory. Let me tell you the Soviets, and all of us—we laughed. How did those stupid Vietnamese intend to damage the United States? The Soviets in fact had advised them temporarily to stop the war or, at least, to focus on the so-called second front, i.e., the political front. But the Vietnamese did prevail.

Q: In your view, what role will low-level warfare operations play in the future?

A: It's now a thoroughly integrated system and it will be gradually implemented with energy but also patience. In democracy, we want everything better yesterday. You know the President is around for four, or if he's lucky, eight years. In the Soviet Union Ponomarev has been at the International Department throughout his life. He sees everything from a very long perspective. The Soviet leaders are sincerely convinced that history is on their side.

Document 2: Testimony of Ladislav Bittman—An Insider's View

L adislav Bittman served in the Czechoslovak Intelligence Service, *Statni bezpecnost* (StB), for about 14 years, rising to the rank of Deputy Chief of StB's Department Eight (unofficially called "D," for "disinformation"), which was involved in the production and coordination of special operations, also known as "active measures."

His statement, published below, is excerpted from "The Role of the Soviet Bloc Intelligence in International Terrorism: The View From Inside"—his contribution to the April 1985 gathering on this topic sponsored by the International Security Studies Program of the Fletcher School of Law and Diplomacy.

In considering the phenomenon of international terrorism and its connections to Eastern Europe, many Western analysts mistakenly separate terrorism from other forms of Soviet "active measures." The KGB's involvement is covered by several protective layers of tight security rules and so-called help from the international proletariat. Even the members of terrorist organizations are unaware of their assigned role in Soviet plans.

Terrorist organizations would not be able to survive for long periods without outside support. The Soviet Union, the German Democratic Republic, Czechoslovakia, Bulgaria, and Cuba have provided various kinds of assistance to terrorists, including weapons, ammunition and explosives, military training, financing, and sanctuaries where they could plan their operations undisturbed or communicate safely with other terrorist groups.

The Weather Underground in the United States maintained contact with Communist intelligence for years, particularly Cuban, East German, and North Korean. They supported the Weather Underground with money, equipment, and a safe haven.[1]

The Puerto Rican FALN, a Marxist–Leninist group more or less openly supported by Cuba for years, is another example of support by the Soviet bloc for leftist terrorist groups operating on U.S. territory.[2]

But there is no evidence that the KGB or the DGI directs operations by such terrorist groups as the FALN or the Italian Red Brigades. As a matter of fact, the Soviets deliberately refuse to select terrorist targets or direct individual operations. The reason is obvious. Even a very disciplined underground organization cannot avoid occasional failures and violations of secrecy. Public disclosure of KGB involvement in a major terrorist act would seriously damage Soviet foreign policy and eventually paralyze other important intelligence operations.

However, the KGB and its satellite agencies do provide selected terrorist organizations with specialized training, for example, in handling guns and explosives. The Palestine Liberation Organization has quite openly sent its members to the Soviet Union for training.[3] Czechoslovakia, Cuba, Vietnam, and North Korea have provided similar training to other terrorist organizations.

Many terrorist groups are armed with weapons manufactured in the Soviet Union, Czechoslovakia, or East Germany. Some shipments of East European weapons destined for Western terrorists have been discovered when they were not properly handled.[4]

Weapons have been supplied directly and openly to the Palestinian Liberation Organization, and the secret network, in turn, has distributed them to other groups, such as the Red Brigades. West European police have intercepted some of these secret shipments.[5]

Notes

1. Larry Gratwohl, a former member of the group, explained that Weather Underground members located each other when cut off from the group by using a special code name to telephone the Cuban Embassy in Mexico or Canada. An operative of the Cuban intelligence stationed at the Cuban Embassy would then bring lost members in contact with others in the area.

2. In Communique No. 6 issued on October 27, 1975, the FALN expressed appreciation for the Soviet block support: "We especially acknowledge the moral support given to our organization by the Cuban people and government in a speech by Prime Minister Fidel Castro in August (1975) in which he said that the Cuban government would do all it could to support the FALN."

3. Adnan Jabel, a Palestinian terrorist captured by the Israelis, stated in 1980 that he had received special training in tactics, weapons, and explosives in the Soviet Union.

4. In 1971, for instance, the Dutch police in Amsterdam confiscated a large volume of Czechoslovak weapons scheduled for delivery to the Irish Republican Army. Later shipments handled more discreetly through several intermidiaries made it difficult to trace the country of origin.

5. In January 1983, the Austrian police arrested a Czechoslovak citizen named Petr Bardon. Careful examination of his car revealed 300 undeclared pistols and 7 automatic rifles of Soviet design (Draganov) equipped with special night signs.

Document 3: Testimony of Vladimir Kostov—KGB Penetration of Bulgarian Security Services

V ladimir Kostov, a former senior Bulgarian official with special insights regarding Bulgarian intelligence (*Durzhavna Sigurnost*—DS), provides testimony of the degree to which his service was penetrated by the KGB, to the extent of performing tasks for the latter without other Bulgarian institutions being "in the picture." The evidence presented is particularly important, since the activities of East European intelligence branches in the areas with which this book is concerned have been identified frequently, but the question has been raised from time to time whether the USSR necessarily knew or had approved such operations. Kostov's insights provide a definitive answer to this question.

Source: The material printed here constitutes part of written testimony sent by Kostov to the Oral History Project on July 20, 1985.

The Soviet KGB, the Soviet Military Intelligence, and the Embassy itself each have their own network of Bulgarian informers and collaborators. The Bulgarian regime claims that collaboration with Soviet intelligence services represents a "higher display of proletarian internationalism"...

... One is bound to pose repeatedly the question of the interrelationships between the Bulgarian and the Soviet secret services, in light of the mutual relationship existing between the political leaderships of the two countries. Is Moscow aware of the decisions taken by Sofia? Is Sofia obliged to seek permission from Moscow for any important action it might be contemplating? And, consequently, is it logical automatically to place equal responsibility on Moscow whenever the Bulgarian regime is suspected of or charged with committing some unseemly act in the international arena. The answers to these questions can best be found by examining the relationship that exists between the Bulgarian state security service (*Durzhavna sigurnost* - DS) and the Soviet state security (Committee for State Security - KGB).

How are relations regulated between the DS and the KGB? The Bulgarian state security service is a strictly centralized organization. Each of its units operates within the boundaries set by a superior unit. A vertical structure is thus obtained for the receipt and issuance of instructions as well as for the transmission of information. The highest ring of this structure is top political leadership: the Politburo of the Central Committee of the BCP. In addition, there exists a horizontal structure connected with the Soviet KGB. The Bulgarian state security officials in charge are obliged to inform their KGB counterparts about their activities and to coordinate these activities with them. The Bulgarian state security resident in a foreign country is obliged to provide detailed information about the work of his residency and to coordinate its activities with the KGB resident. In Bulgaria the head of each department and directorate of the DS coordinates his work with the KGB adviser for each department. The Minister of Interior and State Security briefs the KGB representative (usually a minister plenipotentiary) on the Soviet Embassy staff about the work of his ministry and coordinates this work with the Soviet adviser.

All KGB employees who maintain contact with and are responsible for the Bulgarian state security service are a part of the strictly centralized structure of the KGB. The core of the matter is to be found in the relationships established through the horizontal contacts maintained between the DS and representatives of the KGB. The state security official at whatever level has no right to conceal information from the KGB representative. The latter is not, however, obliged fully to inform a Bulgarian state security official. The Soviet representative supplies only that information which he deems essential for performance of the planned missions. The various sections of the state security apparatus have no right to exclude the KGB official from any operation no matter how sensitive and important it may be and regardless of whether or not Soviet interests are involved. The basic principle followed is that on every level the KGB officers are more competent and possess greater knowledge to appraise and ensure the success of an undertaking than are the officials of the Bulgarian security service. Thus on all levels the KGB officials have the right to confiscate any information they want and to act on it on their own, i.e., within the Soviet vertical structure. They proceed from the premise that the KGB functions more efficiently than does the vertical structure of the Bulgarian state security service.

This fundamental difference between the rights and obligations of the Bulgarian DS and the Soviet KGB is compounded by several other factors. For instance, all senior personnel of the Bulgarian state security are obliged to attend KGB training schools. Upon graduating from these schools they swear an oath of allegiance to the Soviet state just as the Soviet graduates do. A second factor is that almost immediately after the establishment of the Communist regime in Bulgaria, the Soviet authorities insisted that the KGB be allowed to set up its own information network in the country, independent of both the Bulgarian party leaders and the state security service. This network was and still is recruited and managed directly by the KGB. Neither at that time nor at any later date did the Bulgarian party leadership ever oppose this Soviet demand for privileged status as far as intelligence matters are concerned. Such are the rules: the party member informs neither his superiors at work nor his party secretary if he is assigned a secret task by a Soviet agency.

The relationship between the DS and the KGB thus requires that the questions raised at the start of this be put somewhat differently when a Bulgarian official — be he or she a diplomat, a technical specialist, or whatever — is suspected of or charged with an action in violation of international law. The fact that the person involved is a Bulgarian official (as a rule a member of the Bulgarian Communist Party) does not necessarily mean that he was acting on instruction of the DS or of some other authoritative Bulgarian body. It is quite possible that he may have been recruited by the KGB and thus have acted under direct instructions from Soviet bodies, without the knowledge of the DS.

However, if the person in question was not directly subordinate to the KGB but acted on instructions of the DS, would the Soviet authorities have been informed of his activity? Most certainly, because at every level a DS operative renders a full account to a KGB representative. Consequently, it is only logical to seek responsibility for every DS action not only among the top political leadership of Bulgaria but also among the Soviet political leadership.

As for the question of the level at which the Bulgarian bodies - DS or the party and state leadership - are informed, here matters are not so clear. The more complex and more important a secret service operation is, the greater the likelihood that the KGB will exclude one and more levels of the DS from it. Even the Bulgarian political leadership can be expected to be kept in the dark in such cases. Situations such as these are, of course, always presented as "temporary measures". Therefore, in such cases DS units and officials may carry out operations in the firm conviction that they are acting on the instructions of Bulgarian bodies while in fact they are merely acting as tools of the KGB.

The relationship between the Bulgarian security service and the KGB had already assumed its present form by the end of the 1960s. This relationship, which has manifested itself in a number of concrete cases in the past, is the epitome of the policy of sovietization.

Document 4: PLO Arms for the Red Brigades

A lready the first of several defectors from the ranks of the Italian terrorist organization *Brigade Rosse* (BR, Red Brigades), pointed to the collaboration between this organization and the PLO. His deposition was later confirmed and amplified by several other defectors.

In statements to Judge Mastelloni, the Investigating Magistrate at the High Court of Venice, three of these defectors testified, independently of each other, that at a meeting in Paris, in Autumn 1978, a formal agreement to cooperate was reached between representatives of the two organizations. The PLO spokesman at this meeting was alleged to have been Yasser Arafat's deputy, the "Minister of the Interior" or Security Chief of the PLO, Saleh Khalaf (alias Abu Iyad).

Material evidence of this cooperation was provided, by the discovery, near Venice, of an arms cache in February 1982. From the markings of these arms it appeared that some of them were at the disposition of the Red Brigades, while others were stored for future use by the PLO.

In consequence of this find and the ensuing investigation, the High Court of Venice issued an arrest warrant not only against Abu Iyad but also against the top leader of the PLO, Yasser Arafat, on the grounds that he must certainly have known of the agreement concluded by his henchman. However, in June 1985, the Supreme Court of the Republic of Italy sustained Yasser Arafat's appeal against the warrant on technical grounds. However, that decision did not invalidate the evidence regarding the arms transfers. What follows is an excerpt from the Prosecutor General's motion to reject the appeal:

Office of the Prosecutor General of the Republic at the Appellate Court
29790/I/84   1838/ORD.

THE PROSECUTOR GENERAL,
having examined the documentary evidence,
STATES:

1. On the 4th of September, 1984 the examining magistrate of the High Court of Venice had issued an arrest warrant against Yasser Arafat Abu Amarr and Khalaf Salah [sic] (alias Abu Ijad or Abu Ajad), both accused of:

a) the crime specified in the articles 110, 112n. 1 C.P. 9L. October 14, 1974, n.497 for having, the first as leader and representative of the organization PLO, acting in conjunction with the second and with unidentified others, and through meetings on French territory between the latter, as representative of the said organization, and the Red Brigades, approved a joint program of cooperation and, in particular, of having authorized, for subversive purposes, the delivery of a huge quantity of arms and munitions (specified below) which was introduced by sea into the territory of the Italian Republic in Venice in September 1979, by Mario Moretti Riccardo Dura, Andrea Varisco, Sandro Galletta, and Massino Gidoni (all members of the Red Brigade and under separate arraignment), said materials having been received on Lebanese territory (150 Sterling machine guns; 5 bazookas; 10 land-air missiles; numerous antitank-and-personnel bombs; several kilograms of plastic explosive; F.A.L. rifles; thousands of cartridges of various calibers; accessories for weapons);

b) The crime specified in the articles 110, 112n. 1, 81 c.p., 10 L., October 14, 1974 n. 497, 21 L. April 18th, 1975 n. 110, 1 L. 10th of January, 1980 n. 15, because, in prosecution of the same criminal design, in their respective qualities of President of the Executive Committee of the PLO the first, and as a functionary of the security services of the majority faction Al Fatah the second, they concurred in the illegal retention of a part of the arms mentioned above (ground-air missiles, Sterling machine guns, rockets, etc.) which were held by the Venetian column of the PLO at the disposition—on Italian territory—of the PLO, specifically at Mestre and later at Valpago Del Montello up to the date of their discovery in February 1982 by the police forces; committing this act for the purposes of terrorism and in particular in order to commit crimes against property and persons.

2. By disposition of October 8, 1984, the High Court of Venice, after reexamination, has confirmed the arrest warrant against the two accused who remain in hiding.

The lawyers for the defense have appealed on three grounds for Yasser Arafat and two for Khalaf Salah (the latter corresponding to the second and third grounds of Arafat).

3. Arafat moves for cancellation of the warrant on the grounds that this warrant violates the immunity which he enjoys as President of the Organization for the Liberation of Palestine (PLO) an entity which has stature in international law and "specific validity as a state", having obtained recognition by the United Nations as the only legitimate representative of the Palestinian people.

The argument is without foundation.

As the presiding magistrate has observed, the PLO is not a sovereign organization, the equivalent by structure and by effectivity of a state entity, because it totally lacks territorial sovereignty, for which forms of control over the refugee camps are no substitute, because these are always exercised with the consent and under the sovereignty of the host state. . . .

. . . .

[Summary] In continuation, the Prosecutor General also rejects the argument of the defense lawyers that the articles of the penal code invoked in the arrest warrant do not apply to political crimes committed abroad. He states that the acts ascribed to the accused must be considered as having been committed on Italian territory. He therefore moves that the appeal be rejected by the Appellate Court, which concurred with his motion [but was overruled, subsequently, on technical grounds, by the Supreme Court of the Republic].

7
Surrogate Actors in Africa

The 1970s witnessed an unprecedented upsurge of Soviet activity in southern Africa. The joint Soviet–Cuban intervention in Angola ensured the victory of the MPLA and was shortly followed by the triumph of FRELIMO in Mozambique. These successes encouraged the Soviet leaders in their belief that the global "correlation of forces" was shifting in their favor and considerably increased their prestige throughout the Third World. Through the training of military forces, intelligence personnel, and political cadres, the Soviet Union and its surrogates made possible the consolidation of power by the MPLA and FRELIMO regimes. Concurrently, aid to other "national liberation movements" in the region, especially SWAPO and the ANC, increased markedly.

The Soviet Union and its surrogates are also heavily involved in East Africa. After a complex series of diplomatic maneuvers, Ethiopia became the chief Soviet client in the region. Cuban troops were employed in defense of the Mengistu regime and, as Document 1 reveals, the Soviet leaders have well-defined plans for the future role of Ethiopia.

The escalation of Soviet-orchestrated support for "national liberation movements" in southern Africa has exacerbated conflict in the region. An extensive international network of "fraternal" states and mutually supporting movements operates on all levels, from military training to political legitimization. The testimony of five recipients of Soviet and Bloc aid is included in Documents 2 through 6. Their stories reveal how young Africans are commandeered, what they learn, and the ends for which they are used. They record in extensive detail how the Soviet apparatus for supporting low-intensity conflict operates in the southern African theater. Their statements contain certain similarities, from the deception and outright coercion used in recruitment to the disillusionment resulting from participation in a movement that uses the cloak of "national liberation" in the pursuit of something quite different.

Document 1: CPSU Report to Ethiopia

T he excerpts below are taken from a Soviet Communist Party report to Ethiopia detailing guidelines for the future course of the regime of Mengistu Haile Mariam. The report calls for the collectivization of the peasantry, a concerted campaign against religion, and the development of the Ethiopian military services into a force able to fulfill its "internationalist duty." The document reveals how Soviet concerns extend beyond simply the internal consolidation of the revolution to the preparation of a surrogate's armed forces for future foreign operations.

Source: This document was smuggled out of Ethiopia and came into the possession of Colin Legum in London. Parts of the report were reproduced in a *Christian Science Monitor* article of 3 June 1985 written by Mr. Legum.

. . . [T]he first task [in the campaign against religion] is to make sure that the masses give up their old outlooks and get divorced from the reactionary influence of religion and completely forget all their ancient customs and traditions. . . .

The Islamic allies of imperialism are using these [petro-] dollars to support their Ethiopian lackeys who will stop nowhere in their attempts to undermine the revolution. . . .

[The peasants] should be made to give up the idea of individual ownership and holding [of land] and espouse the communist ideas of collective farming. . . .

The indoctrination and the nurturing of the armed forces in Marxism–Leninism is the most important point that should be given immediate and due attention. . . . The new revolutionary armed forces should be different from the old. They should neither be chauvinistic nor unduly patriotic. They should be loyal to the revolution, the principles of proletarian internationalism as well as to the socialist community. *The armed forces should be organized and indoctrinated in such a way as would enable them to fulfill their internationalist duty.* . . . [emphasis added]

. . . like all other preceding revolutions, the Ethiopian revolution has erupted in accordance with the principles of Marxist–Leninist theory [and is] an integral part of the international socialist revolutionary movement. The establishment of a Leninist party and the success of socialism in Ethiopia . . . will be a source of moral inspiration . . . for the revolutionary class struggle being waged everywhere in Africa. . . .

[The CPSU] is thus determined more than ever in its commitment to assist in the fulfillment of its mission. . . . [Reactionary elements are trying to] promote anti-Sovietism in Ethiopia . . . By downplaying the material and moral assistance the Soviet Union and other socialist countries render to socialist Ethiopia, they are trying to attach economic and social problems and difficulties, some of which have come about due to natural causes, to the Soviet Union and to discredit communism and thereby encourage the rise of national chauvinism. . . .

Document 2: Testimony of Jeffrey Motutuzele Bosigo

J effrey Motutuzele Bosigo was born in Soweto, South Africa, in 1959. After an encounter with the police, he left South Africa with a friend in 1976. Upon arrival in Botswana, they were detained until an ANC member arranged their release. They traveled to Zambia, believing that the ANC was "an organization which helped South African refugees continue their studies." In Lusaka, an ANC representative told them they could continue their education if they went to Angola. They flew to Luanda and discovered quickly what type of "education" the ANC provided. They were given extensive military training before Bosigo was selected to go to the Soviet Union.

Bosigo's experiences reveal the extent of Soviet support of the ANC network. From Cuban instruction in Angola to advanced studies in the Ukraine with PLO classmates, Bosigo describes in the following excerpts how the ANC and its Soviet sponsor "educates" young Africans.

Source: Senate Hearings before the Subcommittee on Security and Terrorism of the Committee on the Judiciary, *The Role of the Soviet Union, Cuba, and East Germany in Fomenting Terrorism in Southern Africa*, 1982.

"There were about 200 refugees in the camp of whom some had come from Tanzania via Mozambique. . . . During this period I realized for the first time that I would be receiving military training.

"We had been issued uniforms when we arrived in Engineering Camp . . . [some of] which came from Socialist States. . . . While I was in Engineering camp a group of approximately 25 recruits left the camp to go for further training in East Germany. . . . The subjects that we were taught were mainly theoretical. These included classes in:

1. Politics: The history, purpose and assistence of trade unions, political economy, and South African history.
2. Tactics: The planning of ambushes, how to seek cover, reconnaissance, planning of depots and 'dead letter boxes.' We would do some of these

exercises practically by, for example, marching in particular battle formations and checking different places to find an appropriate spot for a 'dead letter box.'

3. Topography: Map reading physical orientation using stars, the Southern cross, sunflowers, and ant heaps to determine direction.
4. Divisional Drill: We did practical drill exercises.
5. Weapons: We handled the following weapons during the course:
   (1) A.K. 47
   (2) AKM
   (3) Papashai
   (4) P.M.K.M.
   (5) RPG 7 rocket launcher
   (6) G.3
   (7) R.1
   (8) UXI"

.   .   .   .

"At the beginning of March 1977 about 200 Umkontho We Sizwe—F.A.P.L.A.—cadres arrived at the base. These were members of Umkontho We Sizwe who had received their training with F.A.P.L.A., the armed forces of the MPLA government in Luanda. About 14 of these cadres had had training in Russia and came from a transit camp called Huambo. The rest of them had only half completed their training and came from camps at Kabella and Funda. They received training at Benguela together . . . for the period that we were still there.

"At the end of May 1977 we moved from Benguela to a new base Nova Cantengue. . . . I was put in Company 1, Platoon 1, Section 2. . . . The Cuban Commander was Arkimedis and the Cuban interpreter was called Eduardo. . . . The other Cubans who assisted with the recruits apart from Arkimedes and Eduardo were Marero, Armando and Gastillo. Gastillo was a mechanic and commanded those recruits who were training to become mechanics. . . .

"Every recruit was required to know the 'Freedom Charter' which was adopted by the African National Congress, the South African Congress of Trade Unions and the South African Communist Party in 1955. We received lectures on Marx, Engels and Lenin and communist ideology. During all lectures the oppression of the black man in South Africa by the whites was emphasized and we were told that we must fight for our freedom from the South African government. . . .

"At the beginning of December 1977 an old A.N.C. . . . Came to our Section and told us that a group of 60 persons would be going to Russia for further training. . . .

"In the Engineering camp in Luanda the group of 60 was divided into five smaller groups, namely Grad P. B. 10, Zeke U, Mortar and Engineering. [In] . . . 1977 our group of 60 traveled to Moscow in an 'Aeroflot' aircraft . . . [and then to] Pirivalnye in the Ukraine. . . .

"During our six months stay in Russia we had training in the following subjects: Grad P—Physical exercises, handling of the AKM, topography and tactics, gas and gas masks. . . .

"During May 1978 the B.10, Engineering and Zeke U groups left the Soviet Union and returned to Luanda in Angola. In the middle of June 1978 my group, the Grad P Group and the Mortar group left the base at Pirivalnye. . . . After three days in Moscow we . . . traveled back to Luanda via Budapest, Cairo and Brazaville. On our arrival at Luanda we were taken directly from the airport to the new camp at Quibaxe. . . .

Bosigo was asked what other groups he trained with while in the Soviet Union. He responded:

"I was in with a group from Palestine; they were from Lebanon and Libya—the group of about 400 to 450 [He later clarified: "It was a PLO group."]. There were about 250 from Angola, and then we had SWAPO— 200; 20 men from the Republic of Oman; that is an Arab Republic."

[It is likely that Bosigo meant Yemen (the PDRY or South Yemen).] He was then asked about the role and selection of political commissars.

. . ."Well, actually, they select from the people who are . . . more educated than the others. So, that means he can understand politics faster than the others, so they select him as a political commissar.

"Mostly, they have been trained in Cuba, Russia and East Germany. The schools they attend, they normally call 'party schools.' Their role is to uplift the morale of the cadres; that is, to teach the cadres to be loyal to the policies of the organization."

Document 3: Testimony of Ephraim Mfalapitsa

E phraim Mfalapitsa was born in 1953 near Swartruggens, South Africa. After the Soweto riots in June 1976, he left South Africa with his cousin and a friend. They contacted an ANC representative in Botswana, received false UN passports, and were transported by air to Tanzania.

In the following excerpts he recounts his experiences, including training he received in East Germany and operations he was involved with after his return. Mfalapitsa also describes the escalation of the conflict initiated just before he left the ANC.

Source: Senate Hearings before the Subcommittee on Security and Terrorism of the Committee on the Judiciary, *The Role of the Soviet Union, Cuba, and East Germany in Fomenting Terrorism in Southern Africa,* 1982.

"Our daily timetable [in Dar-es-Salaam] was:

Physical training . . .

Political discussions . . .

History of the ANC . . .

The Black Workers in S.A. and the SACTU . . .

Military tactics . . .

The singing of freedom songs

Reading ANC literature like the Sechaba, The African Communist, 50 Fighting Years, Mao's History, Mao TseTung on modern guerrilla warfare.

Doing guard duty.

"We were taken on one occasion to the North Korean Embassy to see a film on the Korean Revolution. . . .

"On the 26th November 1976 our group left for Angola by East African Airways. . . . And were then transported by army trucks to the Engineering Camp situated to the east of Luanda. . . . [where] I saw the following persons:

50 Cuban's, who were mostly instructors and engineers,

300 FAPLA troops, waiting to go to their combat areas,

30 trained ANC cadres waiting for missions, and

100 ANC recruits waiting for military training which included a group from Tanzania. . . .

"[At the camp, we] also helped . . . offloading equipment from the docks destined for the ANC in Angola which was usually shipped from Hungary, Bulgaria, Cuba and the U.S.S.R. . . .

"During February 1977 . . . a platoon of 30 of the most disciplined recruits were going to be selected for military training in East Germany (G.D.R.). I was very happy to be one of the few chosen ones.

"The G.D.R. group including myself flew from Luanda Military Airport by East German civilian airline. . . . We flew via Nigeria and landed at East Berlin International Airport on the 25th February 1977. On arrival we were taken by a civilian bus to the outskirts of a town named Rostov. . . . On arriving we were introduced to the following East Germans who were to be our instructors:

WOLFGANG

JORGAN

MORGAN

TITO

". . . About two days later we were each issued with a complete set of East Germany army uniforms including webbing, tracksuits and takkies, and a set of civilian clothing. We were also issued AK 47 assault rifles of which the firing pins were removed.

"Wolfgang who was the course leader explained the basic course rules we were to adhere to, and our planned training program during our stay, which was as follows:

Fire training (instructed by Wolfgang). Theory of the AK 47, Makarov, RPG 7, F1 and RGD 5 handgrenades, and practical use of some.

Field tactics (instructed by Jorgan). We were given lectures on raiding small military bases, ambushing patrols and army convoys, patrol formations, skirmishing and anti-tracking. We later did everything in practice.

Military combat work (instructed by Tito). We were given lectures in urban guerilla warfare, communication by secret writing using invisible ink prepared from certain chemicals. Preparing suitable Dead Letter Boxes, the formation of underground cells etc.

Explosives (instructed by Morgan). This was a very basic course only including Nitropenta and T.N.T. We were also shown how to use electric detonators and mechanical detonators. We in fact detonated a few charges on the rifle range.

Conspiracy (instructed by Tito). Lectures on underground secrecy, and "the need to know".

The History of the ANC (instructed by . . . , an ANC official . . . from London. . . .

Photography (instructed by a unknown German) including the correct way of taking discreet photographs of people and documents and developing our own photographs.

The structure of the C.I.A. (by an unknown German).

Physical training—every day (by Tito).

"At the beginning of October 1977, we completed our training and flew back to Angola by an East German aircraft. A few East German technicians accompanied us who were all being transferred to Angola. . . .

"Towards the end of October 1977 OUPA and I infiltrated at night into the RSA [Republic of South Africa]. We were both armed with Makarovs and given R200 each. . . .

"I was to be in charge of all ANC weapons in Botswana and help with infiltration [into the RSA]. . . . Whilst in this position, I was also responsible for infiltrations/missions into the RSA, actually carrying out missions myself on occasions. . . .

"During 1979 and 1980 before Zimbabwe's Independence we used to infiltrate cadres from Angola to Zimbabwe. They flew from Angola to Zambia by Angolan Airways or Aeroflot posing as ZAPU cadres. On landing at Lusaka they were transported by ZAPU officials to a ZAPU transit and training camp called CTT camp, of Lusaka.

.   .   .   .

"Botswana would in future be used as a springboard for operations against the RSA. This would take place without permission from the Botswana Government who would in any case not be able to prevent these operations. . . . It had also been decided to amend the existing strategy of the ANC and begin with rural guerrilla operations. This Botswana operation would in future be referred to as "Operation P" [and consisted of] . . . . laying mines on farm roads; attacking farmhouses; ambushing lonely vehicles; and attacking small police stations. By following this strategy the white farmers would leave the area."

.   .   .   .

Mr. Mfalapitsa was asked if he knew of any ANC assassinations of disillusioned or former members. He answered:

". . . I know of two cases, of which I had confirmation before that that people were to be killed. . . . "The first case was a certain man by the name of Pismo, who was involved in operations in African National Congress cadres in Zimbabwe. . . . I [was ordered to] transport this Pismo to an agreed spot where the administrative staff would be waiting, and the man must be stabbed, in the kidneys and immediately be thrown in the hole and buried, and that was done. . . .

"The second man who I know was killed was . . . disillusioned about the ANC, and he told ANC members that he would no longer take part in any activity of the ANC."

He was then asked why he decided to leave the ANC, realizing the personal risk involved. His response indicates his frustration with the direction of the ANC.

"One of the most important points that pushed me into this decision was that the aims and the objectives of the ANC, in reality, were one and the same thing with the objectives of the Communist Party of South Africa.

In their politics, in their language, they have got what they call——they are saying that their strategy is a national liberation strategy; that is, to liberate the black people. Well, that is okay. But they say again that after the national revolution, there will be what they call a socialist revolution. This socialist revolution will commence the dictatorship of the proletariat. . . ."

Document 4: Testimony of Dickson Namolo

D ickson Namolo was born in 1956 at Odibo, Namibia. He left in 1975 to study in Zambia and crossed into Angola near the town of Onjiva. He was told that SWAPO could arrange transportation to Lusaka but instead he was recruited to "liberate Namibia."

Namolo's account also describes the specialized intelligence training he received in the Soviet Union. This type of instruction for a member of a "national liberation movement" illuminates another significant aspect of Soviet support for low-intensity conflict.

After conducting SWAPO intelligence operations for over a year, Namolo was arrested by South African security forces in 1981. SWAPO's practice of executing members that have been captured and released ensured that an already disillusioned Namolo would not return.

Source: Senate Hearings before the Subcommittee on Security and Terrorism of the Committee on the Judiciary, *The Role of the Soviet Union, Cuba, and East Germany in Fomenting Terrorism in Southern Africa,* 1982.

"We took a bus to Onjiva where we met and spoke to the SWAPO representative. We told him that we wanted to go to Zambia to further our education. He agreed to this and said we would leave the following day to Zambia.

"The following day, our group of five and about 60 other SWAPO. . . . spent the night in a barrack of the UNITA organization. We were given food by the UNITA soldiers. . . . We met another SWAPO representative [and] . . . we were told . . . that we would not be going to Zambia but would instead receive military training at Okashapa in Angola. After our training, we would be sent into Namibia to fight in order to liberate Namibia. . . .

"At that stage, the whole group had been under the impression that they were going to Zambia for further academic training. We were all surprised to hear that we were to receive military training but we agreed to go.

"We were taken to a SWAPO base at Okashapa to be trained. This base is situated in Angola near the Angolan/Zambian border. It is very far from the Angolan/Namibian border. Only SWAPO members were present in the camp. . . .

"I received training at Okashapa for 5 months up to September 1975. I received infantry training in the following weapons: AK-47, PPSH, and a carbine that looks like a Mauser. . . .

"We all were taught to march and we had approximately 90 minutes of drilling every day. We also had physical training and political instruction. In our political studies, we studied the geography of Namibia on maps and were told we had to fight to liberate Namibia. We were taught why we were fighting. We were told about the struggle for the Angolan and Mozambican independence. We were taught the history of SWAPO and also were taught about socialism and communism. . . .

"At the beginning of 1978, I was informed . . . that I was to return to Angola. Another SWAPO cadre and I returned to Angola and went to the Ohapeto camp, which is situated approximately 30 kilometers from the Namibian border. There were about 500 trained cadres in the camp under the command of Burumganga. . . .

"At the beginning of May 1978, 12 of us . . . were informed that we were to be sent to the Soviet Union for training. They did not specify what kind of training we were to receive.

"Thereafter, our group of 12 was taken to Luanda where we were accommodated in a warehouse that is used to store some of the SWAPO supplies. There were other people accommodated in the warehouse and we totaled approximately 70.

"The SWAPO members who work in the Luanda office issued our group of 12 with travel documents. . . . We were given air tickets valid for a trip from Luanda to Moscow. On May 4, 1978, we boarded an Aeroflot bound for Moscow. The aircraft refueled at Brazzaville and Budapest. . . .

"We arrived at Moscow on May 5, 1978 . . . a Soviet official called Alexander told us that SWAPO had sent us to Moscow to study underground work and intelligence. He said we were going to study for 6 months.

"Our lectures began on May 7, 1978, with Russian language classes and political classes. . . . In our lectures on political theory, we studied books printed in English on Leninist teachings and political economy. We also studied the origin and development of communism and Leninist teachings.

"We were being trained as intelligence personnel and in underground work. In our course on security and underground measures, we concentrated on physical security—how to protect people as bodyguards.

"We were instructed on the use of the Makarov pistol—stripping, assembling and firing the weapon. In our training on underground work, we were taught how to work with the civilians, how to organize people, get their cooperation and recruit them as informers. Alexander . . . was our instructor in this part of the course. I am of the opinion that he works for Soviet intelligence.

"We started our program at 8 on weekdays. After breakfast, we went to our classes for lectures which lasted for 6 hours—2 hours each for Russian, politics, security and underground measures. We studied 5 days a week for 6 months. Alexander told us that it had been intended to teach us codes, secret writing, and "criminalistics," but that it had been decided at a later stage that it was not necessary to teach us these topics.

"We finished our course near the end of 1978. We were allowed to keep some of our notebooks but had to hand in the rest of our books which we had used for our studies. . . .

"On our return to Luanda, we were taken to the same SWAPO warehouse where we had previously been accommodated. We were instructed to surrender all the notes we had made in Moscow and thereafter were taken to Lubango, where we stayed for a week before moving on to the Matale base. . . .

"In the Northern operational region, I was attached to an information group consisting of 15 trained cadres. Some of us were armed with AK-47's and others with Makarovs. . . . Our task was to debrief SWAPO cadres who returned to Angola from Namibia.

"From early 1979, I was instructed . . . to infiltrate into Namibia to make contact with Ovambo civilians in order to get information on security force movements. I used to cross into Namibia and spend 2 to 3 days at a time, collect the information, and then move out. I had completed about eight missions and on each occasion, I was dressed in civilian clothes and armed with a Makarov pistol. . . ."

Document 5: Testimony of Emanuel Hashiko

E manuel Hashiko was born in 1954 at Edundja, Namibia. He describes his decision to leave Namibia in 1976 and his subsequent experiences. Like Dickson Namolo, he was lured into SWAPO under false pretenses, grew disillusioned, and was afraid to return after his capture by South African Security Forces. Hashiko's training, conducted by Soviet instructors in Angola, supplies further evidence of the direct role played by the Soviet Union in exacerbating the conflict in southern Africa.

Source: Senate Hearings before the Subcommittee on Security and Terrorism of the Committee on the Judiciary, *The Role of the Soviet Union, Cuba, and East Germany in Fomenting Terrorism in Southern Africa,* 1982.

"We decided to go to Angola, join SWAPO, and get further academic training. On SWAPO's radio program over Radio Freedom, the people of Namibia, and especially the young people, were told to leave Namibia and go to Angola to join SWAPO, who would see to it that they received further education. . . .

"On our arrival at Oruma, I found that it was a SWAPO camp with more than 100 SWAPO cadres based there. Nakada was the commander of the camp. Nakada questioned us and told us to forget about academic education because SWAPO had no time for academic education; it only had time for military training.

"He said SWAPO's aim was to liberate Namibia. He said there was only one way to join SWAPO, and that was to go for military training. As we had no choice in the matter, we decided to go for military training. Nakada had informed us that no one had the right to resign from SWAPO. If a person wanted to leave SWAPO, it could only be done in a military way; that means the person has to be killed. . . .

"At the end of December 1976, I was taken in a group of 180 to the Tobias Ha Inyeko Training Center at Lubango for further training. Here, I received 2 months' training as a medical infantryman. Our instructors were mostly Russians. The training concentrated on politics, military combat work, and first aid.

"I attended the following courses: infantry . . . politics . . . military combat work . . . radio . . . medical. . . .

"[In December 1976 we] were then moved to Oiputa base. At that stage, our detachment consisted of 170 men. . . .

"We then broke up into smaller groups. I was in a group of 9 which was later joined by a further 10 SWAPO men. We were instructed to infiltrate into Namibia to check on the roads, waterholes, the terrain, in general, and to try and teach the locals politics in order to get their support. For this purpose, we had two political commissars attached to our platoon. We also had two guides who knew the area and could guide us to the villages.

"In February 1980, we had a contact with the South African Security Forces. One of our political commissars was killed and I and another member were wounded. I had been wounded in both thighs. We were removed by helicopter to a hospital for treatment. I spent a week in the hospital.

"The SWAPO morale, when I was captured, was poor and many of the cadres did not want to fight anymore. Many complained that their aim had been to go for education and not for military training. Many members of SWAPO were deserting. I heard that deserters are regarded by SWAPO as traitors and that they are killed by SWAPO when they are captured."

Mr. Hashiko was asked if he had personal knowledge of SWAPO terrorism. His answer reveals SWAPO "recruitment" practices.

"One day in 1977, I was in a group of 100 men of SWAPO and they were kidnaping some students from Otapi school. . . . We were divided in two groups. One group is supposed to make an ambush by the road because there was a military base nearby that secondary school.

"And after that, when we made an ambush, we cut the telephone wires and the second group was going inside the mission and they took all of the students.

"Many of the children were crying because they did not want to go to Angola. . . . And after that, we bring the students in Angola, up to [Base] Vietnam, where the regional commander stayed. And when Nakada saw the students, he called his political commissar so that he could speak to the students; it means to give them some politics.

"I know all the students were trained as military men or cadres."

Document 6: Testimony of Lt. Adriano Francisco Bomba

Adriano Francisco Bomba was born in 1958 in Matola, Mozambique. He was in his first year of high school when FRELIMO took power. After removal from school, Bomba was trained as a pilot in the Soviet Union. He was commissioned as a lieutenant in the Armed Forces of Mozambique (FAM) in 1980. Disillusioned with both the negative consequences of FRELIMO policies for the people of Mozambique and with the increasing subservience of FRELIMO to the Soviet Union, Lt. Bomba flew his MiG-17 to South Africa and asked for asylum on July 8, 1981.

Source: Senate Hearings before the Subcommittee on Security and Terrorism of the Committee on the Judiciary, *The Role of the Soviet Union, Cuba, and East Germany in Fomenting Terrorism in Southern Africa,* 1982.

"In 1977, when I enrolled for 10th class [grade], pupils were not able to attend school. Amazed at these developments, we sought an explanation which was never given to us. The government had so decided. . . .

"Days later, we were handed over to the Ministry of Defense and only male pupils born in Mozambique were included in the new list drafted by that ministry. We were all examined medically at the military hospital and taken to the camp on March 24, 1977. A group of 75 men, including myself, left for the Soviet Union on March 28.

"We boarded an Aeroflot airplane, called at Dar-es-Salaam, Aden, Cairo, Odessa, and finally landed in Moscow. In Moscow, we boarded another plane to Frunze where, on arrival, we were taken straight to the military camp. The following day, we were welcomed by a Soviet, Colonel Klatchkow, who briefed us on the rights of foreign military students in the Soviet Union, subsidies, and on Soviet history in general. We flew the next day to Djamboul, where our training camp was situated.

"On arrival at the camp in Djamboul, we were divided into two major groups corresponding to our specialities: technicians and pilots. I was included in the group of pilots. Our curriculum included the following subjects: Russian, mathematics, physics, military topography, military administration, Soviet Union, military tactics, massive destruction arms. . . .

"The program for the L-29 air training was restricted to photoshooting and photobombing. On days we did not fly, we had lectures on tactics, Russian, and principles of scientific socialism.

"We were visited by the Mozambican Minister of Defense, Alberto Joaquim Chipande, who happened to be in the U.S.S.R. doing a course at the Soviet Military Academy. It was on this occasion that we were informed that FRELIMO had stipulated that all elements of the group become party members. In August, we were visited by Armando Emilio Guebuza, national political commissar of the FPLM. . . .

". . . we were transferred to Tokmak where we were supposed to start our training on a MiG-17F. Classes started early in December and the prescribed subjects were: air dynamics, air navigation, construction and handling of the engine construction and handling of the airframe, aviation equipment, aviation armament, fighter bomber aviation tactics, Marxist–Leninist philosophy, principles of pedagogics and military psychology, educative work in the armed forces, massive destruction weapons, and Russian. Technical subjects were related to MiG-17F and to UTI MiG-15. . . .

"On our arrival at the camp, we practiced for 15 days on parked aircraft and then started flying training.

"I was a member of the second squadron, and my instructor was Lt. Tchmiwkhow Mikhail Vacilievitch, who was eventually stationed in Mozambique even before the end of the scheduled training. . . .

"We left Moscow on December 4 in the company of the Mozambican minister of defense who completed by then the "Inter-Arms" course at the Vwisstrel Academy. We called at Luanda for refueling and during our short stay we had time to visit Agostinho Neto's mausoleum where the minister placed a wreath. . . .

"Taking a general look at all bases we visited, I should stress that Mozambicans were not the only foreign military trainees, as there were also Angolans, Tanzanians, Congolese, Ethiopians, Somali—they withdrew when the Somali Government cut off diplomatic relations—Libyans, Chadians, Malians, Algerians, Yemenis, Afghans, Vietnamese, Cubans, East Germans, Bulgarians, Romanians.

"In addition to our scheduled classes, we also held meetings to discuss aspects of FRELIMO's history, the history of Marxism–Leninism, and sessions for self-criticism."

Lt. Bomba was asked about Soviet and Bloc advisors in Mozambique and their respective roles.

". . . we have only Soviet advisers in the air force, only Soviet advisers and instructors, only Soviets; in the Navy also; and in the ground forces, but high-level, high-ranking officers, and so forth.

"And civilian personnel, just a few. We have got also Bulgarians, a lot of them. They are more attached to the health services, and in some fields such as agriculture, only Bulgarians.

"East Germans, they are only responsible for the security forces. The Cubans, some in the ground forces, instructors, and some advisers—but they are mainly instructors, the Cubans."

Lt. Bomba was asked to briefly relate the history of FRELIMO.

". . . at the beginning . . . when President Edward Mondlane was alive, FRELIMO was a liberation movement. But the Soviet infiltration transformed FRELIMO into just one puppet of the Soviet Union.

"And after the independence, what happens is that the Soviets, they replaced the Portuguese, and the Soviets are more cruel. I can say, that before the independence in Mozambique, the conditions of life were better. . . .

"This transformation [of FRELIMO] it's not just a coincidence, because the Communists, they have got their ideology and they have got the sequence that must be followed. At the beginning, the liberation movement must fight to have the political power; after they have got the power, they begin with the democratic revolution of the masses, to get influence among the masses, and to have control over all the population.

"After that, what comes is the socialist revolution. That is what happened. In the 3d Congress FRELIMO became a Socialist party, Marxist–Leninist—it was a Communist party at the beginning of the Socialist revolution. . . .

"At the Third Congress, held in February 1977 in Maputo, FRELIMO ceased to be just a liberation front and became a Marxist–Leninist party. Subsequently, the private sector was nationalized in a bid by the Government to restructure the old colonial state machine in accordance with the newly implemented Marxist–Leninist trends and dogmas."

Lt. Bomba was asked what he thought of SWAPO, based on his experience in Namibia after he left Mozambique.

"Like FRELIMO, SWAPO also enjoys full support from the Soviet Union. Well, Soviet support alone isn't bad. Yet history has proven that wherever the Soviet Union has supported those parties or movements more vulnerable and more receptive to Russian power—FRELIMO [Mozambique],

MPLA [Angola], PAIGC [Guinea-Bissau]—this same Soviet aid was accompanied by subtle infiltration of these liberation movements, the end result being the transformation of a genuine nationalist movement into surrogates of the U.S.S.R. in Africa once such movements come to power."

Documents 7 and 8: Lists of Soviet-Bound SWAPO Cadres

T he items below were selected from a large number of documents captured at SWAPO bases in Angola and Namibia outlining the operational role of the Soviet Union and its surrogates in supporting low-intensity conflict in southern Africa. They reveal that Soviet training extends beyond the military sphere of "reconnaissance and sabotage" methods and tactics to include specialized instruction in "political commissarship."

Source: Senate Hearings before the Subcommittee on Security and Terrorism of the Committee on the Judiciary, *The Role of the Soviet Union, Cuba, and East Germany in Fomenting Terrorism in Southern Africa,* 1982.

Document 7

08 07 1977.
Cassinga CHQ

TO BE TRAINED IN RECONNAISSANCE &
SABOTAGE, IN SOVIET UNION, MOSCOW

1. Benjamin   Nangombe   Shakoloka
2. Benhard   Nangolo   Kawali

[8 other individuals named]

Document 8

[Date Illegible]1977
Cassinga CHQ.

COMRADES GOING TO BE TRAINED IN
"POLITICAL COMMISSARSHIP" IN SOVIET UNION, MOSCOW

Home Name		C Name	Std. Ed.
1. Fillemon	Malimo	Lumumba	Form III
2. Darius	Shikongo	Mbolondondo	" I

[8 other individuals named]

Document 9: Statements of "National Liberation Movement" Leaders

T he statements below bear direct witness of the international support network utilized by "national liberation movements." They proclaim the global linkages presented throughout this book from the perspective of the movements' leaders themselves. These statements constitute one more example of public proclamation of the cooperation among different terrorist and insurgent elements.

Source: Senate Hearings before the Subcommittee on Security and Terrorism of the Committee on the Judiciary, *The Role of the Soviet Union, Cuba, and East Germany in Fomenting Terrorism in Southern Africa,* 1982.

"Our revolutionary movement continues to discharge its tasks of solidarity with the Patriotic Front of Zimbabwe, SWAPO of Namibia, the Polisario Front of Western Sahara, [and] the Palestine Liberation Organization. . . .

> ANC Secretary General Alfred Nzo, 1979
> *SECHABA* (official organ of the ANC)
> November 1979

"As natural ideological allies . . . the Socialist countries especially the Soviet Union, the German Democratic Republic, Romania, Poland, Cuba, People's Republic of China, Democratic People's Republic of Korea and the Democratic Republic of Vietnam which give us concrete material assistance, political, diplomatic and moral support."

> SWAPO leader Sam Nujoma, 1976
> Address to SWAPO Central Committee
> Lusaka, Zambia 7 February 1976

8
Surrogate Warfare: The Threat Within

errorism in the United States has not resulted in high loss of human life when compared with other regions of the world. Until now property has been the principal target. Also, North American terrorism has been basically motivated by limited political action goals. However, it should not be concluded that because more deadly tactics have gone unused that they will not occur in the future. Terrorism in the United States has not been considered a serious threat. This is a mistake. Certain domestic terrorist groups have maintained a continuity that far surpasses their counterparts in Western Europe and elsewhere.

The membership of United States terrorist groups has tended to be composed primarily of white females who espouse an "anti-imperialist" ideology which identifies America as its primary enemy. This can be traced back to the Weather Underground Organization (WUO). The WUO claimed responsibility for nearly forty bombings between October of 1969 and September of 1976.[1] One of its leaders, Cathy Boudin, continued underground activities until her capture in the 1981 attempted Brinks robbery in Nyack, New York. Another Weatherperson, Linda Sue Evans, was recently arrested with Brinks fugitive Marilyn Jean Buck on 11 May 1985 in Dobbs Ferry, New York.[2] Evans was a member of the second Venceremos Brigade which traveled to Cuba in 1970.[3] The Venceremos Brigade (VB) has been described in FBI reports as being of vital interest to Cuban intelligence (DGI). The VB provided the DGI with the opportunity to spot, access and recruit its members for intelligence collection in the United States. "A very limited number of VB members have been trained in guerrilla warfare techniques, including use of arms and explosives."[4] The arrest of Buck and Evans led to the identification of a safehouse in Baltimore where a third female was arrested and evidence seized which purportedly links the three to a series of recent bombings in the

This chapter was prepared by Paul M. Joyal. He is a Washington-based expert in North American terrorism and a former federal law enforcement officer.

Washington and New York areas.[5] Possible future bombing plans were also confiscated; these included the White House complex and the Naval Academy.

These factors appear to establish linkages between Weather Underground "actions" and those more recently claimed by the United Freedom Front and the Armed Resistance Unit (see Document 1). The history of these bombings from the sixties through the eighties exhibits continuity in both techniques employed and rhetoric utilized. Additionally, the communiques issued by these groups contain specific international linkages to various causes and Third World "liberation movements." Explicit or implicit in these communiques is the acknowledgement of the international obligations of these entities as revolutionaries. It is this obligation which requires them to conduct "armed actions."

The statements of Susan Lisa Rosenberg reflect the continuity from the early days of the WUO to currently active terrorists in the United States. A reputed member of the May 19th Communist Organization (an offshoot of the WUO), Rosenberg was recently convicted for possession of an arsenal. At her December 13, 1984 arraignment she declared herself to be an international "revolutionary guerrilla . . . captured in the course of building a resistance to this government."[6] When she and an accomplice were convicted in March 1985, she stated that ". . . this was no victory for the U.S. government. The truth that revolutionary resistance fighters were defending the worldwide anti-colonial and anti-imperialist peoples and nations was clear."[7] Statements like these, matched with the communiques themselves, provide an important window into United States terrorist organizations. The analysis of terrorist communiques also provides insight into the profile of these groups. One of the best sources of historical information on the Weather Underground, in which this method is partially utilized, is the formerly top secret FBI report, *Foreign Influence—Weather Underground Organization (WUO)*, declassified for the W. Mark Felt and Edward S. Miller trial. Section III of the report, titled "WUO Underground Communiques and Bombings 1969–1976," has a subsection B which provides "Specific Communiques Showing Continuing Foreign Influence" (see attached excerpts in Document 2).

In February of 1984, an extraordinary compilation of communiques was published with an introduction provided by the May 19th Communist Organization. The title reads: *Armed Propaganda Against the U.S. War Machine: Communiques from the Armed Resistance Unit and the United Freedom Front 1982–1983* (see attached excerpts in Document 3). An analysis of the May 19th Communist Organization introduction provides another window into United States terrorist organizations, calling to mind the Weather Underground communiques from the early 1970s. More important are the Armed Resistance Unit (ARU) and United Freedom Front (UFF) communiques themselves. The ARU's bombing of the United States Capitol in 1983 in response to the Grenada invasion dramatically calls to mind the 1971

Weather Underground bombing of the Capitol in protest of the U.S. invasion of Laos. In both cases "armed actions" were engaged in solidarity with Third World "liberation forces" punishing American military operations.

When one becomes familiar with these communiques and compares them with those of the Weather Underground, it becomes clear that all share a common anti-imperialist orientation and tradition. A simple review of the slogans used indicates that the maintenance of the Nicaraguan revolution, along with the victory of the FMLN/FDR in El Salvador, is a very powerful motivator. Any direct military action by U.S. forces in Central America could provoke a response that heretofore has not been experienced in the United States. Through these communiques, both past and present, we discover the outline of North American terrorism—its parameters and its potential.

Notes

1. Federal Bureau of Investigation *Foreign Influence—Weather Underground Organization (WUO)*, 20 August 1976, pp. 153–56.

2. "Fugitive in $1.6 Million Brink's Holdup Captured," *New York Times*, 12 May 1985, p. 1.

3. Report of the Senate Subcommittee on Internal Security, *The Weather Underground* Washington, D.C.: GPO, 1975, p. 66.

4. Federal Bureau of Investigation, *Foreign Influence—Weather Underground Organization (WUO)*, 20 August 1976, p. 126.

5. "Bomb Plot Evidence Found in Baltimore," *New York Times*, 2 June 1985, p. 22.

6. United Press International, 13 December 1984, PM cycle, pp. 5–6.

7. "Radicals Found Guilty in Federal Trial: 2 Defendants Convicted of Possessing Weapons," *New York Times*, 16 March 1985.

Document 1: Bombings Since 1982 in the New York and Washington Areas

R esponsibility for a series of bombings in the New York and Washington areas have been claimed by groups using the following names: United Freedom Front (UFF), Revolutionary Fighting Group (RFG), Armed Resistance Unit (ARU), Red Guerrilla Resistance (RGR). The targets have included both U.S. government and U.S. corporate facilities. Foreign corporate and diplomatic establishments have also been struck. The dates, targets and group which took responsibility follow.

Source: Dr. Samuel T. Francis, *The Terrorist Underground in the United States* (Washington, D.C., The Nathan Hale Institute, 1984), p. 12; list updated by Paul M. Joyal.

Date	Target	Claimant
16 Dec 82	South African Corporation (Elmont, N.Y.)	UFF
16 Dec 82	IBM Corporation (Harrison, N.Y.)	UFF
28 Jan 83	Federal Building/FBI office (Staten Island, N.Y.)	RFG
26 Apr 83	National War College Ft. McNair (Wash., D.C.)	ARU
12 May 83	Army Reserve Center (Uniondale, N.Y.)	UFF
13 May 83	Navy Reserve Center (Queens, N.Y.)	UFF
17 Aug 83	Navy Computer Facility Navy Yard (Wash., D.C.)	ARU
21 Aug 83	National Guard Armory (Bronx, N.Y.)	UFF
7 Nov 83	U.S. Capitol Building (Wash., D.C.)	ARU
13 Dec 83	Navy Recruiting Center (East Meadows, N.Y.)	UFF

14 Dec 83	Honeywell Corporation (Queens, N.Y.)	UFF
29 Jan 84	Motorola Corporation (Queens, N.Y.)	UFF
19 Mar 84	IBM Corporation (Harrison, N.Y.)	UFF
5 Apr 84	Israeli Aircraft Industries (Manhattan, N.Y.)	RGR
20 Apr 84	Navy Officers Club Navy Yard (Wash., D.C.)	RGR
22 Aug 84	General Electric Corporation (Queens, N.Y.)	UFF
26 Sep 84	South African Consulate (Manhattan, N.Y.)	RGR
26 Sep 84	Union Carbide Corporation (Mount Pleasant, N.Y.)	UFF
23 Feb 85	Police Benevolent Assoc. (Manhattan, N.Y.)	RGR

Document 2: Foreign Influence—Weather Underground Organization

The following excerpts are from a formerly top secret FBI report, *Foreign Influence—Weather Underground Organization (WUO)*, which was declassified for the W. Mark Felt and Edward S. Miller trial. The report's introduction outlines the international connections of the WUO, while Section III provides insight into the WUO's self-proclaimed "internationalist duty" through the use of violent political action, particularly bombings.

Source: FBI Report (CG 100–40903), August 20, 1976; declassified.

UNITED STATES DEPARTMENT OF JUSTICE
FEDERAL BUREAU OF INVESTIGATION

Chicago, Illinois
August 20, 1976

CG 100–40903

FOREIGN INFLUENCE - WEATHER
UNDERGROUND ORGANIZATION (WUO)

INTRODUCTION

From the moment in October, 1967, when Radio Hanoi announced the formation of the South Vietnamese Peoples Committee for Solidarity with American People (by the National Liberation Front (NLF), the political arm of the Viet Cong) with the objective of establishing relations with "progressive organizations and individuals in the United States," a political front was enjoined in behalf of the national interests of the Democratic Republic of North Vietnam (DRV) (and the NLF), the purpose of which was to intensify the anti-war sentiment in the United States. From the initial meeting between the Vietnamese and leading anti-war activists held in Bratislava, Czechoslovakia, in November, 1967, to the July, 1969, meeting with leading Weather-people held in Havana, Cuba, the influence of Vietnamese representatives on the Students for a Democratic Society (SDS) leadership become sharply pronounced. At the same time, the example of the Cuban revolution became the guide for the emerging American student revolutionary. With an increasing number of trips to Havana where the youthful revolutionary could learn at first hand how to create revolution, the influence of Cuba on the developing WUO was enormous. . . .

The WUO obtained their revolutionary methodology from the Cubans and Vietnamese and, importantly, put into practice what they had learned from them. . . . So, when Huynh Van Ba, representative of the Provisional Revolutionary Government of Vietnam (PRG), instructed the WUO to "look for the person who fights hardest against the cops . . . Don't look for the one who says the best thing. Look for the one who fights," the campus base was forgotten and the WUO began to recruit the greasers and assorted oddments who had displayed their hatred of authority in direct combat with police.

The WUO has existed since early 1970. Since then, their ideological statements have developed a more consistent Marxist–Leninist revolutionary stance. . . . Their revolutionary duty lies side by side with the oppressed Third World peoples and the proletariat of the world. Hence, the international character of the WUO and the foreign influence which shaped that character was early defined and has been a constant frame of reference when considering the investigative problem inherent to the WUO.

. . . .

SECTION III

WUO UNDERGROUND COMMUNIQUES AND BOMBINGS
1970–1976

Having entered underground status in February, 1970 and until the issuance of "Prairie Fire" in July, 1974, the political commitment of the WUO was revealed through the issuance of their underground "communiques." These communiques, usually accompanying a bombing and stating the political reason for the bombing, reveal the continuing identification of the WUO as international revolutionaries. As shown in Section I and Section II, their contacts with representatives of the DRV and PRG obliged them to act directly in behalf of the Vietnamese in this country and, the influence of the Cubans on their ideology and their organizational structure was enormous. In addition, the WUO utilized the conceptions of armed struggle against the state as detailed in the "Minimanual of the Urban Guerrilla," by CARLOS MARIGHELLA. MARIGHELLA who was killed in Sao Paulo, Brazil in November, 1969, gave his life in behalf of guerrilla warfare. According to

LARRY GRATHWOHL in his recently issued book, "Bringing Down America," the WUO used MARIGHELLA's Minimanual and DEBRAY's "Revolution In The Revolution?" as their models for guerrilla action. The WUO was not simply engaged in ideological rhetoric but had made the hard commitment to engage in armed struggle, the ultimate purpose of which was to destroy the state.

· · · · · · · · · · ·

B. Specific Communiques Showing Continuing Foreign Influence

Although all of the underground communiques issued by the WUO contain a political rationalization for their "actions", and although most of these communiques reveal what they deem to be their international obligations as revolutionaries, the following communiques have been selected as representative of their commitment to armed struggle. In particular the report which accompanies the WUO statement on their assistance to TIMOTHY LEARY in his escape from prison and his eventual travel to Algeria quite clearly shows their international connections.

· · · · · · · · · · ·

ALL INFORMATION CONTAINED HEREIN IS UNCLASSIFIED EXCEPT WHERE SHOWN OTHERWISE.

Sources whose identities are concealed herein have furnished reliable information in the past except where otherwise noted.

This document contains neither recommendations nor conclusions of the FBI. It is the property of the FBI and is loaned to your agency; it and its contents are not to be distributed outside your agency.

Documents 3–7: Operational Communiques Concerning Acts of Terrorism in the U.S.

T he following communiques of the Armed Resistance Unit (ARU) and the United Freedom Front (UFF) were compiled by an offshoot of the Weather Underground Organization, the May 19th Communist Organization. Together with the introduction prepared by the May 19th Communist Organization, these documents indicate that U.S. domestic terrorist groups act in solidarity with foreign "liberation movements" in attacking the "imperialist" U.S. "war machine".

Source: May 19th Communist Organization

Document 3

ARMED PROPAGANDA AGAINST THE U.S. WAR MACHINE

Communiques from the Armed Resistance Unit
and the United Freedom Front 1982–1983

Compiled with an introduction by the
May 19th Communist Organization

Introduction

Over the past year, armed revolutionary actions have begun to increase inside the U.S. These seven communiques from the Armed Resistance Unit and the United Freedom Front were received by public forces and the mass media after revolutionary actions against the U.S. war apparatus and the U.S. ruling state. Terms for this period of armed activity were defined when the Fuerzas Armadas de Liberacion Nacional (FALN) bombed New York Police headquarters, New York FBI headquarters, and the U.S. Attorney's offices in Brooklyn and Manhattan on December 31, 1982. . . .

These actions have begun to provide revolutionary leadership for those American people who are truly disturbed by the U.S. invasion of Grenada, and for the growing solidarity movements with the peoples of Central America. . . .

The Armed Resistance Unit has made a particular argument in declaring its solidarity with "the peoples of Grenada, Lebanon, Palestine, El Salvador and Nicaragua—who are confronting direct U.S. aggression and those, like the people of Chile and the Philippines, who are struggling to free their nations from U.S. puppet regimes. They are all paying a tremendous price for freedom, and we commit ourselves to fight with the same seriousness. . . . Our actions also carries a message to the anti-imperialist movement here, that we need to resist and fight as people all over the world are doing—with principle, consistency and determination." (from the communique which accompanied the bombing of the U.S. Capitol, November 7, 1983).

·　　·　　·　　·　　·　　·　　·　　·　　·　　·　　·

Document 4

COMMUNIQUE #1

Armed Resistance Unit Bombs War College

April 26, 1983

Tonight we attacked Fort Lesley McNair Military Base in Washington, D.C. Fort McNair houses one branch of the U.S. War College, the National Defense University, and the Inter-American Defense College (IADC). This action was taken in solidarity with the growing liberation movements in El Salvador, in Guatemala, and throughout Central America, and with the socialist government of Nicaragua. This region today is the center of world revolution and the front line in the defeat of U.S. imperialism. For this reason, it is currently the target of the most vicious U.S. counterrevolutionary attacks.

·　　·　　·　　·　　·　　·　　·　　·　　·　　·　　·

COMMANDANTE ANA MARIA (MELINDA ANAYA MONTES) ESTA PRESENTE!
VICTORY TO THE FMLN/FDR!
SOLIDARITY WITH THE PEOPLES OF CENTRAL AMERICA!
BUILD A REVOLUTIONARY RESISTANCE MOVEMENT!
FIGHT U.S. IMPERIALISM!
DEFEND THE NICARAGUAN REVOLUTION!

Document 5

ARMED RESISTANCE UNIT BOMBS THE U.S. CAPITOL

COMMUNIQUE FROM THE ARMED RESISTANCE UNIT
NOVEMBER 7, 1983

Tonight we bombed the U.S. Capitol building. We attacked the U.S. government to retaliate against imperialist aggression that has sent the marines, the CIA and the army to invade sovereign nations, to trample and lay waste to the lives and rights of the peoples of Grenada, Lebanon, El Salvador, and Nicaragua, to carry out imperialism's need to dominate, oppress, and exploit. Every act of the U.S. military—directed by the White House and Congress—has been nothing less than an outright attack on the fundamental right of nations to self-determination, peace and freedom. These acts have been carried out with cynical disregard for life as well as for truth. Reagan calls progress and revolution "terrorism" and tries to portray the true terrorism of imperialist invasion as "democracy" and "freedom." Only a government arrogant enough to believe that its economic and political needs should dominate the whole world can call the invasion of Grenada a "rescue operation," the invasion of Lebanon a "peace-keeping mission," the fascist rulers of El Salvador "democracy's friends," and the contras "freedom fighters."

. . . .

Our action carries a message to the U.S. imperialist ruling class: we purposely aimed our attack at the institutions of imperialist rule rather than at individual members of the ruling class and government. We did not choose to kill any of them at this time. But their lives are not sacred, and their hands are stained with the blood of millions. Let it be as clear to the people of this country as it is to the rest of the people of the world that the U.S. ruling class are war criminals, and they will be held accountable for their crimes.

Document 6

Communique # 2

U.S. OUT OF
EL SALVADOR

HANDS OFF
NICARAGUA

On May 11, 1983 the United Freedom Front bombed the 77th U.S. Army Reserve Command Center, (800th Military Police Group), Hempstead, N.Y. and the U.S. Naval Militia Base, (Naval Reserve Center), Whitestone, Queens, N.Y. . . .

With this action we attack the U.S. imperialist military machine, a machine which has pumped hundreds of millions of dollars in military aid to prop up a military dictatorship, which is in opposition to a just and popular movement of the People of El Salvador.

Document 7

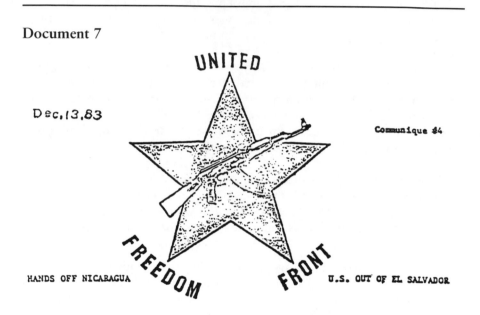

Today armed units of the United Freedom Front continued our attacks on the U.S. military machine with the bombing of the New York District Navy recruiting headquarters, in East Meadow, Long Island, New York. We take this action in solidarity with the People of Central America, especially Nicaragua and El Salvador, who continue to resist U.S. imperialism's escalating acts of war. . . .

Glossary

This glossary is based on part II.

AAPSO Afro-Asian People's Solidarity Organization.

Abu 'Ammar Also Amar. Cover name for Yasser Arafat, head of the al-Fatah.

Abu Iyad Also Ayad or Iyyad. Real name: Saleh Khalaf, Arafat's deputy.

Americas Department Department of the Central Committee of the Cuban Communist Party responsible for supervising subversion in the Western Hemisphere.

ANC African National Congress; formed in 1912 as a black nationalist movement within South Africa. Currently led by Oliver Tambo.

Arce, Bayardo Member of the National Directorate of the FSLN (Nicaragua).

ARU Armed Resistance Unit, an American terrorist group.

Austin, General Hudson Grenada's Secretary of Defense and the Interior, head of the Armed Forces, member of both the Political Bureau and the Central Committee.

Bishop, Maurice Prime Minister of Grenada until October 1983. Head of both the Political Bureau and the Central Committee. Also known as "Comrade Leader."

Borge, Tomas Member of the National Directorate of the FSCN and Minister of the Interior (Nicaragua).

Bourne, Bernard A Minister-Counsellor in Grenada's Embassy in Moscow.

BPR Popular Revolutionary Bloc. Civilian front for the Popular Forces of Liberation (BPR), a Salvadoran guerrilla group.

Carpio, Cayetano Former head of the FPL (Popular Forces of Liberation), one of the Salvadoran guerrilla groups. Code name: Marcial.

Carrion, Luis Member of the National Directorate and head of the DGSE, the Nicaraguan state security apparatus.

CC Central Committee.

Cde. Comrade.

CDS Committees for the Defense of Sandinismo; neighborhood bloc committees in charge of surveillance.

Cerna, Lenin Chief of Counterintelligence in the DGSE.

Chichoneros A Honduran guerrilla group.

CISPES Committee in Solidarity with the People of El Salvador. A communist-led U.S. solidarity group.

CPC Communist Party of Cuba.

CPES Communist Party of El Salvador.

CPUSA Communist Party of the United States.

Cuadra, Joaquin Chief of Staff of the Sandinista Army.

DGI General Directorate of Security. The Cuban state security apparatus.

DGSE General Directorate of State Security. The Nicaraguan state security apparatus.

DOE Department of Special Operations. The department of the Cuban Ministry of the Interior that carries out special operations such as sabotage.

DPEP Department of Propaganda and Political Education. The department of the FSLN in charge of internal propaganda.

DPRK Democratic People's Republic of Korea—better known as North Korea.

DRI Department of International Relations. The department of the FSLN in charge of relations with other communist governments and revolutionary movements.

DRU United Revolutionary Directorate. The political-military coordinating committee of FMLN.

DS Bulgarian State Security.

ERP Popular Revolutionary Army. One of the Salvadoran guerrilla groups.

ETA The Basque terrorist organization.

FALN Armed Forces of National Liberation. A Puerto Rican terrorist organization.

FAM Armed Forces of Mozambique.

FARN Armed Forces on National Resistance. One of the Salvadoran guerrilla organizations.

al-Fatah Also al-Fath. Predominant organization in the PLO [Palestine National Liberation Movement]. Headed by Yasser Arafat.

FDR Revolutionary Democratic Front. The political arm of the FMLN.

Fifth Directorate The intelligence section of the DGSE.

FMLN Farabundo Marti National Liberation Front. The umbrella organization containing the five Salvadoran guerrilla factions.

FMSPS World Front for Solidarity with the Salvadoran People.

FPL Popular Forces of Liberation. One of the Salvadoran guerrilla groups.

FPLM Popular Forces of Liberation of Mozambique; military arm of FRELIMO.

FRELIMO Front for the Liberation of Mozambique; national liberation movement turned Marxist–Leninist vanguard ruling party in Mozambique; currently led by Samora Machel.

FSLN The Sandinista National Liberation Front. The governing party of Nicaragua.

GIS Grenada Information Service.

GPC Grenadian Peace Council.

GPP Prolonged Popular War. One of the three Sandinista factions.

GRU Soviet Military Intelligence.

Handal, Shafik General Secretary of the Communist Party of El Salvador.

Hizballah Also Hezbollah. Party of God. Iranian sponsored Shiite organization based in Lebanon. Led by Mohammed Fadlallah.

ICAP Cuban Institute for Friendship of the Peoples. A government institution taking care of prominent foreign guests.

ID International Department of the Central Committee of the Communist Party of the Soviet Union.

Jacobs, W. Richard Grenada's "roving ambassador" whose assignments included the Soviet Union and Cuba.

James, Liam   Grenada's Director of Internal Security. Also, Central Committee member and Hudson Austin's deputy.

Japanese Red Army   Also Rengo Sekigun. Japanese terrorist group whose members massacred Puerto Rican pilgrims at Lod (Lydda) in 1972.

Farouk Kaddounni   Also Faruqq Quaddumi. Cover name: Abu Lutf. Arafat's chief foreign affairs spokesman.

KGB   Soviet Committee of State Security.

Louison, Major George "Einstein"   Chief of Staff of the Grenadian army and member of both the Central Committee and Politbureau.

M–19   Colombian guerrilla organization.

MIR   Movement of the Revolutionary Left. Chilean terrorist organization.

Montero, Renan   Chief of the intelligence section of the DGSE. Originally, a Cuban citizen.

Montoneros   Argentine terrorist organization.

MPLA   Popular Movement for the Liberation of Angola. Victorious Soviet- and Cuban-supported faction in the three-way struggle for power in Angola led by Agostinho Neto; renamed MPLA—Party of Labor (MPLA–PT); currently led by José Eduardo dos Santos.

National Directorate   The highest political authority of the Sandinista regime. Composed of the Nine Commandantes.

NJM   New Jewel Movement. The ruling party of Grenada. Marxist–Leninist in nature.

Nunez, Carlos   Member of the National Directorate and head of DPEP.

OAS   Organization of American States.

Ortega, Humberto   Member of the National Directorate and Minister of Defense.

PAIGC   African Party for the Independence of Guinea–Bissau and Cape Verde, national liberation movement turned Marxist–Leninist. Ruling party in Guinea–Bissau and Cape Verde.

Pancho, Major   Cuban DGI adviser to the F2 section of the DGSE.

PCC   Communist Party of Cuba.

PCS   Communist Party of El Salvador.

PFLP   Popular Front for the Liberation of Palestine. Formed in 1966. Headed by George Habash. Most powerful organization in the "rejectionist front," which rejects any political resolution of the conflict with Israel. Marxist–Leninist in orientation. Commissioned the Japanese Red Army to attack Lod airport.

PFLP–GC   Popular Front for the Liberation of Palestine—General Command. Parted from the PFLP in 1968. Part of "rejectionist front." Syrian backed.

Pineiro Losada, Manuel   Head of the Americas Department of the Central Committee of the Cuban Communist Party. In charge of coordinating subversion in the Western Hemisphere.

PLAN   People's Liberation Army of Namibia; military arm of SWAPO.

PLO   Palestine Liberation Organization. Umbrella organization of Palestinian factions, formed in 1964. Since 1974 the Arabs have recognized it as "the sole legitimate representative of the Palestinian people." The main governing body is the Palestine National Council, which is chaired by Arafat.

PM   Prime Minister.

Polisario   Sahraoui Liberation Front. Insurgent organization fighting Morocco for control of the western, formerly Spanish, Sahara. Backed by Libya and Algeria.

PRG   People's Revolutionary Government of Grenada.

Proletarians   One of the three factions of the FSLN.

Red Brigades   Italian terrorist organization.

Roberto, General   Chief of all the Cuban intelligence advisers in Nicaragua.

RPG   Rocket-propelled grenade. A bazooka-type weapon.

SACP   South African Communist Party. Formed in 1921, the SACP is the oldest CP in Africa.

SACTU   South African Congress of Trade Unions; a sister organization of the SACP founded in 1955.

al-Sa'iqa   Vanguards of the Popular Liberation War. Formed by Syria in 1968. Second largest group in the PLO. Totally dependent on Syria and acts accordingly.

SI   Socialist International.

StB   Czechoslovak State Security.

SWAPO   South–West African Peoples Organization; formed in 1960 and originally known as Ovambo People's Organization; one of forty-five political parties in Namibia; recognized by the United Nations General Assembly as the "sole and authentic" voice of the Namibian people; currently led by Sam Nujoma.

Terceristas   One of the three factions of the FSLN.

Tirado Lopez, Victor   Member of the National Directorate.

Tupamaros   Uruguayan terrorist organization.

Umkhonto We Sizwe   People's Army of the ANC; also known as MK; formed in 1961.

UNITA   National Union for the Total Independence of Angola; founded in 1966 and led by Jonas Savimbi; currently fighting the MPLA in Angola.

UNIFIL   United Nations Interim Force in Lebanon. Formed after the 1978 Israeli intervention in Lebanon.

VB   Venceremos Brigade, Cuba.

Villalobos, Joaquin   Chief of ERP (Popular Revolutionary Army), one of the Salvadoran guerrilla groups.

WPC   World Peace Council. A Soviet-supported international front organization.

WUO   Weather Underground Organization; formerly the Weathermen, an offshoot of Students for a Democratic Society (SDS).

ZAPU   Zimbabwe African Peoples Union. Soviet backed national liberation movement led by Joshua Nkomo; lost in Rhodesian power struggle to Chinese-backed ZANU (Zimbabwe African National Union) led by Robert Mugabe.

ZS   Czechoslovak Military Intelligence.

Index

This index is based on part I.

About the Authors and Editors

Adda B. Bozeman is Professor Emeritus from Sarah Lawrence University.

William J. Casey is Director of Central Intelligence.

Dr. John J. Dziak is a Senior Soviet Specialist and Staff Director of the International Application Office, Directorate of Foreign Intelligence, Defense Intelligence Agency.

Douglas J. Feith is Special Counsel, International Security Policy, Department of Defense.

Dr. Charles C. Frost is former National Estimates Coordinator, Office of Intelligence, Drug Enforcement Administration, Department of Justice, and President, Frost Commercial Services, Inc.

Ernst Halperin is Professor of Political Science, Boston University, and Adjunct Professor of International Politics at the Fletcher School of Law and Diplomacy.

Paul Henze is Resident Consultant, The Rand Corporation.

Dr. Michael A. Ledeen is former Special Assistant to the [then] Secretary of State, Alexander Haig.

Dr. Neil C. Livingstone is President, Institute on Terrorism and Subnational Conflict.

Igor Lukes is Assistant Professor of Civilization and Foreign Affairs at the Fletcher School of Law and Diplomacy.

Robert L. Pfaltzgraff, Jr. is Shelby Cullom Davis Professor of International Security Studies at the Fletcher School of Law and Diplomacy and President, Institute for Foreign Policy Analysis.

Uri Ra'anan is Professor of International Politics, and Director, International Security Studies Program at the Fletcher School of Law and Diplomacy.

Herbert Romerstein is Senior Policy Officer with the United States Information Agency.

Sam Sarkesian is at the Department of Political Science, Loyola University of Chicago.

Richard H. Shultz is Associate Professor of International Politics at the Fletcher School of Law and Diplomacy.

Claire Sterling is a free-lance journalist.

B. Hugh Tovar is a former Senior Officer with the Central Intelligence Agency.

Sander Vanocur is chief Overview correspondent, ABC News.

Senator Malcom Wallop is former Chairman of the Budget Subcommittee of the Senate Select Committee on Intelligence.